Peter O. Müller, Susan Olsen and Franz Rainer (eds.)
Word-Formation – History, Theories, Units and Processes

This volume is part of a larger set of handbooks to Word-Formation

1   **Word-Formation: History, Theories, Units and Processes**
    Peter O. Müller, Susan Olsen and Franz Rainer (eds.)

2   **Word-Formation: Special Patterns and Restrictions**
    Peter O. Müller, Susan Olsen and Franz Rainer (eds.)

3   **Word-Formation: Semantics and Pragmatics**
    Peter O. Müller, Susan Olsen and Franz Rainer (eds.)

4   **Word-Formation: Language Contact and Diachrony**
    Peter O. Müller, Susan Olsen and Franz Rainer (eds.)

5   **Word-Formation: European Languages**
    Peter O. Müller, Susan Olsen and Franz Rainer (eds.)

Word-Formation
History, Theories, Units and Processes

Edited by
Peter O. Müller, Susan Olsen and Franz Rainer

ISBN 978-3-11-141368-6
e-ISBN (PDF) 978-3-11-142056-1
e-ISBN (EPUB) 978-3-11-142060-8

Library of Congress Control Number: 2025932313

Bibliographic information published by the Deutsche Nationalbibliothek
The Deutsche Nationalbibliothek lists this publication in the Deutsche Nationalbibliografie;
detailed bibliographic data are available on the Internet at http://dnb.dnb.de.

© 2025 Walter de Gruyter GmbH, Berlin/Boston, Genthiner Straße 13, 10785 Berlin
Cover image: BirdHunter591 / iStock / Getty Images Plus
Typesetting: Meta Systems Publishing & Printservices GmbH, Wustermark

www.degruyterbrill.com
Questions about General Product Safety Regulation:
productsafety@degruyterbrill.com

Contents

Hans-Jörg Schmid
1 **The scope of word-formation research** —— 1

Barbara Kaltz and Odile Leclercq
2 **Word-formation research from its beginnings to the 19th century** —— 25

Thomas Lindner
3 **Word-formation in historical-comparative grammar** —— 43

Wolfgang Motsch
4 **Word-formation in structuralism** —— 59

Rochelle Lieber
5 **Word-formation in generative grammar** —— 77

Geert Booij
6 **Word-formation in construction grammar** —— 99

Gary Libben
7 **Word-formation in psycholinguistics and neurocognitive research** —— 119

Pavol Štekauer
8 **The delimitation of derivation and inflection** —— 137

Joachim Mugdan
9 **Units of word-formation** —— 157

Andrew Spencer
10 **Derivation** —— 235

Salvador Valera
11 **Conversion** —— 259

Pavol Štekauer
12 **Backformation** —— 279

Anja Steinhauer
13 **Clipping** —— 293

Susan Olsen
14 **Composition** —— 307

Bernard Fradin
15 **Blending** —— 333

Andrew McIntyre
16 **Particle-verb formation** —— 365

Matthias Hüning and Barbara Schlücker
17 **Multi-word expressions** —— 383

Thomas Schwaiger
18 **Reduplication** —— 405

Elke Ronneberger-Sibold
19 **Word-creation** —— 425

Wolfgang U. Dressler
20 **Allomorphy** —— 445

Index —— 463

Hans-Jörg Schmid
1 The scope of word-formation research

1 Introduction
2 Morphological building blocks and the internal structures of complex lexemes
3 Word-formation patterns
4 Approaches to word-formation research
5 Levels of analysis and description in word-formation research
6 Theoretical models of word-formation
7 Modelling dynamic aspects of word-formation: productivity and lexicalization
8 Conclusion
9 References

Abstract: The first article of this volume presents an introductory survey of the scope of word-formation research. It defines and demarcates the subject-matter of word-formation and explains the basic notions related to the internal structures of complex lexemes and the cross-linguistically important word-formation patterns. Major approaches, analytical and descriptive levels and models in the field of word-formation research are outlined from a bird's eye view. The final section deals with productivity and lexicalization.

1 Introduction

Word-formation research investigates the patterns and regularities underlying the formation of complex lexemes by means of existing building blocks with the aim of formulating rules and other types of generalizations. Complex lexemes (e.g., E. *headteacher* or *trivialize*) are characterized by the fact that they consist of two or more constituents. Unlike most simple lexemes such as *head, teach* and *trivial*, complex lexemes are not entirely arbitrary signs, but instead are morphologically motivated by their constituents and by the semantic links shared with other structurally identical formations. A precise understanding of the nature of this motivation forms the main interest of word-formation research.

The scope of word-formation research in linguistics can be defined by demarcating word-formation from neighbouring fields. The adjacent domain of inflectional morphology deals with elements and operations which produce word-forms

Hans-Jörg Schmid, Munich, Germany

https://doi.org/10.1515/9783111420561-001

of lexemes (e.g., *teaches, teaching, taught*) rather than new lexemes (*teacher, head-teacher, to teamteach*, etc.), as is the case in word-formation. Word-formation and inflectional morphology are not separated by a clear boundary, however (Bybee 1985; Scalise 1988; Plank 1994; Booij 2000 and Stump 2005). A classic example of a delimitation problem is the dispute over whether the English adverb-forming suffix *-ly* as in *really* or *elegantly* should be treated as a derivational, i.e. lexical, or inflectional and thus grammatical morpheme (cf. Giegerich 2012). Syntax, while having emerged as a prominent source of inspiration for theory-building in word-formation, differs from word-formation in that the output of syntactic operations is phrasal and clausal rather than lexical in nature. Needless to say, boundary issues exist as well, e.g., in the distinction of certain types of nominal compounds from noun phrases (e.g., Benveniste 1967; Bauer 1988a and Olsen 2000). Demarcation problems are also very common at the porous boundary to phraseology, for instance when it comes to classifying semi-idiomatic phrases such as *black market* or particle verbs of the type *get up* and *make up for* (see articles 16 on particle-verb formation and 17 on multi-word expressions). Many practitioners of word-formation research distinguish word-formation (in a narrow sense) from ways of extending the lexical resources which do not involve changes in the forms of linguistic signs, mainly metaphorical or metonymic transfers and other forms of lexical change resulting in purely semantic extensions or shifts. Finally, as suggested by the definition given above, *word-formation* can be, but is not always, distinguished from what is referred to as coinage (Lieber 2010: 51), word-creation or word manufacture (Bauer 1983: 239), which does not rely on existing building blocks (see article 19 on word-creation). Frequently quoted examples include product and brand names such as *Kodak* or *Google*.

The subject-matter of word-formation research is also demarcated by the definition provided above. Essentially, four aspects define the remit of word-formation research.

Firstly, word-formation research analyses and describes the internal structures and constituents of complex lexemes and identifies and classifies the forms and meanings of the lexical and morphological building blocks of a given language (see article 9 on units of word-formation). As a part of this segmentation, identification and classification procedure, the lexical building blocks involved in word-formation must be distinguished from inflectional morphemes (see article 8 on the delimitation of derivation and inflection). The results of analytical and classificatory efforts feed into models of word-formation processes.

Secondly, word-formation research identifies, classifies and models the processes underlying the formation of existing and new complex lexemes. This is typically accomplished by segmenting established complex lexemes and describing their grammatical, morphological, semantic and phonological properties as well as those of their constituents. While most researchers in the field agree on a set of basic types of word-formation processes, there has been considerable controversy over the precise way in which they should be modelled.

Thirdly, because of the multifaceted nature of complex lexemes, word-formation research tends to be a multi-level (Lipka 1983) or multi-perspectival endeavour. Traditionally, morphological, syntactic, semantic and phonological aspects have taken centre stage in word-formation research, as these perspectives provide the basis for systematic and parsimonious generalizations regarding word-formation rules and patterns. More recently, sociopragmatic, psycholinguistic, cognitive and textual aspects have been attracting increasing interest (see article 7 on word-formation in psycholinguistics and neurocognitive research).

Fourthly, word-formation research tries to provide adequate models of the creative and dynamic aspects of word-formation. On the level of word-formation rules and patterns, this relates to the changing productivity of word-formation processes and the elements involved in them. On the level of individual complex lexemes, an explanation must be found for how new creations are motivated, how they find their way into the lexicon of a language and how their forms and meanings change in the course of time.

As regards the terminology used to refer to the core interest of word-formation research, the terms *word-formation process*, *word-formation type*, *word-formation model*, *word-formation rule* and *word-formation pattern* will be used interchangeably here, even though they highlight different aspects of the phenomena at hand and have been defined in more specific ways by some authors (e.g., Fleischer and Barz 2012: 67–69; Hansen et al. 1990: 28).

Section 2 of this article will be devoted to the morphological building blocks and internal structures of complex lexemes. Section 3 will provide a survey of cross-linguistically important word-formation patterns. The next three sections will discuss different approaches to word-formation research (section 4), survey the linguistic perspectives included in word-formation research (section 5) and provide a sketch of the major types of theoretical models attempting to capture the nature of word-formation rules and patterns (section 6). Section 7 will focus on research into the temporal and dynamic aspects of word-formation, i.e. the productivity of word-formation patterns and the types of changes that take place as complex lexemes are coined, spread and become part of the lexicon.

2 Morphological building blocks and the internal structures of complex lexemes

Three basic approaches to describing the constituents of complex lexemes can be distinguished: a word-based, a root-based and a morpheme-based approach (see article 9 on units of word-formation).

The first type proceeds from the assumption that words constitute the cores of complex lexemes. Word-formation rules combine several words in the case of compounding, and words and affixes in derivation. This assumption is known as the word-based hypothesis (Aronoff 1976: 21; Scalise 1986: 40–42, 71–78).

In the second approach, roots or stems, rather than full-fledged words, are considered the key constituents of complex lexemes. Terminology is far from uniform in this area, especially regarding the term *stem* (see Chelliah and de Reuse 2011: 314 for a survey). This notion is sometimes used to refer to the base of a word-formation process, i.e. the element to which further morphological material is added, and sometimes to the part which remains constant before inflectional endings are added (Bauer 1988b: 11). According to the first interpretation, *national* would be the stem of (*the company was*) *nationalized*, and according to the second, *nationalize*. To keep these readings apart, some authors (e.g., Hansen et al. 1990: 41) distinguish the *word stem* of a lexeme, *qua* word-form minus inflectional affix, from the *word-formation stem*, i.e. the base of the (final) word-formation process. Whether words or stems are more useful as basic units of word-formation research may well depend on the language being investigated (Bloomfield 1933: 224–226; Kastovsky 1999).

The third approach relies on the notion of morpheme (Baudouin de Courtenay 1895: 10), usually defined as the smallest meaning-bearing units of words (Bloomfield 1926: 155). Morphemes are classified with regard to their distributional properties into (potentially) free morphemes and (obligatorily) bound morphemes, and with regard to their function into grammatical morphemes and lexical morphemes. In English word-formation research (see article 9 on units of word-formation for traditions in other languages), free lexical morphemes, also known as root morphemes, are considered to correspond to simple lexemes (e.g., *hand*, *great*, *eat*); bound grammatical morphemes correspond to inflectional endings, e.g., {genitive -s}, {past tense -ed}, marking word-forms for case, number, tense, etc. Bound lexical morphemes are derivational affixes used for the purpose of word-formation (e.g., *un-*, *-ment*); free grammatical morphemes are function words such as *of*, *to* or *the*, which are orthographically autonomous, serve grammatical functions and are synsemantic rather than autosemantic. Morphemes are theoretical constructs abstracting commonalities over morphs, which are often regarded as perceptible physical events realizing morphological building blocks in actual speech or writing (see article 9 for a critique of this view).

While the notion of morpheme has proved useful for the description of basic constituents of complex lexemes, demarcation problems are rampant, with regard to both the identification of morphemes as such and the classification of morphemes into lexical vs. grammatical and free vs. bound morphemes. The general properties of morphemes are reviewed by Mugdan (1986) and Luschützky (2000), see also article 9 on units of word-formation. Prototypical lexical morphemes, which lie at the heart of word-formation research, have to meet the following morpheme- and lexeme-related criteria:

a) Identifiability: It must be possible to describe each of the potential morphemes precisely in terms of their extent and form and the corresponding meanings.
b) Exhaustive segmentability of complex lexemes into morphemes: It must be possible to segment a given complex lexeme exhaustively into morphemes and other clearly identifiable non-meaning-bearing elements such as linking elements (as in G. *Notenständer* 'music stand' ← {note} + *n* + {ständer}).
c) Autonomy of at least one constituent: Every complex lexeme must consist of at least one free lexical morpheme.
d) Compositionality of complex lexemes: It must be possible to trace the meaning of the complex lexeme back to the meanings of the morphemes.

In practical applications problems tend to arise with regard to all four criteria, resulting in the postulation of different types of pseudo-morphemic, quasi-morphemic or sub-morphemic units (cf. Kubrjakova 2000 and article 9). One notorious challenge are English verbs of Romance origin such as *insist, persist* and *resist* or *ascribe, prescribe* and *subscribe* which suggest an analysis in terms of a prefix (*a-, in-, per-, pre-, re-* and *sub-*) and a stem (*-sist* or *-scribe*). Such an analysis runs into difficulties with criteria a), c) and d), because, at least from a synchronic point of view, it is neither possible to ascribe a meaning to the potential stems *-sist* and *-scribe* nor are these stems free morphemes; as a result, compositionality is also violated. The term *bound root* has been introduced to capture such meaning-bearing units. Neoclassical compounds such as *biology* or *bibliography*, which are found in most European languages, cause partly similar problems. While their parts – *bio-, biblio-, -logy* and *-graphy* – seem to carry identifiable lexical meanings, none of them are free forms, thus violating criterion c). In English and Romance linguistics, the terms *combining form* and *affixoid* have become established to describe this phenomenon; in German linguistics the term

Konfix (Schmidt 1987: 50) is commonly used. Typical lexical blends also defy descriptions in terms of morphemes, as they cause problems for all four criteria. The constituent units of blends, for example *br-* and *-unch* in the case of the classic *brunch*, are known as *splinters* (Lehrer 1996). Furthermore, the particles of English phrasal verbs (*give up, pass out*), German prefix and particle verbs (*beraten, anbahnen*) and similar multi-word lexical items also fall within the scope of morpheme-like building blocks of complex lexemes. The semantic contribution of these elements to the meaning of the multi-word unit is often opaque, however, so that criteria a) and d) are not met. The term *formative* has been suggested either to refer to such minimal units which lack an identifiable meaning, also including linking elements (G. *Fugenelemente*) (Kastovsky 1982: 70; Lipka 2002: 87), or as a superordinate term comprising both morphemes proper and semantically empty morphological building blocks (Bauer 1988b: 24; Bauer, Lieber and Plag 2013: 16). Finally, phonaesthemes (e.g., *fl-* in *flicker, flip, flap, flurry*) are non-arbitrary pairings of phoneme clusters and meanings (Firth 1964: 184–185). Their semantic significance is usually restricted to a limited range of words and their meanings do not go beyond sound-symbolic allusions and associations which are shared by a set of words but are quite difficult to pinpoint. The portions of words that remain when the phonaestheme is segmented do not carry meanings; as a result, the words are non-compositional.

The internal structures of complex lexemes are usually described not in terms of shallow, chain-like sequences of morphemes and morpheme-like elements but as hierarchical structures which follow the principle of binary branching of immediate constituents (cf., e.g., Booij 1977: 32; Lieber 1990: 80; Scalise 1984: 146–151) also prominent in syntactic theorizing. In addition, the right-hand head rule (Williams 1981) states that the two sister constituents on one level are not equipotent but related to each other in a determinans-determinatum (Marchand 1969) or modifier-head relation (cf. also Lieber 1992: 26–76). The determinatum or head is the semantically and, more importantly, grammatically dominant constituent, which is specified by the determinans or modifier.

To conclude this section, Figure 1.1 illustrates the most important concepts introduced here.

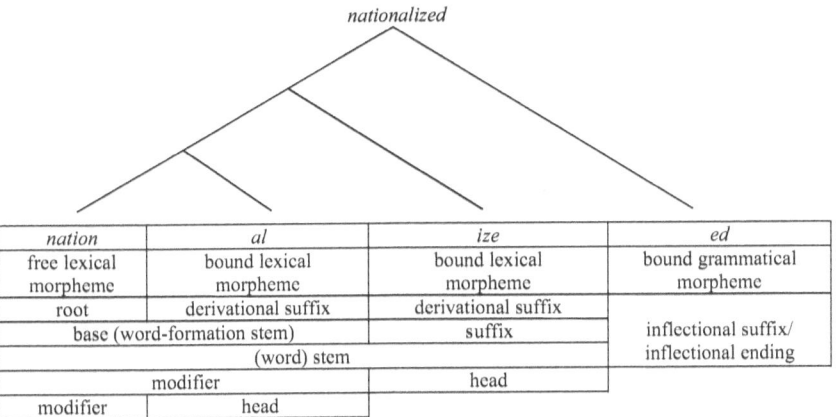

Fig. 1.1: Terms used for the description of the internal structures of complex lexemes.

3 Word-formation patterns

Figure 1.2 represents one of the most common ways of classifying the major types of word-formation patterns found in the languages of the world. While many other classifications are of course possible, depending, among other things, on the type of language and the individual researcher's aims and convictions, the key categories found in Figure 1.2 have proved adequate for the descriptions of the wide range of different languages.

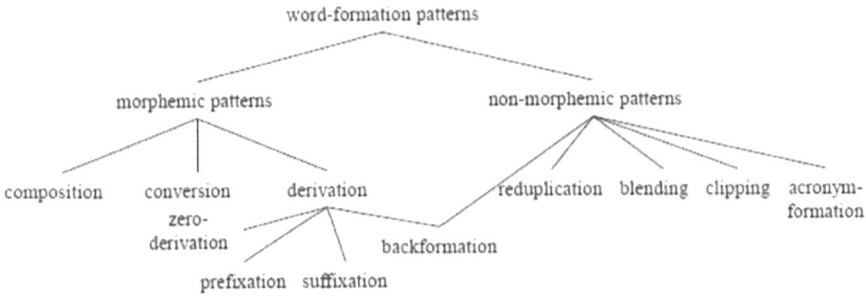

Fig. 1.2: Survey of word-formation patterns.

As all these types of patterns are discussed in greater detail and with reference to a large number of languages, it will suffice here to provide a general survey.

Composition, or compounding, is defined as the combination of (at least) two lexemes or words (Bauer 1988b: 33; article 14 on composition), or stems (Hansen et al. 1990: 43; Fleischer 2000: 889), or bases (Lieber 2010: 43), or free lexical morphemes (Schmid 2011). Many authors explicitly include bound roots or confixes – in addition to free lexical morphemes proper – as potential bases of compounds (Fleischer and Barz 2012: 84 and Plag 2003). Compounds are sub-classified in terms of their semantic structure into endocentric and exocentric compounds, with the former being further divided into determinative and coordinative ones. As regards their forms, root compounds, consisting of only two free lexical morphemes, are distinguished from synthetic (verbal, verbal nexus) compounds, which include bound lexical morphemes (see article 14 on composition). Rules detailing the formation of compounds have to take the word-classes of their constituents into account, granting a prominent role to the head constituent, so that *blackbird* would be referred to as a nominal compound of the form Adj + N.

Derivation (see article 10 on derivation) is the process of adding an affix to a stem, or a bound lexical morpheme to a free one, in order to create a new lexeme. The main forms of derivation are prefixation or prefix-derivation, where the bound morpheme precedes the free one, and suffixation or suffix-derivation where the order is reversed. Rarer types not rendered in Figure 1.2 are infixation and circumfixation. In certain schools of word-formation research mainly in English studies (Marchand 1969; Kastovsky 1982; Hansen et al. 1990), zero-derivation or derivation by zero-morpheme is postulated as a further type of derivation producing new lexemes by the addition of a formally empty zero-morpheme. As indicated by its place in Figure 1.2, the process of backformation (see article 12) straddles the boundary between morphemic and non-morphemic word-formation patterns. In contrast to derivation by means of the addition of an affix, lexemes formed by backformation are the product of the deletion of a bound morpheme or morpheme-like element.

Roughly speaking, conversion (see article 11) is a word-formation process which transposes a lexeme to a new word class without the addition of an overtly marked suffix. As Valera (see article 11) puts it, "the form of the converted item does not change, while its inflectional potential, its syntactic function and its meaning do, such that the item displays inflectional, syntactic and semantic properties of a new word-class". Conversion and zero-derivation – as well as the concept of *paradigmatic derivation* used in work on word-formation in Polish; are essentially competing ways of making sense of the same phenomena. Where the converted item does not acquire the full range of inflectional possibilities (e.g., *the rich*), this is termed *partial conversion* by proponents of the conversion approach and *conversion* by those of the zero-derivation approach.

Morphemic word-formation processes make up the core of word-formation in the sense that they are to a large extent regular and predictable (in hindsight) and therefore amenable to generalizations couched in the format of rules or schemas (see section 7). Equipped with knowledge of such rules, no competent speaker of English who knows the verb *to tweet* will be surprised when confronted with a derived verb such as *to de-tweet*, as this is clearly a potential or possible word (Aronoff 1976: 17–19). The same kind of hindsight predictability does not apply to the group of non-morphemic processes listed in Figure 1.2, which are also known as minor word-formation types. In addition, these processes are more flexible and more creative, which causes difficulties when it comes to attributing a shared meaning to formations of a similar type.

Reduplication (see article 18) is a word-formation process which involves the repetition of a word, word-like element or part of a word either in unchanged form (e.g., *hush-hush*), with a different vowel (e.g., *hip-hop*) or a different consonant (e.g., *boogie-woogie*). Blending (see article 15) is a cover term for a range of processes which, like composition, combine (at least) two lexemes, but, unlike composition, also fuse their forms by either shortening one or both of the input lexemes or by telescoping them into each other at portions where their forms overlap. Unlike all other word-formation processes, clipping and acronym-formation (see article 13) both preserve the denotative meanings of the source lexemes. Both are form-shortening processes only. Clipping, the deletion of initial and/or final portions of words, can be applied to single words, while acronyms, with some variation, are created by deleting everything but initial letters of two-word or longer expressions. Some researchers distinguish between acronyms in a narrow sense, which can be pronounced like normal words, and initialisms, pronounced as series of individual letters.

Needless to say, the description of different word-formation models and the analysis of individual complex lexemes do not stop at this level of granularity. More specific descriptions from a structural perspective tend to consist of at least six types of information. These are illustrated by English deverbal nominalizations in Table 1.1.

Textual, pragmatic and sociolinguistic aspects related to characteristics of the use and frequency of word-formation patterns in different text types and with different functions can complement this information.

Tab. 1.1: Parameters for the description of complex lexemes (inspired by Fleischer and Barz 2012: 73–74).

parameter	exemplified for English deverbal nominalization in *-(a)tion*
a) general morphological properties of the constituents	base: – word-class: transitive verbs, e.g., *explain, combine, describe* – morphological status: free lexical morpheme affix: – morphological status: bound lexical morpheme, suffix – form: *-(a)tion*
b) order of constituents	– base – suffix
c) formal and semantic characteristics of the process	– formal description: [V + *-(a)tion*]$_N$ – semantic description: 'process or product of V-ing'
d) various other characteristics and effects of the complex lexemes generated by the process, especially phonological and graphological ones, sometimes depending on the specific characteristics of the input	– stress movement and vowel change, e.g., /ɪksˈpleɪn/ > /ɛkspləˈneɪʃn/ – possible insertion of <a> /eɪ/ before <tion> /ʃn/
e) restrictions on the nature of the input and on the applicability of the process	– generally not applicable to English words of Germanic origin, cf. *hear* > **hearation*, *eat* > **eatation*
f) degree of productivity	– fully productive, especially in formal contexts

4 Approaches to word-formation research

The study of word-formation has been approached from a variety of angles. Some of these are shared by other linguistic disciplines, while others are specific to word-formation research or manifested in specific forms.

As in other fields of linguistics, we can distinguish between historical approaches and those which investigate the present-day language in its current state. Historical investigations can be carried out in a diachronic manner (cf. Kastovsky 2009) or in a synchronic one. What is specific to word-formation research is that there is always a latent diachronic element in synchronic descriptions, because the very idea that complex lexemes are the products of a formation process actually entails a dynamic perspective (see article 10 on derivation).

While a synchronic description can in principle rely solely on observing paradigmatic relations between words sharing the same apparently productive elements, complex lexemes, much more obtrusively than unmotivated simple lexemes, evoke the impression that they are the effects of a process (cf. Hansen et al. 1990: 31–32).

As in all fields of linguistic inquiry, typological word-formation research compares different languages with the aim of identifying similarities and differences or producing a universally valid description of word-formation in language as such.

Word-formation research has been carried out from a semasiological perspective, which has been the dominant one, but also from an onomasiological one (e.g., Štekauer 1998, 2005). Semasiological investigations aim to describe the structures and meanings of complex lexemes and word-formation patterns. In doing so, they start out from an examination of existing complex lexemes – e.g., *explanation, combination, description* – which share the same morphological structure and are therefore hypothesized, at least metaphorically speaking, to share a common formation history (roughly [V + (a)tion]$_N$). Therefore, it is the analytical aspect of a hearer or reader confronted with a complex lexeme – or indeed the linguist trying to discover structural generalizations – that comes to the fore in semasiological approaches. The complementary onomasiological perspective takes into consideration the fact that competent speakers are not only able to segment complex words into their constituents, but also use the results of such analyses for their own generative potential to create new words. The onomasiological perspective reflects speakers' states of mind while trying to encode a given conceptualization by means of applying a word-formation model. What, for instance, are the speaker's choices when aiming to encode the result of an action by deriving a noun from a verb: -ation as in *transformation* ← *transform*; -ment as in *achievement* ← *achieve*; -ence as in *existence* ← *exist*; -ing as in *painting* ← *paint*; -al as in *denial* ← *deny*; -age as in *blockage* ← *block*? The onomasiological approach thus corresponds to the synthetic aspect of word-formation. The semasiological and the onomasiological approaches differ in terms of their potential to be applied for descriptive purposes. Due to the virtually unlimited range of meanings that can be expressed by means of compounds, especially root compounds, the semasiological perspective has been dominant in this field. Systematic descriptions of prefixation and suffixation can, in principle, be arranged from a semasiological angle, by providing the meanings associated with the different prefixes and suffixes depending on the types of bases, or from an onomasiological one, by listing, for example, the prefixes that encode negation, location or time, or the suffixes that turn verbs into person-denoting nouns.

5 Levels of analysis and description in word-formation research

Due to its position at the interface or crossroads of many different aspects of language, word-formation research potentially includes the full range of linguistic levels, from phonetics and phonology to syntax, semantics, pragmatics and sociolinguistics.

Morphological considerations related to the constituents of complex lexemes and the formation rules and schemas naturally form the core of word-formation research, since a solid understanding of the composition of complex lexemes and their internal structures is required for all other levels of investigation (see article 9 on units of word-formation). Semantic aspects are of key importance not only for the internal segmentation and structural analysis of complex lexemes, but also for describing the semantic links between constituents and the semantic characteristics of word-formation processes and patterns such as compounding or derivation. Phonetic, phonological and morphonological aspects are equally important from a descriptive, an analytical and a heuristic perspective. In the field of derivation, for example, it is crucial to understand and model regularities regarding stem allomorphy, e.g., systematic changes in the stress patterns and vowel qualities of bases and derivatives, as, for example, in English *explain* → *explanation* or *sane* → *sanity* (see article 10 on derivation). Stress is also considered a diagnostic for compound status in English and other languages (cf. Bauer 1988a; Giegerich 2009). Syntactic aspects of word-formation came into focus with attempts to transfer insights from syntactic structures and rules to the internal grammar of words in early generative grammar (see article 5 on word-formation in generative grammar). They also provide important insights into word-class-specific restrictions on word-formation rules and their productivity (cf. Plag 1999).

The remaining levels to be mentioned here hold a less traditional position in word-formation research. This does not mean that they are less important, however. Over the past two or three decades, psycholinguistic and neurolinguistic research has greatly enriched the field of word-formation research by probing the extent to which models of word-formation are realistic and plausible from a psychological and neuronal perspective (see article 7). Questions that have been addressed from this perspective include the way in which novel and lexicalized complex lexemes, especially compounds, derivations and blends, are represented in the mind and the brain, and how they are processed in actual usage (e.g., Libben and Jarema 2006; Schmid 2008). More recently, the cognitive-linguistic perspective focusing on the way in which knowledge of word-formation models and schemas as well as of individual complex lexemes becomes entrenched and is influenced by general cognitive abilities such as categorization and figure-ground segregation has gained in importance (cf., e.g., Ungerer 2002 and 2007; Heyvaerts 2003 and 2009; Onysko and Michel 2010; Schmid 2011). The sociolinguistic perspective looking at word-formation in diverse regional and social varieties (e.g., Biermeier 2008; Braun 2009) and the pragmatic perspective (Downing 1977; Bauer 1979; Clark and Clark 1979; Schmid 2011) highlighting interactional contexts and communicative functions in actual usage-events have also been gaining momentum in the field of word-formation research. This includes the study of lexical creativity in various registers and text-types (Munath 2007) involving a text-related and discourse-related perspective.

6 Theoretical models of word-formation

The articles of this handbook present models of word-formation proposed in different theoretical frameworks, ranging from the historical-comparative tradition to generative grammar, and construction grammar. As one would expect, in each case word-formation is modelled in line with the aims and assumptions typical of the corresponding approaches to linguistics in general. While categorial grammar and generative grammar focus on formal aspects of word-formation, natural morphology, optimality theory, cognitive grammar and construction grammar take a functional stance. As generative grammar favours a modular architecture of language (see article 5), a key issue has been to clarify whether word-formation belongs to syntax or to the lexicon or is an interface or even a module in its own right. Construction grammar (see article 6), on the other hand, favours a holistic conception of word-formation processes which unites morphological, syntactic, semantic, cognitive and even pragmatic aspects.

Supporters of the various theoretical models advocate very different conceptions of how word-formation processes are to be modelled. A frequently quoted early classification of these conceptions was proposed by Hockett (1954), who distinguished between three types of models: item and arrangement, item and process, and word and paradigm. The first approach aims to describe the patterns of word-formation starting out from listing morphemes and describing "the arrangements in which they occur relative to each other in utterances" (Hockett 1954: 212). Secondly, item and process models, as suggested by the term, highlight the procedural aspects of word-formation; they regard the root, rather than the morpheme, as the basic input to morphological processes. Thirdly, word and paradigm models, which tend to focus on inflectional rather than derivational morphology, consider unsegmented words as the basic unit of word-formation and try to disclose paradigmatic similarities by comparing them.

Moving to the present state of the art, the range of current theories which aim to model word-formation patterns and processes can be broadly divided into four types of approaches:
- rule-based models
- schema-based models
- exemplar-based models
- exemplar-cum-schema-based models

The most prominent representatives of rule-based models are the different variants of generative approaches. Much of the research carried out in this framework is concerned with devising general rules applying across different word-formation types as well as type-specific rules or rule schemas, as they are called, in such a way that they can account for the empirical facts largely gleaned from introspection. The precise way in which these rules have been formulated has changed in line with the different stages of generative grammar: transformations and rewriting rules expressed in analogy to the phrase-structure rules of early generative grammar (Chomsky and Halle 1968; Selkirk 1982) were followed by applications of X-bar-theoretical principles (e.g., Scalise 1986) and sets of projection rules compatible with the government-and-binding and the principles-and-parameters approaches (see article 5 on word-formation in generative grammar and Lieber and Mugdan 2000 for more details). What rule-based approaches share is their focus on structural and formal rather than semantic or functional aspects, their commitment to the modularity assumption, giving rise to the need to identify the place where word-formation is situated in the architecture of language and linguistic knowledge, and their goal to formulate maximally generalizable insights and predictions.

Well-known general hypotheses that have been postulated for the field of word-formation include, next to the binary-branching hypothesis and the right-hand head rule already mentioned, the unitary base hypothesis (Aronoff 1976: 47–48; Scalise 1984: 137–146) and the unitary output hypothesis (Scalise 1984: 137), both of which have turned out to be problematic, however. The former states that the syntactic and semantic properties of the bases of derivational rules are clearly specified and unique, which implies that affixes cannot be attached to words of different word-classes. The latter states that affixes must be functionally and semantically unitary in the sense that they cannot be attached to different word-classes and bring about different changes in meaning. In both cases, potential empirical counter-evidence has been dealt with by maximizing the homonymy of affixes. This means, for instance, that the form *-able* in the deverbal adjective *manageable* and the denominal adjective *marriageable* (Bauer, Lieber and Plag 2013: 635–636) and the form *-ese* in the noun *Japanese* and the adjective

Japanese would each have to be considered as two different but homonymic affixes.

As a concrete example of the rule-based approach to describing individual word-formation models, the rule schema proposed by Aronoff (1976: 63) for English adjectival prefixation with *un-* is provided in (1).

(1) *"Rule of negative un#*
    a. $[X]_{Adj} \rightarrow [un\#[X]_{Adj}]_{Adj}$
       semantics (roughly) un#X = not X
    b. Forms of the base
       1. $X_V$en (where *en* is the marker for the past participle)
       2. X_V#ing
       3. $X_V$able
       4. X+y (worthy)
       5. X+ly (seemly)
       6. X#ful (mindful)
       7. X#like (warlike)"
    (Aronoff 1976: 63; original italics)

The endeavours of schema-based models are also directed towards reaching generalizations, but these are not couched in the form of rules, but are instead formulated in terms of (constructional) schemas (see article 6 on construction grammar). These are defined as schematic form-meaning pairings representing lexical and phrasal knowledge and sanctioning concrete uses of complex lexemes. While rules are essentially variable procedural instructions, schemas are unit-like elements containing variable slots (Booij 2010: 41–43). In this way, schemas account for productivity and analyzability as well as creativity in word-formation. Schemas are considered to be connected by formally and semantically motivated hierarchical relations, yielding multi-dimensional networks of schemas and sub-schemas arranged on several levels of specificity (Ryder 1994; Tuggy 2005: 248–264). Schemas on lower levels inherit information from superordinate schemas. In contrast to rule-based approaches, schema-based models subscribe to a holistic, non-modular conception of linguistic knowledge and therefore unite and integrate formal structural, semantic and functional aspects in their accounts of schemas. While rule-based models tend to keep up the strict separation of grammar and usage, schema-based models are compatible with usage-based approaches, which assume that linguistic knowledge emerges from the experience of concrete usage-events in social situations and is subject to the frequencies of occurrence of certain elements (cf., e.g., Kemmer 2003; Bybee 2010). Figure 1.3 provides an idealized

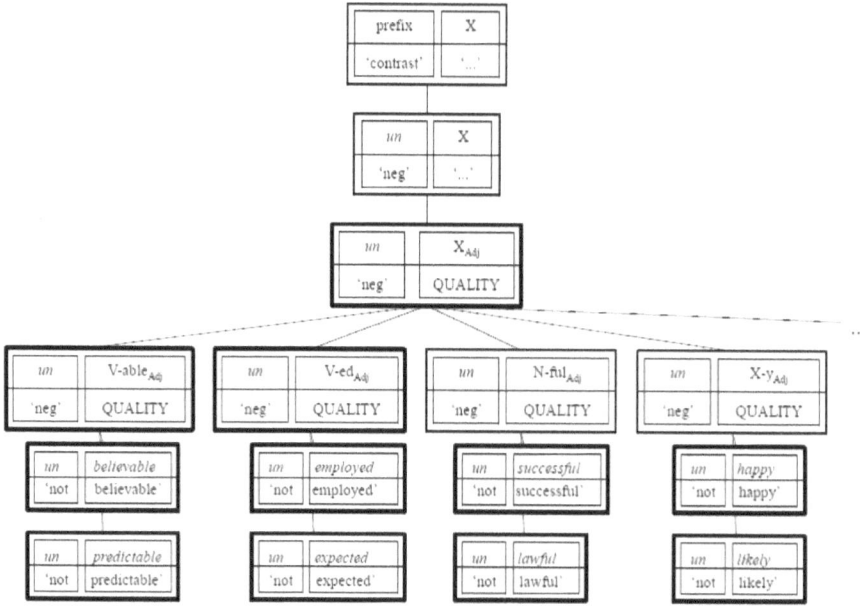

Fig. 1.3: Idealized illustration of a schema-based network for adjectival *un*-prefixation in English.

representation of a schema-based network for *un*-adjective formation inspired by Tuggy (2005) and Booij (2010).

In Figure 1.3, schemas are represented by boxes detailing formal properties above the dividing horizontal lines and meanings below them. Boxes indicate the status of symbolic units, with bolder boxes marking hypothetically more entrenched schemas. The top-level schema in Figure 1.3 represents the most general prefixation schema which is not specified with regard to the form and the meaning of the base. In line with Schmid (2011: 160–162), the meaning of the pattern of prefixation as such, i.e. across different prefixes and different word-classes of the base, is glossed as expressing a contrast to the base. The sub-schemas represent increasingly specific information, from *un*-prefixation applicable not only to adjectives but also verbs and nouns to adjectival *un*-prefixation, different types of *un*-adjectives and, finally, individual words sanctioned by these schemas.

Schema-based and exemplar-based models have more in common than rule-based and schema-based models. Like schema-based models, exemplar-based models (Krott, Schreuder and Baayen 2002; Eddington 2004: 71–98; Bybee 2010: 14–33; 165–193; Bybee and Beckner 2010; Arndt-Lappe 2011) conceive of lexical knowledge and knowledge about word-formation processes in terms of associa-

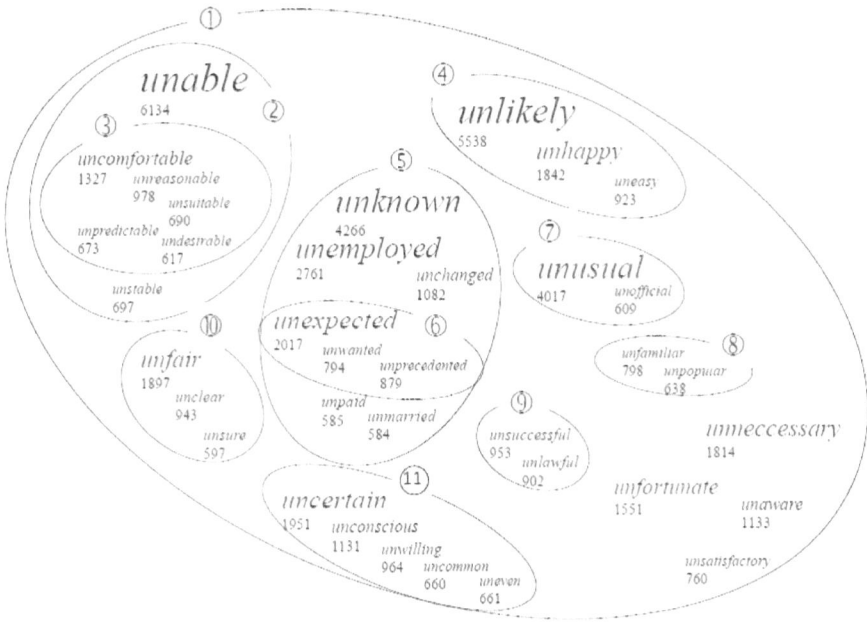

Fig. 1.4: Idealized schema-cum-exemplar-based network representation of English adjectival *un*-prefixation
(Clusters: (1) *un*-Adj; (2) *un-X-able* (various morphological structures); (3) *un-V-able*; (4) *un*-Adj(-*y*) (various morphological structures); (5) *un*-V-D$_2$ (various allomorphs of D$_2$); *un*-V-D$_2$, only /ɪd/ allomorph; (7) *un*-N(-*al*); (8) *un-X-al* (various morphological structures); (9) *un*-N-*ful*; (10) *un*-Adj(monosyllabic); (11) *un*-Adj(bisyllabic, '--').

tive networks that are continuously reorganized under the influence of usage and exposure. The main difference between the two approaches is that strong versions of exemplar-based approaches, especially connectionist ones (e.g., Skousen 1992; Skousen, Lonsdale and Parkinson 2002), deny the existence of symbolic representations such as schemas and assume that linguistic knowledge is only available in the form of representations of individual exemplars stored under the impression of specific usage events. In theory at least, the structures of exemplar-based networks are much more complex than those of schema-based ones, since the nodes are individual exemplars related by means of similarity relations, ideally on all possible levels of description, i.e. meaning, morphological form and phonological form. The structure of networks – in terms of the strengths of nodes and the links between them – is considered to be influenced by probabilistic information extracted from the frequencies of exemplars. Instead of rules or schemas, analogies based on similarities are considered to play the key role of motor and motivation for productive and creative processes.

Some network models (e.g., Bybee 2010) try to reconcile characteristics of schema-based and exemplar-based models. They postulate the existence of schemas representing experience that has been abstracted from usage-events without denying the importance of exemplar-based knowledge and thus argue that multiple and redundant representations on different levels of schematicity co-exist, from general schemas all the way down to individual lexemes. This way, they accommodate the potential to form new complex lexemes both on the basis of productive schemas and also by means of analogical formations based on similarities to stored exemplars (Eddington 2006). Like pure exemplar-based models, such exemplar-cum-schema-based models keep track of usage frequencies of exemplars but have a more differentiated view of the effects of frequency of exposure. While token repetition is considered to reinforce the representation of exemplars, type repetition strengthens schemas sanctioning novel uses (Bybee 2010). Figure 1.4 takes up English adjectival *un*-prefixation once more and provides an exemplary and idealized fragment of an exemplar-cum-schema network indicating form-based clusters of exemplars which are candidates for schemas.

The figure renders information on frequency of occurrence of exemplars in terms of the size of lexeme labels and the frequencies of occurrence in the *British National Corpus*. Clusters are labelled with numbers and glossed in the figure caption. The lexemes not included in clusters are – at least in this illustrative fragment – only related to other exemplars by the very general commonality of *un*-Adj. It should be noted that since exemplar-based networks are multi-dimensional, the figure mirrors only one of a large number of aspects contributing to the coherence of the network.

7 Modelling dynamic aspects of word-formation: productivity and lexicalization

As noted in section 4, word-formation research has an intrinsic dynamic element, since the very notion of word-formation itself evokes the image of a process. Two complementary types of observations reinforce the need to integrate dynamic aspects into word-formation research.

The first type is illustrated by words such as E. *depth*$_N$ (← *deep*$_{Adj}$) and *width*$_N$ (← *wide*$_{Adj}$) or G. *Fahrt*$_N$ 'act of driving, ride, journey' (← *fahren*$_V$ 'to drive') and *Naht*$_N$ 'seam' (← *nähen*$_V$ 'to sew'). While these words are morphologically analysable as bases and suffixes – E. -*th*$_{Adj}$ and G. -*t*$_N$ – it seems unlikely that new words with the help of these suffixes would be formed in present-day English or German, respectively. This suggests that these words were, at some time, formed by means of nominal suffixes for English deadjectival and German deverbal derivation which are no longer productive today.

In its most extreme form, the second type of observation concerns words that are known to be the result of a productive word-formation model but are no longer analysable from today's perspective. English *daisy* (← OE *dæges éage* 'day's eye') or *lord* (← OE *hláfweard* 'loaf keeper') are cases in point. The opacity of such words is usually due to long-term formal, i.e. morphological, phonological and orthographical changes. Semantic developments can bring about the similar, though less extreme effect that "a complex lexeme may be synchronically analysable but no longer motivated" (Lipka 2002: 95), either because the extra-linguistic denotata have changed (e.g., *cupboard*, *blackboard*) or because the meaning itself has undergone changes (e.g., *holiday*, lit. 'holy day').

Research into productivity involves two major facets: firstly, the measurement and description of degrees of the productivity of different word-formation models and patterns. Various attempts have been made to come up with dictionary-based (e.g., Plag, Dalton-Puffer and Baayen 1999) and corpus-based measures of productivity, taking into consideration the number of lexemes manifesting a pattern, i.e. type-frequency (Baayen 1989), the relation of hapax legomena to type frequency (Baayen and Lieber 1991), and the relation of hapaxes to types, while additionally taking into account the distinction between hapaxes that are just rare and hapaxes which are indeed novel formations relying on a pattern (Plag 2006: 542). Corpus-based measures can also be applied to investigate diachronic changes in the productivity of individual patterns (see Scherer 2005; Trips 2009; Schröder 2008, 2011) or of several patterns which are in onomasiological competition, e.g., *-ity* and *-ness* (cf. Gaeta and Ricca 2006; Baeskow 2012). The second major branch of research into productivity tries to provide maximally detailed descriptions of the general or pattern-specific limits or restrictions on productivity. For example, a wide-ranging and in fact somewhat trivial restriction on productivity is that there must be a communicative need for a potential formation. Pattern-specific restrictions can be morphological, semantic, phonological, syntactic and etymological in nature or derive from semasiological or onomasiological competition (blocking) of existing lexemes (Kastovsky 1982: 159–164; Rainer 2005). Recent web-based research (e.g., Schröder and Mühleisen 2010) has indicated that many productivity restrictions are tendencies rather than hard and fast rules.

Research in the field of the lexicalization of individual complex lexemes has been characterized by considerable variation in the choice of terms. Among the terms causing confusion are *lexicalization, institutionalization, idiomatization, conventionalization, diffusion, spread, propagation, listing* and *establishment* (cf. Brinton and Traugott 2005: 32–61). The term *lexicalization* itself, for example, has been conceptualized as "the process by which complex words come to have meanings that are not compositional" (Lieber 2010: 201), i.e. more or less synonymous with *idiomatization*; as "the strength of the lexical representation of a particular lexeme and its forms" (Bauer, Lieber and Plag 2013: 117), i.e. more or less synonymous with *entrenchment*; and by stating that "[w]hen a possible word has become an established word, we say that it has lexicalized" (Booij 2005: 17), i.e. in sociopragmatic terms. As this terminological diversity is partly caused by lumping together different levels of description, it seems desirable to separate these levels both conceptually and terminologically. Schmid (2011: 71–83) therefore proposes that the term lexicalization be reserved for the structure-oriented description of formal processes (fusion, reduction, erosion) and semantic processes (idiomatization) noticeable in the word itself. The sociopragmatic perspective focusing on how a given word spreads in the speech community is captured by the terms *institutionalization* and, more generally, *conventionalization*, while the cognitive perspective describing changes taking place in the mind, such as the strength of a unitary holistic representation or the density of the link to "neighbouring" words, is described in terms of degrees of entrenchment.

8 Conclusion

In keeping with the nature of the opening contribution to any handbook, this article can supply no more than a broad-brush survey of the main issues in word-formation research. In doing so, it aims to chart the terrain for the much more fine-grained explorations offered in the subsequent articles. As has been shown, one of the beauties and challenges of word-formation research is that its ramifications branch out onto all levels of linguistic analysis, description and theorizing. Recently, the field has been marked by an increasing awareness that speakers and writers use the productive and creative resources of their language in a much more flexible and variable manner than had been predicted by rigid and overly reductionist models. Doing justice to this flexibility while upholding the aim to produce valid generalizations could be one of the major challenges to be faced in future research into word-formation.

9 References

Aronoff, Mark (1976): *Word Formation in Generative Grammar.* Cambridge, MA: MIT Press.
Arndt-Lappe, Sabine (2011): Towards an exemplar-based model of stress in English noun-noun compounds. *Journal of Linguistics* 11: 549–585.

Baayen, R. Harald (1989): A corpus-based approach to morphological productivity: Statistical analysis and psycholinguistic interpretation. Ph.D. dissertation, Vrije Universiteit, Amsterdam.

Baayen, R. Harald and Rochelle Lieber (1991): Productivity and English word-formation. A corpus-based study. *Linguistics* 29: 801–843.

Baeskow, Heike (2012): *-Ness* and *-ity*: Phonological exponents of *n* or meaningful nominalizers of different adjectival domains? *Journal of English Linguistics* 40: 6–40.

Baudouin de Courtenay, Jan N. (1895): *Versuch einer Theorie phonetischer Alternationen*. Straßburg: Trübner.

Bauer, Laurie (1979): On the need for pragmatics in the study of nominal compounding. *Journal of Pragmatics* 3: 45–50.

Bauer, Laurie (1983): *English Word-Formation*. Cambridge: Cambridge University Press.

Bauer, Laurie (1988a): When is a sequence of two nouns a compound in English? *English Language and Linguistics* 2: 65–86.

Bauer, Laurie (1988b): *Introducing Linguistic Morphology*. Edinburgh: Edinburgh University Press.

Bauer, Laurie, Rochelle Lieber and Ingo Plag (2013): *The Oxford Reference Guide to English Morphology*. Oxford: Oxford University Press.

Benveniste, Émile (1967): Fondements syntaxiques de la composition nominale. *Bulletin de la Société de Linguistique de Paris* 62: 15–31.

Biermeier, Thomas (2008): *Word-formation in New Englishes. A corpus-based analysis*. Berlin: LIT.

Bloomfield, Leonard (1926): A set of postulates for the science of language. *Language* 2: 153–164.

Bloomfield, Leonard (1933): *Language*. London: Allen & Unwin.

Booij, Geert (1977): *Dutch Morphology. A Study of Word Formation in Generative Grammar*. Dordrecht: Foris.

Booij, Geert (2000): Inflection and derivation. In: Geert Booij, Christian Lehmann and Joachim Mugdan (eds), *Morphology. An International Handbook on Inflection and Word-Formation*. Vol. 1, 360–369. Berlin/New York: de Gruyter.

Booij, Geert (2005): *The Grammar of Words. An Introduction to Morphology*. Oxford: Oxford University Press.

Booij, Geert (2010): *Construction Morphology*. Oxford: Oxford University Press.

Braun, Maria (2009): *Word-Formation and Creolisation. The Case of Early Sranan*. Tübingen: Niemeyer.

Brinton, Laurel J. and Elizabeth Closs Traugott (2005): *Lexicalization and Language Change*. Cambridge/New York: Cambridge University Press.

Bybee, Joan L. (1985): *Morphology. A Study of the Relation between Meaning and Form*. Amsterdam/Philadelphia: Benjamins.

Bybee, Joan (2010): *Language, Usage and Cognition*. Cambridge/New York: Cambridge University Press.

Bybee, Joan L. and Clay Beckner (2010): Usage-based theory. In: Bernd Heine and Heiko Narrog (eds.), *The Oxford Handbook of Linguistic Analysis*, 826–855. Oxford: Oxford University Press.

Chelliah, Shobhana L. and Willem J. de Reuse (2011): *Handbook of Descriptive Linguistic Fieldwork*. Dordrecht: Springer.

Chomsky, Noam and Morris Halle (1968): *The Sound Patterns of English*. New York: Harper and Row.

Clark, Eve and Herbert H. Clark (1979): When nouns surface as verbs. *Language* 55: 767–811.

Downing, Pamela (1977): On the creation and use of English compound nouns. *Language* 53: 810–842.

Eddington, David (2004): *Spanish Phonology and Morphology. Experimental and Quantitative Perspectives*. Amsterdam/Philadelphia: Benjamins.

Eddington, David (2006): Spanish diminutive formation without rules or constraints. *Linguistics* 40: 395–419.

Firth, John R. (1964): *The Tongues of Men & Speech*. Oxford: Oxford University Press.
Fleischer, Wolfgang (2000): Die Klassifikation von Wortbildungsprozessen. In: Geert Booij, Christian Lehmann and Joachim Mugdan (eds.), *Morphology. An International Handbook on Inflection and Word-Formation*. Vol. 1, 886–897. Berlin/New York: de Gruyter.
Fleischer, Wolfgang and Irmhild Barz (2012): *Wortbildung der deutschen Gegenwartssprache*. 4th ed. Berlin/Boston: de Gruyter.
Gaeta, Livio and Davide Ricca (2006): Productivity in Italian word formation. A variable-corpus approach. *Linguistics* 44: 57–89.
Giegerich, Heinz J. (2009): Compounding and lexicalism. In: Rochelle Lieber and Pavol Štekauer (eds.), *The Oxford Handbook of Compounding*, 178–200. Oxford: Oxford University Press.
Giegerich, Heinz J. (2012): The morphology of *-ly* and the categorial status of 'adverbs' in English. *English Language and Linguistics* 16: 341–359.
Hansen, Barbara, Klaus Hansen, Albrecht Neubert and Manfred Schentke (1990): *Englische Lexikologie*. 2nd ed. Leipzig: Enzyklopädie.
Heyvaert, Liesbeth (2003): *A Cognitive-Functional Approach to Nominalization in English*. Berlin/New York: Mouton de Gruyter.
Heyvaert, Liesbeth (2009): Compounding in cognitive linguistics. In: Rochelle Lieber and Pavol Štekauer (eds.), *The Oxford Handbook of Compounding*, 233–254. Oxford: Oxford Univerity Press.
Hockett, Charles F. (1954): Two models of grammatical description. *Word* 10: 210–231.
Kastovsky, Dieter (1982): *Wortbildung und Semantik*. Düsseldorf: Bagel & Francke.
Kastovsky, Dieter (1999): English and German morphology. A typological comparison. In: Wolfgang Falkner and Hans-Jörg Schmid (eds.), *Words, Lexemes, Concepts – Approaches to the Lexicon. Studies in Honour of Leonhard Lipka*, 39–52. Tübingen: Narr.
Kastovsky, Dieter (2009): Diachronic perspectives. In: Rochelle Lieber and Pavol Štekauer (eds.), *The Oxford Handbook of Compounding*, 323–340. Oxford: Oxford Univerity Press.
Kemmer, Suzanne (2003): Schemas and lexical blends. In: Hubert Cuyckens, Thomas Berg, René Dirven and Klaus-Uwe Panther (eds.), *Motivation in Language. Studies in honor of Günter Radden*, 69–97. Amsterdam/Philadelphia: Benjamins.
Krott, Andrea, Robert Schreuder and R. Harald Baayen (2002): Analogical hierarchy: Exemplar-based modeling of linkers in Dutch noun-noun compounds. In: Royal Skousen, Deryle Lonsdale and Dilworth B. Parkinson (eds.), *Analogical Modeling*, 181–206. Amsterdam/Philadelphia: Benjamins.
Kubrjakova, Elena S. (2000): Submorphemische Einheiten. In: Geert Booij, Christian Lehmann and Joachim Mugdan (eds.), *Morphology. An International Handbook on Inflection and Word-Formation*. Vol. 1, 417–426. Berlin/New York: de Gruyter.
Lehrer, Adrienne (1996): Identifying and interpreting blends: An experimental approach. *Cognitive Linguistics* 7: 359–390.
Libben, Gary and Gonia Jarema (eds.) (2006): *The Representation and Processing of Compound Words*. Oxford: Oxford University Press.
Lieber, Rochelle (1990): *On the Organization of the Lexicon*. New York/London: Garland.
Lieber, Rochelle (1992): *Deconstructing Morphology. Word Formation in Syntactic Theory*. Chicago: Chicago University Press.
Lieber, Rochelle (2010): *Introducing Morphology*. Cambridge: Cambridge University Press.
Lieber, Rochelle and Joachim Mugdan (2000): Internal structure of words. In: Geert Booij, Christian Lehmann and Joachim Mugdan (eds.), *Morphology. An International Handbook on Inflection and Word-Formation*. Vol. 1, 404–416. Berlin/New York: de Gruyter.

Lipka, Leonhard (1983): A multi-level approach to word-formation. Complex lexemes and word semantics. In: Shirô Hattori and Kazuko Inoue (eds.), *Proceedings of the XIII*[th] *International Congress of Linguists, Tokyo 1982*, 926–928. Tokyo: The Committee.

Lipka, Leonhard (2002): *English Lexicology. Lexical Structure, Word Semantics and Word Formation.* Tübingen: Narr.

Luschützky, Hans Christian (2000): Morphem, Morph und Allomorph. In: Geert Booij, Christian Lehmann and Joachim Mugdan (eds.), *Morphology. An International Handbook on Inflection and Word-Formation.* Vol. 1, 451–462. Berlin/New York: de Gruyter.

Marchand, Hans (1969): *The Categories and Types of Present-Day English Word-Formation. A Synchronic-Diachronic Approach.* 2nd ed. München: Beck.

Mugdan, Joachim (1986): Was ist eigentlich ein Morphem? *Zeitschrift für Phonetik, Sprachwissenschaft und Kommunikationsforschung* 39: 29–43.

Munat, Judith (ed.) (2007): *Lexical Creativity, Texts and Contexts.* Amsterdam/Philadelphia: Benjamins.

Olsen, Susan (2000): Compounding and stress in English: A closer look at the boundary between morphology and syntax. *Linguistische Berichte* 181: 55–69.

Olsen, Susan (2014): Delineating Derivation and Compounding. In: Rochelle Lieber and Pavol Štekauer (eds.), *The Oxford Handbook of Derivational Morphology*, 26–49. Oxford: Oxford University Press.

Onysko, Alexander and Sascha Michel (eds.) (2010): *Cognitive Perspectives on Word-Formation.* Berlin/New York: Mouton de Gruyter.

Plag, Ingo (1999): *Morphological Productivity. Structural Constraints in English Derivation.* Berlin/New York: Mouton de Gruyter.

Plag, Ingo (2003): *Word-Formation in English.* Cambridge: Cambridge University Press.

Plag, Ingo (2006): Productivity. In: Bas Aarts and April McMahon (eds.), *The Handbook of English Linguistics*, 537–556. Oxford: Blackwell.

Plag, Ingo, Christiane Dalton-Puffer and Harald Baayen (1999): Morphological productivity across speech and writing. *English Language and Linguistics* 3: 209–228.

Plank, Frans (1994): Inflection and derivation. In: Ronald E. Asher (ed.), *Encyclopaedia of Language and Linguistics.* Vol. 3, 1671–1678. Oxford: Pergamon.

Rainer, Franz (2005): Constraints on productivity. In: Pavol Štekauer and Rochelle Lieber (eds.), *Handbook of Word-Formation*, 335–352. Dordrecht: Springer.

Ryder, Mary Ellen (1994): *Ordered Chaos. The Interpretation of English Noun-Noun Compounds.* Berkeley: University of California Press.

Scalise, Sergio (1984): *Generative Morphology.* Dordrecht: Foris.

Scalise, Sergio (1986): *Generative Morphology.* Berlin/New York: de Gruyter.

Scalise, Sergio (1988): Inflection and derivation. *Linguistics* 26: 561–581.

Scherer, Carmen (2005): *Wortbildungswandel und Produktivität. Eine empirische Studie zur nominalen -er-Derivation im Deutschen.* Tübingen: Niemeyer.

Schmid, Hans-Jörg (2008): New words in the mind: Concept-formation and entrenchment of neologisms. *Anglia* 126: 1–36.

Schmid, Hans-Jörg (2011): *English Morphology and Word-formation. An Introduction.* Berlin: Schmidt.

Schmidt, Günter Dietrich (1987): Das Affixoid. Zur Notwendigkeit und Brauchbarkeit eines beliebten Zwischenbegriffes der Wortbildung. In: Gabriele Hoppe, Alan Kirkness, Elisabeth Link, Isolde Nortmeyer, Wolfgang Rettig and Günter Schmidt (eds.), *Deutsche Lehnwortbildung. Beiträge zur Erforschung der Wortbildung mit entlehnten WB-Einheiten im Deutschen*, 53–101. Tübingen: Niemeyer.

Schröder, Anne (2008): Investigating the morphological productivity of verbal prefixation in the history of English. *Arbeiten aus Anglistik und Amerikanistik* 33: 47–69.

Schröder, Anne (2011): *On the Productivity of Verbal Prefixation in English. Synchronic and Diachronic Perspectives*. Tübingen: Narr.
Schröder, Anne and Susanne Mühleisen (2010): New ways of investigating morphological productivity. *Arbeiten aus Anglistik und Amerikanistik* 35: 43–58.
Selkirk, Elisabeth (1982): *The Syntax of Words*. Cambridge, MA: MIT Press.
Skousen, Royal (1992): *Analogy and Structure*. Dordrecht: Kluwer.
Skousen, Royal, Deryle Lonsdale and Dilworth B. Parkinson (eds.) (2002): *Analogical Modeling*. Amsterdam/Philadelphia: Benjamins.
Štekauer, Pavol (1998): *An Onomasiological Theory of English Word Formation*. Amsterdam/Philadelphia: Benjamins.
Štekauer, Pavol (2005): Onomasiological approach to word-formation. In: Pavol Štekauer and Rochelle Lieber (eds.), *Handbook of Word-Formation*, 207–232. Dordrecht: Springer.
Stump, Gregory T. (2005): Word-formation and inflectional morphology. In: Pavol Štekauer and Rochelle Lieber (eds.), *Handbook of Word-Formation*, 49–71. Dordrecht: Springer.
Trips, Carola (2009): *Lexical Semantics and Diachronic Morphology. The development of -hood, -dom and -ship in the history of English*. Tübingen: Niemeyer.
Tuggy, David (2005): Cognitive approach to word-formation. In: Pavol Štekauer and Rochelle Lieber (eds.), *Handbook of Word-Formation*, 233–265. Dordrecht: Springer.
Ungerer, Friedrich (2002): The conceptual function of derivational word-formation in English. *Anglia* 120: 534–567.
Ungerer, Friedrich (2007): Derivational morphology and word-formation. In: Dirk Geeraerts and Hubert Cuyckens (eds.), *The Oxford Handbook of Cognitive Linguistics*, 991–1025. Oxford: Oxford University Press.
Williams, Edwin (1981): On the notions of 'lexically related' and 'head of a word'. *Linguistic Inquiry* 12: 245–274.

Barbara Kaltz and Odile Leclercq

2 Word-formation research from its beginnings to the 19th century

1 Introduction
2 Greek and Roman antiquity
3 The German tradition (16th–19th century)
4 The French tradition (16th–19th century)
5 References

Abstract: In Greco-Latin grammatical theory as well as in the first grammars of European vernacular languages, word-formation was treated within the presentation of word classes. This article aims to show how specific theories of derivation and composition were progressively developed by grammarians of German and French.

1 Introduction

This article starts with a brief survey of research on word-formation in Greek and Roman antiquity (Aristarchus, Dionysius Thrax, Quintilian, Varro). The following sections treat theories developed in modern times by major grammarians of German (Schottelius, Adelung, Becker, Grimm, Paul) and French (Meigret, Arnauld and Lancelot, Beauzée, Butet de la Sarthe, Darmesteter). Our overall focus lies on salient aspects, such as the distinction between derivation and composition and the place of word-formation in grammatical theory.

2 Greek and Roman antiquity

The assumption that there are two basic processes of word-formation, derivation and composition, still widely held in contemporary linguistics (Lallot 2008: 63; McLelland 2010: 13), may be traced back to ancient Greek linguistic thought (Vaah-

Barbara Kaltz, Freiburg, Germany
Odile Leclercq, Aix-en-Provence, France

tera 1998: 60–76). Aristarchus's analysis of complex words in Greek is based upon the distinction between derivatives and compounds. The latter are formed by combining two or more autonomous words, the first by adding derivational suffixes (considered to be non-autonomous) to a word (Matthaios 1999: 254–272; summarized in Matthaios 2004: 16–20). This idea was later developed more fully by Dionysius Thrax (Τέχνη, ed. Lallot 1998). It must be stressed that ancient Greek grammarians did not view word-formation as a separate domain; rather, they treated it within the framework of word class theory, on the basis of categories describing properties ("accidents", e.g., number and gender) of word classes (Matthaios 2004: 8–9). Of these accidents, two are specific to word-formation, "εἶδος" [species] and "σχῆμα" [figure]. Both were attributed to various word classes; the most detailed description was made for the nominal class (Matthaios 2004: 11–16). The category species allows for a distinction between "primary" and "derived" lexical items, while figure is the basis for distinguishing "simple", "composed" and "decompound" words, the latter term designating nominal derivatives from compounds. (Greek grammarians used the term "parasyntheta", in Latin grammar this latter term was rendered as "decomposita"). This view of word-formation as part of word class theory, including the fundamental dichotomy composition – derivation, was then adopted by grammarians of classical Latin, who latinized the Greek terms pertaining to word-formation (e.g., "species primitiva"/"derivativa", "figura simplex"/"composita"/"decomposita"). A discussion of complex words in classical Latin is to be found in writings by Quintilian, Priscian, and Varro, among others (Fögen 2008; Lindner 2002). Classical and medieval Latin grammaticography (entitled "De partibus orationis") is characterized by a canonized system of "parts of speech" (word classes), word-formation is considered strictly within this framework, with a focus on derivation. In early modern times, this word class system in turn constituted the theoretical framework for the process of "grammatisation" (Auroux 1992: 11–64) of vernacular languages (Kaltz 2000: 693–698).

3 The German tradition (16th–19th century)

The development of word-formation theory in German grammaticography from the 16th to the 19th century may be briefly summarized as follows. In the first stage of the "grammatisation" process (16th–early 17th century), grammarians deal with derivation and composition strictly in terms of the categories "species" and "figura", defined as accidents of word classes of German (see section 3.1). 17th-century grammarians generally continue to present German word-formation within the section on word classes ("etymologia", "Wortforschung") though some (Ratke,

Schottelius) begin to conceive of word-formation as being a grammaticographical topic in its own right (see section 3.2). In the 18th century, theories of word-formation in German gradually gain more independence from the Latin tradition, particularly with Mäzke, Heynatz, and Adelung (see section 3.3). 19th-century linguists (Becker, Grimm, Paul, among others) contribute to further development and refinement of word-formation theory as a domain of its own (see section 3.4).

3.1 16th–early 17th century

Early grammars of German, mostly written in Latin (e.g., Albertus, Ölinger, Clajus) closely adhere to the conventions of Latin grammar. The focus is on derivation by "terminationes" ('endings') while authors of grammar books pay little attention to composition. Complex words formed by the addition of "praepositiones", i.e. either separable or inseparable prefixes, are analyzed as compounds, as are "decomposita", resulting from both prefixation and suffixation: "gerecht" ("figura simplex"), "ungerecht" ("figura composita"), "Ungerechtigkeit" ("figura decomposita"; Clajus 1894 [1578]: 43). Albertus occasionally refers to the notion of "radix" ("root"; 1573 [1895]: 66, 74); originally elaborated by grammarians of Hebrew, unknown to the tradition of Greek and Roman grammar (Kaltz 2005: 107–111), this notion was to become a key concept in Schottelius's theory (see section 3.2).

3.2 17th century

While the latinizing tradition is still present in early 17th-century German grammaticography (Padley 1985: 98; note 44), more grammarians now make use of the vernacular, for pedagogical reasons (e.g., Brücker 1620: 5; Ratke 1959 [1612–1615], 1959 [1630]) as well as ideological motives (legitimation of the German language; e.g., Schottelius 1641). In his *Wortbedeütungslehr* [Treatise on the meaning of words], Ratke redefines the traditional categories "Art" [species] and "Gestalt" [figura], arguing that derivation and composition are essential means by which the proper and necessary meaning of discourse is grasped ("wesentliche Mittel [...] darauß die Bedeütung der Rede eigentlich vnd nothwendig erkennet wird"; 1959 [1630]: 277). This work, "the first attempt to provide a semantically based theory of word derivation applied to the vernacular" (Padley 1985: 112), is also the first to deal with word-formation not just in the framework of "Wortforschung", but rather as a topic in its own right (Kaltz 2005: 113–116).

The central figure among 17th-century German grammarians is undoubtedly Schottelius (cf. Gützlaff 1989; McLelland 2010, 2011); he had a major impact on late 17th and early 18th-century grammaticography and lexicography (Kaltz 2005: 117–125). While Schottelius (1663) follows tradition by discussing derivation and composition within the section on word classes ("Wortforschung"), he also addresses the topic of word-formation separately. In three *Lobreden* [discourses of praise], he praises the German language for its abundance of "Stammwörter" or "Wurzelen" [root words], which are monosyllabic, he claims. This section of his grammar may be seen as the first attempt to describe the constituents of complex words in a somewhat systematic manner. Schottelius analyses both derivatives and compounds as being formed on the basis of root words (1663: 49–103); the first result from the addition of "Haubtendungen", i.e. derivative suffixes, which are now differentiated from inflectional ones ("zufällige Endungen"). The binary structure of compounds, formed by combining "Stammwörter" with suffixes, prefixes or other root words, is described by the terms "Beygefügtes/vorderstes Glied des Wortes" ([attributive/first element of the word]; i.e. determiner) and "Grund/Haubtglied" ([basis], [main element]; i.e. primary word; 1663: 75). According to Schottelius, there are four "Verdoppelungs=arten" [types of compounds] in German. The first class, formed by nouns only ("welche aus lauter Nennwörteren entstehet"; 1663: 77), includes determinative compounds as well as copulative ones (e.g., *Freudenpein*; 1663: 79); compounds of the structure "Nennwort + Zeitnennwort" (i.e. a deverbal noun) form the second (e.g., *Mordbrenner, Taglöhner*; 1663: 84). The third class assembles compounds formed by adding a preposition to verbs or nouns ("wan durch die Vorwörter (Praepositiones) die Verdoppelung geschiehet"; primarily verbs such as *erheirathen, einbrokken, vertieffen*, but nouns as well, e.g., *Gezisch, Gesäusel*; 1663: 88 f.) while combinations of one or two *Haubtendungen* with one or two root words constitute the last ("wan mit einem oder zweyen Stammwörtern eine oder zwo Haubtendungen der abgeleiteten verdoppelt werden", e.g., *weibisch, Jüngling, Hofnung, Gottseligkeit*; 1663: 90). Contrary to present-day linguistics, "Ableitung" [derivation] refers to suffixation only here (1663: 318) whereas the term "Verdoppelung" [composition] is used for composition proper and prefixation, and includes the formation of complex verbs with inseparable prefixes.

3.3 18th century

Among early 18th-century grammarians, Longolius is worth mentioning as he maintains the distinction between "Primitiva" [root words], "Derivativa", and "Composita" (also labelled "zusammengestückte Wörter"; 1715: 63) but rejects the idea of the monosyllabic nature of root words (1715: 617 f.). Following Schottelius, he considers the last word ("das letzte Wort") to be the main element ("Grund"), which is merely restricted and determined by the [word] added ("welchen das beygefügte nur gewisser Maaßen restringiret und determiniret"; 1715: 623). His analysis of nominal compounds, however, is somewhat more elaborate than that of Schottelius; in particular, Longolius notes that verb stems may be first constituents of nominal compounds: "Ein Teutsches Substantivum, das mit einem Verbo componiret ist/bedeutet eine Sache von einem Vermögen zu derjenigen Verrichtung/so besagtes Verbum anzeigen" [a German noun that is combined with a verb denotes the ability to perform the action referred to by the said verb], e.g., *Lockvogel, Heuchelchrist, Hakkebret* (1715: 623 f.). The term *Decomposita* is used here for complex compounds such as *Erzpfaffenfreund* and *stockpechdickfinster* (1715: 627).

Like his predecessors, Aichinger (1754) differentiates "Stammwörter" [root words] and "abstammende" [derivatives], "einfache" [simple words] and "zusammengesetzte" [compounds] (Kaltz 2005: 130); he also discusses the "Gattung" and "Gestalt" of complex words in the traditional manner as accidents of word classes (1754: 136 f., 157). Aichinger points out an essential difference between derivation and composition in German: "niemand [darff] leicht sich selber deriuativa schmieden, ausser den Dichtern" ([with the exception of poets, no one has the right to form derivatives]; 1754: 139); on the other hand, he notes that speakers of German have the liberty to create new compounds every day ("die Freyheit, alle Tage neue zusammengesetzte Wörter zu machen"; 1754: 104).

In the late 18th century, significant changes in the theory of word-formation occur as grammarians progressively turn away from the traditional perspective. Heynatz (1777 [1770]: 121) deserves special mention for his analysis of monosyllabic, non-suffixed deverbal derivatives such as *Druck, Schlag, Trieb*, while Mäzke (1776: 5 f.) criticizes the use of the traditional term "praepositiones inseparabiles" for inseparable German prefixes such as *be, er, ent* (Kaltz 2005: 132 f.). Adelung, the most interesting and most influential 18th-century grammarian of German, no longer argues in terms of "figura" and "species". Just as many linguists nowadays, he considers prefixation to be a type of derivation: "Die Ableitung der Wörter geschiehet entweder durch Vorsylben oder durch Nachsylben, oder durch beide zugleich" ([derivation of words occurs either by prefixes or suffixes, or both]; 1784: 97 f.). Derivatives are described in detail within the context of word class theory while composition is dealt with in a separate lengthy section (Adelung 1782: II, 209–274). Adelung stresses the special importance of compounds in German, noting that this has been a much neglected topic due to the excessive weight accorded to the Latin tradition (Kaltz 2002; 2005: 131). As some of his predecessors, he insists upon the binary structure of (determinative) compounds, including complex ones such as *Fastnachtspiel*, which he describes with the terms "Grundwort" [basic/primary word] and "Bestimmungswort" ([determiner]; 1782: II, 215), still commonly used in modern studies of word-formation in German. Copulative compounds (e.g., *Fürst=Bischof*), on the other hand, are analyzed as a type of apposition (Adelung 1782: II, 229).

3.4 19th century

Throughout the 19th century, word-formation was a much discussed topic in general grammar as well as in pedagogical (e.g., Becker 1831) and historical-comparative grammar (e.g., Grimm 1878 and article 3 on word-formation in historical-comparative grammar). Becker, who represents both general and pedagogical grammar (Jankowsky 2004; Forsgren 2008: 134–135), is the author of the first comprehensive study dealing exclusively with word-formation in German (*Deutsche Wortbildung*, 1824; Kaltz 2005: 136). The author establishes a distinction between "Begriffswörter" and "Formwörter" ([notional words] vs. [form words]) on the one hand, "Wurzelwort" [root word] and "abgeleitetes Wort" [derivative] on the other. There are two types of derivatives, "Stamm" ([primary form], e.g., *Bund*) and "Sproßform" ([secondary form], e.g., *bündig*). Composition, Becker argues, must be seen as "wahrhafter Ableitungsvorgang" ([true process of derivation]; Becker 1824: 369 f.) since compounds are new words for new concepts formed on the basis of existing linguistic material ("Stoff"), the same way as derivatives stricto sensu are formed by "Ablautung" [ablauting] and "Umendung" ([change of ending], [suffixation]). In other words, Becker uses "Ableitung" as the comprehensive term for both derivation and composition. The terms "Bestimmungswort" and "Grundwort", introduced by Adelung for the constituents of compounds, are reinterpreted by Becker: the first constituent of compounds is the principal one: "Hauptwort" [main word] whereas the second one is defined as "Beziehungswort" [relational word]. He does follow Adelung, however, as far as the principle of the binary structure of compounds is concerned, noting that it applies to complex compounds as well (e.g., *Nußbaum-holz, Schneider-handwerk, Herzbeutel-wassersucht*; Becker 1831: 45).

J. Grimm had a major impact on 19th- as well as early 20th-century grammar; in fact, he was perceived as the initiator of scientific word-formation theory: "Die wissenschaftliche Wortbildungslehre ist [...] eine Schöpfung J. Grimms" (Paul 1896: 17). Grimm starts out by observing that word-formation theory in particular has been unduly neglected in traditional grammar ("zumahl die wortbildungslehre [ist] ungebührlich verabsäumt worden"; 1878: VI). Word-formation, he argues, occurs "durch innere änderung oder durch äußere mehrung der wurzel" [through internal change or external addition to the root]. "Zusammensetzung" and "Ableitung" differ as follows: "Zusammensetzung kann vorne oder hinten an der wurzel eintreten, ableitung nur hinten" ([composition may occur by combining elements preceding or following the root, derivation by elements following the root only]; 1878: 1). In contrast to "innere wortbildung" ([internal word-formation]; 1878: 1), derivation (i.e. suffixation only) and composition are dealt with in great detail (Kaltz 2005: 144–146). Grimm's classification of compounds is based upon the distinction between "eigentliche" and "uneigentliche composition" ([proper]/[improper composition]; e.g., *wein-stock*, *gras-grün* vs. *tages-licht*; 1878: 386). In spite of his sharp criticism of traditional grammar, he does retain the term "decomposita" for both complex compounds (e.g., *schlafkammer-thürhüter*) and complex derivatives such as *un-absehlich* (1878: 383, 912). Similarly to Adelung, Grimm stresses the binary structure of determinative compounds (including "decomposita"; 1878: 912), but does not give much consideration to copulative compounds such as *christkind*, *tier-mensch* and *fürst-bischof*, which result from "appositionelle verhältnisse" ([appositional relations]; 1878: 416).

Grimm's theory of word-formation was later refined by Paul and other Neogrammarians ("Junggrammatiker"; Fleischer 1983). As his 18th-century predecessors Mäzke and Adelung, Paul insists that it is impossible to draw a sharp line between inflection, derivation, and composition: "Die Scheidelinie zwischen Kompositionsglied und Suffix kann nur nach dem Sprachgefühl bestimmt werden" ([linguistic intuition is the only way to decide between a compound constituent and a suffix]; 1880: 348); "auf die gleiche Weise wie die Ableitungssuffixe entstehen Flexionssuffixe. Zwischen beiden gibt es ja überhaupt keine scharfe Grenze" ([inflectional suffixes arise the same way as derivational suffixes. In fact, there is no sharp line separating both]; 1880: 349). While the focus is on morphological aspects here, Paul later argues that more consideration should be given to semantics in word-formation theory; when analyzing complex words, "Funktionen" [functions] representing meaning, not "Bildungsweisen" [word-formation types] ought to be the primary criterion (1896: 18). In his *Deutsche Grammatik* (1920), Paul further distances himself from Grimm by rejecting the categories of "proper" and "improper" composition for nominal compounds as they are motivated by morphological considerations. Instead, referring explicitly to the classification of compounds in Sanskrit grammaticography (Brocquet 2008: 19), he now argues that the logical relation between constituents as well as that between the compound as a whole and its constituents must be decisive when classifying compounds ("nach dem logischen Verhältnis der Glieder zueinander und des Ganzen zu den Gliedern"; 1920: 6). This principle leads him to differentiate three types of nominal compounds (Kaltz 2005: 150): a) "kopulative" or copulative compounds (e.g., *Prinzregent*, *Fürstbischof*; = "dvandva" in Indian grammar; 1920: 7), b) "solche, in denen das zweite Glied durch das erste bestimmt wird" [compounds in which the second constituent is determined by the first], such as *Senfsauce*, *Mit-*

bürger (1920: 9, 23), and c) "possessive Zusammensetzungen" or possessive compounds (e.g., *Lügenmaul, Rotkehlchen*; = the Indian "bahuvrihi"; 1920: 30). With respect to the place of word-formation, Paul notes that 19th-century grammarians have chosen various options: following "Flexionslehre" [theory of inflection] and preceding syntax (e.g., Grimm), or preceding the former. Paul argues that the status of inflectional suffixes may change as a result of processes of isolation and that their syntactic function changes as they become "Wortbildungssuffixe" [word-formation suffixes]. Compounds, on the other hand, result from syntactic structures. Therefore, he suggests that the most appropriate way is to discuss word-formation in a separate section, following syntax (1920: 3f.). In 20th-century German linguistics, the separate treatment of word-formation became predominant with the gradual shift from the historical perspective to the synchronic, though some grammarians still choose the traditional position by integrating word-formation into the description of the word class system (Kaltz 2005: 152).

4 The French tradition (16th–19th century)

The history of word-formation theories in France from the 16th to the 19th century may be summarized as follows. In the first grammars of French, written in Latin or French, word-formation is studied using the conceptual framework of Latin grammar. The richest developments on lexical morphology are undoubtedly to be read in the first grammar of French written in French, *Le Trętté de la grammęre françoęze* (Meigret 1980 [1550]) (see section 4.1). 17th-century grammarians of French no longer refer to the Latin categories of "espèce" [species] and "figure" [figure]. Even if the contrasts between primitive and derivative or between simple and compound are sometimes mentioned, general grammar assigns the task of dealing with derivation and composition to the dictionary (see section 4.2). Word-formation is then reintroduced into the field of grammar with Beauzée's theses. The encyclopaedist's approach to derivation and composition – based on the theory of the sign specific to general grammar – had a long-standing influence (see section 4.3). In the 19th century, word-formation theories are mostly developed outside the field of grammar, first and foremost in Darmesteter's works (see section 4.4).

4.1 16th century

From Sylvius's *Grammatica latino-gallica* (1531) to Ramus's *Grammaire* (1572), derivation and composition were regarded as word accidents, in compliance with the

Greco-Roman tradition, with the consequence that word-formation was integrated into grammar but had no real autonomy: it was included in the presentation of word classes. The species implies an opposition between "primitifs" and "dérivatifs" and corresponds to suffixal derivation whereas the figure opposes "simples" and "composés" and describes combinations of at least two words considered as autonomous words. Both the species and the figure are discussed along with the other word accidents – essentially morphosyntactic variations. The parts devoted to noun formation are by far the most developed and some elements pertaining to lexical morphology can also be read into the description of the category of "diminutif" [diminutive], traditionally dealt with separately from other suffixed derivatives. 16th-century grammarians pay variable attention to the species and the figure, most of them simply asserting the two dichotomies and exemplifying them. The processes of composition are sometimes studied more precisely. Estienne, for example, distinguishes three types of formations taken up from Donat (Colombat 1999: 243): two "whole words" ("mots entiers"; e.g., *malheur*), a "whole word" and a "corrupted word" ("mot corrompu"; e.g., *ennemi*), a "corrupted word" and a "whole word" (e.g., *chascun*; 1557: 17). Meigret, known for his interest in morphology (Glatigny 1985), added a fourth pattern based on the association of two corrupted words (e.g., *benivole*; 1980 [1550]: 49). But *Le Trętté*, which uses French as metalanguage for the first time, deals above all with derivation in long and detailed discussions in chapter 8 ("Des noms") and chapter 12 ("Des dénominatifs", that is to say proper nouns derived from nouns but nouns derived from verbs, for example, are addressed in the same chapter as well). Meigret attempts to identify different classes built, in particular, on semantico-referential categories: French derivatives can result from names of "affections et qualités" ([affections and qualities]; e.g., *fiévreux*), "arts et sciences" ([arts and sciences]; e.g., *mathématicien*), "chefs de disciplines et sectes" ([heads of disciplines and sects]; e.g., *platonique*), etc. But the classification is primarily organized around suffixes, which are extensively listed. It appears that suffixal derivation is one of the privileged features enabling the differentiation between Latin and the vernaculars. The linguistic filiation is indeed systematically studied in the chapter "Des noms": it must also be observed that all the Latin derivatives ending in *cus*, or Greek derivatives ending in *cos* become *qe* or *çien* ("Il faut aussi entendre que nous tournons en *qe* ou *çien* tous les dérivatifs que nous tirons de la langue latine terminés en *cus*, ou de la grecque en *cos*"; 1980 [1550]: 27). However, it is also important to highlight the specificities of the French language: the Latin ending *-arius* becomes *-ęre* in French, but in the case of *Censorius*, it becomes *Çęnsorin* and not *Çęnsoęre*: because it does not sound right ("au regard de *Censorius*, nous le tournons en *Çęnsorin* et non pas *Çęnsoęre*: parce qu'il sonne mal à l'oreille"; 1980 [1550]: 28). Meigret tries to shed light on general principles whenever possible (for example, the relation between the grammatical classes of derivative and primitive or between the suffix and the gender of the derivative), but he is also very attentive to restrictions on usage. While the form and the meaning of derivatives are often associated in an attempt at generalisation, the grammarian also remarks that the same suffix does not always have the same meaning and that one meaning can be expressed by different suffixes.

4.2 17th century

After Ramus's *Grammaire*, no more references to the categories of species and figure can be found in the grammars of French. The contrast between primitive and derivative or between simple and compound may be mentioned from time to time in relation to the class of the nouns (Chifflet 1659: 8 and Irson 1662 [1656]: 18–19), but a specific section is no longer devoted to them in the presentation of word classes. However, Irson's *Nouvelle méthode* (1662 [1656]) contains a final section entitled "Les étymologies", which is a list of entries arranged alphabetically. These entries correspond to a collection of comments on both the origin of the words and their derivatives in compliance with etymology in its traditional sense (Delesalle and Mazière 2002). A parallel can be drawn between this insertion of a lexical section at the end of a grammar and 17th-century distribution of the roles of grammar and the dictionary in the treatment of word-formation. This distribution is explicitly asserted by Arnauld and Lancelot's *Grammaire générale et raisonnée* in which we find the following passage (1660: 105): "On n'a point parlé, dans cette Grammaire, des mots dérivés ni des composés, dont il y aurait encore beaucoup de choses très-curieuses à dire, parce que cela regarde plutôt l'ouvrage d'un *Dictionnaire général*, que de la *Grammaire Générale*" [derived and compound words are not mentioned in this grammar even though a great many fascinating things remain to be said on the subject but they belong in a *General Dictionary* rather than in a *General Grammar*]. The authors of the *Grammaire générale*, however, assume a certain form of derivation – between substantives and adjectives – by contrasting "signification" and "manière de signifier" [manner of signifying]. All nouns which appear independently in discourse ("subsistent par eux-mêmes dans le discours") – which represents their "manner of signifying" – are called nouns, even if they signify "accidents" (e.g., *rougeur*). Conversely, if the element expressing "connotation" – which implies that an adjective cannot be self-sufficient in discourse – is added to a noun which signifies a substance, the process results in the creation of an adjective (e.g., *humain*; Delesalle 1990). As shown, morphological regularity depends above all on the mental conceptions of things, which is consistent with the programme of French general grammar:

Arnauld and Lancelot show that derivation is a linguistic fact contributing to the expression of thought. Furthermore, only the transformation leading to the creation of an adjective noun from a substantive noun is regarded as enabling generalization. When the link between form and meaning in the lexicon can no longer be systematized, the reader is invited to turn from grammar to the dictionary, or in other words not to expect a rule but to consult a list of items.

The Port-Royal logic and linguistic theory were taken up in the *Dictionnaire de l'Académie française* (1694) with a view to applying them to a particular language. This dictionary, which aims at showing the creativity of the French language, is important for lexical morphology for two reasons. Firstly, at a microstructural level, it enables the emergence of morphosemantic definitions (Mazière 1996; Leclercq 2002). The syntactic forms and semantic categories used at the beginning of the definitions attest to the remarkable stability characterizing the definitions of derivative words. These recurring syntactico-semantic patterns allow an organization of the definition which renders the link between the base form and the derivative explicit. Secondly, at a macro-structural level, not only does the dictionary set up a morphological arrangement of entries but – more importantly – it imposes constraints (explained in the preface) on this classification, which shows that derivation and composition are perceived in synchrony, regardless of etymology (Leclercq 2002). Essentially, the arrangement is used only if a French primitive word is attested: *construire* and *destruire*, for example, are regarded as independent since Latin *struere* has not come down to French ("n'a point passé en français"). To be taken into account in the nomenclature, the formal structure of the derivation must be observable in the French language from a synchronic point of view. It should be noted that the academician Regnier-Desmarais, in his grammar published in the early 18th century, distinguished between the etymon and the base form in synchrony: Simple or primitive nouns [...] are those which do not derive their origin from another noun of the same language, but owe their signification to the first institution of this language ("Les noms simples ou primitifs [...] sont ceux qui ne tirent point leur origine d'un autre nom de la même langue, mais qui doivent leur signification à la première institution de cette langue"; 1705: 179).

4.3 18th–early 19th century

Régnier-Desmarais is one of the few 18th-century grammarians of French who devoted a substantial discussion to derivatives and compounds (both are studied in the section dealing with the noun). As in the 17th century, word-formation was very rare in particular grammars. However, Beauzée reintroduced it into the grammarian's field of studies, integrating it into general grammar. He didn't address the question in his *Grammaire générale* (1767), but in several articles of the *Encyclopédie* (1751–1765). Through a series of subdivisions (article "Grammaire", cf. Beauzée 1751–65b), word-formation was made a part of "etymology", which was itself a part of "lexicology" (a term which, according to Beauzée, was introduced by Girard), lexicology in its turn being included in grammar. Word-formation groups together composition, derivation and inflection (derivation and inflection are both derivational processes that use "inflexions", the first being called "philosophical derivation" and the second "grammatical derivation"). But in the article "Formation" (cf. Beauzée 1751–65a; probably written with Douchet; Bourquin 1980a: 25), Beauzée blames the grammarians who preceded him for having preferred inflection at the expense of derivation. According to him, the explanation lies in the widespread position that grammar may legitimately restrict its focus to ready-made words ("les mots tout faits"). The encyclopaedist justifies the reintegration of the lexical aspects of word-formation into grammar using an argument compatible with the principles of general grammar: derivation and composition not only suppose a uniformity in processes ("uniformité de procédés") within a language, but also some feature common to all languages (article "Formation"). More precisely, the link between form and meaning is interpreted as a regular phenomenon: "Nous disons en premier lieu, que *ces terminaisons sont soumises à des lois générales,* parce que telle terminaison indique invariablement une même idée accessoire" [First of all we believe that these endings are subject to general laws, because an ending invariably indicates the same accessory idea]. The theory of word-formation is incorporated into the theory of the sign that characterizes general grammar: both derivation and composition allow a "primitive" or "fundamental" idea to be modified due to an accessory idea. However, despite the grammarian's asserting the principle of generality, it should be noted that most of the examples given by Beauzée are in Latin and the author explicitly points out that French has fewer regularities in this field than ancient languages.

In the early 19th century, influenced by the work of etymologists (especially de Brosses and Le Bel) and probably inspired by the intense activity of lexical creation that characterized the revolutionary period (Dougnac 1982; Steuckardt 2008), Butet de la Sarthe developed and above all implemented Beauzée's rationalist theory. He produced a new "science of words" (1801: 2), as he called it in his *Abrégé d'un cours complet de lexicologie*. We can consider this book as the first systematic description of formation processes in French (le "premier traitement systématique des procédés de formation en français"; Schlieben-Lange 2000: 31). This book isolates "lexicology" from grammar and gives it autonomy. However this autonomy is relative in fact since suffixal derivation and inflection are considered jointly, as was the case in Beauzée's work. The systematic approach inaugurated by Beauzée and Douchet is reinforced. Butet, who taught physics, exposes not simply a metaphor but an analogy between the combinations that give rise to words and the molecules of matter assembled into bodies: both obey laws and are reducible to formulae. His theses on word-formation aim at implementing a semantic structuring of the lexicon and are fundamentally based on the compositionality of meaning. He takes up his predecessor's theory of the sign: "prepositions" and "endings" are "accessory ideas" which change the main idea expressed by the "root". However, the classification of the resulting words that is proposed is tripartite and no longer bipartite. Indeed Butet distinguishes between "radical constructions" ("constructions radicales"), which only consist of "roots", that is to say elements used to represent the "main idea" ("primitive" or "simple"), "prepositive constructions" ("constructions prépositives") and "postpositive constructions" ("constructions postpositives", which comprise suffixal derivation and inflection). So composition is divided and organized with a view to singling out "compound words", as they are called nowadays. The effort of completeness and systematicity is otherwise remarkable, even though the classification of suffixes, which is based on meaning rather than form, does not take into account the diachrony-synchrony opposition: the formation of French words is put next to that of Latin words and French words resisting analysis are placed on the same footing as French derivatives (words like *instant* or *protéger* constitute examples of prepositive constructions).

4.4 19th century

In the 19th century, grammarians dealing with word-formation did not innovate and generally adopted a pedagogical perspective: suffixal derivation, related to etymology, is mainly seen as a way of focusing on the meaning of words and above all their spelling from a didactical point of view (Jullien 1849: 150). Word-formation is still not clearly separated from etymology and priority is always given to meaning, in compliance with the tradition of general grammar. During this period, progress is made above all in books which are outside the field of grammar. One example is the case of synonym dictionaries that offer a systematic description of suffixes through the study of morphologically related synonyms. It is exemplified by the work of Lafaye (1858 [1841]). Already addressed by Roubaud (1785) and taken up by Guizot (1809), this systematic description is taken one step forward by Lafaye, the author of the *Dictionnaire des synonymes de la langue française* (1858 [1841]). He introduces a distinction between synonyms formed from different stems and grammatical synonyms. With the latter, whose "prefixes" or "endings" constitute the main difference (e.g., *renunciation* and *renoncement*), it is possible to extend the difference found in a particular example to all others sharing the same modification ("faire servir la différence trouvée dans un exemple particulier à la distinction de tous les autres qui présentent la même modification"; 1858 [1841]: 26). Thus synonym dictionaries create lists of suffixes that were taken up during the 19th century.

But the pivotal work of the century is of course Darmesteter's. While associated with historical grammar (his *Cours de grammaire historique de la langue française* was posthumously published from 1891 on), along with Raynouard and Diez, the author breaks new ground by dealing with "today's language", "living language" and by defining a field of study centered on the creativity of the French lexicon. His aim is to separate it from the historical study of word-formation. In his book *De la création actuelle des mots nouveaux dans la langue française*, he proposes to shift the point of view on the language: he concentrates on word-formation seen as a creative process in progress and not on the historical development of French vocabulary (1877: 1–2). Darmesteter takes into consideration three strategies of lexicon enrichment: a) "French formation", lexical constructions created from French "stems" (the term "popular formation" is used but rejected by Darmesteter), b) "learned formation", corresponding to borrowings from Greek or Latin and derivatives and compounds derived from Greek and Latin stems and c) borrowing from modern languages. Concern for the observation of the "real language" is also noticeable in the expansion of the notion of demotivation: a derived word can be considered as a single word if it does not express a "double-idea" (1877: 70), that is to say if compositionality of meaning is no longer obvious. Darmesteter's theories are also characterized by a detailed classification of the different modes of formation. Derivation is split into "dérivation propre" (using a suffix) and "derivation impropre" (covering the processes now called "conversion" and "back formation"). Composition (to which he devotes a separate work entitled *Traité de la formation des mots composés dans la langue française*, 1894 [1875]), which is defined by its ability to create a conceptual unity which obliterates the specific meanings of the elements, implies a division between compounds formed by juxtaposition ("les composés formés par voie de juxtaposition"; e.g., *plafond, arc-en-ciel*), compounds formed with particles, viz. adverbs or prepositions ("les composés formés à l'aide de particules"; e.g., *surprendre, malaise*) and compounds formed by composition as such ("les composés formés par composition proprement dite"; e.g., *chou-fleur, timbre-poste*). Although isolated, prefixation is therefore still regarded as being part of composition and the term of "parasynthesis", taken over from the Greek grammatical tradition, is introduced with its meaning of "résultat d'une composition et d'une dérivation agissant ensemble sur un même radical" [result of a composition and a derivation acting together on the same stem] (1894 [1875]: 96). The opposition between the two remaining sets is founded on the nature of the syntactic relationships between the various elements of the compounds, with the use of the notion of "ellipsis": the composition as such is indeed elliptical, the compound is in this case a "proposition en raccourci" – "*timbre-poste* ne veut pas dire simplement *timbre* et *poste*, mais *timbre de la poste, timbre pour la poste*" (1890: 72) [*postage-stamp* doesn't mean just *stamp* and *postage*, but *stamp for postage*] – while composition by juxtaposition follows the usual syntactic construction. This innovative syntactic theory of composition was taken up widely in the 20th century, especially in a transformational perspective (particulary in Guilbert's and Dubois's works). More generally, Darmester's theses and categories came down with minor changes through the first half of the 20th century and are still used today, despite Saussure's reflections on synchrony and analogy (Kerleroux 2000).

Acknowledgements

We are most grateful to Helmut Puff (University of Michigan, Ann Arbor) and Wilfrid Andrieu (Université de Provence) for their valuable help with the English version.

5 References

Adelung, Johann Christoph (1782): *Umständliches Lehrgebäude der Deutschen Sprache. Zur Erläuterung der Deutschen Sprachlehre für Schulen*. Vol. 2. Leipzig: Breitkopf. [Repr. Hildesheim: Olms, 1971].
Adelung, Johann Christoph (1784): Gebrauch und Mißbrauch der Etymologie. *Magazin für die Deutsche Sprache* II(2): 96–121.
Aichinger, Carl Friedrich (1754): *Versuch einer teutschen Sprachlehre, anfänglich nur zu eignem Gebrauche unternommen, endlich aber, um den Gelehrten zu fernerer Untersuchung Anlaß zu geben, ans Liecht gestellt von C.F.A*. Frankfurt/Leipzig: Kraus. [Repr. Hildesheim: Olms, 1972].
Albertus, Laurentius (1573 [1895]): *Teutsch Grammatick oder Sprach-Kunst*. Augsburg: Manger [*Die deutsche Grammatik des Laurentius Albertus*. Ed. by Carl Müller-Fraureuth, 1895, Straßburg: Trübner].
Arnauld, Antoine and Claude Lancelot (1660): *Grammaire générale et raisonnée*. Paris: Le Petit.
Auroux, Sylvain (1992): *Histoire des idées linguistiques*. Vol. 2: *Le développement de la grammaire occidentale*. Liège: Mardaga.
Beauzée, Nicolas (1751–65a): Formation. In: Denis Diderot and Jean Le Rond d'Alembert (eds.), *Encyclopédie ou Dictionnaire raisonné des sciences, des arts et des métiers*. Vol. 7, 172–176. Paris/Neuchâtel: Le Breton.
Beauzée, Nicolas (1751–65b): Grammaire. In: Denis Diderot and Jean Le Rond d'Alembert (eds.), *Encyclopédie ou Dictionnaire raisonné des sciences, des arts et des métiers*. Vol. 7, 841–847. Paris/Neuchâtel: Le Breton.

Beauzée, Nicolas (1767): *Grammaire générale*. Paris: Barbou.
Becker, Karl Ferdinand (1824): *Die Deutsche Wortbildung oder die organische Entwickelung der deutschen Sprache in der Ableitung*. Frankfurt/M.: Hermann'sche Buchhandlung. [Repr. Hildesheim: Olms, 1990].
Becker, Karl Ferdinand (1831): *Schulgrammatik der deutschen Sprache*. Frankfurt/M.: Hermann'sche Buchhandlung.
Bourquin, Jacques (1979): La place et la fonction de la morphologie dérivationnelle dans la grammaire scolaire au XIXe siècle. *Langue française* 41: 60–76.
Bourquin, Jacques (1980a): La dérivation suffixale (théorisation et enseignement) au XIXe siècle. Thèse présentée devant l'Université de Besançon (1977). Lille: Université de Lille III.
Bourquin, Jacques (1980b): La terminologie du lexique construit (dérivation suffixale et préfixation). *Langue française* 47: 33–47.
Brocquet, Sylvain (2008): Les mots non simples dans la tradition indienne paninéenne. In: Barbara Kaltz (ed.), *Regards croisés sur les mots non simples*, 11–33. Lyon: ENS Editions.
Brücker, Jacob (1620): *Teutsche Grammatic / das ist / Kurtzer Vnterricht / wie eyner etlicher massen recht reden und schreiben lehrnen solle*. Frankfurt/M.: Jennis.
Butet de la Sarthe, Pierre Roland François (1801): *Abrégé d'un cours complet de lexicologie à l'usage des élèves de la quatrième classe de l'Ecole polymathique*. Paris: Renouard.
Chifflet, Laurent (1659): *Essai d'une parfaite grammaire française*. Anvers: van Meurs.
Clajus, Johannes (1894 [1578]): *Die deutsche Grammatik des Johannes Clajus. Nach dem ältesten Druck von 1578 mit den Varianten der übrigen Ausgaben*. Ed. by Friedrich Weidling. Freiburg: Trübner.
Colombat, Bernard (1999): *La grammaire latine en France à la Renaissance et à l'Age classique*. Grenoble: ELLUG (Université Stendhal).
Corpus de textes linguistiques fondamentaux: http://ctlf.ens-lyon.fr
Darmesteter, Arsène (1877): *De la création actuelle de mots nouveaux dans la langue française*. Paris: Vieweg.
Darmesteter, Arsène (1894 [1875]): *Traité de la formation des mots composés de la langue française*. Paris: Vieweg.
Darmesteter, Arsène (1895): *Cours de grammaire historique de la langue française*. Vol. 3: *Formation des mots et vie des mots*. Paris: Delagrave.
Delesalle, Simone (1990): De la définition du nom et du verbe dans la *Logique* et la *Grammaire* de Port-Royal. In: Jacques Chaurand and Francine Mazière (eds.), *La définition*, 72–77. Paris: Larousse.
Delesalle, Simone and Francine Mazière (2002): La liste dans le développement des grammaires. *Histoire Epistémologie Langage* 24(1): 65–92.
Dictionnaire de l'Académie française (1694): Paris: Coignard.
Dougnac, Françoise (1982): La néologie. *Histoire Epistémologie Langage* 4(1): 67–72.
Estienne, Robert (1557): *Traité de la grammaire française*. Genève: Estienne.
Fleischer, Wolfgang (1983): Zur Geschichte der germanistischen Wortbildungsforschung im 19. Jahrhundert: Jacob Grimm und die Junggrammatiker. In: Wolfgang Fleischer (ed.), *Entwicklungen in Wortbildung und Wortschatz der deutschen Gegenwartssprache*, 74–100. Berlin: Akademie der Wissenschaften der DDR – Zentralinstitut für Sprachwissenschaft.
Fögen, Thorsten (2008): La formation des mots et l'enrichissement de la langue vus par quelques auteurs latins. In: Barbara Kaltz (ed.), *Regards croisés sur les mots non simples*, 65–84. Lyon: ENS Editions.
Forsgren, Kjell-Åke (2008): La conception de la formation des mots selon Karl Ferdinand Becker. In: Barbara Kaltz (ed.), *Regards croisés sur les mots non simples*, 131–149. Lyon: ENS Editions.

Glatigny, Michel (1985): L'exception dans le système morphologique de L. Meigret. *Langue française* 66: 9–19.

Grimm, Jacob (1878): *Deutsche Grammatik. Zweiter Theil*. Besorgt durch Wilhelm Scherer. 2nd ed. Berlin: Dümmler. [Repr. Hildesheim: Olms, 1989].

Gützlaff, Kathrin (1989): *Von der Fügung Teutscher Stammwörter. Die Wortbildung in J. G. Schottelius' 'Ausführlicher Arbeit von der Teutschen HaubtSprache'*. Hildesheim: Olms.

Guizot, François (1809): *Nouveau dictionnaire universel des synonymes*. Paris: Payen.

Heynatz, Johann Friedrich (1777 [1770]): *Deutsche Sprachlehre zum Gebrauch der Schulen*. 3rd ed. Berlin: Mylius.

Irson, Claude (1662 [1656]): *Nouvelle méthode pour apprendre facilement les principes et la pureté de la langue française contenant plusieurs traités*. 2nd ed. Paris: Beaudouin.

Jankowsky, Kurt R. (2004): Karl Ferdinand Becker's (1775–1849) concept of word formation within the framework of his general linguistic theory. In: Kjell-Åke Forsgren and Barbara Kaltz (eds.), *Studien zur Geschichte der Wortbildungstheorien*, 89–106. Münster: Nodus.

Jullien, Bernard (1849): *Cours supérieur de grammaire*. Paris: Hachette.

Kaltz, Barbara (2002): Zur Entwicklung der Wortbildungstheorie in der deutschen Grammatikographie 1750–1800. *Beiträge zur Geschichte der Sprachwissenschaft* 12(1): 27–47.

Kaltz, Barbara (2005): Zur Herausbildung der Wortbildungslehre in der deutschen Grammatikographie: Von den Anfängen bis zum Ende des 19. Jahrhunderts. In: Peter Schmitter (ed.), *Sprachtheorien der Neuzeit III/1*, 105–162. Tübingen: Narr.

Kerleroux, Françoise (2000): France and Switzerland. In: Geert Booij, Christian Lehmann and Joachim Mugdan (eds.), *Morphology. An International Handbook on Inflection and Word-Formation*. Vol. 1, 138–145. Berlin/New York: de Gruyter.

Lafaye, Pierre Benjamin (1858 [1841]): *Dictionnaire des synonymes de la langue française*. 2nd ed. Paris: Hachette.

Lallot, Jean (1998): *La grammaire de Denys le Thrace. Traduite et annotée*. 2nd ed. Paris: Editions du CNRS.

Lallot, Jean (2008): De Platon aux grammairiens: Regards grecs sur la structure des mots non simples. In: Barbara Kaltz (ed.), *Regards croisés sur les mots non simples*, 51–63. Lyon: ENS Editions.

Leclercq, Odile (2002): Aspects grammaticaux d'un dictionnaire de langue: Deux traitements de la morphologie par le *Dictionnaire de l'Académie* (1694). *Histoire Epistémologie Langage* 24(1): 107–118.

Lindner, Thomas (2002): *Lateinische Komposita. Morphologische, historische und lexikalische Studien*. Innsbruck: Institut für Sprachwissenschaft.

Longolius, Johann Daniel (1715): *Einleitung zu gründlicher Erkäntniß einer ieden / insonderheit aber Der Teutschen Sprache / Welcher man sich Zu accurater Untersuchung jeder Sprache / und Besitzung einer untadelhafften Beredsamkeit in gebundenen und ungebundenen Reden / Wie auch besonders In Teutschen für allerley Condition, Alter und Geschlechte / Zu einem deutlichen und nützlichen Begriff der Mutter=Sprache / bedienen kan*. Budissin [Bautzen]: Richter.

Mäzke, Abraham Gotthelf (1776): *Grammatische Abhandlungen über die Deutsche Sprache*. Breslau: Meyer.

Matthaios, Stephanos (1999): *Untersuchungen zur Grammatik Aristarchs. Texte und Interpretation zur Wortartenlehre*. Göttingen: Vandenhoeck & Ruprecht.

Matthaios, Stephanos (2004): Die Wortbildungstheorie in der alexandrinischen Grammatik. In: Kjell-Åke Forsgren and Barbara Kaltz (eds.), *Studien zur Geschichte der Wortbildungstheorien*, 5–22. Münster: Nodus.

Mazière, Francine (1996): Un événement linguistique: La définition des noms abstraits dans la première édition du *Dictionnaire de l'Académie* (1694). In: Nelly Flaux, Michel Glatigny and Didier Samain (eds.), *Les noms abstraits. Histoire et théories. Actes du colloque international "Les noms abstraits" (Dunkerque, sept. 1992)*, 161–174. Lille: Presses Universitaires du Septentrion.

McLelland, Nicola (2010): Justus Georgius Schottelius (1612–1676) and European linguistic thought. *Historiographia Linguistica* 37(1): 1–30.

McLelland, Nicola (2011): *J. G. Schottelius·s Ausführliche Arbeit von der Teutschen Haubtsprache (1663) and its place in early modern European vernacular language study*. Oxford: Blackwell.

Meigret, Louis (1980 [1550]): *Le traité de la grammaire française*. Ed. by Franz Josef Hausmann. Tübingen: Narr.

Padley, George Arthur (1985): *Grammatical Theory in Western Europe 1500–1700. Trends in Vernacular Grammar I*. Cambridge: Cambridge University Press.

Paul, Hermann (1880): *Prinzipien der Sprachgeschichte*. Halle/S.: Niemeyer. [Repr. Tübingen: Niemeyer, 10th ed. 1995].

Paul, Hermann (1896): Ueber die Aufgaben der Wortbildungslehre. In: *Sitzungsberichte der philosophisch-philologischen und der historischen Classe der k.b. Akademie der Wissenschaften zu München*, 692–713. [Repr. in: Leonhard Lipka and Hartmut Günther (eds.), *Wortbildung*, 17–35. Darmstadt: Wissenschaftliche Buchgesellschaft, 1981].

Paul, Hermann (1920): *Deutsche Grammatik*. Vol. 5: *Wortbildungslehre*. Halle/S.: Niemeyer.

Ramus, Petrus (1572): *Grammaire*. Paris: Wechel.

Ratke, Wolfgang (1959 [1612–1615]): *Sprachkunst*. In: Erika Ising (ed.), *Wolfgang Ratkes Schriften zur deutschen Grammatik*. Vol. 2, 7–22. Berlin: Akademie Verlag.

Ratke, Wolfgang (1959 [1630]): *Die WortbedeütungsLehr der Christlichen Schule [...]*. In: Erika Ising (ed.), *Wolfgang Ratkes Schriften zur deutschen Grammatik*. Vol. 2, 269–318. Berlin: Akademie Verlag.

Régnier-Desmarais, François Séraphin (1705): *Traité de la grammaire française*. Paris: Coignard.

Rey, Alain (1970): *La lexicologie*. Paris: Klincksieck.

Roubaud, Pierre-Joseph (1785): *Nouveaux synonymes françois*. Paris: Moutard.

Schlieben-Lange, Brigitte (2000): La révolution française. In: Sylvain Auroux (ed.), *Histoire des idées linguistiques*. Vol. 3, 23–34. Liège: Mardaga.

Schottelius, Justus Georg (1641): *Teutsche Sprachkunst [...]*. Braunschweig: Gruber.

Schottelius, Justus Georg (1663): *Ausführliche Arbeit Von der Teutschen HaubtSprache*. Braunschweig: Zilliger. [Repr. Tübingen: Niemeyer 1967; online].

Schulz, Matthias (2002): Wortbildung in Wörterbüchern und Texten des 17. Jahrhunderts. In: Mechthild Habermann, Peter O. Müller and Horst Haider Munske (eds.), *Historische Wortbildung des Deutschen*, 269–288. Tübingen: Niemeyer.

Steuckardt, Agnès (2008): Présentation. In: Pierre-Nicolas Chantreau, *Dictionnaire national et anecdotique*. 1790. Reprint ed. by Agnès Steuckardt, 9–91. Limoges: Lambert-Lucas.

Štichauer, Jaroslav (2005): *Amatrice, autrice, cantateur* (le discours sur les féminins en *-trice* aux XVIIe et XVIIIe siècles). *Écho des études romanes* 1(1): 7–14.

Štichauer, Jaroslav (2014): *Etudes sur la formation des mots en français préclassique et classique*. Prague: Karolinum Press.

Sylvius, Jacobus Ambianus (1531): *Grammatica Latino-Gallica*. Paris: Estienne.

Vaahtera, Jaana (1998): *Derivation. Greek and Roman Views on Word Formation*. Turku: Turun Yliopisto.

Vlassov, Serge (2006): Le traitement des diminutifs dans les grammaires et les remarques sur la langue française aux XVIe et XVIIe siècles. In: Françoise Berlan (ed.), *Langue littéraire et changement linguistique*, 89–104. Paris: Presses de l'Université Paris-Sorbonne.

Warnke, Stefanie (2008). *Jacob Grimms Wortbildungslehre aus der Sicht der gegenwärtigen Morphologie*. München: GRIN.

Thomas Lindner
3 Word-formation in historical-comparative grammar

1 Terminological preliminaries
2 Word-formation immediately before the rise of the historical-comparative method
3 Historical-comparative descriptions
4 Descriptions based on semantic criteria
5 Compounding in comparative grammar
6 References

Abstract: Word-formation in historical-comparative linguistics emerged on the one hand from Classical and German studies at the turn of the 18th and 19th centuries and on the other hand from Indian grammar which had become known in Europe early in 1800. The present article tries to delineate the main developments from the 19th century to the present.

1 Terminological preliminaries

1.1 Basic terminology

Morphological terms such as *root*, *stem* or *affix* as well as the segmentation of words and the consciousness of word-formational processes which they imply represented fundamental linguistic insights that provided concepts of morphological analysis which Indo-European studies, but also other grammatical traditions, could no longer do without. Nevertheless, in comparison with terms relating to syntax, parts of speech or case they are not really old: they do not, as one might be inclined to think, reach back to antiquity, nor were they well-established elements of traditional terminology at the outset of Indo-European studies. Morphological analysis was neglected in ancient grammar: the procedures of analyzing words which are now so familiar to linguists and which Bopp (1824–31) referred to as dissection [*Zergliederung*] were unknown to the ancient grammarians, concepts such as 'root', 'stem' or 'affix' were also completely unfamiliar to them.

Thomas Lindner, Salzburg, Austria

https://doi.org/10.1515/9783111420561-003

In the wake of the Indian grammatical tradition, Franz Bopp was the first to recognize that Indo-European words could generally be broken down into the structure root + derivational affix + inflectional affix. The identification of what was indistinctly called *Grundform* 'basic form', *Stammform* 'stem form', *Stamm* 'stem' or *Thema* 'theme', was so new and groundbreaking at the time that Bopp felt obliged to provide the following clarifications:

> Die Indischen Grammatiker fassen die Nomina (sowohl Substantive, als Adjektive, Pronomina und Zahlwörter), in ihrem absoluten, von allen Casusverhältnissen unabhängigen, und von allen Casuszeichen entblößten Zustande auf, und nehmen daher eine Grund- oder Stammform an, zu welcher der Nominativ und die obliquen Casus der drei Zahlen sich als abgeleitet verhalten. Diese Grundform kommt häufig in zusammengesetzten Wörtern vor, indem die ersten Glieder eines Compositums aller Casusendungen beraubt, und somit identisch mit der Grundform sind. (Bopp 1827: 23)

> [The Indian grammarians conceived of nouns (substantives, adjectives, pronouns and numerals) in their absolute state, independent of all relations and markers of case, assuming the existence of a basic or stem form, from which the nominative and the oblique cases of all three numbers were derived. This basic form often appears in compound words, the first members of compounds being deprived of all case endings and therefore identical with the basic form.]

These stem forms of the old Indo-European languages thus have only been recognized in the Western world since Bopp and his disciples (cf. Lindner 2012: 121). However, Jacob Grimm in his *Deutsche Grammatik* (1819 ff.) did not yet recognize the stem principle: In the analysis of the first members of compounds, where it should have been most obvious, he resorted to the concept of a "composition vowel" (*Compositionsvocal*) which would haunt Indo-European studies until the early Neo-Grammarians (cf. Lindner 2012: 115). German linguists soon adopted Bopp's analysis, first and foremost among them was Eberhard Gottlieb Graff (cf. Lindner 2012: 122), but the classical handbooks continued to perpetuate the old view codified over the centuries in school grammars of Latin and Greek. Philipp Buttmann was the first to use and differentiate the concepts of root (*Wurzel*), stem (*Stamm*) and theme (*Thema*), but he did not recognize that the first members of compounds were stems, calling them declensional or nominal endings, or linking vowels (cf. Lindner 2012: 124). Nevertheless, he was the first classical philologist who had recognized, at least theoretically, the role of the stem in the segmentation of Greek nominal inflection, especially of the third declension. However, he did not yet recognize clearly the amalgamation of stem vowels and inflectional desinences, which is why segmentation did not find its way into school grammars for still quite some time. We will have to wait until well into the second half of the 19th century to see Bopp's insight establish itself in grammars of the classical languages, essentially thanks to the indefatigable endeavors of his disciple Georg

Curtius. It was especially the precise conceptual distinctions in Curtius' *Griechische Schulgrammatik* (1852) which eventually enhanced general consciousness regarding morphological structure.

As we have seen, only comparative linguistics and, hesitantly, classical grammar started differentiating on the one hand *root* (Germ. *Wurzel*) and *stem* (*Stamm*), and on the other *ending* (*Endung*) and *termination* (*Ausgang*). The latter distinction has become established in school grammars and has lived on in scientific discourse until the present day. As a consequence *Ausgang* still refers to the amalgamated combination of a stem-forming element and an inflectional morpheme and probably constitutes the ending *par excellence* for the unsophisticated speaker (cf. Lindner 2012: 138). Alongside the terms *root, stem,* (*inflectional*) *ending*, and *termination*, which became established as late as around 1870 in scientific morphology, Hermann Perthes introduced *Wortstock* 'root or stem, respectively' exclusively for pedagogical purposes from 1875 onwards (cf. Lindner 2012: 138). As this terminology was becoming popular in school grammars of the classical languages in the last quarter of the 19th century, an umbrella term for morphological elements was introduced around 1880 in entirely different scientific contexts, viz. *morpheme*. It had been coined by Jan Baudouin de Courtenay in the Kazan school of linguistics towards the end of the decade of 1870, taking as a model the term *phoneme* which was already in use (cf. Lindner 2012: 140). *Thema*, originally a synonym of *Stamm* 'stem' in morphology, also shows an interesting conceptual evolution: In the course of the 20th century in Old German studies it has narrowed its meaning and become equivalent to *Stammbildungsvokal* 'stem-forming vowel' or *Formans* (cf. Lindner 2012: 140–143).

1.2 The ambiguity of *Wortbildung* 'word-formation'

In the second half of the 19th century there was also some confusion concerning the notion *Wortbildung* 'word-formation' itself. The early Neogrammarians used *Wortbildung* in the sense of 'inflection', while what is called *Wortbildung* today went under the term *Stammbildung* 'stem-formation':

> Es zerfällt demnach die wortbildungslehre (formen-, flexionslehre) in die lehre von der bildung der nomina und in die lehre von der bildung der verba. Jenen liegen nominal-, diesen verbalstämme zu grunde. Die lehre von der bildung der nomina nennt man declination, die lehre von der bildung der verba conjugation. (Miklosich 1876: 1; vgl. Miklosich 1875)
>
> [Word-formation (the study of forms, of inflection) therefore comprises the formation of nouns and verbs. The former are derived from noun stems, the latter from verb stems. The

study of the formation of nouns is called declension, the study of the formation of verbs conjugation.]

Die Suffixe theilt man ein in Wortbildungssuffixe oder Flexionssuffixe im engern Sinne, wozu einerseits die Casusendungen [...], anderseits die Personalendungen [...] gehören, und Stammbildungssuffixe [...]. Eine scharfe Grenze zwischen beiden Suffixgattungen ist nicht zu ziehen, da manches Element, das ursprünglich nur ableitend (stammbildend) war, mit den wortbildenden Suffixen [= Flexionsendungen, Th. L.] auf gleiche Linie gekommen ist. (Brugmann 1886: 15)

[Suffixes are divided into word-formational or inflectional suffixes in the narrow sense, which on the one hand comprise case endings [...] and on the other personal endings, and stem-forming suffixes [...]. It is impossible to draw a sharp line between the two kinds of suffixes, because some elements that originally were derivational (stem-forming) have turned into word-forming suffixes [i.e. inflectional endings; Th. L.].]

This interpretation as well as the arrangement of word-formation before inflection in grammars goes back to Schleicher's *Compendium*, who subsumed both "roots and stems" (stem-formation) as well as word-formation (inflection) under the heading *Morphologie* 'morphology' (cf. Lindner 2012: 94). Brugmann in turn, in the first edition of his *Grundriß* (1892), subsumed both stem-formation and inflection under word-formation. This arrangement met with criticism on the part of Hermann Paul (1896: 692), which is why it was later on abandoned again (also by Brugmann in his final edition of the *Grundriß* in 1906). At the latest in the first decades of the 20th century the traditional terminology had again become standard, cf. Debrunner's preface to his *Griechische Wortbildungslehre*:

Noch ein Wort über die Begrenzung des Stoffs: Das Büchlein soll die Wortbildung, nicht die Formenbildung behandeln. Ausgeschlossen ist also die gesamte Deklination und Konjugation [...]. (Debrunner 1917: IX)

[Just one more word concerning the demarcation of the subject: the book is intended to treat word-formation, not form-formation. All declensions and conjugations are therefore excluded [...].]

The very fact that Debrunner felt obliged to make such a remark, however, shows that the term *Wortbildung* could still provoke uncertainties, otherwise he would not have made it. We have come full circle, returning to the usage of early historical-comparative grammar (and earlier traditions), when word-formation was used in the sense it has today and was located after inflection (cf. Lindner 2012: 94–95, with references).

2 Word-formation immediately before the rise of the historical-comparative method

At the beginning of the 19th century important insights had been gained with respect to the approaches of the ancient grammarians which had been in use in grammars and textbooks until around 1800. Before Buttmann, nobody talked of word-internal structure, only of "endings" (*Endungen, Endigungen*). Especially first elements of compounds were still treated in the traditional way by regarding them as case-forms or mutilations thereof; Christian August Lobeck, for example, continued this tradition of analysis well into the 19th century (cf. Lindner 2012: 125). The systematization of derivational, especially suffixal, word-formation and composition was still in its infancy. Until the 18th century the poorly developed word-formational analysis of the ancient grammarians was treated in the etymological parts of grammars, i.e. those dealing with words and parts of speech, under the headings of *species* and *figura* (*etymologia* had the meaning of 'word analysis', cf. Lindner 2011: 29 and article 2 on word-formation research from its beginnings to the 19th century). Only towards the end of the 18th century could a new orientation be observed that manifested itself in a separate treatment of word-formation, especially composition, by Adelung in his *Umständliches Lehrgebäude* (1782a: 216–236, 1782b: 209–274). In classical grammar that was considered as a revolution, which is why Trendelenburg could write in the second edition of his *Griechische Grammatik*:

> Ueberhaupt, hoffe ich, wird man nicht leicht einen Theil der Sprachlehre an vorhin unbekannten Bemerkungen ganz leer finden [...] Als Beispiel nenne ich nur das eilfte Kapitel [...], in welchem ich einen Versuch gemacht habe, die Wortbildung genauer, wie bisher, auseinander zu setzen. Wenigstens glaube ich mir den zweiten Abschnitt [...] von der Zusammensetzung der Wörter mit Recht zueignen zu können. Denn ich erinnere mich nicht, in irgend einem grammatischen Werke über diesen Theil der Wörter, an welchen das Griechische so außerordentlich reich ist, etwas gelesen zu haben, was die Grundsätze und die Analogie, welche die Sprache in Zusammensetzung der Wörter befolgt, nur einigermaßen auseinandersetzte. Alle Sprachlehrer haben sich bloß auf den mechanischen Theil, auf die Art und Weise, wie zwei Wörter an einander gefügt werden, eingeschränkt [...]. Ich erwehne dieses Versuchs, besonders deswegen, um Freunde von dergleichen Untersuchungen zu bitten, so wol die Grundsätze, welche ich hier angenommen habe, zu prüfen und, wo es nöthig ist, zu berichtigen, als auch gelegentlich das Ihrige dazu beizutragen, diese Lehre mit neuen Bemerkungen zu bereichern, welche sich in diesem Theil der Sprache besonders bei der Vergleichung des Griechischen mit dem Deutschen darbieten werden. (Trendelenburg 1790: VI f.)

> [I hope that one will hardly find any part of this grammar devoid of hitherto unknown observations [...] I would just like to mention Chapter XI [...], where I have tried to deal

with word-formation in more detail than is usual. I think that at least the second section [...] about composition is mostly original work. I do not remember having read in any grammatical treatise about this kind of words which abound in Greek anything that would explain the principles and the analogy which the language follows in compounding. All grammarians have limited themselves to the purely mechanical part of the question, the way in which two words are put together [...]. I mention this essay particularly because I would like to invite friends of this kind of research to assess and, where necessary, correct the principles I have assumed and to enrich this analysis with new observations that one will not fail to make in this area of language especially by comparing Greek and German.]

One should also point out the progress made in the treatment of Greek wordformation by Buttmann, from the short chapter of the first, second and third editions (1805: 266–268, Von der Zusammensetzung) of his *Griechische Grammatik* to the extensive chapter in the fourth and fifth editions (1808, 1810: 399–419, Wortbildung durch Endungen, 420–428, Wortbildung durch Zusammensetzung):

Der bedeutendste größere Zusatz [...] ist der Abschnitt von der Wortbildung, der mich zwar noch keineswegs befriedigt, von welchem ich aber doch hoffe, daß er auch so schon seinen Zweck in der Hauptsache erreichen wird. (Buttmann 1810: X)

[The most important substantial addition [...] is the section on word-formation, which is still far from satisfying me completely, but which hopefully will also attain its main aims as it stands.]

Die Wortbildung im vollen Verstande des Wortes liegt außerhalb der Grenzen der gewöhnlichen Sprachlehre. Denn da die Analogien in dem älteren Theile des Wortvorrathes [...] vielfältig zerrissen und verdunkelt sind [...], [wird daher] eine gewisse Masse von Wörtern lexikalisch voraus[gesetzt] [...]. Gewisse Arten der Ableitung jedoch, von welchen man eben deswegen annehmen kann, daß sie neuer sind, haben sich so vollständig und innerhalb gewisser Grenzen durchgehend erhalten, daß sie mit Sicherheit zusammen gestellt werden können; und diese Vereinigung derselben unter einem Gesichtspunkt erleichtert und beschleunigt die Kenntnis der Sprache [...]. (Buttmann 1810: 399)

[Word-formation in the full sense of the word lies outside ordinary grammar. Since in the older part of vocabulary the analogies [...] have often been broken and are now opaque [...], a certain number of words must be considered as lexically primitive [...]. However, some kinds of derivation, which for that very reason may be considered as younger, have been preserved so fully and completely within certain limits, that they can be put together without question; and assembling them from one specific viewpoint makes knowledge of the language easier and more rapid [...].]

Formal analogies were also decisive for early comparative grammar which built on these forerunners. At the beginning, derivational word-formation was formally oriented exclusively according to the "endings", i.e. stem-forming suffixes:

Bei der Anhängung der Endungen [*scil.* Wortbildungssuffixe] walteten zwei Prinzipe vor, das Bestreben gleichartige Bedeutungen durch einerlei Endung auszudrücken, und das Be-

> streben, die Endung der Form des Stammworts möglichst anzupassen. Allein durch die Kollision dieser Prinzipe entstand zweierlei Verwirrung der Analogie: 1) ist dieselbe Art der Bedeutung häufig unter verschiedene Formen vertheilt; 2) Endungen, die ursprünglich nur von gewissen Formen des Stammworts gebildet wurden [...], gingen, wenn eine gewisse Bedeutung bei mehreren Wörtern gleichen Ausgangs fühlbar geworden war, auch auf andere Stammwörter über, deren Form nicht dazu paßte [...]. (Buttmann 1810: 400)

> [Two principles preside over the attachment of endings [i.e. derivational suffixes], the endeavor to express the same meaning with the same ending, and the endeavor to adapt the ending to the form of the stem as far as possible. Through the collision of these two principles analogy became confused in two ways: 1) often the same meaning is distributed among different forms; 2) endings that had originally been attached only to stems of a certain form came to be attached to other stems whose form was inappropriate as soon as more words with the same ending were felt to form a semantically coherent group [...].]

It still took quite some time before word-formation would also be analysed according to "sameness of meaning", i.e. according to semantic derivational categories. At the beginning, all treatments of word-formation were organized according to formal parameters concerning the suffixes.

Shortly before the publication of Grimm's monumental German word-formation (1826), Becker published his *Deutsche Wortbildung* (1824). In this first monographic treatment of German derivation and composition Becker analyzed the "formation of verbs" (71–261), "derivation by suffixes" (262–368) and "composition" (369–451). Concerning derivation, Becker speaks of *Kernformen* ('nuclear forms', i.e. bases) and *Sproßformen* ('offshoot forms', i.e. derivatives); the process of derivation is called *Umendung* 'change of ending'. *Ableitung* 'derivation' for him is the hyperonym, which leads him to distinguish derivation by change of ending from derivation by composition. In the realm of composition he builds on Adelung's criteria (1782b: 215 ff.) distinguishing *Verschmelzung* 'fusion', the amalgamation of two words into a conceptual unit, and *Zusammenfügung* 'putting together', the syntactic union of two words. These distinctions can also be found in his *Organism* (1827) and in his *Deutsche Grammatik* (1829), placed in the context of a wider grammatical system.

3 Historical-comparative descriptions

3.1 19th century

Jacob Grimm (1826) represents the historical-comparative turn in German word-formation: "The scientific study of word-formation is [...] a creation of J. Grimm" (cf. Paul 1896: 692). He takes into account older stages of the language and provides abundant comparisons with other Germanic and non-Germanic material. First, he distinguishes derivation in the more restricted sense and composition:

> *ableitung* heißt die zwischen wurzel und flexion eingeschaltete, an sich selbst dunkle mehrung des wortes, kraft welcher der begriff der wurzel weiter geleitet und bestimmt wird. [...] die ableitung unterscheidet sich von der zusammensetzung [...] letztere verbindet zwei lebendige oder doch deutliche wurzeln miteinander [...]. (Grimm 1826: 89–90)
>
> [*Derivation* refers to the in itself opaque material that comes between the root and the inflection and which develops and determines the concept expressed by the root. [...] Derivation must be distinguished from composition [...] the latter combines two roots that are still distinctly felt to be such [...].]

Grimm then goes on to differentiate formal patterns of "vocalic" and "consonantic" derivations (92–386), the semantics of which is briefly touched upon (395–398). The latter part is constituted by composition (405–985). Here Grimm introduces the concept of *Compositionsvocal* 'composition vowel', which he did not identify as a stem vowel and which would live on for a long time in German school grammars. Only around 1840 does Grimm abandon this doctrine after harsh criticism from comparatists (cf. Lindner 2012: 117). His distinction of *eigentliche* (*echte*) and *uneigentliche* (*unechte*) *Komposition* (407 f.; cf. Lindner 2011: 15–20), compounding proper and univerbation, on the other hand, has stood the test of time.

Franz Bopp treats Old-Indian word-formation for the first time in his *Ausführliches Lehrgebäude*, where he introduces the Indian terms for types of compounds which are used up to the present day (1827: 268 ff., 310 ff.; cf. section 5). In a comparative context he does the same in the fifth volume of his *Vergleichende Grammatik* (1833–52: 1072 ff., 1410 ff.), classifying derivation according to the form of suffixes and composition according to the Indian categories. Already before Bopp, August Friedrich Pott in his *Etymologische Forschungen* (1836: 351 ff.) had treated word-formation from a comparative perspective, but in a rather casuistic and unsystematic manner.

In the meantime Friedrich Diez had published a treatise of Romance word-formation in the second volume of his *Romanische Grammatik* (1838: 219 ff.). The treatment of derivation follows the formal criterion of the form of suffixes (244 ff.), that of composition is by parts of speech following the example of Grimm (334 ff.). A book that was to become important for the analysis of word-formation, especially of Ancient Greek, by the early Neogrammarians was Curtius' *De nominum Graecorum formatione linguarum cognatarum ratione habita* (1842), dedicated to his teacher Bopp.

In Neogrammarian times the theoretical manifesto, also for word-formation, was Hermann Paul's *Prinzipien* (1880: 161 ff., ^{5}1920: 325 ff.). In turn, the model up to the present day for all descriptively oriented treatises of the word-formation of individual Indo-European languages is constituted by the monumental volume on word-formation in Brugmann's *Grundriß*. The second edition of 1906 set the standard and continues to be indispensable due to the wealth of its comparative material and its comprehensive description. The introduction discussing the structure of Indo-European word-forms as well as the motives and kinds of word-formation processes (1–49, Allgemeines) is followed by a description of composition (49–120) and thereupon the listing of *Stammbildungsformantien* based on formal criteria (120–582; the relevant literature on word-formation is summarized on pp. 49 ff. and 120 ff.). In the concluding section the material is arranged according to semantic groups (582–685, Bedeutung der Nominalstämme). What is worth highlighting is Brugmann's rejection of the affix-terminology and his introduction of the term *Formans* 'formative' to refer to a derivational affix (1906: 8 ff.).

3.2 20th century

The reference works on the word-formation of old Indo-European languages published during the 20th century can only be enumerated here (further references can be found in the bibliographies of the works cited as well as in Heidermanns 2005, Lühr and Balles 2008 and Lühr and Matzinger 2008): from a comparative perspective Brugmann (1906) (esp. Delbrück 1900: 139 ff. and Brugmann 1904: 297 ff., 1906: 49 ff.); for Old Indian: Wackernagel (1905) (Wackernagel and Debrunner 1957), Debrunner (1954); for Avestan: Duchesne-Guillemin (1936), Kellens (1974); for Greek: Debrunner (1917), Chantraine (1933), Schwyzer (1939) as well as Risch (1974) for the language of Homer, for Latin: Leumann (1977), Kircher-Durand (2002) and Lindner (1996, 2002a), for Germanic: Paul (1920), Meid (1967) and Carr (1939). I would also like to draw attention to the part dedicated to word-formation in the on-going project of the *Indogermanische Grammatik* published by Winter in Heidelberg: Lindner (2011 ff.) on compounding, Sadovski (forthc.) on derivation, both with exhaustive bibliographies.

4 Descriptions based on semantic criteria

The first scholar to take a semantic category, viz. verbal abstracts, as point of departure was Karl von Bahder (1880), subordinating the formal side to the semantic perspective:

> Ich hoffe, dass es mir gelungen ist, einige neue gesichtspuncte für die wortbildung aufzudecken [...] Abschliessende resultate wird kein billig denkender von einem versuche for-

dern, der als der erste einer zusammenhängenden betrachtung einer wortkategorie [...] wol bezeichnet werden darf. (von Bahder 1880: I f.)

[I hope to have been able to discover some new viewpoints for word-formation [...] It would be unfair to expect definitive results from an essay that may probably be called the first one to treat a word-category from a coherent perspective.]

In his *Nominale Stammbildungslehre* (1886) Friedrich Kluge followed this model for all categories. He was the first to abandon the prevailing formal approach in a comprehensive treatise of word-formation and to proceed according to the meanings of the formatives; those belonging together from a semantic point of view were treated together in special chapters (suffixes for personal nouns, diminutive suffixes, collective suffixes, suffixes for inanimate concrete nouns, abstract nouns, etc.). Cf.:

Freilich schließe ich mich in der gruppierung des stoffes nicht an linguistische vorbilder an; ich habe nicht die lautform, wie es bisher üblich war, zum ausgangspunkte für die anordnung gemacht. (Kluge 1886: VIII)

[In my arrangement of the material I do not follow existing models; I did not take as the point of departure the phonic form, as has been done up to now.]

This way of proceeding was to become widely accepted. Wilhelm Meyer-Lübke, for example, followed Kluge's arrangement in his *Italienische Grammatik* (1890):

Wenn so von Seiten einer streng historischen Grammatik die italienischen Fachgenossen, die an der Quelle sitzen, mein Buch werden vielfach ergänzen können, so ist das in noch höherm Grade der Fall bei der Wortbildungslehre. Die Darstellung derselben, wie ich sie im III. Kapitel gegeben habe, hat die Unkömmlichkeit, dass sie einmal viele Suffixe nicht bespricht, und sodann, dass manche Erscheinungen, wie die Verknüpfung verschiedener Suffixe, die Präpositionalbildungen, die Suffixvertauschungen nicht zur Sprache kommen. Allein ich habe nicht den historischen Entwicklungsgang geben wollen, mir lag hauptsächlich daran, eine Darstellung zu bieten, wie sie meines Wissens noch für keine romanische Sprache geboten ist. Die begriffliche Seite ist für diesen Theil der sprachlichen Biologie ebenso wichtig wie die formale, und um dies hervorzuheben, habe ich die letztere fast ganz beiseite gelassen, um so eher, als bei der einseitig aufs Formale gerichteten Aufmerksamkeit der romanischen Forschung eine Ergänzung nach dieser Seite hin nicht schwer fällt. (Meyer-Lübke 1890: ix–x)

[Colleagues working on Italian from a strictly historical perspective on the basis of more abundant material will certainly be able to complete the present book, especially regarding word-formation. My description in chapter III has the disadvantage of not treating many suffixes and that some phenomena such as the combination of different suffixes, prepositional formations, or suffix exchange are not mentioned. However, my intention was not to present the historical development, I wanted to provide a description which, to the best of my knowledge, does not yet exist for any Romance language. The conceptual side is as important for this part of linguistic biology as the formal side. In order to highlight this fact, I have almost completely left aside the latter, all the more so as the one-sided attention of research in Romance on the formal side easily allows completing it in that respect.]

Brugmann's *Grundriß* (1892, 1906) eventually combined both a formal and functional perspective. Furthermore, Paul (1896) is an important contribution to the semantic aspects of word-formation categories and their diachronic developments.

5 Compounding in comparative grammar

The formally-oriented doctrine of compounding of the ancient grammarians (cf. Lindner 2002a: 181) remained unchallenged until the 18th century. But when Sanskrit appeared on the scene of European scholars in the last decades of the 18th century, the Western world became acquainted with the approach and terminology of Indian grammarians, who had been led early on by the high productivity of compounding in Sanskrit to develop a syntactico-semantic, functional typology of compounds which *mutatis mutandis* is still in use today (cf. Lindner 2011: 20–21).

The first interface between the Indian tradition and its transmission in Europe can be found in the first Sanksrit grammars printed in Europe at the end of the 18th and the beginning of the 19th century (Lindner 2012: 148). Bopp eventually coined the latinized versions of the Indian terms that are still in use: 1. Copulative compounds, called *dvandva*; 2. possessive compounds, called *bahuvrīhi* ("the compounds of this class are adjectives or common nouns denoting the possessor of what the parts of the compound mean, so that the notion of possessor always has to be supplemented. That is why I call them 'possessive compounds'"); 3. Determinative compounds, called *karmadhāraya* ("The last member of this class of compounds is a noun or adjective, which is determined or described more precisely by the first member"); 4. Dependency compounds (*Abhängigkeits-Composita*), called *tatpuruṣa* ("this class comprises compounds whose first member depends on or is governed by the second one, always realizing some oblique case relation"); 5. Collective compounds, called *dvigu*; 6. Adverbial compounds, called *avyayībhāva* (Bopp 1827: 311 ff., 1833–52: 1427 ff.).

This classification remains practically unchanged over the next decades, excepting order and denomination. The insight that the determinative compounds comprised both *karmadhāraya* and *tatpuruṣa* was formulated somewhat later, by Theodor Benfey in his *Vollständige Grammatik der Sanskritsprache* (1852), who did not follow the six-class-system of the Indian grammarian Vopadeva directly (as most Europeans before him), but another tradition going back directly to Pāṇini, who calls *karmadhāraya* and *dvigu* subclasses of *tatpuruṣa*; this system, however, has not always been adopted by later research on compounding (cf. Benfey 1852: 245 ff.: 1ˢᵗ class: Copulative compounds (*dvandva*); 2ⁿᵈ class: Determinative compounds (*tatpuruṣa*), subdivided into: 1ˢᵗ species: case-determined compounds (*tatpuruṣa stricto sensu*), 2ⁿᵈ species: apposition-determined compounds (*karmadhāraya*), 3ʳᵈ species: numeral-determined compounds (*dvigu*), which he eventually sees as a special case of the second species, in which the appositional determination is realized by a numeral; 3ʳᵈ class: relative compounds (*bahuvrīhi*). Benfey goes as far as to consider the *bahuvrīhi* as a special kind of compounding of the second class).

At the beginning of the decade of 1860 an important study was published that would set standards for the later research on compounds in general and Indo-European linguistics, Ferdinand Justi's *Über die Zusammensetzung der Nomina in den indogermanischen Sprachen* (1861). What is at issue here is genetic and typological comparison based on material also from non-Indo-European languages, with a wealth of examples that would form the basis of Neogrammarian research some fifteen or twenty years afterwards. I would like to draw attention particularly to the first in-depth analysis of the *bahuvrīhi* type, interpreted as "a higher kind of compounding" condensing a relative clause into a word, a stance that gave rise later on to a controversial discussion about the origin of possessive compounds leading to different theories (cf. Lindner 2002b: 269–273). Chronologically the first one was Justi's relative-clause theory, which was further developed and expanded by Jacobi (1897):

> Es gibt nun eine art wortzusammensetzung, welche einen ganzen bezüglichen satz zu éinem wort vereinigt, das aber wie der ganze satz ebenfalls bezügliche, relative bedeutung hat. Statt zu sagen ἐφάνη Ἠὼς ᾗτινι οἱ δάκτυλοι ὥστε ῥόδα εἰσίν, zieht man den ganzen relativsatz zusammen und bringt ihn in numerale, casuelle und geschlechtliche congruenz mit dem nomen, auf das er sich bezieht, und sagt also ἐφάνη Ἠὼς ῥοδοδάκτυλος, welches aber genau aufgelöst bedeutet ‚Eos, welcher finger wie rosen sind'. – *ibid.* Der bahuvrîhi (sic!) ist nun die bildung, in welcher die wortzusammensetzung den gipfel ihrer vollendung erreicht hat; sie ist ebenso schön wie kurz und bündig [...]. (Justi 1861: 117)

> [There is one kind of composition that condenses a whole relative clause into one word, which however also has a relative meaning like the whole clause. Instead of saying ἐφάνη Ἠὼς ᾗτινι οἱ δάκτυλοι ὥστε ῥόδα εἰσίν, the whole relative clause is pulled together and made agree with the noun it is predicated of in number, case and gender, saying ἐφάνη Ἠὼς ῥοδοδάκτυλος, whose explicit meaning however is: 'Eos, whose fingers are like roses'. [...] The bahuvrihi is that kind of formation where compounding has reached its epitome; it is as beautiful as it is concise [...].]

The question of the nature, history, and origin of stem composition has also become the subject of controversy (cf. Lindner 2012: 88–121, 2013: 149–154). Furthermore, the general and philosophical aspects of compounding first addressed by

Justi have been elaborated in Ludwig Tobler's book *Über die Wortzusammensetzung nebst einem Anhang über die verstärkenden Zusammensetzungen* (1868). Moreover, Justi's book stimulated further research on Greek and Latin compounds published in shorter essays (cf. Lindner and Oniga 2005; Lindner 2011: 12, 2012: 131–134).

Apart from such smaller contributions, one has to mention the comprehensive descriptions of syntactic compounds by Francis Meunier (1872) – we usually call them *Juxtaposita* in Indo-European studies (cf. Lindner 2011: 18) –, as well as Leopold Schröder's great monograph *Über die formelle Unterscheidung der Redetheile im Griechischen und Lateinischen mit besonderer Berücksichtigung der Nominalcomposita* (1874). In this first near-exhaustive description of the dispersed material Schröder rightly criticizes that one defect of his predecessors was "that they were far from complete in their empirical coverage, being content with single examples where complete enumerations would be highly desirable" (cf. Schröder 1874: 194). What is more, he coined the terms "synthetic compound" (1874: 206; *synthetisches Kompositum*) as well as *composita immutata* and *mutata* (1874: 208) to replace Justi's "lower" and "higher" formations. Some fifteen years later the present term "exocentric compounds" was introduced. It is first attested in Aleksandrow (1888: 110), going back probably to Baudouin de Courtenay (Lindner 2009: 190–192): *exocentric compounds* ("compounds whose semantic center is not located in its members") and *esocentric compounds* ("composition whose semantic center corresponds to one of the members"), the latter, nowadays called *endocentric*, further subdivided into *bicentric* (= dvandva) and *monocentric* compounds (with the subtypes *primocentralia* and *alterocentralia*, depending on whether the center coincides with the first or the second member). On the history of this terminology cf. Lindner (2009) and (2011: 27–28); on reference works of the 20th and 21st century concerning Indo-European composition as well as further literature see section 3.2 as well as Lindner (2002a: 322–323, 2003: 134), and (2011: 51–53).

6 References

Adelung, Johann Christoph (1782a): *Umständliches Lehrgebäude der Deutschen Sprache, zur Erläuterung der Deutschen Sprachlehre für Schulen.* Vol. 1. Leipzig: Breitkopf.

Adelung, Johann Christoph (1782b): *Umständliches Lehrgebäude der Deutschen Sprache, zur Erläuterung der Deutschen Sprachlehre für Schulen.* Vol. 2. Leipzig: Breitkopf.

Aleksandrow, Aleksander (1888): *Litauische Studien I. Nominalzusammensetzungen.* Dorpat: Hermann.

Bahder, Karl von (1880): *Die Verbalabstracta in den germanischen Sprachen ihrer Bildung nach dargestellt.* Halle/S.: Niemeyer.

Becker, Karl Ferdinand (1824): *Die Deutsche Wortbildung oder die organische Entwickelung der deutschen Sprache in der Ableitung.* Frankfurt/M.: Hermann.

Becker, Karl Ferdinand (1827): *Organism der Sprache als Einleitung zur deutschen Grammatik.* (Deutsche Sprachlehre, Vol. 1.) Frankfurt/M.: Reinherz. [2nd ed. 1841].

Becker, Karl Ferdinand (1829): *Deutsche Grammatik* (Deutsche Sprachlehre, Vol. 2). Frankfurt/M.: Hermann/Kettembeil. [2nd ed. 1836, 3rd ed. 1842].

Benfey, Theodor (1852): *Vollständige Grammatik der Sanskritsprache* (Handbuch der Sanskritsprache, Vol. 1). Leipzig: Brockhaus.

Bopp, Franz (1824–31): Vergleichende Zergliederung des Sanskrits und der mit ihm verwandten Sprachen. 5 Abhandlungen. In: *Abhandlungen der historisch-philologischen Klasse der Königlichen Akademie der Wissenschaften zu Berlin*, Jg. 1824–1831.

Bopp, Franz (1827): *Ausführliches Lehrgebäude der Sanskrita-Sprache.* Berlin: Dümmler.

Bopp, Franz (1833–52): *Vergleichende Grammatik des Sanskrit, Zend, Griechischen, Lateinischen, Litthauischen, [Altslawischen,] Gothischen und Deutschen.* 6 Vol. Berlin: Dümmler.

Brugmann, Karl (1886): *Grundriß der vergleichenden Grammatik der indogermanischen Sprachen.* Vol. 1: *Einleitung und Lautlehre.* Straßburg: Trübner.

Brugmann, Karl (1892): *Grundriß der vergleichenden Grammatik der indogermanischen Sprachen.* Vol. 2: *Wortbildungslehre (Stammbildungs- und Flexionslehre).* Straßburg: Trübner.

Brugmann, Karl (1904): *Kurze vergleichende Grammatik der indogermanischen Sprachen.* Straßburg: Trübner.

Brugmann, Karl (1906): *Vergleichende Laut-, Stammbildungs- und Flexionslehre nebst Lehre vom Gebrauch der Wortformen der indogermanischen Sprachen.* Vol. 1: *Lehre von den Wortformen und ihrem Gebrauch.* Part 1: *Allgemeines, Zusammensetzung (Komposita), Nominalstämme.* 2nd ed. Straßburg: Trübner.

Buttmann, Philipp (^{3}1805, ^{5}1810): *Griechische Grammatik.* Berlin: Mylius.

Carr, Charles T. (1939): *Nominal Compounds in Germanic.* London: Milford.

Chantraine, Pierre (1933): *La formation des noms en grec ancien.* Paris: Klincksieck [Reprint 1979].

Curtius, Georg (1842): *De nominum Graecorum formatione linguarum cognatarum ratione habita.* Berlin: Dümmler.

Curtius, Georg (1852): *Griechische Schulgrammatik.* Prag: Tempsky.

Debrunner, Albert (1917): *Griechische Wortbildungslehre.* Heidelberg: Winter.

Debrunner, Albert [and Jacob Wackernagel] (1954): *Altindische Grammatik.* Vol. 2,2: *Die Nominalsuffixe.* Göttingen: Vandenhoeck & Ruprecht.

Delbrück, Berthold (1900): *Vergleichende Syntax der indogermanischen Sprache.* Vol. 3. Straßburg: Trübner.

Diez, Friedrich (1838): *Grammatik der romanischen Sprachen.* Vol. 2. Bonn: Weber. [5th ed. 1882].

Duchesne-Guillemin, Jacques (1936): *Les composés de l'Avesta.* Liège/Paris: Droz.

Grimm, Jacob (1819): *Deutsche Grammatik.* Vol. 1. Göttingen: Dieterich. [2nd ed. 1822].

Grimm, Jacob (1826): *Deutsche Grammatik.* Vol. 2. Göttingen: Dieterich. [= 3. Buch: *Von der Wortbildung*]. [2nd ed. 1878].

Heidermanns, Frank (2005): *Bibliographie zur indogermanischen Wortforschung. Wortbildung, Etymologie, Onomasiologie und Lehnwortschichten der alten und modernen indogermanischen Sprachen in systematischen Publikationen ab 1800.* 3 Vol. Tübingen: Niemeyer (also available as CD-ROM).

Jacobi, Hermann (1897): *Compositum und Nebensatz. Studien über die indogermanische Sprachentwicklung.* Bonn: Cohen.

Justi, Ferdinand (1861): *Ueber die zusammensetzung der nomina in den indogermanischen sprachen.* Göttingen: Dieterich.

Kellens, Jean (1974): *Les noms-racines de l'Avesta.* Wiesbaden: Reichert.

Kircher-Durand, Chantal (ed.) (2002): *Grammaire Fondamentale du latin. Tome IX: Création lexicale: la Formation des noms par dérivation suffixale.* Louvain: Peeters.
Kluge, Friedrich (1886): *Nominale Stammbildungslehre der altgermanischen Dialekte.* Halle/S.: Niemeyer. [3rd ed. 1926].
Leumann, Manu (1977): *Lateinische Laut- und Formenlehre.* Vol. 1 of Manu Leumann, Johann Baptist Hofmann and Anton Szantyr *Lateinische Grammatik.* München: Beck. [1st ed. 1926–28].
Lindner, Thomas (1996): *Lateinische Komposita. Ein Glossar, vornehmlich zum Wortschatz der Dichtersprache.* Innsbruck: Institut für Sprachwissenschaft.
Lindner, Thomas (2002a): *Lateinische Komposita. Morphologische, historische und lexikalische Studien.* Innsbruck: Institut für Sprachen und Literaturen.
Lindner, Thomas (2002b): Nominalkomposition und Syntax im Indogermanischen. In: Heinrich Hettrich (ed.), *Indogermanische Syntax. Fragen und Perspektiven,* 263–279. Wiesbaden: Reichert.
Lindner, Thomas (2003): Aspekte der lateinisch-romanischen Kompositaforschung. *Moderne Sprachen* 47: 115–141.
Lindner, Thomas (2009): A Note on 'endocentric'. *Historiographia Linguistica* 36(1): 190–192.
Lindner, Thomas (2011): *Komposition* (Indogermanische Grammatik 4/1). Lieferung 1. Heidelberg: Winter.
Lindner, Thomas (2012): *Komposition* (Indogermanische Grammatik 4/1). Lieferung 2. Heidelberg: Winter.
Lindner, Thomas (2013): *Komposition* (Indogermanische Grammatik 4/1). Lieferung 3. Heidelberg: Winter.
Lindner, Thomas (2015): *Komposition* (Indogermanische Grammatik 4/1). Lieferung 4: *Exkurse zur Wissenschaftsgeschichte der Linguistik.* Heidelberg: Winter.
Lindner, Thomas (2016–2018): *200 Jahre Indogermanistik.* 2 Vol. Salzburg/Wien: Tandem.
Lindner, Thomas (2018): *Komposition im Aufriß* (Indogermanische Grammatik 4/2). Heidelberg: Winter.
Lindner, Thomas (2019): *Historische Metalinguistik.* Vol. 1: *Indogermanische Kompositionslehre.* Salzburg/Wien: Tandem.
Lindner, Thomas (2023): *Historische Metalinguistik.* Vol. 2: *Exegetische Noten.* Salzburg/Wien: Tandem.
Lindner, Thomas (2024): *Komposition* (Indogermanische Grammatik 4/1). Lieferung 5. Heidelberg: Winter.
Lindner, Thomas and Renato Oniga (2005): Zur Forschungsgeschichte der lateinischen Nominalkomposition. In: Gualtiero Calboli (ed.), *Lingua Latina! Proceedings of the Twelfth International Colloquium on Latin Linguistics, Bologna 2003,* 149–160. Roma: Herder.
Lühr, Rosemarie and Irene Balles (2008): *Nominale Wortbildung des Indogermanischen in Grundzügen. Die Wortbildungsmuster ausgewählter indogermanischer Einzelsprachen.* Vol. 1: *Latein, Altgriechisch.* Hamburg: Kovač.
Lühr, Rosemarie and Joachim Matzinger (2008): *Nominale Wortbildung des Indogermanischen in Grundzügen. Die Wortbildungsmuster ausgewählter indogermanischer Einzelsprachen.* Vol. 2: *Hethitisch, Altindisch, Altarmenisch.* Hamburg: Kovač.
Meid, Wolfgang (1967): *Wortbildungslehre.* Vol. 3 of Hans Krahe and Wolfgang Meid *Germanische Sprachwissenschaft.* Berlin: de Gruyter.
Meunier, L.-Francis (1872): *Les composés syntactiques en grec, en latin, en français et subsidiairement en zend et en indien.* Paris: Durand et Pedone-Lauriel.
Meyer-Lübke, Wilhelm (1890): *Italienische Grammatik.* Leipzig: Reisland.
Miklosich, Franz (1875): *Vergleichende Grammatik der slavischen Sprachen.* Vol. 2: *Stammbildungslehre.* Wien: Braumüller.

Miklosich, Franz (1876): *Vergleichende Grammatik der slavischen Sprachen*. Vol. 3: *Wortbildungslehre*. 2nd ed. Wien: Braumüller [1st ed. 1856 as Vol. 3: *Formenlehre*].

Paul, Hermann (1880): *Prinzipien der Sprachgeschichte*. Halle/S.: Niemeyer. [5th ed. 1920].

Paul, Hermann (1896): Über die Aufgaben der Wortbildungslehre. In: *Sitzungsberichte der philosophisch-philologischen und historischen Classe der k. b. Akademie der Wissenschaften zu München*. Jahrgang 1896, Heft 4, 692–713. München: Verlag der K. Akademie. [Reprinted in: Leonhard Lipka and Hartmut Günther (eds.) 1981: Wortbildung, 17–35. Darmstadt: Wissenschaftliche Buchgesellschaft].

Paul, Hermann (1920): *Deutsche Grammatik*. Vol. 5: *Wortbildungslehre*. Tübingen: Niemeyer.

Pott, August Friedrich (1836): *Etymologische Forschungen auf dem Gebiete der Indo-Germanischen Sprachen, insbesondere des Sanskrit, Griechischen, Lateinischen, Littauischen und Gothischen*. Vol. 2: *Grammatischer Lautwechsel und Wortbildung*. Lemgo: Meyer.

Risch, Ernst (1974): *Wortbildung der homerischen Sprache*. 2nd ed. Berlin/New York: de Gruyter.

Sadovski, Velizar (forthc.): *Derivation* (Indogermanische Grammatik 4/2). Heidelberg: Winter.

Schröder, Leopold [von] (1874): *Über die formelle Unterscheidung der Redetheile im Griechischen und Lateinischen mit besonderer Berücksichtigung der Nominalcomposita*. Leipzig: Köhler.

Schwyzer, Eduard (1939): *Griechische Grammatik*. Vol. 1: *Allgemeiner Teil, Lautlehre, Wortbildung, Flexion*. München: Beck.

Tobler, Ludwig (1868): *Über die Wortzusammensetzung nebst einem Anhang über die verstärkenden Zusammensetzungen. Ein Beitrag zur philosophischen und vergleichenden Sprachwissenschaft*. Berlin: Dümmler.

Trendelenburg, Johann Georg (1790): *Anfangsgründe der griechischen Sprache*. 3rd ed. Leipzig: Barth. [1st ed. 1782].

Wackernagel, Jakob (1905): *Altindische Grammatik*. Vol. 2,1: *Einleitung zur Wortlehre. Nominalkomposition*. Göttingen: Vandenhoeck & Ruprecht [New impression ²1957 with additions by Albert Debrunner].

Wackernagel and Debrunner (1954): see Debrunner 1954.

Wackernagel and Debrunner (1957): see Wackernagel 1905.

Wolfgang Motsch
4 Word-formation in structuralism

1   Overview
2   Ferdinand de Saussure
3   Directions in structuralism
4   Word-formation in structuralist schools
5   References

Abstract: The subsumption under the designation *structuralism* of directions in linguistic research from the first half of the 20th century which were very different in detail refers to efforts to found a linguistic theory which meets the demands of mathematical requirements. The guiding impulses for this development stem from F. de Saussure with his establishment of the language system as an autonomous subject of linguistics which is independent of and a precondition to all other aspects of the study of language. The language system was seen as a hierarchy of levels, the units of which are connected to one another through specific relations. The scientific ideal demanded a strict formal, inherent differentiation of levels, units and classes of the language system. The analysis was applied primarily to phonemes and morphemes. The suggested theoretical approaches established guiding foundations for phonology, morphology, and for syntactic dependency or constituent structure grammars. Word-formation played a rather marginal role. This can be explained by the strict methodological postulates.

1 Overview

At the beginning of an, in a narrow sense, scientific study of natural languages stood language comparison and language history. The systematic comparison of languages lead to insights regarding the family relationships among natural languages. There was also a central interest in cultural similarities and differences. The investigation of the history of individual languages was also originally motivated by ethnological interest. With the neogrammarians, this phase of linguistics reached its zenith. Both language comparison as well as the study of the history of individual languages were, however, only based on individual linguistic forms,

Wolfgang Motsch, Berlin, Germany

in particular in the context of the word. The characteristics which constitute the essence of natural language were not systematically investigated. The historical-comparative linguistics of the 19th century could carry out its program with a rather undifferentiated concept of grammar. Linguistic research was oriented towards models which had been developed for classical languages.

As a fundamental criticism of this one-sided direction of research, the idea emerged at the beginning of the 20th century that language comparison and language history are only possible on a scientific basis when a theory is proposed which describes the actual core of natural language. Since human languages are by their nature sign systems, i.e. systems which link sounds with their meanings and thus make possible communication between people, a linguistic theory must describe fundamental characteristics of linguistic sign systems. All other phenomena linked with language presuppose such a theory. The results of preceding linguistic research were, thus, not rejected on principle, but merely seen as provisional and inadequate.

The goal of the directions in linguistics collectively designated as *structuralism* was to lift linguistic research to the level of natural sciences such as physics, chemistry and biology. The requirements for theoretical languages for these precise empirical sciences were also discussed in contemporaneous language philosophy. The Vienna Circle, in particular Rudolf Carnap, Hans Reichenbach, and Herbert Feigl, played a decisive role in the formulation of a program which rationally reconstructed the theories of empirical sciences with the help of mathematical logic. The model was Gottlob Frege's attempt to reconstruct mathematics within the framework of logic. Logical empiricism demanded that all meaningful statements be either directly reduced to observation sentences, or that they are at least able to be brought into a logical relation to observation sentences, so that they can be verified and confirmed by accepted observation sentences.

Structuralism is the designation for a phase in the development of linguistics which is quite varied in its details. The common features which led to this designation are, above all, of methodological nature. Similar stages of development can also be found in the history of the humanities, in psychology, economics, and in other social sciences. The debates on methodology in linguistics had a strong influence on anthropology, ethnology, psychology and literary studies, cf. Levi-Strauss (1958).

The main motivator behind the new direction in linguistics was the Genevan linguist Ferdinand de Saussure (1857–1913). His posthumously published work *Cours de linguistique générale* decisively influenced the development of all structuralist lines of research. The questions he raised led directly to those of the European schools which have gone down in history as the Geneva school, the Copenhagen school and the Prague school. But also the directions in American linguistics which fall under the designation of structuralism were decisively characterized by Saussure's ideas and formulations of the problem.

The term *structure* is only rarely used by Saussure. His central term is *system*. Especially in the Prague school and in American linguistics, the term *structure* is found more often. Structuralism can be seen as the true onset of scientifically founded investigation of human language if one considers the introduction of strict, i.e. verifiable, methodological postulates as characteristic of scientific activity. In any case, the linguistic research of the following period would be inconceivable without structuralist approaches. The current widely accepted organization of possible topics in the scientific study of human languages was already outlined by Saussure. Even the methodological foundations of linguistic research developed by Noam Chomsky can be seen as an extension and a more precise rendering of Saussure's ideas, cf. Motsch (2006).

2 Ferdinand de Saussure

Ferdinand de Saussure initially started his career with historical linguistic research in neogrammarian circles, but then sharply criticized the research of his time. He proposed the outline of a theory of language which differed substantially in its fundamental assumptions from historical-comparative linguistics. In this theory, he demands a fundamental departure from the atomistic study of language details and emphasizes the importance of an examination of the relationships into which the individual units enter with one another within the framework of a system. Only in this way can one arrive at a complex system which consists of units of different levels and their mutual relationships, strictly speaking, a system of subsystems. Language is, according to Saussure, by its very nature a system of values, of units of different levels which mutually condition each other and are only determined through their position in the system. This basic idea was taken up and developed further in, to some extent, very different variations in the linguistic research of the following period.

Beginning with a basic model of linguistic signs, Saussure attempts to differentiate various levels of observation which determine separate objects of research. Central to this endeavor is the distinction between *langue* and *parole*. The *langue* corresponds to a sign system which is used by the speakers or writers of a social community to transmit messages to members of this community. The processes which take place during the transmission and the reception of messages compose the *parole*. They are individual in nature in contrast to the social character of the *langue*. The *langue* is the sign system that determines a particular individual language. A further generalization comprises the assumption of a sign system which underlies all human languages. For this, Saussure introduces the term *langage*, the human language faculty. Although the *langue* has social and psychological facets – it must be accepted by a language community and it is situated in the human brain – according to Saussure it can and must be described completely independently of these perspectives. Even meanings may only be included from the formal point of view of the system. The thoughts or ideas which stand behind the meanings, the substance of the content, form an amorphous mass which does not belong to the subject matter of the description of the system of a language. This means: the essential properties of the sign system which underlies a language are independent both of analyses of the substance of the content, the psychological existence and the social use of this system, as well as of the processes of the formation and comprehension of utterances. One can of course investigate the relationships between the sign system of a language and questions of language philosophy or its existence in the human brain, just as one can, e.g., investigate the influence of social factors on the structuring of a language into a standard language and regional and social variants, or on the vocabulary of a language. But in any case, such studies presume a description of the sign system which is completely independent of these kinds of questions. Thus an investigation of the processes of the formation and understanding of utterances, i.e. the *parole*, demands a knowledge of the system of a language and additionally the inclusion of psychological questions and theories as well as the consideration of the given context.

According to Saussure, if one sees the sign system as a fundamental prerequisite for communication among the members of a speech community, a separation of the description of this system from an investigation of the history of this system follows automatically. Linguistic signs are *valeurs*, values in a system in which they coexist with other signs. The coexistence is only possible on the axis of simultaneity (*axe des simultanéités*). Change in the sign system is irrelevant for the user of the sign system. It arises only from the perspective of the linguist. Saussure views every natural language as very much simultaneously a contemporary institution and a product of the past (Saussure 1916: 24). But studying the relationships is only possible if the *inner organism* of the language is initially described without reference to society and history (Saussure 1916: 40, 124). These considerations led Saussure to the dichotomy of *synchrony* and *diachrony*.

The observations thus outlined strengthen Saussure's assumption that the *langue* must be the central subject matter of linguistics. It is the only autonomous topic within the scope of the overall phenomenon of language which is not investigated by any other discipline and which is always assumed in the investigation of other aspects of language. This train of thought decisively influenced the further development of linguistics. It forms the methodological basis for almost all directions in modern linguistic research.

Saussure provided stimulating guidelines with respect to the internal structure of linguistic sign systems. Especially his distinction between *syntagmatic* and *paradigmatic* relations was taken up and expanded upon by other structuralist schools. Saussure differentiates between relations into which units of the system enter *in praesentia*, i.e. with other linguistic units at the same level, e.g., in syntactic chains, as well as *associative relations* (Saussure 1916: 170); these are units which can occupy the same position in a syntagm. This differentiation forms the basis for the assumption of syntactic categories and levels of sentence structure. Syntagm and paradigm are complementary concepts. The language system thus consists of sets of units (phonemes, words, word groups) and a small quantity of very general patterns in which phonemes and words can be inserted under certain conditions. Every linguistic unit can thus also be characterized through the relationships into which it can enter with other units at the same level, cf. Wells (1947) and Jäger (2006).

3 Directions in structuralism

The Geneva school: Immediately following Saussure are his students and colleagues Charles Bally, Albert Sechehaye, Henri Frei, Sergej Karcevski and Robert Godel. Their work was discussed in the Genevan Cercle F. de Saussure and was published primarily in the series *Cahiers F. de Saussure*. In these papers, Saussure's thoughts and arguments are expanded upon and further developed, and misunderstandings are cleared up.

Special attention is due Lucien Tesnière, also considered part of the Geneva school, who in his book "Éléments de syntaxe structurale" (Tesnière 1959), sketched in 1934 and only released posthumously in 1959, published a model of syntactic analysis which was later extended as *dependency grammar*.

An overview of Tesnière and the further development of his ideas can be found in Godel (1961), Kunze (1975), Baumgärtner (1976), Baum (1976), Heringer, Strecker and Wimmer (1980) and Hudson (1980).

The Copenhagen school: Head of the Copenhagen school was Louis Hjelmslev, who in 1943 published a programmatic work in Danish *Omkring sprogteoriens grundlæggelse*. An English translation appeared in 1961 under the title *Prolegomena to a Theory of Language*. To the Copenhagen school belong further Hans Jørg Uldall, Viggo Brøndal, Berta Siertsema, Henning Spang-Hanssen, Knut Togeby, and Paul Diderichsen.

This approach refers to itself as *glossematics*. The goal of this approach is to create an immanent algebra of language, a general calculus for the description of texts in a natural language. Hjelmslev initially only proposes prolegomena of such a linguistic theory, i.e. methodological principles and a few basic assumptions about fundamental properties of the system which underlies natural languages. He emphasizes that a linguistic theory cannot be a sum of hypotheses; it must rather be a system of premises and definitions which is arbitrary, yet suitable for the description of generally accepted and empirically verified data. When establishing the calculus, direct reference to either phonetic or ontological concepts is not allowed.

To the premises which determine the central properties of the theory belong the distinction between *expression* and *content* as well as between *form* and *substance*. This corresponds to distinctions which had already been made by Saussure: *signifié* [signified] and *signifiant* [signifier] as well as *forme* [form] and *substance* [substance]. The calculus must take into consideration the character of natural languages as sign systems as well as the distinction between syntagmatic and paradigmatic relations. It must also permit hierarchical relations.

The glossematic algebra is, as are calculuses of formal logic, a system of dependencies (functions) between terms, which are only determined through their mutual dependencies. Units must be the result of an analytic procedure, a deduction. Hjelmslev thus does not accept the *discovery procedures* which were later suggested in American approaches.

Hjelmslev's analysis does not lead to a separation of syntax and morphology. To a degree, the distinction between paradigmatic and syntagmatic relations corresponds to these components in other linguistic theories. Most applications of glossematics relate to areas which belong to phonology or morphology in other theories. Products of word-formation are only used as examples for general morphological questions. Glossematic grammar corresponds rather more to a dependency grammar than to a constituent structure grammar.

An overview of glossematics is provided by i.a. Martinet (1946), Siertsema (1955), and Spang-Hanssen (1961). A comparison of glossematics with American linguistic theories can be found in Haugen (1951) and Garvin (1954).

The Prague school: In 1926, Vilém Mathesius, Bohuslav Havránek, Jan Mukařovský, Bohumil Trnka and Josef Vachek founded the Cercle linguistique de Prague. At the first International Linguistic Congress, which took place in 1928 in The Hague, Roman Jakobson, Sergej Karcevski and Nikolai S. Trubetzkoy presented theses in the name of this circle, cf. Jakobson, Karcevski and Trubetzkoy (1929). In these theses, theoretical positions on phonology, morphology including word-formation, and on the functional view of linguistic phenomena are presented. In these theses as well, the basis is Saussure's requirement of investigating language as an autonomous system, i.e. independently of philosophy, psychology, acoustics, sociology and other disciplines. But members of the Prague school also concern themselves with topics that go beyond the language system. In contrast to other structuralist schools, the Prague school stipulates a *functional* approach to the language system, taking the path from function to form, cf. Mathesius (1929).

Typical for the Prague school is a broadly based interest in language phenomena. Besides phonology, morphology and syntax, i.e. the areas which belong to the language system, problems of literary texts, text analysis, language acquisition, and a structurally oriented historical linguistics are also discussed.

American approaches: The actual father of American structuralism is considered to be Leonard Bloomfield, whose groundbreaking work *Language* was published in 1933. His most important successors are Zellig S. Harris, Bernard Bloch, Rulon S. Wells, Charles F. Hockett and Charles C. Fries.

As did the European schools originating with Saussure, the American structuralists tried to find methods which permit the identification of linguistic units and their organization into classes by purely formal means. Bloomfield, who stands at the beginning of this movement, refers principally to Saussure. Through Jakobson and Martinet, ideas of the Prague school reached the Linguistic Circle of New York in the 30s. The focal points were initially phonology and morphology. The distributionalists, especially Harris, also systematically include syntax in their linguistic analysis. Characteristic for American structuralism is the search for *discovery procedures*, i.e. for procedures which permit the determination of the grammatical structure of sentences after a finite number of steps.

With Leonard Bloomfield, theoretical linguistics in the United States reached a new level. All following language researchers are in Bloomfield's debt. Bloomfield's methodological premises are influenced by the dominating physicalistic scientific ideal of his time. He only recognizes such data that can be discovered through direct observation and immediate experience. Mentalistic procedures which in principle permit reference to the linguistic knowledge of speakers/hearers of a language are excluded. Of course Bloomfield doesn't deny the character of natural languages as sign systems, he only excludes the explicit reference to meanings in the definition of grammatical concepts. However, he states that the ability of native speakers to decide whether two forms are the same or not must be permitted (Bloomfield 1933: 77). The meanings associated with linguistic forms are, in Bloomfield's view, not accessible to scientific description, at least not for the current state of linguistic research. They must be investigated according to principles which the behaviorist psychology of his time applied in the study of the behavior of animals. He gives an example of how one should proceed according to these principles in order to make scientifically founded statements about mental phenomena such as linguistic meaning. With this example, he would like to demonstrate that even the application of behavioristic methods to the analysis of linguistic meanings is practically impossible.

We owe a significant further development of Bloomfield's approaches to Zellig S. Harris. Harris viewed linguistics, similarly to Hjelmslev and later Chomsky, as applied mathematics (Harris 1968: 1). His first great work was published in 1951 under the title *Methods in Structural Linguistics*. He is the founder of distributionalism. The task of linguistics is, according to his conception, "to describe the distribution or arrangement within the flow of speech of some parts or features relatively to each other". There are three tasks to be solved: 1. The units of different levels must be segmented, 2. The resulting segments must be classified by means of an observation of their distribution. The appearance of segments in the same context means membership in the same class. 3. The relations between the resulting classes must be determined (Harris 1951: 20).

Harris assumes that these tasks can be completed via an effective procedure which after a finite number of steps determines the grammatical structure of linguistic utterances. This procedure must be possible without explicitly taking into account the meaning or the sounds of linguistic units. "In exact descriptive linguistic work […] considerations of meaning can only be used heuristically, as a source of hints, and the determining criteria will always have to be stated in distributional terms" (Harris 1951: 365 fn. 6). In fact Harris must also allow for a native speaker who only answers the questions: *Is that the same?* and *Is that possible?* Harris is however of the opinion that this only makes short cuts possible which otherwise abbreviate very elaborate procedures. "It may be presumed that any two morphemes having different meanings also differ somewhere in distribution" (Harris 1951: 365 fn. 4). The assumption of effective discovery procedures generated great interest, but was also seriously questioned. In particular two points are controversial: are the assumed procedures really effective, i.e. do they lead to an acceptable conclusion? And is the justification for the acceptability of short cuts acceptable? The tenor of the criticism is: it is practically impossible to investigate all segments in every possible context. In phonology this is in any case simpler than in morphology or syntax. For the *substitution-in-frames-procedures* suggested by Harris, it cannot be theoretically proven that it delivers the desired definitions after a finite number of steps (Lees 1957). Problems which arise for the definition of the concept of morpheme are also pointed out by Bierwisch (1961).

The background of distributionalistic thinking is immediate constituent grammar. This type of grammar assumes a very clear and manageable schema involving a strictly hierarchical structuring of the sentence. A sentence consists of phonemes. The combination of phonemes yields morphemes. The combination of morphemes yields words and word groups. The combination of word groups yields sentences (Postal 1964).

As most structuralists, Harris also follows Saussure's view that only an immanent linguistic description of language can be the foundation for "historical linguistics, dialect geography, for relations of language to culture and personality, to phonetics and semantics and for the comparison of language structure with systems of logic" (Harris 1951: 3).

4 Word-formation in structuralist schools

In a description of the history of research on English word-formation, Valerie Adams notes that American structuralism was only interested in questions of word-formation in the context of morphological and syntactic problems, since its adherents focused their main interest on units which are smaller or larger than words. Furthermore, Saussure's distinction between synchrony and diachrony discredited the primarily historically oriented research on word-formation of the 19th century (Adams 1973: 5). It also applies to the European schools that typical phenomena of word-formation were not systematically followed up on by the founders of structuralist schools. Only to the extent that means of word-formation are associated with the analysis of morphemes or with syntactic operations were they taken into consideration.

Hockett discusses, for example, models according to which words can be segmented into morphemes (Hockett 1958: 393). He prefers an item-and-arrangement model, i.e. the segmentation of expressions in units and the determination of types of arrangements of these units. The German verb form *sucht* 'searches' can, for example, be segmented in *such* + *t*. The unit *such* also combines with other units: *Such+e* 'search', *Ver+such+ung* 'temptation', *such+te* 'searched'. All of these units are morphemes, i.e. the smallest grammatical units which are combined with a meaning. Problems are caused by words such as Engl. *cran+berry*, which contain units with which no meaning is associated, words with ablaut (Engl. *took* : *take*, Ger. *zieh* : *zog* 'pull : pulled' and other problematic cases in which words can be segmented into grammatical units which do not correspond to a segmentation of the word into morphemes (Engl. *worse*, *bad* + comparative, Ger. *Lauf* 'walk', *lauf* + nominalization). Problems of this type are associated both with inflectional forms of words as well as with products of word-formation, cf. *zieh* 'to pull' : *Zug* 'pull, train', *seh* 'to see' : *Sicht* 'sight'. To describe these phenomena, Bloomfield suggests an item-and-process model. Bloomfield also discusses relationships between compounds and syntactic expressions (Bloomfield 1933:

227–32). He differentiates *semisyntactic compounds* from *asyntactic compounds*. Syntactic compounds have syntactic expressions as direct parallels, cf. *house keeper: keep house, blue-eyed: blue eyes*. For asyntactic compounds, no syntactic constructions exist in which the members of the compound are constituents, cf. *door knob*. This distinction makes clear Bloomfield's physicalistic scientific ideal. The members of a compound must be able to be immediately adjacent to each other in syntactic constructions. Without syntactic argumentation, he rejects parallels such as *knob of a door* or *door has a knob*.

Tesnière includes products of word-formation which function as translatives in his syntactic theory. Characteristic of sentence structure in Tesnière's model is the possibility to transfer words with a specified grammatical category into words with another grammatical category. In the French construction *le livre rouge* 'the red book', *rouge* 'red' is a word categorized as an adjective. But also in *le livre de Pierre* 'the book of Peter', *de* transfers the noun *Pierre* to an adjective. *De* is a translative and *Pierre* a translate; *de Pierre* and *rouge* are syntactically equivalent. The noun *Pierre* becomes an adjective via the preposition *de* in *de Pierre*. Adjectives can be transferred to verbs with the help of *être* 'to be', e.g., *La maison est neuve* 'The house is new'. Bound morphemes can also function as translatives. In Latin *Venit Romam* '(He/she) came to Rome' the accusative morpheme *-am* causes the transfer of a noun to an adverb. The use of German *gut* 'good' in the syntactic position *Er schläft gut* 'he sleeps well' makes the adjective an adverb without a translative. Verbs are seen as the basic category. But they can also be transferred to other categories. Thus, the subordination of relative clauses is a translation from a structure with verb into an adjective. An object clause makes a structure with verb into a noun. Means of word-formation can also be means of recategorization. The German verb *erobern* 'to conquer' becomes a noun via the suffix *-ung*, as does the adjective *frei* 'free' via the suffix *-heit*.

The reserved attitude toward a systematic search for rules for new words is, strictly speaking, an expected consequence of the methodological principles assumed by the individual schools:

1. Strict synchrony;
2. Mathematical regularity of the combination of linguistic expressions;
3. Meanings may only be taken into consideration via purely formal methods;
4. A mentalistic capturing of data, i.e. reference to the linguistic knowledge of native speakers, is not permitted, with the exception of strictly regulated exceptions;
5. Language use does not influence statements about the language system;
6. These requirements cause concepts such as affixoid, unproductive rule, degree of productivity of a rule, lexicalized word, ad-hoc formation, or accept-

ability of a new formation to be excluded from the analysis of the system. They require a reference to historical contexts or to language use.

Saussure already distinguishes suffixes from other morphemes. He assumes semantic and grammatical functions for suffixes. This is permissible, because the question of whether a morpheme is connected with a meaning or not is acceptable, just as is the question of the function of a form within a syntagm. The suffixes of word-formation (derivational suffixes) are associated with meanings, other suffixes (inflectional suffixes) are markers for grammatical relations. But problems are caused by products of word-formation which entered the lexicon of a language in historic times, cf. Ger. *Brom+beere* 'blackberry', *Dick-icht* 'thicket', *Fahr-t* 'ride', *Klang* 'sound' (nominalization of *kling* via ablaut). In this case, neither the question of whether the suffixes have their own meaning, nor the question of why there are no comparable new formations can be decided on the basis of the principles considered to be permissible. It should generally be noted that the syntactic aspect preferred in the structuralist theories only concerns a portion of word-formation patterns. Except for the syntactic categorization of complex words, recategorization with the help of patterns of word-formation, and the few cases of syntactic restructuring, the principles for the formation of new words are of a semantic nature, cf. Fanselow (1987) and Motsch (2000).

A systematic investigation of the regularities of word-formation within the framework of the methodological principles of most structuralist schools would have led to relatively uninteresting, strongly overgeneralized statements. For example: all words occurring in texts can be divided into derivatives and compounds. Derivatives are combinations of words and affixes. Affixes are suffixes or prefixes. In contrast to words, which can occur alone, affixes are bound to words. Affixoid is strictly speaking not a permissible concept, since it assumes historical or semantic concepts. Affixes are signs, and thus carry meaning. Some suffixes have an innergrammatical function; they indicate the change in category of a word, cf. Ger. *prüf* 'to test' : *Prüf+ung* 'test', *frei* 'free' : *Frei+heit* 'freedom'. Suffixes and prefixes are bound to word categories which are to be syntactically defined. We must however note that, for example, a rule "N+ig yields a possible adjective in German" is much too undifferentiated. Although there are many words for which this rule applies, cf. *sandig* 'sandy', *eckig* 'angular; lit. edgy', *steinig* 'stony', *staubig* 'dusty', *wolkig* 'cloudy', for many other words, this statement is problematic, cf. **tischig* 'tabley', **stuhlig* 'chairy', **zimmerig* 'roomy', **tagig* 'day-y', **hausig* 'housey', **dorfig* 'villagey', **knopfig* 'buttony'. Even if more specific statements about the meanings of affixes were permitted and subclassifications of base words were possible, the problem of overgeneralized statements would remain, cf. Motsch (2011). Compounds are combinations of words which belong to specific word categories. Whether formations with syntactic constructions as a first member – cf. Ger. *warm-herz+ig* 'warm hearted; lit. warm hearty', *kurz-atm+ig* 'short winded; lit. short breathy', *Zwei-zu-eins-Sieg* 'two-to-one-win' – can be satisfactorily described in the framework of the principles of structuralist theories would need to be clarified. Compounds can be differentiated through the category membership of their constituents. Beyond that, only parallels to syntactic constructions can be noted. Probably even the classic, semantically based differentiation between determinative, copulative and exocentric compounds could not be reproduced.

It is not surprising that word-formation in European languages was primarily investigated by scholars who placed more moderate conditions on methodological principles. This includes in particular the work of Marchand (1969), Dokulil (1968), and Fleischer (1969). Synchronic analysis is the focus of this work as well. Many suggestions of structuralist approaches are adopted, although in a weakened form. The greatest impact was from Saussure's requirement of separating synchrony and diachrony. Apart from a few historical references, one doesn't find systematic historical investigations in the large body of works containing descriptions of word-formation. Thus, for example, an investigation of derivational affixes following the assumptions of Jacob Grimm that they trace back to independent words was almost completely lost. Grimm's distinction between proper compounds (echte/eigentliche Komposita) and improper compounds (unechte/uneigentliche Komposita) no longer plays a systematic role either, see article 3 on word-formation in historical-comparative grammar.

Particularly worth mentioning in this context is also Coseriu's (1970) attempt to determine the structure of the vocabulary of a language. He assumes thereby ideas of the classical structuralists, in particular the postulate that all linguistic units, and therefore also the meanings of linguistic expressions, enter into syntagmatic and paradigmatic relations. He follows up on ideas of Hjelmslev, who, parallel to the segmentation of morphemes into phonemes, suggested a decomposition of the meanings of the content plane in figurae. According to Coseriu, the phenomena of the expression plane correspond to *semes*, with the help of which semantic relations between lexemes in the lexicon can be described. Word-formation patterns are seen as special means for the establishment of semantic relations in the lexicon of a language.

Generative grammar also directed attention to structural connections which appear to point out new directions for research on word-formation. Thus Lees (1960) uses transformations in the first version of a generative grammar for the analysis of compounds formed by two nouns. He establishes a connection between syntactic constructions and compounds which makes it possible to highlight differences in meaning. The problem nevertheless remains whether all prominent phenomena of word-formation can be described in the context of a stricter theory of grammar, cf. Motsch (2011). The mentalistic perspective taken by Chomsky and the idea of a modular organization of systems of knowledge adopted from cognitive psychology freed the way for the systematic integration of semantic and pragmatic aspects in the analysis of word-formation. However, for central questions of the theory of grammar, word-formation still remains as a whole of marginal interest. Chomsky (1982: 96) took the view in a discussion with Henk van Riemsdijk that "where we have options to get an infinite vocabulary, it appears to be through pretty trivial mechanisms".

In any case, it is fair to say that structuralist schools have made great contributions to the analysis of the elementary structure of words. Fundamental concepts were worked out for analyzing the internal structure of words and their role in the combination of words to phrases and sentences. We thank structuralist approaches for concepts such as *stem morpheme*, *derivational* and *inflectional morpheme*, *discontinuous morpheme*, and *free* and *bound morpheme*. Bloomfield, Harris and Hockett contributed greatly to these results. It would be impossible to imagine modern research in morphology and word-formation without the preliminary work of the structuralists.

As an example for the influence of classical structuralist schools on research in word-formation, the influential theory of Hans Marchand will be briefly illustrated here.

Marchand's *The Categories and Types of Present-Day English Word-Formation* was first published in 1960 and appeared in a second edition in 1969. As one of his most well-known students, Dieter Kastovsky, writes, this book is even today "the most comprehensive synchronic description of Modern English word-formation" (Kastovsky 1999: 29). Marchand had already developed the theoretical basis of his work in the 1940s of the last century. He bases his important points on European structuralist thought, especially on the basic ideas of Saussure and extensions of these ideas by Charles Bally. But he also takes American structuralists into account. The confrontation with the word-formation theory of Robert Lees led to an extensive reworking of his book, which appeared in a second edition in 1969.

In contrast to the largely neogrammarian orientation of the linguistics of his time, Marchand emphasizes the priority of a synchronic description. References to historical contexts do not have a systematic character. To the foundation of his theory of word-formation belong the concepts *syntagm* and *motivation*, which can be traced back to Saussure and Bally, cf. Bally (1944). The subject matter of word-formation are regular formations which can be analyzed as a syntagm which consists of two morphemes. Morphemes are seen as linguistic units with the character of a sign. According to Saussure, the bond between the two components of the sign, the form and the meaning, is fundamentally arbitrary and unmotivated. Complex linguistic expressions, syntagms, are on the other hand principally motivated, since they can be semantically interpreted on the basis of their constituents and a grammatical pattern. Marchand draws from this the conclusion that meaning is just as important as form, since the smallest linguistic signs, the morphemes, must be interpreted as signs (Marchand 1969: 1). He thus does not accept the trend to a purely distributional definition of linguistic units in American linguistics and makes, as did later Chomsky, the mentalistic assumption that the speakers of a language know the meanings of linguistic expressions and that this aspect of linguistic competence must be taken into consideration in an adequate theory, even though there were at the time no fully-developed proposals as to how linguistic meanings should be described in an appropriate theoretical form.

This approach results in important consequences for determining the subject matter of a theory of word-formation. There are words that form a syntagm, i.e. which are formed from morphemes. Among these are, according to Marchand, compounds, prefixations, suffixations, zero-derivatives and backformations. Other analyzable words cannot be reduced to syntagms. This includes onomatopoeia (Ger. *Schnick-Schnack* 'tittle-tattle'), blends (Ger. *Kurlaub* 'medical treatment holiday', from *Kur* 'cure' and *Urlaub* 'vacation'), words with ablaut (Ger. *Zug* 'train' : *zieh(en)* 'to pull'). Words with parts which do not have a meaning or for which there are no recognizable patterns also do not belong to synchronic descriptions of word-formation (Engl. *cran+berry*). In contrast to the distributionalists, Marchand rejects analyses such as Engl. *re-ceive*, *de-ceive*, *con-ceive*, etc., since neither the prefixes nor the bases have a recognizable meaning. He regards such words as monomorphemic. Word-formation is based on bimorphemic syntagms, which must be productive to a certain degree, i.e. are the basis for new formations. In contrast to Harris, who completely excludes productivity from grammatical analysis, Marchand uses this phenomenon for the definition of word-formation patterns. Harris (1951: 255) writes with theoretical consequence from his methodological premises, "The methods of descriptive linguistics cannot treat the degree of productivity of elements". The term, to be defined by language use, offers, together with the concept of syntagm, the possibility of excluding certain lexicalized formations, but it remains out of place in a, in principle, syntactically grounded theory.

Problematic is also the assumption of a zero-morpheme. Verbs such as *to dirty, to clean, to tidy* have a meaning which is composed of the meaning of the homonymous adjective and the meaning of *make*. They thus stand in relation to the pattern 'adj. + -*ize*', which underlies the forms *legal+ize, national+ize, steril+ize*. According to Marchand, one can on this basis assume morphemes which do not have a phonological form. The strict concept of syntagm is noticeably softened here, as signs are assumed which do not have a phonological form. The justification based on parallel patterns with suffixes is also not convincing. In German, we have denominal verbs such as *geigen* 'to (play the) fiddle', *trompeten* 'to (play the) trumpet', *kämmen* 'to comb', *angeln* 'to fish; lit. to fishing-rod', *hämmern* 'to hammer', the meanings of which can be rendered with 'to do something typical with N'. But there are no parallel patterns with an affix. Phenomena of this type demand a semantically based concept of word-formation pattern.

Characteristic for Marchand's theory of word-formation is the relationship of word-formation patterns to syntactic syntagms. Bally and Bloomfield have also pointed out such connections. Marchand thus sees the relationship of compounds such as *house-keeping* to syntactic constructions such as *keep the house*. He notes, that "Cpds [compounds] are chiefly based on a 'predicate/object' relation, but as such cpds are, on principle, nominalised sentences" (Marchand 1969: 29). He highlights further connections to syntactic relations in his analysis of zero-nominalizations and denominal verbs. He rejects, however, the description of such relations through special restructuring rules, or transformations.

The assumption of zero-morphemes makes clear that Marchand is still deeply bound to the item-and-arrangement model. Since units at the lowest syntactic level are segmented in morphemes, and morphemes are the smallest units which have meaning, in problematic cases an identity in meaning of word components is assumed as sufficient justification for the existence of signs without phonetic marking. Only the assumption of semantic patterns which are linked in different ways with phonological indices is a theoretically satisfying alternative.

According to Marchand, composites, words which have been assembled, are syntagms which consist of a determinant and a determinatum. This is the case for compounds and derivatives. In *head-ache*, *father-hood*, and *un-do*, the first member determines in each case the second. It is typical of prefixations and suffixations that the affix also occurs with other stems: *father-hood*, *mother-hood*, *boy-hood*; *un-do*, *un-fasten*, *un-roll*. This aspect was later discussed under the perspective of head of a construction.

Backformations such as the verb *peddle*, which is later attested than the noun *peddler*, are only peculiar from a historical perspective; from a synchronic point of view they must be dealt with like the noun *writer*, which is derived from the verb *write* on the basis of a pattern.

5 References

Adams, Valerie (1973): *An Introduction to Modern English Word-Formation.* London: Longman.
Bally, Charles (1944): *Linguistique générale et linguistique française.* 2nd ed. Bern: Francke.

Baum, Richard (1976): *Dependenzgrammatik. Tesnières Modell der Sprachbeschreibung in wissenschafts-geschichtlicher und kritischer Sicht*. Tübingen: Niemeyer.
Baumgärtner, Klaus (1976): Konstituenz und Dependenz: Zur Integration der beiden grammatischen Prinzipien. In: Hugo Steger (ed.), *Vorschläge für eine strukturale Grammatik des Deutschen*, 52–77. Darmstadt: Wissenschaftliche Buchgesellschaft.
Bierwisch, Manfred (1961): Über den theoretischen Status des Morphems. *Studia grammatica* 1: 51–89. Berlin: Akademie Verlag.
Bloomfield, Leonard (1933): *Language*. New York: Holt.
Chomsky, Noam (1982): *On the Generative Enterprise. A Discussion with Riny Huybregts and Henk van Riemsdijk*. Dordrecht: Foris.
Coseriu, Eugenio (1970): *Einführung in die strukturelle Betrachtung des Wortschatzes*. Tübingen: Niemeyer.
Dokulil, Miloš (1968): Zur Theorie der Wortbildungslehre. *Wissenschaftliche Zeitschrift der Karl Marx Universität Leipzig. Gesellschafts- und Sprachwissenschaftliche Reihe* 17: 203–211.
Fanselow, Gisbert (1987): Gemeinsame Prinzipien von Wort- und Phrasensemantik. In: Brigitte Ansbach-Schnitker, Herbert E. Brekle and Johannes Roggenhofer (eds.), *Neuere Forschungen zur Wortbildung und Historiographie der Linguistik*, 177–194. Tübingen: Niemeyer.
Fleischer, Wolfgang (1969): *Wortbildung der deutschen Gegenwartssprache*. Tübingen: Niemeyer.
Garvin, Paul L. (1954): Review of Prolegomena to a Theory of Language by Louis Hjelmslev. *Language* 30(1): 69–96.
Godel, Robert (1961): L'École saussurienne de Genève. In: Christine Mohrmann, Alf Sommerfelt and Joshua Whatmough (eds.), *Trends in European and American Linguistics 1930–1960*, 294–299. Utrecht/Antwerpen: Spectrum.
Harris, Zellig S. (1951): *Methods in Structural Linguistics*. Chicago: Chicago University Press.
Harris, Zellig S. (1968): *Mathematical Structures of Language*. New York: Wiley Interscience.
Haugen, Einar (1951): Directions in modern linguistics. *Language* 27: 211–222.
Heringer, Hans Jürgen, Bruno Strecker and Rainer Wimmer (1980): *Syntax: Fragen – Lösungen – Alternativen*. München: Fink.
Hjelmslev, Louis (1943): *Omkring sprogteoriens grundlæggelse*. Copenhagen: Munksgaard.
Hjelmslev, Louis (1961): *Prolegommena to a Theory of Language*. Madison: University of Wisconsin Press.
Hockett, Charles F. (1958): *A Course in Modern Linguistics*. New York: Macmillan.
Hudson, R.A. (1980): Constituency and Dependency. *Linguistics* 18: 179–198.
Jakobson, Roman, Sergej Karcevski and Nikolai S. Trubetzkoy (1929): *Proposition au Premier Congrès International de Linguistes à La Haye, 10–15 avril 1928*, 33–36. Leiden: Sijthoff.
Jäger, Ludwig (2006): *Ferdinand de Saussure zur Einführung*. Hamburg: Junius.
Jespersen, Otto (1942): *A Modern English Grammar on Historical Principles*. Vol. 6: *Morphology*. London/Copenhagen: George Allen & Unwin.
Kastovsky, Dieter (1999): Hans Marchand's theory of word-formation: Genesis and development. In: Uwe Clark and Peter Lucko (eds.), Form, Function and Variation in English. Studies in Honor of Klaus Hensen, 19–39. Frankfurt/M.: Lang.
Kunze, Jürgen (1975): *Abhängigkeitsgrammatik für das Deutsche*. Berlin: Akademie Verlag.
Lees, Robert (1957): Review of Syntactic Structures. *Language* 33: 375–408.
Lees, Robert (1960): *The Grammar of English Nominalizations*. The Hague: Mouton.
Lévi-Strauss, Claude (1958): *Anthropologie Structurale*. Paris: Plon.
Marchand, Hans (1969): *The Categories and Types of Present-Day English Word-Formation. A Synchronic-Diachronic Approach*. 2nd ed. München: Beck.

Martinet, André (1946): Au sujet des fondaments de la théorie linguistique de L. Hjelmslev. *Bulletin de la Société Linguistique de Paris* 124: 19–43.
Mathesius, Vilém (1929): Zur Satzperspektive im modernen Englisch. *Archiv für das Studium der neueren Sprachen und Literaturen* 155: 200–210.
Motsch, Wolfgang (2000): Syntaktische Konsequenzen von Wortbildungsmustern. In: Josef Bayer and Christine Römer (eds.), *Von der Philologie zur Grammatiktheorie: Peter Suchsland zum 65. Geburtstag*, 289–302. Tübingen: Niemeyer.
Motsch, Wolfgang (2006): Methodologische Aspekte der neueren Sprachforschung. In: Kristel Proost and Edeltraud Winkler (eds.), *Von der Intentionalität zur Bedeutung konventionalisierter Zeichen. Festschrift für Gisela Harras zum 65. Geburtstag*, 327–336. Tübingen: Narr.
Motsch, Wolfgang (2011): Grammatische und sprachpsychologische Aspekte der Wortbildung. In: Hilke Elsen and Sascha Michel (eds.), *Wortbildung im Deutschen zwischen Sprachsystem und Sprachgebrauch. Perspektiven – Analysen – Anwendungen*, 43–72. Stuttgart: ibidem.
Postal, Paul (1964): *Constituent Structure*. The Hague: Mouton.
Saussure, Ferdinand de (1916): *Cours de linguistique générale*. Ed. by Charles Bally and Albert Séchehay. Paris/Lausanne: Payot.
Siertsema, Berta (1955): *A Study of Glossematics*. The Hague: Mouton.
Spang-Hansen, Henning (1961): Glossematics. In: Christine Mohrmann, Alf Sommerfelt and Josua Whatmough (eds.), *Trends in European and American Linguistics 1930–1960*, 128–164. Utrecht/Antwerpen: Spectrum.
Tesnière, Lucien (1959): *Élements de syntaxe structurale*. Paris: Klincksieck.
Trubetzkoy, Nikolai S. (1939): *Grundzüge der Phonologie*. Prag: [Harrassowitz].
Wells, Rulon S. (1947): De Saussure's system of linguistics. *Word* 3: 1–3.

Rochelle Lieber
5 Word-formation in generative grammar

1 Introduction
2 Early generative grammar
3 The beginnings of generative morphology as a separate discipline
4 The heyday
5 Reactions to classic generative morphology
6 Conclusion
7 References

Abstract: This article traces the treatment of word-formation in generative grammar from the early days of the theory in which word-formation, if discussed at all, is treated either as a matter of syntax or phonology to the present. We look at the beginnings of the theory in the work of Halle (1973) and Jackendoff (1975) and its heyday in the 1970's and 1980's with the work of Aronoff (1976), Lieber (1980), Williams (1981), and Selkirk (1982). Of special interest is the placement of rules of word-formation with respect to other components of the grammar as well as the issue of lexical integrity. Later developments, such as the return to a syntactic theory of word-formation and the fragmenting of generative morphology into a variety of different approaches are covered as well.

1 Introduction

We use the term generative grammar to refer broadly to the various theoretical frameworks that have arisen from the work of Noam Chomsky, Morris Halle, and their students in the 1950's and 1960's (Chomsky 1957, 1968, 1981, 1995; Chomsky and Halle 1968). Generative grammar has gone through many phases in its more than six decades of existence. Here we will not provide a general overview of the framework, as this can be found elsewhere (e.g., Newmeyer 1986). What is critical for the purposes of this article are the philosophical and psychological foundations of generative grammar which have remained constant over the history of the theory. Those foundational assumptions are: first, that linguistics is a fundamentally mentalist enterprise in the sense that the linguist must attempt to model

Rochelle Lieber, Durham, NH, USA

the native speaker's mental representation of the grammar; second, that the grammar must be able to generate all and only acceptable utterances in the language under study; and third, that all humans are born with some set of linguistic universals, by which we mean mental constructs that allow them to acquire language, and indeed that determine the form of the grammars that they acquire. The formalization of rules, the organization of the grammar, and the assumed nature of linguistic universals have all changed in various ways over the years, but these foundational assumptions have not.

In its early years, generative grammar was largely concerned with syntax and phonology, which can to some extent be interpreted as a natural reaction to the American Structuralist tradition that preceded it. The latter tradition was at least partly built on the attempt in the early part of the twentieth century to document what we would now call understudied and endangered languages, and was quite heavily concerned with the description of morphology and phonology, and much less so with syntax. In contrast, in its early years generative grammar had very little to say directly about morphology, and especially about word-formation, by which we mean here derivation, compounding, and conversion.

Here we will focus on the treatment of word-formation in generative grammar. We will approach our subject from two directions. Our overall treatment of generative morphology will be historical, looking at the treatment of word-formation in the earliest works on generative grammar, at the rise of generative morphology as a discipline in its own right, and at the many ways in which generative morphology has subsequently developed. But we will also treat several themes that have been prominent since the inception of generative grammar, among them the status of the morpheme as a linguistic construct, the nature of rules and the organization of the mental lexicon.

2 Early generative grammar

Although early work in generative grammar did not recognize word-formation as a topic of study per se, word-formation did figure obliquely in both syntactic and phonological theory. We will illustrate this here by looking briefly at two representative works that deal with different aspects of derivation and compounding. On the syntactic side, we take up Lees's (1960) *The grammar of English nominalizations* and on the phonological side Chomsky and Halle's (1968) *Sound Pattern of English* (henceforth, *SPE*).

2.1 Syntactic approaches

Lees's *The grammar of English nominalizations* is typical of the treatment of derivation and compounding in early generative grammar. In the earliest versions of generative theory, the grammar consisted of a set of phrase-structure rules that determine basic constituent structure and a set of transformational rules that modify initial phrase structure trees in various ways, including the addition, deletion, and reordering of morphemes and indeed whole constituents. Lees used this basic framework to explore the relationship between nominal compounds like *pronghorn* (a kind of sheep) and the sentential underlying structure from which they were presumed to derive, in this case the sentences *The sheep has a horn. The horn is like a prong*. In his derivation, a generalized transformation first combines the two base sentences and then a series of simple transformations reduces that structure to the compound, as follows (Lees 1960: 156):

(1) a. The sheep has a horn. The horn is like a prong. →
    b. The sheep has a horn which is like a prong. →
    c. The sheep has a horn like a prong. →
    d. ... sheep with a horn like a prong ... →
    e. ... sheep with a pronghorn ... →
    f. ... pronghorn...

The actual compound formation transformation which Lees calls NPN effects the change from (1d) to (1e), deleting a central preposition or verb, reordering the nouns on either side, and inducing the distinctive left stress pattern typical of English compounds; NPN in its simplest form is stated as in (2):

(2) $x_1 + x_2 + x_3 \rightarrow \acute{x}_3 + \grave{x}_1$

A further process of ellipsis takes us from (1e) to the compound in (1f).

Lees's analysis of compounds obviously uses the theoretical devices at the disposal of early generative theory, but it also reflects the major question with which generative theory was preoccupied at that moment, specifically the derivational relationship between semantically "equivalent" sentences or complex words. It is important to keep in mind that in the first blush of theoretical exuberance, the power of transformational rules was not yet an issue for generative grammar.

2.2 Phonological approaches

Chomsky and Halle's SPE is a comprehensive effort to apply the principles of generative grammar to phonology and has little explicit to say about morphology. But as a great deal of English phonology is specific to particular derivational patterns, SPE of necessity requires some implicit assumptions about complex words. Several sorts of derivational complexity are recognized in SPE and are coded in lexical representations with three different sorts of boundaries. The # symbol is used to represent word boundaries, but it is also deployed to represent the boundary between a root and a so-called "neutral" affix, by which Chomsky and Halle mean an affix that does not affect the stress placement of its base (-*like*, -*able*, -*ish*, -*ness*, etc.). Non-neutral affixes, that is, those which affect stress like -*ity*, -*ic*, -*al*, and -*ive* are signalled by a + boundary. Finally, Latinate formatives like *ceive, pel, mit, scribe*, and so on are separated from the prefixes with which they occur (as in, for example, *deceive, repel, transmit, prescribe*) by a special boundary represented as =. Chomsky and Halle are not generally concerned with how affixes and bases are put together, but passing remarks give an idea of how complex words might be constructed: neutral affixes are "syntactically distinguished" (1968: 86), being "assigned to a word by a grammatical transformation [...]". Non-neutral affixes, on the other hand, are "largely, internal to the lexicon."

3 The beginnings of generative morphology as a separate discipline

The treatment of word-formation as a special subdiscipline of generative morphology is generally said to have its origins in Chomsky's (1970) *Remarks on nominalization*. In this seminal article, Chomsky notes that whereas a gerundive form exists for any given verb (3), derived nominals are far more idiosyncratic in terms both of the form of the derived noun and the productivity of the process with which the noun is formed (4).

(3) a. John's refusing the offer
    b. John's criticizing the book
(4) a. John's refusal of the offer
    b. John's criticism of the book

Given the formal and semantic regularity of the gerundive construction, a transformational derivation is conceivable, but the derived nominals, Chomsky argues, are a matter for the lexicon. The subject of what exactly the lexicon looks like is not broached in that article, but Chomsky's proposal that complex words might be a matter for the lexicon clearly suggested to researchers of the time that the internal structure of the lexicon merited further thought.

Halle (1973) takes up the structure of the lexicon in his *Prolegomena to a theory of word-formation*. In that article, Halle sketches a separate morphological component of the grammar which consists of a list of bases and affixes, a set of word-formation rules, and a dictionary which contains idiosyncratic information concerning semantics and phonology as well as a feature [–lexical insertion] that applies to words produced by the word-formation rules that are not "actual" words. The dictionary thus serves not only to store item-familiar words, but to filter out items that do not exist. The actual form of word-formation rules is left vague, although Halle mentions the possibility of stating them in the form of templates (1973: 10).

Jackendoff's (1975) *Morphological and semantic regularities in the lexicon* is another early effort to flesh out the internal structure of the lexicon. Jackendoff proposes that the lexicon should consist of lexical entries fully specified for syntactic, phonological, and semantic information about words. Lexical entries are related to one another by "lexical redundancy rules", essentially formal devices that evaluate the degree to which those entries overlap: for example, the lexical entry for the derived word *decision* will be "cheaper" to the grammar to the extent that it overlaps with the entry for *decide* (1975: 642–643):

(5) $$\begin{bmatrix} /\text{dec}\bar{\text{i}}\text{d}/ \\ +V \\ +[NP_1 \_\_ on\ NP_2] \\ NP_1\ \text{DECIDE ON}\ NP_2 \end{bmatrix} \longleftrightarrow \begin{bmatrix} /\text{dec}\bar{\text{i}}\text{d} + \text{ion}/ \\ +N \\ +[NP_1\text{'s} \_\_ on\ NP_2] \\ \text{ABSTRACT RESULT OF ACT} \\ \text{OF}\ NP_1\text{'S DECIDING ON}\ NP_2 \end{bmatrix}$$

Lexical redundancy rules are conceived as part of the evaluation metric of a grammar, that is, the mechanism by which the simplicity of the grammar is assessed. The more redundancy, the simpler the grammar, simplicity, of course, being highly valued in a generative grammar. The creative aspect of word-formation is not a central concern in Jackendoff's article, although he does note that to the extent that new forms may be derived, the lexical redundancy rules are permitted to function as generative devices.

Both proposals are very much products of their times. Both display an emphasis on formalism that has characterized generative grammar throughout its existence. And both also exhibit a somewhat prescriptive stance towards the lexicon, starting from the assumption that there is something we might characterize as "the existing words of a language". Perhaps the most important point that they have in common, however, is simply the fact that they identify morphology as a component of the grammar distinct from both phonology and syntax, and worthy of study in its own right.

4 The heyday

The mid-1970's saw the publication of the first monograph on generative morphology, Aronoff's (1976) *Word-formation in generative grammar*, and this was quickly followed by a number of developments that set the stage for discussions of word-formation within generative grammar for the next two decades. We have in mind here the work of Siegel (1974, 1977), Allen (1978), Lieber (1980), Williams (1981), Kiparsky (1982), Selkirk (1982), Scalise (1984) and Di Sciullo and Williams (1987), among others. Rather than look chronologically at key works of generative morphology within this period, we will approach our review thematically in this section, looking at the overall architecture of the theories, including the status of the morpheme as a theoretical construct, the formal nature of rules of word-formation, and the relationship among components of the grammar, and then at a number of specific proposals that form some of the foundational claims of generative morphology.

4.1 Morphology and the architecture of the grammar

As the first full-length monograph treating morphology in the generative tradition, Aronoff's work set the stage for the set of issues that dominated generative morphology in its first decade. Prominent among these was the status of the morpheme and its role in the theory of word-formation. The morpheme is typically defined as the minimal meaningful unit of which words are constituted. Aronoff (1976) begins by pointing out the major issue with this classic definition, namely that there are bits of words that can be formally isolated but are not meaningful (so-called *cran*-morphs, Latinate formatives like *pel*, *mit*, and *ceive*). He therefore rejects the traditional definition of morpheme, and this move in turn leads him to the proposal that, "All regular word-formation processes are word-based. A new word is formed by applying a regular rule to a single already existing word" (1976: 21). Word-formation rules (WFRs) are conceived of formally as phonological operations on a designated set of bases. In addition to changing the phonological form of the base, WFRs specify a syntactic category and subcategorization, a semantic representation for their output, and a set of appropriate bases. (6) is Aronoff's WFR for negative *un-* (1976: 63):

(6) Rule of negative un#
   a) $[X]_{Adj} \rightarrow [un\#[X]_{Adj}]_{Adj}$
      semantics (roughly) un#X = not X
   b) Forms of the base
      1. $X_V$en   (where en is the marker for the past participle)
      2. X_V#ing
      3. $X_V$able
      4. X+y   (worthy)
      5. X+ly   (seemly)
      6. X#ful   mindful)
      7. X#like   (warlike)

For cases in which the base to which an affix attaches is not apparently a surface word (for example, *nomin* in *nominee* or *proscrip* in *proscription*), Aronoff proposes rules of truncation or readjustment. The form *nominee*, for example, starts out as *nominate* + *ee*, with the *-ate* affix being removed by truncation. As we will see shortly it is important that WFRs in Aronoff's theory look formally very much like phonological rules, albeit with a wider range of restrictions.

Subsequent generative models of this classic period can be divided into those that embrace Aronoff's word-based framework and those that do not. Scalise (1984), for example, falls into the former camp, although in a slightly different form: he rightly points out that the notion of 'word' needs to be modified to 'stem' for highly inflected languages like Latin where the bases to which WFRs apply are never themselves free forms. On the other hand, the theories of Lieber (1980), Williams (1981) and Selkirk (1982) explicitly reject the word-based model and assume the traditional morpheme as a legitimate unit of analysis. In all three theories affixes are treated as lexical items on a par with bases as units having lexical entries. Affixes and bases are assembled by rules formally analogous to the phrase-structure rules of generative grammar; the three proposals differ in the technical characterization of the word-structure rules that create complex words; Selkirk's and Williams's rules, for example, look like the phrase-structure rules in the standard theory of generative grammar (7a). Lieber's rules are more like the rules of the later principles and parameters model, with lexical entries like (7b) for morphemes that are then inserted into unlabeled binary-branching word trees to which percolation conventions (see below) apply.

(7) a. A → N A^{Af}
    (Selkirk 1982: 66)
  b. -ize (phonological representation)
          semantic representation: causative
          category/subcategorization:]$_N$ __]$_V$
          insertion frame: NP __ (NP)
          diacritics: Level II

These theories make slightly different predictions, but in many ways they are comparable.

A second issue that forms part of the landscape of generative morphology concerns the relationship among the components of the grammar. The vast majority of generative morphologists professed some form of what has come to be called the strong lexicalist hypothesis or the lexical integrity hypothesis. Lapointe (1980: 8), for example, proposes what he calls the generalized lexicalist hypothesis, which states that "[n]o syntactic rule can refer to elements of morphological structure". This version of the hypothesis in effect rules out early generative analyses like Lees's (1960) as well as Levi's (1978) transformational analysis of complex nominals. Selkirk's version, the word structure autonomy condition (1982: 70), is similar. Di Sciullo and Williams' version is the atomicity thesis, which is a bit more explicit: "Words are 'atomic' at the level of phrasal syntax and phrasal semantics. The words have 'features', or properties, but these features have no structure, and the relation of these features to the internal composition of the word cannot be relevant in syntax [...]" (1987: 49). A corollary of the strong lexicalist hypothesis is Botha's (1983) no phrase constraint, which prevents syntactic phrases from being the input to rules of derivation and compounding.

An important consequence of the lexicalist hypothesis is that generative morphologists like Lieber, Selkirk, and Williams treat both inflection and word-formation as part of a single morphological component of the grammar. Lieber's argument in favor of this arrangement of the grammar hinges on the behavior of inflectional allomorphy, specifically that in highly inflected languages stem allomorphs that figure in inflectional paradigms also form the input to rules of derivation. Anderson (1982), in contrast, advocates a division between inflection and word-formation; arguing on the basis of case marking and agreement in Breton, for example, he suggests that inflectional features must be generated as part of the syntactic component, with features being associated with phonological forms only after syntactic operations have taken place. This separation between word-formation, which takes place in the morphological component, and inflection, which is part of the syntax, has come to be known as the weak lexicalist hypothesis.

Classical generative morphology also saw the formulation of a number of theoretical restrictions on word-formation or word-structure rules, among them the *righthand head rule*, *feature percolation conventions*, the *unitary base hypothesis*, the *unitary output hypothesis*, the *atom condition*, and the *adjacency condition*.

One of the most influential proposals to come out of classical generative morphology is the righthand head rule. Borrowing the concept of "head" from syntactic theory, the head of a word was defined as that morpheme that determines the category and morphosyntactic features of the word as a whole. According to Williams (1981), the rightmost morpheme in a complex word is the head, a principle that is known as the righthand head rule (RHHR). While the RHHR is largely correct for English word-formation, it is problematic in at least two ways. Lieber (1980) points out that is not necessarily true in other languages: for example, Vietnamese is a language that has left-headed compounds. Moreover, there are clear exceptions in English as well, where, for example, the prefix *de-* can be category-changing and therefore are at least apparently heads, and where several affixes like *-dom*, *-hood*, and *-ship* do not change category, and therefore are righthand elements that cannot be considered heads.

An alternative to the RHHR is what Lieber (1980) refers to as *percolation conventions*. In Lieber's version of generative morphology, features belonging to an affix percolate (in other words are attributed to) the derived word as a whole whether the affix is a prefix or a suffix. Most, but not all, prefixes in English lack categorial and other morphosyntactic features, which accounts for why English is mostly but not entirely right headed. While feature percolation is clearly a weaker proposal than the RHHR, it is cross-linguistically more supportable.

Another important theoretical proposal is Aronoff's (1976) *unitary base hypothesis* which require that WFRs be stated to apply to a single sort of base. According to the unitary base hypothesis, WFRs cannot be formulated, for example, to apply to both nouns and verbs. Clear counterexamples can be found in English and in many other languages, however. For example, the suffix *-er* in English can attach to verbs to form agent or instrument nouns like *writer* or *computer*, but it also attaches to nouns to form personal or instrument nouns like *villager* or *freighter*. To the extent that the semantic contribution of *-er* seems to be the same in both instances, this looks like evidence against the unitary base hypothesis. Cases like this can be circumvented only by claiming that what appears superficially to be a single affix is actually two homophonous affixes. Aronoff's example is the suffix *-able*, which he argues is in fact two suffixes, one that attaches to nouns (*marriageable*) and another to verbs (*washable*). Scalise (1984) points out an obvious problem with this fix: since nearly every prefix in English attaches to multiple syntactic catgories, we would therefore be forced into the untenable conclusion that we have two or more homophonous affixes for the vast majority of prefixes.

Scalise also proposes what he calls the *unitary output hypothesis*, which states that WFRs must have as their output words of a single morphosyntactic category. Like the unitary base hypothesis, the unitary output hypothesis has potential counterexamples; for example, the prefix *un-* in English attaches to adjectives (*unhappy*) to form adjectives and to verbs (*unwind*) to form verbs, but has nevertheless been argued to be a single negative prefix (Horn 1989; Lieber 2004).

Several proposals in generative morphology are concerned with the locality of word-formation rules. The *atom condition* proposed by Williams (1981) and the *adjacency condition* proposed by both Siegel (1977) and Allen (1978) all prohibit the statement of morphological rules from seeing any but the outermost layer of structure. In other words, in a structure like [[x]y], a rule can refer to information contained in y but not x. As in the case of the other restrictions we have reviewed here, there are possible counterexamples. Aronoff (1976: 52–53) mentions the case of the suffix *-ment*. Nouns in *-ment* can generally only be made into adjectives by suffixing *-al* if *-ment* is itself attached to a bound base (*ornamental, regimental*). If *-ment* is attached to a free verb base, the adjective in *-al* is generally not possible (**discernmental, *containmental*). If we were to state a restriction to this effect on suffixation of *-al*, we would need to refer to x in the configuration [[x]y], which is ruled out by the atom condition and the adjacency condition.

Although it is true that the majority of theorists that contributed to the early period of generative morphology were based in North America, we should not forget that there were theorists in Europe, South Africa, and Asia that early adopted a generative stance, among them Booij (1977), Scalise (1984), Botha (1983), and Kageyama (1982).

4.2 Morphology and phonology

At the same time that classical generative morphologists were interrogating the relationship between morphology and syntax, the relationship between morphology and phonology was also of great interest, giving rise to both the framework of lexical phonology and morphology and to prosodic morphology.

Lexical phonology and morphology, developed in work by Siegel (1974, 1978), Allen (1978), Kiparsky (1982), Halle and Mohanan (1985), Mohanan (1986), among many others, begins from the premise that morphology and phonology are not distinct components, with word-formation strictly preceding the operation of phonological rules. Instead, rules of morphology and phonology are organized into a series of strictly ordered levels with rules of word-formation and phonological rules interspersed within each level. Affixes are introduced by rules that specify the phonological form of the affix and the environment into which they are inserted. They do not themselves have lexical entries. In Kiparsky's (1982) classic version of the theory, English morphology, for example, consists of three levels. Level 1 includes morphological rules involving what SPE called "non-neutral" derivational affixes, as well as rules for irregular inflectional forms. Level 2 contains rules that add # boundary affixes (what SPE calls "neutral" affixes) and rules that create compound words. Level 3 includes the rules for regular inflection. Each level is associated with its own set of phonological rules. These three levels are distinct from the syntax, which is subject to its own set of phonological rules referred to as postlexical rules. Rules that apply to an earlier level cannot apply to the output of a later level. It is this strict ordering of levels that accounts for the generalizations that non-neutral affixes cannot occur outside neutral ones, that phonological rules that apply to non-neutral affixes do not affect words formed with neutral affixes, that inflection is outside of both types of derivational affix, and so on. Kiparsky's illustration of the model (1982: 5) is given in (8):

(8)
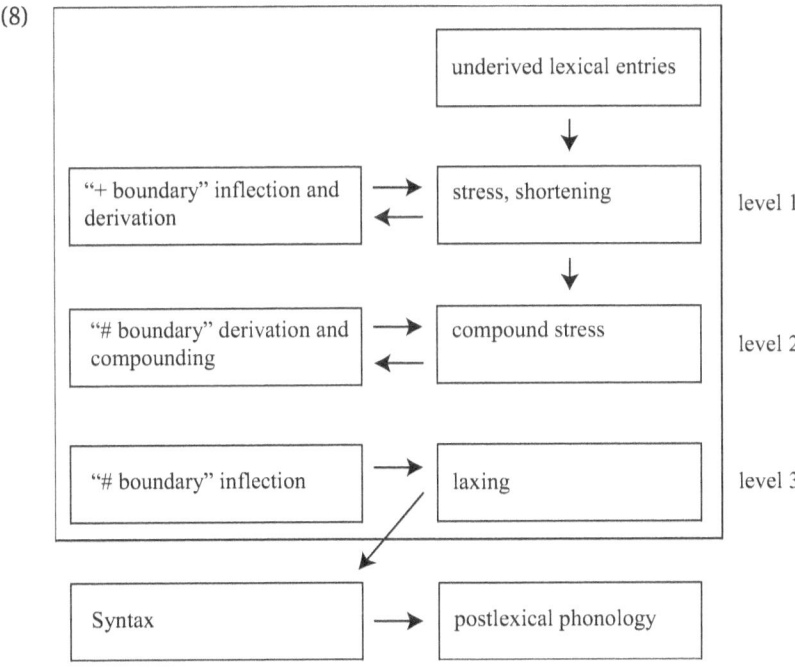

Lexical phonology and morphology was an enormously influential theory, but it was beset by problems from the start, prominent among them the need to introduce loops allowing words formed on later levels to be cycled back to earlier levels; for example, Giegerich (1999: 3) cites examples like *systems analyst*, where a regularly inflected form appears as the first element in a compound.

Prosodic morphology, also known as autosegmental morphology, was another theory that developed from generative roots. Originating in the work of McCarthy (1979), prosodic morphology essentially sought to apply the principles of autosegmental phonology to the treatment of non-concatenative processes of word-formation. Autosegmental phonology postulates that phonological segments are not unstructured lists of distinctive features, but rather are organized into a number of tiers that are themselves composed into hierarchically organized prosodic structures (syllables, feet, prosodic words). Prosodic morphology capitalizes on this hierarchical organization by postulating that morphemes can consist of segmental tiers or prosodic constituents, and not just of sequences of whole segments as is typical of generative morphology. This sort of organization makes it possible to treat non-concatenative word-formation processes more on a par with conventional affixation and compounding. McCarthy's seminal work was on the root and pattern morphology of the Semitic languages, but the theory was soon applied to reduplication (Marantz 1982) and processes of vowel and consonant mutation (Lieber 1984, 1987). McCarthy's now-classic analysis of the Arabic conjugation partitions each verb into three tiers. One tier consists of a pattern of organization of consonants and vowels that corresponds to what Hebrew grammarians call "binyanim". A second tier contains the consonantal root, which carries the central lexical meaning of the complex word. Finally a third tier contains vowels that typically signal aspect and voice:

(9)

'write'

binyan 9

perfective active

A major result of the work of this period on prosodic morphology was a substantial deepening of our knowledge of the scope and limits of non-concatenative word-formation cross-linguistically.

5 Reactions to classic generative morphology

By the mid 1980's the time was ripe for reconsidering the assumptions of classic generative morphology. We begin with a consideration of the anti-lexicalist reaction and then consider a number of post-generative frameworks that can be said to have their roots in the generative movement.

5.1 The resyntacticization of morphology

By the mid 1980's morphology was clearly established in the generative framework as a legitimate area of study. This newly established legitimacy allowed theorists of the period to reconsider the organization of the grammar and revive the possibility that some or all of morphology could be treated as a matter of syntax; that is, one could claim morphology as a legitimate area of research interest without committing oneself to a separate component of morphology in the grammar. The rejection of morphology as a separate component did not, however, mean a return to the sort of analysis proposed by Lees in the early days of generative grammar. By the 1980s the theoretical landscape of generative syntax was very different from Chomsky's early theory. The move back to syntactic morphology took place in the context of the theory that has come to be known alternatively as government-binding theory or the principles and parameters model (Chomsky 1981).

It is in the context of this theory that Fabb (1984), Sproat (1985), Roeper (1988), Baker (1988), and Lieber (1992) adduce several sorts of evidence to call even the weak form of the lexicalist hypothesis into question. By the early 1980's the nature of argument structure had become a topic of great interest in generative syntax, giving rise within the principles and parameters model to case theory on the one hand and theta theory on the other. Since both derivational affixes and synthetic compounds exhibit argument structure effects – for example, the propensity for a derived word in *-er* to denote the external argument of its base verb or the interpretation of the first element of a synthetic compound as the internal argument of the second element's base – it was natural that these types of word-formation come under special scrutiny and that attempts be made to put them in line with the syntactic theory of the time.

Fabb (1984), for example, splits derivational affixes into two sorts, what he calls syntactic affixes and lexical affixes. The former are productive, regular, and subject to case theory. They generally (but not always) attach to verbs and either allow the projection of verbal arguments (for example, gerundive *-ing*) or affect the verbal projection in some regular way (for example, the suffix *-er* which is associated with the external theta role of the verb in the sense that derived *-er* words denote whatever the thematic role of the subject of a given verb would be). The lexical affixes are less productive and the forms derived with them are associated with idiosyncratic properties. What is problematic about Fabb's proposal is that there are lexicalized forms derived from most affixes, which leads to the conclusion that most affixes must have both syntactic and lexical versions. Sproat's (1985) proposal is much stronger than Fabb's, abandoning the lexicalist hypothesis entirely. He uses the existence of so-called bracketing paradoxes like *unhappier* to argue for postulating two levels of analysis for derived words, a syntactic level and a phonological level; there is no separate morphological component. He argues that bracketing paradoxes can be resolved by assuming that on the syntactic level, *-er* is attached to the negative adjective *unhappy*, from which we can derive the appropriate semantic representation. On the phonological level, negative *un-* is attached to the comparative form *happier*; with the latter bracketing, we are able to maintain the phonological restriction that comparative *-er* attaches to words of no more than two syllables. The two levels are associated to each other via mapping principles.

Baker (1985, 1988) adduces a different sort of evidence for the syntactic treatment of word-formation. He formulates what he calls the the mirror principle, which says that "[m]orphological derivations must directly reflect syntactic derivations (and vice versa)" (1985: 375). This principle allows him to account for facts of languages like Chichewa in which it is possible either to apply a process of applicativization to a passive sentence, or alternatively to passivize an applicative sentence. In the former case, the passive morpheme appears inside the applicative and in the latter the applicative appears inside the passive, the order of the morphology reflecting the ordering in which the operations are performed (example from Baker 1988: 14; abbreviations used in examples (10) and (11) are as follows: SP = subject prefix, PASS = passive, APPL = applicative, ASP = aspect, 3M = third person masculine, 3N = third person neuter, DET = determiner, SUF = nominal inflection suffix):

(10) a. *Mpiringidzo un-na-perek-edw-a   kwa mtsikana ndi mbidzi*
    Crowbar   SP-PAST-hand-PASS-APPL-ASP to   girl   by zebras
    'The crowbar was handed to the girl by the zebras.'
 b. *Mtsikana a-na-perek-er-edw-a   mpiringidzo ndi mbidzi*
    girl   SP-PAST-hand-APPL-PASS-ASP crowbar   by zebras
    'The girl was handed the crowbar by the zebras.'

Baker (1988) also brings to the discussion the process of noun-incorporation in which it appears that a syntactic object can become part of a complex verb. Examples like (11) from Mohawk are prima facie persuasive, as they appear to illustrate that a noun stem can be extracted from an NP leaving behind its possessor (1988: 20):

(11) a. *Ka-rakv   ne sawatis hrao-nuhs-a?*
       3N-be.white DET John   3M-house-SUF
       'John's house is white.'
    b. *Hrao-nuhs-rakv   ne sawatis*
       3M-house-be.white   DET John
       'John's house is white.'

Both the mirror principle and the syntactic analysis of noun incorporation have not been uncontroversial, however. Grimshaw (1986), for example, argues that the facts accounted for by the mirror principle can be better explained without assuming a syntactic analysis. Similarly, Rosen (1989) argues against a syntactic treatment of noun-incorporation.

In the context of this discussion, synthetic compounds also were taken to suggest the syntactic treatment of morphology. Arguing on the basis of facts concerning control and aspect, Roeper (1988) proposes that compounds like *rock-throwing* in English should be analyzed as the output of a syntactic operation of head movement that starts out with a sentential structure. Roeper's derivation of the compound *rock-throwing* is illustrated in (12).

(12)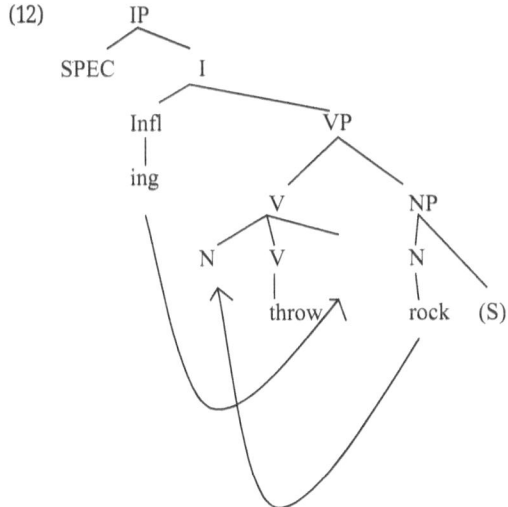

The N *rock* is incorporated into the verb and the *-ing* suffix is lowered onto the complex verb from an Infl node. As part of the derivation Roeper assumes that the IP undergoes a category-change to an NP, with a PRO subject under SPEC, thus explaining why in a sentence like *John enjoyed rock-throwing for hours*, the rock-thrower is typically interpreted as John. The Infl node in the underlying structure of the same sentence accounts for the progressive interpretation of the synthetic compound.

Lieber (1992) continues in the effort to apply principles of syntax to word-formation. Lieber starts from the premise that the existence of phrasal compounding and derivation suggests that morphology and syntax cannot be separated into distinct components. She then attempts, on the grounds of simplicity, to develop a theory in which the principles of morphology and syntax are in fact the same. As part of this program she tries to derive the ordering of affixes from the normal settings of the X-bar parameters, an attempt that is in the end undermined by the difficulty of applying terms like complement and specifier to morphemes in complex words.

All of these proposals have come under criticism and the relative merits of counting word-formation as a part of syntax or as a distinct component are still being debated (see, for example, Lieber and Scalise 2006). Di Sciullo (2005) is notable in this regard: although she seeks to apply the principles of the minimalist program to word-formation, Di Sciullo nevertheless continues to maintain that the mechanisms that apply to word-formation are distinct in key ways from syntactic principles.

5.2 The fragmentation of generative morphology

Up to the early 1990's it is possible to think of the theory of generative morphology as a single framework united not so much by specific principles or a set of formal mechanisms espoused by any specific theorist, but by the set of foundational assumptions mentioned at the outset. What has characterized the study of morphology in generative grammar over the last two decades has been an increasing specialization of theory. In this section we look at some of the outgrowths of generative morphology, giving most attention to those that have focused on word-formation as opposed to inflection.

5.2.1 A digression on inflection

Although the subject of this article is word-formation in generative grammar and not inflection, it is difficult to continue a discussion of more recent developments without at least passing mention of frameworks whose primary focus is inflection.

Anderson's (1992) a-morphous morphology and Stump's (2001) paradigm function morphology both have their roots in Matthews' (1972) word-and-paradigm framework which begins from the observation that the relationship between meaning/morphosyntactic features and phonological representation is rarely one to one. When looking at complex inflectional systems, we often find on the one hand that a single morphosyntactic feature is expressed by more than one morpheme (so-called multiple exponence), and on the other that a single morpheme can express more than one morphosyntactic feature. Anderson (1992) takes this observation as a point of departure for a theory consisting of rules that associate bundles of features (sometimes with internal structure) with phonological forms; like Aronoff's classic theory, Anderson's framework is word-based, but his rules do not introduce inflectional features, as Aronovian-style rules would, but rather associate phonological form with sets of features. Stump's (2001) paradigm function framework differs in formal details from Anderson's, but is based on a similar premise. What is important for our purposes is that both Anderson's and Stump's frameworks are conspicuous in that they have almost nothing to say about word-formation (each contains only a brief chapter or part of a chapter devoted to the subject).

Another highly influential framework that was proposed in the early 1990's is distributed morphology (DM) (Halle and Marantz 1993; Harley and Noyer 1999). Like a-morphous morphology and paradigm function morphology, the main emphasis in this framework has been on the analysis of inflection, with relatively little attention devoted to word-formation. DM is conceived broadly as a part of the larger minimalist program (Chomsky 1995). Morphology proper is part of the syntax. Nodes in a syntactic tree are associated with bundles of features, and bundles of features can undergo movement rules from one structural position to another. Only after the syntactic derivation is complete are bundles of features associated with phonological forms and subjected to certain sorts of readjustment rules, an arrangement that is referred to as "late insertion"; DM thus embraces Beard's separation hypothesis. Roots – the lexical bases to which affixes attach – are inherently categoryless, and are associated with a syntactic category as part of the syntactic derivation; versions of the theory differ on whether roots as well as affixes are subject to late insertion. Attempts have been made within DM to extend the discussion at least to compounding (Harley 2009), but it remains to be seen how the theory might be adapted to account for derivational word-formation.

5.2.2 Lexeme morpheme base morphology

Most of the syntactic models discussed in section 5.1 take for granted that the morpheme should be taken as the standard unit of analysis. Beard (1995), however, takes as a point of departure the same lack of a one to one correspondence between meaning and form that motivates Anderson's and Stump's theories and explores the consequences of this observation for derivation. The result is what he calls lexeme morpheme base morphology. One of Beard's most important achievements is to bring the issue of semantics into the discussion of word-formation by observing that derivation, like inflection, often involves mismatches between form and meaning. Beard's solution to these mismatches is to treat the semantics of derivation on a par with that of inflection. For Beard, word-formation consists in the addition of derivational features like [Agent] to a lexemic base. The agentive nouns corresponding to the verbs *write* and *account* would both be the same at this stage of derivation. However, these two representations are spelled out with different phonological forms, resulting in the one case in the form *writer* and in the other the form *accountant*. The disjunction between the semantic representation of a word and its ultimate phonological form is what Beard calls the separation hypothesis. A major question that arises from Beard's theory, however, is whether the semantics of derivation can really be accounted for with a featural system analogous to that needed for inflection.

5.2.3 The lexical semantics of word-formation

Beard's solution to the mismatch between morphology and semantics is essentially an architectural one: by designing a theory that separates the semantic part of word-formation from its phonological realization he is able to address the important issue of meaning-form mismatches. Lieber (2004) agrees that such mismatches must be accounted for, but argues that the success of any treatment depends on having an explicit theory of lexical semantics that accounts for derivation, compounding, and conversion, as well as the lexical semantics of free morphemes. Beginning from the well known observation that the affix *-er* not only forms agent nouns like *writer*, but also instrument nouns (*printer*), location nouns (*diner*), and even patient nouns (*loaner*), she proposes a framework of lexical semantic representation that allows her to explain why derivational affixes are so often wildly polysemous. Beard relies on inflectional categories like [agent], [means] (the feature Beard uses for instruments), or [location] to characterize the meanings of derivational morphemes, thus making it seem accidental that a suffix like *-er* can express all these meanings. Lieber's lexical semantic representations consist of hierarchical arrangements of features and their arguments. Features cover broad aspects of lexical meaning, such as for example the characteristic of being concrete or abstract, which Lieber encodes in the feature [+/–material] and eventive or non-eventive, encoded in the feature [+/–dynamic]; features are deployed across syntactic categories, so that nouns may be characterized as eventive or non-eventive, just as verbs are. Both affixes and bases in her theory have lexical semantic representations, indeed the same sorts of representations. When these representations are combined, arguments of the affix may be linked to arguments of the base via what Lieber calls a principle of co-indexation:

(13) a. write   [+dynamic [( ), ( )]]
     b. -er   [+material, dynamic ([ ], <base>)]
     c. writer   [+material, dynamic ([$_i$], [+dynamic([$_i$], [ ])])]

The polysemy of an affix like *-er* falls out in her theory not so much from the architecture of the grammar but from the extent to which the semantic representation of the affix is underspecified.

6 Conclusion

Active study of word-formation continues in the generative tradition. However, the emphasis in recent years has to some extent changed. For many years, generative morphology focused on a broad-brush characterization of the architecture of the theory and relied on formalism and principles modeled on the syntactic or phonological theory of the moment. In recent years we have seen a gradual movement towards a line of thinking that does not essentially piggyback on syntactic or phonological theory. One reason for this change in emphasis is the welcome convergence of theoretical approaches to morphology in the generative tradition with an independent thread of psycholinguistic study of word-formation that has gone on almost in parallel. Represented in the work of Taft (1988), Marslen-Wilson et al. (1994), Baayen, Dijkstra and Schreuder (1997), De Vaan, Schreuder and Baayen (2008), Kuperman, Bertram and Baayen (2010), among many others, this line of research has attempted on the basis of psycholinguistic experiments to model the extent to which complex words are stored as wholes in the mental lexicon as opposed to generated on line. This line of research as well as the increased attention to the issue of productivity in word-formation (for example, Plag 1999; Bauer 2001), has brought home to many current morphologists that words are different from sentences. Words persist in the mental lexicon in a way that sentences typically don't. Further, the increasing availability of searchable corpora like the British National Corpus or the Corpus of Contemporary American English gives theorists today the means to track productivity and the semantics of complex words in context, and this will certainly lead to new insight into the organization of the mental lexicon.

7 References

Allen, Margaret (1978): Morphological investigations. Ph.D. dissertation, University of Connecticut, Storrs.
Anderson, Stephen (1982): Where's morphology? *Linguistic Inquiry* 13(4): 571–612.
Anderson, Stephen (1992): *A-morphous Morphology*. Cambridge: Cambridge University Press.
Aronoff, Mark (1976): *Word-formation in Generative Grammar*. Cambridge, MA: MIT Press.
Baayen, Harald, Ton Dijkstra and Robert Schreuder (1997): Singulars and plurals in Dutch: Evidence for a parallel dual-route model. *Journal of Memory and Language* 17(1): 94–117.
Baker, Mark (1985): The mirror principle and morphosyntactic explanation. *Linguistic Inquiry* 16(3): 373–415.
Baker, Mark (1988): *Incorporation*. Chicago: University of Chicago Press.
Bauer, Laurie (2001): *Morphological Productivity*. Cambridge: Cambridge University Press.
Beard, Robert (1995): *Lexeme Morpheme Base Morphology*. Albany: State University of New York Press.
Booij, Geert (1977): *Dutch Morphology*. Lisse: Peter De Ridder Press.
Botha, Rudolph (1983): *Morphological Mechanisms*. Oxford: Pergamon Press.
Chomsky, Noam (1957): *Syntactic Structures*. The Hague: Mouton.
Chomsky, Noam (1968): *Aspects of the Theory of Syntax*. Cambridge, MA: MIT Press.
Chomsky, Noam (1970): Remarks on nominalization. In: Roderick A. Jacobs and Peter S. Rosenbaum (eds.), *Readings in English Transformational Grammar*, 184–221. Waltham, MA: Ginn.
Chomsky, Noam (1981): *Lectures on Government and Binding*. Dordrecht: Foris.
Chomsky, Noam (1995): *The Minimalist Program*. Cambridge, MA: MIT Press.
Chomsky, Noam and Morris Halle (1968): *The Sound Pattern of English*. New York: Harper and Row.
De Vaan, Laura, Robert Schreuder and Harald Baayen (2008): Regular morphologically complex neologisms leave detectable traces in the mental lexicon. *The Mental Lexicon* 2(1): 1–24.
Di Sciullo, Anna Maria (2005): *Asymmetry in Morphology*. Cambridge, MA: MIT Press.
Di Sciullo, Anna Maria and Edwin Williams (1987): *On the Definition of Word*. Cambridge, MA: MIT Press.
Fabb, Nigel (1984): Syntactic affixation. Ph.D. dissertation, MIT Cambridge, MA.
Giegerich, Heinz (1999): *Lexical Strata in English*. Cambridge: Cambridge University Press.
Grimshaw, Jane (1986): A morphosyntactic explanation for the mirror principle. *Linguistic Inquiry* 17(4): 745–749.
Halle, Morris (1973): Prolegomena to a theory of word formation. *Linguistic Inquiry* 4(1): 3–16.
Halle, Morris and K. P. Mohanan (1985): Segmental phonology of Modern English. *Linguistic Inquiry* 16(1): 57–116.
Halle, Morris and Alec Marantz (1993): Distributed morphology and the pieces of inflection. In: Keneth Hale and Samuel Jay Keyser (eds.), *The View from Building 20*, 111–176. Cambridge, MA: MIT Press.
Harley, Heidi (2009): Compounding in distributed morphology. In: Rochelle Lieber and Pavol Štekauer (eds.), *The Oxford Handbook of Compounding*, 129–144. Oxford: Oxford University Press.
Harley, Heidi and Rolf Noyer (1999): Distributed morphology. *Glot International* 4(4): 3–9.
Horn, Laurence (1989): *A Natural History of Negation*. Chicago: University of Chicago Press.
Jackendoff, Ray (1975): Morphological and semantic regularities in the lexicon. *Language* 51: 639–671.

Kageyama, Taro (1982): Word formation in Japanese. *Lingua* 57(2-4): 215-258.
Kiparsky, Paul (1982): Lexical phonology and morphology. In: In-Seok Yang (ed.), *Linguistics in the Morning Calm*, 3-91. Seoul: Hanshin Publishing Company.
Kuperman, Victor, Raymond Bertram and Harald Baayen (2010): Processing trade-offs in the reading of Dutch derived words. *Journal of Memory and Language* 62(2): 83-97.
Lapointe, Steven (1980): A theory of grammatical agreement. Ph.D. dissertation, University of Massachusetts, Amherst.
Lees, Robert (1960): *The Grammar of English Nominalizations*. Bloomington, IN: Indiana University Press.
Levi, Judith (1978): *The Syntax and Semantics of Complex Nominals*. New York: Academic Press.
Lieber, Rochelle (1980): On the organization of the lexicon. Ph.D. dissertation, MIT Cambridge, MA. [Published 1981 Bloomington, IN: Indiana University Linguistics Club and 1990 New York: Garland Publications.]
Lieber, Rochelle (1984): Consonant gradation in Fula: An autosegmental approach. In: Mark Aronoff and Richard Oehrle (eds.), *Language Sound Structure*, 329-345. Cambridge, MA: MIT Press.
Lieber, Rochelle (1987): *An Integrated Theory of Autosegmental Processes*. Albany: State University of New York Press.
Lieber, Rochelle (1992): *Deconstructing Morphology*. Chicago: University of Chicago Press.
Lieber, Rochelle (2004): *Morphology and Lexical Semantics*. Cambridge: Cambridge University Press.
Lieber, Rochelle and Sergio Scalise (2006): The lexical integrity hypothesis in a new theoretical universe. *Lingue e Linguaggio* 5(1): 7-32.
Marantz, Alec (1982): Re reduplication. *Linguistic Inquiry* 13(3): 435-482.
Marslen-Wilson, William, Lorraine Tyler, Rachelle Waksler and Liane Olde (1994): Morphology and meaning in the English mental lexicon. *Psychological Review* 101(1): 3-33.
Matthews, Peter H. (1972): *Inflectional Morphology*. Cambridge: Cambridge University Press.
McCarthy, John (1979): Formal problems in Semitic phonology and morphology. Ph.D. dissertation, MIT Cambridge, MA.
Mohanan, K.P. (1986): *The Theory of Lexical Phonology*. Dordrecht: Reidel.
Newmeyer, Frederick (1986): *Linguistic Theory in America*. New York: Academic Press.
Plag, Ingo (1999): *Morphological Productivity. Structural Constraints in English Derivation*. Berlin: Mouton de Gruyter.
Roeper, Thomas (1988): Compound syntax and head movement. In: Geert Booij and Jaap Van Marle (eds.), *Yearbook of Morphology 1988*, 187-228. Dordrecht: Foris.
Rosen, Sara (1989): Two types of noun incorporation: A lexical analysis. *Language* 65(2): 294-317.
Scalise, Sergio (1984): *Generative Morphology*. Dordrecht: Foris.
Selkirk, Elisabeth (1982): *The Syntax of Words*. Cambridge, MA: MIT Press.
Siegel, Dorothy (1974): Topics in English morphology. Ph.D. dissertation, MIT Cambridge, MA.
Siegel, Dorothy (1977): The adjacency condition and the theory of morphology. In: Mark J. Stein (ed.), *Proceedings of the Eighth Annual Meeting of the North East Linguistic Society*, 189-197. Amherst, MA: GSLA.
Sproat, Richard (1985): On deriving the lexicon. Ph.D. dissertation, MIT Cambridge, MA.
Stump, Gregory (2001): *Inflectional Morphology*. Cambridge: Cambridge University Press.
Taft, Marcus (1988): A morphological-decomposition model of lexical representation. *Linguistics* 26: 657-67.
Williams, Edwin (1981): On the notions 'lexically related' and 'head of a word'. *Linguistic Inquiry* 12(2): 245-274.

Geert Booij
6 Word-formation in construction grammar

1   Introduction
2   The hierarchical lexicon
3   Holistic properties of word structure
4   Phrasal and phrase-based lexical items
5   Form-meaning asymmetries
6   Conclusions
7   References

Abstract: The notion "construction" that plays a central role in construction grammar, is an indispensable notion for the analysis of word-formation patterns. In the study of word-formation, we investigate the systematic correspondences between form and meaning at the word level. Constructional schemas provide an adequate format for expressing these systematic correspondences. Moreover, they are part of a hierarchical lexicon in which both complex words and morphological patterns of various levels of abstraction can be specified. An important advantage of the construction morphology approach is that it can express the relevant similarities between morphological and phrasal lexical expressions, and the paradigmatic relations between morphological and phrasal schemas. Thus, lexical knowledge is characterized as a complicated network between words and phrasal expressions on a range of levels of abstractions, varying between individual words and completely abstract patterns.

1 Introduction

Word-formation is the domain of linguistics in which systematic correspondences between the form and meaning of complex words are studied. Consider the following sets of English adjectives:

(1) steady   unsteady
     social   unsocial

Geert Booij, Leiden, Netherlands

https://doi.org/10.1515/9783111420561-006

suitable   unsuitable
stressed   unstressed
sympathetic unsympathetic

The meaning of the adjectives in the column on the right can be circumscribed as 'not A', where A is the meaning of the corresponding adjective in the column on the left. That is, there is a systematic correspondence between the presence of un- and the meaning component 'not'. Therefore, we consider the adjectives in the rightmost column as complex words, with the word structure $[un[x]_A]_A$, where x is a variable for a phonological string. Thus, we assign morphological structure to words on the basis of systematic paradigmatic relations with other words.

The structure $[un[x]_A]_A$ is part of the following constructional schema in which the correspondence between form and meaning of a morphologically defined class of words is specified:

(2) $<[un[x]_{Ai}]_{Aj} \leftrightarrow [\text{NOT SEM}_i]_j>$

The angled brackets demarcate a constructional schema. The correlation between form and meaning is expressed by the double-arrowed symbol ↔. The meaning contribution of the base word on the right of the arrow is co-indexed with the relevant part of the formal structure on the left of the arrow. The schema thus represents the meaning of these un-adjectives as a compositional function of that of their base words. The format of these schemas derives from the parallel architecture framework, as developed in work by Ray Jackendoff (Jackendoff 2002; 2009; 2010; 2013). The meaning (SEM) of the base words is specified independently in the lexicon, whereas the meaning contribution of affixes is specified in constructional schemas, since their meaning is not accessible outside of the morphological structure in which they occur. Note, moreover, that the meaning of un- depends on the kind of morphological structure it occurs in. In the structure $[un[x]_N]_V$ for instance, the meaning of un- is 'reversative action', as in the denominal verbs un-cork and un-root. Hence, the meaning of the prefix un- cannot be specified in isolation of the morphological structure of which it forms a part.

Word-formation patterns can thus be considered constructions at the word level, and the individual complex words that instantiate these patterns are (morphological) constructs. The constructional schema in (2) differs from the format of the word-formation rule as used in traditional generative morphology (Aronoff 1976) in that it is neutral as to production or perception. This schema is a declarative statement that characterizes a set of existing English complex adjectives, and at the same time indicates how new adjectives of this type can be formed. This type of morphological knowledge can be used both in language perception and in language production, and therefore, it is quite appropriate for morphological regularities to be expressed in declarative form.

The notion "construction" has been shown to be essential for a proper characterization of the syntax of natural languages, and this theoretical stance is referred to as construction grammar (Goldberg 2006). The use of the notion "construction" in the domain of morphology has been argued for in my monograph *Construction Morphology* (Booij 2010). In this article I will present a number of arguments in favour of a construction morphology approach to word-formation. In section 2 the concept of the hierarchical lexicon is introduced. In section 3 holistic properties of complex words are shown to be an argument for constructional schemas at the word level. Section 4 argues that there is no sharp boundary between lexicon and grammar, a basic idea of construction grammar, and that constructional schemas can be used in order to express the parallelisms between morphological and syntactic constructs. In section 5 we will see that we need the concept of paradigmatic relationships between constructional schemas in order to account for form-meaning asymmetries in complex words. Section 6 presents a summary of the argumentation for a construction morphology approach to word-formation.

2 The hierarchical lexicon

The acquisition of word-formation patterns is based on knowledge of memorized complex words. Once a pattern has been discovered, this can be expressed in a constructional schema that dominates the individual instantiations of this schema. The schema and its instantiations co-exist, as the discovery of a schema will not lead to removal from one's memory of the set of complex words that formed the basis of the constructional schema. This insight can be expressed in a hierarchical lexicon, in which abstract schemas dominate their instantiations. For instance, the following substructure can be assumed for the English lexicon:

(3) $\quad <[un[x]_{Ai}]_{Aj} \leftrightarrow [\text{NOT SEM}_i]_j>$

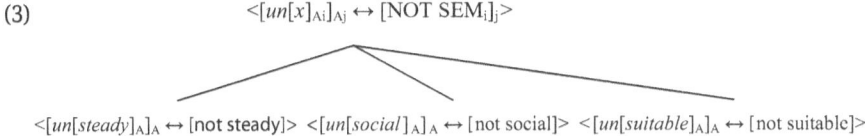

$<[un[steady]_A]_A \leftrightarrow [\text{not steady}]> \quad <[un[social]_A]_A \leftrightarrow [\text{not social}]> \quad <[un[suitable]_A]_A \leftrightarrow [\text{not suitable}]>$

The information about these three adjectives is almost completely redundant, as their properties are inherited from the general schema by which these adjectives are dominated, and the meaning of their independently specified base words. The only non-redundant information about these complex adjectives is that they exist, that is, that they are conventionalized complex words of present-day English.

The partial structure of the English lexicon specified in (3) has only one level of abstraction above the level of the individual complex words. However, it might be necessary to have more levels of abstraction. A clear case for this necessity can be found in the domain of compounding in Germanic languages. The most general statement about Germanic compounds is that they are right-headed. This can be expressed at the topmost level of the substructure of the lexicon for compounds. However, the various classes of compounds may also have specific properties of their own. Examples are that verbal compounding is unproductive in languages like Dutch, English, and German, and that in Dutch AN compounds, unlike NN compounds, the non-head tends to be simplex. For instance, whereas the AN compound *hoog-bouw* 'high-building, high rise building' is a correct compound of Dutch, a compound like *huizenhoog-bouw* 'houses-high building, very high rise building', with the complex adjective *huizen-hoog* lit. 'houses high, very high' as modifier, is ungrammatical. Hence, the following partial hierarchy is relevant for Dutch AN-compounds:

(4) $<[X_i\ Y_j]_{Yk} \leftrightarrow [SEM_j$ with relation R to $SEM_i]_k>$
  |
  $<[A_i\ N_j]_{Nk} \leftrightarrow [SEM_j$ having property $SEM_i]_k>$ Condition: A_i = simplex

The lower schema is an instantiation of the upper schema, with the category variables specified as A and N, and the nature of the semantic relation R specified as 'having property'; moreover, a restriction on the complexity of the non-head constituent applies.

Another argument for the use of intermediate levels of abstraction for the description of regularities in compounds is that constituents within compounds may have lexicalized, yet productive meanings. That is, they may have bound meanings dependent on their occurrence in compounds. An example from Dutch is the use of the noun *dood* 'death' as a modifier in NA compounds, with the meaning 'very, to a high degree' as in:

(5) dood-gewoon   'very normal'
     dood-moe   'very tired'
     dood-simpel   'very simple'
     dood-stil   'very quiet'

This productive use of the bound meaning 'very' of the noun *dood* can be expressed in a subschema for NA compounds that is dominated by the NA compound schema that in its turn is dominated by the general schema for adjectival compounds:

(6)   <[[dood]$_{Ni}$ [x]$_{Aj}$]$_{Ak}$ ↔ [very$_i$ SEM$_j$]$_k$>

In this schema one of the slots is lexically specified, and hence this is a constructional idiom (Jackendoff 2002). The semantic specification for *dood* in (6) overrules the literal meaning 'death' of *dood* when used as an independent word.

Words with bound meanings are often referred to as affixoids, as they are similar to affixes in having bound meanings. By making use of the concept of 'constructional idiom' we can avoid introducing a new morphological category for word constituents besides words and affixes. A constructional idiom is a constructional schema in which at least one slot is lexically fixed, and at least one slot is open.

We need this type of constructional schema for another form of boundedness as well. Consider the German word *Macher* 'maker', discussed in detail in Joeres (1995). Joeres' observation is that -*macher* with the regular meaning 'maker' is a very productive constituent of compounds, whereas it has a lexicalized meaning when used as an autonomous lexeme, namely 'strong personality who achieves a lot'. Hence, Joeres (1995: 151) concluded that -*macher* can be qualified as a "Halbsuffix", that is, an affixoid. Note, however, that *macher* is not one morpheme, as was the case for the affixoids discussed above, but consists of two, the verbal stem *mach*- 'to make' and the agentive suffix -*er*. Examples of this type of compounding in German are:

(7)   *with A as first constituent*:
      Fit-macher   'fit-maker'
      Krank-macher   'ill-maker'
      Wach-macher   'awake-maker'

      with N as first constituent:
      Baby-macher   'baby-maker'
      Eis-macher   'ice-maker'
      Programm-macher   'program-maker'

Different from what is at stake with the noun *dood*, the meaning of *macher* in these words is completely regular: it has the meaning 'entity that causes or creates something'. This meaning, however, is only productive within compounds, and not available for the word *Macher* in isolation, which only has the lexicalized meaning mentioned above. In order to account for its bounded productivity, we may assume the following constructional idioms for this class of compounds:

(8) <[[A$_i$ [mach]$_{Vj}$]$_V$ er]$_{Nk}$ ↔ [who [CAUSE TO BE]$_j$ SEM$_i$]$_k$
<[[N$_i$ [mach]$_{Vj}$]$_V$ er]$_{Nk}$ ↔ [who [CREATE]$_j$ SEM$_i$]$_k$

These structures presuppose that the -*er*-nouns are derived from potential but non-existing verbal compounds of the type AV and NV respectively. For instance, *Fit-macher* can be seen as a derivation from *fit machen* 'to make fit'. Thus, it is predicted that in these complex words, *macher* has the expected, fully regular meaning of causer or creator. The schemas in (8) will be dominated by the general schema for deverbal nouns in -*er* in German.

The schema format proposed here makes it possible to account for the co-occurrence of word-formation patterns. In (8) we saw a case of the productive co-occurrence of verbal compounding and deverbal -*er*-derivation in German. Normally, verbal compounding in German is unproductive. That is, this is a case of "embedded productivity" (Booij 2010: ch. 3). Language users may use more than one word-formation process at the same time, in order to construct a multiply complex word. There are, for example, quite a number of English *un*-adjectives listed in Van Dale's *English–Dutch dictionary* for which the base adjective in -*able* is not listed as well, for instance:

(9) *listed*   *not listed*
     un-beat-able   beat-able
     un-comment-able   comment-able
     un-crush-able   crush-able
     un-say-able   say-able

We can account for the formation of *un-V-able* adjectives from verbal bases without the intermediate word, a deverbal adjective in -*able*, being in existence, by assuming that word-formation schemas can be unified and have "a life of their own". The following unified schema accounts for the adjectives in the left column of (9):

(10) [*un*[V-*able*]$_A$]$_A$

To conclude, the schema format is an appropriate format for characterizing word-formation processes and sets of complex words as parts of a hierarchical lexicon.

3 Holistic properties of word structure

One of the motivations for construction grammar is that constructions may have holistic properties that cannot be reduced to properties of their individual constituents. This applies to morphological constructions as well. A clear example is that reduplication structures often indicate some form of increase of a semantic property denoted by the base word. For instance, in Malay the plural form of nouns is created by adding a full copy of the base noun (e.g., *buku* 'book' – *buku-buku* 'books'). The meaning of plurality does not derive from one of the constituents *buku*, but is evoked by the copying configuration as such.

An example from Dutch is the semantic interpretation of numerals discussed in detail in Booij (2010: ch. 8). The numeral *drie* '3' and *honderd* '100' can be concatenated in both orders, but with different interpretations: *drie-honderd* '300', *honderd-drie* '103'. Hence, the nature of the semantic relation between the two numeral constituents (multiplication or addition) is determined by the order in which the lower and the higher numeral appear. That is, the semantic interpretation is partially a holistic property of the complex numeral as a whole.

A prototypical example of holistic properties in word-formation is the interpretation of nominal VN compounds in Romance languages, which denote agents, instruments, or both, and sometimes other semantic categories such as events. Here are some examples from Italian:

(11) apri-concerto   'open-concert, opening act'   (event)
      apri-scatole   'open-cans, can opener'   (instrument)
      lancia-fiamme   'throw-flames, flame thrower'   (instrument)
      lava-piatti   'wash-dishes, dish washer'   (agent or instrument)
      spazza-neve   'plough-snow, snow plough'   (instrument)
      porta-bagagli   'carry-luggage, luggage carrier / (agent or instrument)
                       roof rack'

The semantic component of these VN compounds that is not expressed by either of their constituents is the meaning 'agent / instrument / event'. It is this meaning that is evoked by the morphological configuration as a whole. Note that the lexical category N of these compounds is also a holistic property as these compounds are exocentric, and the N constituent is not the head of the compound, neither formally nor semantically. These holistic properties can be captured by a constructional schema of the following type:

(12) $<[V_i N_j]_{Nk} \leftrightarrow [\text{Agent/Instrument/Event of ACTION}_i \text{ on SEM}_j]_k>$

This schema specifies a meaning component for which no explicit constituent is available.

In conclusion, holistic properties of word-formation constructions support the construction morphology approach to word-formation.

4 Phrasal and phrase-based lexical items

An important argument for construction morphology is that it is able to express the parallelisms between complex words and phrasal expressions with similar functions. A class of phrasal lexical items that is very relevant for a proper analysis of the syntax-morphology interaction is formed by particle verbs in Germanic languages (Los et al. 2012). These particle verbs function as names for verbal concepts (events, actions). They are phrasal in nature since the particle can be separated from the verb. In German and Dutch, for instance, root clauses have a word order in which the finite verb appears in second position, whereas the particle appears at the end of the clause. Particle verbs are therefore phrasal lexical units, but similar in function to prefixed verbs. An example is the class of Dutch particle verbs with the particle *door*. These verbs express continuative aspect:

(13) *verb* *phrasal verb*
 eten 'to eat' door eten 'to continue eating'
 fietsen 'to cycle' door fietsen 'to continue cycling'
 zeuren 'to nag' door zeuren 'to continue nagging'

The crucial observation is that the word *door* has a productive, yet bound meaning when combined with a verb into a phrasal verb, namely that of continuative aspect. The following constructional schema expresses this semantic property:

(14) <[door$_i$ V$_j$]$_k$ ↔ [continue$_i$ SEM$_j$]$_k$>

This schema specifies redundant properties of existing particle verbs with *door*, and how new particle verbs of this type can be coined. The schema in (14) is a good example of a constructional idiom (Jackendoff 2002), a schema with both variable and lexically filled positions.

In probably all European languages we find phrases with coordination that are semantically transparent, but have a fixed order, such as English *salt and pepper, father and son, ladies and gentlemen*. These conventionalized expressions have to be listed because of the fixed order in which the two words appear. On the other hand, they instantiate regular and productive phrasal patterns, and we should express this in our description. Therefore, the syntactic coordination schema [N and N]$_{NP}$, which is a sub-case of English coordination, dominates its instantiations, phrases such as *salt and pepper*. The only non-redundant information concerning these *N and N* phrases is that they exist (that is, are conventionalized), and the order in which the two words appear. Thus, there is no principled difference between complex words and phrases with respect to the division of labour between storage and computation. There is massive empirical evidence for prefabs, word combinations stored in memory (Erman and Warren 2000; Kuiper et al. 2007; Sprenger 2003; Sprenger, Levelt and Kempen 2006; Tremblay and Baayen 2010; Wray 2002; 2008).

Romance languages use various types of phrases as names for concepts. For example, in French the patterns *N à N* and *N de N* (as in *moulin à vent* 'windmill' and *salle de bains* 'bathroom' respectively) are used for constructing names for entities. This means that French NPs with the form [N [à/de N]$_{PP}$]$_{NP}$ have a lexical status, and function as constructional idioms (Booij 2009).

A correct prediction of the position that both words and phrases are stored as lexical units is that we will find competition and blocking effects between synonymous phrases and words. For instance, the existence of the Dutch AN compound *zuur-kool* 'sour-cabbage, sauerkraut' impedes using the AN phrase *zure kool* 'sour cabbage' for this type of cabbage, and inversely, the existence of the AN phrase *rode kool* 'red cabbage' impedes the coinage of the AN compound *rood-kool*. Related languages may differ in the choice between synonymous but structurally different options. For instance, whereas German is characterized by a very frequent use of AN compounds, Dutch speakers tend to prefer AN phrases (as in German *Rotwein* 'red wine' versus Dutch *rode wijn* 'red wine' (Booij 2002; Hüning 2010)). Interestingly, it has been shown that the choice between AN compound and AN phrase in German for a new concept depends on the family of related expressions. For instance, since there are many AN compounds with *Milch* 'milk' as their head, a new AN expression for a new kind of milk will most probably be a compound (Schlücker and Plag 2011). This shows that new AN expressions are made on analogy to constituent families, the sets of existing AN compounds or phrases that share a constituent.

In Polish, nouns followed by a denominal relational adjective are used extensively, where English would have NN compounds (Szymanek 2010):

(15) a. kość [[słoni]$_N$-ow]$_A$-a
    bone elephant-ADJ-FEM.SG
    'ivory, lit. elephant bone'
  b. sok [[jabłk]$_N$ow]$_A$-y
    juice apple-ADJ-MASC.SG
    'apple juice'

Lexically stored collocational restrictions between A and N in AN phrases may also affect inflection. In Dutch, the prenominal adjective that is normally inflected and ends in the suffix -e /ə/ may be used without an ending when the AN phrase is a lexicalized name, as in *het stoffelijk overschot* 'the mortal remains', where the expected schwa ending is omitted (Speelman, Tummers and Geeraerts 2009).

The consequence of these observations is that there is no sharp boundary between grammar and lexicon. Both at the level of the word and the level of the phrase, the grammar contains schemas that dominate their lexicalized instantiations. Thus, the lexicon becomes a "constructicon".

The absence of a sharp boundary between lexicon and syntax is also manifested by the fact that phrases may feed word-formation. It is in particular compounding that appears to be permissive in this respect. As far as Dutch is concerned, it is far less common to use phrasal units as bases of derivation, although this is possible for a few suffixes, such as denominal -*er* '-er' and denominal -*achtig* 'like'. The denominal suffix -*er* in Dutch combines easily with classifying phrases:

(16) [[derde klass]$_{NP}$ er]$_N$ 'third form pupil'
 [[17de-eeuw]$_{NP}$ er]$_N$ 'person living in the 17th century'
 [[doe-het-zelv]$_S$ er]$_N$ 'do it yourself-er'

In the linguistic literature one finds an extensive debate on the consequences of phrasal compounds for our view of the architecture of the grammar (Meibauer 2007). Wiese claimed that "a mechanism such as quotation must be held responsible for the existence of phrasal compounds" (Wiese 1996). Meibauer (2007) objected to this claim, and noted that often the use of phrases within compounds has an expressive function, and does not always lead to conventionalization into lexical units. Expressiveness is not, however, a formal precondition for using phrases as building blocks of words, as we will see below.

The expressive function of this type of word-formation is dominant when sentences are embedded in compounds, as in the following English examples:

(17) Don't ask, don't tell policy
 (US army policy of dealing with gay soldiers)

 One-size-fits-all-education
 (*Boston Globe* 6 March 2010)

 I understand the whole 'live it up, you're only in college once' thing
 (*Tufts Daily* April 7, 2010)

 The eat-your-spinach-approach to education
 (*Boston Globe* 13 March 2010)

The sentential constituents in these compounds can be characterized as "fictive interaction" (Pascual and Janssen 2004), and they have indeed a strong expressive character. Some of these compounds with a sentential constituent are conventionalized, as is the case for the following Dutch compounds:

(18) God-is-dood-theologie
'God is dead theology'

blijf-van-mijn-lijf-huis
lit. 'stay away from my body-house, house for threatened women'

Not all phrasal compounds possess the property of expressiveness, however. What one may expect is that when a particular phrasal pattern is used systematically for the purpose of classification (that is, for naming concepts), the resulting type of phrasal compound will be quite normal, and will not carry a particular expressive value. This is indeed the case for right-headed phrasal compounds with AN phrases as their left constituent, as is illustrated here for Dutch:

(19) $[[blinde_A\ darm_N]_{NP}[ontsteking]_N]_N$ 'blind intestine inflammation, appendicitis'
$[[centrale_A\ verwarmings_N]_{NP}[monteur]_N]_N$ 'central heating technician'
$[[derde_A\ wereld_N]_{NP}[land]_N]_N$ 'third-world country'
$[[ronde_A\ tafel_N]_{NP}[conferentie]_N]_N$ 'round table conference'
$[[vrije_A\ tijds_N]_{NP}\ kleding]_N]_N$ 'free time clothing, casual dress'
$[[zwarte_A\ kousen_N]_{NP}][kerk]_N]_N$ 'black stockings church, orthodox church'

In these examples, the AN phrase is a conventional lexical unit. However, it is not the case that Dutch AN phrases can only feed compounding when they are conventional names for concepts. The crucial property of AN phrases as parts of compounds is that they can function as classifiers. Hence, there are also phrasal compounds in which the left AN constituent is not a conventional lexical unit by itself. This is the case for the following Dutch phrasal compounds:

(20) $[[drie_{NUM}\ sterren_N]_{NP}[hotel]_N]_N$ 'three stars hotel'
$[[lange_A\ afstands_N]_{NP}[loper]_N]_N$ 'long distance runner'
$[[twee_{NUM}\ componenten_N]_{NP}[lijm]_N]_N$ 'two components glue'
$[[vier_{NUM}\ kleuren_N]_{NP}[druk]_N]_N$ 'four colours print'
$[[witte_A\ boorden_N]_{NP}[criminaliteit]_N]_N$ 'white collars criminality'

For instance, there is no lexical unit *drie sterren* 'three stars' in Dutch. Crucially, these AN phrases embedded in compounds do not function as referring expressions, but specify the type of N, where N is the head of a compound. This is also why the NP modifier in these compounds cannot contain a determiner, as this would imply a referential interpretation of the modifying NP. It is revealing to compare this absence of a determiner to the use of AN combinations such as *blinde darm* 'appendix; lit. blind intestine' when not embedded in a compound. Since *darm* 'intestine' is a count noun, it must be preceded by a determiner, and the determinerless phrase *blinde darm* is therefore ill-formed, unless it is embedded in a word. Yet, these AN sequences are phrases, since the adjective is inflected. The ending *-e* in *blinde*, for instance, is required since *darm* is a singular common noun, and Dutch adjectives agree in gender and number with their head noun. Agreement is a clear indication of phrasal status, since there cannot be agreement between parts of words, as this would go against lexical integrity, the defining property of wordhood.

We thus observe that a particular type of word structure, compounding, licenses a particular type of phrasal structure: AN phrases headed by count nouns but without determiners. This once more underscores the point that schemas for morphological structure and those for phrasal structure are interdependent in the formation of lexical units.

5 Form-meaning asymmetries

In section 4 we saw that phrases can feed word-formation. This strengthens the position that morphology and syntax cannot be completely separated. But what happens if a word-formation process does not take phrases as bases for affixation? Consider the following examples from Italian:

(21) chitarra elettrica   'electric guitar'
     chitarrista elettrico 'electrical guitarist'

  flauto barocco   'baroque flute'
  flautista barocco 'baroque flute player'

  tennis da tavolo   'tennis table'
  tennista da tavolo 'table tennis player'

The word sequences on the left and the right are NPs of the form A + N or N Prep N. The phrase *chitarrista elettrico* denotes someone who plays the electric guitar.

However, the phrase *chitarra elettrica* lit. 'guitar electric' is not the formal base for the attachment of *-ista*, a suffix that is used in Italian to create personal nouns. This is clear from the word order (the suffix is not attached at the right edge, **chitarra elettricista*), and from the fact that the adjective *elettrico* agrees in number and gender with the masculine noun *chitarrista*, and not with the feminine noun *chitarra*. This asymmetry between form and meaning ("bracketing paradox") is the same as that in the famous English example *transformational grammarian* discussed in Spencer (1988). In the case of English, one might consider the suffix *-ian* to be formally attached to the phrase *transformational grammar*, an option that is available due to English word order and the poor inflection of English. Such an analysis is obviously impossible in the case of Italian, which only allows for a phrasal interpretation:

(22) [[chitarr-ista]$_N$ [elettrico]$_A$]$_{NP}$

This suggests that the adjective *elettrico* has semantic scope over a part of the complex phrasal head *guitarrista*, and that the internal morphological structure of the modified head word is accessible. In example (22), the adjective *elettrico* modifies the nominal base of the head noun. In the following examples AN phrases used as modifiers are turned into AA sequences, in order to fit the canonical phrase structure of Italian (examples provided to me by Daniele Vergilitto):

(23) energia solare 'solar energy'
impianto$_N$ energetico$_A$ solare$_A$ 'solar power plant'

chirurgia$_N$ estetica$_A$ 'aesthetic surgery'
intervento$_N$ chirurgico$_A$ estetico$_A$ 'aesthetic surgery intervention'

The same type of bracketing paradox has been observed for Polish. In Polish relational adjectives follow the head noun. Hence, the structural paradox is the same as for Italian (Szymanek 2010):

(24) chirurgia plastyczna 'plastic surgery'
chirurg plastyczny 'plastic surgeon'

praca fizyczna 'manual work'
pracownik fizyczny 'manual worker'

In these examples the post-nominal relational adjectives agree in gender with the preceding head noun. Hence the variation in form of the relational adjectives *plastyczn-* and *fizyczn-*.

Let us look at these facts from the perspective of how to encode meaning. When an Italian speaker knows the lexical phrase *guitarra elettrica*, and (s)he wants to construct the lexical unit for denoting a person playing an electric guitar, the suffix *-ista* that is used for creating personal names cannot be attached to the phrase *guitarra elettrica* because this suffix is attached to words only: the noun *gitarra-elettric-ista* is ill-formed. The alternative is a phrase with a form-meaning mismatch in which the (stem forms of the) relevant lexemes (*guitarra* and *elettrico*) that form a lexical collocation, are inserted in the available slots in a schema that complies with the restriction that *-ista* does not accept phrasal bases. This is the schema [[N-*ista*]$_N$ A]$_{NP}$. The semantic property to be specified is that the adjective has semantic scope over the base-N only.

Productive patterns with this kind of asymmetry can be accounted for by specifying a paradigmatic relationship between two phrasal schemas (Booij 2010), where ≈ denotes a paradigmatic relationship:

(25) <[N$_j$ A$_k$]$_{NPi}$ ↔ SEM$_i$> ≈

      <[[N$_j$-ista]$_N$ A$_k$]$_{NPl}$ ↔ [PERSON with relation R to [SEM$_i$]]$_l$>

Another example of form-meaning asymmetries is formed by words derived from particle verbs in Scandinavian languages. In the Mainland Scandinavian languages Danish, Norwegian, and Swedish, the particle follows the verb, as is the case for English. However, the particle precedes the verb in past and present participles which have both verbal and adjectival properties, and in deverbal nouns (Allan, Homles and Lundskaer-Nielsen 1995; Faarlund, Lie and Vannebo 1992; Holmes and Hinchcliffe 2003). Here are some examples of participles of particle verbs in these three languages:

(26) *particle verb*   *past participle*

 Danish
 falde ned   'to fall down'   ned-faldne (æbler)   'windfall (apples)'

 Norwegian
 bring ud   'to deliver'   Posten bliver ud-bragt   'The mail is being delivered'

 Swedish
 köra om   'to overtake'   den om-körda lastbilen   'the overtaken lorry'
 ring up   'to phone'   upp-ringd   'phoned'

In the following deverbal nouns in Norwegian (Faarlund, Lie and Vannebo 1992), we see again the reversal effect:

(27) *particle verb*   *nominalization*
    binde inn   'to bind (a book)'   inn-bind-ing   'book cover'
    rydde opp   'to tidy up'   opp-rydd-ing   'tyding up'
    skrive av   'to copy'   av-skrif-t   'copy'
    trekke opp   'to pull up'   opp-trekk-er   'cork screw'

The deverbal suffixes cannot be attached to the particle since it is not a verb, or part of a verb. If the suffix were attached to the verb, we would get forms like *bind-ing-inn*. As there are no particle nouns, particles cannot occur after a noun. And since Norwegian compounds are right-headed, *bind-ing-inn* cannot be interpreted as a compound. Therefore, the nominalizations have the form of a compound, consisting of a particle followed by the deverbal head noun. Hence, the formal base of these nominalizations is not the particle verb as such, even though the meaning of these nominalizations is a compositional function of the (often idiomatic) meaning of the corresponding particle verb. In the nominalizations, the lexical collocation of the particle and the verb is preserved, but inserted in the reverse order, in the slots of the available compound type [X N]$_N$, which is the general template for nominal compounds in Germanic languages. There is a form-meaning asymmetry, since the particle verb is not a (non-discontinuous) subconstituent of the nominalization. Yet, the meaning of these nominalizations is regular and transparent as they relate in a systematic, yet paradigmatic way to the corresponding particle verbs.

The same explanation can be invoked for the reversal effect in participles of particle verbs. Since participles are adjectives, the only possible shape of adjectival forms of particle forms is that of a right-headed adjectival compound.

The following form-meaning asymmetries have been observed in relation to particle verbs in English, Dutch, German, and Italian (Booij 2010: 189):

(28) a. English particle verbs may carry the suffixes *-er* and *-ing* on their verbal head: *look-er-on, runn-er-up, digg-ing up, switch-ing off the lights*;
   b. the past participle of Dutch particle verbs is formed by prefixing *ge-* and suffixing *-t/-d/-en* to the stem form of the verbal head: *aan-val* 'to attack' – *aan-ge-vall-en*, *op-bellen* 'to phone up' – *op-ge-bel-d*; *ge-*nominalization also applies to the head: *rond-spring* 'jump around' – *rond-ge-spring* 'jumping around';
   c. when German particle verbs undergo nominalization with the affix combination *ge-e*, this affix combination is attached to the verbal head of the particle verb: *herum-hops-en* 'to jump around' – *Herum-ge-hops-e* 'jumping around' (Müller 2003; 2006);

d. in Italian, nominalizing suffixes are attached to the verbal head (Francesca Masini, pers. comm.): *venire giù* 'to come down' – *la venuta giù* 'the coming down', *mangiare fuori* 'to eat out' – *la mangiata fuori* 'the meal at a restaurant'.

In all cases, canonical morphological forms are used for creating denominal forms of particle verbs. Note that, since Italian has left-headed compounds, the particle can appear after the deverbal noun, unlike what is the case for Germanic languages such as Norwegian, where a compound like [[*bind-ing*]*inn*] is ill-formed. The relevant patterns can be accounted for in terms of paradigmatic relations between schemas. For example, the relation between German *herumhopsen* and *Herumgehopse* in (28c) can be expressed by a paradigmatic relationship symbolized by the sign ≈ between two schemas:

(29) <[Part$_i$ V$_j$]$_k$ ↔ [SEM]$_k$> ≈ <[Part$_i$ [ge-V$_j$-e]$_N$]$_{Nl}$ ↔ [NOM SEM$_k$]$_l$

NOM stands for the semantic operator of event nominalization. The structure [Part$_i$ [*ge*-V$_j$-*e*]$_N$]$_N$ in (29) is a right-headed compound structure of the type [XN]$_N$, in which the head is a deverbal noun with the discontinuous affix *ge…e*. What is special about the structure of these compounds is that its semantic correlate requires reference to the semantics of a paradigmatically related structure, that of particle verbs. In (29) we specify that this event nominalization of German particle verbs is formally a head operation: it is the verbal head that is nominalized, but the nominalizing element has semantic scope over the particle verb as a whole.

In conclusion, the flexibility in encoding lexical units for denoting concepts is greatly enhanced by allowing for certain types of asymmetries between form and meaning, mismatches that can be resolved by the language user on the basis of paradigmatic relationships between (morphologically or syntactically) complex expressions. These observations also show that the internal structure of a lexical unit is not by definition opaque as an effect of storage: conventional lexical units may preserve their formal and semantic transparency.

6 Conclusions

The notion "construction" that plays a central role in construction grammar, is indispensable for the analysis of word-formation patterns as well. In the study of word-formation, we investigate the systematic correspondences between form and meaning at the word level. Constructional schemas provide an adequate format for expressing these systematic correspondences. Moreover, they are part of a hierarchical lexicon in which both complex words and morphological patterns of various levels of abstraction are specified.

An important advantage of the construction morphology approach is that it can express similarities between morphological and phrasal lexical expressions, and the paradigmatic relations between morphological and phrasal schemas. Thus, lexical knowledge is characterized as a complicated network between words and phrasal expressions at a range of levels of abstractions, varying between individual words and completely abstract patterns.

7 References

Allan, Robin, Philip Holmes and Tom Lundskaer-Nielsen (1995): *Danish. A Comprehensive Grammar*. London/New York: Routledge.
Aronoff, Mark (1976): *Word Formation in Generative Grammar*. Cambridge, MA: MIT Press.
Booij, Geert (2002): Constructional idioms, morphology, and the Dutch lexicon. *Journal of Germanic Linguistics* 14: 301–327.
Booij, Geert (2009): Phrasal names: a constructionist analysis. *Word Structure* 3: 219–240.
Booij, Geert (2010): *Construction Morphology*. Oxford: Oxford University Press.
Booij, Geert (ed.) (2018): *The Construction of Words. Advances in Construction Morphology*. Cham: Springer.
Booij, Geert (2023): Paradigmatic relations in Construction Morphology: the case of Dutch Noun+Verb compounds. *Zeitschrift für Wortbildung / Journal of Word formation* 7(2): 13–33.
Booij, Geert and Francesca Masini (2015): The role of second order schemas in the construction of complex words. In: Laurie Bauer, Livia Körtvélyessy and Pavel Štekauer (eds.), *Semantics of Complex Words*, 47–66. Cham: Springer.
Diessel, Holger (2023): *The Constructicon. Taxonomies and Networks*. Cambridge: Cambridge University Press.
Erman, Britt and Beatrice Warren (2000): The idiom principle and the open choice principle. *Text* 20: 29–62.
Faarlund, Jan Terje, Svein Lie and Kjell Ivar Vannebo (1992): *Norsk Referansegrammatikk*. Oslo: Universitetsforlaget.
Goldberg, Adele (2006): *Constructions at Work. The Nature of Generalization in Language*. Oxford: Oxford University Press.
Hein, Katrin (2015): *Phrasenkomposita im Deutschen. Empirische Untersuchung und konstruktionsgrammatische Modellierung*. Tübingen: Narr Francke Attempto.
Hein, Katrin and Sascha Michel (eds.) (2023): Wortbildung und Konstruktionsgrammatik/Word Formation and Construction Grammar. Sonderheft/Special Issue. *Zeitschrift für Wortbildung / Journal of Word Formation* 7(2): 1–190.
Holmes, Philip and Ian Hinchcliffe (2003): *Swedish. A Comprehensive Grammar*. London/New York: Routledge.

Hüning, Matthias (2010): Adjective + Noun constructions between syntax and word formation in Dutch and German. In: Alexander Onysko and Sascha Michel (eds.), *Cognitive Approaches to Word Formation*, 195-218. Berlin: Mouton de Gruyter.
Jackendoff, Ray (2002): *Foundations of Language*. Oxford: Oxford University Press.
Jackendoff, Ray (2009): Compounding in the parallel architecture and conceptual semantics. In: Rochelle Lieber and Pavol Štekauer (eds.), *The Oxford Handbook of Compounding*, 105-129. Oxford: Oxford University Press.
Jackendoff, Ray (2010): *Meaning and the Lexicon. The Parallel Architecture 1975-2010*. Oxford: Oxford University Press.
Jackendoff, Ray (2013): Formal CxG: Constructions in the parallel architecture. In: Thomas Hoffmann and Graeme Trousdale (eds.), *The Oxford Handbook of Construction Grammar*, 70-92. Oxford: Oxford University Press.
Jackendoff, Ray and Jenny Audring (2020): *The Texture of the Lexicon. Relational Morphology and the Parallel Architecture*. Oxford: Oxford University Press.
Joeres, Rolf (1995): *Wortbildungen mit -macher im Althochdeutschen, Mittelhochdeutschen und Neuhochdeutschen*. Heidelberg: Winter.
Köpcke, Klaus-Michael, Sarah Schimke and Verena Wecker (2021): Processing of German noun plurals: Evidence for first- and second-order schemata. *Word Structure* 14: 1-24.
Kuiper, Koenraad, Marie-Elaine Van Egmond, Gerard Kempen and Simone Sprenger (2007): Slipping on superlemmas: Multi-word lexical items in speech production. *The Mental Lexicon* 2: 313-357.
Los, Bettelou, Corrien Blom, Geert Booij, Marion Elenbaas and Ans Van Kemenade (2012): *Morphosyntactic Change. A Comparative Study of Particles and Prefixes*. Cambridge: Cambridge University Press.
Masini, Francesca (2019): Compounds and Multi-word Expressions in Italian. In: Barbara Schlücker (ed.), *Complex Lexical Units: Compounds and Multi-word Expressions*, 153-187. Berlin: De Gruyter.
Meibauer, Jörg (2007): How marginal are phrasal compounds? Generalized insertion, expressivity, and I/Q-interaction. *Morphology* 17: 233-259.
Müller, Stefan (2003): The morphology of German particle verbs: Solving the bracketing paradox. *Journal of Linguistics* 39: 275-325.
Müller, Stefan (2006): Phrasal or lexical constructions? *Language* 82: 850-883.
Pascual, Esther and Theo Janssen (2004): Zinnen in samenstellingen. Presentaties van fictieve verbale interactie. *Nederlandse Taalkunde* 9: 285-310.
Schlücker, Barbara and Ingo Plag (2011): Compound or phrase? Analogy in naming. *Lingua* 121: 1539-1551.
Speelman, Dirk, José Tummers and Dirk Geeraerts (2009): Lexical patterning in a construction grammar: The effect of lexical co-occurrence patterns on the inflectional variation in Dutch attributive adjectives. *Constructions and Frames* 1: 87-118.
Spencer, Andrew (1988): Bracketing paradoxes and the English lexicon. *Language* 64: 663-682.
Sprenger, Simone A (2003): *Fixed Expressions and the Production of Idioms*. Nijmegen: Max-Planck-Institut für Psycholinguistik.
Sprenger, Simone, Willem J. M. Levelt and Gerard Kempen (2006): Lexical access during the production of idiomatic phrases. *Journal of Memory and Language* 54: 161-184.
Szymanek, Bogdan (2010): *A Panorama of Polish Word-formation*. Lublin: Wydawnictwo KUL.
Tremblay, Annie and R. Harald Baayen (2010): Holistic processing of regular four-word sequences: A behavioral and ERP study of the effects of structure, frequency, and probability on immediate free recall. In: David Wood (ed.), *Perspectives on Formulaic Language. Acquisition and Communication*, 151-173. London: The Continuum International Publishing Group.

Van de Weijer, Jeroen, Weiyun Wei, Yumeng Wang, Guangyuan Ren and Yunyun Ran (2020): Words are constructions, too: A construction-based approach to English ablaut reduplication. *Linguistics* 58: 1701–1735.
Wiese, Richard (1996): Phrasal compounds and the theory of word syntax. *Linguistic Inquiry* 27: 183–193.
Wray, Alison (2002): *Formulaic Language and the Lexicon*. Cambridge: Cambridge University Press.
Wray, Alison (2008): *Formulaic Language. Pushing the Boundaries*. Oxford: Oxford University Press.

Gary Libben
7 Word-formation in psycholinguistics and neurocognitive research

1   Introduction
2   An in-depth look at a seminal study
3   Word-formation and the functional architecture of the mental lexicon
4   Morphological parsing and constituent activation
5   Linguistic and psycholinguistic isomorphism: assumptions and new alternatives
6   Conclusion
7   References

Abstract: Most words of a language will contain more than one morpheme. Thus, word-formation is central to the understanding of how words are represented in the mind and brain, how they are created, and how acts of word-formation, diachronically in the history of the language and synchronically in acts of language processing, are linked to cognitive processes and patterns of brain activity. Early studies on morphological processing in the visual domain revealed that morphological constituents are activated. It is also the case, however, that effects of the characteristics of whole-word forms have been found. These have given rise to models that capture the processing of multimorphemic words as both fully integrated units and as decomposed representations. Recent proposals have called into question the extent to which traditional theoretical constructs such as morpheme, morphological structure, and mental lexicon actually play a role in lexical representation and processing from a psycholinguistic and neurocognitive perspective. It has been suggested that we need to recast those constructs in a manner that accords with a more dynamic view of words in the mind and brain and the role that learning and experience play in shaping how multimorphemic words are represented.

1 Introduction

In linguistic terms, word-formation can be seen as the means by which the vocabulary of a language is expanded through the use of existing language elements

Gary Libben, St. Catharines, ON, Canada

https://doi.org/10.1515/9783111420561-007

and patterns to create new words. Thus, the compound word *blueberry* is based on the individual lexical components *blue* and *berry* and accords with the general patterns of compounding in English. It also accords with patterns found in related English compounds such as *blackberry* and *strawberry*. Similarly, affixed word pairs such as *untwist* and *twistable* and pairs such as *elevator* and *elevation* are formed through the combination of existing elements in a manner that is consistent with both general language patterns and patterns associated with individual elements.

We might begin the discussion of word-formation in psycholinguistic and neurocognitive research with the term *psycholexical* to capture the psychological issues associated with those constructs that we commonly call words. Assuming that the scope of word-formation encompasses derivation and compounding, but does not include inflection, the psycholinguistic and neurocognitive approach is one that connects those lexical categories to the two fundamental psycholexical questions:
a) How are words represented in the mind/brain?
b) How are they processed during acts of language production and comprehension?

The psycholexical research issue is thus the extent to which the word-formation status of a word is required to adequately understand how it is represented in the minds/brains of language speakers and how it is processed when those speakers engage in acts of language comprehension and production.

Consider, as an example, a word with a word-formation history such as *elevator*. There are good reasons to describe this word as multimorphemic. The focus of research from a psycholexical perspective is thus the extent to which the representation and processing of this word might differ from the mental representation and processing of similarly sounding comparison words without clear morphological components in English (e.g., *elephant* or *alligator*).

The term *psycholexical* itself is also a potentially useful springboard to framing the issues. Some readers may be familiar with the term in the context of personality theory of the late nineteenth and mid twentieth centuries. For many readers, however, it is likely a new word. In the context of this article, I assume that this word will be much more useful to the reader than a completely novel form such as, say, *pomapel*. The reason for this is that upon first reading, the language comprehender is able to identify and make use of the major components *psycho-* and *-lexical* in order to arrive at an interpretation of the novel string. How is this done? What computational processes are involved? What knowledge structures are required? And, if the word remains in the vocabulary of readers, is it encoded in terms of the constituents that were first used to scaffold its comprehension? Are those units (i.e. *psycho-* and *-lexical*) stored in the mind? Does the morphological analysis that identified those constituents also result in the decomposition of the string *lexical* into the morphological units *lex*, *ic* and *al*?

Finally, is it the case that in the mind/brain, it is reasonable to claim that a form such as *psycholexical* has morphological structure at all? Might it be the case that that which we call morphological structure simply falls out from lexical association, in which *psycholexical* might be interpreted by analogy to existing elements, including both the forms *lexical* and *psychological*? These are among the key issues that can be addressed through psycholinguistic and neurocognitive research.

2 An in-depth look at a seminal study

Speculation on how morphologically complex words are represented in the mind can be traced back to antiquity (Libben 2010). However, there is no doubt that the paper of Taft and Forster (1975) represented a pivotal moment in the development of the psycholinguistic study of the relation of word-formation to online lexical processing. As I will discuss below, many of the issues that guided the research agenda in subsequent decades had their beginnings in the details of the three experiments that Taft and Forster reported in their initial study. Accordingly, I review those experiments in some depth below.

The experiments reported by Taft and Forster (1975) employed a visual lexical decision paradigm in which participants are presented with a target string on a computer screen and must decide as quickly as possible whether that target string is in fact a word of their language, by pressing either a button labeled "yes" or a button labeled "no". Response time and response accuracy served as their dependent variables.

There is no doubt about the fact that the lexical decision task (introduced into the literature by Meyer and Schwanefeldt 1971) has been a cornerstone of research on lexical processing and our ability to probe the manner in which multimorphemic words are processed (see Libben and Jarema 2000; Libben, Westbury and Jarema 2012). Indeed Henderson (1982) has claimed that the ascendency of the field of psycholinguistics is very much linked to the success of the lexical decision task.

Because the lexical decision task requires participants to press either a "yes" or "no" response button, it necessitates the presence of nonwords in the experiment (typically the balance of words to non-words is 50 %, to ensure that the experiment does not produce a response bias). It is most often the case that it is the real words in a lexical decision experiment that are the primary focus, and lexical decision latencies are interpreted as representing the speed with which words are recognized. In Taft and Forster's (1975) paper, however, it was the nonwords that were the primary object of study. Specifically, they examined the differences in lexical decision speed and accuracy for words such as *juvenate* vs. *pertoire*. Critically, both these nonwords are substrings of the words *rejuvenate* and *repertoire* respectively. Both of these words begin with the string (and possible prefix) *re-*. Taft and Forster (1975) found that response times to produce a "no" response for strings such as *juvenate* were longer than those for strings such as *pertoire*. The explanation that they provided for this result set the stage for a great deal of the reasoning and debate in the field of psycholinguistics on the role of word-formation in mental representations and lexical processing. The explanation that they presented has two components. The first is that online lexical processing contains an in-built morphological analysis procedure that is obligatory and non-discriminating. The second is that the mental lexicon contains not just words, but also morphological substrings such as *juvenate* (the possible presence of a suffix in the string did not receive special attention in this early work of Taft and Forster). Thus, in the case of *rejuvenate*, the potential prefix *re-* would be stripped from the string during processing. The string *juvenate* would then be looked up in the mental lexicon and found to exist. The same procedure would occur for *repertoire*, except that in this case, after the potential prefix *re-* is stripped from the stimulus and the string *pertoire* is looked up in the mental lexicon, no representation for *pertoire* is found. This, according to Taft and Forster (1975), is the reason why participants can reject *pertoire* more quickly than *juvenate* in a lexical decision task.

There was an unintended way in which the examples of *rejuvenate* and *repertoire* used in the Taft and Forster (1975) study highlights a key challenge in bringing together the linguistics of word-formation and the psychology of lexical processing. Taft and Forster were likely quite right in noting that *rejuvenate* is understood as containing the prefix *re-*. As it turns out, however, etymologically, *repertoire* also contains the prefix *re-*. In this case, it is likely the Latin intensifying prefix *re-*, attached to the archaic Latin form *parire* 'to produce'. Thus, from the very beginning, we were forced to grapple with the problem of the potential mismatch between the diachrony of a word in the history of a language and its synchrony in the minds of native speakers in the *psycholexical* approach to word-formation. From a psycholexical perspective, *rejuvenate* has morphological structure, because the language user has experience with the formally and semantically related string *juvenile*.

The case that Taft and Forster (1975) presented for obligatory and automatic prefix stripping in the reading of English words and for the representation in the mental lexicon of stems that are not free-standing words was strengthened by their use of stimuli such as *dejuvenate* vs. *depertoire* in a subsequent lexical decision experiment reported in the same study. These stimuli are formed by taking what Taft and Forster claimed to be existing elements of the mental lexicon (e.g., *juvenate*) as compared to representations that do not exist in the mental lexicon (e.g., *pertoire*) and attaching the prefix *de-* to each, resulting in the creation of nonwords such as *dejuvenate* and *depertoire*. They found that participants took longer to reject the former as compared to the latter. Again, they took this to support the argument that the prefix *de-* was automatically and obligatorily stripped from the input string. Following that operation, *juvenate* would be found in the mental lexicon, creating the response uncertainty that would be manifested in more errors (i.e. false "yes" responses) and elevated responses times.

Finally, a third experiment in the seminal Taft and Forster (1975) study set the stage for another key issue in the study of morphological processing and the mental lexicon. That is the issue of competition within the mental lexicon. In Experiment 2 of their report, they focused on strings such as *vent*. This is a monomorphemic free-standing word in its own right, but is also part of prefixed words such as *invent*, *prevent*, and *circumvent*. Taft and Forster compared lexical decision latencies for words such as *vent* to latencies for words such as *coin*, which is only a free-standing word. They also contrasted *vent*, for which the bound form is more frequent than the free form, to words such as *card*, which also has a bound variant (*discard*). In the case of *card*, however, the frequency of the free form is higher than that of the bound form. The results showed that "yes" response times for words such as *vent* were longer than those for matched free-form-only words such as *coin*. However, there was no difference between response times to words such as *card* and their matched free-only counterparts (e.g., *fist*). They concluded that the reason for this is that *card* has its own representation in the mental lexicon as a bound stem and that bound stems and free forms can be in competition. In the lexical decision task, the presentation favours the free form. Therefore, an interference effect is found only for words in which the bound variant is more frequent than the free one and therefore "gets in the way".

To summarize, the seminal study of Taft and Forster (1975) created the background to many of the fundamental psycholexical questions that were to dominate research programs of the next decades. The study also provides an interesting contrast to the kinds of issues that have become dominant in just the last few years and which promise to play a role in the next steps of psycholexical research.

The first issue concerns a shift from viewing the mental lexicon as a static knowledge store that is composed of discrete items to one that is a dynamic network that changes through the lifespan. As will be discussed in section 3, there has been a clear development in models of the mental lexicon. It now seems clear that the mental lexicon is likely not a monolithic knowledge structure. And, it is very unlikely to have the characteristics of a list. Moreover, it is unlikely that the mental lexicon of a person can be equated with the lexicon of a language. Generally speaking, vocabulary knowledge grows in both size and richness of association through the lifespan. And, most people in the world speak more than one language. Therefore, in psycholexical terms, the more common organization of the mental lexicon across the population is one that can support multilingual activity.

The second issue concerns the processes of morphological analysis itself. The original Taft and Forster proposal posited a process of prefix stripping that would enable a multimorphemic word to be accessed through its stem in reading. It is less clear how morphological analysis takes place in the case of suffixed words. And, compound words offer a particularly challenging problem because there is no "short list" of affixes that morphological parsing can make use of to identify constituent elements. Moreover, as will be discussed in section 4, it seems that the morphological processing system is not simply a parser. It is more likely that morphological parsing falls out from the interaction of many variables that operate within a system that has as its goal the maximization of opportunity for meaning creation. In most cases, by maximizing opportunity for meaning creation, the psycholexical processing system will produce a parse of an input stimulus that accords with a morphological description of that stimulus. For some cases, it does not. And, it is precisely from these cases of morphological misanalysis in processing that we can learn a great deal about the characteristics of the psycholexical system.

The third issue, which is discussed in section 5, is the issue of linguistic and psycholinguistic isomorphism. In the original Taft and Forster study, and indeed in very many studies that have followed, researchers have, as a matter of metaphorical convenience, described psycholexical representations and processes in a manner that implicitly assumes that the elements (e.g., morphemes) that are used as constructs in linguistic analyses are also constructs that are relevant in the psychological domain. Thus we speak, for example, of "the activation of morphemes in the mind". However, whether human minds represent morphological structures, or represent morphemes at all, is an empirical question that has substantial consequences for how we view the relation among the "vocabularies" of linguistic, psycholinguistic, and ultimately neurolinguistic approaches to language.

3 Word-formation and the functional architecture of the mental lexicon

The notion of a mental lexicon is at the heart of our understanding of how language is represented in the mind. It has also served as a construct that has, perhaps more than any other, brought together research on formal linguistics, psycholinguistics, neurolinguistics, and aphasiology.

Of course, we must bear in mind that the notion of a mental lexicon is itself a theoretical construct. There has never been any direct observation of the mental lexicon. In addition, there is no *a priori* reason to expect that the neurological instantiations of an individual's vocabulary store will have a single localized representation in the brain (Freud 1953 [1891]; Pulvermüller 2013; Pulvermüller, Cappelle and Shtyrov 2013). So, for the most part, descriptions of the functional architecture of the mental lexicon should be considered to be metaphors regarding the nature of a theoretical construct.

The metaphor that Taft and Forster (1975) used was that of a frequency-ordered list of entries (Forster 1976). In this view, the list is accessed from beginning to end, and is ordered in terms of frequency, with more frequent lexical entries being closer to the top of the list than less frequent ones. It is clear that the particular metaphor of a serial list was influenced by the ways in which it was common to frame hypotheses concerning cognitive representations and processing in terms of the data structures that were then current in the development of computer applications. Nevertheless, a review by Forster (2007) speaks to the way in which a frequency-ordered mental lexicon provides an elegant answer to the question of why lower frequency items are slower to recognize (see, however, Baayen 2010 for an alternative view of the fundamental nature of the frequency effect).

A rather different approach to constructing a metaphor concerning how words are represented in the mind has its origins in work by Selfridge (1959) and Selfridge and Neisser (1960) (see also Grainger, Rai and Dufau 2008). In Selfridge's approach, mental representations for features can be seen as units which he termed *demons*, highlighting their active and independent status. This approach can be seen as a precursor to the logogen model of Morton (1969) in which logogens are characterized as evidence-collecting units of representation that have specific and independent activation thresholds that result from individual experience.

Irrespective of whether representations in the mental lexicon are seen as elements in a list or as quasi-independent processing units, the question that is most important for a consideration of the role of word-formation is the question of whether the nature of lexical units is constrained or affected by the word-formation history of an item. Thus, we ask whether words such as *legal, illegal,* and *illegality* have separate representations as full forms or whether they are, at some fundamental level, represented in terms of their constituent morphemes. The hypothesis of a morphologically decomposed representation has, of course, storage efficiencies associated with it, because there are many fewer morphological elements than there are possible combinations of those elements into morphologically complex words.

It seems at the present time uncontroversial to claim that the consensus in the field is that there are mental representations for both multimorphemic words and what we term morphological constituents. This consensus has been driven largely by data from a variety of experimental paradigms that have shown that response patterns to the presentation of multimorphemic words are driven both by characteristics of the whole word (e.g., its lexical frequency) as well as the lexical characteristics of morphological stems (e.g., their lexical frequency). Such findings required the postulation of models of lexical access and of representation that could accommodate an assertion that multimorphemic words do have representations in the mental lexicon and that those representations are structured so that they embody morphological constituency. The supralexical model of Giraudo and Grainger (2000) provided a framework that claimed that constituent morphemes are accessed through their multimorphemic full word forms, rather than the other way around, as suggested by Taft and Forster (1975).

Another issue that arose following the early work of Taft and Forster (1975) is whether it is appropriate to assume that representations in the mental lexicon are likely to be structurally homogenous. Might it be the case, for example, that some prefixed words are processed through their constituent morphemes, while others are processed and represented as full forms? Such questions were accommodated in a family of dual-route models that posited competing decomposition routes to the recognition of multimorphemic words and whole-word processing routes. These processing alternatives were visualized as pathways in a flowchart. Such an approach was represented by the augmented addressed morphology (AAM) model (e.g., Burani and Caramazza 1987; Burani and Laudanna 1992). A related approach claimed that the processing alternatives are carried out by routes that operate in parallel (e.g., Bertram, Schreuder and Baayen 2000; Schreuder and Baayen 1995). In this type of model, the online processing of multimorphemic words was seen as a type of horserace. In this horserace, one route conducts a morphological analysis of a multimorphemic word. The other route processes it as a whole. The process that reaches the finish line first is the one that is employed.

The early models of the mental lexicon that have been outlined above have their origins in the initial conceptualization of the mental lexicon as a memory store with a relatively well-defined architecture and with relatively well-defined units of representation. The issue of whether or not this is a good starting point for modeling the mental lexicon has been central to more recent discussions. Researchers such as Elman (2011) have argued that the notion of a mental lexicon is not required to explain lexical processing phenomena. He proposes that we see words not as elements of a mental lexicon, but rather as stimuli that alter mental states in lawful ways. This proposal has as its core the dynamic nature of processing and the fact that lexical processing in a natural setting is contextualized in sentences, discourses and situations.

Another recent perspective on the nature of morphemes and lexical representations has been advanced in the context of naive discrimination learning (NDL) (Baayen et al. 2011; Baayen, Hendrix and Ramscar 2013). This model is based on the Recorla-Wagner learning equations (Wagner and Recorla 1972) and has the notions of discrimination and learning at its core. As has been demonstrated by Baayen, Hendrix and Ramscar (2013), the NDL model can account for lexical frequency effects without recourse to explicit morphological representations for prefixed, suffixed or compound words.

As the above new approaches to lexical processing demonstrate, there is considerable challenge to the notion of a mental lexicon as an inert knowledge store. We can expect that the mental lexicon will increasingly be characterized as a dynamic cognitive system that allows for lexical activity. And, a key component of this activity is the lexical creativity associated with understanding new affixed and compound forms and producing them in a manner that will be understood by others.

If the ability to produce and understand novel multimorphemic words resides in the domain that we call the mental lexicon, it is necessary that we consider that domain to be more active and more flexible than we have in the past. To exemplify this activeness and flexibility, let us return, for example, to the word *repertoire* that Taft and Forster (1975) used as a monomorphemic contrast to the multimorphemic form *rejuvenate.* The word *repertoire,* is very likely monomorphemic in the minds of most native speakers of English. But now, what happens psycholexically in the following scenario: Imagine that a concert pianist is asked to play a familiar piece of music. However, she declines the request, saying: "I don't play that anymore. It used to be part of my *repertoire*, but now I would say that it is part of my *ex-pertoire*". It is quite likely that the coinage will be easily understood in that context as a piece of music no longer played. But now, imagine a slightly different scenario: In this version, a concert pianist is also asked to play a familiar piece of music. But now she says: "I have never played that piece well enough. I have tried, but I guess it will never be part of my *expert-oire*." Here, it seems that the ability to interpret the novel word as referring to "part of an individual's repertoire that is played particularly well" is scaffolded by the existence of the lexical items *repertoire*, *expert*, and *expertise*.

Both the example cases above are intended to demonstrate that the word *repertoire* is not morphologically inert. Perhaps it is the case that no representation in the mental lexicon is morphologically inert. Rather, psycholexically, as soon as there are multiple representations in an individual's vocabulary, and those representations are linked, new word-formation possibilities are built as expressions of human creative ability. Thus, it is appropriate to see the mental lexicon not simply as the repository of lexical elements (i.e. morphemes) and not simply as a repository of the results of word-formation (i.e. whole multimorphemic words), although it most likely contains representational information for both. The key feature of the mental lexicon is its dynamic nature and the manner in which it can connect lexical knowledge in order to make word-formation possible and in order to make the comprehension of the results of word-formation possible. Moreover, because the mental lexicon of an individual will very likely encompass lexical knowledge of more than one language, adequate models need to be able to account for the ways in which linguistic variation in morphological patterns and constraints can be accommodated.

4 Morphological parsing and constituent activation

The discussion above of the dynamic nature of the mental lexicon and the need to have an architecture that can encompass lexical creativity and the results of word-formation brings to the foreground the issue of how morphological decomposition is actually achieved. That is, how do listeners or readers actually find the constituent morphemes in existing and novel multimorphemic words? This is an issue that is weighted toward the comprehension side of morphological processing (although there are significant computational issues to be considered in production as well).

As was the case for conceptions of the mental lexicon, we can trace research on morphological parsing and activation back to the very early work by Taft and Forster in the mid 1970s. As has been discussed above, Taft and Forster (1975) provided an explicit proposal for how prefixed words of English are parsed in order for them to be looked up in the mental lexicon in terms of their stems. In a publication in the following year, Taft and Forster (1976) addressed the matter of how compound words are processed. Their proposal was that, during single-word reading, compound words are looked up in the mental lexicon in terms of their first constituents. They assumed a left-to-right parse of compound words and further assumed that the prefix stripping approach that was employed for prefixed words could not work for compound words, because there is no "short list" of compound initial constituents that would be analogous to the relatively "short list" of prefixes that exist in English.

Taft and Forster's (1976) evidence for the claim that compound words were accessed in terms of their initial constituents came from lexical decision "no" latencies to nonwords (as was the case in their 1975 study). They contrasted stimuli such as *footmilge* as compared to *trowbreak*. The crucial difference here is that in the case of *footmilge*, the initial constituent is a real word and the final constituent is a nonword. In the case of *trowbreak*, the nonword is in initial position. Taft and Forster found that it took participants longer to reject *footmilge* and suggested that compounds are processed from left to right in English in a manner that allowed lookup in terms of the initial constituent. Subsequent work by Libben (1994) proposed a compound parsing algorithm in which compounds are scanned in a recursive beginning-to-end manner. Libben, Derwing and de Almeida (1999) extended this work to consider "challenging" cases such as the ambiguous English novel compounds *cartrifle* (which can be parsed as either *car-trifle* or *cart-rifle*). Evidence from words such as these suggests that morphological parsing does not yield a single univocal parse. Rather, all constituents that can be activated will be activated. Thus, Libben, Derwing and de Almeida (1999) found that a stimulus such as *cartrifle* generated activation of *car*, *cart*, *rifle*, and *trifle*. Additionally, participants showed evidence of mis-parses such as *cart-trifle.*

The theme of morphological mis-parsing and mis-activation has been a dominant one in the morphological processing literature, generating a string of papers with the general title "Is there an X in X?". Sample papers in this genre include "Is there a hat in that" (Bowers, Davis and Hanley 2005), "The broth in my brother's brothel" (Rastle, Davis and New 2004), and a set of studies that investigate whether there is *corn* in *corner* (e.g., Longtin, Segui and Hallé 2003; Morris, Grainger and Holcomb 2008; Lehtonen, Monahan and Poeppel 2011; Lavric, Elchlepp and Rastle 2012).

There is still considerable controversy in the field regarding the means by which recognition of a word *corner* will also activate the representation for *corn*, and how such effects can be accommodated in models of lexical representation and processing. If we accept, however, that such mis-activations do occur, this presents important consequences for the linking of theories of word-formation to psycholexical theories of morphological processing. The first is that the term morphological processing itself is perhaps inappropriate. The reason for this is that the processing of *corner* into *corn+er* is not a true morphological analysis. Extracting the lexical representation for *broth* out of *brothel* is certainly not, and extracting *hat* from *that* seems to be rather maladaptive from a morphological point of view. Yet, from a psycholexical perspective, all of these may be fully adaptive in terms of the function of the system as a whole. It is important to bear in mind that if there is a goal in the processing of words, that goal is to create meaning, not just to perform a linguistic or morphological analysis of an input string. Under this view, the overarching characteristic of the human lexical processing system is that it seeks to maximize the opportunity for meaning creation (Libben 2010, 2014). In this way, we might imagine that if multimorphemic words are indeed analyzed morphologically, it is likely not in order to facilitate their lookup in the mental lexicon under this or that access key. Rather, it is so that activation can occur under any and all access keys. It may be the case that this, the overlapping access to as many morphological sub-elements as possible, is the core characteristic of morphological processing. The means by which this can be achieved will differ from language to language, depending on morphological patterns within the language and, in the case of reading, the conventions that govern its expression in writing and print. But despite the potential homogenizing effects of those conventions, we can expect that morphological processing will be relatively unconstrained, resulting in many "false positive" activations, such as those that enable *corn* to be activated in *corner*.

Finally, it should be noted that this type of over-activation moves us yet further away from a view of the mental lexicon as an inert list. It seems that, in the case of multimorphemic words, it is likely to be a dynamic place which is characterized by considerable conflict. The activation of *corn* interferes with, rather than accords with, the interpretation of *corner*. The activation of all the potential constituent morphemes in the ambiguous form *cartrifle* will, at some point in the interpretation of the ambiguous word, require that some potential constituents be deactivated. And finally, for words that we can characterize as semantically opaque (e.g., *honeymoon*, *humbug*), the maximization of opportunity for meaning creation will result in over-activation and the need to resolve the cognitive conflict that may result.

5 Linguistic and psycholinguistic isomorphism: assumptions and new alternatives

As is often the case in the history of psycholinguistics, the foundational research in the field of morphological processing demonstrated the extent to which categories and constructs that play a role in theoretical linguistics also play a role in online processing. Such investigations may be considered as coming under the general heading of "psychological reality studies". Derwing (1973) argued that in each such case, the adequacy of a linguistic construct to the psychological domain must be tested against psycholinguistic data. Authors such as Myers (2007, 2016) have outlined both the opportunities and challenges associated with employing the terminology of linguistics in the psycholinguistic domain.

As the discussions in the sections above have underlined, psycholinguistic and neurocognitive research on the representation and processing of multimorphemic words has been moving to a much more dynamic conceptualization of the mental lexicon and a much less categorical conceptualization of morphological processing. Thus, if there has been an assumed isomorphism between linguistic and psycholinguistic constructs in the past, this is likely to come under a great deal more scrutiny in the future. Indeed indications at present are that the fundamental notions of a morpheme, a word, and multimorphemic structure are likely to be re-thought.

An anticipation of this re-thinking might prompt us to consider the fundamental question of why that which we call morphological constituency would be activated or built up during online lexical processing at all. One approach to this question is to suggest that morphemes are activated because words have morphological structure. However, if we adopt a psycholexical approach, that simply becomes a tautological statement. From a psycholexical perspective, words do not have any properties that are not fundamentally psychological in nature.

Another approach, one that requires fewer assumptions and that is situated in the psycholexical domain, is that, because our minds are organized to maximize the opportunity for meaning creation, we cannot but recognize subunits of multimorphemic strings when they correspond to elements for which we already have representations (i.e. those with which we already have experience). So in the case of *elevator*, there is activation of *elevate*. In the case of *illegal* there is activation of *legal*. When there is less transparency, for example in the case of *illegality*, in which there is associated stress change, we might assume that activation of *legal* is made somewhat more difficult. It is important to note here that using the term "experience" may have advantages. Consider a compound example such as *blueberry*. It seems that there are two kinds of experiences that are relevant here. One is experience with the free form *berry*. The other is experience with the compound head *-berry*. That latter experience is the one that is more relevant to the processing of *blueberry*. But at the same time, it is the principle of maximization of opportunity that also gives rise to the activation of *berry* as a free-form. So, depending on the weighting of those competing experiences, i.e. their relative frequency, we will see interference effects rather than facilitation effects between the experience that a language user has with the free form *berry* and that user's experience with the compound head *-berry*, which we can assume to have psycholexical status as a positionally defined bound item.

The maximization of opportunity places us in a situation where strict rules of morphological constituency cannot be automatically related to psycholinguistic phenomena. At the outset of this article, multimorphemic forms such as *elevator* were contrasted with monomorphemic forms such as *alligator* that are similar sounding and of comparable length. But as we have noted with the form *pertoire* above, morphological structure, from a psychocentric perspective, is a matter of experience. And, that experience grows and changes throughout the lifespan. Consider how the clipping *gator* is used, both as a shortening for *alligator* and as a compound head in the famous drink *Gatorade*. This experience could easily give rise to a novel compound *alloygator*, drawing by analogy on *alligator*, but using *-gator* as a compound head. Indeed, a Google search will reveal that such a novel compound has been used commercially as the name for an automobile alloy wheel protector. The novel compound builds on the whole-word form *alligator* (the picture of the product shows an alligator biting the rim of a wheel). It may also be the case that the product name is trading on the activation of *gate* (with the connotation of protection). And, if so, this would be entirely consistent with the notion of maximization of opportunity and a psycholexical conceptualization of morphological activation. It would be less consistent with the view of morphological processing that is focused on the formal morphological analysis of the string.

The kind of lexical processing and activation that we have claimed may occur in the comprehension of the novel compound *alloygator* accords with the observation by Singh (2006) that it is much more common for compounds to be formed by switching out individual elements (creating compound families) than by bringing together two free morphemes in an entirely novel construction.

The reason for this from a psycholexical perspective is that it is easier to draw on positional experience. And, it is likely that when such positional experience is activated, it is not only the form, but many other experiences associated with that form that are also activated. These would include the semantic relations that have been examined by Gagné and Spalding (2007, 2009).

An additional important component in the re-thinking of complex and compound words in the mind/brain involves addressing the question of whether lexical representations themselves can be said to be fixed. Libben (2014) presents a framework in which they are not. Rather, it is suggested within that framework that those representations that we typically refer to as morphemes and which take part in complex and compound representations, develop as a result of the lexical experience of the language user, into what Libben (2014) calls *morphologi-*

cal superstates. The construct of a morphological superstate draws metaphorically on the notion of superposition in quantum physics. As applied to morphological processing, the notion suggests that the experience that a language user has with a lexical form (e.g., the word *board*) creates new morphological possibilities. So, if those experiences include the use of the form *board* as a compound modifier (e.g., *boardroom*) and a compound head (e.g., *keyboard*), these develop as new positionally bound morphological elements in the mental lexicon. It is claimed that the new morphological representation for *board* can be seen to generate a proliferation of morphological elements in the mind/brain. This proliferation may be less efficient from the perspective of storage efficiency in the mental lexicon, but it is much more effective from the perspective of maximizing the opportunity for meaning creation. It is claimed that these alternative uses of a form such as *board* are potentially in competition in the mental lexicon. One of the ways in which this potential conflict is reduced is for morphological forms with different morphological and semantic functions to be represented in a superstate form which has specific morphological manifestations (e.g., free lexeme, compound modifier, compound head) depending on specific usage needs. These manifestations may come into conflict in specific situations. One of those situations would be a constituent priming paradigm in which a word such as *board* is followed immediately by a compound such as *boardroom* or *keyboard* that contains the same string, but with a different morphological function.

6 Conclusion

In this article we have traced the role of word-formation in psycholinguistic and neurocognitive research from its beginnings in the work of Taft and Forster (1975, 1976) to investigations of the electrophysiological correlates of affixation and pseudoaffixation in Lavric, Elchlepp and Rastle (2012) and, finally, to models that call into question whether morphemes are useful constructs at all (e.g., Baayen, Hendrix and Ramscar 2013) and models that challenge the notion of morpheme as a univocal mental structure (Libben 2014).

It has been almost 40 years since the seminal work of Taft and Forster. Over that period, there have been very substantial advances in methodology in the field, and a great deal more is known about how multimorphemic words are processed across languages, across specific word forms within languages, and among individuals. Yet there remains a great deal to be accomplished. In the next years, a key domain of exchange and advancement will be to find the transdisciplinary language that brings together insights from the study of morphology, the psycholexical study of morphological processing, and the neurocognitive study of brain correlates in the production and comprehension of multimorphemic words. Bringing these domains together will enable the integration of the notion of word-formation as something that takes place in a language and also something that takes place in a mind and between minds. Indeed, the question could be framed in the following manner: "If a new word is formed in the forest and there is nobody there to hear it, is it really a new multimorphemic word?"

This question may contain within it the challenges for the next decade of psycholinguistic and neurocognitive research on word-formation. In some sense, the answer must be "yes, a new word is formed". But, on the other hand, the simple enactment of the word-formation ability of a single language user seems to fail to satisfy the notion of what it means for something to be "a new word". A new multimorphemic word is associated with patterns of interpretation in a linguistic community. It is linked to other representations in the mental lexicons of language users, and it instantiates the links that must exist across language users in order for communication to take place. These are very likely to be among the next psycholexical research issues concerning word-formation and the central role that it plays in language production, comprehension and creativity.

7 References

Baayen, R. Harald (2010): Demythologizing the word frequency effect: A discriminative learning perspective. *The Mental Lexicon* 5: 436–461.

Baayen, R. Harald, Peter Hendrix and Michael Ramscar (2013): Sidestepping the combinatorial explosion: Towards a processing model based on discriminative learning. *Language and Speech* 56: 329–347.

Baayen, R. Harald, Petar Milin, Dusica Filipovic Durdevic, Peter Hendrix and Marco Marelli (2011): An amorphous model for morphological processing in visual comprehension based on naive discriminative learning. *Psychological Review* 118: 438–482.

Bertram, Raymond, Robert Schreuder and R. Harald Baayen (2000): The balance of storage and computation in morphological processing: The role of word formation type, affixal homophony, and productivity. *Journal of Experimental Psychology: Learning, Memory & Cognition* 26: 489–511.

Bowers, Jeffrey, Colin Davis and Derek A. Hanley (2005): Automatic semantic activation of embedded words: Is there a 'hat' in 'that'? *Journal of Memory and Language* 52: 131–143.

Burani, Cristina and Alfonso Caramazza (1987): Representation and processing of derived words. *Language and Cognitive Processes* 2: 217–227.

Burani, Cristina and Alessandro Laudanna (1992): Units of representation for derived words in the lexicon. In: Ram Frost and Leonard Katz (eds.), *Orthography, Phonology, Morphology and Meaning*, 361–376. Amsterdam: North-Holland.

Derwing, Bruce (1973): *Transformational Grammar as a Theory of Language Acquisition. A study in the empirical, conceptual and methodological foundations of contemporary linguistics.* Cambridge: Cambridge University Press.

Elman, Jeffrey L. (2011): Lexical knowledge without a mental lexicon? *The Mental Lexicon* 60: 1–33. [doi:10.1075/ml.6.1.01elm].

Forster, Kenneth (1976): Accessing the mental lexicon. In: Roger J. Wales and Edward Walker (eds.), *New Approaches to Language Mechanisms*, 257–287. Amsterdam: North-Holland.

Forster, Kenneth (2007): Visual word recognition: problems and issues. In: Gonia Jarema and Gary Libben (eds.), *Core Perspectives on the Mental Lexicon*, 56–78 Oxford: Elsevier.

Freud, Sigmund (1953 [1891]): *On Aphasia. A critical study.* New York: International University Press.

Gagné, Christine and Thomas Spalding (2007): The availability of noun properties during the interpretation of novel noun phrases. *The Mental Lexicon* 2: 239–258.

Gagné, Christine and Thomas Spalding (2009): Constituent integration during the processing of compound words: Does it involve the use of relational structures? *Journal of Memory and Language* 60: 20–35.

Giraudo, Hélène and Jonathan Grainger (2000): Prime word frequency in masked morphological and orthographic priming. *Language and Cognitive Processes* 15: 421–444.

Grainger, Jonathan, Arnaud Rey and Stéphane Dufau (2008): Letter perception: From pixels to pandemonium. *Trends in Cognitive Sciences* 12(10): 381–387.

Henderson, Leslie (1982): *Orthography and Word Recognition in Reading.* New York: Academic Press.

Lavric, Aureliu, Heike Elchlepp and Kathleen Rastle (2012): Tracking hierarchical processing in morphological decomposition with brain potentials. *Journal of Experimental Psychology Human Perception & Performance* 38: 811–816. [DOI:10.1037/a0028960]

Lehtonen Minna, Philip Monahan and David Poeppel (2011): Evidence for early morphological decomposition: Combining masked priming with magnetoencephalography. *Journal of Cognitive Neuroscience* 23: 3366–3379. [DOI:10.1162/jocn_a_00035]

Libben, Gary (1994): How is morphological decomposition achieved? *Language and Cognitive Processes* 9(3): 369–391.

Libben, Gary (2010): Compounds, semantic transparency, and morphological transcendence. In: Susan Olsen (ed.), *New Impulses in Word-formation*, 212–232. Hamburg: Buske.

Libben, Gary (2014): The nature of compounds: A psychocentric perspective. *Cognitive Neuropsychology* 31: 8–25. [DOI:10.1080/02643294.2013.874994]

Libben, Gary, Bruce Derwing and Roberto de Almeida (1999): Ambiguous novel compounds and models of morphological parsing. *Brain and Language* 68: 378–386.

Libben, Gary and Gonia Jarema (2002): Mental lexicon research in the new millennium. *Brain and Language* 81: 1–10.

Libben, Gary, Chris Westbury and Gonia Jarema (2012): Embracing complexity. In: Gary Libben, Gonia Jarema and Chris Westbury (eds.), *Methodological and Analytic Frontiers in Lexical Research*, 1–12. Amsterdam/Philadelphia: Benjamins.

Longtin, Catherine-Marie, Juan Segui and Pierre A. Hallé (2003): Morphological priming without morphological relationship. *Language and Cognitive Processes* 18: 313–334.

Meyer, David and Roger Schvaneveldt (1971): Facilitation in recognizing pairs of words: Evidence of a dependence between retrieval operations. *Journal of Experimental Psychology* 90: 227–234.

Morris, Joanna, Jonathan Grainger and Phillip Holcomb (2008): An electrophysiological investigation of early effects of masked morphological priming. *Language and Cognitive Processes* 23: 1021–1056. [DOI:10.1080/01690960802299386]

Morton, John (1969): Interaction of information in word recognition. *Psychological Review* 76: 165–178.

Myers, James (2007): Generative morphology as psycholinguistics. In: Gonia Jarema and Gary Libben (eds.), *The Mental Lexicon. Core perspectives*, 105–128. Amsterdam: Elsevier.

Myers, James (2016): Psychological reality of linguistic structure. In: Rint Sybesma, Wolfgang Behr, Yueguo Gu, Zev Handel, James Huang and James Myers (eds.), *Encyclopedia of Chinese Language and Linguistics*. Vol. 3, 94–100. Leiden: Brill.

Pulvermüller, Friedemann (2013): How neurons make meaning: Brain mechanisms for embodied and abstract-symbolic semantics. *Trends in Cognitive Sciences* 17(9): 458–470. [DOI: 10.1016/j.tics.2013.06.004]

Pulvermüller, Friedemann, Bert Cappelle and Yury Shtyrov (2013): Brain basis of words, constructions, and grammar. In: Thomas Hoffmann and Graeme Trousdale (eds.), *The Oxford Handbook of Construction Grammar*, 397–416. Oxford: Oxford University Press.

Rastle, Kathleen, Mathew H. Davis and Boris New (2004): The broth in my brother's brothel: Morpho-orthographic segmentation in visual word recognition. *Psychonomic Bulletin and Review* 11: 1090–1098.

Schreuder, Robert and R. Harald Baayen (1995): Modeling morphological processing. In: Laurie B. Feldman (ed.), *Morphological Aspects of Language Processing*, 131–154. Hillsdale, NJ: Erlbaum.

Selfridge, Oliver (1959): Pandemonium: A paradigm for learning. In: D. V. Blake and A. M. Uttley (eds), *Proceedings of the Symposium on Mechanisation of Thought Processes*, 511–529. Her Majesty's Stationary Office.

Selfridge, Oliver and Ulric Neisser (1960): Pattern recognition by machine. *Scientific American* 203: 60–68.

Singh, Rajendra (2006): Whole Word Morphology. In: Keith Brown (ed.), *Encyclopedia of Language and Linguistics*. Vol. 13, 578–579. 2nd ed. Oxford: Elsevier.

Taft, Markus and Kenneth Forster (1975): Lexical storage and the retrieval of prefixed words. *Journal of Verbal Learning and Verbal Behavior* 14: 630–647.

Taft, Markus and Kenneth Forster (1976): Lexical storage and retrieval of polymorphemic and polysyllabic words. *Journal of Verbal Learning and Verbal Behavior* 15: 607–620.

Wagner, Allen and Robert A. Rescorla (1972): A theory of Pavlovian conditioning: Variations in the effectiveness of reinforcement and nonreinforcement. In: Abraham H. Black and William F. Prokasy (eds.), *Classical Conditioning II*, 64–99. New York: Appleton-Century-Crofts.

Pavol Štekauer
8 The delimitation of derivation and inflection

1 Introduction
2 Reasons for fuzziness
3 Criteria for the distinction between derivation and inflection
4 Conclusions
5 References

Abstract: This article establishes that the relation between inflectional morphology and derivational morphology is that of cline. The main reasons for this situation are briefly outlined. The fuzzy nature of the boundary between the two areas of morphology is illustrated by means of selected criteria for their delimitation that are each confronted with counter-examples taken from various languages of the world.

1 Introduction

Recent decades have witnessed a profound change in evaluating the relationship between linguistic categories and disciplines. It was cognitive linguistics, in particular, that highlighted their fuzzy nature. The attention of linguists was thus shifted to the problems of vague boundaries, prototypes and peripheries, good exemplars and poor exemplars. The situation within the traditional discipline of morphology is no exception. A number of morphologists, making use of the invaluable contribution of cross-linguistic typological research, have come to the conclusion that "the inflection/derivation distinction is not absolute but allows for gradience and fuzzy boundaries […] we are dealing with a continuum from clear inflection to clear derivation with ambiguous cases in between" (Haspelmath 1996: 47).

What are the reasons for this situation within morphology? A brief summary of these reasons is outlined in the first part of the article, followed by an overview of criteria proposed in the literature for the distinction between derivation and inflection. It will be demonstrated that none of these criteria are of universal validity due to numerous counter-examples from the languages of the world.

Pavol Štekauer, Košice, Slovakia

2 Reasons for fuzziness

2.1 The concept of new word

While it is generally accepted that derivational morphology deals with the formation of new words, i.e. with giving names to yet unnamed objects, it is not quite as clear *what a new word actually is*. Is a clipping or an acronym a new word? They do not denote a new object; instead they denote an "old" one by means of a reduced form. Even more evident is the fuzziness in numerous quantity-related categories. Thus, for example, do diminutives and augmentatives refer to new "objects", like Slovak *bežkať* in (1)?

(1)   *bežkať*   ←   *behať*
       'to run+DIM'   'to run'

If so, then the comparative and the superlative degrees of adjectives should also be treated as derivational forms, although they are mostly discussed within inflectional morphology. And what about various *aktionsart*-categories, like frequentatives, duratives, intensifications, as in the following example from Wichi (Verónica Nercesian, pers. comm.),

(2)   *n'-yahin-pej*
       1SUB-look-ITER
       'I look many times'

that are usually considered to be of inflectional nature? While Beard (1982) gives arguments in favour of the derivational status of the category of Plural in general, and Robins (1971) argues that number in Japanese is derivational, the plural of verbs has been perceived as a prototypical inflectional category. But there are also pluractional verbs like those in the Chadic language Hausa (3) and the Austronesian language Karao (4):

(3)   *tuntùnā*
       RED~tunàa
       PL.ITER~remind
       'to remind many or often'
       (Newman, pers. comm.)

(4) *manbabakal*
    man-CV~bakal
    RECIP.IMPFT-PL-fight
    'to fight each other' (indicates that more than 2 participants are involved in the action)
    (Brainard, pers. comm.)

When discussing the situation in Kwakw'ala Anderson (1985: 30) argues in favour of the derivational status of affixes expressing tense, aspect, voice, modality and plurality, because they are (a) optional, and present only where necessary for emphasis or disambiguation; and (b) equally applicable to words of any syntactic function or word class. Anderson shows that, for example, $x^wak^wəna$ 'canoe' has a future form $x^wak^wənaλ$ 'canoe that will be, that will come into existence'. Its recent past form is $x^wak^wənaxdi$ 'canoe that has been destroyed'. In addition, Štekauer, Valera and Körtvélyessy (2012) point out that, compared to the "simple, inflectional" plural meaning 'more than one', pluractional verbs have, in principle, an additional meaning, like 'repeated action', 'extent/degree of action', 'simultaneity of action', etc.

2.2 Language dependence

This brings us to another problematic point revealed by cross-linguistic research. In particular, *one and the same category may be inflectional in one language and derivational in another*, as pointed out, e.g., by Katamba with respect to diminutives (1993: 212). Let us furthermore call attention to the so-called D-element which in some languages, such as Hupa, a Na-Dene language spoken in North America, is mostly derivational, while in other languages, like Koyukon, it is more inflectional and productive (Thompson 1996: 353), or passivization in Udihe, an Altaic language, by the suffix *-u* (Nikolaeva and Tolskaya 2001: 287, 307) which – in contrast to the situation in the majority of languages – is formed by derivation from a restricted class of transitive verbs (5):

(5) *ana-u*
    to.push-PASSIVE
    'to be pushed'

2.3 Crossing the inflection-derivation borders

Third, inflections may be *borrowed by the derivational system*, or they even may gradually acquire derivational status. Examples of the "borrowing" of inflectional affixes by derivation to produce new words are numerous. Sapir (1965: 57) reports a few instances of inflectional markers in Kujamaat Joola functioning as derivational affixes. So, for example, the passive suffix *-i* combines with *-wɔl* 'to give birth' to form *kawɔli* 'birth$_N$' and the negative *-ut* can be combined with the theme *-ju̱* 'to be in good health' to form *-ju̱:t* 'to be sick'. The status of *-ut* as a derivative is assured by its position. Sapir points out that the phrase *əju:təlenore-rit* 'he never pretends to be sick' would be impossible if *-ut* in the double derivative formation *-ju̱:təlenor* 'to pretend to be sick' was functioning in its normal capacity as mood marker.

A change of inflectional paradigm is a device used in a number of genetically unrelated languages as illustrated in (6):

(6) a. *shoN*$_N$ 'old age' ← *joN*$_v$ (*D+shoN*) 'to be old' (Rice) Slavey
    b. *shaya* 'to work' ← 'work' (Bril) Nêlêmwa
    c. *frumosul* 'beauty' ← 'beautiful' (Iacob and Măciucă) Romanian
    d. *nợ* 'debt' ← 'to owe' (Thái Ân) Vietnamese

2.4 Affixal ambiguity

Ambiguous affixes also contribute to the fuzziness of the inflection/derivation distinction. Beck (pers. comm.) points out the abundance in Upper Necaxa Totonac of quasi-inflectional affixes. While these affixes are fully productive and thus carry a typical feature of inflectional affixes, they do not express obligatory morphological categories and do not constitute a paradigm (unlike prototypical inflectional morphemes). An example of one such affix expressing repetition is in (7):

(7) *tsa:lapa:la:niÔ:tsá*
    flee–RPT–PF=now
    'he had fled again'

2.5 Systematic ambiguity

While in most languages the inflection/derivation ambiguities are restricted to individual cases/categories, the situation in Ket and all the other Jenissej languages is much more complex. Werner (1998) demonstrates that *the whole system* of verbs in these languages is fuzzy in this respect. Belimov (1991: 25) even assumes that word-formation and inflection are in fact a single process of forming new lexical units. Werner refers to verbs in Ket, derived by infixation, which have complete inflectional paradigms but lack an infinitive as a basic citation form:

(8) ti‹j›vij   'southerly wind blows'
     ti‹j-lˌ›vij   'southerly wind blew'
     ur‹a›vij   'northerly wind blows'
     ur‹ɔ-nˌ›vij   'northerly wind blew'
     (Werner 1998: 135)

Interestingly, the potential infinitives are identical to nominal compounds given in (9).

(9) tivej   'southerly wind'
     udbej   'northerly wind'
     ɛsˌbej   'upward-rising smoke'
     (Werner 1998: 135)

2.6 Serving two masters

Some affixes *serve two masters*. The following example from Karao (Brainard, pers. comm.) shows that polysemy/homonymy can cross the inflection/derivation boundary (also because, on a more general level, the boundary between polysemy and homonymy is rather fuzzy). The Karao affix *pan-/impan-* can be a nominalizing affix, it can express, e.g., iterative action on a verb (10) but it can also signal imperative mood (!) as exemplified in (11):

(10) *pan-chinel-an   mo-ak*
     ITER-depend.on-IPFV.PAT   ERG.2SG-ABS.1SG
     'You can always depend on me'

(11) *pan-dotho   ka!*
     IMPER-cook   ABS.2SG
     'Cook!'

To give a more familiar example, the English form *-er* can express the comparative degree of adjectives as well as various semantic roles, such as Agent (*teacher*), Instrument (*cooker*), Patient (*foreigner*), and a number of other meanings.

3 Criteria for the distinction between derivation and inflection

The following brief overview surveys various criteria recently proposed in literature and shows that, while prototypically the criteria are effective, they face counter-examples and/or various degrees of validity indicating their cline-like nature. Most of them draw on Dressler (1989), Scalise (1988), ten Hacken (1994) and Plank (1994).

3.1 Function

While derivational morphology has a semiotic function and contributes to lexical enrichment, inflectional morphology has the relational function of serving syntax or marking syntactic constructions with special word forms.

While inflectional morphology is obligatory in a syntactic construction, derivational morphology is not.

Apart from the counter-examples given in (6), one should mention conversion in the Slavic languages which is viewed as the derivation of a new word by changing its inflectional paradigm (Filipec and Čermák 1985: 104), and therefore labeled *transflexion* by Dokulil (1982). Stump (2005: 64) refers to Sanskrit, where the derivation of causative verbs is a productive process, but this process is simply based on the shifting of a verb from one conjugational category to another. Thus, the derivation of the causative verb from the verb *dviṣ* 'to hate' is based on shifting it from the second to the tenth conjugation. In Swahili, both diminutives and augmentatives are formed very productively by the change of paradigm (noun class) (Contini-Morava, pers. com.). A change of inflectional paradigm is a device used in Datooga where causatives are formed by the conversion of a verb from class 1 to class 2 (Kießling, pers. comm.):

(12) *noos* (class 2) 'to stick, fasten' ← *noos* (class 1) 'to be stuck'

While inflection, unlike derivation, is required by syntactic operations (Bybee 1985: 81–83; Matthews 1991: 50), Booij (2006: 655) maintains that "[t]his does not mean [...] that inflection is always governed by syntax". As an example, Booij (2006: 655–656) refers to the accusative form of the Latin word *Roma* 'Rome', i.e. *Romam*, which can express either a direct object, or an adverbial phrase ('to

Rome'). The use of the adverbial form is not required by syntax. On the other hand, derivation is also of syntactic relevance when it changes a syntactic category. We can generalize Booij's position by saying that, prototypically, inflection is *affected* by syntax while derivation *affects* syntax.

3.2 Range of categories

Inflectional morphology typically involves smaller meaning changes than derivational morphology.

This meaning-related criterion is closely related to the distribution of derivational and inflectional morphemes and their respective functions. Since the basic function of derivation is the formation of names for new "objects" it is "natural" that a derivational morpheme is positioned next to the particular lexical morpheme. Since the basic function of inflection is to express grammatical relations between words it is natural that inflectional morphemes are placed at the periphery immediately before/after the neighbouring word. Thus, prototypically, there is an opposition between lexical (conceptual) meaning and grammatical meaning.

But there are at least two points that need to be taken into account. First, Beard (1981, 1995) postulates 44 fundamental Indo-European functions which underlie both derivation and inflection and which are realized in various languages differently (or, are not realized at all). If this hypothesis is true, the semantic distinctions between inflection and derivation, at least, historically, become obliterated. This hypothesis may be supported by instances where a category which is commonly used by derivation is, in some languages, integrated in the inflectional system, and vice versa.

The second aspect of the problem concerns Bybee's assumption that the derivational/inflectional status of morphological items correlates with their *semantic relevance* for the root and *generality* of their meaning: "[a] meaning element is *relevant* to another meaning element if the semantic content of the first directly affects or modifies the semantic content of the second" (1985: 13). In addition, Bybee assumes that "the greater the difference between the meaning of the derived word and the meaning of the base, the greater the likelihood that the affix is derivational" (1985: 5). Bybee's approach necessarily leads to a semantic cline, with various degrees of semantic change and semantic relevance.

3.3 Transparency

Inflectional morphology is usually semantically and formally more transparent than derivational morphology.

Laca's claim (2001: 1218) that irregularity in derivational morphology manifests itself in the many-to-one and one-to-many relationships between form and meaning appears to be too strong. These types of relationships seem to be equally typical of inflectional morphology, at least in fusional languages which are characterized by numerous cases of cumulative exponence and syncretism. As an example, each inflectional morpheme in each of the Slovak paradigms is a portmanteau morpheme expressing three fundamental meanings: case, number, and gender. Extensive syncretism in Slavic paradigms may be illustrated with the inflectional morpheme *-om* in *chlap-om*, which can mean either singular, instrumental, masculine noun of the pattern *chlap* 'man', or plural, dative, masculine noun of the same pattern. This syncretism runs across paradigms, and so *-om* expresses the same grammatical meanings in the (different) paradigm *dub* 'oak'.

Ricca (2005: 198–211) refers to portmanteaux morphemes which combine derivational and inflectional categories, this being an important argument against strict separation of inflectional and derivational morphology. For illustration, French denominal adjectives in -[al] as in *national* 'national' form masculine plural by -[o] (*nationaux*). The suffix not only derives denominal adjectives but also combines the inflectional categories of masculine and plural (Ricca 2005: 207). Zwarts (2007, pers. comm.) shows that in Endo, a Southern Nilotic language, the derivation process based on changing a vowel from [−ATR] (i.e. non-advanced (retracted) tongue root) to [+ATR] (advanced (retracted) tongue root) results in agent nouns in plural:

(13) *kwaang* 'to cook' → *kwääng* 'cooks'

Interestingly, its singular is derived through the singulative suffix *-ün*, to give *kwäängün*.

Derzhanski (2005) provides additional cross-linguistic evidence of the derivation+inflection type of cumulative exponence, in particular, by giving examples of the plural+diminutive cumulation in languages of various families (e.g., Bulgarian (Slavic), Fula (Atlantic-Congo), Swahili (Bantu), Asmat (Trans-New Guinea)).

On the other hand, Plank (1994: 1675) aptly relates the lack of transparency in some derived words to the process of lexicalization to which inflected forms are usually not exposed. But examples of a semantic shift in inflected forms do occur, like *air-s* 'unnatural manner or action intended to impress'; *damage-s* 'money claimed from a person for causing damage'; *work-s* 'moving parts of a machine'. And finally, also derivation may be highly transparent as is the case with, for example, derivation of adverbs from adjectives in English.

3.4 Productivity and regularity

While rules of inflectional morphology are typically highly productive, the productivity of derivational morphology is restricted.

While inflection is regular, derivation is fraught with idiosyncrasies.

These two criteria reflect the deep-rooted belief of a number of morphologists and syntacticians, at least since Chomsky's *Remarks on Nominalization* (1970), that the productivity and regularity of word-formation processes are much lower than that of syntactic and inflectional processes. However, this has been called into question in recent decades (Anderson 1982; Strauss 1982; Di Sciullo and Williams 1987; Štekauer 1998; Plag 1999). Plag (1999: 2) emphasizes that "derivational processes are much more regular than previously conceived", and Anderson (1992: 78) notes that "even a completely productive process can still, arguably, be derivational, such as the formation of English nominals in *-ing* from verbs". On the other hand, some inflectional paradigms are incomplete, defective (cf. singularia tantum, pluralia tantum, mass nouns, proper names; non-gradable adjectives, etc.).

The bias against productivity and regularity in word-formation seems, however, to rest on *unequal criteria*.

While the productivity of inflection is usually assessed on the basis of categorial meanings expressed by the categories of gender, plural number, case, tense, etc., the lack of productivity in derivation is usually argued for on the basis of purely formal criteria (cf. Bauer 2000: 37). Štekauer (1998: 83–85) shows that it is not important in what way (by suffixation, compounding, conversion, etc.), for example, AGENTIVE meaning is expressed. What matters is that, if required, such an AGENTIVE name can be produced for any AGENTIVE concept. Furthermore, while it is true that the suffix *-ion*, for example, does not combine with all verbs, it is also true that not all verbs can be used in the sentence structure *noun – verb – object*. The constraint permits only transitive verbs to be inserted in the relevant slot. Both restrictions (syntactic and derivational) are based on the same principle of combinability of structural units. And, to give one more example from the field of inflection, the productivity of the Slovak plural suffix *-ovia* (as in *hrdinovia* 'heroes') – as one of many plural affixes in Slovak – is restricted to one of 12 different substantival paradigms, notably plural of masculine animate nouns ending in a vowel. From this point of view, however, the assumption of "full productivity" of inflection vs. significantly restricted productivity of derivational processes does not seem to be so persuasive.

3.5 Word class

While prototypical inflectional morphology does not change word class, derivational morphology often does.

Obviously, this criterion is not applicable to cases in which affixation does not change word class. As counterevidence, our examples of transflexion in section 3.1 above show the class-changing function of inflection in some languages. In addition, Stump (2005: 53–54) shows that an inflectional category can affect the word class. He refers to cases like present participles (i.e. inflected forms of verbs), for example *discouraging*, which can also function as attributive adjectives, as in the phrase *the most discouraging news*. While one might hypothesize a separate word-formation process, the non-derivational nature of the attributive use of the participle can, in Stump's view, be supported by evidence from many other languages, in which present participles never appear without declensional morphology which is unmistakably that of an adjective.

Furthermore, Booij (1994) and van Marle (1995) argue that the so-called *inherent inflection* (numerous examples of plural nouns in various languages; infinitives, participles and comparatives in Dutch) can feed word-formation, and that inherent inflection "expresses like derivation, a certain amount of independent information, whereas the information expressed by contextual inflection is redundant, and only reflects certain aspects of the syntactic structure of the sentence" (Booij 1994: 30).

Van Marle's examples from Dutch show that "derivational forms may develop inflection-like properties [...] and that inflectional forms may display derivation-like properties" (Van Marle 1995: 78) as exemplified in (14) and (15):

(14) $[[X]_{Quant}\_\_]_{NP},$

where the slot can be filled by adjectives compulsorily taking -*s*:

(15) *iets groen-s*   'something green'
      niets waar-s   'nothing true'
      een heleboel slecht-s 'a lot of bad things'

The -*s*-suffixation is automatic, and the resulting forms do not occur as independent words: they can only occur as a part of a construction with the above-given structure. These are typical inflectional characteristics. The point is, however, that the suffixed forms are noun-like in contrast to their adjectival bases: (a) at least in some cases, nouns (without -s) may fill the empty slot in (14), the -s forms are sometimes used as nouns, and some of them have become lexicalized as nouns (*lekkers* 'sweets', *nieuws* 'news'). This suggests that "inflectional forms may develop properties which are usually primarily associated with derivation: the ability to change category. The -s forms indicate, then, that category changing operations can be found in the realm of inflection as well [...]" (Van Marle 1995: 74).

Last but not least, Haspelmath (1996) gives ample evidence that word-class changing inflection (for example, German participles, Lezgian verbal nouns) exists in numerous languages, which authorizes him to conclude that "the myth that word-class-changing inflection does not exist is no more than a myth [...]" (Haspelmath 1996: 50).

3.6 Recursiveness

While rules of derivational morphology can be reapplied, rules of inflectional morphology are not recursive.

While the order of derivational affixes reflects the order of semantic operations, the order of inflectional affixes is fixed and/or semantically irrelevant: only one order is available.

As pointed out by ten Hacken (1994: 156 ff.) the criterion of recursiveness may be interpreted in various ways: it may refer to multiple application of different derivational/inflectional rules, or to the reapplication of one and the same rule. The former criterion is not of much relevance. In derivation it is very common. An extreme case may be illustrated by West Greenlandic where there "are around 400 productive affixes in use [...]. They may combine with each other iteratively, producing a prodigious potential for the derivational expansion of simple stems; up to ten or more affixes in succession before the inflectional ending is not particularly unusual [...]" (Fortescue 1984: 313). On the other hand, at least agglutinative languages admit more than one inflectional affix in a word (resulting from the application of more than one inflectional rule) as in the following example from Hungarian:

(16) *ház-a-ink-ban*
 ház-ak-ink-ban
 house-PL-POSS.PL-DATIVE
 'in our houses'

That the prediction of the non-existence of recursive application of the same rule in inflection, as compared to the cyclic application of derivational rules, is not absolute follows from Dressler's (1989: 8) example taken from Turkish:

(17) *ev-ler-de-ki-ler-de*
      house-PL-LOC-that/which/who-PL-LOC
      'in those which are in the houses'

As to the related criterion specified in this section, Anderson (1985: 33) gives an example from Kwakw'ala by referring to the suffixes *-amas* 'to cause' and *-exsd* 'to want'. From the verb *ne'nak^w* 'to go home', we can form *ne'nak^w'exsd* 'to want to go home'. By attaching the suffix *-amas* we obtain *ne'nak^w'exsdamas* 'to cause to want to go home'. On the other hand, from *q'aq'oλa* 'to learn' we can make *q'aq'oλaamas* 'to cause to learn, teach' and, from this, *q'aq'oλamadzexsd* 'to want to teach' can be formed in turn. In these examples, the same suffixes appear in opposite orders corresponding to different meanings 'to cause to want' vs. 'to want to cause'.

3.7 Paradigms

While inflectional morphology is typically organized into paradigms and inflectional classes, the paradigmatic organization of derivational morphology is much weaker.

While this criterion reflects another deep-rooted false belief (see also, for example, Katamba 1993) van Marle rejects the view that "paradigmatics is of little or no importance to derivational morphology. The only justifiable conclusion is that, in derivation, paradigmatic structure may manifest itself in a fundamentally different way from the way it does in inflection" (1994: 2929). This stance may be further supported by Vallés' view that "word-formation patterns emerge from paradigmatic relations" (2003: 14). Let us also direct our attention to the highly elaborated conceptions of derivational paradigms in Dokulil (1962: 7–18) and Furdík (2004). They show that the derivational system is in fact based on paradigmatic relations reflecting the internal structure of the word-formation system of a language as a whole and that word-formation relations cannot be reduced to those between the motivating and the motivated words. Rather, each such pair of words is the basis for much more complex relations, including *clusters* relating a motivating word with a set of motivated words. Thus, to take Dokulil's (1962) example, the Czech word *list* 'leaf' as a motivating word is related to a large number of motivated words like *lístek* 'small leaf', *listina* 'document', *listář* 'dossier', *olištěný* 'provided with leaves', *listnatý* 'deciduous', *listovní* 'concerning a letter', *listovat* 'to browse', *listopad* 'November', etc.

A word can also be related to a series of words whose neighbouring members are related by motivation:

(18) list   lístek   lístkový   lístkovitý   lístkovitost
     'leaf'   'leaflet'$_N$ 'leaflet'$_A$ 'having leaflets'$_A$ 'property of having leaflets'$_N$

This brings us to what might be called a derivational paradigm in a narrow sense, corresponding to the concept of proportional series:

(19) list   'leaf'   →   líst-ek   →   lístk-ový   →   lístkov-itý
     květ   'flower'   →   kvít-ek   →   kvítk-ový   →   kvítkov-itý
     zub   'tooth'   →   zoub-ek   →   zoubk-ový   →   zoubkov-itý
     roh   'corner'   →   růž-ek   →   růžk-ový   →   růžkov-itý
     smrk   'spruce'   →   smrč-ek   →   smrčk-ový   →   smrčkov-itý etc.

3.8 Mental lexicon

While accepted derived words are likely to be stored as wholes in memory, inflected word forms are unlikely to be so.

Booij (2006: 659) refers to the contradictory results of recent psycholinguistic experiments some of which suggest that derived words, even regular ones, are always stored, while only irregular inflections are stored in the lexical memory (Clahsen, Sonnenstuhl and Blevins 2003). Plag (1999: 11) refers to psycholinguistic and structural linguistic arguments according to which regular complex words can also be stored in the lexicon. Furthermore, experiments by Stemberger and MacWhinney (1988), and Baayen, Lieber and Schreuder (1997) indicate that regular inflectional forms of high frequency of occurrence are also stored.

3.9 Distribution

Inflectional affixes typically have a more peripheral position in the word form than derivational affixes.

This criterion is, in fact, a paraphrase of Greenberg's Universal 28: "If both the derivation and inflection follow the root, or they precede the root, the derivation is always between the root and the inflection" (Greenberg 1966: 93) and has been justified within various theoretical frameworks (cf. Dressler 1989 for the arguments in favour of this criterion from the position of natural morphology, Kiparsky 1982a, b and Mohanan 1986 for arguments within lexical phonology, and Anderson 1992, Perlmutter 1998, and Booij 2006 for the arguments based on the theory of split morphology). There are, however, important exceptions to this criterion. They may concern individual cases or follow from the existence of languages whose system as such is an exception to the general expectations. It is this latter type that suggests that not all exceptions belong to the periphery of a language system as believed by Scalise (1988: 566–567). As for the first type of exception, let us mention the well-known English examples like *worsen, betterment, unhappier*, or Hebrew *ʔimahut* 'motherhood' formed from the plural of *ʔem* 'mother', i.e. pl. *ʔimahot* by means of the suffix *-ut* (Schwarzwald 2001: 29). The other type of exception may be illustrated with Ket. Vajda (pers. comm.) demonstrates that it is difficult to separate derivational and inflectional affixes in the finite verb: they are interspersed in between one another in a rigid template of eight prefix position classes:

(20) subject 8
    incorporated root 7
    subject or object 6
    derivational consonant 5
    tense/mood affix 4
    neuter class subject or object 3
    tense/mood consonant 2
    subject or object affix 1
    verb root 0

Another example is provided by the agglutinating verbal morphology of Kujamaat Jóola. Fudeman (in Aronoff and Fudeman 2005: 96) notes that the derivational suffix *-u* 'from' can follow inflectional markers, as exemplified in (21):

(21) nə-   riŋ-   e   -u   -riŋ
    3AGR- arrive- HAB- from- redup
    'He habitually arrives from'

Rubino (pers. comm.) gives an example of interspersed derivational and inflectional affixes in Ilocano, an Austronesian language:

(22) *nagkinnaawatanda*
    n-ag-ka(inn)-awat-an-da
    PERF-AV-COMIT(RECIP)-understand-NML-3p
    'they understood each other'

where *ag-* is derivational (AV- agentive voice), *n-* is inflectional based on *ag-* (perfective), *ka-* is derivational (comitative), and *-inn-* is inflectional (reciprocal). A similar situation can be found in Udihe (Nikolaeva and Tolskaya 2001), an Altaic language. Let us also mention productively formed noun + noun compounds in the Dravidian language Telugu (Pingali, pers. comm.) with a plural suffix inside them, for example:

(23) *paLLapoDi*
    tooth-PL.NON.NOM-powder
    'toothpowder'

(where *pannu* 'tooth' takes the plural marker which, due to a process of retroflexion becomes *paLLu*. Its non-nominative form is *paLLa*. All other case markers and postpositions attach to this form).

3.10 Headedness

Only derivational suffixes can function as heads.

This issue has been much discussed in the literature, ranging from Marchand's (1960, 1967) idea of a determinant–determinatum structure of the word-formation syntagma, through Williams' (1981) righthand head rule, Lieber's (1981) feature percolation conventions, Selkirk's (1982) revised right-hand rule or Di Sciullo and Williams' (1987) concept of relativized head, with the latter two allowing inflectional morphemes to function as heads, up to Bauer's (1990) head-related skepticism and Štekauer's counter-argument, to name only few of a number of various approaches to the concept of headedness which differ substantially in their treatment of the concept of head. A picture coming out of these different treatments suggests that (a) the concept of head depends on the particular theoretical approach, and (b) that some of these approaches assign the status of head also to inflectional morphemes.

3.11 Exponents

While the positioning and the segmental, suprasegmental, syllabic, and morphemic structure of the exponents of inflectional categories are relatively similar, those of derivational categories are dissimilar.

While analyzing the categories of verbal 3rd person singular agreement and nominal number, Plank (1994: 1676) maintains that (a) exponents of inflectional categories, if expressed by affixes, are exclusively suffixes; (b) they are phonetically similar; (c) they are mostly expressed by monosyllabic or nonsyllabic exponents; (d) they neither carry nor change the position of stress. While this is true of English, it does not hold universally, and there are languages which express inflectional categories by means of prefixes as well. An example from Upper Necaxa Totonac (Beck, pers. comm.) is given in (24):

(24) nakinka:tala'hx'a:te:lhaniya:ntunká
 na-kin-ka:-ta-la'h-x'a:-te:lha-ni-ya:-n-tunká
 FUT-1OBJ-PL.OBJ-3PL.SUBJ-DIST-husk.corn-AMB-BEN-IMPF-2OBJ-very
 'They will go around husking lots of corn for us.'

A similar example comes from Zulu (Van der Spuy, pers. comm.):

(25) *be-si-nga-sa-zu-m-biz-a*
 PAST-we-NEG-still-FUT-him/her-call-VERB
 'We were no longer going to call him/her.'

Neither does the issue of phonetic similarity hold universally. Inflectional languages provide ample counter-examples, for example, various plural markers for various substantival paradigms, to name just one of them. On the other hand, derivational affixes may show homonymy too: consider the polysemous/homonymous suffixes standing for AGENTS, INSTRUMENTS, PATIENTS, etc. in English, but not only there.

3.12 Bases

While inflectional morphemes are typically added to existing bases, derivation can also make use of non-existing bases.

For illustration, as pointed out by Newman (pers. comm.), Hausa agentives are (usually) formed from verbs. Many of these verbs are formed from simple nouns by means of the suffix -taa, e.g., *aikìi* 'work', *aikàtaa* 'to work', *ma'àikàcii* 'worker'. However, some agent nouns are based on non-existing verbs. The verb *zinaata does not actually occur as such, but one has to postulate it as a step in the derivation to make any sense of what is happening:

(26) *mazìnàacī* 'adulterer' ← *zìnā* 'adultery'

The Tzotzil suffix -*tik* 'it's a place of' combines with intransitive stems which never occur independently (Cowan 1969: 102–103) as in (27):

(27) *té²-tik*
tree/stick-it.is. a.place.of
'a place of trees'

Bauer (2009: 407) refers to some compounds in Danish one constituent of which has no independent existence:

(28) a. *bom-uld*
?-wool
'cotton'
b. *jom-fru*
?-woman
'virgin'

Contrary to postulate 12, there are, however, plural forms in English without any corresponding singular (*belonging-s*, *outskirt-s*, *particular-s*, etc.). Similarly, the comparative of *good*, i.e. *bett-er*, is also based on a non-existing base.

4 Conclusions

Not all of the criteria proposed in literature could be mentioned here for reasons of space. However, this brief overview provides adequate support for the view that it is not possible to draw a clear-cut borderline between inflection and derivation and that the relation between these two areas of morphology is best treated "as a *cline* rather than a dichotomy" (Katamba 1993: 217), with prototypical cases at both ends of the cline.

5 References

Anderson, Stephen R. (1982): Where's morphology. *Linguistic Inquiry* 13(4): 571–612.
Anderson, Stephen R. (1985): Typological distinctions in word formation. In: Timothy E. Shopen (ed.), *Language Typology and Syntactic Description*. Vol. 3: *Grammatical Categories and the Lexicon*, 4–56. Cambridge: Cambridge University Press.
Anderson, Stephen R. (1992): *A-Morphous Morphology*. Cambridge: Cambridge University Press.
Aronoff, Mark and Kirsten Fudeman (2005): *What is Morphology?* Oxford: Blackwell.
Baayen, Harald, Rochelle Lieber and Robert Schreuder (1997): The morphological complexity of simplex nouns. *Linguistics* 35: 861–877.
Bauer, Laurie (1990): Be-heading the word. *Journal of Linguistics* 26: 1–31.
Bauer, Laurie (2000): What you can do with derivational morphology. In: Sabrina Bendjaballah, Wolfgang U. Dressler, Oskar E. Pfeiffer and Maria D. Voeikova (eds.), *Morphology 2000. Selected Papers from the 9th Morphology Meeting. Vienna, 24–28 February 2000*, 37–48. Amsterdam/Philadelphia: Benjamins.
Bauer, Laurie (2009): Compounding in Danish. In: Rochelle Lieber and Pavol Štekauer (eds.), *Oxford Handbook of Compounding*, 400–416. Oxford: Oxford University Press.
Beard, Robert E. (1981): *The Indo-European Lexicon. A Full Synchronic Theory*. Amsterdam: North-Holland.
Beard, Robert E. (1982): The plural as a lexical derivation. *Glossa*. 16(2): 133–148.
Beard, Robert E. (1995): *Lexeme-Morpheme Base Morphology. A General Theory of Inflection and Word Formation*. Albany, NY: State University of New York Press.
Belimov, Èduard I. (1991): *Ketskij sintaksis. Situacija, propozicija, predloženie*. Novosibirsk: Izdat. Novosibirskogo universiteta.
Bonami, Olivier and Denis Paperno (2018): Inflection vs. derivation in a distributional vector space. *Lingue e Linguaggio* 2: 1–23.
Booij, Geert E. (1994): Against split morphology. In: Geert Booij and Jaap van Marle (eds.), *Yearbook of Morphology 1993*, 27–49. Dordrecht: Kluwer.
Booij, Geert E. (2006): Inflection and derivation. In: Keith Brown (ed.), *Encyclopedia of Language and Linguistics*. 2nd ed., 654–661. Oxford: Elsevier.
Bybee, Joan L. (1985): *Morphology. A Study of the Relation between Meaning and Form*. Amsterdam/Philadelphia: Benjamins.
Chomsky, Noam (1970): Remarks on nominalization. In: Roderick Jacobs and Peter Rosenbaum (eds.), *Readings in English Transformational Grammar*, 184–221. Waltham, MA: Ginn.
Clahsen, Harald, Ingrid Sonnenstuhl and James P. Blevins (2003): Derivational morphology in the German mental lexicon: A dual mechanism account. In: Harald Baayen and Robert Schreuder (eds.), *Morphological Structure in Language Processing*, 125–157. Berlin/New York: Mouton de Gruyter.
Cowan, Marion M. (1969): *Tzotzil Grammar*. Norman: Summer School of Linguistics of the University of Oklahoma.
Derzhanski, Ivan A. (2005): On diminutive plurals and plural diminutives. In: Geert E. Booij, Emiliano Guevara, Angela Ralli, Salvatore Sgroi and Sergio Scalise (eds.), *Morphology and Linguistic Typology*. On-line Proceedings of the Fourth Mediterranean Morphology Meeting (MMM4_) Catania 21–23 September 2003, University of Bologna, 2005. [http://morbo.lingue.unibo.it/mmm/].
Di Sciullo, Anna-Maria and Edwin Williams (1987): *On the Definition of Word*. Cambridge, MA: MIT Press.

Dokulil, Miloš (1962): *Tvoření slov v češtině. 1. Teorie odvozování slov.* Prague: Nakladatelství Československé akademie věd.
Dokulil, Miloš (1982): K otázce slovnědruhových převodů a přechodů, zvl. transpozice. *Slovo a slovesnost* 43: 257–271.
Dressler, Wolfgang U. (1989): Prototypical differences between inflection and derivation. *Zeitschrift für Sprachwissenschaft und Kommunikationsforschung* 42: 3–10.
Filipec, Josef and František Čermák (1985): *Česká lexikologie.* Praha: Academia.
Fortescue, Michael (1984): *West Greenlandic.* London: Croom Helm.
Furdík, Juraj (2004): *Slovenská slovotvorba.* Prešov: Náuka.
Greenberg, Joseph H. (1966): Some universals of grammar with particular reference to the order of meaningful elements. In: Joseph H. Greenberg (ed.), *Universals of Grammar,* 73–113. Cambridge, MA: MIT Press.
Haspelmath, Martin (1996): Word-class changing inflection and morphological theory. In: Geert E. Booij and Jaap van Marle (eds.), *Yearbook of Morphology 1995,* 43–66. Dordrecht: Kluwer.
Haspelmath, Martin (2024): Inflection and derivation as traditional comparative concepts. *Linguistics* 62(1): 43–77.
Katamba, Francis (1993): *Morphology.* London: MacMillan.
Kiparsky, Paul (1982a): Lexical morphology and phonology. In: In-Seok Yang (ed.), *Linguistics in the Morning Calm. Selected Papers from SICOL-1981,* 3–91. Seoul: Hanshin.
Kiparsky, Paul (1982b): From cyclic phonology to lexical phonology. In: Harry van der Hulst and Norval Smith (eds.), *The Structure of Phonological Representations.* Part I, 131–175. Dordrecht: Foris.
Laca, Brenda (2001): Derivation. In: Martin Haspelmath, Ekkehard König, Wulf Oesterreicher and Wolfgang Raible (eds.), *Language Typology and Language Universals,* 1214–1227. Berlin/New York: de Gruyter.
Lieber, Rochelle (1981): On the organization of the lexicon. Ph.D. dissertation, MIT. Bloomington, IN: Indiana University Linguistics Club.
Marchand, Hans (1960): *The Categories and Types of Present-Day English Word-Formation.* Wiesbaden: Harrassowitz.
Marchand, Hans (1967): Expansion, transposition, and derivation. *La Linguistique* 1: 13–26.
Matthews, Peter H. (1991): *Morphology. An Introduction to the Theory of Word-Structure.* 2nd ed. Cambridge: Cambridge University Press.
Mohanan, Karuvannur P. (1986): *The Theory of Lexical Phonology.* Dordrecht: Reidel.
Nikolaeva, Irina and Maria Tolskaya (2001): *A Grammar of Udihe.* Berlin/New York: Mouton de Gruyter.
Perlmutter, David M. (1988): The split morphology hypothesis: evidence from Yiddish. In: Michael Hammond and Michael Noonan (eds.), *Theoretical Morphology. Approaches in Modern Linguistics,* 79–100. San Diego, CA: Academic Press.
Plag, Ingo (1999): *Morphological Productivity. Structural Constraints in English Derivation.* Berlin/New York: Mouton de Gruyter.
Plank, Frans (1994): Inflection and derivation. In: Ronald E. Asher (ed.), *Encyclopaedia of Language and Linguistics.* Vol. 3, 1671–1678. Oxford: Pergamon.
Ricca, Davide (2005): Cumulative exponence involving derivation. In: Wolfgang U. Dressler, Dieter Kastovsky, Oskar E. Pfeiffer and Franz Rainer (eds.), *Morphology and its Demarcations. Selected Papers from the 11th Morphology Meeting, Vienna, February 2004,* 197–214. Amsterdam/Philadelphia: Benjamins.
Robins, Robert H. (1971): *General Linguistics. An Introductory Survey.* London: Longman.

Sapir, David J. (1965): *A Grammar of Diola-Fogny. A Language Spoken in the Basse-Casamance Region of Senegal*. Cambridge: Cambridge University Press.
Scalise, Sergio (1988): Inflection and derivation. *Linguistics* 26: 561–581.
Schwarzwald, Ora (2001): *Modern Hebrew*. Munich: LINCOM Europa.
Selkirk, Elisabeth O. (1982): *The Syntax of Words*. Cambridge, MA: MIT Press.
Spencer, Andrew (2016): Two morphologies or one? Inflection versus word-formation. In: Andrew Hippisley and Gregory Stump (eds.), *The Cambridge Handbook of Morphology*, 27–49. Cambridge: Cambridge University Press.
Štekauer, Pavol (1998): *An Onomasiological Theory of English Word-Formation*. Amsterdam/Philadelphia: Benjamins.
Štekauer, Pavol (2001): Beheading the word? Please, stop the execution. *Folia Linguistica* 34(3-4): 333–355.
Štekauer, Pavol, Salvador Valera and Lívia Körtvélyessy (2012): *Word-Formation in the World's Languages. A Typological Survey*. Cambridge: Cambridge University Press.
Stemberger, Joseph P. and Brian MacWhinney (1988): Are inflected forms stored in the lexicon? In: Michael Hammond and Michael Noonan (eds.), *Theoretical Morphology. Approaches in Modern Linguistics*, 101–116. Orlando: Academic Press.
Strauss, Steven L. (1982): On 'relatedness paradoxes' and related paradoxes. *Linguistic Inquiry* 13: 695–700.
Stump, Gregory T. (2005): Word-formation and inflectional morphology. In: Pavol Štekauer and Rochelle Lieber (eds.), *Handbook of Word-Formation*, 49–71. Dordrecht: Springer.
ten Hacken, Pius (1994): *Defining Morphology. A Principled Approach to Determining the Boundaries of Compounding, Derivation, and Inflection*. Hildesheim: Olms.
Thompson, Chad (1996): The Na-Dene middle voice: An impersonal source of the D-element. *International Journal of American Linguistics* 62(4): 351–378.
Vallés, Teresa (2003): Lexical creativity and the organism of the lexicon. *Annual Review of Cognitive Linguistics* 1: 137–160.
van Marle, Jaap (1994): Paradigms. In: Ronald E. Asher (ed.), *Encyclopaedia of Language and Linguistics*. Vol. 6, 2927–2930. Oxford: Pergamon.
van Marle, Jaap (1995): The unity of morphology: On the interwovenness of the derivational and inflectional dimension of the word. In: Geert E. Booij and Jaap van Marle (eds.), *Yearbook of Morphology 1995*, 67–82. Dordrecht: Kluwer.
Werner, Heinrich (1998): *Probleme der Wortbildung in den Jenissej-Sprachen*. München/Newcastle: LINCOM Europa.
Williams, Edwin (1981): On the notions 'lexically related' and 'head of a word'. *Linguistic Inquiry* 12(2): 245–274.

Joachim Mugdan
9 Units of word-formation

1 Introduction
2 Sign, morpheme, morph
3 Word and lexeme
4 Root, stem, affix
5 Types of affixes
6 Morphological processes
7 Inputs and outputs of word-formation rules
8 References

Abstract: The article discusses the notion of word and the smaller units that words are composed of (morph and morpheme, root and affix, stem). It provides surveys of different types of affixes and morphological processes (in particular, reduplication, substitution and subtraction), with a focus on terms and definitions. It also addresses the question of which units can be inputs to word-formation rules, with special attention to inflected forms and phrases as well as the role of word classes.

1 Introduction

The term *word-formation* suggests that the fundamental unit of this linguistic subdiscipline is the word. *Formation* implies that we are dealing with rules that "form" (create, generate, derive) words. But what exactly does *word* mean (see section 3)? And is it always true that word-formation is the "formation of longer, more complex words from shorter, simpler words", e.g., *unfriendly* from *friend* (McArthur 1998: s. v. *word-formation*)? That is, is it always the case that the output of a word-formation rule is a word and that the input to such a rule must be a word as well (see section 7)? And if the word *unfriendly* is built up from *friend*, a survey of the units of word-formation must include elements such as *un-* and *-ly* (see sections 2, 4–5) as well as processes that serve a similar purpose (see section 6).

The units of word-formation, in particular the word and its components, are essentially the same as the units of morphology in general (for a brief survey, cf.

Joachim Mugdan, Münster, Germany

Mugdan 1994), and some concepts that are relevant to word-formation presuppose certain notions of inflectional morphology. Therefore, neither the theoretical discussion nor the examples can be strictly confined to word-formation to the exclusion of inflection. Although most examples come from European languages (unless otherwise noted, they are taken from standard grammars and dictionaries), some phenomena must be illustrated with languages from other parts of the globe.

The exact nature of word-formation rules and their place in a model of grammar have been the subject of a great deal of debate. Some linguists describe word-formation by means of bidirectional static relations (alias redundancy rules or constructional schemas) between items in the lexicon rather than unidirectional dynamic rules or processes with words as their output. Others assume that *unfriendly* is not derived from or related to *friendly* by some kind of rule but simply consists of the elements *friend, un-* and *-ly*; the meaning and other properties of the whole must then be somehow inferred from the parts (see also section 6.5). In the present article, I do not espouse a specific theory of word-formation; if I follow conventional practice and speak of word-formation "rules" and the like, it is merely for the sake of convenience. Adherents of other approaches should be able to translate this into their own terminology, and although the various theories of word-formation differ somewhat in the units they posit, the present discussion should be of relevance to all of them. Generally, I will refrain from considering individual approaches or "schools" and their theory-internal problems, focussing on broader issues instead.

2 Sign, morpheme, morph

2.1 Linguistic sign

In a European tradition that goes back to Ferdinand de Saussure (1916: 99–101 [97–99]), words are viewed as linguistic signs – two-sided entities with a *signifiant* (signifier, *signans*) and a *signifié* (signified, *signatum*) or, to use the less confusing terms introduced by Louis Hjelmslev (1961: 47–48), an expression and a content. These can be represented by a string of phonemes or graphemes (or the corresponding elements of sign languages) and a bundle of semantic features, respectively. When we mention a sign, we note its expression as a string of phonemes between slashes /.../ or as a sequence of sound segments (irrespective of their phonological status) in square brackets [...]; graphemes are enclosed in angle brackets ⟨...⟩ or italicized. Many linguists use standard orthography or, for foreign scripts, a transliteration although an element of the spoken language is meant, possibly even together with its content. An indication of the content is typically placed in single quotation marks '...'. For abstract grammatical meanings, special terms or their abbreviations are available; they are frequently written in capitals or small capitals, e.g., 'PLURAL' or 'PL'. Otherwise, synonyms, paraphrases or translations may be employed. Where this is relevant to the discussion, complex signs are analyzed into their components (e.g., according to the Leipzig Glossing Rules, http://www.eva.mpg.de/lingua/resources/glossing-rules.php; cf. also Lehmann 2004).

Some authors regard information on how the sign can combine with others (word class, subcategorization features, etc.) as a third side of the sign (e.g., Mel'čuk 1982: 40, 2006: 385), but it is equally possible to include it in the content – there is no cogent reason to restrict the term *content* to "meaning" in a narrow sense. (*Expression* can be understood more broadly as well, cf. section 6.5.) It must be emphasized that, like all linguistic units, both expressions and contents are not observable realities in the extra-linguistic world but abstractions which belong to the language system as a theoretical construct.

An American approach pioneered by Leonard Bloomfield regards a word as one type of linguistic form, where a form "*is* a recurrent vocal feature", i.e. a string of phonemes, and "*has* meaning" (Bloomfield 1926: 155, emphasis J. M.). The meaning thus remains external to the form. Whether a string of phonemes is a form or not depends on whether it has meaning, but it should not be relevant which meaning it has: -*er* in *great-er* and -*er* in *writ-er* should be the same form despite the difference in meaning ('COMPARATIVE' vs. 'AGENT NOMINALIZER'), whereas -*er* in *winter* does not qualify as a form since one cannot ascribe any meaning to it. In actual fact, Bloomfield assumed that forms can be different although they are "alike [...] as to vocal features", i.e. phonologically identical, giving -*er* 'COMPARATIVE' and -*er* 'AGENT NOMINALIZER' as an example (1926: 157). Such a statement presupposes that the meaning is an integral part of these elements. The failure to distinguish clearly between signs and their expressions, between two-sided and one-sided elements, is characteristic of much that is said about morphological units, even in textbooks and handbooks. In order to achieve greater clarity and consistency, I will work with the concept of the bilateral linguistic sign.

2.2 Minimal sign

Linguistic signs come in various sizes, from entire texts down to parts of words. But if we segment a text into progressively smaller signs, we eventually reach a point where no division on the expression side matches a division on the content side and vice versa. For instance, English *filly* has an expression that consists of the phonemes /f/, /ɪ/, /l/ and /i/ and a content that can be decomposed into 'young', 'female' and 'horse'. A comparison with *colt* 'young male horse', *mare* 'adult female horse', etc. shows that it is impossible to associate any of the phonemes of *filly* with any of the meaning components – *filly* 'young female horse' is a *minimal sign*, a sign that cannot be segmented into smaller signs. Less common alternative terms are *simple sign* and *elementary sign*; in the 1970s, several German linguists appropriated Hjelmslev's term *plereme* for this purpose, but without much success. Quite often, *morph* or *morpheme* are used in this sense but these terms can also refer to sets of minimal signs (see section 2.3).

In order to show that a sign is complex, i.e. not minimal, consisting of the signs A and C, we should ideally be able to find two further signs B and D that can be substituted for A and C, respectively, such that all the combinations are signs and satisfy the proportion AC : BC :: AD : BD on both the expression side and the content side, forming a "square". If A is *eat-* and C *-ing*, we can use *walk-* as B and *-s* as D to complete the proportion *eating* : *walking* :: *eats* : *walks* (cf. Greenberg 1957: 20). A "perfect square" meets two conditions:
a) The expressions of both parts of the sign to be segmented recur elsewhere, i.e. alone or in combination with other signs, and
b) their content in these other occurrences is the same as in the sign under analysis.

If only one of these conditions is met, it may still be appropriate to decompose the sign. The famous word *cranberry* violates condition a) since there is no X such that *cranberry* : *blueberry* :: *cranX* : *blueX*. Yet, *cranberry* seems to have the same structure as *blueberry*. We would therefore like to isolate *cran-* as a minimal sign, perhaps with the content "whatever it is which differentiates cranberries from these other kinds of berries" (Hockett 1958: 126). Such non-recurrent signs are called *unique*; other terms are *remnant*, *cranberry morph[eme]*, *blocked morph[eme]* or *pseudomorph[eme]* and the more specific *uniroot* and *unifix* (cf. Mel'čuk 1982: 66, 87–88) for unique roots and unique affixes (see section 4.1).

Condition (b) is violated by the following square:

(1)		-ceive	-sist	-tain	-vert
	per-	perceive	persist	pertain	pervert
	re-	receive	resist	retain	revert
	con-	conceive	consist	contain	convert

The parts *per-*, *re-*, *con-* and *-ceive*, *-sist*, *-tain*, *-vert* recur in many combinations, but their content is not constant and, in fact, highly elusive. From a semantic point of view, nothing is gained by decomposing *perceive*, etc., but the systematic relationship between *-ceive* and *-cep-* (in *perception, reception, conception*) or *-vert* and *-vers-* (in *perversion, reversion, conversion*) is an argument for recognizing *-ceive*, *-vert*, etc. as morphological elements (cf. Aronoff 1976: 11–14; see also article 10 on derivation, section 4.3). Such a recurrent part without clear content but with some morphological function has been called *quasi-sign* or *quasi-morph[eme]*. *Submorph[eme]* and *submorphemic [element, unit]* may be restricted to quasi-signs but can also be cover terms for a wider variety of morphological units that lack certain properties of canonical minimal signs (cf. Kubrjakova 2000: 417).

The terms *pseudomorph[eme]*, *quasi-morph[eme]*, *submorph[eme]*, etc. should be taken as labels that point to certain difficulties but do not refer to well-defined types of units. The same applies to the expressions *defectively segmentable* and *conditionally segmentable* which have been suggested to describe signs that pose formal or semantic problems, as illustrated by *cranberry* and *perceive*, respectively (cf. Kubrjakova 2000: 419). Faced with the question "to segment or not to segment?", we must ultimately make a decision. Elevating doubtful cases to the status of entities of a special kind avoids the issue and does not lead to greater clarity (see also section 4.2).

Apart from the question of whether to segment and if so, where (cf. also Spencer 2012), a more fundamental difficulty is that expression and content are often not in a simple 1:1 relationship (cf. Coates 2000). A well-known example is that of English nouns:

(2)

	SINGULAR	*root* /ruːt/	*loop* /luːp/	*proof* /pruːf/	*goose* /guːs/	*tooth* /tuːθ/
	PLURAL	*roots* /ruːts/	*loops* /luːps/	*proofs* /pruːfs/	*geese* /giːs/	*teeth* /tiːθ/

Since the first three plural forms clearly consist of two parts, the second of which is /s/ 'PLURAL', we would like to analyze /giːs/ and /tiːθ/ similarly, as combinations of /guːs/ and /tuːθ/ with a minimal sign that has the content 'PLURAL'. However, the segmentation procedure outlined so far does not allow this in a straightforward way. Some linguists have responded to the challenge by abandoning the initial assumption that the expression of a sign must be a continuous sequence of segments, while others have rejected the building-block model entirely (see section 6.5).

2.3 Morpheme and morph

The segmentation problem on the syntagmatic axis – is this item a single element or a sequence of two? – has a parallel in the classification problem on the paradigmatic axis: Are these items two different elements or instances of the same element? At one level of analysis, the minimal signs /s/ 'PLURAL', /z/ 'PLURAL' and /ɪz/ 'PLURAL' that we can identify in *proofs* /pruːf-s/, *grooves* /gruːv-z/ and *nooses* /nuːs-ɪz/ are different because they differ in expression (cf. section 2.1). On the other hand, they have the same content and can therefore be considered variants of a single element at a different level of analysis. Such an element, a set of minimal signs with the same content, is a *morpheme* (for other meanings of this term, see section 2.5), and the members of the set are its *allomorphs* (see section 2.4). Conversely, /s/ 'PLURAL' can be grouped together with /s/ '3RD PERSON SINGULAR' in *writes* /raɪts/ and /s/ 'POSSESSIVE' in *Jack's* /dʒæks/; such a set of minimal signs with the same expression is a *morph*. As defined here, allomorphs are minimal signs and not morphs, although often only their expression is given. According to this terminology, both morphs and morphemes are sets and are defined in mirror-image fashion – morphs by identity of expression, morphemes by identity of content –, but there is no simple term for minimal signs. Alternatively, *morph* can be used for the minimal sign (cf. Mel'čuk 1982: 63, 2006: 388), in which case the unit "set of minimal signs with the same expression" has no name – a tolerable gap since this unit is of far less interest than the morpheme. The correspondence between concepts and terms can be summarized as in (3).

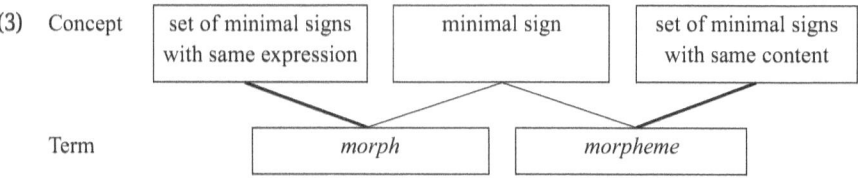

(3) Concept: set of minimal signs with same expression | minimal sign | set of minimal signs with same content

Term: *morph* | *morpheme*

Unfortunately, it is often not clear which of the meanings of *morph* is intended, i.e. whether *-s* in *proofs* and *-s* in *writes* are regarded as the same morph or as two different ones. Worse still, many textbook authors introduce the term *morpheme* in connection with the demonstration that complex words can be decomposed into several minimal signs, giving, say, *-s* in *books* as an example (where *-s* is evidently a shorthand notation for the minimal sign /s/ 'PLURAL'), but at some later point they describe this *-s* as one of the variants or allomorphs of the plural morpheme (i.e. the set of minimal signs with the content 'PLURAL'), without making explicit that this amounts to a redefinition of the term *morpheme* (for a typical case, see Fromkin, Rodman and Hyams 2013: 37–38, 63–64, 225–228).

The allomorphs of a morpheme should be distributed according to sufficiently simple and general rules, i.e. we should be able to state under which conditions each of the allomorphs occurs (see also section 2.4). As I see it, this requirement is not an integral part of the definition of *morpheme* (as in Mel'čuk 1982: 88, 2006: 24, 388); like the principles for the identification of morphemes that have been developed in American structuralism (e.g., Nida 1948: 419–438, 1949: 6–61), it serves to clarify the notion of sameness of content. In inflectional morphology, where we are dealing with morphosyntactic properties such as 'SINGULAR' and 'PLURAL' in tightly structured paradigms, contents are generally easier to determine than in derivational morphology, where it often happens that an affix has two or more closely related functions (e.g., *-er* in *bak-er* 'person who bakes' and in *grind-er* 'instrument that grinds') or that several affixes have more or less the same function (e.g., *-er* in *bak-er* and *-ist* in *typ-ist* 'person who types'), making it difficult to decide whether we are dealing with (allomorphs of) a single morpheme or with different morphemes.

A morpheme is typically written in braces (curly brackets) {...}, which can be taken as a reminder that it is a set (cf. Mel'čuk 2006: 388). Ideally, the braces should enclose an indication of the defining characteristic, the content. For grammatical meanings, we can employ the conventional labels {PLURAL} or {PL}, etc. Where such a label is not available, we can use the expression of one of the allomorphs, e.g., {hoof} for the set {/hu:f/ 'hoof', /hu:v/ 'hoof'} (as in *hoof, hooves*), but we must bear in mind that in reality we mean the content. There is no generally accepted notation for morphs as defined here; one possibility is to use {'...'} for morphemes and {/.../} for morphs (cf. Bergenholtz and Mugdan 1979a: 50–51), e.g., {'PLURAL'} and {/ər/} (for the set with the members /ər/ 'AGENT NOMINALIZER', /ər/ 'COMPARATIVE', etc.). In the following, I will retain the simpler notation {...} (without quotation marks) for morphemes and resort to {/.../} for morphs when needed.

Although morphs are defined in terms of expression and morphemes in terms of content, the morph {/ər/} is not identical with the phoneme sequence /ər/ (cf. section 2.1 on *winter* vs. *great-er, writ-er*), and the morpheme {PLURAL} must be distinguished from the content feature 'PLURAL' (so that this definition of *morpheme* is not purely content-oriented). This can be seen in the following forms of the Polish noun *miasto* 'town':

(4)

	SINGULAR	PLURAL
NOMINATIVE	miast-o	miast-a
DATIVE	miast-u	miast-om

Here, number and case are always expressed simultaneously, a phenomenon known as *cumulative exponence* or *cumulation*. (It normally concerns inflectional categories, cf. Coates 2000: 619–620; for examples involving derivation, not all of them fully convincing, see Ricca 2005. The terms *fusion* and/or *portmanteau* are sometimes used for cumulation, but they are better reserved for cases where the simultaneous expression of two or more content elements is a deviation from the normal pattern.) In the nominative plural *miasta*, for instance, -*a* expresses both 'PLURAL' and 'NOMINATIVE'. While Polish has these content features, it does not have distinct morphemes {PL} and {NOM} but a single morpheme {NOM;PL}.

The Polish example (4) also illustrates another important point. Since only neuter nouns have a nominative plural in -*a*, one might consider including 'NEUTER' ('N' for short) in the content of -*a*. I prefer to say that 'N' is a feature of *miast-* which prompts the choice of -*a* (see also section 2.4 on morphological conditioning). Thus, the content of a linguistic sign does not necessarily include all the information that can be gathered from its occurrence. It need not be a full specification of its meanings and uses either. For example, there is no necessity to distinguish a perfect participle as in *She has written the letter* and a passive participle as in *The letter was written* for every English verb. In my view, *written* is the same participle everywhere (whether we label it 'PERFECT PASSIVE PARTICIPLE', 'PAST PARTICIPLE' or whatever), and the fact that the constructions in which this participle occurs with the auxiliaries *have* and *be* are grammatical idioms, i.e. have meanings that cannot be deduced from their components, is not a matter of morphology.

While it is true that a morpheme is more "abstract" than its allomorphs, in the sense that it abstracts away from the differences in their expressions, this does not mean that allomorphs or morphs are "concrete" or somehow more "real". Attempts at equating the distinction between morpheme and (allo)morph with dichotomies such as *langue* vs. *parole*, form vs. substance or system vs. text are untenable (cf. Mugdan 1986: 33–34). Similarly, it is potentially misleading to describe the relationship between them as one of "realization" (Bauer 2003: 17, 334–335) or to discuss allomorphs under the heading "the pronunciation of morphemes" (Fromkin, Rodman and Hyams 2013: 225–228). Just as a toy building block retains its identity whether it is in its box or serves as part of an edifice, so too a linguistic element remains the same whether we look at it as a component of the language system or of a text. The building-block analogy is not entirely accurate, however, inasmuch as a given linguistic element can occur an unlimited number of times in a text. If we are asked how many words there are in *They might or they might not*, we can answer 6, counting the two occurrences or *tokens* of *they* and *might* separately, or 4, counting *they* and *might* only once each, as a *type*. This distinction is applicable to linguistic units at all levels; the difference between type and token is unrelated to that between *X-eme* and *allo-X*. As regards the latter pair, the essential point is that certain differences which are taken into account at the *allo-X* level are ignored at the *X-eme* level (cf. Mel'čuk 1982: 120–122, 2006: 400), and this is what the definition of an *X-eme* as a set of *allo-X*s is intended to capture.

2.4 Allomorphy

When describing morphemes and their allomorphs, three aspects must be taken into consideration: conditioning, relatedness and domain. My focus will be primarily on terminology; for a fuller treatment and more examples, see article 20 on allomorphy.

a) Conditioning: Which factor determines the occurrence of one allomorph rather than the other(s)? A basic distinction is that between *phonological conditioning*, where only the expression side is relevant, and *morphological conditioning*, where features of content are decisive. Typical phonological conditioning factors are segments or features in the context, word stress or tone, syllable structure, etc. (for surveys of various subtypes and issues, see Neef 2000a; Nevins 2011; Bonet and Harbour 2012: 220–234); sometimes, the distribution of allomorphs is best described by an "output constraint", i.e. with reference to the resulting structure (cf. Booij 1998).

Some linguists distinguish between *grammatical conditioning* (or *morphological conditioning* in the narrower sense) and *lexical conditioning*, but rarely with sufficient clarity; many explanations mix criteria and the common denominator behind the examples given is often not obvious. In particular, the distinction seems to be drawn according to whether the conditioning factor is
– an affix or a stem (cf. "grammatical element" vs. "word" in Katamba and Stonham 2006: 30–31; on the notions affix and stem, see sections 4.1 and 4.3),
– an independently motivated morphosyntactic feature (e.g., [masculine] in a language with gender agreement) vs. a special "diacritic feature" or "index" that must be recorded in the lexicon just to account for the allomorphy in question, such as [conjugation class 2] or [undergoes rule X] (cf. Haspelmath and Sims 2010: 26) or
– a feature that defines a larger class of items vs. one that marks individual exceptions (cf. Bauer 2003: 327, where inflection class is cited as an instance of grammatical rather than lexical conditioning).

A more comprehensive typology of morphological conditioning must take into account all of these factors as well as some others, such as conditioning by a morpheme vs. by a specific allomorph.

Whether *syntactic conditioning*, i.e. conditioning by the syntactic structure in which a morpheme appears or by the syntactic function it has, should be admitted as a further type is controversial. Even examples that allegedly show that the assumption of syntactic conditioning is inevitable (cf. Neef 2000b: 482–483) are open to alternative analyses that do not involve allomorphy at all; in any case, they do not pertain to word-formation.

Finally, two or more allomorphs of a given morpheme may occur in the same context: The plural of /ruːf/ 'roof' can be /ruːf-s/ or /ruːv-z/. This phenomenon is known as *free variation*, but the variants are rarely freely interchangeable. They often differ in stylistic value or correlate with differences in the speaker's age, regional background or social status. Even where such factors are not detectable, one of the variants is likely to be more frequent – and the statistics may differ from item to item (cf. Meder and Mugdan 1990: 92–99).

b) Relatedness: Are the allomorphs of a morpheme "similar" to one another or not? Or rather, are they phonologically related in a systematic way (which does not necessarily imply easily recognizable surface similarity)? In generative phonology, phonological relatedness is shown by setting up an underlying representation, here indicated by vertical lines |...|, which may or may not coincide with one of the surface allomorphs and from which the (other) surface allomorphs are derived by means of phonological rules, possibly with some morphological conditions attached. If we assume the underlying representation |z| 'PL', we can derive /s/ 'PL' by a rule of devoicing and /ɪz/ 'PL' by a rule of /ɪ/-insertion that both operate only in certain phonological environments. In this approach, important questions are how to choose the underlying representation, how "abstract" (i.e. how far removed from the surface forms) it may be, which kinds of rules are permissible and how they may interact. Depending on the answers, a given pair of allomorphs may be considered related or not (for some discussion, see Bonet and Harbour 2012: 201–204).

It is quite common for several morphemes to exhibit the same kind of allomorphic variation: One Bashkir adverbializer has the allomorphs /sɑ/ 'ADVR' (after a back vowel) and /sæ/ 'ADVR' (after a front vowel), and the same difference between back /ɑ/ and front /æ/ with the same conditioning is found in the allomorphs of numerous other morphemes, e.g., the negative /mɑ/ 'NEG' and /mæ/ 'NEG'. In such a case, we speak of a (*phonological* or *morphophonemic*) *alternation* between /ɑ/ and /æ/ that can be symbolized as /ɑ/~/æ/. The Prague school suggested a new type of unit, the *morphophoneme*, for a set of alternating phonemes or phoneme sequences (not to be confused with the *archiphoneme*, an element at the phonemic level that is not specified for certain features). Thus, one can set up a morphophoneme //A// for the alternation /ɑ/~/æ/; at the morphophonemic level, /sɑ/ and /sæ/ will then have the same representation //sA//. Although morphophonemes are no longer in vogue, capital letters have been retained as a convenient notational device that obviates the need to list all surface allomorphs.

Allomorphs that are not phonologically related in a regular way are called *suppletive*. We speak of *weak suppletion* if some similarity is discernible, which could mean either that native speakers feel a connection or that etymologically the allomorphs go back to the same source. For example, the allomorphs /faɪv/ and /fɪf/ 'five' in English *five, fivish* vs. *fifth, fifty* are similar but exhibit irregular alternations. The term *strong suppletion* is used where the allomorphs are highly dissimilar and/or have different etymological origins. In English, /gʊd/ 'good' and /bɛt/ 'good' (in the comparative *better* /bɛt-ə/ 'good-CMPR') stand in a relationship of strong suppletion. *Bad* /bæd/ 'bad' and *worse* /wɜːs/ 'bad.CMPR' illustrate a different kind of suppletion, occasionally called *portmanteau suppletion* as opposed to *allomorphic suppletion*; here, two phonologically unrelated signs exhibit a regular difference in content (cf. also Perlmutter 1988: 85, where this is called *full suppletion* vs. *stem suppletion*; for a detailed discussion of suppletion, see Mel'čuk 2006: 405–467).

Phonological conditioning frequently coincides with phonological relatedness and morphological conditioning with suppletion, as with English /s/, /z/ and /ɪz/ 'PL' as opposed to /ən/ 'PL' in *oxen*. This is, however, not necessarily so: /huːf/ and /huːv/ 'hoof' (as in *hoof, hooves*) are phonologically related but morphologically conditioned, and the often overlooked phenomenon of phonologically conditioned suppletion is solidly attested in many languages, predominantly in inflection (cf. Carstairs 1988; Nevins 2011).

c) Domain (also known as *internal conditioning*): If several morphemes have phonologically related allomorphs that exhibit the same alternation, which morphemes show this pattern? In a language with front/back vowel harmony (e.g., Bashkir), we will ideally find that every affixal morpheme with a front-vowel allomorph has a corresponding back-vowel allomorph and vice versa. But it is often not predictable which morphemes exhibit a certain pattern of allomorphy so that they must be listed. The alternation between voiceless /f/ and voiced /v/ is a case in point: It occurs in *hoof/hooves* but not in *proof/proofs* or *groove/grooves*.

2.5 Notes on terminology

The term *morpheme* was coined in its Russian form *morfema* by the Polish linguist Jan Baudouin de Courtenay. While *phoneme*, on which it was modelled, goes back to a Greek word, *phōnēma* 'voice' (cf. Mugdan 2011: 96–99), *morpheme* was a new word-formation and established the extremely popular pattern of terms in *-eme* for linguistic units. *Morfema* is first attested in 1880 as a parenthesized alternative to *morfologičeskaja čast'* 'morphological part'; in Baudouin's later publications, the elements he calls *morpheme* sometimes correspond to a minimal sign, sometimes to a set of minimal signs with the same content (cf. Mugdan 1986: 30–31). This ambiguity persisted for decades, even among American structuralists who strove for conceptual clarity. A first attempt at resolving it was made by Zellig Harris, who suggested *morpheme alternant* and *morpheme unit* (1942: 170–171; in the following, I will sometimes use *alternant* as a neutral expression where other terms would prejudge a terminological issue). Charles Hockett proposed the more successful pair *morph* and *morpheme* instead (1947: 322), but it remained unclear whether homophones such as /sɛl/ 'sell' and /sɛl/ 'cell' should be counted as different morphs or as the same morph (cf. Hockett 1958: 272 vs. 1961: 32). As for *allomorph*, Eugene Nida was believed to have originated the term because his note "[m]orphemic alternants can conveniently be called *allomorphs*" sounded like a proposal (1948: 420 n13), but it is now known that the word already appears in an earlier paper by Paul Garvin (1945: 253).

Some limit the term *allomorph* to a situation where a morpheme has two or more alternants (e.g., Bonet and Harbour 2012: 196, 218), and this is also the implicit practice of those who would call, say, /s/ 'PL' and /z/ 'PL' in English "allomorphs" of each other. It is, however, normally assumed that all morphemes have at least one allomorph.

Traditionally, "[t]here are absolutely no limits to the degree of phonological difference between allomorphs" (Nida 1949: 44), but there are a number of linguists who require the allomorphs of a morpheme to be "similar" in expression, i.e. phonologically related in a regular way (e.g., Booij 1998: 145). Possibly, they were influenced by the condition that allophones of a phoneme must have some phonetic resemblance (but in one case, the requirement of "similarity" resulted from a misinterpretation of Leonard Bloomfield's definition of *morpheme*, cf. Mugdan 1986: 34–35). Sometimes, phonological conditioning is brought into play, presumably under the erroneous assumption that this excludes suppletion. If allomorphs must be phonologically related, English /s/, /z/ and /ɪz/ 'PL' belong to one morpheme but /ən/ 'PL' belongs to a different one, and there is no term for a unit that comprises both of them. Conversely, others apply *allomorph* only to those (underlying) alternants that are not phonologically related (e.g., Booij 2002: 174;

see also Bonet and Harbour 2012: 199–201, where terminological choices are mistaken for theoretical approaches; for a discussion of whether only affixes or also roots exhibit "allomorphy" in this sense, see Bonet and Harbour 2012: 214–218). Again, this is occasionally confused with lack of phonological predictability, i.e. conditioning (see also De Belder 2011: 137, where allomorphs may be neither phonologically conditioned nor strongly suppletive). As a new term for phonologically related alternants, *(phonological) variant* may be used; in this parlance, the English plural morpheme has, among others, the allomorphs |z| 'PL' (with the variants /s/, /z/ and /ɪz/) and /ən/ 'PL'. Terminological consistency is, however, a rare virtue, and it is not uncommon for authors to vacillate between different uses of *morpheme* and *allomorph* or to give vague explanations that leave open what is really meant.

In a French tradition that goes back over a century (cf. Mugdan 1986: 32), *morphème* is used only for minimal signs with grammatical meaning; those with lexical meaning may then be called *sémantème* or *lexème* (not to be confused with *lexeme* as defined in section 3.4), with *monème* as a cover term (cf. Martinet 1960: 20 [15–16]). As an offshoot of this usage, Louis Hjelmslev employed *morphème* for an individual grammatical meaning, i.e. a morphosyntactic property (1961: 25–26). Presumably independently, some English-speaking scholars did so as well (e.g., Lyons 1968: 189–191; cf. also Mugdan 1986: 36–37). The difference between this terminology and that adopted here becomes apparent in cases of cumulative exponence, as in the Polish example (4), where these authors would speak of 'PL' and 'NOM' as "morphemes". Another term for grammatical (and specifically inflectional) content elements, used chiefly by Russian linguists, is *grammeme* (cf. Mel'čuk 1982: 30, 2006: 23); although it also has various other uses, it is a convenient alternative that makes it unnecessary to redefine *morpheme* in this way.

3 Word and lexeme

3.1 The universality of the word

The word, "that most elusive of all units encountered in the segmentation of utterances" (Malkiel 1966: 310), is nonetheless "the unit *par excellence* of traditional grammatical theory" (Lyons 1968: 194) and the basis of the conventional distinction between morphology and syntax according to which morphology deals with the internal structure of words and syntax with their external combinations. While it is conceivable that some languages do not have words and hence no distinction between morphology and syntax, there is no convincing evidence that this is indeed the case. (My remark that "some languages evidently lack a word level altogether", Mugdan 1994: 2552, should have been formulated more cautiously.) The word is therefore generally assumed to be universal although this cannot be proven. Interestingly, not all languages have a word for 'word' and non-linguists are not necessarily conscious of words, especially if they do not use a writing system that marks word boundaries (cf. Dixon and Aikhenvald 2002: 2–4, 32–33).

For a language to "have words" means that a unit *word* is to be distinguished from both morpheme and phrase (cf. Bauer 2000a: 255). In languages that are said to be of the isolating type, the average number of morphemes per word approaches 1 but still remains a little higher so that words and morphemes cannot be equated. In Vietnamese, for instance, the ratio in a text sample of 100 words was found to be 1.06 (Greenberg 1960: 193) – and subject to how one defines compounds, it may well be considerably higher. As for polysynthetic languages, the impressive textbook examples of extremely long words that correspond to fairly complex English sentences should not be taken to imply that all sentences (or all phrases) in such languages consist of a single word.

It is notoriously difficult to provide a universal definition of the unit *word*. Since there are different criteria that do not necessarily converge, the notion of the word is neither a predictive concept such that being a word entails a number of logically independent properties (cf. Jacobs 2011), nor is it a comparative concept, i.e. we cannot be sure that what we call *word* in language A is "the same thing" as what we call *word* in language B (cf. Haspelmath 2011). But, as even those who raise these objections admit, this does not invalidate the usefulness of the concept in practice, especially in the description of individual languages.

3.2 The word in orthography, phonology and the lexicon

The answer to the question "is this one word or a sequence of two?" will depend on whether we consider orthography (section 3.2.1), phonology (section 3.2.2), semantics (section 3.2.3) or grammar (section 3.3). More detailed surveys and discussions of the various criteria can be found in textbooks (e.g., Lyons 1968: 199–206; Bergenholtz and Mugdan 1979a: 12–29; Booij 2012: 283–296), handbook articles (e.g., Bauer 2000a; Julien 2006) and other publications devoted to the topic of the word (e.g., Peškovskij 1925; Dixon and Aikhenvald 2002: 10–25; Haspelmath 2011).

3.2.1 Orthography

In many but by no means all writing systems, words are bounded by spaces or, more rarely, some other symbol (cf. Daniels 2013: 66–67). An exact definition of the *orthographic word* is not trivial, however. It must take into account various special symbols (punctuation marks, digits, etc.) and will have to be different not only for different writing systems but even for different languages that employ the same writing system (e.g., English, French and German, which differ slightly in the use of spaces in conjunction with punctuation marks). Moreover, orthographic words do not necessarily correspond to units of phonology or grammar. Even orthographies devised with the participation of linguists (e.g., the German spelling reform adopted in 1998) are not fully convincing in this regard. Apart from that, detailed official rules do not eliminate uncertainty and fluctuation in practice.

3.2.2 Phonology

The *phonological word* (or *prosodic word*, *p-word*, ω) is a constituent between the syllable (or the foot) and the phonological phrase in a hierarchy of prosodic units, i.e. units on the expression side. Its defining properties are language-specific and the various criteria need not coincide (cf. Dixon and Aikhenvald 2002: 13–18). For some languages, we may therefore have to assume more than one type of phonological word; for others the notion may not be useful (cf. Schiering, Bickel and Hildebrandt 2010). Nonetheless, phonological descriptions often presuppose some concept of "word". First, there are certain features that characterize an entire word rather than an individual segment. Words typically have one primary stress or accent (but even if it falls on a particular syllable, e.g., the first or the penultimate, one cannot infer word boundaries from stress position unambiguously, as is often assumed, e.g., Dixon and Aikhenvald 2002: 16; cf. Mugdan 1994: 2551). Tone patterns may be associated with words rather than syllables, and other *suprasegmental features* or *prosodies* such as [+back] or [–back] (in languages with vowel harmony), nasalization, etc. may extend throughout a word (or over a domain defined in terms of the word). Second, there are phenomena that occur specifically at word boundaries. In particular, the phonological oppositions, allophones or segment clusters that are found word-initially or word-finally may differ from those found word-medially. Third, the internal syllabic or segmental structure of phonological words may be restricted. For example, words in some languages must have a minimum number of syllables or must end in a vowel. Fourth, if we convert underlying representations into surface representations by means of phonological rules (cf. section 2.4), some of these rules may operate only within a word or only across a word boundary.

In word-formation, stress patterns are often invoked in order to distinguish compounds from phrases, e.g., *bláckbird* vs. *blàck bírd* (Bloomfield 1933: 180), but this criterion has only limited applicability (cf. Giegerich 2009) and the constituents of compounds as defined by stress are often distinct phonological words in other respects. In Hungarian, the name of the capital *Budapest* (which was created out of two cities) has one main stress on the first syllable but violates vowel harmony: *Buda* has back vowels and *Pest* a front vowel. In Dutch and other languages, there are reasons to regard not only members of compounds but also certain affixes (see section 4.1) as prosodic words (cf. Booij 2002: 168–174). This is especially true of prefixes, which is one of the reasons why some studies of word-formation in European languages treat prefixation as a variety of compounding or as a process that differs essentially from both compounding and suffixation (cf. Montermini 2008: 13–24, 41–45).

Often, an element which is phonologically part of a word must be viewed as a distinct word from a grammatical perspective. In Czech, where main stress falls on the first syllable, certain prepositions form a phonological word together with the following item, e.g., a noun as in *na stromě* /ˈnastromɲe/ 'on [a/the] tree' – but the fact that an adjective can intervene, as in *na velkém stromě* /ˈnavelkeːm ˈstromɲe/ 'on [a/the] big tree', shows that *na* is a separate word in a syntactic sense (see section 3.3.2). Elements of this kind are known as *clitics*, but the term has been applied to a wide variety of other borderline phenomena as well (the vast literature on the topic cannot be summarized here – for a brief introduction, see Nevis 2000). Unless a narrower definition is chosen, clitics do not constitute a third type of linguistic unit between word and affix but rather a residual category for cases where criteria are in conflict (cf. Nevis 2000: 388; see also section 4.2 on affixoids).

3.2.3 Lexicon

If the lexicon is understood as the repository of irregularities, we expect it to contain simple words because their meanings are arbitrary but not phrases because their meanings can be deduced from the meanings of their parts and the meaning of the construction. Such *compositionality of meaning* is lacking in many compounds so that they must be listed in the lexicon, too. Although there is some semantic relation between the meanings of the parts, it can be almost any relation: *Book house* (a compound by the criterion of stress) could mean 'a house that contains many books', 'a house where books are produced', 'a house where books are sold', 'a house in the shape of a book', etc.; as a rule, only one of these possibilities is conventionalized. It is often said that "many complex words are semantically compositional in exactly the same way as phrases and clauses" (Haspelmath 2011: 36). But while it is true that we can easily understand numerous word-formations we have never encountered before, we often need contextual, pragmatic or extralinguistic knowledge to select the correct interpretation among those that are conceivable. Still, some complex words do have fully predictable meanings (e.g., most English derived adjectives with *un-*), which would mean that they are not listed in the lexicon. Conversely, numerous phrases are not semantically compositional, e.g., idioms such as *beat about the bush* 'avoid the point at issue' or so-called particle verbs such as *put up* 'provide food and lodging' (see also article 17 on multi-word expressions). Verbs with "separable prefixes" resemble derivatives to a greater degree because there are constructions in which the element in question behaves both syntactically and phonologically like part of a word, e.g., Dutch *op* in *ik moet [hem] opbellen* 'I must ring [him] up', but since there are other constructions in which *op* clearly is a separate particle, e.g., *ik bel [hem] op* 'I ring [him] up', such verbs must be regarded as idiomatic word combinations, too. In cases such as Portuguese *moinho de vento* 'mill of wind (windmill)', which are sometimes classified as compounds, the fact that plural is marked on the first constituent (*moinhos de vento*) suggests that they are likewise idiomatic syntactic constructions rather than complex words. Some linguists extend the term *lexeme* (see section 3.4) to multi-word expressions, but it is preferable to use a different term for an item that must be listed because its properties cannot be inferred from those of its parts; a highly successful suggestion is *listeme* (Di Sciullo and Williams 1987: 3). *Lexical item* is more neutral and also applicable in models which allow the lexicon to contain redundant information, in particular a semantically compositional whole as well as its parts.

3.3 The word in grammar

In syntax, the word is located on the lowest rung of a hierarchy of units that traditionally reaches up to the sentence, with at least phrase and clause in between. It is generally assumed that this lowest syntactic unit is simultaneously the highest morphological unit so that a suitable term for it is *morphosyntactic word*, whereas *grammatical word* is also used in another sense (see section 3.4). Morphosyntactic words are said to be characterized by external autonomy and internal cohesion; more specifically, this may mean:
– Words can be uttered in isolation, parts of words cannot (section 3.3.1).
– A word cannot be interrupted by pauses or "other forms" (Bloomfield 1933: 180), but it is possible to separate the words in a sentence from one another in this way (section 3.3.2).
– The parts of a word cannot be reordered whereas the order of words in a sentence can be changed (section 3.3.3).
– Syntax does not have access to the internal structure of words (section 3.3.4).

3.3.1 Minimum sentence

Since a higher-level element can, in the limiting case, consist of a single lower-level element, the word is often defined as a minimum sentence (or minimum utterance); this is also what is meant by "minimum free form" (Bloomfield 1933: 178). However, many items that we generally call words are not used by themselves as sentences, e.g., in reply to a question. For instance, the answer to *What do you see there?* can be *Paw-marks* (in the plural) but not *Paw-mark* (in the singular, without an article), and while *Hunting* is a possible response to *What are you doing?*, one would be hard put to find a question which can be answered with the present-tense form *Hunts* alone. (There are languages in which sentences can consist of a bare count noun in the singular or a bare finite verb, but the set of minimum free forms is still smaller than that of words in the traditional sense.) If we admit photo captions such as *Paw-mark* or book titles such as *Hunted* and the like, the range of minimum free forms will be larger, but even this will not help in many cases. Evidently, the minimum sentence criterion is at best a sufficient but not a necessary one. Moreover, it might lead us to regard *paw-mark* as a sequence of two words (cf. Haspelmath 2011: 39), and it is doubtful whether the problem can be solved satisfactorily by pointing to the fact that *mark* in isolation has stronger stress than in *paw-mark* (cf. Bloomfield 1933: 180).

3.3.2 Uninterruptability

In spontaneous speech, pauses and hesitation phenomena do not necessarily coincide with word boundaries. It has therefore been suggested that the determination of points at which pausing is possible should be based on slow and careful speech (Hockett 1958: 166–167), but this version of the criterion is still problematic. When dictating for a transcriber, literate speakers will be influenced by conventional orthography, whereas the points at which speakers of unwritten languages pause seem to depend on the language type; apart from that, pauses tend to be more closely related to phonological than to morphosyntactic word boundaries (cf. Dixon and Aikhenvald 2002: 11–12, 23–24).

As regards interruptability by "other forms", we must specify which forms we mean. Surely, we do not want to say that *interrupt* consists of two words because we can insert *-cept* and *dis-* to give *intercept* and *disrupt*. Also, morphemes may certainly interrupt a word: In Polish, the insertion of the comparative marker *-sz-* into *młod-y* 'young-NOM.SG.M' results in *młodszy* 'younger'. It seems, then, that the inserted material must consist of whole words (cf. Vardul' 1991: 22) so that the criterion presupposes the unit it is meant to identify (see already Peškovskij 1925:

124–125). This circularity can be eliminated if we determine words in stages, first those with the highest degree of autonomy (minimum sentences) and then those with lesser degrees of autonomy (cf. Plungjan 2003: 18–28; see also Bloomfield 1933: 179). Then the criterion can be reformulated as "a word cannot be interrupted by other words that have already been identified as such"; conversely, the fact that *the paw-mark* can be interrupted by *small* demonstrates that this is a phrase even though *the* cannot be used alone.

Allegedly, some cases of noun incorporation violate this principle, e.g., Pawnee (Oklahoma, USA) *tā-tu-k^ut* 'I have cut it for you', which can be interrupted by *rīks* 'arrow', resulting in *tā-tu-rīks-k^ut* 'I have cut your arrow' (Haspelmath 2011: 45, slightly modified from Julien 2002: 34–35; this version differs in several details from the original source, Boas 1911: 31, and the freestanding noun actually needs an absolutive suffix *-u*, cf. Parks 1976: 97–99 – but examples of this kind are, in principle, possible). If so, should we perhaps argue that English *doors* consists of two words because it can be interrupted by *knob* (in *doorknobs*)? As with the definition of the word as a minimum sentence (see section 3.3.1), the difficulties posed by compounding, including the subtype known as incorporation, can be partially overcome by showing that the stem which occurs in the compound is not fully identical with the corresponding freestanding word. One can also argue that the incorporation of nouns into verbs is much more restricted than the insertion of words into a phrase (even sequences of words such as *unusually large* can come between *the* and *paw-mark*) and that verbs with incorporated nouns behave essentially like simple verbs (cf. Julien 2002: 35 with reference to Boas 1911: 31–32, where the line of reasoning is, however, somewhat different).

If words are uninterruptible, the notion of "discontinuous word" is untenable so that *has come* and *will stop* must be phrases rather than bipartite word forms as is sometimes maintained (see also section 3.4 on the status of so-called periphrastic forms). One of the more difficult cases is Russian *nikto* 'nobody' with the genitive *nikogo* 'of nobody' and the instrumental *nikem* 'by nobody', which are interrupted by prepositions, as in *ni do kogo* 'to nobody' and *ni s kem* 'with nobody' (cf. Vardul' 1991: 25), but an obvious solution is to regard *ni* as a clitic, i.e. a distinct morphosyntactic word (see section 3.2.2). Other apparent counterexamples can be dealt with in the same way.

3.3.3 Fixed vs. variable order

One proof that *I said* consists of two morphosyntactic words is that they can occur in either order, as in *"I'll try," I said* and *"Then I will go on," said I*. On the other hand, the permutation test demonstrates that *paw-mark* is a single word because the opposite order *mark-paw* is impossible. Since the order of words in a phrase is often quite rigid, this is, however, another subsidiary criterion of limited applicability: We cannot transpose *I'll try*, and the five constituents of *Then I will go on* occur in only a few of the theoretically possible 120 orders.

Conversely, there are cases where the parts of a word can be reordered. Many compounds are reversible, normally with a semantic difference as in *boathouse* vs. *house-boat*. Frequently, differences in the order of affixes correlate with differences in meaning and hierarchical structure, i.e. the order in which the affixes are added in the derivational history of the word (cf. Rice 2011: 174–176; see also article 10 on derivation, section 3.1). In Dutch, for instance, some verb prefixes can appear in either order, although minimal pairs are quite rare. One of them is *veronzekerd* 'made unsure (disconcerted)' vs. *onverzekerd* 'uninsured', both derived from *zeker* 'sure'. In *veronzekerd*, the negative prefix *on-* has scope over *zeker*. The addition of *ver-* to *on-zeker* 'unsure' leads to *ver-on-zeker[en]* 'to make unsure (disconcert)' (the bracketed *en* is the infinitive suffix of the citation form) with the past participle *ver-on-zeker-d*. In *onverzekerd*, the order of derivation is *zeker* 'sure' → *ver-zeker[en]* 'to make sure (insure)' → *ver-zeker-d* 'insured' (past participle) → *on-ver-zeker-d* 'uninsured'. It has been suggested that the function of an affix determines its position if it is derivational but not if it is inflectional (Stump 2001b: 713); depending on how one defines the distinction between derivation and inflection (see article 8), the existence of contrasting scope relationships among tense/mood/aspect affixes either contradicts this assumption or shows that these affixes are not inflectional in the language concerned (cf. Korotkova and Lander 2010: 306, 310, 314–315 on Adyghe).

Because of such examples, the principle that the order of morphemes in a word cannot be varied is often restricted to free variation without a semantic difference (e.g., Dixon and Aikhenvald 2002: 20). This generalization is sometimes called "Perlmutter's universal" or "Postal and Perlmutter's universal" (cf. Perlmutter 1970: 234). Again, some counter-examples can be dismissed, more or less plausibly, as involving clitics rather than affixes – but not all (cf. Bickel et al. 2007; see also Good and Yu 2005). In fact, the existence of variable order should not come as a surprise. If there is no scopal relationship between affix A and affix B or if affix A can have semantic scope over affix B but not vice versa, the order of A and B does not matter; it may therefore be fixed arbitrarily, vary freely (cf. also Rice 2011: 185–187) or be governed by some external condition (for factors that can be relevant, see Manova and Aronoff 2010: 111–112; Ryan 2010; Rice 2011). Order may also be immaterial if it makes hardly any semantic difference whether A has scope over B or B over A (cf. Korotkova and Lander 2010: 305–306 on Adyghe). But even if A can have scope over B and B over A with a clear contrast in meaning (e.g., 'I'll want to make her eat' vs. 'I'll make her want to eat'), we occasionally find that either order is possible and compatible with both interpretations (cf. Caballero 2010; see also Rice 2011: 187–188). As for the constituents of compounds, free variation is highly unusual but does occur: Vietnamese, where the native order (modifier second) coexists with the Chinese order (modifier first), sometimes allows both options without any apparent difference in meaning, e.g., in combinations with *trưởng* 'leader' such as *trưởng-lớp* or *lớp-trưởng* 'leader of a group' (Bisang 2001: 199).

3.3.4 Invisibility of internal structure

It is commonly assumed that parts of words are not accessible to syntax. (This does not apply to models in which the basic building blocks of syntax are morphemes rather than words; cf. Julien 2002: 8–11, 27–28 for some discussion.) In particular, the member of a compound that semantically modifies the other cannot be referred to with a pronoun; this has been expressed in the slogan that words are "anaphoric islands" (Postal 1969: 205). In the "interpretable but mildly unsettling" utterance *I went baby-sitting last night. Boy, was she ugly!*, which might look like a counter-example, the referent of *she* is not established grammatically, via the compound-member *baby*, but rather pragmatically, by our knowledge about the situation (Mithun 1984: 871; apart from its rudeness, the problem with the utterance seems to be the ambiguity of *she*, which could also refer to the baby's mother).

Secondly, it should not be possible to modify a part of a complex word by an external attribute. Here, exceptions are not difficult to find (see also article 10 on derivation, section 3.4). For instance, a German cookery book from the late 1950s published by a manufacturer of refrigerators has the title *Kalte Küchenkniffe* 'cold cuisine_tricks', where *kalte* semantically modifies the compound-internal constituent *Küche* but agrees in number with the plural *Kniffe* (the singular would be *ein kalter Küchenkniff* 'a cold cuisine_trick'). While native speakers find this a bit amusing, a much-discussed English example involving derivation is perfectly normal: *nuclear physicist* does not mean 'physicist who is nuclear' but 'specialist in nuclear physics'. Such discrepancies between grammatical and semantic structure are known as *bracketing paradoxes* or *morphosemantic mismatches*. A suggestion that would eliminate the mismatch is to analyze cases of this kind as compounding with or derivation from a phrase (*kalte Küche, nuclear physics*), but many reject this as theoretically unacceptable or empirically inadequate (see section 7.1).

A third corollary is that words can be coordinated but parts of words cannot. It appears to be falsified by Dutch *hoofd- of nevenaccent* 'main [stress] or secondary stress', *zicht- en tastbaar* 'vis[ible] and tangible', *ijs- en bruine beeren* 'ice [bears] (polar bears) and brown bears' (cf. Booij 2002: 171–172) and analogous constructions in other languages (cf. Haspelmath 2011: 47–49). These expressions could, however, be derived from *hoofdaccent of nevenaccent*, etc. by ellipsis. Even if the idea that this is a purely phonological phenomenon (cf. Booij 2002: 172–173) may be an over-simplification, we are not dealing with coordination below the word level (cf. also Chaves 2008).

In summary, the generalizations about words as grammatical units are partly theory-dependent and partly open to objections that require further fine-tuning of the criteria. If the tests for word status give intuitively undesirable results, we have a choice between developing alternative interpretations of the data and giving up our preconceived notions. Where there is room for legitimate disagreement as to whether a given element is a morphosyntactic word or part of one, the final decision should be guided by overall structural considerations but may often well be a matter of taste.

3.4 Word-form, grammatical word, lexeme

As regards the classification problem – are we dealing with two different morphosyntactic words or instances of the same word? –, we can draw a distinction that is similar to that between minimal sign, morpheme and morph (see section 2.3) but involves an additional pair of concepts, *morphosyntactic category* and *morphosyntactic property* (cf. Matthews 1974: 66, 136). A morphosyntactic category is a set of two or more mutually exclusive morphosyntactic properties, i.e. content elements, one of which must be chosen for each word of a certain class. English has a morphosyntactic category number with the two properties 'SINGULAR' and 'PLURAL', and all nouns are specified for one of these properties when used in a text. The term *morphosyntactic* indicates that the properties in question are relevant to syntax and are expressed by morphological means, more specifically by inflection. Therefore, *inflectional category* is frequently used instead; *morphological category* and *grammatical category* should be broader notions but often serve as synonyms of *inflectional category*. Some define morphosyntactic categories more narrowly as those involved in government or agreement (notably case, number, gender and person); categories that are not relevant to syntax in this particular sense but encode semantic distinctions (e.g., tense, aspect, mood, voice/diathesis) are then called *morphosemantic* (Kibort 2010: 64, 80–83). One of the alternatives to the term *(morphosyntactic) property* that has already been mentioned is *grammeme* (see section 2.5). Confusingly, *(inflectional) category* is sometimes used as the hyponym, with a somewhat idiosyncratic hyperonym such as *complex of categories* (Wurzel 1989: 52) or *inflectional dimension* (Haspelmath 2002: 60–61). The most important rival to the pair *category/property* is *feature/value* (e.g., Haspelmath and Sims 2010: 81–83; Kibort 2010: 66; cf. also Stump 2001a: 38–39). However, *feature* can also refer to an individual morphosyntactic property (e.g., Matthews 1991: 40). Besides, features do not always correspond one-to-one to categories if we postulate that features must have exactly two values. Thus, the category person, which typically comprises the properties '1ST PERSON', '2ND PERSON' and '3RD PERSON', can be captured by two binary features, [±me] and [±you], such that the three properties are reanalyzed as the combinations [+me, –you], [–me, +you] and [–me, –you], respectively. As this example shows, we usually enclose feature names in square brackets. Values are indicated by + and – (if there are two) or by numbers (if there are more). Some linguists prefer a format like [NUM: sg], where NUM stands for the feature number and sg for its value 'SINGULAR' (e.g., Zwicky 1985: 374; Stump 2001a: 39–41). An affix or process (see sections 5–6) which expresses a morphosyntactic property (or a bundle of properties) is called *exponent* (cf. Matthews 1974: 144, 1991: 175) or *marker* (cf. Wurzel 1989: 51), and the relationship between morphosyntactic properties and exponents is known as *exponence* (for different types of exponence, see Coates 2000).

Words that differ only in their morphosyntactic properties but otherwise have the same meaning, e.g., *book* 'book.SG' and *books* 'book.PL', can be viewed as different words or as variants of the same word, depending on whether the differences in morphosyntactic properties and the corresponding differences in expression are taken into account or not. Widely-used terms for these two senses of *word* are *grammatical word* and *lexeme*. (For other meanings of these terms, see sections 2.5, 3.2.3, 3.3. *Lexeme* is attested in the Russian form *leksema* since the 1920s, cf. Peškovskij 1925: 138.) A lexeme is a set of grammatical words which have the same content, save for their morphosyntactic properties. While grammatical words are linguistic signs, a characterization of lexemes as signs (cf. Aronoff 1994: 9; Montermini 2010: 86) deprives this term of its meaning. Occasionally, a grammatical word is called *lex* or, in relation to the lexeme it belongs to, *allolex* (in analogy to *allomorph*, see section 2.3). Lexemes are usually indicated by small capitals, e.g., BOOK for the set {*book* 'book.SG', *books* 'book.PL'}. If necessary, one can add a subscript in order to distinguish the noun BOOK_N from the verb BOOK_V. The latter has, among others, the grammatical words *booked* 'book.PST' and *booked* 'book.PST.PTCP', which we distinguish because the past tense and the past participle of other verbs differ in expression (e.g., *I booked/chose my flight two weeks ago* and *I have already booked/chosen my flight*). If, however, we focus on the expression side, *booked* 'book.PST' and *booked* 'book.PST.PTCP' can be regarded instances of the same word. The term *word form* may be used for this third sense of *word*, i.e. a set of grammatical words with the same expression. (The three-way distinction between *lexeme*, *grammatical word* and *word form* goes back to Matthews 1972: 160–161; conceptually, it is already formulated in Lyons 1968: 196–197. According to one definition, a word form comprises not only grammatical words of the same lexeme but also grammatical words of different lexemes, such as *books* 'book.PL' as in *Linguistics books are expensive* and *books* 'book.3SG.PRES' as in *She always books early*; cf. Carstairs-McCarthy 2000: 595.) Some use *word form* instead of *grammatical word* or do not state clearly whether *booked* 'book.PST' and *booked* 'book.PST.PTCP' are the same word form or different ones (e.g., Booij 2012: 3; Lieber 2010: 7; cf. section 2.3 on the analogous ambiguity of *morph*). Sometimes, *word* without further specification is restricted to one of the three senses, e.g., lexeme (Donalies 2005: 19) or grammatical word (Matthews 1974: 26, 1991: 31; I will follow this practice for the sake of brevity). It is often said that lexemes are abstract units which are "realized" in texts by concrete word forms – but both lexemes and word forms (or grammatical words) are elements of the system as well as the text, and all linguistic units are abstractions (see section 2.3 on the relationship between morpheme and morph). As defined here, the concept of lexeme is not confined to the "major lexical categories", the word classes noun, verb and adjective/adverb (as in Aronoff 1994: 9–10). It should be noted that words of minor categories, e.g., determiners or prepositions, may be inflected, requiring a distinction between lexeme and grammatical word. And just as the notion of morpheme is motivated by the existence of variation but can be extended to cases of non-variation (see section 2.5 on *allomorph*), so too can we allow a lexeme to consist of a single grammatical word so that the notion is applicable to all words.

The grammatical words which belong to a given lexeme form a pattern that is defined by the morphosyntactic categories and properties involved and can be represented as a multi-dimensional array. The Lower Sorbian nouns DUB 'oak' and ŽONA 'wife', for instance, are inflected for two categories, number and case, and their grammatical words form a 3 × 6 grid:

(5)		SINGULAR		DUAL		PLURAL	
	NOMINATIVE	dub	žon-a	dub-a	žon-je	dub-y	žon-y
	GENITIVE	dub-a	žon-y	dub-owu	žon-owu	dub-ow	žon-ow
	DATIVE	dub-oju	žon-je	dub-oma	žon-oma	dub-am	žon-am
	ACCUSATIVE	dub	žon-u	dub-a	žon-je	dub-y	žon-y
	INSTRUMENTAL	dub-om	žon-u	dub-oma	žon-oma	dub-ami	žon-ami
	LOCATIVE	dub-je	žon-je	dub-oma	žon-oma	dub-ach	žon-ach

The term *paradigm* can refer not only to such an array filled by the grammatical words of a specific lexeme (e.g., the paradigm of DUB) but also to an array filled by the markers that express these morphosyntactic properties in a particular inflection class (e.g., the paradigm of one subset of noun lexemes that includes ŽONA, characterized by *-a* in the nominative singular, *-y* in the genitive singular, etc.) or an array that is empty except for the morphosyntactic properties that define the cells (e.g., the Lower Sorbian noun paradigm; cf. Carstairs-McCarthy 2000: 596–597, where it is recommended that *paradigm* should be used only in this last sense).

There is a further morphosyntactic category that is relevant to a Lower Sorbian noun lexeme, that of gender. But in contrast to number and case, for which its grammatical words vary, each noun has an invariable gender property that is specified in the lexicon; DUB is masculine, ŽONA feminine. Adjectives, however, are inflected for gender in agreement with the noun they modify, e.g., *strowy dub* 'healthy oak' vs. *strowa žona* 'healthy wife'. Using the feature/value terminology, we can thus distinguish between fixed and variable features of a lexeme. As regards the latter, the values of some features are selected for semantic reasons, e.g., number, which generally corresponds to the quantity of entities the speaker wants to refer to. Others are dictated by syntax, especially government and agreement; in this case, the feature is called *imposed* (Zwicky 1986: 85) or *contextual* (Booij 1994: 28, 1996: 2–3). *Inherent* often serves as a cover term for fixed and selected features (Zwicky 1986: 85; Kibort 2010: 73–77) or refers to selected features only (Booij 1994: 28, misquoting Anderson 1988: 25; Booij 2012: 103–104). This is a rather unfortunate terminological choice because *inherent* suggests invariance (and is, in fact, used for fixed features by some authors, e.g., Anderson 1988: 25). The hypothesis that selected and imposed features behave differently with regard to word-formation needs to be investigated further (see section 7.2).

Among the grammatical words of a lexeme, one is the *citation form* that is conventionally used to refer to the lexeme as a whole. For nouns inflected for case and number, it is normally the nominative singular, which serves to name or label entities and is semantically unmarked (least specific), e.g., *dub* and *žona* in our Lower Sorbian examples. The criterion of semantic markedness is less helpful for verbs, where typical citation forms are the infinitive (e.g., in Russian), the first person singular present (e.g., in Latin) or the third person singular present (e.g., in Macedonian). Frequently, the citation form is also a *base form* in a morphological sense, i.e. one that is morphologically unmarked and can be regarded as underlying the entire paradigm; this is true of *dub* (which does not have a suffix) but not of *žona* (which has one). A slightly different notion is that of *diagnostic forms*, traditionally known as *principal parts*. They are a subset of the grammatical words of a lexeme from which the rest of the lexeme's paradigm can be deduced (cf. Wurzel 1989: 112–121). It should be remembered that a lexeme is not identical with its citation form; this is particularly important when describing derivational relationships. For example, the Italian lexeme SICUREZZA 'security' is not derived from the citation form *sicuro* of the lexeme SICURO 'secure'; hence, the suffix *-o*, which is inflectional, need not be deleted before *-ezza* can be added (see also section 7.2 on the input to word-formation rules). It is also incorrect to identify the lexeme with the "root or underlying form" (Dixon and Aikhenwald 2002: 6–7) or rather the stem, which is, roughly speaking, that part which all the grammatical words of a lexeme share, e.g., *dub* and *žon-* (see sections 4.1–4.3).

A fundamental question that has major repercussions for word-formation is what exactly should be included in an inflectional paradigm (see also article 8 on the delimitation of derivation and inflection). One problem can be illustrated by the following partial paradigm of the Latin verb ARO 'to plow' (to simplify matters, only 3rd person present indicative forms are shown):

(6)

	ACTIVE		PASSIVE	
IMPERFECTIVE	*arat*	'plows'	*aratur*	'is [being] plowed'
PERFECTIVE	*aravit*	'plowed'		

Latin verb lexemes do not have a grammatical word with the properties 'PERFECTIVE' and 'PASSIVE'; instead, 'has been plowed' must be expressed by the construction *aratus est*. For the sake of symmetry, this so-called *periphrastic form* is often included in the paradigm, but the definition of *lexeme* given here does not allow such a solution (for some discussion of periphrasis and paradigms, cf. Haspelmath 2000). The participle *aratus* 'plowed' raises a second question. Like a Latin adjective, it is inflected for gender, number and case and can be used attributively, e.g., *ager aratus* 'plowed field' (nominative singular masculine), *terrarum aratarum* 'of plowed lands' (genitive plural feminine), etc. Do all these grammatical words belong to the paradigm of the verb ARO (cf. Haspelmath 1996 for a defence of "word-class changing inflection")? Or should we maintain that a verb paradigm cannot contain an adjective paradigm because inflection can never change the word class (cf. Scalise 1984: 103)? If so, the formation of participles (and, for that matter, noun-like infinitives) must be derivation despite its regularity – a conclusion that is somewhat unusual but by no means unreasonable (cf. Plungjan 2003: 122; see also Motsch 1999: 21, 312–313). There is a problem of circularity here, however: If lexeme classes, i.e. morphological as opposed to syntactic word classes (cf. Bergenholtz and Mugdan 1979a: 137–141), are defined by paradigms, we cannot distinguish inflection from derivation in terms of preservation vs. change of word class.

4 Root, stem, affix

4.1 Root vs. affix

Minimal signs fall into two classes which are relevant to the definition of compounding or composition (see article 14) as opposed to derivation (see article 10), namely *root* (German *Wurzel*, French *radical*, Russian *koren'*, etc.; the concept was borrowed from Hebrew linguistics, cf. Lindner 2012: 144–146) and *affix*. For example, *book-s* 'book-PL' is generally considered to consist of a root *book* and an affix *-s*. It is, however, not so easy to name the criteria on which the distinction is based.

According to one explanation, roots are *free* and affixes are *bound*. Here, *free* does not mean "can be uttered by itself" (as in the definition of the word as a "minimum free form", see section 3.3.1) but "can occur as a word by itself"; by contrast, a bound minimal sign cannot constitute a word except in conjunction with another sign. It is therefore more accurate to speak of *potentially free* and *obligatorily bound*. This criterion may work reasonably well for English, but the Lower Sorbian example (5) shows that the matter is not so simple. While *dub* is potentially free (since it forms a word by itself in the nominative and accusative singular), there is no cell in the paradigm of ŽONA in which *žon-* appears alone. Even *dub* is not free if we assume zero affixes in the nominative and accusative singular (cf. Mel'čuk 1982: 75; see also section 5.9). How then can we uphold the traditional view that both *dub* and *žon-* are roots? One option is to accept that while potentially free minimal signs are always roots, obligatory bound ones can be either roots or affixes, but this requires additional criteria. Alternatively, we can classify a minimal sign as free even if it must always be combined with some inflectional affix (cf. Donalies 2005: 20).

According to a related distributional criterion, roots are obligatory components of a word but affixes are not (cf. Vardul' 1991: 29). There are, however, a number of potential counter-examples to the assumption that every word contains at least one root (cf. also Dixon and Aikhenvald 2002: 22). They include Hebrew /bəxa/ 'in you', where a prefix seems to be combined with a suffix, cf. /bə-ʃir/ 'in-song', /ʃir-xa/ 'song-POSS.2SG (your song)', and Hungarian *nálad* 'with/near you', where the suffix *-nál* 'ADESSIVE' seems to be combined with the suffix *-ad* 'POSS.2SG', cf. *ház-nál* 'house-ADESSIVE (at [a] house)', *ház-ad* 'house-POSS.2SG (your house)'. We might want to say that *nál* is a root in *nálad* but an affix in *háznál* (for examples from other languages, some of which may be open to other analyses, cf. Volodin and Chrakovskij 1991: 110; see also section 3.2.3 on "separable prefixes") – but there are linguists who exclude such a possibility on principle (e.g., Vardul' 1991: 31).

Another distinction that is frequently appealed to is that between *lexical meaning* and *grammatical meaning*. It is based on a variety of factors (cf. Croft 2000: 258–260); putting it simply, lexical meanings have something to do with entities, properties and states of affairs in the extra-linguistic world, and grammatical meanings are relational or structural. This can also be expressed by the terms *autosemantic* (having meaning by itself) and *synsemantic* (having meaning only in conjunction with another item), whereas the characterization of lexical meanings as *concrete* and of grammatical meanings as *abstract* is too vague to be helpful. A definition of root and affix via lexical vs. grammatical meaning is, however, somewhat problematic. One difficulty is that there are many meanings that can be expressed – in different languages or even within the same language – either by a root or an affix as defined on distributional grounds (cf. Volodin and Chrakovskij 1991: 109; Croft 2000: 258). Secondly, it is unclear how to classify certain kinds of meanings in a given language. Derivational elements are by definition affixes (cf. Booij 2005: 109) but their meanings are sometimes regarded as grammatical (e.g., Fleischer and Barz 2012: 63), sometimes as lexical (e.g., Fleischer and Barz 1992: 26). Conversely, some potentially free minimal signs have a meaning that is evidently grammatical, e.g., uninflected particles such as English *with*, *because*, etc. and inflected determiners such as Slovene *moj* 'my(NOM.SG.M)' / *moj-ega* 'my-GEN.SG.M', etc. (as in *moj mož* 'my husband', *mojega moža* 'of my husband'). If we nonetheless want to uphold the definition of roots as minimal signs with lexical meaning, we have to give up the simple bipartition root/affix and introduce additional classes of minimal signs (cf. Bergenholtz and Mugdan 1979a: 119–121).

Some linguists feel that the term *root* should be reserved for a diachronic concept (cf. Chelliah and de Reuse 2011: 314) or avoid it for some other reason. Among the alternatives are *base morpheme* (German *Grundmorphem* or *Basismorphem*) and *core morpheme* (German *Kernmorphem*). Certain definitions of *root* are, in fact, definitions of what is normally called *stem* (see section 4.3; cf. Stump 2001a: 33; Aronoff 2012: 29–30; see also Matthews 1974: 40).

4.2 Neither root nor affix?

One response to delimitation problems is to abandon an exhaustive subdivision into mutually exclusive classes in favour of prototypes which are characterized by a certain bundle of properties. Items can now be assigned to points on a continuum between the prototypes, based on their similarity to the latter. These points need not include the prototypes themselves, which then remain ideals that are never attained in practice. In our case, we can describe minimal signs as more root-like or more affix-like, and we may or may not find elements that have all the properties of prototypical roots or prototypical affixes. Such a gradual distinction is, of course, more accurate but may not be very useful for practical purposes. Another solution is to introduce an intermediate category, e.g., semi-affix, between root and affix – but this means that instead of one delimitation problem, root vs. affix, we now have two, root vs. semi-affix and semi-affix vs. affix. For this reason, many linguists are reluctant to increase the number of categories although they may use a special label for a group of problematic cases (see also section 3.2.2 on clitics as an additional category between affixes and particles).

The terms *affixoid* or *semi-affix* (and the more specific *prefixoid*, *suffixoid*, etc., see section 5.2) are commonly applied to an element that poses a semantic problem: Although it seems to be identical with a free minimal sign, it does not have the same meaning (cf. Fleischer and Barz 2012: 58–61; Booij 2005: 114–117). A standard example are German nouns with the component *-tag* that denote assemblies (as events and/or institutions), e.g., *Juristentag* 'lawyer assembly' (an organization of lawyers and its annual meeting) and *Bundestag* 'federation assembly' (the German parliament). One can discern some semantic connection with the word *Tag* 'day', but unlike ordinary compounds such as *Herbsttag* 'autumn day', these complex words do not fit the pattern 'AB is a (kind of) B'. Another characteristic of "affixoids" that is regularly mentioned is their high degree of productivity, but that does not necessarily distinguish them from ordinary compound members. We can therefore classify them as roots if we allow for the possibility that certain meanings of a root occur only in word-formations (see also section 7.3 on compounding stems). It is well known, however, that roots can develop into affixes, and an affixoid is sometimes described as an element that may diachronically be in the process of becoming an affix (e.g., Donalies 2005: 24–25). The term *affixoid* has also been used in a completely different sense, for sound sequences that resemble affixes "without qualifying for that rank", e.g., *-er* in *hammer* (Malkiel 1966: 323).

A second kind of minimal sign, often called *confix* (for a different use of this term, see section 5.1), poses a formal problem: It has lexical meaning but is not free (in the broader sense that it does not constitute a word by itself or in combination with an inflectional affix), occurring only in word-formations. The stock example are elements of Greek or Latin origin such as *phob(e)* in *phobia* and *xenophobe*, but the term *confix* has also been applied to native elements like *step-*

in *stepmother*. Typically, the neo-classical minimal signs were free in the donor language but were borrowed only in combinations with other signs and later recombined into new words that did not exist in the classical languages. In many (mostly Indo-European) languages of Europe, neo-classical word-formation constitutes a special subsystem that is largely independent of these languages (cf. Montermini 2008: 31–32). This exceptional situation hardly justifies the introduction of novel units; despite certain difficulties, a division into roots and affixes seems sufficient.

4.3 Stem

The term *stem* (German *Stamm*, French *thème*) is used in slightly different ways in different traditions (cf. the comparative table in Chelliah and de Reuse 2011: 314; for its history, see Lindner 2012: 135–144). It is frequently defined as what remains when inflectional affixes are removed from a grammatical word (e.g., Anderson 1992: 71; Lieber 2010: 35). Accordingly, the stem of the plural noun *books* is *book* because -*s* 'PL' is an inflectional affix. But what about the singular noun *book* where there is nothing to be removed? It might be clearer to say that a stem is something to which an inflectional affix can be added (e.g., Stump 2001a: 33; Bauer 2003: 341). That would mean that *book* has a stem because -*s* can be added, while uninflected words such as *because* do not have one. We may therefore want to amend the definition a little (cf. Schpak-Dolt 2010: 37) so that all words consist of a stem and possibly one or more inflectional affixes. It should be noted, however, that something to which inflectional affixes can be added does not necessarily lack inflectional affixes altogether so that the two definitions are not equivalent (as is sometimes mistakenly assumed, e.g., Donalies 2005: 19–20). If we remove all inflectional affixes from the Bashkir word /awɤl-dar-ɤbɤð-ðan/ 'village-PL-1PL.POSS-ABL (from our villages)', we arrive at the stem /awɤl/ 'village'. But if we consider the signs to which inflectional affixes can be added, then /awɤldar/ 'villages' and /awɤldarɤbɤð/ 'our villages' are stems as well, and stem is a recursive category: A stem can contain a stem. Even if we decide that only something without any inflectional affixes should be called *stem*, we may want to say that the derivational affix /-daʃ/ 'co-' turns the stem /awɤl/ 'village' into the stem /awɤldaʃ/ 'co-villager (inhabitant of the same village)', which occurs in /awɤldaʃtarɤbɤððan/ 'from our co-villagers', etc. (see also section 7.3. on word-formation as stem formation) – and if we insist that a word has only one stem and assign /awɤl/ to a different category when it occurs in the derivative /awɤl-daʃ/, that category will have to be recursive (e.g., *Stammteil* 'stem part' in Bergenholtz and Mugdan 1979a: 123–125).

In the Lower Sorbian example (5), the stems of DUB 'oak' and ŽONA 'wife' can easily be identified as *dub* and *žon-*. Often, it is more difficult to draw the boundary between stem and affix (cf. Spencer 2012 for some discussion), and the operation "omit all inflectional affixes" need not give the same result for all the grammatical words that belong to a lexeme. Lower Sorbian KOTEŁ 'kettle' has the nominative singular *koteł*, the genitive singular *kotła* and the locative singular *kotle*, and removal of the inflectional affixes, if any, leads to three different remainders, *koteł*, *kotł-* and *kotl-*. In such a situation, some say that the lexeme has a single stem with several *stem alternants* (cf. Halle 1953: 46) or *stem forms* (cf. Fuhrhop 1998: 22; Aronoff and Fuhrhop 2002: 454–456). Others speak of different stems (e.g., Stump 2001a: 33); one can then call the set of all stems and their distribution *stem space* (cf. Bonami, Boyé and Kerleroux 2009: 106–108). It may be desirable to distinguish multiple stems from mere variants of a stem, for which the term *allostem* suggests itself (which has, however, also been used for stem alternants of all kinds) so that a lexeme can have several stems which can in turn have several allostems (cf. Spencer 2012: 98). What exactly should count as an allostem needs to be clarified, but the extent to which phonological factors are involved (see section 2.4 on conditioning, relatedness and domain) certainly plays a decisive role. In the following, I will use *stem alternant* as a neutral term where I do not want to commit myself as to whether we are dealing with multiple stems or allostems of a single stem.

A typology of stem alternations will also need to consider the information content and the distribution of the alternants. The following partial paradigms of the cognate verbs VARFA 'to throw' in the Bosco Gurin dialect of Walser German (Ticino, Switzerland) and WERFEN 'to throw' in Standard German serve to illustrate these points:

(7)		Bosco Gurin	Standard German	
		PRESENT	PRESENT	PAST
	1SG	varf-a	vɛrf-ə	varf
	2SG	verf-ʃt	vɪrf-st	varf-st
	3SG	verf-t	vɪrf-t	varf
	1PL	varf-a	vɛrf-ən	varf-ən
	2PL	varf-at	vɛrf-t	varf-t
	3PL	varf-an	vɛrf-ən	varf-ən

In Bosco Gurin, certain verbs have a special stem alternant with the vowel /e/ instead of /a/ in the second and third person singular, but the affixes /-ʃt/ and

/-t/ are unambiguous exponents of these morphosyntactic properties so that the information provided by the stem alternation is redundant. Standard German has a similar alternation between /ɛ/ and /ɪ/, but here the third person singular and the second person plural, /vɪrf-t/ and /vɛrf-t/, have the same affix /-t/ and are distinguished only by the stem alternants. Nonetheless, we may still regard this as allo-variation, i.e. as a side effect without meaning, because the vast majority of Standard German verbs have the same word form in these two cells. By contrast, the main difference between the present and past tense forms cited lies in the stem so that the content of /varf/ includes the feature [+past]. Such a stem which encodes one or more morphosyntactic properties in addition to the lexical meaning may be named *portmanteau stem* (cf. Stump 2001a: 208–211; the hypothesis that stems never serve as exponents of morphosyntactic properties, cf. Spencer 2012: 89, 98, presupposes a different analysis of /varf/).

With regard to the distribution of stem alternants, the question is whether the cells in which they occur form a *natural class* in the sense that they can be characterized by a morphosyntactic feature or combination of features that is associated with all of these cells and only these cells. Standard German /vɪrf/ and /varf/ occur in cells that form natural classes since they can be identified by the features [–me, –pl, –past] and [+past], respectively. This is also expressed by traditional labels such as *past (tense) stem*, which are often extended to morphologically complex stems such as German /ʃɛrf-t/ 'sharpen-PAST' in /ʃɛrf-t-ə/ 'sharpen-PAST-1SG ([I] sharpened)', etc. with the regular affix /-t/ 'PAST'. For a stem alternant which appears in cells that do not form a natural class, the term *morphomic* has become fashionable (cf. Aronoff 1994: 25). A well-known case are French verbs of the type PUNIR 'punish'. In the present tense, they have an extended stem in -*iss* (e.g., *puniss*-) in both the indicative and the subjunctive mood except for the singular of the indicative – a distribution that cannot be captured by any feature specification. Another stock example is the Latin "third stem" or "participial stem". But there is often no need to resort to morphomic stems if morphosyntactic properties are not taken to be full specifications of meanings and functions (see section 2.3) or if derivational processes are allowed to delete or change morphosyntactic properties (cf. Mel'čuk 2006: 293–294).

If a lexeme has several stem alternants, word-formation rules may operate on more than one of them (see also sections 7.2–7.3). For example, French *punition* 'punishment' is derived from the simple stem *puni*-, *punissable* 'punishable' from the extended stem *puniss*-. It is an open question which kinds of stem alternants may serve as inputs to derivation or compounding. Furthermore, alternations in derivatives are not always due to different inputs. Some have a phonological explanation, others result from different affixes having partially the same effect, as in the case of German umlaut (roughly, vowel fronting): A number of verbs with the basic stem vowel /ɑː/ have /ɛː/ (orthographically *ä*) in the second and third person singular present, e.g., *trag-en* 'carry-INF' – *träg-t* 'carry-3SG'. The noun *Träg-er* 'carry-AGNR (carrier)' might seem to be derived from the stem alternant *träg-*, but a comparison with *fahr-en* 'drive-INF' – *fähr-t* – *Fahr-er*, *jag-en* 'hunt-INF' – *jag-t* – *Jäg-er* and *frag-en* 'ask-INF' – *frag-t* – *Frag-er* shows that the occurrence of /ɛː/ in the derived noun is independent of its occurrence in the verb forms (cf. also Eschenlohr 1999: 89–96 on umlaut in German derived verbs).

4.4 Templatic and hierarchical word structure

Words can have numerous affixes, and there are essentially two ways of accounting for the possible combinations: templates and hierarchical structures. (Additional constraints that have been suggested, e.g., that affixes may belong to mutually exclusive levels, see article 5 on word-formation in generative grammar, section 4.2, or that certain affixes prevent further affixation will not be considered here.) A template consists of a series of slots (also known as position classes) for the root or stem and the affixes that can precede or follow it (cf. Stump 2006; Rice 2011: 188–193). In each of the affix slots, there is a choice between a limited number of mutually exclusive affixes. Some of these slots must be filled while others may remain empty. There may be certain co-occurrence restrictions, e.g., "if slot *i* is filled, slot *j* must be filled as well" or "if slot *i* is filled with item *x*, slot *j* may not be filled with item *y*", but by and large the slots are filled quasi-simultaneously and each affix makes its own contribution to the content of the whole word independently of the others. Sometimes, the order of the affixes in a template may seem arbitrary (e.g., when derivational and inflectional affixes are not neatly separated), but it often follows from some more general principles (e.g., "inflection comes outside of derivation", see section 7.2 and article 8 on the delimitation of derivation and inflection).

Hierarchical structures can be generated by rewrite rules and are represented by tree diagrams or bracketings as in syntax. Here, affixes are added in a certain order and typically have semantic scope over the structure they attach to: If we start from *roll* and first add *-able* and then *un-*, we arrive at [un[rollable]] 'not able to be rolled', but if we attach the affixes in the opposite order, the result is [[unroll]able] 'able to be unrolled' (see also section 3.3.3 on Dutch *onverzekerd* vs. *veronzekerd*). The principle that all trees are binary branching is usually taken for granted; cases where three or more constituents seem to be of equal rank (e.g., *blue*, *white* and *red* in *the blue-white-red flag*) are fairly rare and their analysis is controversial. A question which has played a major role in debates about certain types of word-formations is whether all the intermediate steps in a hierarchical structure have to be actual words. A well-known case are English and German verbs of the type *endanger* 'to expose to danger' and *bestuhl[en]* 'to furnish with chairs' (← *Stuhl* 'chair'; the bracketed *-en* is the infinitive suffix of the citation form), where some linguists would rather assume the nonexisting verbs **danger* and **stuhl[en]* as intermediate steps than allow prefixes to change word class (cf. Eschenlohr 1999: 106–108; Donalies 2005: 120–121).

Templates may be more suitable for some morphological systems or subsystems than for others. In general, templatic structures are typical of inflection and some highly constrained patterns of derivation, whereas most word-formation creates hierarchical structures. Therefore, the two models can often be combined so that complex stems are built up hierarchically but the combination of stems with inflectional affixes conforms to a template.

5 Types of affixes

5.1 Criteria

Types of affixes are frequently defined in terms of their position relative to a root, but affixes can also attach to more complex structures. Depending on the exact definition of *stem* (see section 4.3), it may be more correct to describe their positions with respect to a stem (cf. Stump 2001b: 708), but it is best to use the neutral term *base* for whatever it is that the affix attaches to (cf. Matthews 1991: 131; Bauer 2004: 21). We can then classify affixes according to whether or not they disrupt the base, making it discontinuous, and whether or not they themselves are disrupted (cf. Mel'čuk 1963: 34–37, 1982: 82–87, 1997: 147–177, 2006: 299–300, with further examples). This gives the four types in (8); affixes that are neither disrupting nor disrupted are subclassified by position, before the base (*prefix*), after the base (*suffix*) or between two bases (*interfix*).

(8)	continuous base	discontinuous base
continuous affix	prefix, suffix, interfix	infix
discontinuous affix	circumfix	transfix

There is no generally accepted superordinate term for prefixes and suffixes (and interfixes, which are often not taken into account). *Confix*, which was proposed in connection with this classification, is also used in another meaning (see section 4.2). *Adfix* has the advantage of being parallel to *adposition*, the generally accepted cover term for prepositions and postpositions, but it occurs primarily in contradistinction to *infix*, and it is not always clear whether it includes only prefixes and suffixes or also interfixes and/or circumfixes. *Exfix* (Marušič 2003: 1) and *extrafix* (cf. Hoeksema and Janda 1988: 204) are rare and have both been used for other purposes as well.

Another classification recognizes prefixes, suffixes and infixes as basic types and describes discontinuous affixes as combinations of these: A *circumfix* is a combination of a prefix and a suffix, whereas *transfix*, if defined as in (8), covers any combination of an infix with one or more other affixes of any type, prefix, suffix or infix. It is only if *transfix* is understood more narrowly (cf. section 5.5) that *circumfix* and *transfix* leave a "descriptive gap" (Bauer 1988: 17) that could be filled by additional terms, e.g., *parafix* for infix plus prefix or infix plus suffix (Blevins 1999: 383–384). A number of cover terms for affix combinations in general have been suggested, including *polyaffix* (Plungjan 2003: 95–97) and *simulfix* (Bickel and Nichols 2007: 200), both of which are also attested in other senses. *Synaffix* has been proposed for combinations which involve affixes and/or internal modification (Bauer 1988: 23), and *multifixation* for morphological processes of any kind (cf. section 6) that operate simultaneously (Hoeksema and Janda 1988: 216). If such a cover term is needed at all (see section 6.6 for approaches to multiple marking), *multifix* would seem the best choice; *polyaffix* and *synaffix* are rather odd word-formations.

5.2 Prefix and suffix

The terms *prefix* and *suffix* were coined around 1600 (for details, cf. Lindner 2012: 146–147) and are firmly established, notwithstanding the fact that the opposite of *pre-* 'before' is *post-* 'after' and not *sub-* 'under' (cf. *preposition* vs. *postposition*). Some linguists do use *postfix* instead of *suffix*; others, especially Slavicists, employ *postfix* for a derivational suffix that follows inflectional suffixes (cf. Haspelmath 1990: 63, where *antefix* is suggested for a pre-inflectional prefix and *extrafix* as a cover term for affixes outside of inflectional affixes). In some languages, native equivalents of *prefix* and *suffix* (e.g., Dutch *voorvoegsel/achtervoegsel*, Icelandic *forskeyti/viðskeyti*, Polish *przedrostek/przyrostek*, Bulgarian *predstavka/nastavka*) are quite common. German *Vorsilbe* and *Nachsilbe* are based on *Silbe* 'syllable', which is highly misleading because affixes do not need to coincide with syllables. English *ending*, German *Endung*, French *désinence*, Russian *okončanie*, etc. are often used instead of *suffix*, but these terms can also refer to a phonological string at the end of a word regardless of its morphological status (cf. also Lindner 2012:

138). Some distinguish between *suffix* as derivational and *ending* as inflectional, and others use *ending*, etc. for a sequence of one or more inflectional suffixes (Schpak-Dolt 2010: 36–37; cf. Mel'čuk 1997: 147; see also Aronoff 2012: 48 for the unsubstantiated claim that *ending* refers specifically to the last inflectional element in a word).

Cross-linguistically, prefixes are far less common than suffixes (cf. Stump 2001b: 709–711; Montermini 2008: 49–59). This holds true of Europe, too, where a number of languages are exclusively or almost exclusively suffixing. In this region, prefixes do, however, often play a significant role in derivational morphology, as a rule without a change in word class (see also section 7.4). The verb systems of Indo-European languages as well as Hungarian and many Caucasian languages make extensive use of prefixes (known as *preverbs* in some grammatical traditions). They often signal local or directional meanings or metaphoric extensions of these, but numerous prefix-stem combinations have a meaning that is not predictable from the parts. In a number of languages, prefixes can derive verbs with a specific aktionsart (e.g., Germanic) or aspect (e.g., Slavic). Prefixes also occur on nouns and adjectives, where they express a wide variety of meanings (e.g., *ex-president, co-worker, postmodern, decentral*, etc.); one frequent function is the formation of antonyms (e.g., Albanian *pa-barazi* 'in-equality', Faroese *ó-vanligur* 'un-usual', Welsh *an-aml* 'in-frequent'). There are other meanings for which suffixes are clearly preferred, among them diminution (e.g., West Frisian *tún-tsje* 'garden-DIM', Romanian *mic-uț* 'small-DIM'). Such correlations between different derivational meanings and prefixing vs. suffixing need to be explored further.

5.3 Circumfix

A *circumfix* consists of two parts, one that precedes the base and one that follows it, as in Georgian *sidide* 'size' from *did-i* 'large-NOM'. (According to the Leipzig Glossing Rules, one should write *si-did-e* 'NR-large-NR', where the repetition of the gloss NR, short for NOMINALIZER, indicates the circumfix. A more convincing notation, which is more in line with that for infixes, is *si⟩di⟨de* '⟨NR⟩large' with the gloss NR arbitrarily given for the prefixal part only, cf. Lehmann 2004: 1853.) Less common terms are *simulfix, confix, ambifix* and *parasynthesis* (cf. Hagège 1986: 26; Vardul' 1991: 54; Greenberg 1966: 92 and Malkiel 1966: 314.)

How can we distinguish this type of affix from a situation where a prefix and a suffix are attached in one step (or even in two)? According to one definition, neither of the members of a circumfix "ever appears alone" (Rubba 2001: 679), which should presumably be taken to mean that neither of them occurs elsewhere with a meaning that one could also attribute to it in the combination. Another definition requires that the parts "together have a single unitary meaning" and that they "must occur together to provide that meaning" (Bauer 2004: 29). Such conditions exclude a number of standard examples, e.g., that of the German past participle: In *gefragt* 'ask.PST.PTCP' (cf. *frag-en* 'ask-INF'), *ge-...-t* is often said to be a circumfix. However, *ge-* can also combine with *-en* in some irregular verbs, e.g., *getragen* 'carry.PST.PTCP' (cf. *trag-en* 'carry-INF'), and verb stems with an unstressed first syllable do not have *ge-*, e.g., *erfrág-t* 'ascertain-PST.PTCP' and *ertrág-en* 'bear-PST.PTCP' (cf. *erfrág-en* 'ascertain-INF', *ertrág-en* 'bear-INF'). This shows that the prefixal and suffixal parts are independent of each other. The main reason for positing a circumfix seems to be that we cannot easily assign any meaning to *ge-*, but this does not preclude an interpretation of *ge-...-t* as a prefix-suffix combination (cf. Wiese 1996a: 89–98). Sometimes, a more sophisticated analysis allows us to determine the distinct functions of the prefixal and suffixal parts even though they do not have a "single meaning" in the conventional sense (cf. Anderson 1992: 137–145 on agreement markers in Georgian).

In derivational morphology, the assumption of circumfixes may rest on the premise that all intermediate steps must be actual words (see section 4.4; cf. Lieber 2010: 78). Thus, one could argue that the Russian verb *doždat'sja* 'to wait until [the desired result]' is derived from *ždat'* 'to wait' with a circumfix *do-...-sja* because neither **do-ždat'* nor **ždat'-sja* exists (Brown 2011: 494–495). But then again, *dokatit'sja* 'to roll (intr.) until [the goal]' must be derived from *katit'* 'to roll (tr.)' with a prefix *do-* 'until' and a suffix *-sja* 'REFLEXIVE' because *dokatit'* 'to roll (tr.) until [the goal]' and *katit'sja* 'to roll (intr.)' are both in the Russian lexicon. If derivations via potential but unattested words are permitted, this discrepancy disappears and there is no need for a circumfix. Another fundamental decision affects the interpretation of a type of word-formation exemplified by the Slovak adjective *pod-kož-n-ý* 'under-skin-ADJECTIVIZER-NOM.SG.M (subcutaneous)' and the Serbo-Croat noun *do-vrat-ak* 'next_to-door-NOMINALIZER.NOM.SG (doorpost)'. If phrases are allowed to be inputs to word-formation rules (see section 7.1), a derivation from the prepositional phrases *pod kož-ou* 'under [the] skin-INS.SG' and *do vrat-a* 'next_to [the] door-GEN.PL' is plausible; otherwise, the circumfixes *pod-...-n* and *do-...-ak* are an option.

When derivational patterns are stated in terms of citation forms, it must be remembered that the inflectional affixes of these forms are not part of the pattern (see also section 3.4). For example, Belarusian has a verb *uprygožyc'* 'to beautify' from *prygož-y* 'beautiful-NOM.SG.M'. Here, the infinitive suffix *-yc'* must not be mistaken for the suffixal part of a derivational circumfix *u-...-yc'*. It is equally unsatisfactory to set up a circumfix *u-...-y* if the infinitive suffix is taken to consist of *-c'* only. Rather, the only overt affix involved is a prefix, irrespective of how one accounts for the fact that the end result is a verb which belongs to the inflection class with the infinitive suffix -yc' or the theme vowel y (on this issue, see section 4.4 on English *endanger*, etc.; cf. also Schpak-Dolt 2010: 129–134 for a discussion of various analyses of French examples that leads to a different conclusion).

Some linguists believe that all alleged circumfixes can be reanalyzed as affix combinations (e.g., Vardul' 1991: 54–55), while others explicitly prefer one discontinuous affix to two continuous ones (e.g., Mel'čuk 2006: 316). Even according to the second opinion, convincing examples of derivational circumfixes are hard to find in the languages of Europe, and it is therefore impossible to make any general statements about their functions.

5.4 Infix

Infixes are far less common than prefixes and suffixes and it is a generally accepted universal that a language does not have them unless it also has prefixes and/or suffixes (cf. Greenberg 1966: 92). Europe is one of the regions where infixes are very rare. English "expletive infixation" as in *fan-blooming-tastic* is often cited, but it is more of a language game than a word-formation pattern – insertion of an entire word is not a normal form of infixation. A language with several typical derivational infixes is Khmer (Cambodia). One of them, *-n-*, is inserted after the first consonant of the base and serves, among other things, as an instrument nominalizer, e.g., /koah/ 'to raise' → /k⟨n⟩oah/ '⟨INSTNR⟩raise (lever)', /reəŋ/ 'to obstruct' → /r⟨n⟩eəŋ/ '⟨INSTNR⟩obstruct (screen, curtain)'. (In accordance with the Leipzig Glossing Rules, infixes are enclosed in angle brackets ⟨...⟩; the gloss 'INSTNR' appears at the edge near which the infix is located, hence before 'raise' and 'obstruct'.)

Contrary to the definition in (8), the term *infix* is sometimes used for an affix which occurs closer to the root than others. In some descriptions of Swahili (East Africa), for instance, the verb form *a-li-ni-ambia* '3SG.SBJ-PST-1SG.OBJ-tell (he told me)' is said to contain the infixes *li* and *ni* because only the leftmost affix is counted as a prefix. Others call *ni* an infix but *li* a prefix; the reason seems to be that a verb form must contain a tense marker but not necessarily an object agreement marker. In the terminology adopted here, *a-*, *ni-* and *li-* are all prefixes. Some uses of *infix* are motivated by specific assumptions about the derivational history of a word, e.g., that German *entscheidungs-un-freudig* 'decision-NEG-happy (reluctant to make decisions)' should be derived from *entscheidungs-freudig* 'decision-happy (happy to make decisions)' – but it could also be a compound with the second component *unfreudig* (cf. Donalies 2005: 34; see also Moravcsik 2000:

546; Paster 2009: 28). What these alleged infixes have in common is that they occur at a word-internal morph boundary, and this possibility is not excluded if we define an infix as an affix that disrupts a base of any kind. We might therefore want to specify that infixes (and transfixes) are inserted into a root, while prefixes, suffixes and circumfixes attach to stems irrespective of their degree of complexity (cf. Helmbrecht and Lehmann 2008: 281–282). But this is not always true, as the verb *tawagan* 'to call' in Tagalog (Philippines) shows (the suffix -*an* marks directional focus in the indicative and is not relevant here). From this neutral aspect form, the perfective aspect is obtained by infixing -*in*- after the first consonant *t* (*t⟨in⟩awagan*) and the contemplated aspect by reduplicating the first consonant and vowel *ta* (*ta~tawagan*; see section 6.2 on reduplication). In the imperfective aspect, the infix -*in*- appears inside the reduplicative prefix: *t⟨in⟩a~tawagan*. In order to account for such cases, we could define an infix as an affix which occurs inside a base that consists of a single minimal sign (alias morph or morpheme), be it a root or an affix (cf. Moravcsik 2000: 546). It may be more appropriate, however, to say that Tagalog -*in*- is inserted into the entire stem *ta~tawagan*. The best solution, then, may be to retain the original definition according to which an infix occurs inside the base, be it morphologically simple or complex. Unfortunately, the proviso "such that the preceding and following portions are not meaningful by themselves" (Moravcsik 2000: 545) is not correct, as shown by the aspectual infix -*h*- in Choctaw (Oklahoma, USA; cf. Stemberger and Bernhardt 1999: 613–614; Paster 2009: 35–36). It is placed to the right of the penultimate vowel of the stem, and that point is sometimes within a morph (root or prefix) and sometimes at a morph boundary (between prefix and root or between root and suffix). Ultimately, common sense must decide what should count as an infix and what should not.

It has been suggested that all infixes are underlyingly prefixes or suffixes but move in from the edge of the word because of "phonological pressures" (Ussishkin 2007: 457), especially constraints on syllable structure. A favourite example cited in support of this position is the Tagalog agent-focus affix *um*, which appears to be a prefix with vowel-initial stems such as *alis* 'to depart' (*um-alis*) but an infix with consonant-initial stems such as *sigaw* 'to shout' (*s⟨um⟩igaw*), where a better syllable structure – CV rather than VC – is achieved by placing *um* after the first consonant of the base. Phonologically, however, the supposedly vowel-initial stems begin with a glottal stop so that -*um*- is always infixed. Although the case for an underlying prefix would be stronger if it sometimes surfaced as such, this is not essential – but infixes do not always yield phonological structures that are more optimal than those with the corresponding prefix or suffix (cf. Yu 2007: 27–31). It seems, therefore, that genuine infixes do exist (see Yu 2007 for a comprehensive survey and Moravcsik 2000 for a brief overview).

5.5 Transfix

The term *transfix* is not very common and typically refers to vowel patterns in Semitic languages that combine with a root consisting solely of consonants to form a stem with a particular inflectional or derivational meaning. (Terms that one can occasionally find instead include *intercalated affix* and – contrary to normal usage – *interfix*; cf. Stump 2001b: 708; Ussishkin 2007: 463–465.) The Modern Hebrew root /g-d-l/, for instance, can be combined with -a-a-, -a-e-, -a-o- and -o-e- to give the verb forms /ga'dal/ '[he] grew' and /ga'del/ '[he] is growing', the adjective /ga'dol/ 'big' and the noun /'godel/ 'size'. In the examples that are normally given, all the vowels occur between the root consonants, and some definitions of *transfix* explicitly require this (cf. Helmbrecht and Lehmann 2008: 282). A vowel preceding the first or following the last root consonant is, however, sometimes clearly part of the transfix and not a prefix or suffix with an identifiable meaning, e.g., in Maltese *ifqar* 'poorer.M.SG' (cf. *faqar* 'poverty'), where *i--a-* marks the comparative. In addition, Semitic transfixes may consist of a single vowel, i.e. strictly speaking an infix, e.g., in *fqir* 'poor.M.SG'. Since a transfix *-Ø-i-* with a zero vowel (cf. Mel'čuk 1997: 175) is not to everyone's liking, it may be advisable to use a special term for the Semitic vowel patterns, e.g., *diffix*, leaving *transfix* for other affixes that are both disrupted and disrupting (cf. Plungjan 2003: 95). The verb forms *ftaqar* '[he] became poor' and *faqqar* '[he] made poor' pose a further problem: Should the infixed *t* in *ftaqar* and the gemination of the second root consonant in *faqqar* be regarded as part of the transfix? While this is a debatable point, it is clearly not appropriate to decompose *ftaqartu* '[you] became poor' into *f-q-r* and a transfix *-ta-a-tu* (cf. Bossong 2001: 667); rather, the form contains a transfix *-ta-a-* (or a transfix *-a-a-* as well as an infix *-t-*) and the suffix *-tu* '2.PL'. Transfixes must also be distinguished from an intercalation of affix and base that results from phonological metathesis. For instance, the /t/ of the Hebrew prefix /hit/ changes places with a sibilant, as in /hiʃtadel/ '[he] tried hard' from the root /ʃ-d-l/ vs. /hitgadel/ '[he] made himself big (boasted)' from /g-d-l/ (for similar examples with suffixes, cf. Stemberger and Bernhardt 1999: 616–618; Paster 2009: 32).

Transfixes are not a generally recognized type of affix because several other analyses are possible (cf. Broselow 2000; Rubba 2001). Instead of starting from a consonantal root, one could take a specific stem with vowels as basic, e.g., Hebrew /ga'dal/ '[he] grew', and derive the others, e.g., /ga'del/ '[he] is growing' and /gi'del/ '[he] raised', from it by changing the vowels (see section 6.3; cf. also Ussishkin 2007: 464–468 for a slightly different approach). This may be the reason why *transfixation* has also been used for "an alternation at multiple sites throughout the domain" that affects all eligible segments, as in the Basque affective diminutive /poʎica/ from /polita/ 'pretty', which involves palatalization of all coronals (Bye and Svenonius 2012: 431 – but this is not an instance of a transfix as defined in (8). Another approach, that of autosegmental morphology, holds that in a given type of inflected or derived Semitic word both the consonantal root and the vowel pattern must be linked to a template, a skeleton of slots for vowels and consonants, possibly with some pre-specified segments. In this model, Maltese *ftaqar* and *faqqar* must conform to the templates CtVCVC and CVCCVC, respectively; the *-t-* in *ftaqar* is simply part of the template and gemination of *q* in *faqqar* is the answer to the question of how to match up three root consonants with four C slots.

Transfixes play a major role in Maltese, the only Semitic language of Europe (if we exclude Hebrew and Arabic as the languages of liturgy and study in Judaism and Islam, respectively). I am not aware of other European languages with discontinuous affixes that disrupt the base.

5.6 Ambifix

The term *ambifix*, which is sometimes used for a circumfix (cf. Greenberg 1966: 92), normally refers to an affix which can be either prefixed or suffixed. Such an element has also been called *variable-direction affix* (Ussishkin 2007: 460), *mobile affix* (Paster 2009: 34) or, in German, *Wechselaffix* (Bossong 2001: 667). The position of an ambifix may vary freely or it may be determined by phonological, morphological or syntactic conditions (for examples, see Mel'čuk 1997: 162–163; Marušič 2003: 4–9; Paster 2009: 34–36; Rice 2011: 177–178); the existence of phonologically conditioned affix placement is, however, a matter of dispute (see also section 3.3.3). One of the few ambifixes in a European language is the Lithuanian reflexive marker *si*, which appears as a final suffix if the stem is not prefixed but as a prefix immediately before the root if the stem is prefixed, e.g., imperfective *perk-a-si* 'buy-3SG-REFL ([he] buys for himself)' vs. perfective *nu-si-perk-a* 'PERF-REFL-buy-3SG'. Affixes may also occur as prefix and infix or as infix and suffix or even in all three positions (for some examples, cf. Blevins 1999; Marušič 2003: 9–12; Paster 2009: 20; Rice 2011: 177–178; Bye and Svenonius 2012: 470, 475–476); one European instance of three-way variation, that of gender agreement markers in some Northeast Caucasian languages is inflectional.

5.7 Interfix

According to one definition, an *interfix* is an affix that is placed between two roots which together form a compound (Mel'čuk 1982: 86, 1997: 150, 157, 2006:

298–300), but in some of the examples given it actually occurs after a derivational suffix and/or before a derivational prefix. In Russian *social'n-o-ėkonomičeskij* 'social-LINK-economic', for instance, the interfix *-o-* comes after a derivational suffix, the adjectivizer *-n*. The definition must therefore be amended to "between two stems". It is often stressed that an interfix has no meaning in the conventional sense. Although this is sometimes viewed as a defining property (e.g., Haspelmath and Sims 2010: 332), it is not a logical necessity (cf. Mel'čuk 1997: 150). Whether or not "meaningless" elements are signs and belong to a morpheme is an entirely different issue (*pace* Helmbrecht and Lehmann 2008: 279–280). If they do not qualify as signs, not all words can be exhaustively decomposed into signs (or morphemes) or into roots and affixes. This consequence can be avoided by recognizing an interfix as an *empty sign* (one whose meaning is an empty set, cf. Mel'čuk 1982: 51–52, 1997: 15–21) or by regarding the function of indicating the connection between the two stems as its content, as reflected in the gloss 'LINK' (cf. Bergenholtz and Mugdan 1979a: 71). Originally, *interfix* was suggested for an empty sign between a stem and a derivational affix (Lausberg 1953: 229), as in the Spanish diminutive *avion-c-ito* 'airplane-LINK-DIM', which has an additional *-c-* not present in *reloj-ito* 'watch-DIM'. This usage is still widespread in Romance linguistics, but according to the terminology adopted here, an element such as *-c-* is a suffix (if it is recognized as a separate affix at all).

Even after the introduction of *interfix*, empty signs in both compounding and derivation are still occasionally called *infix*, but this usage has been rightly criticized. The terms *linking element* or *linker* (German *Fugenelement*, also *Fugenzeichen* 'linking sign', *Fugenmorphem* 'linking morpheme' or simply *Fuge*) frequently serve as synonyms of *interfix* as defined here, but some authors who employ *linking element* for empty signs in compounding use *interfix* for similar elements in derivation (e.g., Fuhrhop 1998: 24; cf. also Donalies 2005: 44) or as a cover term for both (e.g., Fleischer and Barz 1992: 32–33). Occasionally, two or more of the terms *interfix*, *linking element*, *linking morpheme*, etc. are applied to different subtypes of interfixes.

Interfixes frequently go back to inflectional affixes, especially markers of case and/or number, and are often formally identical with them; the historical developments may, however, be a good deal more complex (cf. Nübling and Szczepaniak 2013: 68–74 on German). Some linguists maintain that compounds can indeed contain certain inflectional affixes, which are then excluded from the category of interfixes (cf. Wiese 1996a: 144–145; Donalies 2005: 45–48 on German), whereas others (including myself) are of the opinion that the erstwhile inflectional markers no longer have that status synchronically so that all elements at the boundary between compound members should be treated in the same way (see section 7.2). An interfix is called *paradigmatic* if it coincides with an inflectional affix that occurs in the paradigm of the lexeme in question. In Icelandic, the interfix -s- in *ávarp-s-fall* 'address-LINK-case(NOM.SG.) (vocative)' is paradigmatic because ÁVARP has a genitive singular in -s. In *kúpling-s-disk-ur* 'clutch-LINK-disk-NOM.SG', -s- is non-paradigmatic because KÚPLING does not have any word form with the suffix -s. Some interfixes have no synchronic connection to inflectional affixes, either because it never existed, as in the case of Greek and Slavic "linking vowels" (cf. Bauer 2000b: 702) or the Iranian "ezafe", or because the inflectional affixes they developed from were lost (e.g., the genitive -s in Dutch, cf. Booij 2002: 34–35, 178–179).

In languages with a variety of interfixes (e.g., many Germanic languages), there are often no hard and fast rules for their distribution, but one can detect statistical tendencies that are primarily based on phonological, morphological or semantic properties of the first compound member. To the extent that interfixes have functions that go beyond holding the compound together, they likewise tend to have more to do with the left than with the right constituent. Phonologically, too, interfixes are more closely connected with the first member of the compound. In view of these facts, an alternative analysis suggests itself: Linking elements in compounds are not distinct linguistic signs (and hence not affixes) but part of the first stem, which thus has two or more alternants (cf. also Fuhrhop 1998: 187). In the Icelandic examples, this means that we should segment *ávarps-fall* and *kúplings-disk-ur*, with *ávarps-* and *kúplings-* as alternants of the stems *ávarp* and *kúpling* – so-called *combining forms* or *compounding stems* (see section 7.2). We could then still describe -s as a linking element, with the understanding that it is a phonological stem extension, but *interfix* or *linking morpheme* would no longer be appropriate. Analogous considerations apply to an empty suffix before a genuine derivational suffix, e.g., -ul in Romanian *frunz-ul-iț-ă* 'leaf-LINK-DIM-SG' from *frunz-ă* 'leaf-SG' (vs. *grădin-iț-ă* 'garden-DIM-SG' from *grădin-ă* 'garden-SG', without -ul), where we have the additional option of assuming allomorphic variation between -iț and -uliț 'DIM' (for arguments in favour of and against the different solutions see Malkiel 1966: 318–319 on Spanish; Wiese 1996a: 100–103 and Motsch 1999: 14 on German). Instead of trying to eliminate interfixes by drawing the morphological boundaries differently, some linguists go in the opposite direction and posit a zero linking element in every compound that does not have an overt one – but if *zero* means 'nothing', it means nothing (see section 5.9).

5.8 Suprafix

Inflectional and derivational meanings can be expressed not only by strings of segmental phonemes but also by suprasegmental features, especially stress and tone (cf. Hyman and Leben 2000). A well-known example are the English verb/ noun pairs that differ in their stress pattern: *imprínt* vs. *ímprint*, *recóil* vs. *récoil*, etc. Tonal morphology plays hardly any role in Europe but is very common in Africa. An oft-quoted example is that of verbs in Ngbaka (DR Congo), which are not specified for tone, e.g., /kpolo/ 'to return'. Different tone patterns are added to them, as in /kpòlò/, /kpōlō/, /kpòló/, /kpóló/ (where ´ marks high tone, ¯ mid tone and ` low tone), to express tense/aspect distinctions (Nida 1949: 63, 66; this description is not quite correct inasmuch as the tense/aspect values are co-determined by the tone of the subject pronoun, by a vowel alternation, here /kpolo/~/kpula/, and by postverbal particles, while it is difficult to assign a unitary meaning to the tone patterns on the verb; cf. Maes 1959: 13, 24–25). The term *suprafix* was proposed for a suprasegmental affix which is added to a neutral base (Nida 1949: 69; cf. also Matthews 1974: 133). *Superfix* is often given as a synonym but originally referred to the stress pattern of a word considered as a "special kind of affix" by which a base and its prefixes and suffixes are "combined and unified" (Trager 1948: 157). Of course, suprasegmental features are not arranged "above" or "below" segmental phonemes but are simultaneous with them so that *simulfix* might seem a better term (Hockett 1954: 212) – but instead of replacing *suprafix*, *simulfix* was put to a variety of other uses, none of which were ever broadly accepted (see sections 5.1, 5.3, 6.3).

Although one could conceivably decompose *imprínt* and *ímprint* into a stressless and word-class neutral stem *imprint* and a suprafix – ´– 'VERB' or ´ – – 'NOUN', an analysis that is more in keeping with the overall structure of English takes the verb as basic and derives the noun by means of a stress shift, i.e. a process and not an affix in the usual sense (see section 6.3). Some linguists define *suprafix* or *superfix* as referring to such a suprasegmental change (e.g., Bauer 2003: 342, 2004: 98; cf. also Rubba 2001: 680, where *suprafix* is extended to multiple segmental changes). It is not always easy to decide whether modification or addition of suprasegmental features is involved.

Suprasegmental alternations are not necessarily due to a direct change of features. Sometimes, it is more plausible to assume an affix with an expression that consists solely of a "floating" tone which then affects the tones of the base (cf. Hyman and Leben 2000: 589 for examples; see also Akinlabi 2011: 1945, 1957–1961). In some languages, stress placement can be described in terms of stress-relevant properties of the constituents of words, and derivational processes can change these properties. One such language is Abkhaz, where each element of a word (CV, V or C) is either dominant or recessive and stress falls on the last of an uninterrupted sequence of dominant elements. In the masdar (verbal noun) /aṣa'ra/ 'dawning', the general definite prefix ("article") /a-/, the root /ṣa/ and the masdar suffix /-ra/ are all dominant and therefore /-ra/ is stressed. When an abstract noun is formed from the masdar, /-ra/ becomes recessive, which has the effect of moving the stress back: /aˈṣara/ 'dawn' (cf. Hewitt 2005: 101, 117), but the application of "make /-ra/ recessive" does not result in an overt difference between the masdar /aˈdərra/ 'knowing' and the abstract noun /aˈdərra/ 'knowledge'. Here, root-initial /də/ is dominant and root-final /r/ recessive so that stress must fall on /də/ and cannot be affected by the properties of /-ra/ (George Hewitt, p.c.).

5.9 Zero

Returning once again to the inflectional paradigms of Lower Sorbian nouns in (5), we can observe that all grammatical words of the lexemes DUB and ŽONA have a case/number affix – except for the nominative and accusative singular of DUB. This anomaly can be rectified if we allow the expression of a linguistic sign to be zero (i.e. an empty set; cf. Mel'čuk 1982: 48). We can then postulate the *zero affixes* -Ø 'NOM.SG' and -Ø 'ACC.SG', which are *zero allomorphs* of the morphemes {NOM.SG} and {ACC.SG}. Importantly, these morphemes have non-zero allomorphs as well, e.g., -*a* 'NOM.SG' and -*u* 'ACC.SG' in *žon-a* and *žon-u*. English nouns, though, never have an overt affix in the singular, and if we analyze *book* as *book*-Ø 'book-SG' as opposed to *book-s* 'book-PL', the morpheme {SG} is a *zero morpheme*, one that has no non-zero allomorphs. Since the introduction of zero elements opens a Pandora's box, various principles have been formulated with the aim of preventing an uncontrolled proliferation of zeros, e.g.,
– zero morphemes are not allowed;
– one may not "treat overt distinctions as meaningless and covert distinctions [between zero and nothing, JM] as meaningful" (Nida 1948: 415);
– zero elements must be recognizable.

Helpful though such guidelines are, each of them excludes some reasonable analyses, and in the end we have to rely on our good judgment (cf. Bergenholtz and Mugdan 2000: 440–443; see also Mel'čuk 2006: 469–516). We should bear in mind, however, that *zero* is not just a more fancy word for *nothing*: A zero affix is a linguistic element and not the same thing as an unfilled affix slot.

In word-formation, zero elements are much more difficult to justify than in inflection, and some linguists do not allow derivational zero affixes at all (e.g., Volodin and Chrakovskij 1991: 129; Mel'čuk 2006: 504–505). *Zero derivation*, i.e. derivation by means of a zero affix, is frequently invoked in cases where lexemes of different word classes (or subclasses, e.g., genders) have homonymous stems, e.g., *cook* as in *please cook the vegetables* and *she is a good cook* or Latvian *direktor-*, the stem of a masculine and a feminine noun which take different case/number suffixes, *direktor-s* 'headmaster-NOM.SG' vs. *direktor-e* 'headmistress-NOM.SG', etc. If the verb *cook* is basic, the noun could be derived from it by means of the affix -Ø 'AGNR' (short for 'AGENT NOMINALIZER'). A major argument in favour of this zero affix is the existence of overt nominalizers with the same function, e.g., *-er* in *baker*. This approach leads to a multitude of zeros with different contents (cf. Bergenholtz and Mugdan 2000: 445–446) and it is not always clear which overt affix should be taken as the analogue. For example, does Dutch *zuiver-* 'to make pure' (here shown without the infinitive suffix *-en* of the citation form) from *zuiver* 'pure' have a zero suffix because of *blond* 'blond' → *blondeer-* 'to make blond (bleach)' or a zero prefix because of *warm* 'warm' → *verwarm-* 'to make warm' or perhaps both? There are two major theoretical alternatives to zero derivation of this type: *conversion* (see article 11) and *multifunctionality*. Although often equated with zero derivation, conversion is by no means the same thing: It is a process that changes syntactic (and possibly also semantic) features and leaves no "visible" traces. Hence, a verb that was converted from a noun should have the same properties as a primary verb. By contrast, a zero affix is a linguistic element and should behave like an overt affix, be it that where overt affixes cannot attach, zero affixes cannot attach either, be it that word-formation processes can distinguish between zero-affixed and primary stems (which does not seem to be the case; cf. Meder and Mugdan 1990: 100–102; Eschenlohr 1999: 60–63, 221). Both zero derivation and conversion effect a *transposition* from one word class to another (or *motion* from one gender to another), on the premise that one member of the pair is basic and the other derived. Multifunctionality, on the other hand, means that English is assumed to have a single stem *cook* which can serve as both a noun stem and a verb stem without any intervening word-formation process (see also section 7.4). These three analyses are not only conceptually quite different and make different empirical predictions but may describe different phenomena that can co-exist in the same language (cf. van Lier 2012).

While those who speak, indiscriminately, of "conversion or zero derivation" attach little importance to the mechanism involved, more theoretically minded linguists have deliberately postulated zero affixes in order to uphold their hypotheses. For instance, if one believes in the principle that, at least in English, prefixes may not change word class (cf. sections 4.4, 5.3), one can dismiss counter-examples such as *endanger* by positing a zero suffix that supplies the feature 'VERB'. It goes without saying that zeros of this kind are highly suspect.

6 Morphological processes

6.1 Typology of processes

As the comparison of *goose/geese* with *proof/proofs*, etc. in (2) has already shown, affixation (see section 5) is not the only means of expressing a grammatical meaning. Intuitively, we would say that *geese* is formed from *goose* by changing the vowel /u:/ to /i:/, i.e. by a *morphological process* (Mel'čuk 1997: 325–350, 2000, 2006: 288–320) – also known as *morphological operation* (Booij 2012: 35–42) or *morphophonological operation* (Spencer 1998) – which changes the expression side of the base (for the theoretical consequences of this analysis, see section 6.5). If we confine ourselves to segmental expressions, there are four ways in which a string of segments can be altered:
– addition: one or more segments are added;
– substitution: one or more segments are replaced by others;
– permutation: the segments are rearranged in a different order (apparently, the only type that occurs in natural languages is metathesis, where two segments change places);
– subtraction: one or more segments are deleted.

Each of these changes can occur as the exponent of a grammatical meaning but also as a purely phonological process or a diachronic sound change. Sometimes, the same term serves for both morphological and phonological processes (e.g., *metathesis*), sometimes the terminologies diverge (e.g., *infixation* vs. *epenthesis* and *subtraction* vs. *elision, apocope*, etc.). Among the morphological processes, substitution (see section 6.3) is next in importance to addition (affixation). Subtraction is rare but has generated a great deal of interest (see section 6.4). While metathesis as a phonological process is not uncommon (see section 5.5 for a Hebrew example), it is marginal as a morphological one (cf. Becker 2000; see also Mel'čuk 1997: 296–297; Spencer 1998: 138–140) and will not be discussed further.

Many enumerations of morphological processes include compounding. This is defensible if *morphological process* is understood in a broader sense, but compounding differs from the others in that it does not express a grammatical meaning (cf. Mel'čuk 2006: 288–290, 297–299); it is therefore not included here. Suppletion, which appears in various lists (e.g., Matthews 1991: 139), is not a process but a relationship (cf. Mel'čuk 2000: 531, 2006: 309), and it is not correct to say that, for instance, the English comparatives *better* and *worse* are "formed by suppletion". One process that does belong here is reduplication but it does not easily fit into the above classification. (This issue and some terminological matters are addressed in section 6.2; for general overviews from different perspectives, see article 18 on reduplication as well as Wiltshire and Marantz 2000; Raimy 2011; for attempts at more rigorous definitions, cf. Mel'čuk 1996: 41–52, 1997: 273–288; Stolz, Stroh and Urdze 2011: 1–70.)

6.2 Reduplication

The term *reduplication* suggests that something is doubled or repeated, and this is indeed how reduplication is typically described. Such an explanation will do in simple cases, such as Chuvash total reduplication as in *şĕr* 'hundred' → *şĕrşĕr* 'hundreds', *pin* 'thousand' → *pinpin* 'thousands', and Aghul partial reduplication as in *ʕafú* 'five' → *ʕá~ʕafu* 'DISTR~five (five each)', *jerxí* 'six' → *jé~jerxi* 'DISTR~six (six each)'. (According to Rule 10 of the Leipzig glossing rules, "reduplication" – which apparently means partial reduplication – "is treated similarly to affixation" but marked by a tilde ~ instead of a hyphen.) Here, it seems that a certain string of segments is copied and appended to the base. The copy is often called *reduplicant*. The highly similar term *reduplicand* has been suggested for the "original" that is copied; if it is adopted, it is advisable not to use *reduplicant* but some other term, e.g., *image* or *replicate*, for the copy (cf. Mel'čuk 1996: 41–42, 2006: 301; Stolz, Stroh and Urdze 2011: 40). The *reduplicative base* is that string from which the reduplicant may copy. (On the relationship between the reduplicative base and the entire base to which the reduplicant attaches, see Hogoboom 2003; Haugen 2009; Inkelas 2012: 357–359.) Another term for the string within which reduplication applies is *domain* (Mel'čuk 1996: 41–42; cf. Stolz, Stroh and Urdze 2011: 43–44). In partial reduplication, the reduplicant is frequently viewed as a special type of affix that is defined only in terms of its prosodic constituents (or, for the sake of simplicity, as a sequence of vowel and consonant slots). *Duplifix* has sometimes been understood as a term for such reduplicative affixes although this was not its original meaning (see below). *Parafix* (see also section 5.1) was proposed for a specific mechanism to describe reduplication (by means of an affix that is attached in parallel to the stem and only later linearized, Clements 1985: 47) but has also come to be employed for reduplicative affixes in general. The picturesque term *chameleon morph*[eme] (Hockett 1950: 79) underscores that the expression of a reduplicative affix is determined by its environment.

A number of observations suggest that reduplication is not necessarily plain repetition.

a) The reduplicant need not be adjacent to the reduplicative base: In Temiar (Malaysia), the continuative aspect of a triconsonantal verb stem $C_1.C_2VC_3$ is formed by inserting a copy of the last consonant just before the final syllable,

resulting in $C_1C_3.C_2VC_3$, e.g., s.lɔg 'to lie_down' → sg.lɔg (periods indicate syllable boundaries).
b) The segments to be copied need not be contiguous (before or after reduplication has applied; cf. Hogoboom 2003: 177–179 on copying from both sides): If a Temiar verb stem has the shape C_1VC_2, the consonants are copied without the vowel and are prefixed to give $C_1C_2.C_1VC_2$ in the continuative aspect, e.g., gəl 'to sit_down' → gl.gəl.
c) The copy may diverge from the original string: Karaim uses a reduplicant CV*p*- to express a high degree of a property, as in *kap~kara* 'very~black', *top~tolu* 'very~full'. In Akan (Ghana), pluractional verbs have a prefixal reduplicant that consists of the first consonant of the base and a vowel which agrees with the first vowel of the base in the features [±back] and [±tense] but is always [+high], e.g., /sɛʔ/ 'resemble' → /sɪ~sɛʔ/, /saʔ/ 'cure' → /sɪ~saʔ/, /soʔ/ 'seize' → /su~soʔ/. From the perspective of the reduplicative base, this is *inexact reduplication*; viewed from the reduplicant, this type of reduplication is characterized by prespecified or fixed segments (e.g., Karaim *p*) or features (e.g., Akan [+high]). Reduplication with so-called *fixed segmentism* (Alderete et al. 1997; why *-ism*?) has occasionally been regarded as a combination of reduplication and affixation (e.g., Bergenholtz and Mugdan 1979a: 73) and a special term, *duplifix*, has been suggested for it (Haspelmath 2002: 24), but given that reduplication with a fixed segment is merely the limiting case of prespecification, it is not reasonable to single it out.

These forms of reduplication can still be described by means of an underspecified affix which acquires the missing features by copying them from the base, and if we assume that reduplication first creates a full copy that is subsequently truncated and/or attribute certain surface oddities to the workings of phonological rules, we can perhaps even maintain that the underlying operation is repetition. But if reduplication is to be a subtype of affixation, we must be able to specify the affix involved. This is possible if the reduplicant has a constant shape, as in Aghul, where it is always a CV sequence that is reduplicated, whether it is a syllable of the base (*ʃá~ʃa.fu*) or not (*jé~jer.xi*). There are, however, cases where the base rather than the reduplicant determines how much is copied, e.g., in Yaqui (Mexico). Here, habitual verbs are formed by copying a complete syllable, be it CV as in *vu.sa* 'awaken' → *vu.vu.sa* or CVC as in *vam.se* 'to hurry' → *vam.vam.se* (cf. Haugen 2009: 507–508). Sometimes, it is the entire output which must have a certain shape – this is true of Temiar, where the continuative conforms to the template CC.CVC for both bi- and triconsonantal stems (cf. Gafos 1998: 234–249; see also Inkelas 2012: 366–371). Such facts lend support to the view that reduplication is not a special kind of addition but a type of modification on a par with substitution, etc. (e.g., Mel'čuk 2006: 294–298) or a process *sui generis*.

Reduplication as a morphological process, and specifically as a productive process of word-formation, must be distinguished from

- syntactic doubling with a non-repetitive meaning (syntactic total reduplication, cf. Stolz, Stroh and Urdze 2011: 3, 26–29) as in Biblical Hebrew *'īš 'īš* 'man man (each man)', where doubled phrases, e.g., *yōm laš-šānāh yōm laš-šānāh* 'day for.the-year, day for.the-year (a day for each year)', provide additional evidence that this is not a matter of word-formation;
- iterative affixation as in Polish *dom* 'house' → *dom-ek* 'house-DIM (little house)' → *dom-ecz-ek* 'house-dim-DIM (tiny house)', where *-ecz* and *-ek* are allomorphs of the same morpheme (cf. Stolz, Stroh and Urdze 2011: 34–36 on Hungarian and Turkish);
- reduplicative roots and stems which do not follow a pattern that is regular on both the expression and the content side, as in English *zigzag*, where the parts *zig* and *zag* do not occur by themselves and have no meaning (cf. Stolz, Stroh and Urdze 2011: 33–34 on Maltese), or Yiddish *pile-plóim* 'great wonders', which has lost the phrasal structure of its Hebrew source *pil'ēj pəlā'īm* 'wonders.of wonders' and is synchronically neither morphologically segmentable nor regularly related to *péle* 'wonder'.

Unfortunately, these distinctions are not always observed, and what studies of word-formation in individual languages describe under the heading "reduplication" varies greatly.

6.3 Substitution

The substitution of segments as in *goose* → *geese* or of suprasegmental features as in *recóil* → *récoil* (see section 5.8) is also called *replacement* or *internal modification* (e.g., Bauer 2004: 57–58; for an overview of types of substitution and a discussion of theoretical issues, see Lieber 2000). The term *apophony* is used either for any substitution or specifically for a vowel change (Bauer 2004: 17–18). In a wider sense, *apophony* includes subtraction and metathesis as well (cf. Mel'čuk 1982: 98–102, 2006: 302–304). Other terms that can similarly be applied more broadly or to specific phenomena in individual languages include *mutation*, *gradation* and, for vowels, *ablaut*. Vowel changes due to assimilation, in particular fronting before a high front vowel in the following syllable, are known as *umlaut*; historically, English *goose* → *geese* belongs to this type. In German linguistics, there is a tradition of calling derivational vowel changes (as in *sing* → *song*) *implicit deriva-*

tion as opposed to explicit derivation with an affix (e.g., Fleischer and Barz 1992: 51; Donalies 2005: 132–133).

Attempts at construing substitution as an additive process operate with a "mutating" infix that manifests itself only through its effect (Bossong 2001: 667) or with a featural affix that coalesces with one or more segments of the base (Akinlabi 2011; Bye and Svenonius 2012: 443–451; cf. also Volodin and Chrakovskij 1991: 116–117). Such an affix has been called *simulfix* (cf. Wallis 1956), but the term is sometimes extended to substitutions in general irrespective of whether they are analyzed in this way (cf. Lieber 2010: 79; see also section 5.8 on other meanings of *simulfix*).

In European languages, substitution quite often accompanies affixation (see section 6.6); more rarely, it is the only or primary exponent of a grammatical meaning. Productive substitution is largely confined to inflection, e.g., plural formation of nouns in several Germanic and Romance language varieties which originally had a suffix that conditioned palatalization of the preceding consonant or fronting/raising of the preceding vowel. Loss of the suffix resulted in morphologization of the alternation, which could then be analogically extended to lexemes that did not have it originally. In derivational morphology, a number of non-productive substitution patterns can be observed; in some descriptions, they appear under "conversion" on the assumption that the substitution is merely a side-effect. Verb/noun pairs similar to English *sing/song* occur in Germanic, Romance and Balto-Slavic languages; for example, the verb 'to fly' and the noun 'flight' (without inflectional suffixes) are /vul-/ and /vɔwl/ in the Bolognese dialect of Italian, /letɕ-/ and /lot/ in Polish, /skrìd-/ (past tense stem) and /skrĩ:d-/ in Lithuanian. Causative verbs that are derived from intransitive verbs by a vowel change, e.g., English *fall* → *fell* 'to cause to fall', are found in other Germanic languages as well. In the Circassian branch of Northwest Caucasian, intransitive and transitive verb roots often differ only in the vowel, /a/ vs. /ə/, e.g., Kabardian /txa-/ 'to be involved in writing' vs. /txə-/ 'to write [something]', and this may be a case of substitution /a/ → /ə/.

The limited role of substitution as a morphological process can be attributed to its lack of constructional iconicity or diagrammaticity: Additional content is not matched by additional expression. Languages of the agglutinating type (represented in Europe by Turkic, Mongolian and, to a lesser extent, Uralic) value iconicity very highly and therefore avoid substitution, whereas the Indo-European languages exploit its main advantage, brevity, to a limited degree. Where affixation and substitution can express the same grammatical meaning, e.g., past tense in Germanic weak and strong verbs such as *sin/sinn-ed* vs. *sing/sang*, one might think that a preference for the economy of substitution over the iconicity of affixation should correlate with a high text frequency of the lexemes. In actual fact, the relationship between frequency and irregularity is much more complex (cf. Meder and Mugdan 1990: 87–89 on German).

6.4 Subtraction

Subtraction expresses a grammatical meaning by deleting part of the base, prototypically the final segment (for a survey, cf. Dressler 2000). An example that seems to be more convincing than most comes from Tohono O'odham (Arizona): Perfective verbs are formed from imperfective ones by deleting the last C or, in certain cases, VC, e.g., /hihim/ → /hihi/ 'to laugh', /hi:nk/ → /hi:n/ 'to bark', /gɨgoṣid/ → /gɨgoṣ/ 'to feed' (Kosa 2008: 18). The decisive reason for assuming this direction of derivation is that otherwise there would be a number of imperfective suffixes, /-m/, /-k/, /-id/, etc., with an unpredictable distribution. The same argument has been applied to adjectives in spoken French, where the shorter masculine form is predictable from the longer feminine form but not vice versa, e.g., /ot/ → /o/ 'high', /lurd/ → /lur/ 'heavy'. Here, a simple phonological solution preserves the semantically more plausible derivation of the feminine from the masculine: If the underlying representations are |ot| 'high(M)' and |ot-ə| 'high-F' (cf. the spellings *haut* and *haute*), the surface forms can be obtained by applying deletion of the final consonant and deletion of final /ə/ in that order. In fact, most alleged instances of subtractive morphology have been reanalyzed in one way or another (cf. Kosa 2008: 5–15); some are non-productive and concern a very small number of items, some are better interpreted as derivation of the longer form from the shorter one and some may involve an opposition between an explicit affix and zero (e.g., Bolognese Italian /skra:na/ 'chair' vs. /skra:n/ 'chairs', /do:na/ 'woman' vs. /do:n/ 'women', where /-a/ may be a singular suffix, cf. /raga:sa/ 'girl' vs. /raga:si/ 'girls').

In derivational morphology, subtraction must be distinguished from phenomena that are sometimes conflated with it, namely clipping and other shortening processes (see article 13) and backformation (see article 12). The latter is not a morphological process at all but a diachronic development: Sometimes a word that contains a derivational affix (or looks as if it did) exists in the lexicon without an underived counterpart and is therefore not fully segmentable (see section 2.2). This was true of the English noun *sculptor* when it was borrowed in the 17th century without a base verb. Backformation consisted in the creation of the verb *sculpt*, and when it entered the lexicon (according to the *Oxford English Dictionary*, it is first attested in 1864), *sculptor* became a word derived from *sculpt* notwithstanding the fact that it existed before its base. The argument that backformation "must be allowed for in a synchronic grammar if it is still a current method of forming lexemes" (Bauer 1983: 65) is fallacious; it is based on a misinterpretation of synchrony vs. diachrony as "current" vs. "former" and does not distinguish the technique of backformation that is available to native speakers from the derivational relationships that hold between items in the lexicon at a given point in time.

Unlike backformations, clippings such as *bike* from *bicycle* and name truncations such as *Liz* from *Elizabeth* (which should perhaps not be lumped together) are indeed synchronically derived from the longer forms by truncation. These processes are often said to differ from subtraction in that they do not change the meaning. However, they frequently signal endearment, contempt and the like and thus resemble derivations with hypocoristic or pejorative affixes. The relevant difference seems to be a formal one: Subtraction deletes a specified part of the base (e.g., the last consonant), whereas templatic truncation (clipping, etc.) deletes whatever is needed to arrive at a specified shape (e.g., a single closed syllable); when this is taken into account, another alleged difference between subtraction and clipping, regularity vs. unpredictability, cannot serve as a criterion either (cf. Alber and Arndt-Lappe 2012).

In addition to backformation and templatic truncation, we must eliminate two further patterns that sometimes figure as derivational "subtraction" in the literature. Both can be illustrated by Russian *lirika* 'lyric_poetry' → *lirik* 'lyric_poet'. First, we must bear in mind that *lirika* has an inflectional suffix *-a* 'NOM.SG', whereas *lirik* has none (or -Ø): The stems are identical, and only the citation forms create the illusion of subtractive word-formation. Second, it could be argued that *lirik* contains the same derivational suffix *-ik* as many other personal nouns; if so, stem-final *-ik* is truncated before derivational *-ik* just as it is truncated before *-izm* in *lir-izm* 'lyricism'. Truncation of the base in conjunction with affixation is quite common and can affect both phonological strings (see section 6.6 on German) and morphological units, e.g., the verbal suffix *-ate* in *nominate* → *nominee* (cf. Aronoff 1976: 88–97, where *truncation* refers specifically to this type). In the latter situation, one could also speak of the replacement of one affix by another, so-called "paradigmatic word-formation" (cf. Booij 2002: 6–7, 102–103). At any rate, we are not dealing with subtraction as the primary exponent of a derivational meaning.

For the remaining examples of derivational subtraction that have been cited, alternative analyses can be offered. In pairs such as Serbo-Croat *Hrvatsk-a* 'Croatia-NOM.SG' / *Hrvat* 'Croat(NOM.SG)' (inhabitant name), the direction of derivation is debatable: Is a Croat someone who lives in Croatia or is Croatia the country of the Croats? Apart from that, the great diversity of formal relations between the names of countries, regions and cities on the one hand and inhabitant names on the other (which can be observed in many European languages, with remarkable cross-linguistic differences in detail) makes one wonder whether derivational rules are at play at all. Moreover, in *Hrvatska* → *Hrvat* as well as in the patterns exemplified by French /fotografi/ 'photography; photograph' → /fotograf/ 'photographer' and Bulgarian *mišk-a* 'mouse-SG' → *miš-i* 'mouse's-M.SG' (adjective as in *miši zăb* 'mouse tooth', etc.), the deleted material is not phonologically defined as it should be in true subtraction. Rather, it is a derivational affix (although in Bulgarian, in contrast to Russian *myš* 'mouse' → *myška* 'mouse.DIM', only the derived form *miška* exists), and one might consider the possibility that both members of each pair are derived from a common base and not one from the other. In sum, in derivational as in inflectional morphology, there are no uncontested instances of subtraction. This is not surprising: As a counter-iconic process in which more content is coupled with less expression, subtraction is clearly the worst option.

6.5 Elements and operations

Substitution and subtraction present a challenge to building-block models of morphology. American structuralists therefore came up with the idea that *goose* and *geese* have a discontinuous stem /g...s/ and infixes /u:/ 'SG' and /i:/ 'PL' or that *geese* consists of an allomorph of {goose} and a zero suffix Ø 'PL'. These counter-intuitive analyses, the second of which would work for subtraction as well, were soon abandoned in favour of the tenet that a "morpheme", i.e. the expression of a linguistic sign, can be either a string of segments or a process that manipulates such a string (see also Mel'čuk 2006: 295–297, where both entities and operations are sign-expressions but are systematically kept apart). In this way, all morphology involves the concatenation of signs, and terms such as *replacive morph*[*eme*] and *subtractive morph*[*eme*] (cf. Nida 1948: 440–441), *simulfix* (see section 6.3) and *disfix* (Hardy and Montler 1988: 389) are symptomatic of the reinterpretation of processes as entities. (*Subtractive morph*[*eme*] is sometimes erroneously used for what is subtracted – it is, however, not the deleted material but the process of deletion that expresses a grammatical meaning.) Such approaches stem from the belief that affixation is more "natural" (although there is some experimental evidence that speakers can learn stem changes as easily as affixes, cf. Bybee and Newman 1995) or follow from specific assumptions about the modular structure of grammar (cf. Bye and Svenonius 2012: 428, where non-concatenative effects are attributed to the phonological component).

At the other extreme, we find models that reinterpret entities as processes and do away with inflectional affixes as linguistic elements: Morphosyntactic features trigger certain string manipulations, among which addition has no pride of place. On this view, (inflectional) morphology is "a-morphous" in the sense that it operates without (affixal) morphs, i.e. minimal signs (cf. Anderson 1992: 1–2). The two models are not mutually exclusive, however, inasmuch as the second describes how one can get from a lexeme with a set of morphosyntactic feature values to the corresponding word form (e.g., the 1st person plural past indicative of the Catalan verb CANTAR 'to sing' is expressed by *cantàvem*), which is the perspective of the speaker, while the first shows how one can infer the meaning of a complex word from the meanings of its constituents (e.g., the combination of *cant-* 'sing', *-av* 'PAST.IND' and *-em* '1PL' gives 'we sang'), which is part of the task of the hearer.

6.6 Multiple processes

Very often, a given grammatical meaning seems to be expressed by several morphological processes simultaneously – this has been called *extended exponence* (Matthews 1974: 149–150; cf. Coates 2000: 622–623, where extended and multiple exponence are distinguished). For instance, German diminutives are characterized by a suffix *-chen* (e.g., *Leiter* 'ladder' → *Leiterchen*) and possibly one or more of the following:

– umlaut, a vowel substitution, orthographically a→ä, o→ö, u→ü (e.g., *Nagel* 'nail' → *Nägelchen*);
– truncation of stem-final *-e* /ə/ or *-en* (e.g., *Riemen* 'strap' → *Riemchen*); this can be treated as a purely phonological phenomenon (according to another opinion, stem-final *-e* and *-en* are always derivational suffixes and do not occur when another noun-forming suffix does, cf. Wiese 1996a: 26);
– insertion of *-el* after the velars *g*, *ng* /ŋ/, *ch* /x/ but not *k* (e.g., *Strich* 'line' → *Strichelchen*; *Kuchen* 'cake' → *Küchelchen* illustrates the combination of all processes).

In such a situation, many linguists – tacitly or, more rarely, expressly – follow the "principle of a single morphological process" (cf. Mel'čuk 1982: 79–80, 2000: 533–534, 2006: 314–318) and select one of the morphological processes as the exponent of the content in question, relegating the others to the status of "meaningless" side effects. There are two major reasons why in our example the suffix *-chen* should be regarded as the exponent of 'DIMINUTIVE'. One is that, other things being equal, an affix is the preferred exponent because addition ranks higher on a hierarchy of naturalness than substitution and subtraction. More importantly, *chen*-suffixation is the process that always occurs; umlaut, *e(n)*-truncation and *el*-insertion are obligatory when the phonological preconditions are met but are not applicable to all bases. An even stronger case for the "meaninglessness" of umlaut can be made with agent nominalizations in -*er*, where some of the eligible bases exhibit umlaut and others don't (see section 4.3 on *Träger* 'carrier' vs. *Fahrer* 'driver').

Other morphologists – again tacitly or expressly – reject the idea that 'DIMIN-UTIVE' has the suffix -*chen* as its only exponent or marker, whereas it triggers umlaut, *e(n)*-truncation and *el*-insertion without being expressed by them (e.g., Wurzel 1989: 51; Stump 2001a: 3–7, 10–11); this tends to go hand in hand with the rejection of building-block models. Instead, it is assumed that all the morphological processes taken together express the content in question – with the corollary that morphologically conditioned stem allomorphy (see section 2.4) is logically impossible. Some who take this position weaken it by admitting that the processes are not equal in rank and identify one of them as the main exponent (e.g., Matthews 1991: 181).

Suprasegmental processes that accompany segmental ones in inflection are often best described separately; the complex stress alternations in some Balto-Slavic languages, for instance, constitute stress paradigms that are fairly independent of the affix paradigms (see section 3.4). Derivational affixes, on the other hand, are typically characterized by a particular behaviour with regard to stress or tone: Some are neutral and preserve the stress or tone of the base, whereas others impose their own pattern or modify the pattern of the base in a certain way.

7 Inputs and outputs of word-formation rules

Before we can turn to the general questions as to which linguistic units serve as inputs and outputs of word-formation rules (section 7.3) and whether they are specified for word class (section 7.4), we have to address two specific issues: Can phrases (section 7.1) and inflectional forms (section 7.2) be constituents of complex words? Examples of both phenomena have been reported for well over a century (cf. Baudouin de Courtenay 1869 on Polish) and have generated substantial controversy. Non-morphological inputs, notably letters and syllables (see article 13 on clipping, sections 3.3–3.4), and word-formation that is not rule based (see article 19 on word-creation) will not be considered here.

7.1 Phrases as input

It is frequently claimed that phrases can serve as inputs to word-formation rules. What counts as a phrasal compound or a phrasal derivative is, however, often not clearly defined but simply taken for granted, and the phenomena that have been subsumed under these rubrics are quite varied. A phrasal input is most likely to be posited if typical traits of a phrase are still present in the output, as in Dutch *hetelúchtballon* 'hot air balloon', which seems to preserve the agreement suffix *-e* of *hete̲ lúcht* 'hot air' as well as the phrasal stress pattern. However, a phrasal base has also been assumed for compounds like Dutch *róodbuikpapegaai* 'red belly parrot', where the constituent *róodbuik* lacks the *-e* of *rode búik* 'red belly' and has compound stress, and for derivatives like *red-bellied* in the corresponding English name *Red-bellied Parrot*. Function words are another characteristic of phrases that appears to occur word-internally, e.g., the conjunction *en* 'and' in Dutch *peper-en-zout-stel* 'pepper and salt set' and the preposition *für* 'for' in German *Wort-für-Wort-Übersetzung* 'word for word translation'. In other compounds, comparable relations remain unexpressed, as in Swedish *öst-väst-konflikt* 'East-West conflict', which can be paraphrased as *konflikt mellan öst och väst* 'conflict between East and West'. For some morphologists, *öst-väst* is nonetheless a compound member of the same kind as *peper-en-zout*, be it a phrase or a compound (cf. Booij 2002: 146–151).

Often, a phrase is postulated as the input to a word-formation rule if the constituents that belong together semantically do not form an existing word (see section 4.4 on unattested intermediate steps). Dutch *heteluchtballon*, for instance, cannot consist of *hete* 'hot' and *luchtballon* 'air balloon' (both of which are attested words) because it does not mean 'air balloon that is hot' but 'balloon that operates with hot air'. But although *hetelucht* must be regarded as one of the immediate constituents for semantic reasons, it does not occur as a word by itself.

Many linguists reject phrasal inputs to word-formation rules altogether because the model of grammar they advocate does not allow the kinds of interactions between syntax and morphology that would be required. In order to maintain this "No Phrase Constraint", alleged examples of phrasal compounds and derivatives must be analyzed differently. The alternatives that can be pursued include the following:

a) The complex word has a different bracketing. For example, instead of regarding a so-called "synthetic compound" such as Dutch *groenogig* 'green-eyed' as a derivative from the phrase *groen-e og-en* 'green-PL eye-PL' (with plural suffixes that do not occur in the derivative), we could view it as a compound with a second component that does not occur as a word, viz. **ogig* 'eyed' (for some discussion, cf. Booij 2002: 158–160 and Donalies 2005: 91–93).

b) The supposed phrasal constituent is a compound. For the type *roodbuikpapegaai*, for instance, one can argue that *roodbuik* is a compound rather than a phrase. Since compounds like *roodbuik* are not productive except as first members of compounds, this analysis presupposes that possible words are

admissible as constituents of complex words (see section 4.4; cf. Booij 2002: 148–151).
c) The supposed complex word is a syntactic construction. This option is available in languages such as English where so-called compounding often consists in mere juxtaposition. While some regard *local body elections* as a compound, others classify it as an entity between a noun (N) and a full noun phrase (NP), with *local body* being a nominal modifier of *elections* (cf. Carstairs-McCarthy 1998: 213).
d) The complex word is created in a single step. In particular, simultaneous application of compounding and derivation is a solution for *groenogig*, etc. that avoids the need to posit constituents **groen-oog* or **og-ig* that do not exist as independent words. A variant of this approach is to assume a template [A [N-*ig*]$_A$]$_A$ 'having N with property A', a conflation of the independently motivated templates [A A]$_A$ and [N-*ig*]$_A$ (cf. *lichtgroen* 'light green' and *kleurig* 'colourful'). While it has the bracketing suggested in (a), it takes into account that A has semantic scope over N only and not over N-*ig* and that N-*ig* is not necessarily an attested word (cf. Booij 2002: 159–160, 2005: 128–129).
e) The phrase is quoted. It might seem, for example, that *no phrase constraint* itself disproves the constraint because *no phrase* is a phrase, but one could counter that in this case *no phrase* is being mentioned rather than used (cf. Carstairs-McCarthy 1998: 214). This analysis is supported by the occasional use of quotation marks, as in the German newspaper example *die „Sicherer-als-Bargeld"-Idee* 'the "safer than cash" idea' (Lawrenz 2006: 72) and by compounds with foreign-language items or non-alphabetic signs, e.g., German *ihre C'est-la-vie-Haltung* 'her c'est-la-vie attitude' (with a French clause) and *das @-Zeichen* 'the @-sign' (Wiese 1996b: 186–187), which demonstrate that linguistic elements of any kind can be quoted as part of a complex word.

7.2 Inflectional forms as input

In many descriptions of individual languages, certain derivatives and compounds are said to contain inflectional forms, for instance Icelandic *orð-a-bók* 'word-GEN.PL-book (dictionary)' and Yiddish *mishpokhe-s-vayz* 'family-PL-wise (by families)'. This assumption contradicts Joseph Greenberg's Universal 28: "If both the derivation and inflection follow the root, or they both precede the root, the derivation is always between the root and the inflection" (1966: 93). The generalization can be reformulated in hierarchical rather than purely linear terms so that it applies even to markers on opposite sides of the root: Inflection has scope over derivation (cf. Rainer 1996: 83) and likewise over compounding. If so, word-formation and inflection can be handled by distinct components of grammar that operate strictly in this order. A different architecture of the grammar is required if compound-internal inflection and inflection within derivation are allowed. While some linguists explicitly defend this option, others offer alternative interpretations so as to avoid a loop from inflection back into word-formation or a conflation of the two components, and some try to reduce the problem by permitting only certain types of inflection to feed derivation, e.g.,

– only irregular inflectional forms, on the grounds that they are listed in the lexicon (cf. Anderson 1988: 41; see also Perlmutter 1988: 89), a stock example being English *mice-infested* vs. *rats-infested;
– only "inherent" inflection, i.e. selected features such as number as opposed to imposed features such as case (see section 3.4; cf. Booij 1996; see also Gallmann 1999: 178–179, 183; Motsch 1999: 8).

These generalizations are, however, either aprioristic or based on too few examples and should not be accepted without further empirical evidence.

Compounds and derivatives that seem to be built on inflectional forms can be reanalyzed in a number of ways:

a) The supposed compound is a phrase. This solution is particularly convincing if other phrasal properties are present as well. In West Frisian, for example, the "genitive compound" *koken-s-doar* 'kitchen-GEN-door (door of the kitchen)' has certain phonological and semantic characteristics which it shares with phrases but not with regular compounds such as *koken-doar* 'kitchen-door (door of a kitchen)'. But even if a construction with a case marker is otherwise quite similar to a complex word, it may qualify as a phrase. For instance, Kalmyk /ykr-æ maxn/ 'cow-GEN meat (beef)' seems to consist of two words – so that it is not of the same type as the compound /hol maxn/ 'centre meat (fillet)' – although it differs from normal phrases in that the components appear in a fixed order and cannot be modified (cf. Pavlov 1983: 88). Even semantic non-compositionality as in the case of Khinalug /pt:-e xu/ 'eye-GEN$_2$ water (tear)' is not sufficient evidence against phrase status. Other phenomena that may very well be phrases include close-knit combinations with case-marked objects, e.g., Icelandic *fán-um prýdd-ur* 'flag-DAT.PL decorate.PST.PTCP-NOM.SG.M (decorated with flags)' and Hungarian *iskolá-ba jár* 'school-ILLAT go (attend school)' with the nominalization *iskolá-ba jár-ás* 'school-ILLAT go-NR (school attendance)', and instances of "internal inflection" as in English *brother-in-law* (plural *brothers-in-law*).
b) The alleged inflectional marker is derivational. This is a possible response to the claim that comparatives and superlatives are typical examples of "inher-

ent inflection" (cf. Booij 1996: 5–6) which can feed word-formation, as in the Ukrainian derived verb *žovt-iš-a-ty* 'yellow-CMPR-VR-INF (become more yellow)' ← *žovt-iš-yj* 'yellow-CMPR-NOM.SG.M' ← *žovt-yj* 'yellow-NOM.SG.M'. Infinitives and participles occur in derivatives and as both first and second members of compounds, e.g., Dutch *slap-en-s-tijd* 'sleep-INF-LINK-time (bed time)', *begrens-d-heid* 'limit-PAST.PTCP-NR (limitedness)', *boek-bind-en* 'book-bind-INF (bookbinding)' and *computer-ge-stuur-d* 'computer-Ø-control-PST.PTCP (computer controlled)'. But in these complex words they behave like nouns and adjectives, as is evident from the linking *-s* in *slapenstijd* and the non-existence of finite forms of **boekbind-* and **computerstuur-* (cf. Booij 1996: 7). One can therefore either say that infinitives and participles are always derivatives rather than part of the inflectional paradigm of the verb or that they undergo conversion to nouns and adjectives before further word-formation rules apply (see also sections 3.4 and 7.4).

c) What looks like an inflectional form is a homonymous special stem or combining form. For two reasons, special stems that are used only in word-formations must be assumed in any case. First, not all linking elements resemble inflectional markers and those that do sometimes appear even in cases where the lexeme in question does not have a form with this marker. One example is that of Icelandic *-s*, which is identical with one of the genitive singular suffixes but is also found in compounds of the type *kúplings-diskur* 'clutch-disk' although the genitive singular of KÚPLING 'clutch' is *kúplingar* (see section 5.7). Secondly, constituents of compounds or derivatives often coincide with an inflectional form for which there is no semantic motivation (cf. also Fuhrhop 1998: 192–194; Eschenlohr 1999: 195–206 on German). In Latvian, for instance, the nominalizer *-ums* is described as attaching to the past tense stem of verbs, e.g., *mēģinājums* 'attempt' (cf. *mēģināj-u* 'try.PST-1.SG', *mēģin-u* 'try.PRS-1.SG'), but the feature [+past] is not reflected in the meaning of the resulting nouns (for a similar case involving [+feminine]). One could allow word-formation rules to delete morphosyntactic properties or devise a mechanism that prevents certain features from contributing to the meaning of the complex word or simply posit that they are not carried over (cf. Mel'čuk 2006: 293–294; Wiese 1996a: 144–145; Augst 1975: 83, 133), but this leaves unexplained why inflectional forms should occur in complex words to begin with. A further problem is that, for no apparent reason, similar word-formations often exhibit different inflectional forms of the same lexeme. For example, Finnish *sade-kappa* 'rain-coat' and *sateen-varjo* 'rain-shade (umbrella)' seem to contain the nominative singular *sade* and the genitive singular *sateen* of SADE 'rain', respectively, although the semantic relationship between the compound members is the same. Thus, there is good reason to regard Finnish *sade-* and *sateen-*, Latvian *mēģināj-* and the like as special word-formation stems that are merely homonymous with inflectional forms or stems but cannot be equated with them. (Alternatively, one could assume "morphomic" stems that occur in an arbitrary set of inflectional forms, compounds and/ or derivatives; crucially, such stems are not specified for morphosyntactic properties either, see section 4.3.) In other cases, the evidence in favour of regarding certain word constituents as inflectional forms is stronger but still not compelling:

- There are numerous complex words with a constituent which not only looks like an inflectional form but apparently has the grammatical meaning associated with that form. In German *Häuserreihe* 'row of houses', for instance, the first member *Häuser* is identical with the plural of *Haus* 'house' and could be argued to be semantically plural because a row involves more than one item (cf. Booij 1994: 36–37, 2002: 147 on Dutch) – but compounds with *Reihe* 'row' do not always contain a plural form, e.g., *Lochreihe* 'row of holes' (← *Loch* 'hole', plural *Löcher*). Even if *Loch-* is not viewed as a singular form but as a stem which is not specified for number (cf. Booij 2002: 145), this demonstrates that the plural reading required by *Reihe* is independent of number marking on the other constituent. Conversely, some compound members that must be semantically singular are plural in form, e.g., *Eier-schale* 'egg-shell' (← *Ei* 'egg', plural *Eier*) as opposed to *Ei-gelb* 'egg-yellow (yolk)'. Although the percentage of such mismatches may be rather small (see August 1975: 145–152 for some statistics), their existence raises the question of whether it is really so obvious that *Häuser-* in *Häuserreihe* is an inflectional form.
- Psycholinguistic experiments concerning the Dutch linking element *-en*, which is homonymous with a productive plural suffix (cf. Booij 2002: 24, 180), show that a first compound member with *-en* is more likely to be interpreted as plural than as singular (Hanssen et al. 2013) and that informants prefer *-en* to no linking element in contexts that suggest a plural meaning (Banga et al. 2013) – but a look at the figures reveals that both tendencies are not particularly pronounced.
- There are minimal pairs such as German *Volkskunde* 'folklore (as a discipline)' vs. *Völkerkunde* 'ethnography' (← *Volk* 'people', plural *Völker*) and Dutch *stedenraad* 'council of cities' vs. *stadsraad* 'city council' (← *stad* 'city', plural *steden*; see Booij 2002: 179). Their number is, however, quite small, their meanings are not fully predictable in terms of singular vs. plural and other pairs with such a formal difference are synonymous, e.g., the German regional variants *Rindsbraten* and *Rinderbraten* 'beef roast' (← *Rind* 'bovine', plural *Rinder*).

It is therefore generally possible to assume word-formation stems without morphosyntactic properties instead of treating some word constituents as inflectional forms and others as stems. While the choice of one word-formation stem rather than another can have a bearing on the semantic interpretation of the complex word, it is only one of many factors involved and can be accounted for without recourse to inflectional meanings.

7.3 Words, lexemes, roots or stems?

Compounds are sometimes defined as containing two or more roots (e.g., Jackson 2007: 29), and a classification of affixes according to their position relative to a root (see section 5.1) implies that derivation likewise operates on roots. While this is true in the simplest of cases, it must be remembered that the output of a word-formation rule can serve as the input to another (or even the same) word-formation rule. Danish *sprogvidenskabelig* 'linguistic', for example, is a derivative based on the compound *sprogvidenskab* 'linguistics', which in turn consists of *sprog* 'language' and the derivative *videnskab* 'science' (← *viden* 'knowledge' ← *vid-* 'to know'). A characterization of word-formation rules as operations on roots is therefore inadequate.

According to another definition, word-formation forms words from words (see section 1); in particular, a compound is said to be "a word which consists of two or more words" (Fabb 1998: 66). Since *word* has a number of different meanings (see section 3), we must clarify which of them is intended here. The output is definitely a lexeme as a whole and not one of its grammatical words with certain morphosyntactic properties, and it is sometimes explicitly stated that the "word" which a word-formation rule takes as its input is a lexeme as well (e.g., Booij 2002: 141; Bonami, Boyé and Kerleroux 2009: 124; Montermini 2010: 86). One handbook article that offers such an explanation adds: "The implication of this is that the forms in which the individual subwords appear may be differently defined in different languages: a citation form in one, a stem in another, a specific compounding form in yet a third, a word form in a fourth" (Bauer 2006: 719). While this statement does not logically follow, it leads to an important point: As a set of grammatical words, a lexeme cannot appear as such but must be represented either by a specific word form or by a stem (cf. also Montermini 2010: 87). There is no need to single out the citation form since it is simply one of the word forms; if it coincides with the bare stem, it is better analyzed as such, unspecified for morphosyntactic properties (cf. Booij 2002: 145). If a lexeme is allowed to have stems that occur only in word-formations (which requires a slight revision of the definition of *stem* in section 4.3), the "specific compounding form" is not a separate case either. On the premise that compounds and derivatives do not contain inflectional forms (see section 7.3), only one of the four options mentioned in the above quotation remains: The input to a word-formation rule is a lexeme, represented by a word-formation stem.

While special word-formation stems are not a novel idea (cf., e.g., Bloomfield 1933: 229), the implications for the paradigms of lexemes require further study. The suggestion that lexemes (or at least German nouns, verbs and adjectives) have a stem paradigm which always contains at least one derivational stem and one compounding stem in addition to the inflectional stem(s) (Fuhrhop 1998: 22–26; Aronoff and Fuhrhop 2002: 454–456) is not convincing because the distinction between derivation and compounding may or may not play a role in the distribution of word-formation stems. The principle that all lexemes of a given word class have a fixed number of stems (many of which have the same expression in certain inflection classes) with the same distribution for each lexeme is feasible for inflectional paradigms (cf. Bonami, Boyé and Kerleroux 2009: 107–108) – but when word-formation stems are included (cf. Bonami, Boyé and Kerleroux 2009: 120–123), it becomes unwieldy. It seems more realistic to allow lexemes to have a variable number of word-formation stems with distributions that do not necessarily have a parallel in other lexemes. For example, numerous Finnish nouns have two word-formation stems, one homonymous with the nominative singular and one homonymous with the genitive singular (e.g., *sade-* and *sateen-* 'rain-', see section 7.2), but there are no firm rules as to when which of them is used. Such systematic homonymy between word-formation stems and inflectional forms requires a further refinement of the model: It must permit the expression side of a stem to be deduced not only from another stem but also from a specific cell in the inflectional paradigm.

A word-formation stem may be special not only in expression but also in content. It does not necessarily have the full range of meanings of the lexeme it belongs to, and its meaning in a complex word may well depend on the constituent it combines with; so-called affixoids (cf. section 4.2) can be viewed simply as word-formation stems with meanings that the simplex word does not have. On the practical side, this implies that dictionaries should have (sub-)entries for word-formation stems with a description of the most common patterns in which they occur and the meanings they have there (for some suggestions, cf. Mugdan 1984: 298–303). Furthermore, one can allow for the possibility that the only stems of a lexeme are word-formation stems, e.g., *phon-* and *-ology* in *phonology*, etc. (cf. section 4.2 on "confixes"). Then, a distinction between word-formations at different levels, e.g., root, stem and word (cf. Wiese 1996a: 131 on German), is not needed (cf. Montermini 2010: 82, 87).

7.4 The role of word classes and subclasses

Word-formation rules are commonly stated in terms of word classes or lexical categories (noun, verb, adjective, etc.). In particular, it is often assumed
- that roots are specified for word class,
- that derivational rules operate on bases of a specific word class ("unitary base hypothesis", cf. Aronoff 1976: 47–48) and
- that they generate lexemes of a specific word class ("unitary output hypothesis", cf. Scalise 1984: 137).

The unitary base hypothesis and the unitary output hypothesis lie behind the popular characterization of derivatives as denominal verbs, deadjectival nouns, etc. Proponents of the unitary output hypothesis additionally require that the output should be uniform with regard to subclass (e.g., gender of nouns, transitivity of verbs), inflectional class and perhaps semantics (cf. Plag 1999: 49–50); the unitary base hypothesis is usually not interpreted quite so strictly.

The unitary output hypothesis is widely accepted but exceptions are easy to find. Italian *-ista* and *anti-*, for example, create words that function as both nouns and adjectives (cf. Montermini 2008: 182–183), e.g., *ottimista* 'optimist/optimistic' (← *ottim-o* 'optimal-SG'), *antifurto* 'burglar alarm/anti-theft' (← *furt-o* 'theft-SG'). Here, it is difficult to justify two homonymous affixes or a conversion from noun to adjective or vice versa (see also De Belder 2011: 152–170 on Dutch). Frequently, derivational affixes which violate the unitary output hypothesis violate the unitary base hypothesis as well and are "transparent" with regard to word class or subclass. Evaluative suffixes in Romance and Slavic languages which preserve the gender of the base and can sometimes be used with words of different classes are a typical example, e.g., the Kashubian diminutive *-k* in the masculine noun *grzibk* ← *grzib* 'mushroom', the feminine noun *gąbka* ← *gãba* 'face' (with the nominative singular suffix *-a*) and the verb *róbkac* ← *robic* 'to work' (with the infinitive suffix *-c* preceded by a theme vowel). Yet, evaluative suffixes do not always behave in this way. For instance, the diminutive affixes of Dutch, Frisian and German attach to nouns of any gender but the output is always neuter, in conformity with the unitary output hypothesis; Albanian has diminutive suffixes which are gender-specific with regard to both input and output, *-th* for masculine nouns as in *djalëth* ← *djalë* 'boy' and *-z* for feminine nouns as in *arkëz* ← *arkë* 'box'. On the other hand, suffixes that are transparent to gender are not necessarily evaluative; one example is Breton *-ad* as in *tasad* 'cupful(M)' ← *tas* 'cup(M)', *bolad* 'bowlful(F)' ← *bol* 'bowl(F)'. Prefixes do not constitute a systematic exception either. Many are transparent to word class, but some do conform to the unitary output hypothesis and determine the word class of the output, e.g., English *en-* in *endanger* (unless one resorts to one of the debatable analyses mentioned in sections 4.4 and 5.9). Thus, it is not predictable which derivational affixes obey the unitary output hypothesis and which do not, and perhaps the possible outputs should not be characterized in terms of output word classes at all (cf. De Belder 2011: 170–195).

The unitary base hypothesis is almost impossible to falsify because of two immunization strategies that can be employed if a given affix attaches to bases of different word classes (cf. Plag 1999: 47–48, 2004: 198):

a) If the word classes in question form a natural class, the latter can be regarded as a unitary base. For example, if nouns are defined as [+N,–V], adjectives as [+N,+V] and verbs as [–N,+V], an affix that attaches to both nouns and adjectives, e.g., *-en* in *strengthen* and *deepen*, has the unitary underspecified base [+N] and one that attaches to both verbs and adjectives, e.g., *-th* in *growth* and *warmth*, has the base [+V].

b) If the word classes in question do not form a natural class, e.g., nouns and verbs in the feature system given in a), one can assume homonymous affixes, e.g., *-ful$_1$* in *thoughtful* and *-ful$_2$* in *forgetful*.

These strategies are highly problematic. First, the featural decomposition of word classes is somewhat arbitrary; for instance, one can easily devise a system in which nouns and verbs do go together. Second, it is frequently not clear whether one should assume underspecification or homonymy. Faroese *-lig*, for example, can be combined with nouns, adjectives or verbs, as in *andlig-* 'spiritual' (← *and-* 'spirit$_N$'), *blídlig-* 'kind' (← *blíð-* 'kind$_A$') and *dámlig-* 'pleasant' (← *dám-* 'like$_V$'; the obligatory inflectional affixes are not shown). Should one set up three distinct affixes or only two – and if so, which? Third, the assumption of homonymy is often not convincing because all the meanings of the affix in question are closely related and are not fully determined by the word class of the base (cf. Plag 2004: 213–214, 217–218 on English *un-*). Generally, less subjective criteria for the distinction between polysemy and homonymy would be desirable (see De Belder 2011: 132–152 for a proposal).

A number of case studies (e.g., Plag 2004: 202–216 on English) lead to the conclusion that restrictions on the input to word-formation rules are primarily semantically based and not word-class based. This is supported by the observation that a derivational affix which prototypically takes bases of a particular word class may be applied to other bases, too, as long as the output can be interpreted in a similar way. For example, German adjectives in *-bar*, which are often used with the negative prefix *un-*, are normally based on transitive verbs, e.g., *(un)trinkbar* '(un)drinkable' (← *trink-en* 'drink-INF'). In 1990, an advertising campaign for reusable PET bottles introduced *unkaputtbar* 'unbreakable', from the informal adjective *kaputt* 'broken'. This was followed by *unplattbar* (← *platt* 'flat') for a bicycle tyre that cannot be punctured, and although the pattern was originally deviant and could therefore serve as an attention-getting device, it may well become productive and unremarkable in the course of time. Such developments are amply attested (cf. also Eschenlohr 1999: 120–122 on German *er-* and De Belder 2011: 191–195 on Dutch nonce formations). An important prerequisite for the success of *un-A-bar* 'cannot be made A' was its close resemblance to *un-V-bar* 'cannot be V-ed'; at a more abstract level, both instantiate the same pattern. Thus, word-formation patterns or schemas form a hierarchy, and newly created compounds and derivatives need not follow the most specific schema (see also article 6 on word-formation in construction grammar, section 2).

The specification of roots for word class runs into difficulties when lexemes of different classes have identical roots, e.g., SAW$_N$ as in *he plays music on a saw* and SAW$_V$ as in *she sawed the fish with a knife*. Many linguists take one of the lexemes as basic and derive the other(s) by means of conversion or zero derivation (see section 5.9). Leaving aside the diachronic question as to which lexeme is attested earlier, there are a number of criteria for determining the direction of derivation (cf. Marchand 1964; Umbreit 2010: 308–314). The most important among them is semantic dependence as shown by a paraphrase test: Since, so the argument goes, the meaning of the verb *saw* must be explained with the help of the noun ('to cut with a saw') but not vice versa (one need not describe a saw as 'instrument for sawing'), the noun is basic and the verb derived (cf. Marchand 1964: 12). In reality, it is often debatable which paraphrase is superior to the other (cf. Umbreit 2010: 310) and typically both of them have their weaknesses. It has also been noted that lexeme A is not necessarily semantically dependent on lexeme B in all of its meanings (cf. Marchand 1964: 12; Plank 2010). For these and other reasons, native speakers often disagree about which lexeme is derived from the other (cf. Bergenholtz and Mugdan 1979b: 350–352).

In many cases of alleged conversion, it is not necessary to posit a change of word class at all. The Russian term for the grammatical subject, *podležaščee* (literally 'that which underlies'), is a typical example. It is the nominative singular neuter form of the present active participle of *podleža-t'* 'underlie-INF', with adjectival inflection and the syntactic functions of nouns (head of a noun phrase, etc.). On some accounts, the participle as a form of the verb is converted into an adjective and the adjective into a noun. The first step is unnecessary because one can regard the participle as an adjective derived from the verb (see section 3.4). The second step is unnecessary if we distinguish between two kinds of word classes, morphological word classes (lexeme classes) defined in terms of inflectional paradigms and syntactic word classes defined in terms of syntactic functions (cf. Bergenholtz and Mugdan 1979a: 133–141). Russian adjectives (lexemes inflected for gender, number and case) can generally serve the same syntactic functions as nouns (lexemes with inherent gender, inflected for number and case) but not vice versa. If conversion is admitted as a process of word-formation, it should involve a change in lexeme class, e.g., from the adjective *dobr-yj* 'good-NOM.SG.M' (neuter *dobr-oe* with the genitive *dobr-ogo*) to the abstract noun *dobr-o* 'good(N)-NOM.SG' (with the genitive *dobr-a*), whereas the syntactic behaviour and the semantic specialization of *podležaščee* do not involve the formation of a different lexeme.

An alternative to conversion or zero derivation is to give the lexemes in question equal status by means of underspecification or multiple specification of the root (cf. Eschenlohr 1999: 70–71). For English *saw*, underspecification means that it is neither noun nor verb, being unspecified for the feature that distinguishes the two word classes. Of course, this presupposes a suitable feature system. Multiple specification means that *saw* is both verb and noun. One drawback which this solution shares with the conversion approach is that one must decide for each derivative on which of the roots it is based – and this is often not obvious (cf. also Malkiel 1966: 358). For example, *uncork* has been described as a denominal verb with the meaning 'to remove a cork' (Plag 2004: 213); with equal justification, it could be a deverbal verb with the meaning 'to reverse the corking', of the same type as *unbind*. Similarly, the first member of the German compound *Kaufangebot* could be either the noun *Kauf* 'purchase' or the verb *kauf-en* 'buy-INF' so that it could be paraphrased as 'to offer for purchase' or 'to offer to buy'.

A radical counter-hypothesis, which was developed for German without a claim to universality, is that roots are not specified for word class: The language system allows all lexical roots to be combined with nominal, verbal and adjectival inflections and it is a matter of language use if not all the possibilities are exploited (cf. Bergenholtz and Mugdan 1979a: 155–167, 1979b). This proposal was rejected as failing to account for systematic restrictions, e.g., that German adjectives can be converted into verbs but not into nouns or that some derivational affixes with similar meaning differ precisely in the word class of their bases (see Olsen 1986: 121–124; cf. also Eschenlohr 1999: 69–70). But as we have seen, such restrictions are normally not absolute and cannot fully account for what is possible in a language and what is not (see also De Belder 2011: 174–195 on grammatical rules vs. "convention" as the factor that restricts some derivational affixes to certain output word classes). In keeping with an increasing recognition of fuzziness and irregularity in language, a more flexible compromise position seems to be called for. A pilot study indicates that languages differ with regard to how category-specific their roots and stems are (cf. Lehmann 2008), and within a given language, roots may differ in categoriality so that some are specified for a single word class and others for several or perhaps for none. Similarly, derivational processes may differ as to how choosy they are with regard to their input. Thus, it has been suggested that the derivational affixes of agglutinating languages are more likely to be transcategorial, attaching to bases of different word classes, than those of inflectional languages (cf. Plungian 2001: 674–677). The semantic relations between lexemes that share a root may range from more bidirectional to more unidirectional (cf. Umbreit 2010: 323–325), and in a model that does not shun redundancy, the lexicon may contain compounds and derivatives alongside their constituents, with an intricate web of connections at various levels.

8 References

Akinlabi, Akinbiyi (2011): Featural affixes. In: Marc van Oostendorp, Colin J. Ewen, Elizabeth Hume and Keren Rice (eds.), *The Blackwell Companion to Phonology*. Vol. 4: *Phonological Interfaces*, 1945–1971. Chichester: Wiley-Blackwell.

Alber, Birgit and Sabine Arndt-Lappe (2012): Templatic and subtractive truncation. In: Jochen Trommer (ed.), *The Morphology and Phonology of Exponence*, 289–325. Oxford: Oxford University Press.

Alderete, John, Jill Beckman, Laura Benua, Amalia Gnanadesikan, John McCarthy and Suzanne Urbanczyk (1999): Reduplication with fixed segmentism. *Linguistic Inquiry* 30: 327–364 [originally 1997 in *Rutgers Optimality Archive*, available at http://roa.rutgers.edu/files/226-1097/roa-226-alderete-1.pdf].

Anderson, Stephen R. (1988): Inflection. In: Michael Hammond and Michael Noonan (eds.), *Theoretical Morphology. Approaches in Modern Linguistics*, 23–43. San Diego, CA: Academic Press.

Anderson, Stephen R. (1992): *A-Morphous Morphology*. Cambridge: Cambridge University Press.

Aronoff, Mark (1976): *Word Formation in Generative Grammar*. Cambridge, MA/London: MIT Press.

Aronoff, Mark (1994): *Morphology by Itself. Stems and Inflectional Classes*. Cambridge, MA/London: MIT Press.

Aronoff, Mark (2012): Morphological stems: What William of Ockham really said. *Word Structure* 5: 28–51.

Aronoff, Mark and Nanna Fuhrhop (2002): Restricting suffix combinations in German and English: Closing suffixes and the monosuffix constraint. *Natural Language and Linguistic Theory* 20: 451–490.

Augst, Gerhard (1975): Über das Fugenmorphem bei Zusammensetzungen. In: Gerhard Augst, *Untersuchungen zum Morpheminventar der deutschen Gegenwartssprache*, 71–155. Tübingen: Narr.

Banga, Arina, Esther Hanssen, Anneke Neijt and Robert Schreuder (2013): Preference for linking element *-en-* in Dutch noun-noun compounds: Native speakers and second language learners of Dutch. *Morphology* 23: 33–56.

Baudouin de Courtenay, Jan (1869): Wortformen und selbst sätze, welche in der polnischen sprache zu stämmen herabgesunken sind. *Beiträge zur vergleichenden Sprachforschung* 6(2): 204–210 [volume dated 1870].

Bauer, Laurie (1983): *English Word-formation*. Cambridge: Cambridge University Press.
Bauer, Laurie (1988): A descriptive gap in morphology. In: Geert Booij and Jaap van Marle (eds.), *Yearbook of Morphology*, 17–27. Dordrecht/Providence, RI: Foris.
Bauer, Laurie (2000a): Word. In: Geert Booij, Christian Lehmann and Joachim Mugdan (eds.), *Morphology. An International Handbook on Inflection and Word-Formation*. Vol. 1, 247–257. Berlin/New York: de Gruyter.
Bauer, Laurie (2000b): Compounding. In: Geert Booij, Christian Lehmann and Joachim Mugdan (eds.), *Morphology. An International Handbook on Inflection and Word-Formation*. Vol. 1, 695–707. Berlin/New York: de Gruyter.
Bauer, Laurie (2003): *Introducing Linguistic Morphology*. 2nd ed. Washington, DC: Georgetown University Press [1st ed. 1988].
Bauer, Laurie (2004): *A Glossary of Morphology*. Washington, DC: Georgetown University Press.
Bauer, Laurie (2006): Compound. In: Keith Brown (ed.), *Encyclopedia of Language and Linguistics*. Vol. 2, 719–726. 2nd ed. Amsterdam: Elsevier.
Becker, Thomas (2000): Metathesis. In: Geert Booij, Christian Lehmann and Joachim Mugdan (eds.), *Morphology. An International Handbook on Inflection and Word-Formation*. Vol. 1, 576–581. Berlin/New York: de Gruyter.
Bergenholtz, Henning and Joachim Mugdan (1979a): *Einführung in die Morphologie*. Stuttgart: Kohlhammer.
Bergenholtz, Henning and Joachim Mugdan (1979b): Ist Liebe primär? Über Ableitung und Wortarten. In: Peter Braun (ed.), *Deutsche Gegenwartssprache. Entwicklungen, Entwürfe, Diskussionen*, 339–354. München: Fink.
Bergenholtz, Henning and Joachim Mugdan (2000): Nullelemente in der Morphologie. In: Geert Booij, Christian Lehmann and Joachim Mugdan (eds.), *Morphology. An International Handbook on Inflection and Word-Formation*. Vol. 1, 435–450. Berlin/New York: de Gruyter.
Bickel, Balthasar, Goma Banjade, Martin Gaenszle, Elena Lieven, Netra Prasad Paudyal, Ichchha Purna Rai, Manoj Rai, Novel Kishore Rai and Sabine Stoll (2007): Free prefix ordering in Chintang. *Language* 83: 43–73.
Bickel, Balthasar and Johanna Nichols (2007): Inflectional morphology. In: Timothy Shopen (ed.), *Language Typology and Syntactic Description*. Vol. 3: *Grammatical Categories and the Lexicon*, 169–240. 2nd ed. Cambridge: Cambridge University Press.
Bisang, Walter (2001): Syntax/morphology asymmetry in Vietnamese – a consequence of contact by writing between Vietnamese, Chinese and Standard Average European Languages. In: Birgit Igla and Thomas Stolz (eds.), *"Was ich noch sagen wollte …". A Multilingual Festschrift for Norbert Boretzky on Occasion of His 65th Birthday*, 189–201. Berlin: Akademie Verlag.
Blevins, Juliette (1999): Untangling Leti infixation. *Oceanic Linguistics* 38: 383–403.
Bloomfield, Leonard (1926): A set of postulates for the science of language. *Language* 2: 153–164.
Bloomfield, Leonard (1933): *Language*. New York: Holt [British edition London: Allen & Unwin 1935].
Boas, Franz (1911): Introduction. In: Franz Boas (ed.), *Handbook of American Indian Languages*. Part 1, 1–83. Washington, DC: Government Printing Office.
Bonami, Olivier, Gilles Boyé and Françoise Kerleroux (2009): L'allomorphie radicale et la relation flexion-construction. In: Bernard Fradin, Françoise Kerleroux and Marc Plénat (eds.), *Aperçus de morphologie du français*, 103–125. Saint-Denis: Presses Universitaires de Vincennes.
Bonet, Eulalia and Daniel Harbour (2012): Contextual allomorphy. In: Jochen Trommer (ed.), *The Morphology and Phonology of Exponence*, 195–235. Oxford: Oxford University Press.
Booij, Geert (1994): Against split morphology. In: Geert Booij and Jaap van Marle (eds.), *Yearbook of Morphology 1993*, 27–49. Dordrecht: Kluwer [dated ©1993].

Booij, Geert (1996): Inherent versus contextual inflection and the split morphology hypothesis. In: Geert Booij and Jaap van Marle (eds.), *Yearbook of Morphology 1995*, 1–16. Dordrecht: Kluwer.
Booij, Geert (1998): Phonological output constraints in morphology. In: Wolfgang Kehrein and Richard Wiese (eds.), *Phonology and Morphology of the Germanic Languages*, 143–163. Tübingen: Niemeyer.
Booij, Geert (2002): *The Morphology of Dutch*. Oxford: Oxford University Press.
Booij, Geert (2005): Compounding and derivation. Evidence for Construction Morphology. In: Wolfgang U. Dressler, Dieter Kastovsky, Oskar E. Pfeiffer and Franz Rainer (eds.), *Morphology and its Demarcations. Selected Papers from the 11th Morphology Meeting, Vienna, February 2004*, 109–132. Amsterdam/Philadelphia: Benjamins.
Booij, Geert (2012): *The Grammar of Words. An Introduction to Linguistic Morphology*. 3rd ed. Oxford: Oxford University Press [1st ed. 2005].
Bossong, Georg (2001): Ausdrucksmöglichkeiten für grammatische Relationen. In: Martin Haspelmath, Ekkehard König, Wulf Oesterreicher and Wolfgang Raible (eds.), *Language Typology and Language Universals*. Vol. 1, 657–668. Berlin/New York: de Gruyter.
Broselow, Ellen (2000): Transfixation. In: Geert Booij, Christian Lehmann and Joachim Mugdan (eds.), *Morphology. An International Handbook on Inflection and Word-Formation*. Vol. 1, 552–557. Berlin/New York: de Gruyter.
Brown, Dunstan (2011): Morphological typology. In: Jae Jung Song (ed.), *The Oxford Handbook of Linguistic Typology*, 487–503. Oxford: Oxford University Press.
Bybee, Joan L. and Jean E. Newman (1995): Are stem changes as natural as affixes? *Linguistics* 33: 633–654.
Bye, Patrik and Peter Svenonius (2012): Non-concatenative morphology as epiphenomenon. In: Jochen Trommer (ed.), *The Morphology and Phonology of Exponence*, 427–495. Oxford: Oxford University Press.
Caballero, Gabriela (2010): Scope, phonology and morphology in an agglutinating language: Choguita Rara'muri (Tarahumara) variable suffix ordering. *Morphology* 20: 165–204.
Carstairs[-McCarthy], Andrew (1988): Some implications of phonologically conditioned suppletion. In: Geert Booij and Jaap van Marle (eds), *Yearbook of Morphology*, 67–94. Dordrecht/Providence, RI: Foris.
Carstairs-McCarthy, [Andrew] (1998): [Contribution to] Discussion of the papers by Sadock and Baker. In: Steven G. Lapointe, Diane K. Brentari and Patrick M. Farrell (eds.), *Morphology and Its Relation to Phonology and Syntax*, 213–215. Stanford, CA: CLSI.
Carstairs-McCarthy, Andrew (2000): Lexeme, word-form, paradigm. In: Geert Booij, Christian Lehmann and Joachim Mugdan (eds.), *Morphology. An International Handbook on Inflection and Word-Formation*. Vol. 1, 595–607. Berlin/New York: de Gruyter.
Chelliah, Shobhana L. and Willem J. de Reuse (2011): *Handbook of Descriptive Linguistic Fieldwork*. Dordrecht: Springer.
Chaves, Rui P. (2008): Linearization-based word-part ellipsis. *Linguistics and Philosophy* 31: 261–307.
Clements, G[eorge] N. (1985): The problem of transfer in nonlinear morphology. *Cornell Working Papers in Linguistics* 7: 38–73.
Coates, Richard (2000): Exponence. In: Geert Booij, Christian Lehmann and Joachim Mugdan (eds.), *Morphology. An International Handbook on Inflection and Word-Formation*. Vol. 1, 616–630. Berlin/New York: de Gruyter.
Croft, William (2000): Lexical and grammatical meaning. In: Geert Booij, Christian Lehmann and Joachim Mugdan (eds.), *Morphology. An International Handbook on Inflection and Word-Formation*. Vol. 1, 257–263. Berlin/New York: de Gruyter.

Daniels, Peter T. (2013): The history of writing as a history of linguistics. In: Keith Allan (ed.), *The Oxford Handbook of the History of Linguistics*, 53–69. Oxford: Oxford University Press.

De Belder, Marijke (2011): *Roots and Affixes. Eliminating Lexical Categories from Syntax*. Utrecht: LOT. Available at http://www.lotpublications.nl/publish/articles/004300/bookpart.pdf.

Di Sciullo, Anna Maria and Edwin Williams (1987): *On the Definition of Word*. Cambridge, MA/London: MIT Press.

Dixon, R[obert] M. W. and Alexandra Y. Aikhenvald (2002): Word: A typological framework. In: R. M. W. Dixon and Alexandra Y. Aikhenvald (eds.), *Word. A Cross-Linguistic Typology*, 1–41. Cambridge: Cambridge University Press.

Donalies, Elke (2005): *Die Wortbildung des Deutschen. Ein Überblick*. 2nd ed. Tübingen: Narr [1st ed. 2002].

Dressler, Wolfgang U. (2000): Subtraction. In: Geert Booij, Christian Lehmann and Joachim Mugdan (eds.), *Morphology. An International Handbook on Inflection and Word-Formation*. Vol. 1, 581–587. Berlin/New York: de Gruyter.

Eschenlohr, Stefanie (1999): *Vom Nomen zum Verb. Konversion, Präfigierung und Rückbildung im Deutschen*. Hildesheim: Olms.

Fabb, Nigel (1998): Compounding. In: Andrew Spencer and Arnold M. Zwicky (eds.), *The Handbook of Morphology*, 66–83. Oxford: Blackwell.

Fleischer, Wolfgang and Irmhild Barz (1992): *Wortbildung der deutschen Gegenwartssprache*. Tübingen: Niemeyer.

Fleischer, Wolfgang and Irmhild Barz (2012): *Wortbildung der deutschen Gegenwartssprache*. 4th ed. Berlin/Boston: de Gruyter.

Fromkin, Victoria, Robert Rodman and Nina Hyams (2013): *An Introduction to Language*. 10th ed. Independence, KY: Cengage Learning [dated ©2014, 1st ed. 1974].

Fuhrhop, Nanna (1998): *Grenzfälle morphologischer Einheiten*. Tübingen: Stauffenburg.

Gafos, Diamandis (1998): Eliminating long-distance consonantal spreading. *Natural Language and Linguistic Theory* 16: 223–278.

Gallmann, Peter (1999): Fugenmorpheme als Nicht-Kasus-Suffixe. In: Matthias Butt and Nanna Fuhrhop (eds.), *Variation und Stabilität in der Wortstruktur. Untersuchungen zu Entwicklung, Erwerb und Varietäten des Deutschen und anderer Sprachen*, 177–190. Hildesheim: Olms.

Garvin, Paul L. (1945): Pure-relational suffixes and postpositions in Hungarian. *Language* 21: 250–255.

Giegerich, Heinz J. (2009): The English compound stress myth. *Word Structure* 2: 1–17.

Good, Jeff and Alan C. L. Yu (2005): Morphosyntax of two Turkish subject pronominal paradigms. In: Lorie Heggie and Francisco Ordóñez (eds.), *Clitic and Affix Combinations. Theoretical Perspectives*, 315–341. Amsterdam/Philadelphia: Benjamins.

Greenberg, Joseph H. (1957): *Essays in Linguistics*. Chicago, IL: University of Chicago Press.

Greenberg, Joseph H. (1960): A quantitative approach to the morphological typology of language. *International Journal of American Linguistics* 26: 178–194.

Greenberg, Joseph H. (1966): Some universals of grammar with particular reference to the order of meaningful elements. In: Joseph H. Greenberg (ed.), *Universals of Language*, 73–113. 2nd ed. Cambridge, MA/London: MIT Press [1st ed. 1963].

Hagège, Claude (1986): *La langue palau. Une curiosité typologique*. München: Fink.

Halle, Morris (1953): The German conjugation. *Word* 9: 45–53.

Hanssen, Esther, Arina Banga, Robert Schreuder and Anneke Neijt (2013): Semantic and prosodic effects of Dutch linking elements. *Morphology* 23: 7–32.

Hardy, Heather K. and Timothy R. Montler (1988): Alabama radical morphology: H-infix and disfixation. In: William Shipley (ed.), *In Honor of Mary Haas. From the Haas Festival Conference on Native American Linguistics*, 377–409. Berlin: Mouton de Gruyter.
Harris, Zellig S. (1942): Morpheme alternants in linguistic analysis. *Language* 18: 169–180.
Haspelmath, Martin (1990): The grammaticization of passive morphology. *Studies in Language* 14: 25–72.
Haspelmath, Martin (1996): Word-class-changing inflection and morphological theory. In: Geert Booij and Jaap van Marle (eds.), *Yearbook of Morphology 1995*, 43–66. Dordrecht: Kluwer.
Haspelmath, Martin (2000): Periphrasis. In: Geert Booij, Christian Lehmann and Joachim Mugdan (eds.), *Morphology. An International Handbook on Inflection and Word-Formation*. Vol. 1, 654–664. Berlin/New York: de Gruyter.
Haspelmath, Martin (2002): *Understanding Morphology*. London: Arnold.
Haspelmath, Martin (2011): The indeterminacy of word segmentation and the nature of morphology and syntax. *Folia Linguistica* 45: 31–80.
Haspelmath, Martin and Andrea D. Sims (2010): *Understanding Morphology*. 2nd ed. London: Hodder Education.
Haugen, Jason D. (2009): What is the base for reduplication? *Linguistic Inquiry* 40: 505–514.
Helmbrecht, Johannes and Christian Lehmann (2008): Hočank's challenge to morphological theory. In: K. David Harrison, David S. Rood and Arienne Dwyer (eds.), *Lessons from Documented Endangered Languages*, 271–315. Amsterdam/Philadelphia: Benjamins.
Hewitt, George (2005): North West Caucasian. *Lingua* 115: 91–145.
Hjelmslev, Louis (1961): *Prolegomena to a Theory of Language*. 2nd ed. Translated by Francis J. Whitfield. Madison: University of Wisconsin Press [1st ed. 1953, originally Danish 1943].
Hockett, Charles F. (1947): Problems of morphemic analysis. *Language* 23: 321–343.
Hockett, Charles F. (1950): Peiping morphophonemics. *Language* 26: 63–85.
Hockett, Charles F. (1954): Two models of grammatical description. *Word* 10: 210–234.
Hockett, Charles F. (1958): *A Course in Modern Linguistics*. New York: Macmillan.
Hockett, Charles F. (1961): Linguistic elements and their relations. *Language* 37: 29–53.
Hoeksema, Jack and Richard D. Janda (1988): Implications of process-morphology for categorial grammar. In: Richard T. Oehrle, Emmon Bach and Deirdre Wheeler (eds.), *Categorial Grammars and Natural Language Structures*, 199–247. Dordrecht: Reidel.
Hogoboom, S. L. Anya (2003): Definition of the base. *Proceedings of the [...] Annual Meeting of the Berkeley Linguistics Society* 29(1): 173–183.
Hyman, Larry M. and William R. Leben (2000): Suprasegmental processes. In: Geert Booij, Christian Lehmann and Joachim Mugdan (eds.), *Morphology. An International Handbook on Inflection and Word-Formation*. Vol. 1, 587–594. Berlin/New York: de Gruyter.
Inkelas, Sharon (2012): Reduplication. In: Jochen Trommer (ed.), *The Morphology and Phonology of Exponence*, 355–378. Oxford: Oxford University Press.
Jackson, Howard (2007): *Key Terms in Linguistics*. London/New York: Continuum.
Jacobs, Joachim (2011): Grammatik ohne Wörter? In: Stefan Engelberg, Anke Holler and Kristel Proost (eds.), *Sprachliches Wissen zwischen Lexikon und Grammatik*, 345–372. Berlin/Boston: de Gruyter.
Julien, Marit (2002): *Syntactic Heads and Word Formation*. Oxford: Oxford University Press.
Julien, M[arit] (2006): Word. In: Keith Brown (ed.), *Encyclopedia of Language and Linguistics*. Vol. 13, 617–624. 2nd ed. Amsterdam: Elsevier.
Katamba, Francis and John Stonham (2006): *Morphology*. 2nd ed. Basingstoke/New York: Palgrave Macmillan [1st ed. by Francis Katamba 1993].

Kibort, Anna (2010): Towards a typology of grammatical features. In: Anna Kibort and Greville G. Corbett (eds.), *Features. Perspectives on a Key Notion in Linguistics*, 65–106. Oxford: Oxford University Press.
Korotkova, Natalia and Yury Lander (2010): Deriving affix ordering in polysynthesis: Evidence from Adyghe. *Morphology* 20: 299–319.
Kosa, Loredana Andreea (2008): An argument for process-based morphology. Subtractive morphology in Tohono O'odham (Uto-Aztecan). M.A. Thesis, Department of Linguistics, Simon Fraser University. Available at http://summit.sfu.ca/item/8989.
Kubrjakova, Elena S. (2000): Submorphemische Einheiten. Übersetzung und Bearbeitung Joachim Mugdan. In: Geert Booij, Christian Lehmann and Joachim Mugdan (eds.), *Morphology. An International Handbook on Inflection and Word-Formation*. Vol. 1, 417–426. Berlin/New York: de Gruyter.
Lausberg, Heinrich (1953): [Brief notice on Malkiel 1949.] *Romanische Forschungen* 65: 229–230.
Lawrenz, Birgit (2006): *Moderne deutsche Wortbildung. Phrasale Wortbildung im Deutschen. Linguistische Untersuchung und sprachdidaktische Behandlung*. Hamburg: Kovač.
Lehmann, Christian (2004): Interlinear morphemic glossing. In: Geert Booij, Christian Lehmann, Joachim Mugdan and Stavros Skopeteas (eds.), *Morphology. An International Handbook on Inflection and Word-Formation*. Vol. 2, 1834–1857. Berlin/New York: de Gruyter.
Lehmann, Christian (2008): Roots, stems and word classes. *Studies in Language* 32: 546–567.
Lieber, Rochelle (2000): Substitution of segments and features. In: Geert Booij, Christian Lehmann and Joachim Mugdan (eds.), *Morphology. An International Handbook on Inflection and Word-Formation*. Vol. 1, 567–576. Berlin/New York: de Gruyter.
Lieber, Rochelle (2010): *Introducing Morphology*. Cambridge: Cambridge University Press.
Lindner, Thomas (2012): *Indogermanische Grammatik, Band IV/1. Komposition*. Lieferung 2 [pages 71–148]. Heidelberg: Winter.
Lyons, John (1968): *Introduction to Theoretical Linguistics*. London: Cambridge University Press.
Maes, V[édaste] (1959): *Dictionnaire ngbaka-français-néerlandais précédé d'un aperçu grammatical*. Tervuren: Musée Royal du Congo Belge.
Malkiel, Yakov (1949): Studies in the Hispanic infix -*eg*-. *Language* 25: 139–181.
Malkiel, Yakov (1966): Genetic analysis of word formation. In: Thomas A. Sebeok (ed.), *Current Trends in Linguistics*. Vol. 3: *Theoretical Foundations*, 305–364. The Hague/Paris: Mouton.
Manova, Stela and Mark Aronoff (2010): Modeling affix order. *Morphology* 20: 109–131.
Marchand, Hans (1964): A set of criteria for the establishing of derivational relationship between words unmarked by derivational morphemes. *Indogermanische Forschungen* 69: 10–19.
Martinet, André (1960): *Éléments de linguistique générale*. Paris: Colin [later editions with different pagination].
Marušič, Franc (2003): **Aff-STEM-ix*: On discontinuous morphology. Available at http://www.ung.si/~fmarusic/pub/marusic_2003_cirkumfixi.pdf.
Matthews, P[eter] H. (1972): *Inflectional Morphology. A Theoretical Study Based on Aspects of Latin Verb Conjugation*. Cambridge: Cambridge University Press.
Matthews, P[eter] H. (1974): *Morphology. An Introduction to the Theory of Word-Structure*. Cambridge: Cambridge University Press.
Matthews, P[eter] H. (1991): *Morphology*. 2nd ed. Cambridge: Cambridge University Press.
McArthur, Tom (1998): *Concise Oxford Companion to the English Language*. Online edition. Oxford: Oxford University Press. Available at http://www.oxfordreference.com/view/10.1093/acref/9780192800619.001.0001/acref-9780192800619 [last access 10 Sept 2014].

Meder, Gregor and Joachim Mugdan (1990): Alle reden von Häufigkeit .... Anmerkungen zum Thema „Frequenz" in der Morphologie. In: A[rmin] Bassarak, D[agmar] Bittner, A[ndreas] Bittner and P[etra] Thiele (eds.), *Wurzel(n) der Natürlichkeit. Studien zur Morphologie und Phonologie IV*, 87–108. Berlin: Zentralinstitut für Sprachwissenschaft.

Mel'čuk, I[gor'] A. (1963): O "vnutrennej fleksii" v indoevropejskich i semitskich jazykach. *Voprosy jazykoznanija* 12(4): 27–40.

Mel'čuk, I[gor] A. (1982): *Towards a Language of Linguistics*. Ed. by Ph[ilip] Luelsdorff. München: Fink.

Mel'čuk, Igor (1996): *Cours de morphologie générale (théorique et descriptive)*. Vol. 3/3: *Moyens morphologiques / Quatrième partie. Syntactiques morphologiques*. Montréal: Presses de l'Université de Montréal; [Paris:] CNRS Éditions.

Mel'čuk, Igor (1997): *Cours de morphologie générale (théorique et descriptive)*. Vol. 4/5: *Cinquième partie. Signes morphologiques*. Montréal: Presses de l'Université de Montréal; [Paris:] CNRS Éditions.

Mel'čuk, Igor (2000): Morphological processes. In: Geert Booij, Christian Lehmann and Joachim Mugdan (eds.), *Morphology. An International Handbook on Inflection and Word-Formation*. Vol. 1, 523–535. Berlin/New York: de Gruyter.

Mel'čuk, Igor (2006): *Aspects of the Theory of Morphology*. Ed. by David Beck. Berlin/New York: Mouton de Gruyter.

Mithun, Marianne (1984): The evolution of noun incorporation. *Language* 60: 847–894.

Montermini, Fabio (2008): *Il lato sinistro della morfologia. La prefissazione in italiano e nelle lingue del mondo*. Milano: FrancoAngeli.

Montermini, Fabio (2010): Units in compounding. In: Sergio Scalise and Irene Vogel (eds.), *Cross-Disciplinary Issues in Compounding*, 77–92. Amsterdam/Philadelphia: Benjamins.

Moravcsik, Edith A. (2000): Infixation. In: Geert Booij, Christian Lehmann and Joachim Mugdan (eds.), *Morphology. An International Handbook on Inflection and Word-Formation*. Vol. 1, 545–552. Berlin/New York: de Gruyter.

Motsch, Wolfgang (1999): *Deutsche Wortbildung in Grundzügen*. Berlin/New York: de Gruyter.

Mugdan, Joachim (1984): Grammatik im Wörterbuch. Wortbildung. In: Herbert Ernst Wiegand (ed.), *Studien zur neuhochdeutschen Lexikographie V*, 237–308. Hildesheim: Olms.

Mugdan, Joachim (1986): Was ist eigentlich ein Morphem? *Zeitschrift für Phonetik, Sprachwissenschaft und Kommunikationsforschung* 39: 29–43.

Mugdan, Joachim (1994): Morphological units. In: R[onald] E. Asher (ed.), *The Encyclopedia of Language and Linguistics*. Vol. 5, 2543–2553. Oxford: Pergamon Press.

Mugdan, Joachim (2011): On the origins of the term *phoneme*. *Historiographia Linguistica* 38: 85–110.

Neef, Martin (2000a): Phonologische Konditionierung. In: Geert Booij, Christian Lehmann and Joachim Mugdan (eds.), *Morphology. An International Handbook on Inflection and Word-Formation*. Vol. 1, 463–473. Berlin/New York: de Gruyter.

Neef, Martin (2000b): Morphologische und syntaktische Konditionierung. In: Geert Booij, Christian Lehmann and Joachim Mugdan (eds.), *Morphology. An International Handbook on Inflection and Word-Formation*. Vol. 1, 473–484. Berlin/New York: de Gruyter.

Nevis, Joel A. (2000): Clitics. In: Geert Booij, Christian Lehmann and Joachim Mugdan (eds.), *Morphology. An International Handbook on Inflection and Word-Formation*. Vol. 1, 388–404. Berlin/New York: de Gruyter.

Nevins, Andrew (2011): Phonologically conditioned allomorph selection. In: Marc van Oostendorp, Colin J. Ewen, Elizabeth Hume and Keren Rice (eds.), *The Blackwell Companion to Phonology*. Vol. 4: *Phonological Interfaces*, 2357–2382. Chichester: Wiley-Blackwell.

Nida, Eugene A. (1948): The identification of morphemes. *Language* 24: 414–441.
Nida, Eugene A. (1949): *Morphology. The Descriptive Analysis of Words*. 2nd ed. Ann Arbor: University of Michigan Press [1st ed. 1946].
Nübling, Damaris and Renata Szczepaniak (2013): Linking elements in German: Origin, change, functionalization. *Morphology* 23: 67–89.
Olsen, Susan (1986): *Wortbildung im Deutschen. Eine Einführung in die Theorie der Wortstruktur*. Stuttgart: Kröner.
Parks, Douglas R. (1976): *A Grammar of Pawnee*. New York/London: Garland.
Paster, Mary (2009): Explaining phonological conditions on affixation: Evidence from suppletive allomorphy and affix ordering. *Word Structure* 2: 18–47.
Pavlov, Dordži A. (1983): Imja suščestvitel'noe. In: *Grammatika kalmyckogo jazyka. Fonetika i morfologija*, 67–131. Èlista: Kalmyckoe knižnoe izdadel'stvo.
Perlmutter, David M. (1970): Surface structure constraints in syntax. *Linguistic Inquiry* 1: 187–255.
Perlmutter, David M. (1988): The split morphology hypothesis: Evidence from Yiddish. In: Michael Hammond and Michael Noonan (eds.), *Theoretical Morphology. Approaches in Modern Linguistics*, 79–100. San Diego, CA: Academic Press.
Peškovskij, A[leksandr] M. (1925): Ponjatie otdel'nogo slova. In: A. M. Peškovskij, *Sbornik statej. Metodika rodnogo jazyka, lingvistika, stilistika, poètika*, 122–140. Leningrad/Moskva: Gosudarstvennoe izdatel'stvo.
Plag, Ingo (1999): *Morphological Productivity. Structural Constraints in English Derivation*. Berlin/ New York: de Gruyter.
Plag, Ingo (2004): Syntactic category information and the semantics of derivational morphological rules. *Folia Linguistica* 38: 193–225.
Plank, Frans (2010): Variable direction in zero-derivation and the unity of polysemous lexical items. *Word Structure* 3: 82–97.
Plungian [= Plungjan], Vladimir A. (2001): Agglutination and flection. In: Martin Haspelmath, Ekkehard König, Wulf Oesterreicher and Wolfgang Raible (eds.), *Language Typology and Language Universals*. Vol. 1, 669–678. Berlin/New York: de Gruyter.
Plungjan, Vladimir A. (2003): *Obščaja morfologija. Vvedenie v problematiku*. 2nd ed. Moskva: URSS [1st ed. 2000].
Postal, Paul M. (1969): Anaphoric islands. *Papers from the Regional Meeting of the Chicago Linguistic Society* 5: 205–239.
Raimy, Eric (2011): Reduplication. In: Marc van Oostendorp, Colin J. Ewen, Elizabeth Hume and Keren Rice (eds.), *The Blackwell Companion to Phonology*. Vol. 4: *Phonological Interfaces*, 2383–2413. Chichester: Wiley-Blackwell.
Rainer, Franz (1996): Inflection inside derivation: Evidence from Spanish and Portuguese. In: Geert Booij and Jaap van Marle (eds.), *Yearbook of Morphology 1995*, 83–91. Dordrecht: Kluwer.
Ricca, Davide (2005): Cumulative exponence involving derivation: Some patterns for an uncommon phenomenon. In: Wolfgang U. Dressler, Dieter Kastovsky, Oskar E. Pfeiffer and Franz Rainer (eds.), *Morphology and Its Demarcations. Selected Papers from the 11th Morphology Meeting, Vienna, February 2004*, 197–213. Amsterdam/Philadelphia: Benjamins.
Rice, Keren (2011): Principles of affix ordering: An overview. *Word Structure* 4: 169–200.
Rubba, Johanna (2001): Introflection. In: Martin Haspelmath, Ekkehard König, Wulf Oesterreicher and Wolfgang Raible (eds.), *Language Typology and Language Universals*. Vol. 1, 678–694. Berlin/New York: de Gruyter.
Ryan, Kevin M. (2010): Variable affix order: Grammar and learning. *Language* 86: 758–791.

Saussure, Ferdinand de (1916): *Cours de linguistique générale*. Publié par Charles Bally et Albert Sechehaye avec la collaboration de Albert Riedlinger. Lausanne/Paris: Payot [later editions with different pagination].
Scalise, Sergio (1984): *Generative Morphology*. Dordrecht/Cinnaminson, NJ: Foris.
Schiering, René, Balthasar Bickel and Kristine A. Hildebrandt (2010): The prosodic word is not universal, but emergent. *Journal of Linguistics* 46: 657–709.
Schpak-Dolt, Nikolaus (2010): *Einführung in die französische Morphologie*. 3rd ed. Berlin/New York: de Gruyter [1st ed. 1992].
Spencer, Andrew (1998): Morphophonological operations. In: Andrew Spencer and Arnold M. Zwicky (eds.), *The Handbook of Morphology*, 123–143. Oxford: Blackwell.
Spencer, Andrew (2012): Identifying stems. *Word Structure* 5: 88–108.
Stemberger, Joseph P. and Barbara Handford Bernhardt (1999): Contiguity, metathesis, and infixation. In: Kimary Shahin, Susan Blake and Eun-Sook Kim (eds.), *The Proceedings of the Seventeenth West Coast Conference on Formal Linguistics*, 610–624. Stanford, CA: Center for the Study of Language and Information.
Stolz, Thomas, Cornelia Stroh and Aina Urdze (2011): *Total Reduplication. The Areal Linguistics of a Potential Universal*. [Berlin]: Akademie Verlag.
Stump, Gregory T. (2001a): *Inflectional Morphology. A Theory of Paradigm Structure*. Cambridge: Cambridge University Press.
Stump, Gregory T. (2001b): Affix position. In: Martin Haspelmath, Ekkehard König, Wulf Oesterreicher and Wolfgang Raible (eds.), *Language Typology and Language Universals*. Vol. 1, 708–714. Berlin/New York: de Gruyter.
Stump, G[regory] T. (2006): Template morphology. In: Keith Brown (ed.), *Encyclopedia of Language and Linguistics*. Vol. 11, 559–562. 2nd ed. Amsterdam: Elsevier.
Trager, George L. (1948): Taos I: A language revisited. *International Journal of American Linguistics* 14: 155–160.
Umbreit, Birgit (2010): Does *love* come from *to love* or *to love* from *love*? Why lexical motivation has to be regarded as bidirectional. In: Alexander Onysko and Sascha Michel (eds.), *Cognitive Perspectives on Word Formation*, 301–333. Berlin/New York: De Gruyter Mouton.
Ussishkin, Adam (2007): Morpheme position. In: Paul de Lacy (ed.), *The Cambridge Handbook of Phonology*, 457–472. Cambridge: Cambridge University Press.
van Lier, Eva (2012): Reconstructing multifunctionality. *Theoretical Linguistics* 38: 119–135.
Vardul', I[gor'] F. (1991): Morfema v tipologičeskom issledovanii. In: I. F. Vardul' (ed.), *Morfema i problemy tipologii*, 6–85. Moskva: Nauka.
Volodin A[leksandr] P. and V[iktor] S. Chrakovskij (1991): Tipologija klassifikacij morfem. In: I[gor'] F. Vardul' (ed.), *Morfema i problemy tipologii*, 108–134. Moskva: Nauka.
Wallis, Ethel (1956): Simulfixation in aspect markers of Mezquital Otomi. *Language* 32: 453–459.
Wiese, Richard (1996a): *The Phonology of German*. Oxford: Oxford University Press.
Wiese, Richard (1996b): Phrasal compounds and the theory of word syntax. *Linguistic Inquiry* 27: 183–193.
Wiltshire, Caroline and Alec Marantz (2000): Reduplication. In: Geert Booij, Christian Lehmann and Joachim Mugdan (eds.), *Morphology. An International Handbook on Inflection and Word-Formation*. Vol. 1, 557–567. Berlin/New York: de Gruyter.
Wurzel, Wolfgang Ullrich (1989): *Inflectional Morphology and Naturalness*. Translated by Manfred Schentke. Berlin: Akademie Verlag; Dordrecht: Kluwer [originally German 1984].
Yu, Alan C. L. (2007): *A Natural History of Infixation*. Oxford: Oxford University Press.

Zwicky, Arnold M. (1985): How to describe inflection. In: Mary Niepokuj, M. V. Clay, V. Nikiforidou and D. Feder (eds.), *Proceedings of the 11th Annual Meeting of the Berkeley Linguistics Society*, 372–386. Berkely, CA: Berkeley Linguistics Society.

Zwicky, Arnold M. (1986): Imposed versus inherent feature specifications, and other multiple feature markings. In: *The Indiana University Linguistics Club Twentieth Anniversary Volume. Papers*, 85–104. Bloomington: Indiana University Linguistics Club.

Andrew Spencer
10 Derivation

1   Introduction
2   Formal aspects: how derivation is realized
3   Syntagmatic and paradigmatic aspects of derivational processes
4   Semantico-syntactic aspects
5   References

Abstract: The article summarizes the principal formal, syntagmatic and semantic aspects of derivational morphology. The formal aspects include stem formation and selection as well as affixational and non-affixational operations. Under syntagmatic aspects we consider the internal structure of derived words, including affix ordering, morphophonological restrictions and paradigmatic aspects. In the semantico-syntactic aspects we include the prototypical semantic categories of derivation, as well as argument structure alternations, such as causatives, applicatives and passives, derivational relationships that do not involve any semantic component, and evaluative morphology (diminutives/augmentatives).

1 Introduction

I shall assume without comment that derivation relates lexemes. As such, derivation is part of the much wider phenomenon of lexical relatedness. It is often assumed that derivation takes a lexeme (the base lexeme) as input and delivers another lexeme (the derivate). This implies a metaphor of temporal processing in which the derivate in some sense "comes after" the base. Indeed, this is implied in the term *word-formation* itself. In some theoretical models, derivational morphology is derivational in the technical sense that it is formalized in terms of a set of generative rules or principles operating as a sequence rather than as a set of well-formedness constraints on arbitrarily defined structures (see article 5 on word-formation in generative grammar for further discussion). This has led to a debate over whether morphology in general and especially derivational morphology should be defined by means of a derivational generative engine (as in the work of Aronoff 1976; Halle 1973; Lieber 1992; Selkirk 1982; and many others)

Andrew Spencer, Essex, UK

https://doi.org/10.1515/9783111420561-010

or whether it should be defined in terms of static well-formedness statements (Jackendoff 1975; Bochner 1993; Stump 2001), perhaps arranged as a multiple inheritance tree (as in Riehemann 1998). The static conception of lexical relatedness leaves open the question of how a genuinely new lexeme comes to be coined by means of derivational morphology. Koenig (1999) provides important discussion of this problem, deploying the notion of on-line type construction.

Although derivates are generally coined historically from a pre-existing base we often find that a language borrows a morphologically complex form and only coins the apparent base lexeme much later (sometimes hundreds of years later; see article 12 on backformation. In general, we cannot rely on etymology for guidance on this matter. Although I shall continue to use the derivational metaphor it should be borne in mind that a static interpretation of lexical relatedness is also valid.

I take a lexeme to be minimally a three-dimensional object uniting form properties, syntactic properties, and a semantic representation. Form properties include a specification of the pronunciation of the root, a set of stems or a representative word form from the lexeme's inflectional paradigm ("leading form"). In addition, it is often necessary to include information such as inflectional class, irregular morphological forms, idiosyncratic subcategorization/selection properties and so on. The syntactic properties of a lexeme can often be projected from its semantic representation. For instance, in English a lexeme denoting a dynamic event relating two participants will typically take the form of a transitive verb (e.g., HIT). However, in many cases syntactic properties such as government or even word class have to be stipulated. Likewise, in many cases the morphological properties of a word can be predicted from its syntactic properties. For instance, we can deduce by default that the verb HIT has a past and non-past form (though we cannot predict exactly what those forms will be). However, there are many instances of mismatch. Thus, in Russian the word for a cafeteria or dining room, STOLOVAJA, is a noun syntactically and semantically, but it inflects like a feminine gender adjective. Thus, the default morphological specifications for this lexeme have to be overridden and the lexicon has to refer us to the inflection of adjectives to specify the word forms of the lexeme (see Spencer 2007, 2010, 2013).

There are always two aspects to derivation. The first is the formal aspect: what are the morphophonological operations that realize the derivational relationship? The second is the semantic aspect: how does the meaning of the derived lexeme relate to that of the base lexeme? In addition, derivational morphology often has a third aspect: a specification of how the syntactic properties of the derived lexeme relate to those of the base. The formal operations define what is sometimes called a "derivational type" (for instance, "deverbal nominal in -er" vs. "deverbal nominal in -ant") and the semantic relations define a "derivational category" (for instance "agentive deverbal noun" vs. "causative verb") (see Szymanek 1989 for discussion of the type/category distinction in the context of English word-formation).

As Štekauer (article 8 on the delimitation of derivation and inflection) points out, one of the main differences between inflection and derivation is that derivation (typically) increases the lexical stock of the language. That article uses the term "derivation" in a wide sense. Here I concentrate mainly on the morphological means by which new lexemes can be formed, recognizing that it is very difficult to individuate lexemes in practice. At the end of the article I briefly discuss evaluative morphology, which appears to create pragmatically modified versions of a lexeme rather than a new lexeme as such.

Although derivation typically creates a new lexeme, it is difficult to use this as a hard-and-fast criterion because there is no way of deciding when two words constitute distinct lexemes as opposed to two usages of one and the same lexeme. This can be thought of as the central problem of lexicology. In particular, it is often difficult to know whether a new lexeme has been created when new meanings are coerced. For instance, in English it is often possible to coerce a count meaning from a mass term (and hence allow that term to be pluralized: *three coffees* meaning 'three cups of coffee', the "Universal Packager"), or to coerce a mass meaning from a count noun (*there's egg on your tie*, the "Universal Grinder"). However, this coercion relation is limited to specific lexemes, in general, and is therefore not a fully productive part of the language. It is therefore difficult to know whether we are dealing with different allowable ways of using a single lexeme (mass/count 'coffee', 'egg') or whether we have a lexically restricted derivational category expressed by conversion giving rise to systematic polysemy (mass 'coffee' → count 'coffee'). Similar problems arise, for instance, with intransitive/transitive verb alternants such as BREAK: *The vase broke* vs. *Tom broke the vase* and a whole host of other lexical relations (see also article 11 on conversion).

In this connection we must bear in mind that in some respects polysemous variants of a lexeme very frequently behave like distinct lexical entries with respect to word-formation. To give just one simple example, from the adjective *poor* we can create the property noun *poverty* but only where *poor* means 'not rich (in something)', either concrete (*the poverty of the unemployed*) or abstract (*the poverty of the stimulus*). Where *poor* means just 'bad' we have to use the nominal form *poorness*: *the poorness/*poverty of the team's performance*. This suggests we have two distinct lexemes (see also Plank 2010 on German *fett* 'fat'). Abundant examples can be found in deverbal actional nominals. Thus, *commit (a crime)* gives *commission*, *commit (to trial)* gives *committal* while *commit (oneself to something)* gives *commitment* (Carstairs-McCarthy 1992a). It may turn out that we can use such derivational patterns as a test of lexemehood.

2 Formal aspects: how derivation is realized

2.1 Stems

It is customary to define the root of the base lexeme as the starting point for derivational processes. However, in practice, we usually find that the interesting generalizations about derivation (and inflection) are defined over sets of stems (the root is often the default stem form). Traditionally, a stem is what remains when we remove inflections, though this definition hinges on us being able to distinguish inflectional formatives from stem formatives (see Spencer 2012 on segmenting stems and inflections).

In the descriptive tradition a stem is often associated with a meaning or inflectional property ('the oblique case stem', 'the imperfect stem' and so on). However, Aronoff (1994) introduces the notion of 'morphomic stem'. This is a form that does not realize a meaning or morphosyntactic property in itself, and which is used as the basis for inflectional, derivational and sometimes compounding morphology. Aronoff illustrates this notion with the third stem in Latin. A regular 1st conjugation verb (AMO 'I love') has a first ('imperfect') stem ending in the conjugation theme vowel (*ama:*) and a second ('perfect') stem derived by adding -*v* to the first stem: *ama:-v-*. For some verb classes there are irregularities and subregularities. For example, the 3rd conjugation REGO (*reg-*) 'I rule, govern', lengthens the root vowel and adds -*s*: *re:ks-i:* (= *re:gsi:*) 'I ruled'.

Latin verbs also distinguish a third stem in -*t*: *ama:-t* '(having been) loved'. This stem is not necessarily passive in meaning, however, because it is the base for another stem, that of the future active participle in -*u:r-*: *ama:-t-u:r-(us)* 'being about to love (-M.SG.NOM)'. This derivation is found with irregular verbs, too: e.g., the suppletive: FERO 'I carry', infinitive *ferre*, 3rd stem *la:t-* 'carried', future active participle *la:tu:rus*. It would be incorrect to think of the third stem as purely inflectional, however, because it is the basis of several derivational processes, including the agent nominal in -*or*: *ama:re* → *ama:t-or* 'lover', an event nominal in -*io(n-)*: *cogita:re* 'to think' → *cogita:t-io(n-)* 'thought' and an iterative verb in -*it*: *scri:bere* > *script-* > *scriptit-* 'write often'.

It is sometimes thought (mistakenly) that stems are typically irregular in form (partly because discussion tends to focus on irregular stems) but the three Latin stems are entirely regular for regular verbs: [root + theme vowel], [root + theme vowel + w-] and [root + theme vowel + t]. On the other hand, in many languages stems are irregular in the important sense that they consist of two or more discontinuous parts, whose combination is unpredictable. Typically, this is found with verbs and is the result of grammaticalizing a verb root with an adverbial, an incorporated root or whatever. Athapaskan languages illustrate this pattern (see Spencer 1991: 208–211 for examples from Navajo) as does the very distantly related Siberian (Yenisseian) language Ket. Verbs in Ket can become very complex, being extended by a host of prefixes. Here I follow the position class description in Vajda (2004: 45), shown in (1). (Vajda calls agreement markers "valence" markers. For a more complex analysis of Ket position classes see Werner 1997.)

(1) Ket position class template

P8	P7	P6	P5	P4	P3	P2	P1	P0	P–1
agr	incor-porate	agr	adpos	dur/ or agr	agr	past/ imp	agr	base	agr

The crucial positions are P0, the position of the basic root, P5 and P7. All but about 100 simplex verbs, and all productive patterns, require an overt element in position P7. This may be a productively incorporated element, for instance a direct object, an instrument, or a meaningless element, sometimes accompanied by a (meaningless) element (noted as "L") in P5. In some words none of the components of the stem can be assigned any meaning, as in (2), where "MS" is a "morphotactic separator", a meaningless connector, and the P7, P0 elements are both cranberry morphs:

(2) déqsàq   'I hear'
    di^8 eq^7 (s)   aq^0
    1SG.SUBJ^8 L^7 (MS)   L^0

2.2 Morphological devices realizing derivation

In addition to standard patterns of affixation, a number of European languages (especially English) employ conversion (see article 11). Infixation is uncommon (though it seems to have been an exponent of derivation in earlier stages of Indo-European). Reduplication (see article 18) is found, though not in the derivational morphology of Indo-European languages. (However, a type of reduplication process has entered conversational French evaluative morphology: *bête* 'stupid' → *bébête* 'a bit stupid'.) Turkic languages and languages of other groups influenced by Turkic often have full or partially reduplicated forms akin to English *bye-bye* or *higgeldy-piggeldy*, what is sometimes referred to as the *mışmaş*-type, after Turkish. Such formations are almost always onomatopoeic or evaluative/expressive in character. Unlike many language groups outside Europe we don't find, say, reduplication of the first syllable of a root to express prototypical derivational relations such as subject nominalization or causative verb in typical European languages. However, in some Daghestanian languages reduplication does have a genuine derivational function, for instance, verb root reduplication to express aktionsarten or aspectual categories in Tsezic languages.

In inflection, languages may deploy non-affixational or non-concatenative formal devices. These include ablaut/apophony (change in the root vowel), consonant mutation (change usually in the initial or final consonant(s) of the root), and prosodic alternations, including alternations in stress, accent, or tone, segment length (gemination/lengthening or shortening of consonants or vowels), word-domain prosodies such as nasality, palatality, or advanced tongue root. Non-affixational devices seem to be less common and less systematic in (canonical) derivation, but it is not uncommon to find such devices being used as part of the systematic morphology. For instance, in English there are noun-verb pairs related only by stress shift: *a cóntrast ~ to contrást, tránsport ~ to transpórt*. This only affects disyllabic verbs which are etymologically of the form prefix-stem and it reflects a tendency for disyllabic nouns to be forestressed (*sýntax*) and disyllabic verbs to be endstressed (*reláx*).

In a number of language groups we see non-concatenative morphology, in which morphological properties are realized by changing the disposition or the length of vowels and consonants in the root rather than by affixation. The most well-known systems are often referred to as 'root-and-pattern' morphology (also called "transfixation" by Bauer 1988). It is in the Afro-Asiatic languages and especially the Semitic languages such as Hebrew and especially Arabic that we see well-developed systems of this kind. The system is described in any handbook of Arabic (and many textbooks of morphology) but a convenient summary of Modern Standard Arabic (with transcribed examples) is presented in Kaye (2007). Of the languages of Europe, Maltese preserves a good many of these patterns.

Derivational relations are often expressed by multi-word expression (see article 17) and in the course of grammaticalization the grammatical components of such expressions often become more affix-like. Thus, Toivonen (2003) argues that in English the particle of particle-verb constructions (see also article 16) such as *turn on* or *throw out* has become a suffix when it appears after the verb and before the direct object (turn#on the light, where # represents an affix boundary). In post-verb position, however, (turn the *light on*) the particle is a non-projecting word, that is, a word which cannot form the head of a multi-word phrase. If this analysis is correct it shows that we have a morph which is sometimes an affix and sometimes a syntactically independent form. This complicates the morphological definition of "derivation" somewhat.

A particularly interesting set of cases is represented by preverbs in languages such as German and especially Hungarian (Ackerman and LeSourd 1997), in which the separable preverb can attach as a prefix to the verb stem and the whole construction can then undergo further derivation. For example, from Hungarian *old* 'to dissolve' we obtain *meg-old-* 'to solve (a problem)' (with the (meaningless) preverb *meg-*), from which we can derive the adjective *megold-hatatlan* 'unsolvable' (Ackerman and LeSourd 1997: 89).

Even in languages in which the preverb is always fixed to the verb stem morphologically we find that the preverb may not cohere as tightly to the base as we would expect from a bona fide prefix. Languages such as Greek and Sanskrit exhibit interesting instances of inflection between the preverb and the verb. The so-called Greek augment is a case in point. In (3) we see examples of present and past tense verb forms (Holton, Mackridge and Philippaki-Warburton 1997: 161 f.):

(3) Prefixation in Greek verbs
Present		Past Imperfective
grafo	'write'	e-grafa
epivalo	'impose'	ep-e-vala
sim-veni	'happen'	sin-e-vi
ep-ana-lamvano	'repeat'	ep-an-e-lava

The tense prefix is *e-* but the derivational prefixes *epi-*, *sim-*, *ana-* appear external to that tense marker. This is an instance of what Stump (2001: chapter 4) refers to as head-marking morphology, because the inflections effectively ignore the non-head, prefixal, part of the representation.

Another type of word-formation that is not mediated through affixes as traditionally defined is illustrated by verbs with reflexive pronominal clitics. In a number of Slavic languages weak pronominal forms, including reflexives, are realized as second position (Wackernagel) clitics. As in many of the world's languages, reflexive verbs have a generally detransitivizing function, but the meanings of the reflexive can be very varied, ranging from a straightforward pronominal object (*The children washed themselves*) to no discernible meaning change whatever. One familiar function is that of a passive voice as seen in (4) from Czech, where the verb *kosit* 'to mow' is used in an imperfective passive sense (the examples are adapted from Šmilauer 1972):

(4) Obilí se kosí
    corn REFL mow.3SG
    'The corn is being mown.'

This represents word-formation to the extent that you believe that a regular passive alternation is a species of derivation. A very common use of reflexive forms is to detransitivize causatives:

(5) a. *Zavírat   dveře*   Czech
      close.INF.IPFV doors.ACC
      'to close the doors'
   b. *Dveře   se   zavírají*
      Doors.NOM REFL close
      'The doors are closing.' [warning on Prague underground railway]

This process can give rise to reflexiva tantum interpretations, as in (6c) compared with (6a, b):

(6) a. *Zlomil   větev*   Czech
      broke.M.SG branch
      'He broke the branch.'
   b. *Větev   se   zlomila*
      branch(F) REFL broke.F.SG
      'The branch broke.'
   c. *Zlomil   se   mu   hlas*
      broke.M.SG REFL him.DAT voice(M)
      'His voice broke.'

Another use of reflexive forms common in Slavic is to create a kind of intensive aktionsart (often accompanied by prefixation). Such constructions can sometimes be difficult to render in languages such as English, cf. the Czech examples in (7):

(7) *spát* 'to sleep' ~ *vyspát se* 'to sleep off, get a good night's sleep'
     dělat 'to do, make' ~ *nadělat se nepříjemností* 'to create a lot
     of unpleasantness'

There are a good many reflexiva tantum in Czech, including some very common verbs such as *bát se* (+genitive) 'to fear, be afraid of', *smát se* 'to laugh', *ptát se* 'to ask', *zdát se* 'to dream (of); seem'. In some cases, or in some meanings, the reflexive is optional, as with *blýskat (se)* 'to flash (e.g., lightning)', or *začít (se)* 'to begin' and *skončit (se)* 'to finish'.

The examples so far have all illustrated the accusative form of the reflexive clitic pronoun, *se*. Czech also has a dative reflexive form, *si*, and this, too, participates in word-formation. An example of a dative reflexivum tantum verb is *všímat si* 'to notice', which takes a genitive case complement.

3 Syntagmatic and paradigmatic aspects of derivational processes

By "syntagmatic aspects of derivation" I mean principally the order of stems and affixes. That aspect has been subject to a good deal of discussion. Rice (2011) provides a very good summary of recent research into the determinants of affix ordering cross-linguistically in inflection and also in derivation. Paradigmatic relations are normally discussed in relation to inflection, but some linguists have argued that they can be discerned in derivation, too. Finally, there are phenomena that have both syntagmatic and paradigmatic aspects, which I discuss briefly in the final subsection.

It is often said that derivation is "recursive". What is meant by this is that a word-formation rule gives rise to a lexeme and it is lexemes which are the base of word-formation rules, so the output of such a rule can serve as the input to another rule. Thus, we can find chains of the kind $[_N$ cipher$] \rightarrow [_V$ de $[_N$ cipher$]] \rightarrow [_A [_V$ de $[_N$ cipher$]]$ able$] \rightarrow [_A$ in $[_A [_V$ de $[_N$ cipher$]]$ able$]] \rightarrow [_N [_A$ in $[_A [_V$ de $[_N$ cipher$]]$ abil$]]$ity$]$. However, there are generally phonological, grammatical and semantic restrictions on the applicability of a given word-formation process, so the recursion is not as general as in the case of syntax. Some languages have affixes which are obligatorily word final.

3.1 Affix order and scope

Cross-linguistically, we often find claims that semantic scope determines affix order. However, in European languages there are fewer clear instances of scope-driven ordering. Here I will look briefly at two recent studies which argue for scopal differences in ordering, one for suffixes, the other for prefixes.

Kiefer and Komlósy (2011) discuss the behaviour of the deverbal causative (*-(t)At*) and factitive (*-tAt*) suffixes, the diminutive/iterative suffix (*-gAt*) (actually, a better term would be "attenuative", since this is not an instance of evaluative morphology), and the possibility suffix (*-hAt*) in Hungarian. Kenesei, Vágo and Fenyvesi (1998: 359) treat the causative and factitive suffixes in Hungarian as a single causative suffix. However, Kiefer and Komlósy argue that they should be distinguished because they have different syntax. Their causative only attaches to non-agentive verbs (hence, only to intransitives) behaving rather like a transitivizer, while their factitive behaves more like a standard causative suffix and can causativize transitives. The two can be combined in one word in the order stem < causative < factitive: *mozg-at-tat* 'to make somebody move something'.

Likewise, the factitive can combine with a deadjectival causative verb formed with -*ít*: *nagy-ít* 'to make bigger, enlarge', *nagy-ít-tat* 'to let make bigger, let enlarge'.

The diminutive/iterative suffix can combine with verbs derived with the causative and/or factitive suffix. Either order of diminutive/iterative and factitive is possible, depending on the sense: from *olvas* 'to read' we have *olvas-tat-gat* 'from time to time (*gat*) it is true that x lets (*tat*) y read' vs. *olvas-gat-tat* 'to let read from time to time'. As is generally the case cross-linguistically, the affix furthest from the stem takes the nearer affix in its scope: *olvas-tat-gat* = [[[READ]-CAUSE]-ITERATIVE], *olvas-gat-tat* = [[[READ]-ITERATIVE]-CAUSE].

The possibility suffix -*hAt* behaves rather differently. This suffix always seems to come finally in the word and fails to take most of the verbal inflections expected of a verb stem. Many grammarians treat it as (effectively) inflectional (see, for instance, Kenesei, Vágo and Fenyvesi 1998: 359). Kiefer and Komlósy (2011), however, suggest that this means that the suffix is not (prototypically) inflectional and not (prototypically) derivational.

Bulgarian, like other Slavic languages, has several layers of verb prefixation. Markova (2011) draws the traditional distinction between lexical prefixes, which create entirely new verb lexemes and other types. For instance, from the root *znaja* 'to know' we have the verbs *po-znaja* 'to be acquainted with; guess, tell', *sŭ-znaja* 'to realize', *u-znaja* 'to learn, find out', *pri-znaja* 'to acknowledge, recognize; confess, admit' (Markova 2011: 247; examples given in 3sg present tense form). The semantic contribution of these prefixes is generally non-compositional. However, there are other kinds of prefix which impart aspectual or aktionsart meanings ("supra-lexical prefixes"). Markova argues that there are two sorts, inner and outer (aspectual) prefixes. The inner prefixes modify the verb's argument structure by specifying a spatial/locative, or a causative or a quantificational meaning. Examples of the spatial/locative prefixes are: *bjaga* 'to run' vs. *do-bjaga* 'to run to (place)'; *pluva (v rekata)* 'to swim (in the river)', intransitive vs. *pre-pluva (rekata)* 'to swim (the river)', transitive. A causative prefix is *raz-* as in *plače bebe-to* 'cries baby-the, the baby cries' (intransitive) vs. *raz-plača bebe-to* 'I CAUS-cry baby-the, I make the baby cry' (transitive). The cumulative and distributive suffixes induce quantification over the verb's complement, as in the case of the cumulative *na-*: *gotvja* 'to cook' vs. *na-gotvja supi* 'to prepare a lot of soups'. Markova's outer prefixes have no particular effect on verb arguments but instead introduce aspectual or phasal meanings: *za-plače* 'to start crying (*plače*)', *pri-boli* 'to suddenly start hurting (*boli*)', *po-plače* 'to cry for a little while', *ot-boli* 'to stop hurting', *pre-proda* 'to sell again' (from *pro-da* 'to sell', with the lexical prefix *pro-*). A second set of outer prefixes modulate the intensity of an action, giving intensive or attenuative readings: *pre-jade* 'to eat excessively (*jade*)', *po-jade* 'to eat a little'. Finally, there are prefixes which denote manners: *s-migne* 'to blink rapidly (*migne*)', *raz-vŭrže* 'to untie (*vŭrže*)'.

Up to four prefixes may be found in a single verb form: *iz-po-na-[raz-kaže]* 'to narrate ([raz-kaže]) completely (iz) many (na) stories one by one (po)'. Markova follows Cinque (1999) in assuming that all the different meanings of the inner and outer affixes are represented in a universally fixed hierarchy which gives rise to a strict linear ordering (though some of the prefixes appear in more than one place on the hierarchy). This is said to govern the combinability of the inner and outer prefixes. For example, we can combine the outer prefix *do-* 'completion' and inner prefix *na-* 'many' in that order in *do-na-[pri-gotvja]* 'finishing preparing many (materials)' but not in the reversed order, **na-do-[pri-gotvja]*.

3.2 Morphophonological restrictions

Earlier generative approaches to affix ordering generally, and derivational affix ordering in particular, proposed that affixes in English (and by extension in other languages) can be split into two complementary groups, "Class I" and "Class II" (Siegel 1974; Kiparsky 1982; see the summary in Spencer 1991: 79–81). The Class I affixes, such as *-ity*, trigger and undergo idiosyncratic allomorphy and affect stress while the Class II affixes, such as *-ness*, are morphophonologically inert. According to this "stratal" or "cyclic" model the Class I affixes are always closer to the word root than Class II affixes. Many morphologists were unconvinced by these proposals even for English (Aronoff 1976) and especially for other languages such as Polish (Booij and Rubach 1984, 1987), not least because of contradictions and blatant counterexamples. Fabb (1988) demonstrated that an empirically better solution could be found relying on affix-specific selection restrictions. Hay (2002) argued for a psycholinguistically-based account in terms of "parsability": some affixes are easily integrated into the morphophonology of a word and are therefore hard to identify as affixes. For instance, word forms ending in the past tense suffix allomorph *-t*, such as *sent*, *bent*, *kept* and so on have the same shape as monomorphemic roots such as *dent*, *apt*, but the *-ed* suffix of *jogged*, *rubbed* gives rise to the word final sequences *-gd*, *-bd* which are never found in monomorphemic forms. Thus, the *-d* suffix is easily parsed out of these word forms. Hay argued that the *-ment* in *government* is less parsable in these phonotactic terms than, say, the *-ment* of *bafflement*. For this reason it is easier to treat *government* as a possible base for *-al* suffixation, witness *governmental* vs. *bafflemental. Hay and Plag (2004) demonstrated that a very good empirical fit for English could be obtained by a judicial combination of selection restrictions in the manner of

3.3 Paradigmatic aspects of derivational processes

The most obvious way in which we can speak of paradigmatic relations in derivation is seen with the phenomenon of competing affixation. It is typically the case that a given derivational relationship, say, subject-nominal formation, can be expressed by more than one affix depending on the nature of the base lexeme. Thus, in English, deverbal subject nominals are formed with the suffixes -ant/ent (*claimant, applicant, student, resident*, etc.), by conversion (*cook*), by total suppletion (*pilot* from *fly (an aircraft)*), but mostly by -er suffixation (*driver*). We can think of these various processes as being in paradigmatic opposition to each other, with -er suffixation being the default. In this way, subject-nominal formation is morphologically similar to plural formation.

However, there are more subtle types of paradigmatic relationship, which involve whole words. For instance, Spencer (1988) discusses personal nouns of the type *baroque flautist, electrical engineer, East German*. These are each motivated by two distinct expressions: {*baroque flute, flautist*}, {*electrical engineering, engineer*}, {*East Germany, German*}. The phrasal personal nouns are derived from the nominal expressions *baroque flute*, etc., so that a baroque flautist is 'one who plays the baroque flute (habitually, professionally)'. The morphology of the head noun *flautist*, however, is determined by the head noun. This can lead to a situation in which it appears that the meaning of 'person who' is expressed by a process of truncating the suffix of the phrasal noun's head. However, not all expressions permit such personal nouns. Although most baroque flutes are made out of wood we cannot say of a baroque flautist that she is a wooden flautist. The correct way to think of such constructions is to say that personal noun formation of this sort is completely productive provided that the base expression is a lexicalized expression. Where the base expression is a normal syntactic phrase such as *wooden flute* the paradigmatic lexical relationship no longer holds and the word-formation is not licensed. The linear model of derivation, under which a derivational process creates a new lexeme, which can then further serve as the base of lexeme formation, has difficulty in accounting for those kinds of derivational relationship which appear to be organized paradigmatically (Booij 1997, 2008; Spencer 1988; see Ackema and Neeleman 2004 for a different analysis of these and related constructions in Dutch).

3.4 The internal structure of derived words

The recursive property of word-formation gives the impression that morphologically complex words have a hierarchical organization, representable as a (binary branching) tree structure. However, it has been widely observed that this is misleading because most of the structure is invisible to morphosyntactic or morphosemantic principles ("lexical integrity"). Anderson (1992) argues at length for a model of morphology which eschews such hierarchical structure. A morphological process only has access to its immediate input, not to any deeper layers of structure. Thus, he would argue that it would not be possible to find a word-formation rule of English that, say, added the suffix *-ity* to a word such as *indecipherable* only if it had been constructed using the prefix *de-*.

Interestingly, there are words which seem to counterexemplify Anderson's claims. For instance, the form **indecodeability* is non-existent even though this would mean more or less the same as *indecipherability*. Rather, we use the negative prefix *un-*: *undecodeability*. But now it looks as if the *in-/un-* selection principle can "see inside" the structure of [[de[code]]able] and access the fact that the base is *code* rather than, say, *cipher*. In fact, what is happening here is that *indecipherable* is itself irregular. Most *-able* adjectives that are not highly lexicalized are negated with *un-*. The word *indecipherable* is therefore an irregular negated form of the whole lexeme *decipherable* (perhaps motivated in part by analogy with words such as *indestructible*). Thus, prefix selection doesn't need to access internal structure.

A related issue is that of lexical integrity (see, amongst many others, the discussion in Lieber and Scalise 2007; Booij 2009). Words are held to be autonomous units at the syntactic level of organization and so syntactic operations such as gapping, movement, topicalization, anaphoric reference by pronouns, modification of word parts by external modifiers and so on should be impossible. Unfortunately, the authors cited already show there is ample evidence for all of these phenomena.

A defence of lexical integrity has been mounted by Ackerman and colleagues in a number of places. A recent statement (and references) can be found in Ackerman, Stump and Webelhuth (2011: 326). They factorize the notion "lexical" into four aspects: morphological form (wordhood), lexical properties (meaning, argument structure/grammatical function inventories, case government), inflectional properties (the morphosyntactic properties expressed by the lexeme's word forms) and finally syntactic make-up. They argue that the first three aspects respect integrity, in that syntactic principles cannot manipulate word internal structure, lexical properties or inflectional properties. However, they argue that it is perfectly possible for a lexeme or for a word form of a lexeme to be comprised of more than one syntactic word (syntactic terminal, atom). In the latter case we have inflectional periphrasis, in the former case we have a periphrastic lexeme (for instance, a phrasal verb).

Nonetheless, there remain troubling cases in which it would appear that a morphologically derived word has parts which are accessible to syntactic principles. A well-known example is that of possessive adjectives in Upper Sorbian. These are similar to possessive adjectives in Slavic languages generally (see section 4.2 below). Thus from *bratr* 'brother' we obtain the adjective *bratrow*. However, the original base noun *bratr* can itself be modified by a possessive pronoun (Corbett 1987: 300):

(8) a. *mojeho   bratr-ow-e   dźěći*
       my.M.GEN.SG. brother(M)-POSS.A-NOM.PL child.NOM.PL
       'my brother's children'
    b. *našeho   wučerj-ow-a   zahrodka*
       our.M.GEN.SG teacher(M)-POSS.A-F.NOM.SG garden(F).NOM.SG
       'our teacher's garden'

These cases are particularly odd because the possessive pronominal adjectives *mojeho, našeho* not only modify the base nouns *bratr* 'brother' and *wučer* 'teacher' but agree with them in number, gender, and in case, as though the noun were in the genitive rather than in the possessive adjective form. Other Slavic languages demonstrate (or used to demonstrate) this type of "category mixing" to a much lesser extent, as reported in detail by Corbett (1987).

Further examples of denominal adjectives whose nominal base is itself modified are found in a number of languages, and especially in the Tungusic group of languages spoken mainly in Russia (Nikolaeva 2008). These languages have a productive category of proprietive adjective, that is, a denominal adjective with the meaning 'having N' (such languages often have privative or caritive adjectives with the meaning 'without, lacking N'; cf. English *headless* 'without a head'). In English proprietive meanings are expressed by compounds such as *short-sleeved* ('having short sleeves'), *blue-eyed*, or by derivations such as *hairy* 'possessing hair', *colourful*, *headed* (as in linguistics terminology: a *headed* (i.e. endocentric) *compound*). Proprietive adjectives in the Northern Tungusic language Evenki (spoken in Russia) are productively derived from nouns with the suffix *-či-*. This adjective can combine with number-inflected nouns and it then agrees in case with the noun it modifies:

(9) *aja-l   oro-l-či-du   asi:-du*
    good-PL reindeer-PL-PROPR-DAT woman-DAT
    'to the woman with good reindeer'

Example (9) shows that the proprietive marker is a lexical suffix, not a clitic or phrasal affix, because it can be shown independently that the case markers are suffixes and not clitics. Moreover, the proprietive marker may be followed by diminutive and augmentative affixes that semantically modify the base noun:

(10) a. *saŋari-či-ka:r*
    hole-PROP.A-DIM
    'with little holes'
  b. *xegdi dere-či-ke:ku:n*
    big   face-PROP.A-AUG
    'with a big face'

Similar constructions can be found in Samoyedic languages of Russia, such as Selkup (Nikolaeva 2008; Spencer 2013) and Nenets (Nikolaeva 2003).

4 Semantico-syntactic aspects

4.1 Primary semantic functions of derivation – examples from Chukchi

The prime role of derivation is to create new lexemes by adding a semantic predicate to that of the base lexeme. For comparison, I describe the derivational patterns found in Chukchi, spoken in the northeastern part of the Russian Federation (Skorik 1961; Dunn 1999). In this language we see a wide variety of derivational meanings expressed mainly by suffixes.

In the Tables below I list the principal derivational affixes of Chukchi, including aktionsart affixes. One noticeable feature is that several of these affixes appear with more than one meaning/function, an instance of "separationism" (Beard 1995). These include: *cik/cek*, *-lʔet/lʔat*, *təmŋe*, *e-...-ke*, *mec/mac-*, *-tku/tko*, *em-/am-*, *-rʔu/rʔo*, *-twa*, *et/at*, *ew/aw*. In addition some aktionsart suffixes are also used to form verbs from nouns: *lʔet/lʔat*, *-rʔu*, *-tku*.

The affixes *ine-/ena-* and *-tku/tko* are particularly polyfunctional. They are used as antipassive markers and also as parts of the transitive agreement paradigms, and in their use as aktionsart markers and in denominal verb formation they are often found as more or less meaningless derivational formatives. The suffix *-tku/tko* additionally has a derivational function meaning 'activity with given object'. In these functions it is distinct morphophonologically from the ho-

Tab. 10.1: Chukchi denominal affixes.

1.	*-et/-at* 'general verbalizer'
2.	*-ew/-aw* 'general verbalizer'
3.	*-twa* 'general verbalizer (for statives)'
4.	*-tku/tko* 'activity with given object'
5.	*-lʔet/-lʔat* 'to travel by N'
6.	*-rʔu/rʔo* 'developing event (of meteorological phenomena)'
7.	*-jp/-ep* 'donning clothing'
8.	*-tw* 'removing clothing'
9.	*-u/o* 'to hunt', 'to eat', 'to remove'
10.	*-ŋit/ŋet* 'to spend period of time'
11.	*te/ta-N-ŋ* 'creation of N'
12.	*r-...-ew/aw* 'causative'
13.	*r-...-et/at* 'causative'
14.	*r-...-twet/twat* 'causative'
15.	*-twi/twe* 'inchoative'

mophonous iterative aktionsart marker (weakened sporadic action), which triggers "palatalization" of /l/, unlike the other occurrences of *-tku/tko*.

In (11) I cite representative examples from Moll and Inenliqej's (1957) dictionary (including some Russian glosses which are especially difficult to translate into English out of context), with the derivational formatives in boldface.

(11) Derived lexemes in Chukchi

rə-təlewək 'to move sth. from one place to another; continue'
[peredvigat'; prodolžat']

ine-n-təlewək 'to lead, carry' [vodit', vozit']
(Note that the transitivizing prefix *rə-* has the allomorph *n* in non-initial position)

ine-n-təlewə-tku-k 'to lead, guide; govern, manage'
[vesti, provodit'; pravit', upravljat']

rə-citkuk 'to govern, manage'
[pravit', upravljat']

ine-n-citkuk 'to govern, manage; rectify, touch up; touch'
[pravit', upravljat'; podpravit'; trogat']

rə-jegtelewək 'to save; leave alive' [spasat'; ostavljat' v živyx]

ine-n-jegtelewək 'to save; preserve life' [spasti; soxranit' žizn']

Tab. 10.2: Chukchi denumeral affixes.

16.	*-qew/qaw* (i.e. ordinal suffix) intransitive verbalizer 'act n times'
17.	*r-...-qew/qaw* transitive verbalizer 'act on s.o./sth. n times'

Tab. 10.3: Chukchi affixes for expression of aktionsarten.

1.	*-lʔet/-lʔat* 'prolonged continuous action'
2.	*-cir* 'prolonged interrupted action'
3.	*-cʔet/-cʔat* 'occasional action'
4.	*-cit* 'alternating action'
5.	*-rʔu/rʔo* 'distributive'
6.	*-sqacet/-sqacat* 'accelerated action'
7.	*tale-/tala-* 'gradual action'
8.	*-jiwə/-iwə* 'intensity'
9.	*-tku* 'weakened sporadic action'
10.	*-ŋŋo* 'inceptive'
11.	*-platku* 'terminative, completive'
12.	*teŋ-/taŋ-* 'extreme completion'
13.	*mec-/mac-* 'incomplete action'
14.	*cik-/cek-* 'partial action'
15.	*em-/am-* 'delimitative'

Tab. 10.4: Related verb forms.

1.	*lagi-/lage-* 'genuine action'
2.	*tamŋe-* 'in vain, not seriously'
3.	*-ca* 'scattered distributive'
4.	*-qeet/-qaat* 'diminutive'
5.	*-cgat* 'augmentative'
6.	*re-/ra-...-ŋ* 'desiderative'

4.2 Transpositions and valency alternations

There are several types of lexical relatedness which border on standard derivation but which some morphologists would regard as a distinct type of relation from derivation proper. It is often difficult to distinguish these other types of relatedness from standard derivation. The kinds of relations I am thinking of are:
- Lexical relatedness which is mediated through addition of a semantic predicate which arguably forms part of the inflectional paradigm ("inherent inflection"),

– Lexical relatedness which is not mediated through addition of a semantic predicate but which involves a change in morpholexical or syntactic word class (transposition).
– Lexical relatedness which is mediated through an alteration in the argument structure of a predicate (usually a verb), either with the addition of a semantic predicate (causative verbs, stative/middle verbs) or without the addition of a semantic predicate (passive and antipassive verb forms, applicative verbs, reflexive/reciprocal verbs).

An example of borderline lexical relatedness is the possessive adjective construction found in many languages, for instance, throughout Slavic. These adjectives are similar to relational adjectives. Relational adjectives, however, simply create an adjectival form of a noun so that it can be used as an attributive modifier, as *prepositional* (from *preposition*) in the phrase *prepositional phrase*. Thus, in Russian the noun *kniga* 'book' gives the adjective *knižnyj* 'pertaining to a book' as in *knižnyj magazin* 'book shop'. In Polish relational adjectives differ syntactically from qualitative adjectives because, provided there is only one of them, it will appear in postnominal position (Szymanek 2010: 82, 85–91). Possessive adjectives, on the other hand, seem to add a meaning component of 'possession' (either alienable or inalienable), though it is very hard to know how to characterize that meaning. Thus, in Russian the nouns *Mama* 'Mummy' or the name *Ivan* form adjectives *mam-in* 'Mummy's', *Ivan-ov* 'Ivan's', as in *mamina ruka/sestra/šapka/mašina/.../problema* 'Mummy's hand/sister/hat/car/.../problem'. The adjective can express more or less any pragmatically mandated relation between the "possessor" and the "possessed". In Russian, possessive adjectives inflect in a different way from ordinary qualitative adjectives (or relational adjectives such as *knižnyj*), but they are clearly denominal adjectives. Russian, like a number of Slavic languages, also has a class of adjectives which are formed from names of animals: *ryba* 'fish' → *ryb-ij* 'pertaining to (a) fish' which has yet another declension pattern (see also Szymanek 2010: 93 for corresponding forms in Polish).

One of the unclear aspects of derivational morphology is the position of argument structure alternations and derivation. There are two ways in which argument structure is important in a classification of derivation. First, it is very common for morphology to target a verbal argument to derive a subject- or object-denoting noun such as English *employer* or *employee* respectively.

A closely related type of derivation is found in languages which permit conversion of adjectives to nouns. In many cases the language preferentially or obligatorily converts an adjective into a noun denoting a person (see Spencer 2002 for discussion). Thus, in Russian the adjective *bol'noj* 'sick, ill' can be used as a noun to mean 'patient'. When such conversion applies to deverbal transpositions we obtain nouns with meanings of the kind 'person that VERBs' or 'person that is VERB-ed', and these have essentially the same function as -*er/ee* nominals in English. Thus, the normal word for 'school pupil/student' is a (reflexive) present participle, inflected as an adjective but functioning syntactically like a noun: *učaščijsja* (from the verb *učit'sja* 'to learn'). Similarly, the word *obvinjaemyj* means '(male) defendant (in a court trial)' and is the present passive participle from the verb *obvinjat'* 'to accuse'. In some cases the present passive morphology is found in the absence of the base verb lexeme, for instance, the word *podsudimyj* 'defendant' (*sud* 'trial', *pod* 'under'). Although the verb *sudit'* 'to judge' exists as well as various prefixed forms, there is no verb **podsudit'*.

Such converted personal nouns are fairly widespread cross-linguistically. For instance, Skorik (1961: 345) describes a "noun-participle" form in Chukchi. This is formed from nouns, verbs, and adjectives with the suffix *-lʔən*. Skorik stresses that such derived forms are indeterminate between attributive modifiers and personal nouns (where they can denote humans), serving to respond to either 'one who is doing what?' or 'which person?'. Skorik provides numerous examples, including *rəjulʔən* 'one who is herding (reindeer); herder', from *rəjuk* 'to herd (reindeer)', *ʔattʔalʔən* 'one who has dogs; dog-owner', from *ʔattʔən* 'dog', *gəntiŋalʔən* 'one who is handsome; handsome person'.

4.3 A-semantic lexical relatedness: meaningless derivation

Aronoff (1976) pointed out that English has a number of verbs derived from Latin or French in the main which appear to consist of a meaningless prefix (such as *con-*, *de-*, *e(x)-*, *per-*, *re-*, *trans-* and others) and a meaningless root (such as *-fer*, *-late*, *-mit*, *-port*). He argued that such words really are morphologically complex on the grounds that the roots show consistent allomorphy, for instance, in their nominalized forms: *com-mit ~ com-mission*, *e-mit ~ e-mission*, *per-mit ~ per-mission*, *trans-mit ~ trans-mission* and so on. Now, it's unclear whether such words really are best thought of as complex (see Carstairs-McCarthy 1992b for discussion). However, there exists a small number of verbs in English with a similar prefix-stem structure for which it's clear that the stem represents a motivating verb which has no semantic relationship to the derived verb: *under-stand*, *with-stand*, *up-hold*, *with-hold* and others. The reason we know such verbs are motivated (formally) by STAND, HOLD is that they share the same irregularity in inflection: *withstood*, *withheld*, etc. Thus, English has verbs which are clearly complex morphologically but in which both the prefix and the base are meaningless ("cranberry") morphs.

This phenomenon is fairly marginal in English, but in other languages the existence of prefixed verbs consisting entirely of cranberry forms is widespread. As a rough approximation I would estimate that at least one third of the verb vocabulary of Slavic languages such as Russian is of this character (Spencer 2000). German is another language whose verb stock is mainly populated with prefixed verbs. A glance at any German dictionary will demonstrate that the majority of German verbs are formed with one of a small number of prefixes such as *be-*, *ein-*, *ver-*. Some of the prefixes, the so-called "separable prefixes", have special behaviour (see below). In many prefixed verbs it is impossible to assign a meaning reliably either to the prefix or to the base or to both.

In many cases it is possible to discern some meaning relationship with the base lexeme. Thus, (*sich*) *ver-sprechen* in its meaning of 'to make a speech error' is motivated by *sprechen* 'to speak' and is likewise related to a small number of other verbs (also in construction with the accusative reflexive pronoun) with a similar meaning: (*sich*) *ver-lesen* 'to misread', *lesen* 'to read'; (*sich*) *ver-schreiben* 'to make a slip of the pen', *schreiben* 'to write', (*sich*) *ver-sehen* 'to overlook', *sehen* 'to see'. In other cases *ver-* seems to function as a deadjectival causative prefix: *sicher* 'sure, certain', *ver-sichern* 'to assure'. In yet other cases, the prefixed verb is essentially synonymous with the unprefixed base lexeme which motivates it but it differs in somewhat subtle ways semantically. Thus, *verändern* 'to change' consists of the morphs *ver-ander-n* (with umlaut of the /a/ of the base form, that is vowel fronting apophony /a/ → /e/), clearly begins with a prefix *ver-* and is clearly derived from the verb *ändern* 'to change'.

In many other cases, however, it is impossible to motivate the *ver-* prefixed verb by its morphological base. Thus, the 'mis-' class of verbs with *ver-* illustrated above all have other (usually more frequent) meanings: *ver-sprechen* 'to promise' (and with a dative, rather than accusative, reflexive pronoun *sich etwas von jemandem/etwas versprechen* 'to have expectations of something'), *verlesen* 'to sort, clean (fruit, salad, etc.)', *verschreiben* 'to prescribe', *versehen* 'to provide with' and so on. In other cases there is no semantic relation between the *ver-* prefixed verb and its base: *geben* 'to give', *ver-geben* 'to award; forgive', *ver-fügen* 'to have at one's disposal, possess', *fügen* 'to place'. In some cases the verb merely has the form of a prefixed verb but there is no (longer any) motivating lexeme: *ver-gnügen* 'to amuse' in the absence of **gnug/gnüg* (though this is presumably related etymologically to the adjective *genug* 'enough').

Languages such as German, Russian and a good many others demonstrate that we need to adopt the distributional approach to word-formation as well as the semantically-based approach if we are to understand how derivation works. Verbs in these languages obey a constructional schema (see article 6 on word-formation in construction grammar) that licenses words of the form prefix-base without necessarily providing a strict set of rules or meanings.

4.4 Evaluative morphology

Evaluative morphology is an expression of the speaker's emotional attitude towards the referent of the word, either positive or negative. Evaluative morphology applied to nominals (nouns or adjectives) tends to derive from morphology realizing size: diminutives and augmentatives. There is a tendency for diminutives to express a degree of endearment ('cute little X') while augmentatives are pejorative ('ugly great X'). Unlike canonical derivational morphology evaluative morphology very frequently applies to proper nouns.

Evaluative morphology retains major word class and in a number of languages it is transparent to such categories as gender or number. For instance, the Spanish diminutive suffix *-(c)it-* passes on the gender of the base lexeme and reflects this by inflectional class membership: *-(c)ito* for masculine nouns and *-(c)ita* for feminine nouns (e.g., *Carmencita* 'little Carmen'). On the other hand, a number of diminutive suffixes in Russian themselves determine the inflectional class of the derived word while remaining transparent to gender. Thus, *-ulja* forms diminutives of declensional class 2, which by default has nouns of feminine gender, such as *mama* 'Mummy', *mamulja*. However, when attached to a masculine noun such as *papa* 'Daddy' it gives a masculine diminutive *papulja* but still of class 2. On the other hand, *-išče* derives augmentatives in class 1b, which is generally for neuter gender nouns, but *domišče* 'ugly great house' is masculine, like its base, *dom* 'house'. In Breton diminutives formed with *-ig* can attach to plural inflected nouns, but then have to be re-inflected for plural: *bag* 'boat', *bag-où* 'boats', *bag-ig* 'little boat', *bag-où-ig-ou* 'little boats' (Stump 1993, 2001: 104). However, in other languages evaluative morphology resembles derivation in that it determines (nearly) all aspects of the derived word's category. Thus, German noun diminutives in *-chen*, *-lein* are always neuter, whatever the gender of the base, and similar neuter gender diminutives are found in Greek.

Evaluative morphology often relates very closely to standard derivation because in many cases evaluative forms such as diminutives are homophonous with derived lexemes. For instance, the Russian word *ruka* 'hand' has a diminutive form *ručka* 'little hand' or 'hand (endearing)'. By metaphorical extension of the 'little hand' meaning the word has come to mean 'handle'. In some cases the base has been lost or has acquired a different meaning, so that the diminutive becomes a base lexeme in its own right. For instance, Russian *čaška*, which is the normal word for 'cup', is morphologically the diminutive of *čaša* 'goblet', which is historical/archaic, and likewise German speakers regard *Mädchen* as simply the word for 'girl', not the diminutive of *Magd* 'maid' (its historical source). Russian *čaška*, moreover, can undergo further diminutive formation: *čašečka* 'little cup'.

The existence of evaluative morphology can be one of the reasons why it's difficult to distinguish inflection from derivation, in that evaluative morphology adds semantic or pragmatic content to the lexeme, like derivation, but it doesn't change word class and may preserve a number of other grammatical and lexical properties of the base lexeme, just as inflectional morphology does.

5 References

Ackema, Peter and Ad Neeleman (2004): *Beyond Morphology. Interface Conditions on Word Formation.* Oxford: Oxford University Press.

Ackerman, Farrell and Philip LeSourd (1997): Toward a lexical representation of phrasal predicates. In: Alex Alsina, Joan Bresan and Peter Sells (eds.), *Complex Predicates*, 67–106. Stanford: CSLI.

Ackerman, Farrell, Gregory T. Stump and Gert Webelhuth (2011): Lexicalism, periphrasis, and implicative morphology. In: Robert D. Borsley and Kersti Börjars (eds.), *Non-transformational Syntax. Formal and Explicit Models of Grammar*, 325–358. Oxford: Blackwell.

Anderson, Stephen R. (1992): *A-morphous Morphology*. Cambridge: Cambridge University Press.

Aronoff, Mark (1976): *Word Formation in Generative Grammar*. Cambridge, MA: MIT Press.

Aronoff, Mark (1994): *Morphology By Itself*. Cambridge, MA: MIT Press.

Baeskow, Heike (2020): Denominal verbs in morphology. In: Rochelle Lieber (ed.), *The Oxford Encyclopedia of Morphology*, 531–550. Oxford: Oxford University Press.

Bauer, Laurie (1988): A descriptive gap in morphology. In: Geert Booij and Jaap van Marle (eds.), *Yearbook of Morphology 1989*, 17–27. Dordrecht: Kluwer.

Beard, Robert (1995): *Lexeme Morpheme Base Morphology*. Stony Brook, NY: SUNY Press.

Bochner, Harry (1993): *Simplicity in Generative Morphology*. Berlin: Mouton de Gruyter.

Booij, Geert (1997): Autonomous morphology and paradigmatic relations. In: Geert Booij and Jaap van Marle (eds.), *Yearbook of Morphology 1996*, 35–54. Dordrecht: Kluwer.

Booij, Geert (2008): Paradigmatic morphology. In: Bernard Fradin (ed.), *La raison morphologique. Hommage à la mémoire de Danielle Corbin*, 29–37. Amsterdam/Philadelphia: Benjamins.

Booij, Geert (2009): Lexical integrity as a formal universal: A constructionist view. In: Sergio Scalise, Elisabetta Magni and Antonietta Bisetto (eds.), *Univerals of Language Today*, 83–100. Dordrecht: Springer.

Booij, Geert and Jerzy Rubach (1984): Morphological and prosodic domains in lexical phonology. *Phonology Yearbook* 1: 1–27.

Booij, Geert and Jerzy Rubach (1987): Postcyclic versus postlexical rules in lexical phonology. *Linguistic Inquiry* 18: 1–44.

Carstairs-McCarthy, Andrew (1992a): *Current Morphology*. London: Routledge.

Carstairs-McCarthy, Andrew (1992b): Morphology without word-internal constituents: A review of Stephen R. Anderson's A-Morphous Morphology. In: Geert Booij and Jaap van Marle (eds.), *Yearbook of Morphology 1992*, 209–234. Dordrecht: Kluwer.

Cinque, Guglielmo (1999): *Adverbs and Functional Heads. A Cross-Linguistic Perspective*. Oxford: Oxford University Press.

Corbett, Greville G. (1987): The morphology-syntax interface. *Language* 63: 299–345.
Dunn, Michael (1999): A grammar of Chukchi. Ph.D. dissertation, Australian National University, Canberra.
Fabb, Nigel (1988): English suffixation is constrained only by selectional restrictions. *Natural Language and Linguistic Theory* 6: 527–539.
Halle, Morris (1973): Prolegomena to a theory of word formation. *Linguistic Inquiry* 4: 3–16.
Hay, Jennifer (2002): From speech perception to morphology: Affix ordering revisited. *Language* 78: 527–555.
Hay, Jennifer and Ingo Plag (2004): What constrains possible suffix combinations? On the interaction of grammatical and processing restrictions in derivational morphology. *Natural Language and Linguistic Theory* 22: 565–596.
Holton, David, Peter Mackridge and Irene Philippaki-Warburton (1997): *Greek. A Comprehensive Grammar of the Modern Language*. London: Routledge.
Jackendoff, Ray S. (1975): Morphological and semantic regularities in the lexicon. *Language* 51: 639–671.
Kaye, Alan S. (2007): Arabic morphology. In: Alan S. Kaye (ed.), *Morphologies of Asia and Africa*. Vol. 1, 211–247. Winona Lake, IA: Eisenbrauns.
Kenesei, István, Robert M. Vágo and Anna Fenyvesi (1998): *Hungarian*. London: Routledge.
Kiefer, Ferenc and András Komlósy (2011): On the order of word-class preserving derivational suffixes in the Hungarian verb. *Word Structure* 4: 201–214.
Kiparsky, Paul (1982): From cyclic phonology to lexical phonology. In: Harry van der Hulst and Norval H. S. Smith (eds.), *The Structure of Phonological Representations*. Part 1, 131–175. Dordrecht: Foris.
Koenig, Jean-Pierre (1999): *Lexical Relations*. Stanford, CA: CSLI.
Lieber, Rochelle (1992): *Deconstructing Morphology*. Chicago: University of Chicago Press.
Lieber, Rochelle (2016): *English Nouns: The Ecology of Nominalization*. Cambridge: Cambridge University Press.
Lieber, Rochelle (2020a): Nominalization: General overview and theoretical issues. In: Rochelle Lieber (ed.), *The Oxford Encyclopedia of Morphology*, 443–456. Oxford: Oxford University Press.
Lieber, Rochelle (2020b): Derivational Morphology. In: Rochelle Lieber (ed.), *The Oxford Encyclopedia of Morphology*, 427–443. Oxford: Oxford University Press.
Lieber, Rochelle and Sergio Scalise (2007): The lexical integrity hypothesis in a new theoretical universe. In: Geert Booij, Luca Ducceschi, Bernard Fradin, Emiliano Guevara, Angeliki Ralli and Sergio Scalise (eds.), *On-line Proceedings of the Fifth Mediterranean Morphology meeting (MMM5), Fréjus 15–18 September 2005*. Bologna: University of Bologna. http://mmm.lingue.unibo.it/
Lieber, Rochelle and Pavol Štekauer (2014): *The Oxford Handbook of Derivational Morphology*. Oxford: Oxford University Press.
Markova, Angelina (2011): On the nature of Bulgarian prefixes: Ordering and modification in multiple prefixation. *Word Structure* 4: 244–271.
Moll, T. A. and P. I. Inenliqej (1957): *Čukotsko-russkij slovar'*. Leningrad: Nauka.
Nikolaeva, Irina A. (2003): The structure of the Tundra Nenets noun phrase. In: Marianne Bakró-Nagy and Károly Rédei (eds.), *Ünnepi kötet Honti László tiszteletére*, 315–327. Budapest: MTA.
Nikolaeva, Irina A. (2008): Between nouns and adjectives: A constructional view. *Lingua* 118: 969–996.
Olsen, Susan (2019): Innerconnectness and variation of meaning in derivational patterns. *SKASE Journal of Theoretical Linguistics* 16(1): 19–34.

Plag, Ingo and Harald Baayen (2009): Suffix ordering and morphological processing. *Language* 85: 109–152.
Plank, Frans (2010): Variable direction in zero-derivation and the unity of polysemous lexical items. *Word Structure* 3: 82–97.
Rainer, Franz (2014): Polysemy in derivation. In: Rochelle Lieber and Pavol Štekauer (eds.), *The Oxford Handbook of Derivational Morphology*, 338–353. Oxford: Oxford University Press.
Rainer, Franz (2015): Agent and instrument nouns. In: Peter O. Müller, Ingeborg Ohnheiser, Susan Olsen and Franz Rainer (eds.), *Word-Formation. An International Handbook of the Languages of Europe*. Vol. 2, 1304–1316. Berlin/Boston: De Gruyter Mouton.
Rice, Keren (2011): Principles of affix ordering: An overview. *Word Structure* 4: 169–200.
Riehemann, Susanne (1998): Type-based derivational morphology. *Journal of Comparative Germanic Linguistics* 2: 49–77.
Rossdeutscher, Antje and Hans Kamp (2010): Syntactic and semantic constraints in the formation and interpretation of ung-nouns. In: Artemis Alexiadeu and Monika Rathert (eds.), *The semantics of nominalisations across languages and frameworks*, 169–214. Berlin/Boston: De Gruyter Mouton.
Selkirk, Elizabeth O. (1982): *The Syntax of Words*. Cambridge, MA: MIT Press.
Siegel, Dorothy (1974): Topics in English morphology. Ph.D. dissertation, Department of Linguistics and Philosophy, MIT, Cambridge, MA.
Skorik, Pjotr Ja. (1961): *Grammatika čukotskogo jazyka*. Vol. 1. Leningrad: Nauka.
Šmilauer, Vladimír (1972): *Nauka o českém jazyku*. Prague: Státní pedagogické nakladatelství.
Spencer, Andrew (1988): Bracketing paradoxes and the English lexicon. *Language* 64: 663–682.
Spencer, Andrew (1991): *Morphological Theory*. Oxford: Blackwell.
Spencer, Andrew (2000): Morphology. In: Mark Aronoff and Janie Rees-Miller (eds.), *Handbook of Linguistics*, 213–237. Oxford: Blackwell.
Spencer, Andrew (2002): Gender as an inflectional category. *Journal of Linguistics* 38: 279–312.
Spencer, Andrew (2007): Extending deponency: Implications for morphological mismatches. In: Matthew Baerman, Greville C. Corbett, Dunstan Brown and Andrew Hippisley (eds.), *Deponency and Morphological Mismatches*, 45–70. Oxford: Oxford University Press.
Spencer, Andrew (2010): Lexical relatedness and the lexical entry – a formal unification. In: Stefan Müller (ed.), *Proceedings of the HPSG10 conference*, 322–340. Stanford: CSLI.
Spencer, Andrew (2012): Identifying stems. *Word Structure* (Guest editors Olivier Bonami and Gilles Boyé) 5: 88–108.
Spencer, Andrew (2013): *Lexical Relatedness*. Oxford: Oxford University Press.
Stump, Gregory T. (1993.): How peculiar is evaluative morphology? *Journal of Linguistics* 29: 1–36.
Stump, Gregory T. (2001): *Inflectional Morphology. A Theory of Paradigm Structure*. Cambridge: Cambridge University Press.
Szymanek, Bogdan (1989): *Introduction to Morphological Analysis*. Warsaw: Państwowe Wydawnictwo Naukowe.
Szymanek, Bogdan (2010): *A Panorama of Polish Word-Formation*. Lublin: Wydawnictwo KUL.
Toivonen, Ida (2003): *Non-Projecting Words. A Case Study of Swedish Particles*. Dordrecht: Kluwer.
Vajda, Edward J. (2004): *Ket*. München: LINCOM Europa.
Werner, Heinrich (1997): *Die ketische Sprache*. Wiesbaden: Harrassowitz.

Salvador Valera
11 Conversion

1 Introduction
2 Background
3 Conversion as word-class change plus formal identity
4 Conversion as word-class change without formal identity
5 Conversion without word-class change, but with formal identity
6 Conversion in European languages
7 Conclusion
8 References

Abstract: Conversion is recorded throughout the European languages. Its manifestations vary according to the theoretical standpoint on word-formation and of related issues, and also according to the morphological structure of each language. This article reviews the essentials of the concept (section 2), and the cases that are described as conversion in several European languages according to the two conditions that are set in the concept of conversion (sections 3 to 5). An overview of conversion in European languages shows that the well-known difficulties that it poses in certain languages occur in other languages too and are likely to be inherent in the concept of conversion (section 6).

1 Introduction

Derivation is described in article 10 based on the formal, syntactic and semantic features that characterize the relation between base and derivative. According to that framework, and unlike derivation, conversion appears as a word-formation process where the form of the converted item does not change, while its inflectional potential, its syntactic function and its meaning do, such that the item displays inflectional, syntactic and semantic properties of a new word class. The definition of conversion is therefore built upon the conditions of formal identity and word-class change of the base form (Bauer 1983: 32, 2003: 38), as in the following examples borrowed from the *British National Corpus* (at http://corpus.byu.edu/bnc/) and the *Corpus do português* (at http://www.corpusdoportugues.org/), respectively:

Salvador Valera, Granada, Spain

https://doi.org/10.1515/9783111420561-011

(1) *He was put up for sale before the <u>start</u> of this season.* English
    Each time it was a great way to <u>start</u> the season.

(2) *A   <u>planta</u>   tem   folhas   longas   e*   Portuguese
    The plant-FEM.SG have-3.SG.PR leaves.FEM.PL long-FEM.PL and
    estreitas [...]
    narrow-FEM.PL
    'The plant has long and narrow leaves [...]'

   Os   colonizadores   tinham   começado   a   <u>plantar</u>
   The settlers-MASC.PL have-3.PL.PAST start.PAST.PART to plant-INF
   algodão [...]
   cotton
   'The settlers had started to plant cotton [...]'

This article does not discuss the theories of conversion that are available. Partly intended as an overview, it first provides a general background (section 2), and then focuses on different interpretations of the conditions of conversion that are possible in the description of contemporary word-formation in European languages (sections 3 to 5). The interpretations may be a result of different theoretical standpoints and some of them may not be primarily about conversion (e.g., gender as a grammatical or as a lexical category, see section 5). However, they also reflect how one and the same concept can be understood in the context of different languages. Based on the two defining notions of word-class change and formal identity, these interpretations are:
(i) Conversion as word-class change plus formal identity (section 3).
(ii) Conversion without word-class change or formal identity (for convenience, dealt with in section 5).
(iii) Conversion as word-class change without formal identity (section 4).
(iv) Conversion without word-class change, but with formal identity (section 5).

The article closes with an overview of the resulting picture of conversion in European languages (section 6).

2 Background

Conversion has been studied in several European languages (e.g., Vogel 1996; Don 2003; Bauer 2005; Manova and Dressler 2005; Manova 2011). These references show that the interpretation of conversion may differ widely according to the theoretical framework used. It may be interpreted, for example, as formally unmarked derivation by word-class change, as affixation of a zero element, as lexical relisting, and as no derivational process altogether due to multiple functionality of the word in question or to word-class underspecification. The latter has been used especially with regard to four pairs of word classes: noun and verb (e.g., in Whorf 1945; Lipka 1971; Farrell 2001), adjective and verb (e.g., in Siegel 1980: 150), noun and adjective (see below in this section), and adjective and adverb (cf. Feuillet 1991, Hummel 2000 and Bisang 2011 on word-class identification in cross-linguistic research and on word-class separation, specifically of noun/verb contrast). These are the word classes where conversion is usually described, particularly between nouns and verbs and less often between adjectives and adverbs. The differentiation between nouns and adjectives is particularly difficult considering the frequency with which multifunctionality is reported with respect to the categories noun and adjective. This appears to be so, even if multifunctionality sometimes applies not to all the members of these two word classes but to a subclass or several subclasses.

For a review of the theories of conversion, a number of specific analyses are available in the literature which have become classic references themselves for the study of conversion (e.g., Bergenholtz and Mugdan 1979, 2000; Lieber 1981; Pennanen 1984; Sanders 1988; Olsen 1990; Don 1993; Štekauer 1996; Plag 1999).

The concept of conversion is a function of the concept of word-class change, which in turn relies on the concept of word class (Bauer 2005). In cross-linguistic research, the categories inherited from the Western tradition are used as the framework and new concepts are added as necessary, e.g., converbs or masdars as intermediate categories for specific languages. The notion of intermediate categories is closely related to the flexibility with which the categories should be understood. Most current approaches define the separation between categories as a gradient, so the differences between at least some categories, specifically nouns, verbs and adjectives, are of degree, rather than of kind, with respect to the prototype according to which each category has been defined (cf. Daneš 1966; Lipka 1971, 1986; Ross 1972; Croft 1984). In the prototype approach, each word class is defined by canonical members that have the potential to display all the morphological, syntactic and semantic features that are associated with the members of the category (see article 10 on derivation). Category members may deviate from the prototype in various degrees by not displaying all the possible features of the category and taking on instead features of other categories (for a review of word classes as prototype-based categories, cf. van der Auwera and Gast 2011).

There is also the view that the above relativism is unnecessary as regards at least the categories noun, verb and adjective (cf., among others, Colombat 1988; Baker 2003). The combination of properties prototypical of each category is then replaced by a defining feature, e.g., syntactic function in Baker (2003: 301–302), even if it projects into the morphology and the semantics of each category. For ease of reference, but also because the categories in question coincide largely with the ones that have been described as universal (noun, verb and adjective, plus the word class adverb, which has been considered systematically in this handbook), this article uses the conventional system of word classes, even if its categories may not always reflect accurately what they are supposed to represent in different languages (for a review of word classes in cross-linguistic research, cf. Bisang 2011).

Neither of these two views on word classes is without difficulty in the identification of conversion, partly due to the framework, partly due to the operation of related processes. This article does not make the distinction between conversion and processes whose output is synchronically similar to the output of conversion but that may not qualify as conversion diachronically. This is a relevant distinction according to the differences that may be found between actual cases of conversion and processes that may give similar results. The distinction is relevant as regards the process too. The word classes and the type of diachronic process may differ in each language, e.g., nouns and verbs in English, nouns and participles in Hungarian and nouns and verbs in Romanian.

In general, some degree of overlap between conversion and historical processes lies at the core of several Indo-European languages, and is present in languages of several genera, e.g., Danish, French, Turkish and Awar. This overlap is well-known in the literature on conversion in English (cf. Pennanen 1984; cf. also Pennanen 1975 on the connection between conversion and backformation). It is also present in the description of a number of issues in word-formation, e.g., concerning argument-structural restrictions on word-formation patterns and also concerning adverbial categories.

A more relevant separation is between syntactic processes that have as a result a similar profile to conversion and actual lexical conversion (cf. Marchand 1967, 1969; Plag 2003: 113–116; Manova and Dressler 2005; cf. also Eschenlohr 1999 on German and the identification of transposition vs. derivation based on the former's higher productivity, semantic predictability, low lexicalization, resistance to change their inflectional and governmental properties and low availability). These syntactic processes are not usually considered to be lexical conversion, e.g., when nouns premodify other nouns as heads of noun phrases, or when adjectives appear as heads of noun phrases. Of these, the former case (nouns interpreted as adjectives to whatever extent as a result of their prenominal position) is more questionably lexical conversion, even if the literature may have presented it as a case of *partial* conversion. When this position entails not only apparent syntactic change but also semantic change, as in noun-noun compounds in French like *marron* (where the nominal meaning 'chestnut' changes into a colour as an adjective), it can be argued that conversion has occurred.

As to adjectives that appear as heads in noun phrases without nominal inflection, a case for ellipsis is often cited. This structure is well-known in a number of languages of a number of genera, from English or Ukrainian to Khwarshi. The elliptical noun may typically denote a person or thing, and one of these, or a hyponym, is reported to be usually recoverable in the structure:

(3) Les <u>bienheureux</u> sont [...]   French
    'The blessed are [...]'

(4) Die <u>Armen</u> sind [...]   German
    'The poor are [...]'

(5) L'<u>impossibile</u> è [...]   Italian
    'Whatever impossible is [...]'

(6) Lo <u>extranjero</u> es [...]   Spanish
    'Whatever foreign is [...]'

The structure may result in varying degrees of lexicalization. The structure may also reach the point that the adjective acquires the categorial meaning of the noun and the elliptical noun is no longer recoverable because it causes ungrammatical redundancy (e.g., Spanish present participles in *-ante* or *-ente*, as in *amante* or *presidente*; cf. also Ramat and Hopper 1998: 2). A similar situation is reported to be widespread cross-linguistically in article 10 on derivation for Russian and, similarly, there are cases where the present participle remains in this lexicalized form, even if the original verb is no longer present in the language (e.g., Spanish *agente* from *agĕre*). These cases have also been described for Latin. They appear in the literature as plain conversion and as partial conversion. It is usually thought that they do not qualify as complete conversion unless they take on nominal inflection and the categorial meaning of nouns (cf. Marchand 1969: 362; Colombat 1988: 62; Gutiérrez Ordóñez 1994 for the role of syntactic processes, specifically of ellipsis; cf. also Dokulil 1968b: 58 on the descriptive problem that these constructions pose in English and German).

These cases are allegedly less productive than conversion between noun and verb of the type found in Romance languages, but they are at the heart of the interpretation that nouns and at least a subcategory of adjectives (classifying adjectives) are essentially the same word class. The productivity of each type depends on the view of conversion being assumed. In languages like English or Spanish, the restrictions on the type of adjectives that can gain access to the syntactic structure described above are not entirely clear, e.g., with asymmetries between positive and negative predicates, as in Spanish *un tonto* vs. *un inteligente that do not always hold (cf. *un tonto* vs. *un listo*). This structure, where nouns and adjectives converge, is recorded in a number of languages of a range of genera, e.g., Germanic, Romance, Slavic, Indo-Iranian, Uralic, Basque, Turkic and Northeast Caucasian. Actually, the high frequency with which this structure is cited in Indo-European endorses Kruisinga's (1927: 103) claim that conversion of adjectives to nouns is related at least to primitive Indo-European grammar.

A number of other cases can be mentioned here which have not always attracted much attention in relation to conversion. One is conversion from noun to adverb by lexicalization of oblique forms of nouns. This can be found rarely in English, as in *forwards*, and in German, as in *abends* 'in the evenings', and is reportedly present in a number of other languages too, like Lithuanian, Latvian, Lak and Bezhta. Their interpretation depends largely on whether the original inflectional paradigm of the noun is available and the nominal base can take other inflections proper of the original word class. Another case concerns participles, for their borderline status between the categories verb, noun and adjective; cf. Haspelmath (1996). Although participles are reported as input for conversion in a number of European languages, it should first be decided whether these really entail word-class contrast and in which respects, i.e. to what extent this change really means new inflectional, syntactic and/or semantic contrast, or whether participles should be considered an intermediate, multifunctional category.

3 Conversion as word-class change plus formal identity

Canonical conversion requires word-class change and formal identity. This matches the standard profile of conversion in English and the one on which the description of conversion in other languages has been modeled. A number of other European languages can be added to this profile depending on the word classes involved and the direction of conversion. Other aspects of conversion in addition to this profile have achieved a lower degree of unanimity as regards the essential elements involved in the concept, namely the process, the input, the output, the productivity and the relationship.

Whether viewed as a dynamic process with a base and a derivative or not, as is possible in some of the theoretical approaches listed in the introduction, conversion responds to a lexical need. As in the definition used as a starting point for this article, the output retains the form of the input and assumes the inflectional potential, the syntactic function and the categorial meaning of the new word class. The input is usually the citation form of the base, but it can also be an inflected form, as is the case with participles when they are taken to be the result of conversion (see also section 3). The input and especially the output are mainly members of open word classes, although closed word classes and a range of multiword items have also been recorded as input for conversion.

Transfer between nouns and verbs, between adjectives and nouns, and between adjectives and verbs are the usual cases. The first type of transfer is the most common pattern, in either direction, but it is not recorded in every language: the North Caucasian languages Khinalug, Bezhta and Khwarshi are examples of word-class change and formal identity, but none of them involves the word classes noun and verb. Hungarian must also be mentioned here, even if situations become particularly complex with the relationship of one and the same form with nouns, adjectives and participles as in English *-ing* and its interpretation as conversion or as a multifunctional suffix (also with intervening diachronic considerations which may, however, not be entirely a reflex of contemporary word-formation).

The output of conversion tends to come in line with a set of semantic patterns that are specific for the word class of the output (cf. Whorf 1945: 9; Nida 1949: 50; Marchand 1969: 375; Cetnarowska 1996: 17–18; Plag 1999: 219–221). Converted words are versatile and adapt themselves to the context so they may carry different meanings as required by the context in which they are used (cf. Clark and Clark 1979; Cetnarowska 1996; Buck 1997; Plag 1999: 225–226). This is a property of conversion that helps understand its productivity. Conversion may also be related to figures of speech, specifically with metonymy and metaphor. The role of these figures in conversion has received less attention than it deserves, even if they have been cited in the literature occasionally (cf. Stein 1977: 228–230; Kastovsky 1989: 182).

The output of conversion is usually considered a new lexeme (cf. Dokulil 1968b), but not in the interpretation of conversion as word-class underspecification, where no new item is formed and the lexeme limits itself to taking one or the other specification as regards word class. The interpretation of the productivity of conversion varies according to the theoretical position, and specific constraints have been defined in several languages (cf. Don 1993 for Dutch; Plag 1999: 221–222 for English and Neef 1999 and 2005 for German).

The relationship between the base and the derivative is interpreted in terms of formal identity, whether it is homonymy (Lipka 1986, 1990: 140; Saeed 1997: 63–64), polysemy or heterosemy (Goddard 1998: 20), homomorphy (Quirk, Greenbaum, Leech and Svartvik 1985: 70–71; Hockett 1994: 180–181), or zero-derivation (as a relation instead of a process, Sanders 1988: 157), according to the significance granted to the contrast implicit in the word class between the base and the derivative. The interpretation of the relationship between the input and the output as polysemy or as homonymy is by necessity implicit in how conversion-related pairs are recorded in dictionaries: they can be listed under the same entry or under separate entries. It has been claimed that finer distinctions in the analysis of the lexical change involved in conversion are necessary for the identification of conversion-related pairs as one or as several lexemes, e.g., as in the comparison between the noun and the verb *can* and the noun and the verb *corner*, or the noun and the verb *book*, and the semantic contrast that the syntactic difference carries with it in the latter two cases and that may argue against the classification of the latter pairs as one and the same lexeme (cf. Cruse 1986: 79–80).

As regards the relationship between the pairs involved in conversion, the emphasis is otherwise on directionality (for a review of the synchronic and diachronic criteria used in directionality and of their degree of agreement in English, cf. Bram 2011). It has been suggested that the usual approach to directionality needs to identify the base and the derivative by senses rather than by lexemes, because several bases and several derivatives may exist within one and the same lexeme according to the senses of the input and the output (Plank 2010). This multiplies the difficulty inherent in the identification of directionality in conversion, but is consistent with the relative independence of senses within lexemes as regards their use in word-formation, or at least with the fact that derivation can pick up on a specific sense for creation of a new word and not on others within the same lexeme (see article 10 on derivation).

4 Conversion as word-class change without formal identity

4.1 Formal contrast by (supra-)segmental change

Two main types of formal variation are usually accepted in conversion: minor formal changes involving segmental or suprasegmental material (e.g., vowel or consonant alternation, deletion, voicing, stress shift), and formal changes involving morphology that may be considered inflectional or derivational (see section 4.2).

The former types of formal contrast have been regarded as of less importance than other morphologically, syntactically and semantically more relevant variables. They have been included as conversion often, with and without the qualification that they are of a marginal or a special type. Well-known cases are stress shift and the less discussed issue of voicing with and without orthographical reflex in English noun/verb conversion (cf. Kastovsky 1996: 234; Payne 1997: 30; Beard 1998: 63; Carstairs-McCarthy 2006: 752 on different types of internal modification). Formal changes may be in other languages too, e.g., associated stress shift in noun/verb conversion in Lithuanian and, under different circumstances, in Slovene and Greek deadjectival adverbialization (cf. also adjective to noun conversion in Ukrainian):

(7) gãr-as vs. gar-úo-ti Lithuanian
'steam, vapour' 'to evaporate'

(8) lépo vs. lepó Slovene
'beautiful' 'beautifully'

(9) βέβαιος vs. βεβαίως Greek
véveos vevéos
'certain' 'certainly'

Vowel contrasts have also been cited as conversion in German (cf. Neef 1999: 199 on the interpretation of vowel mutation as conversion in German):

(10) Kopf vs. köpfen German
'head' 'to behead'

Ablaut in Frisian may be interpreted to belong synchronically in conversion. The opposite view is possible too, and vowel contrast is understood as outside conversion for Icelandic and presented instead as sound change and as ablaut in Greek.

Other formal changes can also be considered here, e.g., involving consonant and vowel in noun to verb conversion in Danish, the linking morpheme -k or -t in noun to verb conversion in Frisian vowel variation or deletion in adjective to adverb conversion in Albanian and l/r alternation in noun to verb conversion, and internal Sandhi adjective to verb conversion in Basque:

(11) gaffel vs. gafle Danish
'fork' 'to take with a fork'

(12) tún vs. túnkje Frisian
'garden' 'to garden'

(13)	*sinne* 'sun'	vs.	*sintsje* 'to sunbathe'	Frisian
(14)	(*i*) *shpejtë* 'fast_ADJ'	vs.	*së shpejti* 'very soon_ADV'	Albanian
(15)	*afërm* 'close_ADJ'	vs.	*së afërmi* 'close up_ADV'	Albanian
(16)	*aske* 'free'	vs.	*askatu* 'to free'	Basque
(17)	*ugari* 'plenti(ful)'	vs.	*ugaldu* 'to increase'	Basque

These are less well-known than the cases cited for English but fall within the same group as regards formal variation of the citation form of the base and of the derivative. The occurrence of each of these changes needs consideration of each specific case separately, so the description reflects their status as specific processes, or as associated features of conversion.

4.2 Stem-based conversion

The second issue in formal changes and conversion revolves around the question as to whether systematic formal variation is allowed between the base and the derivative. This is partly related to the often cited connection between conversion and English, or to the alleged higher productivity of conversion in English than in other languages, which has been attributed to the loss of inflections since Old English. Viewed from the opposite end, a relation has sometimes been established between inflection and conversion, such that inflectionally rich languages tend to constrain conversion because they mark word classes explicitly (for a review, cf. Pennanen 1984).

This constraint has been rejected in the literature based on the argument that conversion in inflecting languages only manifests itself differently than in non-inflecting languages, i.e. conversion appears according to what the morphology of each language requires and, within that, to what the morphology of each word class requires. Inflecting languages may use stems as their input and then apply deletion of the ending in the base form and/or addition of a new ending, e.g. the classing suffix patterns in Bulgarian and Russian. This appears as a more complex process than word-class change without any subtraction or addition (examples (18) and (20) are from Manova and Dressler 2005: 73–74):

(18)	*vik* 'a cry'	vs.	*víkam* 'I cry'	Bulgarian
(19)	*работа* rabota 'work'	vs.	*работать* rabotat' 'to work'	Russian
(20)	*hod* 'walk, gate, pace'	vs.	*hódati* 'to walk, pace'	Serbo-Croatian

Alternatively, this has also been described as an inflectional method of word-formation. Other terms are *paradigmatic derivation*, or *transflexion*, even if the latter may not always entail word-class change (cf. also Pennanen 1984: 79–80 for the description of morphologically related pairs where one of the pair members by default must take a word-class mark, namely the infinitive mark in terms other than conversion, specifically as *dérivation immédiate, transfert grammatical* or *unmittelbare Ableitung*; cf. also Kastovsky 1994: 104 on the nature of derivational and inflectional endings).

In the case of English, this means that conversion may not be any more frequent than in highly inflectional languages like Spanish or Latin, and that the loss of endings has not resulted in a higher influence on the productivity of conversion, as has been claimed in the literature (Marchand 1969: 362–364; cf. also Quirk and Wrenn 1957: 104–106 for the link between these processes in stem-based morphological frameworks like Old English and word-based morphological frameworks like Modern English, even if both are not explicitly presented as the same process in nouns and adjectives with respect to verbs). The availability of this process, at least for the categories noun and verb, has been reported for highly inflected Indo-European languages like Latin, Sanskrit or Old English (cf. Biese 1941: 18–30; Marchand 1969: 363–364; Pennanen 1984: 88; Sanders 1988: 170; Kastovsky 1992: 392). It is also a profitable process in such highly inflected languages as Italian and Romanian, for example as regards denominal verbs:

(21)	*hoop* 'hope'	vs.	*hopen* 'to hope'	Dutch
(22)	*tanssi* 'dance'	vs.	*tanssia* 'to dance'	Finnish
(23)	*strega* 'witch'	vs.	*stregare* 'to bewitch'	Italian

(24) vorbă   vs.   vorbi   Romanian
      'talk'   'to talk'

The view that this pattern of word-class change is conversion even if it may necessarily mark the derivative as belonging to a specific word class is also consistent with the claim that affixless denominal verbal derivation has been described as deeply engrained in Indo-European languages as well as more common than suffixal derivation (Kastovsky 1994: 94). It should however be noted that what today is described as conversion may historically have been derivation of different word classes from a common root in Indo-European, so there is no actual relationship between those word classes, but a relationship with a common source (Kastovsky 1994: 110). Although this does not necessarily have an effect on synchronic description, it may help to explain the existence of similar difficulties in the description of conversion in Indo-European languages.

The argumentation that word-based and stem-based conversion are not substantially different types of processes except that they manifest themselves differently according to the different morphology of each language finds support from a different perspective in the study of language disorders. Omission of the verbal inflection appears as replacement of the correct inflection with the infinitive ending, i.e. the occurrence of the verbal stem requires the infinitival ending for verbal denominal conversion in Italian but not in English. When morphologically related noun/verb pairs express themselves with and without the same infinitival ending in Italian and English, they do, as in aphasia, as a result of the morphological pattern of each language rather than as a result of different processes.

5 Conversion without word-class change, but with formal identity

The difference between this type and the first case discussed lies in whether change of secondary word class should qualify as conversion and, therefore, as formation of a new word (insofar as conversion is a word-formation process). In this interpretation, the standpoint is that conversion covers unmarked change of secondary word-class categories such as countability or gender in nouns, valency in verbs, or gradability in adjectives, to name some of the most common. If this change involves formal variation too, this is the least frequent of the cases considered in the outline of the introduction, i.e. conversion without word-class change and without formal identity.

The above changes of subclass may entail a new inflectional potential, new structural capacities and a new nuance of meaning as, for example, in the (in-)transitive and reflexive verbs of Mari and in Ukranian, which deals with relational to qualitative adjectives). To the best of our knowledge, the view that this is conversion, even if it is of a secondary type, dates back to Leech (1974: 214–216), but this is not a widespread approach. This view of conversion has been extended to categories which have traditionally been considered to be grammatical categories, like gender in nouns (cf. Spanish, Italian, Polish and Ukrainian), or grammatical categories, as can be argued of Polish aspect:

(25) *líder*   vs.   *líder*   Spanish
     'leader.FEM'   'leader.MASC'

(26) *ragazza*   vs.   *ragazzo*   Italian
     'girl'   'boy'

The semantic contrasts sometimes go as far as involving such specific oppositions as the one between tree vs. its fruit (cf. Spanish and Italian), or proper to common noun as in French:

(27) *naranja*   vs.   *naranjo*   Spanish
     'orange'   'orange tree'

(28) *mela*   vs.   *melo*   Italian
     'apple'   'apple tree'

The implication of this interpretation is that conversion then ceases to be word-class changing derivation by definition (see article 8 on the delimitation of derivation and inflection for several languages where this approach is used). Another implication is that conversion does not necessarily belong to word-formation. Considering the lexical proximity between the two terms of the opposition, secondary word-class conversion may be different uses of one and the same word, i.e. a new meaning structure. When these contrasts are described in terms other than conversion, the literature uses the terms *morphological alteration* or *valency-changing word-formation* (see Payne 1997: 25, 41–43 on some of these changes and their value as derivation).

6 Conversion in European languages

Unlike derivation or compounding, conversion is non-iconic, i.e. the changes in the semantic structure of the input are not represented formally in the output, except for the new inflectional characteristics that the word-class change entails. This property leads to the expectation that conversion should be rarer than other, morphosemantically more transparent word-formation processes (cf. Dressler 1987: 105, 116; Beard 1998: 63). This property also establishes a contrast with derivation or compounding that has been felt since the earliest approaches to word-formation outside grammar in the 19th century. As a result, conversion is often listed along with minor word-formation processes, even if its productivity is usually described as higher than that of those minor word-formation processes, and close to that of derivation and compounding (see article 2 on word-formation research from its beginnings to the 19th century; cf. also Sanders 1988: 165). To the best of our knowledge, no procedure for the measurement of the productivity of conversion has been put forward as there is, for example, for suffixation. Quantitative assessments of the productivity of conversion are therefore not available in the literature. However, conversion is often reported to be productive in Germanic languages, like English and to a lesser extent German, less productive in Romance and Slavic languages and marginal in Uralic languages.

It has been questioned whether conversion is justified outside Indo-European languages, or whether it is as justified as in the languages which have modeled linguistic description. In fact, conversion does not seem to exist in Welsh, Mordvinic, Gagauz, Karaim or Akhwakh, to mention but a few European languages.

Although it does not entail formal contrast to signal the new meaning, conversion stands out among word-formation processes for its formal simplicity (cf. Kerleroux 1999: 100). This formal simplicity, along with its semantic versatility (see section 2) explains its use before other more iconic but also more complex processes (e.g., certain types of affixation), and its wide occurrence over a number of languages.

The range of structures that are presented here as conversion have the disadvantage that some may not qualify as conversion for a number of readers and are thus a lax interpretation. It has the advantage that it exhausts the possibilities of interpretation of conversion in a range of languages. The resulting picture also offers the possibility of viewing conversion as applying to varying degrees as regards the conditions set on the notion. The view of degrees of conversion is frequent where a separation is made between true conversion and the other types of conversion.

The manifestations of conversion may vary because word classes and the properties on which they are defined may vary across languages, and also because the value of formal identity and, more importantly, the degree of freedom in the formal differentiation of words may also vary across languages. In this respect, it should be stressed not only that conversion is difficult to identify cross-linguistically (Kerleroux 1999: 93), but also that English, which has set the pattern for the description of conversion in the less well-known languages, is not the best possible frame of reference for conversion because it is not representative of the morphological framework in which conversion has to operate in other languages.

The essential requirements for the ideal of this word-formation process apply differently not only across languages according to their own morphology, but different types of conversion may also co-exist within one and the same language. This idea lies at the core of specific studies on conversion like Don (2005), where directionality is taken to the fore as a criterion for the identification of different types of conversion between nouns and verbs in Dutch. It is also the conclusion of Bauer's (2005) review of a number of cases of infinitival constructions in a set of languages and of his discussion of what it means to change a lexical class: not all languages may exhibit the canonical type of conversion that certain languages do for a number of cases within certain word classes.

As conversion does not use a different explicit form with which each of its meanings can become associated, it is usually considered to be one and the same process regardless of the base it operates on and regardless of the derivative it forms. However, taking to the extreme the position that finer distinctions are necessary in the study of conversion, it may be argued that these are different types of conversions when different inflectional paradigms, different categorial meanings and/or different semantic patterns within the same new categorial meaning are involved in conversion according to the word classes involved. If different semantic patterns of conversion also display different properties (such as different degrees of productivity, different constraints, etc.), then they must be considered different types of conversion, even if the patterns do not carry different formal markings (as, for example, in Spanish). The same applies as regards directionality as proposed in Don (2005). Deverbal nominal conversion is reportedly less frequent than denominal verbal conversion in several respects. Thus, e.g., in English child language deverbal nominal formation is not mainly by conversion, but by compounding, whereas the opposite, i.e. denominal verbs, are mainly by conversion; in French child language, it is reportedly not productive. The constraints involved in the conversion patterns that exist between nouns and verbs in English have been referred back to the origins of Indo-European (Buck 1997). These patterns belong to different levels of lexis formation, so their differences are more complex than just directionality and involve, for example, different potential for further derivation (as in the case of closing suffixes).

The hypothesis that there are as many different models of conversion as there are word classes and directions of conversion from one word class into another is conversion's counterpart to the diversity of patterns of affixation, again according to the direction of application and the word class. The same goes for compounding. The difference is that in conversion the output does not mark the different meanings (including the different word classes that may be created by the same form). This also goes for the different internal relations that are possible between the base lexemes of compounds but are not marked formally. This does not presuppose formal, syntactic or semantic unity within one process and within one word class, where considerable variation may exist between the inflectional paradigms and the categorial meanings associated with the target word class (e.g., regular vs. irregular patterns as regards inflection, and different semantic patterns within, e.g., noun to verb conversion, even if they all form denominal verbs). The specialized literature does not use this position (cf. Plag 1999: 223–225). In an output-oriented approach, there is no need to consider formal specifications because there are not any, and fairly small sets of semantic patterns can account successfully for the semantic diversity of the output. In a process-oriented approach, the fact that all the examples comply with the general conditions of conversion regardless of the word classes involved, of the formal specifications that are abandoned or taken on, or of the semantic patterns which are used does not mean that they are one and the same process in each case.

7 Conclusion

Conversion has a range of interpretations in European languages. The difficulties of identification reside in the widely varying morphological structures of European languages and in the concept of conversion itself.

Some conceptual agreement exists on the nature of the output of conversion, but otherwise there is considerable conceptual diversity. This is an effect of the dependence of conversion upon the theoretical framework used for the description of word classes or the interpretation of word-formation in general and the concept of formal identity in particular.

Acknowledgements

I would like to thank the editors of this volume for extremely helpful comments on earlier versions of this paper. Special thanks are also due to Prof. Laurie Bauer, Dr. Ana Díaz-Negrillo and Dr. Juan Santana Lario for insightful discussion. I would also like to thank Prof. Nicolas Ballier and Dr. Jesús M. García González for their comments on French and Modern Greek, respectively. Responsibility for all errors remains mine. Preparation of this paper was supported by the Spanish Ministry of Economy and Competitiveness' project with reference FFI2012-39688.

8 References

Auwera, Johan van der and Volker Gast (2011): Categories and protoypes. In: Jae Jung Song (ed.), *The Oxford Handbook of Language Typology*, 167–189. Oxford: Oxford University Press.

Baker, Mark C. (2003): *Lexical Categories. Verbs, Nouns, and Adjectives*. Cambridge: Cambridge University Press.

Bauer, Laurie (1983): *English Word-formation*. Cambridge: Cambridge University Press.

Bauer, Laurie (2003): *Introducing Linguistic Morphology*. 2nd ed. Edinburgh: Edinburgh University Press.

Bauer, Laurie (2005): Conversion and the notion of lexical category. In: Laurie Bauer and Salvador Valera (eds.), *Approaches to Conversion/Zero-Derivation*, 19–30. Münster: Waxmann.

Bauer, Laurie, Rochelle Lieber and Ingo Plag (2013): *The Oxford Reference Guide to English Morphology*. Oxford: Oxford University Press.

Beard, Robert (1998): Derivation. In: Andrew Spencer and Arnold M. Zwicky (eds.), *Handbook of Morphology*, 44–65. Oxford/Malden, MA: Blackwell.

Bergenholtz, Henning and Joachim Mugdan (1979): Ist Liebe primär? Über Ableitung und Wortarten. In: Peter Braun (ed.), *Deutsche Gegenwartssprache*, 339–354. München: Fink.

Bergenholtz, Henning and Joachim Mugdan (2000): Nullelemente in der Morphologie. In: Geert Booij, Christian Lehmann and Joachim Mugdan (eds.), *Morphology. An International Handbook of Inflection and Word-Formation*. Vol. 1, 435–450. Berlin/New York: de Gruyter.

Biese, Yrjö M. (1941): Origin and development of conversions in English. *Annales Academiae Scientiarum Fennicae* B 45(2): 1–495.

Bisang, Walter (2011): Word classes. In: Jae Jung Song (ed.), *The Oxford Handbook of Language Typology*, 280–302. Oxford: Oxford University Press.

Bram, Barli (2011): Major total conversion in English: The question of directionality. Ph.D. dissertation, School of Linguistics and Applied Language Studies, Victoria University of Wellington.

Buck, Rosemary A. (1997): Words that are their opposites: Noun to verb conversion in English. *Word* 48(1): 1–14.

Carstairs-McCarthy, Andrew (2006): Internal modification. In: Keith Brown (ed.), *Encyclopedia of Language and Linguistics*. Vol. 5, 752–755. Oxford: Elsevier.

Cetnarowska, Bożena (1996): Constraints on affixless derivation in Polish and English: The case of action nouns. In: Henryk Kardela and Bogdan Szymanek (eds.), *A Festschrift for Edmund Gussmann from his Friends and Colleagues*, 15–28. Lublin: The University Press of the Catholic University of Lublin.

Colombat, Bernard (1988): Les "parties du discours" (partes orationis) et la reconstruction d'une syntaxe latine au XVIe siècle. *Langages* 92: 51–64.

Clark, Eve V. and Herbert H. Clark (1979): When nouns surface as verbs. *Language* 55(4): 767–811.

Croft, William (1984): Semantic and pragmatic correlates to syntactic categories. In: David Testen, Veena Mishra and Joseph Drogo (eds.), *Papers from the Parasession on Lexical Semantics*, 53–70. Chicago, IL: Chicago Linguistic Society.

Cruse, Alan (1986): *Lexical Semantics*. Cambridge: Cambridge University Press.

Dahl, Eystein and Antonio Fábregas (2017): Zero morphemes. *The Oxford Research Encyclopedia of Linguistics*. Oxford: Oxford University Press.

Daneš, František (1966): The relation of centre and periphery as a language universal. *Travaux Linguistiques de Prague* 2: 9–21.

Dokulil, Miloš (1968a): Zur Frage der Konversion und verwandter Wortbildungsvorgänge und -beziehungen. *Travaux Linguistiques de Prague* 3: 215–239.

Dokulil, Miloš (1968b): Zur Frage der sog. Nullableitung. In: Herbert E. Brekle and Leonhard Lipka (eds.), *Wortbildung, Syntax und Morphologie*, 55–64. The Hague: Mouton.

Don, Jan (1993): Morphological conversion. Ph.D. dissertation, Utrecht University.

Don, Jan (2003): A note on conversion in Dutch and German. In: Leonie Cornips and Paula Fikkert (eds.), *Linguistics in the Netherlands 2003*, 33–43. Amsterdam/Philadelphia: Benjamins.

Don, Jan (2005): Roots, deverbal nouns and denominal verbs. In: Geert Booij, Emiliano Guevara, Angela Ralli, Salvatore Sgroi and Sergio Scalise (eds.), *Morphology and Linguistic Typology. On-line proceedings of the Fourth Mediterranean Morphology Meeting (MMM4). Catania, 21–23 September 2003*, http://mmm.lingue.unibo.it/mmm-proc/MMM4/MMM4-Proceedings-full.pdf [last access 31 May 2012].

Dressler, Wolfgang U. (1987): Word formation as part of natural morphology. In: Wolfgang U. Dressler, Willi Mayerthaler, Oswald Panagl and Wolfgang U. Wurzel (eds.), *Leitmotifs in Natural Morphology*, 99–126. Amsterdam/Philadelphia: Benjamins.

Eschenlohr, Stefanie (1999): *Vom Nomen zum Verb. Konversion, Präfigierung und Rückbildung im Deutschen*. Hildesheim: Olms.

Feuillet, Jack (1991): Adjectifs et adverbes: Essai de classification. In: Claude Guimier and Pierre Larcher (eds.), *Les états de l'adverbe*, 35–58. Rennes: Presses Université de Rennes.

Farrell, Patrick (2001): Functional shift as category underspecification. *English Language and Linguistics* 5(1): 109–130.

Gaeta, Livio (2023): Between derivation and multifunctionality: In search of evidence for conversion. *SKASE Journal of Theoretical Linguistics* 20(4): 20–42.

Goddard, Cliff (1998): *Semantic Analysis. A Practical Introduction*. Oxford: Oxford University Press.

Gutiérrez Ordóñez, Salvador (1994): El artículo sí sustantiva. In: Alegría Alonso González, Beatriz Garza Cuarón and José Antonio Pascual Rodríguez (eds.), *II Encuentro de Lingüistas y Filólogos de España y México*, 483–507. Salamanca: Ediciones de la Universidad.

Haspelmath, Martin (1996): Word-class-changing inflection and morphological theory. In: Geert Booij and Jaap van Marle (eds.), *Yearbook of Morphology 1995*, 43–66. Dordrecht: Kluwer.

Hockett, Charles F. (1994): Conversion: The problem of parts of speech in English. *Études Anglaises* 47(2): 171–181.

Hummel, Martin (2000): *Adverbale und adverbialisierte Adjektive im Spanischen*. Tübingen: Narr.

Iordăchioaia, Gianina (2023): Morphological vs. syntactic conversion: Diagnostics and analytical means. *SKASE Journal of Theoretical Linguistics* 20(4): 57–73.

Iordăchioaia, Gianina and Chiara Melloni (2023): The zero suffix in English and Italian deverbal nouns. *Zeitschrift für Sprachwissenschaft* 42(1): 109–132.

Kastovsky, Dieter (1989): Word-formation. In: René Dirven (ed.), *A User's Grammar of English. Word, Sentence, Text, Interaction*. Vol. 1, 171–214. Frankfurt/M.: Lang.

Kastovsky, Dieter (1992): Semantics and vocabulary. In: Richard M. Hogg (ed.), *The Cambridge History of the English Language*. Vol. 1: *The Beginnings to 1066*, 290–407. Cambridge: Cambridge University Press.

Kastovsky, Dieter (1994): Verbal derivation in English: A historical survey or Much Ado About Nothing. In: Derek Britton (ed.), *English Historical Linguistics 1994. Papers from the 8th International Conference on English Historical Linguistics (8. ICEHL, Edinburgh, 19–23 September 1994)*, 93–117. Amsterdam/Philadelphia: Benjamins.

Kastovsky, Dieter (1996): The place of word-formation in grammar: A historical survey. In: Kurt R. Jankowsky (ed.), *Multiple Perspectives on the Historical Dimensions of Language*, 227–243. Münster: Nodus.

Kerleroux, Françoise (1999): Identification d'un procédé morphologique: La conversion. *Faits de Langues* 14: 89–100.
Kruisinga, Etsko (1927): On the history of conversion in English. *English Studies* 9: 103–108.
Leech, Geoffrey (1974): *Semantics*. Harmondsworth: Penguin.
Lieber, Rochelle (1981): Morphological conversion within a restricted theory of the lexicon. In: Michael Moortgat, Harry van der Hulst and Teun Hoekstra (eds.), *The Scope of Lexical Rules*, 161–200. Dordrecht: Foris.
Lieber, Rochelle (2015): The semantics of transposition. *Morphology* 25(4): 353–369.
Lipka, Leonhard (1971): Grammatical categories, lexical items and word-formation. *Foundations of Language* 7: 211–238.
Lipka, Leonhard (1986): Homonymie, Polysemie und Ableitung im heutigen Englisch. *Zeitschrift für Anglistik und Amerikanistik* 34(2): 128–138.
Lipka, Leonhard (1990): *An Outline of English Lexicology. Lexical Structure, Word Semantics, and Word-Formation*. Tübingen: Niemeyer.
Manova, Stela (2011): *Understanding Morphological Rules. With Special Emphasis on Conversion and Subtraction in Bulgarian, Russian and Serbo-Croatian*. Dordrecht/New York: Springer.
Manova, Stela and Wolfgang U. Dressler (2005): The morphological technique of conversion in the inflecting-fusional type. In: Laurie Bauer and Salvador Valera (eds.), *Approaches to Conversion/Zero-Derivation*, 67–102. Münster: Waxmann.
Marchand, Hans (1967): Expansion, transposition and derivation. *La Linguistique* 1: 13–26.
Marchand, Hans (1969): *The Categories and Types of Present-Day English Word-Formation. A Synchronic-Diachronic Approach*. 2nd ed. München: Beck.
Neef, Martin (1999): A declarative approach to conversion into verbs in German. In: Geert Booij and Jaap van Marle (eds.), *Yearbook of Morphology 1998*, 199–224. Boston/Dordrecht: Kluwer.
Neef, Martin (2005): On some alleged constraints on conversion. In: Laurie Bauer and Salvador Valera (eds.), *Approaches to Conversion/Zero-Derivation*, 103–130. Münster: Waxmann.
Nida, Eugene A. (1949): *Morphology. The Descriptive Analysis of Words*. 2nd ed. Ann Arbor, MI: The University of Michigan Press.
Olsen, Susan (1990): Konversion als kombinatorischer Wortbildungsprozeß. *Linguistische Berichte* 127: 185–216.
Payne, Thomas E. (1997): *Describing Morphosyntax. A Guide for Field Linguists*. Cambridge: Cambridge University Press.
Pennanen, Esko V. (1975): What happens in back-formation? In: Even Hovdhaugen (ed.), *Papers from the Second Scandinavian Conference of Linguistics, Lysebu, April 19–20, 1975*, 216–229. Oslo: University of Oslo.
Pennanen, Esko V. (1984): What happens in conversion? In: Håken Ringbom and Matti Rissanen (eds.), *Proceedings from the Second Nordic Conference for English Studies, Hanasaari/Hanaholmen, 19th–21st May 1983*, 79–93. Åbo: Åbo Akademi.
Plag, Ingo (1999): *Morphological Productivity. Structural Constraints in English Derivation*. Berlin/New York: Mouton de Gruyter.
Plag, Ingo (2003): *Word-Formation in English*. Cambridge: Cambridge University Press.
Plank, Frans (2010): Variable direction in zero-derivation and the unity of polysemous lexical items. *Word Structure* 3(1): 82–97.
Quirk, Randolph, Sidney Greenbaum, Geoffrey Leech and Jan Svartvik (1985): *Comprehensive Grammar of the English Language*. London: Longman.
Quirk, Randolph and C. L. Wrenn (1957): *An Old English Grammar*. 2nd ed. London: Methuen.
Rainer, Franz (2016): Derivational morphology. In: Adam Ledgeway and Martin Maiden (eds.), *The Oxford Guide to the Romance Languages*, 513–523. Oxford: Oxford University Press.

Ramat, Anna Giacalone and Paul J. Hopper (1998): Introduction. In: Anna Giacalone Ramat and Paul J. Hopper (eds.), *The Limits of Grammaticalization*, 1–10. Amsterdam/Philadelphia: Benjamins.

Ross, John Robert (1972): The category squish: Endstation Hauptwort. In: Paul M. Peranteau, Judith N. Levi and Gloria C. Phares (eds.), *Papers from the Eighth Regional Meeting*, 316–328. Chicago, IL: Chicago Linguistic Society.

Saeed, John I. (1997): *Semantics*. Oxford: Blackwell.

Sanders, Gerald (1988): Zero derivation and the Overt Analogue Criterion. In: Michael Hammond and Michael Noonan (eds.), *Theoretical Morphology. Approaches in Modern Linguistics*, 155–175. San Diego, CA: Academic Press.

Ševčíková, Magda (2021): Action nouns vs. nouns as bases for denominal verbs in Czech: A case study on directionality in derivation. *Word Structure* 3: 97–128.

Siegel, Muffy E. A. (1980): *Capturing the Adjective*. New York/London: Garland.

Soares Rodrigues, Alexandra and Salvador Valera (2025): Conversion in the Romance Languages. In: Michele Loporcaro (ed.), *Oxford Encyclopedia of Romance Linguistics* (part of *Oxford Research Encyclopedia of Linguistics* ed. by Mark Aronoff). Oxford: Oxford University Press. [Online available at: https://doi.org/10.1093/acrefore/9780199384655.013.683]

Stein, Gabriele (1977): The place of word-formation in linguistic description. In: Herbert E. Brekle and Dieter Kastovsky (eds.), *Perspektiven der Wortbildungsforschung. Beiträge zum Wuppertaler Wortbildungskolloquium vom 9.–10. Juli 1976*, 219–235. Bonn: Bouvier Verlag Herbert Grundmann.

Štekauer, Pavol (1996): *A Theory of Conversion in English*. Frankfurt/M.: Lang.

Vogel, Petra Maria (1996): *Wortarten und Wortartenwechsel. Zu Konversion und verwandten Erscheinungen im Deutschen und in anderen Sprachen*. Berlin/New York: de Gruyter.

Whorf, Benjamin Lee (1945): Grammatical categories. *Language* 21: 1–11.

Pavol Štekauer
12 Backformation

1 Introduction
2 Approaches to backformation
3 Conclusions
4 References

Abstract: This article discusses the nature of one of the most problematic processes of word-formation that has been traditionally labeled as backformation or back-derivation. It provides an overview of a range of theoretical approaches which differ considerably in their respective accounts of the nature of this process. Finally, a new approach to this phenomenon is proposed.

1 Introduction

According to the theory of natural morphology the most natural process in inflectional and derivational morphology is captured by the principle of diagrammaticity, i.e. *constructional iconicity* (cf. Mayerthaler 1981; Dressler 2005; Dressler, Mayerthaler, Panagl and Wurzel 1987). This principle requires that a new meaning be represented by a corresponding form. Therefore, suffixation and prefixation processes are most natural, while conversion is not natural, and subtraction processes, including backformation, are counter-natural.

This counter-naturalness of backformation is reflected in the limited number of languages that make use of backformation as a (productive) word-formation process. For example, Štekauer, Valera and Körtvélyessy (2012) show that backformation only occurs in 10 out of 55 analyzed languages. What is even more striking, none of these ten languages make use of backformation productively. Examples of backformed words are given in (1):

(1) *kvalitetssäkra*   ←   *kvalitetssäkring*   Swedish
    'to assure quality'   'quality assurance'
    (Olofsson, pers. comm.)

Pavol Štekauer, Košice, Slovakia

stofzuig	←	*stofzuiger*	Dutch
'to vacuum-clean'		'vacuum-cleaner'	
(Booij 2010: 41)			

Cross-linguistic research by Štekauer, Valera and Körtvélyessy (2012) also indicates that backformation is more or less a European phenomenon which occurs in Germanic, Romance and Slavic languages. Backformation in Finno-Ugric languages is non-existing, or very rare. According to Kilgi (pers. comm.), there are some examples of backformation in Estonian as in (2), but it is not a productive word-formation process nowadays. In Finnish it depends on the account of relatively rare compound verbs traditionally explained either as calques or backformations (3) (Laakso, pers. comm.):

(2) *eelis* ← *eelistama* Estonian
'advantage' 'to prefer'
(Kilgi, pers. comm.)

(3) *hiekkapuhaltaa* ← *hiekkapuhallus* Finnish
'to sandblast' 'sand-blasting'
(Laakso, pers. comm.)

There are only three exceptions to the "Eurocentric nature" of backformation in the sample collected for the above-mentioned research (Tamil, Hebrew, and Marathi), here exemplified with a backformed word from Marathi:

(4) *kara* ← *karaNe* Marathi
'hand' 'to do'
(Dixit, pers. comm.)

Thus, the question may be raised as to whether the non-occurrence of backformation in other parts of the world is a methodological issue, i.e. what counts as backformation in European linguistic tradition may be possibly evaluated in a different way (see section 2 for various theoretical accounts), or whether it is not a purely diachronic process as proposed by Marchand. The latter option might suggest that the absence of backformation in the word-formation descriptions of the languages of the world might be related to the lack of historical data, or better, to the absence of this kind of investigation.

While there is a consensus among morphologists that backformation is a word-formation process in which a morpheme or a pseudomorpheme (or even – more generally – "something" (Booij 2010: 40)) is deleted, they differ in accounting for the nature of this process. Therefore, in the following sections various approaches to the concept of backformation will be presented and various answers to the questions raised above will be discussed. Moreover, it will be shown that there are basically two groups of views, those which only admit the diachronic relevance of backformation, and those who stress that, synchronically, it is a productive word-formation process (in English), no matter what its nature stems from.

2 Approaches to backformation

2.1 Backformation as zero-derivation with subsequent clipping

In Marchand's view (1960, 1969), paralleled by the views of, for example, Kastovsky (1968, 1982), Quirk et al. (1972), Aronoff (1976), Kiparsky (1982), the process called back-derivation (backformation) is of diachronic relevance only. That *peddle*$_V$ is derived from *peddler*$_N$ is of historical interest. For synchronic analysis Marchand's equation is

(5) *peddle* : *peddler* = *write* : *writer*

which means that backformation is analyzed analogically with suffixation. In order to adhere to his principle of the syntagmatic nature of word-formation, Marchand suggests that all backformed verbs are zero-derived from their suffixal bases (1960: 310). In other words, the "basic" verb is arrived at through zero-derivation and the subsequent dropping of the (pseudo)morpheme.

Hansen et al. (1982: 135) distinguish between the type *peddle – pedlar/peddler* that can be analyzed as a 'person who peddles', which, synchronically, should be classified as suffix derivation, and the type *burglar – burgle* with the paraphrase 'to act as a burglar', which belongs in the field of backformation owing to the more complex semantic structure of the "backformed" coinage. This brings us to Marchand's assumption that "content must be the final criterion of derivational relationship for any pair of words" (1969: 392). This position is reflected in a series of semantic criteria for determining the direction of derivation (Marchand 1964). For illustration, the verb *saw* is backformed from the noun *saw* because the semantics of the verb *saw* depends on the semantics of the corresponding noun: 'to use a saw, cut with a saw' (ibid.: 12). This idea was later taken over by Nagano (2007).

Marchand's approach suffers from serious problems. Zandvoort calls into question the assumption that backformation is of diachronic relevance only, and, furthermore, claims that "[d]erivation without a derivational morpheme somehow reminds me of Bottom's Dream" (1961: 123). Pennanen (1966, 1975), like Adams (1973: 38–42), shows that, first, a set of semantic criteria designed to determine the direction of zero-derivation is not reliable, with there being many counter-examples (cf., for example, Štekauer 2000). Therefore, no semantic criterion can be the only and primary criterion for backformation. Certainly, semantics cannot be ignored as illustrated with the verb *unwish* which should not be treated as backformed from *unwished* because their meanings do not match ('to revoke, retract, cancel a wish' vs. 'not desired, not wished').

Second, the zero-derivation approach is called into question by many cases in which the backformed verb occurs much earlier than the converted verb from the same base, which means that "it is not conceivable how conversion should have a share in the formation of the BF [backformation, P. Š.]" (Pennanen 1975: 221–222). As an example, *to beg* backformed from *beggar* dates back to 1225 whereas the converted verb *beggar* is first instanced three centuries later in 1528. Moreover, these two verbs have different semantics: *beg* 'to ask for alms', *beggar* 'to make a beggar of, to impoverish, to make look like a beggar'. Consequently, Pennanen, like Bladin (1911: 51 ff.) and Biese (1941: 245) before him, suggests that the reduction of converted verbs be classified as clipping. In addition, while the majority of conversion-backformation pairs differ semantically, the few pairs that are not semantically distinct differ in frequency, register, or grammatical features. For illustration, while the verb *jell* is intransitive, *jelly* is both transitive and intransitive.

The view of the diachronic validity of backformation is also rejected by Szymanek (1998) who draws attention to "one quite productive pattern where backderivation reveals itself as a synchronically powerful device" (1998: 94), in particular, to "compound verbs" like *caretake* ← *caretaker*; *air-condition* ← *air-conditioning*; and *henpeck* ← *henpecked*. In addition, Szymanek points out that Polish has a productive way of deriving augmentative/pejorative nouns on the basis of nouns ending in the suffix *-ka*, which is associated with a diminutive meaning (ibid.: 95):

(6) *beka* 'big barrel' ← *beczka* 'barrel'
    buła 'big roll' ← *bułka* 'roll'

Finally, the "diachronic-only" position is criticized by Bauer (1983) who maintains that "this can be seen not to be true. While it is true that now the paradigms:

meddle   peddle
meddler   peddler

sound identical, and it is not possible to tell that the second was a case of backformation, at the time the form *peddle* was first used as a lexeme, there must have been some synchronic process which allowed the analogy [...]. Backformation must be allowed for in a synchronic grammar, it is still a current method of forming lexemes" (1983: 64–65). All in all, Bauer emphasizes that backformation is a synchronically productive process different from suffixation.

2.2 Backformation as compounding

Kiparsky (1982) also assumes that the term backformation has historical relevance only. This position is supported by the fact that the assumption that backformed verbs are historically derived from nouns and adjectives comes as a surprise to linguistically unsophisticated speakers, it is not accessible to a learner, and it has no structural significance. Diachronically, Kiparsky speaks of the process of reanalysis, where morphologically simple words come to be perceived as derived from verbs:

(7) [beggar]$_N$ reanalyzed as [[beg]$_V$ ar]$_N$
 [injury]$_N$ reanalyzed as [[injur]$_V$ y]$_N$

Synchronically, "backformations" of the *air-condition*$_V$ type are, according to Kiparsky, explained by scheme (8):

(8) [Y Z]$_X$

i.e. as compounds generated by insertion of stems Y and Z into a categorial frame X where X is a verb.

Verbs such as *beg, edit, peddle, eavesdrop, partake, syllabify* are treated by Kiparsky as basic, and the fact that they are historically backformed from nouns and adjectives has no structural significance.

2.3 Backformation as reinterpretation

In relation to word-pairs like *peddler – peddle*, Pennanen (1966, 1975) assumes that the starting point for the process in question is the re-interpretation of a given form as a complex word. Pennanen, like Koziol (1937: 194), maintains that reinterpretation is based on the backward application of a particular derivative pattern. To use Nagano's example (2007: 34), *beggar*$_N$ is originally a monomorphemic word, but is reanalyzed as having the structure [[begg]-ar], based on which backformation takes place and brings about beg_V. The idea of backward application of word-formation rules re-emerges in Aronoff's groundwork of generative grammar (1976).

This approach was rejected by Nagano (2007) who shows that Pennanen's model cannot account for cases of backformation with no corresponding word-formation rules:

(9) a. $surveillance_N$ → $surveille_V$ $peevish_A$ → $peeve_V$
　　b. $bruxism_N$ → $brux_V$ $frivolous_A$ → $frivol_V$
　　c. $liaison_N$ → $liaise_V$ $Bolshevik_N$ → $bolsh_V$

In (a) the deleted part corresponds to an unproductive suffix. In (b) the deletion process has no corresponding word-formation rule because it ignores the categorial selectional property of the deleted suffix. The suffixes -ism and -ous, for instance, cannot attach to a verb in English. In (c) the deleted part (-on, -evik) does not even exist as an affix.

2.4 Backformation as paradigmatic word-formation

Closely related to Pennanen's idea of reinterpretation is Booij's (2010) account of backformation as a prototypical case of paradigmatic word-formation. Like Pennanen, Booij explains the formation of the verb *sculpt* from the Latin borrowing *sculptor* by re-interpretation of the latter as [[sculpt]$_V$or]$_N$, analogically to the existing word-formation pattern (V-or)$_N$. What makes Booij different is his emphasis on the paradigmatic pressure consisting in the assignment to a moneme of an internal morphological structure on the basis of existing verb-noun pairs such as *terminate – terminator*. Reinterpretation is also at play in the case of verbs backformed from compounds, such as English *babysit* and Dutch *stofzuig* 'to vacuum-clean'. The structure of the corresponding nouns *babysitter* and *stofzuiger* 'vacuum cleaner' [[N][V -er]$_N$]$_N$ has been reinterpreted as [[N V]$_V$ -er]$_N$, with subsequent backformation.

Becker (1993), who argues in favour of the synchronic relevance of backformation by refering to its synchronic productivity, places emphasis on the paradigmatic relations of motivation. His paradigmatic rules not only relate actual words but also generate new words for which actual words serve as a model (the rule of proportional analogy). In Becker's view, affixation rules and backformation rules are of the same type; the main difference between them rests in productivity: "A rule is a backformation rule if and only if its inverse is more productive" (ibid.: 8). This is manifested in (10) where the rule of affixation (10a) and the rule of backformation (10b) are of the same nature but, clearly, the affixation rule is more productive in Modern English:

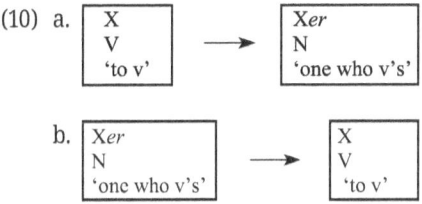

(10) a. [X / V / 'to v'] → [Xer / N / 'one who v's']

b. [Xer / N / 'one who v's'] → [X / V / 'to v']

Becker does not agree with merging these two rules into one bidirectional relation because "this would dissolve the difference between backformation and other formations" (ibid.). This is an important difference from Plag's schema-based model discussed in section 2.5.

2.5 Schema-based model of backformation

Plag calls into question an analysis of backformation based on suffix deletion by pointing out that there is no productive process of suffix deletion in English. In his schema-based model which systematically relates two sets of words, new words can be formed in both directions (hence the bidirectional arrow in the schema below). Plag assumes that "the existence of backformation is to be expected in a schema-based model, because there is no inherent directionality in the relationship between the two sets of words that are related by the schema" (2003: 187). Even though he does not provide any specific schema for backformation one of them might look as follows:

(11) $\begin{bmatrix} <X> \\ /V/ \\ \text{'X'} \end{bmatrix} \longleftrightarrow \begin{bmatrix} <Xer> \\ /N/ \\ \text{'Agent performing X'} \end{bmatrix}$

While this model copes with Nagano's class (a) it still cannot account for the other two problematic classes.

2.6 Backformation as conversion with subsequent clipping

Nagano (2007) accounts for backformation as a kind of conversion rather than zero-derivation. The synchronic relevance of backformation is, in his view, evidenced by the productivity of backformation in English. Nagano resumes Marchand's idea of semantic relationship and, in addition, introduces a quantitative-distributional criterion in order to determine the derivational relationship among the three patterns illustrated in (12) and (13):

(12) $[xvolve]_V \sim [xvolute]_V \sim [xvolution]_N$

circumvolve		circumvolution
convolve	convolute	convolution
devolve	devolute	devolution
evolve	evolute	evolution
intervolve		intervolution
involve	involute	involution
revolve	revolute	revolution

(13) $[xsolve]_V \sim [xsolute]_V \sim [xsolution]_N$

absolve		absolution
dissolve	dissolute	dissolution
exsolve		exsolution
resolve	resolute	resolution
solve	solute	solution

Nagano assumes that the quantitative-distributional criterion makes it possible to identify the derivational relations in the direction $xvolve_V \rightarrow xvolution_N \rightarrow xvolute_V$, and $xsolve_V \rightarrow xsolution_N \rightarrow xsolute_V$, respectively, which gives support to the back-formed nature of the forms $[xvolute]_V$ and $[xsolute]_V$.

Nagano points out that the three problematic classes of backformation (a)–(c) (see section 2.3) are coped with in Marchand's zero-derivation approach because the attachment of zero is followed by clipping a particular phonological sequence, a pseudomorpheme, which has no derivational significance. By implication, as Nagano says, this approach makes it possible to delete a non-productive affix in (a), to ignore the categorial selectional property of an affix in (b), and to delete a non-affixal element in (c).

However, given the extensive criticism of the theory of zero derivation, Nagano comes up with a modified version of Marchand's theory and claims that backformation is a type of conversion with subsequent clipping: "BF results from these two processes. Take the BF pair of the simple-word type $television_N$, $televise_{Vi}$ and the BF pair of the compound type $baby$-$sitter_N$, $baby$-sit_{Vi}, for instance. Just as conversion turns the nouns *catalog* and *chairman* into verbs ($catalog_V$, $chairman_V$), it turns the nouns *television* and *baby-sitter* into verbs ($television_V$, $baby$-$sitter_V$), and just as clipping shortens the forms of the nouns *cocaine* and *doctor* to the forms *coke* and *doc*, it shortens the forms of the verbs *television*$_V$ and *baby-sitter*$_V$ to the forms *televise* and *baby-sit*. The only difference between the converted verbs *catalog*$_V$ and *chairman*$_V$ and the 'back-formed' verbs *televise* and *baby-sit* is that the latter have their forms 'adjusted' by clipping" (2007: 56). While the main reason for clipping can be seen in the universal tendency towards the economy of expression, Nagano assumes that, with backformation, one more reason is at play, in particular, the adjustment of a converted word's form to its category. When, for example, an input has a nominal or adjectival (pseudo) suffix (e.g., *television*$_N$), conversion to a verb yields a categorially verbal but formally nominal/adjectival output (e.g., *television*$_V$). In such cases, conversion uses clipping to remove the categorially obstructive element, i.e. the (supposed) suffix, to adjust the output form to the output category. Nagano (2007: 65) maintains that since clipping is not a systematic grammatical process a backformed verb may have a converted rival as in *usher*$_V$ and *ush*$_V$ for the same reason that we have the doublet nouns *doctor* and *doc*.

Like all the other accounts this one also is not watertight. First, the lack of systematicity in the clipping of converted words can also be used as a counter-argument to the theory of backformation as clipped conversion. The question may be raised as to why the majority of converted words do not undergo the clipping process, and why a few of them co-exist with the clipped counterparts. And why, in fact, one and the same word should exist both clipped and not clipped if they emerge due to the same underlying process, especially in the cases when the backformed and the converted verbs have identical meanings.

Furthermore, the existence of converted verbs whose form has not been categorially adjusted to the category of verbs calls into question the claim that the purpose of clipping in backformation is to adjust the form of the converted word to that without an affix of a different syntactic category.

2.7 Backformation as a synchronically non-rule-based process

Allen (1978) assumes that backformation is not a productive word-formation process because "it is limited to applying only to lexicalized compounds with idiosyncratic meanings (i.e. compounds in the permanent lexicon), and does not apply to productive compounds with a variable range of possible meanings. In other words, there is no rule of English morphology which directly derives non-occurring compound verbs such as *[[furniture][move]]*$_V$, *[[watch][wind]]*$_V$, *[[bracelet][jangle]]*$_V$ or occurring compounds such as *baby-sit, type-write, tape-record*" (1978: 214).

Similarly, Anderson (1992: 191) does not consider backformation of the type *editor – edit* to be a rule-based process; rather, it is a sporadic process. For example, *submersible* falls within the class of *-able* words. A speaker may then presume that inspite of there not being a corresponding base verb, there ought to be one. This "enables" him to produce *submerse*. The coming into existence of *submerse* is, in Anderson's view, a matter of inference, which might be distinguished from the direct application of word-formation rules.

Finally, let us mention Beard (1995) who, in addition to automatic L(exical)-extension rules, introduces another type of L(exical)-rules. They are intentional, conscious, extragrammatical rules. He demonstrates his ideas on the basis of backformations, acronyms, and clippings. Thus, for example, the backderivation of *lase* from *laser* is not an automatic process, it is the product of an individual, non-ideal, speaker. It presupposes the existence of a prior L-extension rule (in this case, the *-er* suffixation rule generating instrumental nouns) to analyze and subsequently backform *lase* in analogy with such words as *shak-er, blow-er*, etc. Consequently, unlike automatic L-rules, instances of backformation are irregular, non-automatic, and unpredictable.

2.8 Onomasiological approach

The so-called backformations are treated in accordance with the general onomasiological model (Štekauer 1998, 2005) on the basis of the principle of morpheme-to-seme assignment that relates the onomasiological and the onomatological levels of the word-formation model. This can be exemplified by *stage-manager* and *stage-manage* in (14) and (15). The examples show that these naming units are produced independently:

(14) Conceptual level: 'a person who manages a stage'
Onomasiological level:
Object ← Action – Agent
stage   manage   er

(15) Conceptual level: 'to manage a stage'
Onomasiological level:
Object ← Action
stage   manage

In the case of naming units of the *peddler*-type only the "longer" word falls within the scope of word-formation. To derive it, one postulates a potential verb *peddle* that, later, became "actualized".

2.9 Noun incorporation?

It may be assumed that what has been traditionally analyzed as backformation (mostly based on diachronic data indicating that the "longer" form appeared historically before the "shorter" one) represents, formally, two different processes. It may be proposed that one of these processes that brings into existence naming units of the N+V structure (*baby-sit, proof-read, brainwash, sheepsteal, housebreak, caretake, fortune-hunt, book-keep, spring-clean, sight-read, strap-hang, sleep-walk, chain-smoke, vacuum-clean, wire-pull, window-shop, air-condition, brainstorm, tape-record, spotweld, factory-automate*, etc.) has developed into a new productive word-formation process in English, i.e. the process of noun incorporation. If noun incorporation is understood as a verb-forming process whereby a nominal stem is fused with a verbal stem to yield a larger, derived verbal stem, and the incorporated noun functions as an argument (usually object) of the predicative verb, all new English "backformed" verbs comply with this definition and most of them have the prototypical direct object–verb structure. Furthermore, if noun incorporation is viewed as a special type of compounding as it combines two stems, this approach is, in principle, in accordance with the above-mentioned conception of Kiparsky. There are at least five reasons for this proposal: (i) compounding is globally, and also in English, a highly productive word-formation process; (ii) it is a concatenative process which better corresponds to the psychological expectations of language users; furthermore, subtractive morphology appears to be an alien element in the overwhelmingly concatenative system of English word-formation; (iii) a high number of new coinages of this kind indicate a high productivity of this process. It may be assumed that noun-incorporation emerged on the basis of analogy (as is usally the case with new word-formation patterns) and later on – with a growing number of instances – it developed into a new word-formation pattern, a situation not unique cross-linguistically in the field of word-formation; (iv) if it is the suffix which is deleted in backformation – as postulated in the "classical" account of backformation – the suffix must have first been – logically – attached to the stem (at least potentially). Thus, what is proposed by the classical account is a cumbersome two stage model in which at first the affix is attached and subsequently it is deleted. The noun-incorporation-based account of these formations is much simpler and more straightforward, corresponding to the principle of constructional iconicity as specified in natural morphology; (v) as demonstrated by Brömser (1985: 101) there are numerous recent N/A+V coinages without a motivating nominal or adjectival basis.

Admittedly, there are views rejecting this option, but they do not seem to be well-founded. Thus, Booij opts for backformation in the case of words like *babysit* because "there is no general process of N + V compounding in English" (2010: 41), a view which, in fact, reiterates Marchand's rejection of this type of compounds (1969: 100). Plag (2003: 154), too, claims that verbal compounds with nouns as non-heads are impossible in English, and that verbs cannot incorporate adjectival/adverbial non-heads. First, it is not quite clear why verbal compounds with nouns as non-heads should be impossible. Each language undergoes changes, and the development of English from Old English to Modern English provides ample evidence that what once may have seemed to be impossible has become reality. Moreover, Brömser (1985) – who also argues in favour of an incorporation-based theory of "backformation" (within the framework of functional grammar) – points out that verbal compounds existed as early as Old English. Second, American Indian languages and some other languages of the world give evidence that it is not only nouns that are incorporated (Hall 1956; Štekauer, Valera and Körtvélyessy 2012).

Therefore, nothing precludes verbs like *merry-make*, *rough-ride*, *white-wash* from being considered adjective incorporations. Semantically, various functions can be fulfilled by the incorporated noun in languages of the world, including the category of Time as in *spring-clean*, the category of manner as in *strap-hang*, etc. Thus, contrary to what is claimed by Plag, nothing prevents the potential incorporations like *book-read*, *car-steal*, *fast-drive*, *slow-move* from becoming actual verbs of English.

All in all, it may be argued that the original process of backformation in English gave rise to numerous analogical formations no longer relying on "longer" counterparts. The growing number of such formations may have triggered a synchronically productive process of noun/adjective incorporation. This view is not new. In 1956, Hall, in a paper with a highly indicative title, *How we noun-incorporate in English*, conclusively argues that noun incorporation is a productive method of English word-formation which has been used for centuries (the fact that contradicts the above-mentioned views of Booij and Plag). A more careful position is taken by Kastovsky (1986: 419) who predicts gradual development of a productive process of noun incorporation, a view recently strengthened in Kastovsky (2009: 338) by saying that "this type has become rather popular in Modern English as a result of the re-interpretation of denominal back-formations". A high productivity of this pattern is also confirmed by Szymanek (2005: 434) who speaks of "considerable growth over recent years". Let us conclude this section by Brömser's words who assumes that "there is no essential difference between English verbal compounds and incorporation constructions in those languages which make use of such a process for the construction of sentences" (1985: 111).

3 Conclusions

This article has provided an overview of various approaches to the phenomenon known in (predominantly) European languages as backformation or back-derivation. It has been shown that there is no agreement in assessing the nature of this process. Differences concern its diachronic vs. synchronic validity, different theoretical approaches to this phenomenon as well as the systematicity vs. idiosyncrasy of the process. It may be surmised that one can hardly describe various aspects of "backformation" by a unified theory. It seems that rather than a single word-formation process we face processes of different sort, including, on the one hand, incorporation, and on the other hand, a mixture of reinterpretation, analogical formation, and clipping, all this clearly connected with the general tendency (especially strong in recent decades) towards the economy of expression. Whether or not, in what way and to what degree this general tendency is implemented appear to depend, primarily, on productivity and the related morphosemantic transparency of the corresponding word-formation rules. No wonder then that about 87 % of English backformed words are verbs (Pennanen 1975). Namely, as Rainer (1993: 86) correctly points out, deverbal derivatives such as action or agent nouns are produced by highly productive rules and generally allow unequivocal reconstruction of the semantics of the base word – the circumstances that establish a favourable framework for the processes in question.

4 References

Adams, Valerie (1973): *An Introduction to Modern English Word Formation*. London: Longman.
Allen, Margaret R. (1978): Morphological investigations. Ph.D. dissertation, University of Connecticut, Storrs, CT.
Anderson, Stephen R. (1992): *A-Morphous Morphology*. Cambridge: Cambridge University Press.
Aronoff, Mark (1976): *Word Formation in Generative Grammar*. Cambridge, MA: MIT Press.
Bauer, Laurie (1983): *English Word-Formation*. Cambridge: Cambridge University Press.
Beard, Robert E. (1995): *Lexeme-Morpheme Base Morphology. A General Theory of Inflection and Word Formation*. Albany: State University of New York Press.
Becker, Thomas (1993): Back-formation, cross-formation, and 'bracketing paradoxes' in paradigmatic morphology. In: Geert Booij and Jap van Marle (eds.), *Yearbook of Morphology 1993*, 1–25. Dordrecht: Kluwer.
Biese, Yrjö M. (1941): *Origin and Development of Conversions in English*. Helsinki: Suomalainen Tiedeakatemia.
Bladin, Wilhelm (1911): *Studies on Denominative Verbs in English*. Uppsala: Alquist and Wiksell.
Booij, Geert (2010): *The Grammar of Words. An Introduction to Morphology*. Oxford: Oxford University Press.
Brömser, Bernd (1985): On the derivation of English verbal compounds. In: Wilfried Kürschner and Rüdiger Vogt (eds.), *Grammatik, Semantik, Textlinguistik*. Vol. 1, 99–113. Tübingen: Niemeyer.

Dressler, Wolfgang (2005): Word-formation in Natural Morphology. In: Pavol Štekauer and Rochelle Lieber (eds.), *Handbook of Word-Formation*, 267–244. Dordrecht: Springer.
Dressler, Wolfgang U., Willi Mayerthaler, Oswald Panagl and Wolfgang U. Wurzel (1987): *Leitmotifs in Natural Morphology*. Amsterdam/Philadelphia: Benjamins.
Hall, Robert (1956): How we noun-incorporate in English. *American Speech* 31: 83–88.
Hansen, Barbara, Klaus Hansen, Albrecht Neubert and Manfred Schentke (1982): *Englische Lexikologie*. Leipzig: VEB Verlag Enzyklopädie.
Kastovsky, Dieter (1968): *Old English Deverbal Substantives Derived by Means of a Zero Morpheme*. Esslingen: Langer.
Kastovsky, Dieter (1982): *Wortbildung und Semantik*. Tübingen/Düsseldorf: Francke.
Kastovsky, Dieter (1986): Diachronic word-formation in a functional perspective. In: Dieter Kastovsky and Aleksander Szwedek (eds.), *Linguistics across Historical and Geographical Boundaries. In Honour of Jacek Fisiak on the Occasion of his Fiftieth Birthday*, 409–421. Berlin/New York: Mouton de Gruyter.
Kastovsky, Dieter (2009): Diachronic perspectives. In: Rochelle Lieber and Pavol Štekauer, (eds.), *The Oxford Handbook of Compounding*, 323–342. Oxford: Oxford University Press.
Kiparsky, Paul (1982): Lexical Morphology and Phonology. In: In-Seok Yang (ed.), *Linguistics in the Morning Calm. Selected Papers from SICOL-1981*, 3–91. Seoul: Hanshin Publishing Company.
Koziol, Herbert (1937): *Handbuch der englischen Wortbildungslehre*. Heidelberg: Winter.
Marchand, Hans (1960): *The Categories and Types of Present-Day English Word-Formation*. Wiesbaden: Harrassowitz.
Marchand, Hans (1964): A set of criteria for the establishing of derivational relationship between words unmarked by derivational morphemes. *Indogermanische Forschungen* 69: 10–19.
Marchand, Hans (1969): *The Categories and Types of Present-Day English Word-Formation. A Synchronic-Diachronic Approach*. 2nd ed. München: Beck.
Mayerthaler, Willi (1981): *Morphologische Natürlichkeit*. Wiesbaden: Athenaion.
Nagano, Akiko (2007): Marchand's analysis of back-formation revisited: Back-formation as a type of conversion. *Acta Linguistica Hungarica* 54(1): 33–72.
Pennanen, Esko (1966): *Contributions to the Study of Back-formation in English*. Tampere: Julkaisija Yhteiskunnallinen Korkeakoulu.
Pennanen, Esko (1975): What happens in back-formation? In: Even Hovdhaugen (ed.), *Papers from the Second Scandinavian Conference of Linguistic*, 216–229. Oslo: Oslo University Department of Linguistics.
Plag, Ingo (2003): *Word-formation in English*. Cambridge: Cambridge University Press.
Quirk, Randolph, Sidney Greenbaum, Geoffrey Leech and Jan Svartvik (1972): *A Grammar of Contemporary English*. London: Longman.
Rainer, Franz (1993): *Spanische Wortbildungslehre*. Tübingen: Niemeyer.
Štekauer, Pavol (1998): *An Onomasiological Theory of English Word-Formation*. Amsterdam/Philadelphia: Benjamins.
Štekauer, Pavol (2000): *English Word-Formation. A History of Research (1960–1995)*. Tübingen: Narr.
Štekauer, Pavol (2005): Onomasiological approach to word-formation. In: Pavol Štekauer and Rochelle Lieber (eds.), *Handbook of Word-Formation*, 207–232. Dordrecht: Springer.
Štekauer, Pavol, Salvador Valera and Lívia Körtvélyessy (2012): *Word-Formation in the World's Languages. A Typological Survey*. Cambridge: Cambridge University Press.
Szymanek, Bogdan (1998): *Introduction to Morphological Analysis*. Warszawa: Wydawnictwo Naukowe PWN.
Szymanek, Bogdan (2005): The latest trends in English word-formation. In: Pavol Štekauer and Rochelle Lieber (eds.), *Handbook of Word-Formation*, 429–448. Dordrecht: Springer.

Anja Steinhauer
13 Clipping

1   Introduction
2   Historical outline
3   General survey of the most common forms of clipping
4   Semantic and pragmatic aspects of clipping
5   References

Abstract: Clipping – including acronyms and hybrid forms of word shortening – has been accepted as a part of word-formation for many years now. This article presents an overview of research history up to modern (prosodic, prototypical, semantic, interdisciplinary) approaches. It also highlights the most common techniques of word shortening in different European languages and focuses on some pragmatic features of word shortening.

1 Introduction

Clipping, in general, refers to a word-formation process in which the cutting of a lexeme (one or more words) does not result in a change of meaning, i.e. the new, condensed word carries the same meaning as the (longer) original. In this article, the term *clipping* (also known as "truncation") is therefore used for a variety of word shortening processes that result in new word-forms, i.e. a new word is produced by abbreviating a longer form. This process is not limited to individual words; in fact, an existing lexeme can also contain several words, and even phrases can be clipped (e.g., *as soon as possible* is commonly clipped to *ASAP* and also to *saspo*). Furthermore, a clipping usually occurs simultaneously with its longer original, at least when it is first being formed. This article describes different results of this clipping process.

There are various other types of word shortening that do not result in new words and that therefore, strictly speaking, do not belong to the field of word-formation (like abbreviations). This article provides an overview of the types of word shortening that generate accepted new words. Unfortunately, the term clipping is not used consistently in the description of word-formation processes. In

---

Anja Steinhauer, Wiesbaden, Germany

https://doi.org/10.1515/9783111420561-013

fact, researchers tend to generally bemoan the simultaneous existence of a variety of definitions. Nevertheless, this drawback has never been resolved.

In order to lay a convenient foundation for the discussion of different kinds of word shortenings, *clipping* should be understood primarily as a general term for word shortening as a word-formation process, comprising lexemes that have retained – at least for a while – (nearly) the same meaning as their longer originals. In the literature, the term clipping is often used only for cases where one part of a word stands for the whole, e.g., *condo(minium)*, *(tele)phone* or *(in)flu(enza)*. Given that a strict classification of all versions of word shortening is hardly possible, it seems helpful to see clipping as the umbrella term for word shortenings in the context of word-formation (for further details of definition and classification see section 3.1).

Section 2 provides a brief overview of the history of research on word shortening. Since the techniques of word shortening differ significantly, the resulting words need to be differentiated as well. In the last decades, numerous attempts have been made to establish a stringent typology of clipped word forms. While no generally accepted typology has been found to date, most scholars agree on the basic terminology. Following a brief presentation of word shortenings that do not belong to clipping, such as blending or backformation, this section also discusses divergent approaches to word shortening and various typologies.

Section 3 presents the most common classes of clipping. Since clipping is to be found in most modern languages today, this article offers examples of word shortenings from a variety of languages, with a concentration on European languages. Kreidler (2000) presents further information on clipping in other languages, including Japanese. A German anthology on linguistic shortness in general (Bär, Roelcke and Steinhauer 2007) includes analyses of "brevity" in various European languages. Thornton (1996) discusses shortenings extensively in Italian, and López Rúa (2004) concentrates on English and Spanish "Acronyms & Co.".

2 Historical outline

2.1 Word shortening and its research

Clipping as a word-formation process is seen as a phenomenon of the late 19th and the 20th and 21st century. While many shortened forms were found in ancient times (like in Latin *IMP.* for *imperator*, *COS.* for *consul*, *INRI* for *Iesus Nazarenus Rex Iudaeorum*, *SPQR* for *senatus populusque romanus*) or in medieval manuscripts (Greule 2007: 121 f.), these were not the result of word-formation; they are not considered autonomous words (see below in section 3.1). In particular, as far as we know today, it seems significant that shortened forms like the abbreviations mentioned above have never been used in spoken language. But even as early as the time when Latin was spoken some examples of real clipping can be found, as ascertained by Biville (1989).

One of the first scientifically-based remarks on contracted word forms that are used in the spoken language as well comes from the German linguist Johann Christoph Adelung, who stated in the year 1790 that contractions are typically found among rather poorly educated people and in some dialects (cf. Steinhauer 2000: 12). With the emergence of technical terminology and specialized languages, an increasing number of short forms have emerged; first within special domains, then in everyday or quotidian language. One of the first fields to make excessive use of shortened words was chemistry. In fact, both the periodic table of the elements with its symbolic language and the chemical nomenclature are based on word shortening (Steinhauer 2000: 105–114). Early in the development of a specific chemical language, namely in 1823, blendings like the name *ethal* (the first two syllables of the words *ether* and *alcohol*) came into existence. The World Health Organization (WHO) and the International Organization for Standardization (ISO) have established numerous examples of chemical terminology like the International Nonproprietary Names (INN) for active pharmaceutical ingredients and the Common Names for ingredients in pesticides – all of them being shortenings of the names of the strict systematic nomenclature.

Already at the end of the 19th century, and increasingly in the 20th century, more and more clipped words found their way into the community at large and into the spoken language of ordinary people to a greater extent. The Industrial Revolution brought forth major changes in agriculture, manufacturing, mining, transportation and technology. With the creation of new technologies, concepts and inventions, the need for new words developed, and the often long and complex existing terms were predestined to be clipped. Kreidler points to an additional aspect that has expedited this new type of word-formation, namely the element of play: "clipping can be an enjoyable linguistic sport" (Kreidler 2000: 959) – which holds true even up to today.

During the first half of the 20th century, administration became ever more relevant in quotidian life, and as a result, increasing amounts of complicated terms found their way into everyday speech. The often long and intricate words and phrases were soon shortened, resulting in the eventual disappearance of the lengthier forms. The described increase in word shortenings, not only in languages for special purposes but also in the common language, led linguists to take a closer look at this relatively new phenomenon. Especially after World War

II, linguistic publications on clipping amplified. (For an overview on research in Germany see Steinhauer 2000: 10–23.)

For the German language, the studies by Bellmann (1980) and Greule (1996) became seminal; the most extensive study on clippings in German overall was published by Kobler-Trill (1994), followed by Steinhauer (2000) who focuses on clippings in languages for special purposes, and Balnat (2011) who specifically investigates clippings in colloquial speech and in sociolects. The most comprehensive discussions of clippings in English are by Kreidler (1979 and 2000) and Cannon (1989), with Cannon offering, in addition, an excellent overview on the history of the scholarship and research of shortenings in English. For an overview of clipping and its research in Spanish see López Rúa (2004), for clippings in Italian Thornton (1996), and in Dutch Leuschner (2008). Since all languages differ in their approaches to word shortening and prefer their own ways of clipping, it is not feasible to discuss all of them here. (For shortening in German, English, French, Italian, Swedish, Danish, Norwegian, Icelandic and Ukrainian see also the adequate articles in Bär, Roelcke and Steinhauer 2007, namely Busse and Schneider 2007, Mayer and Rovere 2007, Nübling and Duke 2007, Sandhop 2007, Schmitt 2007.)

2.2 Typological and terminological variation

For a few decades, scholars mainly concentrated on the shortening process itself, describing what parts of the long form were taken to create the shortened form. This became the basis for handling the phenomenon on a scientific fundament. Miscellaneous publications appeared, each with its own terminology, and often only discernable by minute details. Since there are numerous ways to shorten a word and consequently various different types of clippings, it is immensely complicated to establish a typology that applies to all cases. Accordingly, scholars are usually forced to refer to a great variety of clipping. As López Rúa states, "the multifarious nature of the categories forces them to complete those descriptions with long enumerations of particular cases which do not follow the general rule" (López Rúa 2004: 112).

In the last few years, research has begun to examine the linguistic features that surpass the pure process of shortening, following the trend to leave structuralism in favor of a more pragma- and sociolinguistically oriented approach. Today, research discusses clipping as a phenomenon of "extragrammatical morphology" (cf. Doleschal and Thornton 2000) containing submorphemic elements. Especially the aspect of *prosodic morphology* has surfaced as significant. As early as 1996, scholars began to use the theory of prosodic morphology to explain the strategies of word shortening: Anna M. Thornton underlined the existence of prosodically governed morphological phenomena in Italian (Thornton 1996) and Elke Ronneberger-Sibold examined the "phonotactic and prosodic properties of shortenings in German and French" (Ronneberger-Sibold 1996); for the English language, Ingo Plag discussed clippings in the context of prosodic morphology (cf. Plag 2003). One example illustrates the underlying idea of examining clippings on the basis of prosodic morphology: As Thornton shows in her study, the minimal prosodic word in Italian is disyllabic, has trochaic stress, and ends in a vowel. Various examples in fact support her thesis that this typical minimal word serves as a template for the process of clipping in Italian.

The last decades have elucidated the impracticality of classifying the great variety of existing types of shortening into one typology. Still, the *prototypical approach* (e.g., Lopez Rúa 2002 and 2004; Michel 2006) might offer a solution to this dilemma, since it focuses on the main issue, namely that there are central, peripheral and borderline cases of shortenings that stretch across a kind of continuum – some being more typical than others, and again others being central but not typical. The idea of a continuum matches the need for classification best since it allows for locating any clipping in the appropriate position. Following this method enables observations such as, "the most 'perfect' examples of acronyms (such as *laser*) look like actual words, both in shape and in meaning (that is, speakers use them as words and are no longer aware that they once replaced a whole expression)" (López Rúa 2004: 125).

Another aspect of research on clipping is the semantic approach (cf. Michel 2011): Why are originals actually clipped? What happens to their meaning and the meaning of the clipped form? When do the meanings differ from each other? Other linguists examine clipping from a lexicographical point of view (e.g., Schröder 2000), focus on grammatical aspects (cf. Harley 2004; Ronneberger-Sibold 2007) or employ an interdisciplinary approach (Fandrych 2008a, 2008b).

3 General survey of the most common forms of clipping

3.1 Word shortenings not belonging to clipping

Clipping is different from most types of classic word-formation as it neither accumulates morphemes, nor does it attach something to a base (like in composition and affixation). Rather, it is a process of deleting material but it needs to be distinguished from other cases of shortening a longer base.

First, there are examples of shortening that do not result in a new word, namely the purely graphic abbreviations. These should not be treated in the context of word-formation since they are far from being "real" words. Purely graphic abbreviations that are always dismantled in spoken language cannot count as new words of their own, they are never pronounced in the shortened form, which means that no new word is being formed (like *Mr.* for *Mister* in English, *Hbf.* for *Hauptbahnhof* in German, *qc.* for *quelque chose* in French, *sing.* for *singular, Singular* and *singulier* in all the three languages). As stated earlier, abbreviations constitute a rather old phenomenon that can be traced back to ancient times when writing texts was an intricate and arduous piece of work and authors often felt pressed to shorten words for economical reasons. Also, the numerous abbreviations occurring in medieval handwritings did not find their way into spoken language, and have never become lexemes.

Furthermore, the definition of clipping claims that the clipped form – at least when being created – represents a kind of synonym with its "original", the longer form. This implies that the longer form is a lexeme by itself. This does not apply to blends (see article 15 on blending) and their longer forms: the basis for a blending never existed as only one lexeme itself. The words *breakfast* and *lunch* exist, but not a combination of both, whereas the blend *brunch*, which contains parts of both, is a lexicalized word of its own. Also, backformation (see article 12 on backformation) is not an example of clipping.

On the contrary, formations that result from clipping like the ones often called *acronyms* (*Laser* from *light amplification by stimulated emission of radiation*, *NATO* from *North Atlantic Treaty Organization*, with orthoepic pronunciation, i.e. pronounced as a word) and the ones often called *initialisms* (*CIA* from *Central Intelligence Agency*, pronounced as a series of letters) today are clearly seen as part of word-formation, even if they are not considered to be morphological. Therefore they are treated in this article as well as the "classic" forms of clipping like the ones that are a single subpart of the original.

3.2 Back clipping, fore-clipping, and related forms

Some archetypes of clipping occur in many languages. While various current attempts to explain the phenomenon of clipping concentrate on other issues than the purely formal typology of short forms, an introduction to the great variety of clippings is helpful in order to gain an overview.

In order to avoid further confusion resulting from inconsistent terminology, this article centers on describing only the most common types of clipping, each as a kind of prototype. Terminologically, it follows the majority of research on word shortening by calling the longer form that is reduced the *original*.

The first group of clippings comprises words that consist of one continuous part of the original; they can go back to "back clipping", "fore-clipping" or "middle clipping".

a) Back clipping: The original is clipped at its back and the beginning is retained. Examples in which the original is a simple word are English *ad(vertisement)*, *app(lication)*, *exam(ination)*, *gas(oline)*, *gym(nasium)*, *lab(oratory)*, *mag(azine)*, *math(ematics)*, *recap(itulation)*, *vet(erinarian)*; German *Abi(tur)*, *Dino(saurier)*, *Frust(ration)*, *Perso(nalausweis)*, *Prof(essor)*, *Reha(bilitationsmaßnahme)*, *Uni(versität)*; French *ampli(ficateur)*, *anar(chiste)*, *bac(calauréat)*, *croco(dile)*, *impro(visation)*, *manif(estation)*, *proc(ureur)*, *promo(tion)*; Dutch *bib(liotheek)*, *bios(coop)*, *aso(ciaal)*, *juf* (from *juffrouw)*. The clipping process differs from one language to another: German *Kino* no longer possesses an original, whereas English *cinema* does not have a short form. In comparison, most Romance languages employ both a longer and a shorter form: French *ciné* and *cinéma*, Italian *cinema* and *cinematografo*, Portuguese *cine* and *cinema*, or Spanish *cine* and *cinematógrafo*. In Russian, too, one can find the clipped form and the original: *kino* and *kinoteatr*.

In German, the second part of a complex noun is often deleted, whereas the first morpheme constitutes the clipping. Especially foreign words utilize back clippings: *Auto(mobil)*, *Chiro(praktik)*, *Derma(tologie)*, *Dia(positiv)*, *Echo(lot)*, *Endo(skopie)*, *Ergo(therapie)*, *Foto(grafie)*, *Kilo(gramm)*, *Mammo(graphie)*, *Neuro(logie)*, *Ortho(pädie)*, *Sono(graphie)*. Scandinavian languages similarly favor this kind of clipping, e.g., Swedish *arr(angemang)* and *el(ektricitet)*, Danish *kval(ifikasjonsrunde)* and *stud(erende)*, Norwegian *krim(inalroman)* und *perm(isjon)*. Icelandic, however, rarely uses back clippings, and instead clearly prefers fore-clippings (cf. Nübling and Duke 2007).

Sometimes the clippings lose their link to the original (see section 4) or the original is not recalled at once; this is the reason why some examples of back clipping have a gender different from their original form. Such a change of gender can be registered for instance in German *der Frust* (masculine noun) but *die Frustration* (female noun), *die Mikro* (female noun) but *das Mikrowellengerät* (neuter), *das Foto* (neuter) but *die Fotografie* (female noun).

As evidenced in the examples above, the clippings that result from shortening can be arbitrary parts or existing morphemes; prosodic morphology tries to answer the question why words are clipped in a certain way. Additionally, examples exist in which the original is rather complex and consists of several words: English *cap(ital letter)*, *pub(lic house)*, or German *Zoo(logischer Garten)*. Sometimes the clipped form is slightly adjusted, e.g., in *bike* (*bicycle*) or *coke* (*Coca Cola*).

Following a rather ancient tradition, first names are also often found among clippings: *Al, Ben, Fred, Lu, Nick, Ray*. Furthermore, back clippings of proper names with an additional endearing suffix are popular: *Andy, Benny, Charlie*, also *Lindy* (*Charles Lindberg*), *Oppy* (*Robert Oppenheimer*). In Germany, famous soccer players are honored this way, e.g., *Klinsi* (*Jürgen Klinsmann*) and *Schweini* (*Bastian Schweinsteiger*). In both English and German, a hypocoristic suffix cannot only be added to proper names but to common nouns as well: English *looney* (*lunatic*), *Aussie* (*Australian*), *bookie* (*bookmaker*), *cabby* (*cabman*), *telly* (*television*), German *Compi* (*Computer*), *Knobi* (*Knoblauch*), *Pulli* (*Pullover*), *Schlaffi* (*Schlaffer*), *Studi* (*Student/-in*).

b) Fore-clipping, in which the original is clipped at the beginning and the end of the word is retained, is less common in English – *(we)blog, (omni)bus, (violon)cello, (ra)coon, (alli)gator, (tele)phone, (turn)pike, (aero)plane, (cara)van, (uni)versity*; and very rare in German (there are *Bus* and *Cello*, like in English, and the rather colloquial *Schland* for *Deutschland*), French, and other European languages. Only Icelandic has a greater number of fore-clippings, such as *(automo)bíll, (sósíaldemo)krati, (síga)retta* or *flensa* for *influenza* (cf. Nübling and Duke 2007). First names originating in fore-clipping are, for example, *Bella, Dora, Tilda, Tina, Trix*, with an additional hypocoristic suffix in *Betty* and *Netty*.

Fore-clippings must not be mistaken for similar-looking short forms such as German *Rad* for *Fahrrad* or *Kanzlerin* for *Bundeskanzlerin*. In such cases (frequently found in German) determinative compounds are shortened to their head; no new words are being constructed.

c) Clippings with the middle of the word retained are rather infrequent. *Flu* for *influenza*, *fridge* for *refrigerator* in English, or *níver* for *aniversário* in Portuguese may serve as examples. In German, they are virtually unknown except for some proper names such as *Lisa* (*Elisabeth*) or *Basti* (*Sebastian*); French is merely acquainted with *strass* for *l'administration*. Typically, the term middle clipping is employed in English to describe these formations. Not surprisingly, this expression often leads to confusion, since the terms *back* clipping and *fore*-clipping emphasize the part of the original that is clipped, whereas the term *middle* clipping stresses the part that is retained.

Generally speaking, back clipping surfaces as the rule in most languages when retaining whole parts of the original, while the omission of the first part is much less common. While most of the clipped words are nouns, some adjectives can be found: English *bi(sexual)*, or with hypocoristic suffix *comfy* (*comfortable*) and *loony* (*lunatic*), German *bio(logisch)*, French *sympa(thique)*. In German, for example, the trend for clipping seems to be more dominant in colloquial language or youth slang than in standard language. Often, back and front-clipping is employed to create novel, humorous, or witty words such as the adjectives *schizo* and *phren* (both in use for *schizophren*), or *depri* deriving from *deprimierend*.

3.3 Acronyms, initialisms, and related forms

At first glance, this category appears closed and easily identifiable; it includes shortenings that consist of different separate letters of the original. These are the most frequent word shortenings in all modern languages, with the most common type containing three letters of the original (*FBI*, *JFK*, *UNO*), but also with the possibility for two (*UK*), four (*YMCA*) or more letters (*UNESCO*).

Such words are usually labelled acronyms or initialisms, generally discerned on the basis of their pronunciation: There is first the alphabetic, letter-naming, letter-recitation type, when every letter of the word is pronounced on its own (*EFSF* for English *European Financial Stability Facility* and German *Europäische Finanzstabilisierungsfazilität*, *OON* for *Organizacija Ob"edinennyx Nacij*, the Russian version of *UNO*, or Polish *PKO* for *Polska Kasa Oszczędności*, Poland's largest bank), and there is second the orthoepic, letter-sounding type, in which the shortened form is pronounced as a "normal" word (*NATO* for *North Atlantic Treaty Organization* in English, *OTAN* for *Organisation du Traité de l'Atlantique Nord* in French, *Havo* for *Hoger Algemeen Vormend Onderwijs* in Dutch, *TAP* for *Transportes Aéreos Portugueses* in Portuguese). Very long acronyms characteristically belong to the second category since it would be rather exhausting to spell a word such as *UNESCO*. The orthoepic acronyms are also more likely to be integrated into the lexicon of a language since, typically, the original eventually falls out of the speakers' awareness: Who can remember spontaneously that *UNESCO* stands for *United Nations Educational, Scientific and Cultural Organization*, or *laser* for *light amplification by stimulated emission of radiation*? Even shorter ones like *Aids* and *PISA* are not always known to stem from a longer original, and only few people remember the original (*acquired immune deficiency syndrome* and *Programme for International Student Assessment*).

The distinction between alphabetic and orthoepic acronyms is not always viable. For example, there are cases in which both types of pronunciation can be observed: The acronym *VIP* is pronounced as [vi: ai 'pi:] and as [vip], in German you can speak of the *FAZ* (*Frankfurter Allgemeine Zeitung*) as [ef a: tset] or as [fats] – the latter pronunciations being much more informal. Similarly, the name of the lung disease *SARS* (*severe acute respiratory syndrome*) was pronounced as [es a: er es] when it first emerged in Germany in 2007. After a period of intense media coverage, both the pronunciation and the notation were adjusted to that of other substantives: *Sars*. In fact, there are even words that combine alphabetic and orthoepic pronunciation: *LSAT* (*Law School Aptitude Test*) [ɛl sæt] in English, *CPAM* [ce pam] and *FIDL* [fidɛl] in French, or *EuGH* (*Europäischer Gerichtshof*) [oi ge: ha:] in German. And *WLAN* (*Wireless Local Area Network*) in German is pronounced as a mixture as well [ve: la:n]; in English this short form is not known, it is commonly called *Wi-Fi*, a term resembling the long-established term *Hi-Fi* (for *high fidelity*), but originally not being a short form for *wireless fidelity*. As to the pronunciation of French "sigles", Plénat found out that apart from historical, sociological and lexical factors there are some phonological regularities like the distribution of consonants and vowels ("syllababilité"), the length of the acronym ("taille") and the hiatus that have an impact on the way an acronym is pronounced (Plénat 1998).

The basis for an acronym is most often a complex lexeme, but there are also phrases and even sentences that are shortened this way. Especially electronic communication makes use of acronyms: English *bbs*/*BBS* (*be back soon*) or *lol*/ *LOL* (*laughing out loud*), German *HDL*/*hdl* (*hab dich lieb*) or *wkw* (*Wer kennt wen?*) (for different kinds of word shortening in electronic communication cf. Balnat 2011).

3.4 Hybrid forms of clipping

The problematic lack of a cohesive terminology becomes most evident in the case of word-formations that do not fit into any single category. There are words like, for example, *radar* (*radio detection and ranging*) that take one syllable and three further initials; *Benelux* (*Belgium, Netherlands, Luxembourg*) that takes syllables from different parts of the original; Portuguese *ABRALIN* (*Associação Brasileira de Lingüística*) that takes one letter and two syllables; or German *BaFin* (*Bundesanstalt für Finanzdienstleistungen*) that takes two initials from parts of the first compound and one syllable of the last word.

Syllable clippings such as these occur rather frequently in German and Dutch. They are often called acronymic clippings or clipping compounds: German *Azubi* (*Auszubildender*), *Kita* (*Kindertagesstätte*), *Schiri* (*Schiedsrichter*); and Dutch *doka* (*donkere kamer*), *minco* (*minderwaardigheidscomplex*), *stufi* (*studiefinanciering*). But syllable clippings are found in Russian as well: *politruk* (*političeskij rukoviditel'*), *Komintern* (*Kommunističeskij internacional*), *Minzdrav* (*Ministerstvo zdravooxranenija*), or *zavkaf* (*zavedujuščij kafedroj*). Fascinatingly, German *Kripo* (*Kriminalpolizei*) must be considered such a hybrid clipped form, while the similar-looking *Krimi* for *Kriminalroman* or *Kriminalfilm* as one continuous part of the original counts as a back clipping, a fact that challenges the terminology. Most of these clippings originate in rather informal speech, with many of them becoming increasingly popular and hence incorporated in quotidian language.

Other examples of hybrid forms of clipping are combinations of one letter standing for one part of the original compound with the second word unclipped, such as English *b-day* (*birthday*), *e-mail* (*electronic mail*), *e-zine* (*electronic magazine*), or German *H-Milch* (*haltbare Milch*), *K-Frage* (*Kanzlerfrage*), *O-Saft* (*Orangensaft*), and *U-Haft* (*Untersuchungshaft*).

4 Semantic and pragmatic aspects of clipping

As evidenced, the use of clippings often expresses familiarity and hints at implied social bonds among the people employing them: one needs to belong to the same social group to easily decode the meaning of a clipping. Such groups and their specific languages can be as diverse as languages for special purposes (such as technology, the military, police, medical sciences, linguistics, and countless other disciplines) or, for example, youth slang. Especially slangy or colloquial contexts witness a change of stylistic level between the short form and its original.

Often we find analogies among word shortenings: the term *yuppie* (*young urban professional*), which emerged during the early eighties of the twentieth century, was followed by *dinkie* (*double income no kids*, also *Dink*), *Yettie* (*young, entrepreneurial, tech-based twenty-something*), and lately *Fruppie* (*frustrated urban professional*). Other clippings employed to characterize people are *LOHAS* (*lifestyle of health and sustainability*), or *Lobo* (*Lifestyle of bad organization*).

Gradually, clippings can lose the link to their original, and their initial meaning might be lost as a consequence. This can entail communicative problems, such as attempts of concealment on the side of the user, or misunderstandings on the side of the recipient because of ambiguities, e.g., English *sub*: this clipping can refer to such diverse words as *submarine, substitute, subscription, subeditor* or *substitute teacher*. At the same time, this very phenomenon might help to ease communication when only a short form is vocalized and the listener knows exactly what it signifies. This applies to examples such as *NATO, UNESCO*, or *WHO*. Since communication mostly depends on context, all partners know what they are talking about – they are acquainted with the subject, and hence usually with the meaning of shortened forms. Especially in LSP (languages for special purposes), clippings are indispensable since economic communication is essential.

A formidable communicative advantage of clippings is the possibility of further word-formations. Even German with its characteristic vast compounding possibilities could never assemble words like *OECD-Studie*, or *ARD-Korrespondent* without using clipped forms. Clipping also results in new verbs such as English *to voip* and German *voipen* ('to make a telephone call over the Internet using *Voice over Internet Protocol technology*'), English *to blog* and German *bloggen* ('to maintain or add content to a *blog* = *weblog*'), or German *simsen* ('to send a message via *Short Message Service* on a cell phone').

Often, letters are deliberately chosen in clippings to coin a word that speaks for itself because it coincides with an already existing word; the homonym *CARE* (*Cooperative for American Remittances to Europe*) might serve as an example. Another communicative aspect of clipping is language creativity necessarily employed for (re-)interpreting known clippings. The case of the internationally operating German company *SAP* might serve as an example for a situation in which the holder of a clipped name requires (re-)interpretation: *SAP* originally stood for *Systemanalyse und Programmentwicklung* and can now equally denote the company after it changed its name to *Systems, Applications, and Products in Data Processing*. Similarly, the names of the German companies *AEG* (initially *Allgemeine Elektricitäts-Gesellschaft*) and A&P (formerly *The Great Atlantic and Pacific Tea Company*) grew to be "Aus Erfahrung gut" and "Attraktiv & Preiswert", respectively, in advertising and commercials. And the name *FIAT* (*Fabbrica Italiana Automobili Torino*) came to stand colloquially in Germany for *Fehler in allen Teilen*, *Für Italien ausreichende Technik*, or *Fahre immer am Tag* – all of which insinuate ironically a lack of quality and reliability in the cars.

Especially the last examples point to the huge variety of possibilities word shortening procures. In the future, contrastive research should focus significantly on clipping in different languages. Further investigation following the example of the recent publications concentrating on more than purely structural and formal aspects of clipping (cf. section 2.2) indicates a very promising strategy that allows for analyzing the various aspects – and specifically the semantic role – of word shortening.

5 References

Alber, Birgit and Sabine Arndt-Lappe (2023): Clipping and truncation. In: Peter Ackema, Sabrina Bendjaballah, M. Eulàlia Bonet i Alsina and Antonio Fábregas (eds.), *The Wiley Blackwell Companion to Morphology*. Hoboken, NJ: Wiley-Blackwell. [Online available at: https://doi.org/10.1002/9781119693604.morphcom017]

Balnat, Vincent (2011): *Kurzwortbildung im Gegenwartsdeutschen*. Hildesheim: Olms.

Bär, Jochen A., Thorsten Roelcke and Anja Steinhauer (eds.) (2007): *Sprachliche Kürze. Konzeptuelle, strukturelle und pragmatische Aspekte*. Berlin/New York: de Gruyter.

Bellmann, Günther (1980): Zur Variation im Lexikon: Kurzwort und Original. *Wirkendes Wort* 30: 369–383.
Biville, Frédéric (1989): Un processus dérivationnel méconnu du latin: la dérivation par troncation. *L'Information Grammaticale* 42: 15–22.
Busse, Ulrich and Dietmar Schneider (2007): Kürze im englischen Wortschatz. In: Jochen A. Bär, Thorsten Roelcke and Anja Steinhauer (eds.) *Sprachliche Kürze. Konzeptuelle, strukturelle und pragmatische Aspekte*, 159–180. Berlin/New York: de Gruyter.
Cannon, Garland (1989): Abbreviations and acronyms in English word-formation. *American Speech* 64(2): 99–127.
Doleschal, Ursula and Anna Thornton (eds.) (2000): *Extragrammatical and Marginal Morphology*. München: LINCOM Europa.
Fandrych, Ingrid (2008a): Submorphemic elements in the formation of acronyms, blends and clippings. *Lexis* 2: 105–123.
Fandrych, Ingrid (2008b): Pagad, Chillax and Jozi: A multi-level approach to acronyms, blends, and clippings. *Nawa Journal of Language and Communication* 2: 71–88.
Greule, Albrecht (1996): Reduktion als Wortbildungsprozeß der deutschen Sprache. *Muttersprache* 106: 193–203.
Greule, Albrecht (2007): Kurzwörter in historischer Sicht. In: Jochen A. Bär, Thorsten Roelcke and Anja Steinhauer (eds.), *Sprachliche Kürze. Konzeptuelle, strukturelle und pragmatische Aspekte*, 118–130. Berlin/New York: de Gruyter.
Harley, Heidi (2004): Why is it *the CIA* but not **the NASA*? Acronyms, initialisms, and definite descriptions. *American Speech* 79: 368–399.
Kobler-Trill, Dorothea (1994): *Das Kurzwort im Deutschen. Eine Untersuchung zu Definition, Typologie und Entwicklung*. Tübingen: Niemeyer.
Kreidler, Charles W. (1979): Creating new words by shortening. *Journal of English Linguistics* 13: 24–36.
Kreidler, Charles W. (2000): Clipping and acronomy. In: Geert Booij, Christian Lehmann and Joachim Mugdan (eds.), *Morphology. An International Handbook on Inflection and Word-Formation*. Vol. 1, 956–963. Berlin/New York: de Gruyter.
Leuschner, Torsten (2008): Kurzwortbildung im Deutschen und Niederländischen. Grundlagen und Ergebnisse eines prototypischen Vergleichs. *Germanistische Mitteilungen* 67: 247–261.
López Rúa, Paula (2002): On the structure of acronyms and neighbouring categories: A prototype-based account. *English Language and Linguistics* 6: 31–60.
López Rúa, Paula (2004): Acronyms & Co.: A typology of typologies. *Estudios Ingleses de la Universidad Complutense* 12: 109–129.
Mayer, Maurice and Giovanni Rovere (2007): Kürze im italienischen Wortschatz. In: Jochen A. Bär, Thorsten Roelcke and Anja Steinhauer (eds.), *Sprachliche Kürze. Konzeptuelle, strukturelle und pragmatische Aspekte*, 211–226. Berlin/New York: de Gruyter.
Michel, Sascha (2006): Kurzwortgebrauch. Plädoyer für eine pragmatische Definition und Prototypologie von Kurzwörtern. *Germanistische Mitteilungen* 64: 69–83.
Michel, Sascha (2011): Das Kurzwort zwischen ‚Langue' und ‚Parole' – Analysen zum Postulat der Synonymie zwischen Kurzwort und Vollform. In: Hilke Elsen and Sascha Michel (eds.), *Wortbildung im Deutschen zwischen Sprachsystem und Sprachgebrauch. Perspektiven – Analysen – Anwendungen*, 135–163. Stuttgart: ibidem.
Nübling, Damaris and Janet Duke (2007): Kürze im Wortschatz skandinavischer Sprachen. Kurzwörter im Schwedischen, Dänischen, Norwegischen und Isländischen. In: Jochen A. Bär, Thorsten Roelcke and Anja Steinhauer (eds.), *Sprachliche Kürze. Konzeptuelle, strukturelle und pragmatische Aspekte*, 227–263. Berlin/New York: de Gruyter.

Plag, Ingo (2003): *Word-formation in English*. Cambridge: Cambridge University Press.

Plénat, Marc (1998): De quelques paramètres intervenant dans l'oralisation des sigles en français. *Cahiers d'Etudes Romanes (CERCLID)* 9: 27–52.

Ronneberger-Sibold, Elke (1996): Preferred sound shapes of new roots: On some phonotactic and prosodic properties of shortenings in German and French. In: Bernhard Hurch and Richard A. Rhodes (eds.), *Natural Phonology. The State of the Art*, 261–292. Berlin/New York: Mouton de Gruyter.

Ronneberger-Sibold, Elke (2007): Zur Grammatik von Kurzwörtern. In: Jochen A. Bär, Thorsten Roelcke and Anja Steinhauer (eds.), *Sprachliche Kürze. Konzeptuelle, strukturelle und pragmatische Aspekte*, 276–291. Berlin/New York: de Gruyter.

Sandhop, Martin (2007): Kürze im ukrainischen Wortschatz. In: Jochen A. Bär, Thorsten Roelcke and Anja Steinhauer (eds.), *Sprachliche Kürze. Konzeptuelle, strukturelle und pragmatische Aspekte*, 264–275. Berlin/New York: de Gruyter.

Schmitt, Christian (2007): Kürze im französischen Wortschatz. In: Jochen A. Bär, Thorsten Roelcke and Anja Steinhauer (eds.), *Sprachliche Kürze. Konzeptuelle, strukturelle und pragmatische Aspekte*, 181–210. Berlin/New York: de Gruyter.

Schröder, Marianne (2000): Kurzwörter im Wörterbuch: Lexikographische Aspekte der Kurzwortbildung. In: Irmhild Barz, Marianne Schröder and Ulla Fix (eds.), *Praxis- und Integrationsfelder der Wortbildungsforschung*, 91–105. Heidelberg: Winter.

Steinhauer, Anja (2007): Kürze im deutschen Wortschatz. In: Jochen A. Bär, Thorsten Roelcke and Anja Steinhauer (eds.), *Sprachliche Kürze. Konzeptuelle, strukturelle und pragmatische Aspekte*, 131–158. Berlin/New York: de Gruyter.

Steinhauer, Anja (2000): *Sprachökonomie durch Kurzwörter. Bildung und Verwendung in der Fachkommunikation*. Tübingen: Narr.

Thornton, Anna M. (1996): On some phenomena of prosodic morphology in Italian: Accorciamenti, hypocoristics and prosodic delimitation. *Probus* 8: 81–112.

Susan Olsen
14 Composition

1   Definition of composition
2   Categories of compounds
3   Exceptions to the head generalization
4   Bound compound constituents
5   Compound meaning
6   Conclusion
7   References

Abstract: This article first defines the term composition and explains the major structural properties of compounds. It then sets out to examine the different categories of compounds proposed in traditional works on compounding with the intention of contrasting them with current terminology and checking their coherence. Exceptions to the regular properties of compounds, in particular the head generalization and the criterion of free lexeme constituents, are discussed. A basic reasoning strategy is proposed to explain the broad range of meaning types possible for novel compounds. Finally, general pragmatic limitations on the compounding process deriving from the function and use of compounds are discussed that restrict the nature of compound meaning.

1 Definition of composition

1.1 Historical development of the category

Composition is a major process of vocabulary extension in natural language. It refers to the combination of two or more lexemes (roots, stems or freely occurring words) in the formation of a new, complex word, termed a compound. Over the course of time, the scope of the term composition has shifted somewhat in tandem with a change in content of its major counterpart, derivation. In his diachronically oriented *Deutsche Grammatik* [German Grammar], Jacob Grimm (1826) defined derivation narrowly as the addition of a formative to the end of a root for the purpose of deriving a new word, thus limiting the class of explicit

Susan Olsen, Berlin, Germany

https://doi.org/10.1515/9783111420561-014

derivational processes to suffixation. Prefixes, lacking the transpositional function of suffixes, were considered equivalent in function to the initial constituents of compounds, hence, Grimm called combinations of prefixes with lexemes *Präfixkomposita* [prefix compounds] and treated them together with compounds. Wilmanns and Paul in their diachronic works of 1896 and 1920 respectively, both also entitled *Deutsche Grammatik*, followed Grimm's example in treating prefixations together with compounds and contrasting the class of compounds with explicit derivation, i.e. suffixation. This organization of the major categories of word-formation was adopted by Henzen (1947) in his historical *Deutsche Wortbildung* [German Word-formation] and was also represented in Romance linguistics where the reasoning resembled that found in Grimm, namely the obvious similarity between the set of prefixes and the freely occurring prepositions and adverbs that formed first constituents of compounds, thereby functioning as modifiers of the lexeme they combine with rather than as formatives of new words, cf. Bauer (2005) and article 2 on word-formation research from its beginnings to the 19th century. This view is present in certain relatively contemporary studies of English as well. For example, Marchand (1967) claims that all syntagmas are made up of a determinant and determinatum and represent the two basic word-formation categories of expansions and derivations, depending on whether the determinatum is an independent or a dependent morpheme. The class of compounds is defined in the following manner: "All combinations whose determinata are independent morphemes [...] are expansions. Expansions of which both the determinatum and the determinant are words [...] are called compounds." Thus, compounds form a subclass of the category of expansions to which prefixations also belong: in *rewrite* the independent determinatum *write* is modified by the determinant *re-* (Marchand 1967: 323).

The second edition of Henzen's *Deutsche Wortbildung*, which appeared in 1957, documents a shift in perspective. The class of prefixations was removed from the category composition and assigned an intermediate status of its own between composition and derivation. This reduction in the original scope of composition and new three-way division of concatenative word-formation with prefixation constituting its own category served as the basis of Fleischer's 1969 *Wortbildung der deutschen Gegenwartssprache* [Word-formation of the contemporary German language]. Fleischer's revised work in collaboration with Irmhild Barz in (1992) altered this categorization further to reach the view, already represented in Erben (1983) and generally accepted in theoretical works today, in which suffixation and prefixation together constitute the category of explicit derivation which is set apart from composition.

1.2 Properties of compounds

Composition is a productive process of word-formation in which the component lexemes are chosen from the lexical categories of a language forming a combination in which one constituent functions as the head that is modified by the other constituent. In *cherry tree*, for example, *tree* forms the head determining the nominal category and the related morphosyntactic features of the complex word as well as constituting its general concept, while the first constituent *cherry* modifies the head, creating a complex or subordinate concept whose meaning is a hyponym of the meaning of *tree*. A certain amount of recursion is permitted resulting in hierarchically arranged, binary groupings of constituents as in *rug repair-man* [[rug] [repair + man]], *brass knuckle method* [[brass + knuckle] [method]] or *fruit fly attention span* [[fruit + fly] [attention + span]]. But frequently compounds appear as simple combinations made up exclusively of lexical categories that combine freely with one another. For instance, in the Germanic languages that display regular and highly productive compounding patterns, the compounding process is not restricted by the categorial or selectional properties of the head constituent as is generally the case in their derivational and syntactic configurations (see sections 2.4 and 3 for the more restrictive nature of Slavic and Romance compounds). Because of their lack of functional categories, compounds do not overtly express the grammatical or conceptual relations that exist between their constituents and are, consequently, inherently ambiguous. For instance, a *lawyer joke* can be a 'joke about lawyers', 'a joke thought up by a lawyer' or 'a joke typically told by lawyers', etc.

It is generally the final constituent that functions as the head of a compound transferring its categorial and morphosyntactic features to the whole word; this generalization is captured in Williams' (1981) righthand head rule. The most common heads cross-linguistically are found among the nominal and adjectival categories. Perhaps not quite as common, but certainly possible, are verbal compounds. All the lexical categories occur as the modifier constituent (nouns, adjectives, verbs, adverbs and prepositions) and, occasionally, certain minor categories such as pronouns and focus particles may appear as the nonhead constituent as well, although these are exceptional (cf. *she-wolf, self-indulgence*, G. *Noch-Kanzler* 'still-chancellor'). Compounds with plural and phrasal first constituents are not uncommon, cf. *suggestions box, sky's-the-limit promise*, G. *Mitgliederkarte* 'members card', *Versuch'-Dein-Glück-Spiel* 'try-your-luck game', cf. Johansson (1980) and Meibauer (2007). But, again, these nonlexical categories are only found as nonheads. Since words often carry inflectional markings for case, number, person, etc. and since inflection is expressed on the head constituent (cf. Hoeksma's 1985 head operations), a nonfinal head would be a nonoptimal morphological structure due to the fact that the head inflection (for plural, case, etc.) would break up the structural integrity of the word. But exceptions to the head generalization can be found: there are both compounds without a head and compounds that are left-headed. It is also necessary to distinguish between the formal and semantic aspects of headhood, i.e. there are cases where a constituent serves as the formal but not the semantic head of the compound. These different deviations from the default pattern will be discussed in section 3. In general, composition creates potentially recursive, binary branching, headed word structures or morphological objects (cf. DiSciullo and Williams 1987) that carry a unified accent, have a unique inflection expressed on the head and constitute both formally and semantically a coherent unit in which the individual constituents cannot be separated by other material, establish a referent on their own or be modified independently of one another, cf. Giegerich (2009).

2 Categories of compounds

2.1 Determinative, copulative and possessive compounds

Although compounds are found in most natural languages (cf. Bauer 2001; Dressler 2006), each language determines the parameters that define its particular class of compounds. The Romance and Slavic languages are not highly compounding languages (especially if the default case of lexical combinations of basic stems without formatives or functional categories are the focus of attention, while compounding is much more productive in the Germanic languages. In the early Indic language of Sanskrit compounds were extremely prevalent, so much so that the description of the compound types found in the grammars of Sanskrit was adopted as the descriptive basis for compounds in the historical grammars of Europe (see article 3 on word-formation in historical-comparative grammar). Whitney's (1993) *Sanskrit Grammar* distinguished three classes of compounds, cf. also Mayrhofer (1965: 101–103). The most productive class were the determinative compounds, illustrated in (1a), in which the first constituent depends on or describes the second. These were the *tatpuruṣa* compounds, with the descriptive subclass sometimes referred to separately as *karmadhāraya* compounds. Copulative compounds, illustrated in (1b), are those whose constituents are coordinated such that the relation between them can be rendered explicitly by the conjunctions 'and' or 'or'. They were usually marked for dual number and were termed *dvandva* by the Indic grammarians. Possessive compounds, cf. (1c), had the structure of determinative compounds but were used adjectivally to express possession. This class is also referred to as *bahuvrīhi* compounds, the term itself an example of the class meaning 'having much rice; lit. much-rice', cf. Whitney (1993: 481–511).

(1) a. Determinative: *pādodaka* 'water for the feet'
 maharṣí 'great sage'
 b. Copulative: *candrādityāu* 'moon and sun'
 c. Possessive: *bṛhádratha* 'having great chariots; lit. great-chariot'

Many synchronic treatments of compounds in the European languages make use of this classification as well, sometimes having it serve as a basis of the description (as, e.g., Fleischer and Barz 2012) and others as established terminology deserving some discussion centering around the semantic nature of the coordination. As Wälchli (2005) and Arcodia, Grandi and Wälchli (2010) have pointed out, the coordinative structure of the prevalent class of coordinative compounds in the Standard European languages represents an appositive meaning (an oncologist who is a surgeon) rather than the additive meaning of the Sanskrit *dvandvas* (moon and sun together). The categories are exemplified in (2) again with examples from English and German:

(2) a. Determinative: beach towel / Bierflasche 'beer bottle'
 b. Copulative: oncologist-surgeon / Dichter-Komponist 'poet-composer'
 c. Possessive: tenderfoot / Dickbauch '(person with a) fat belly'

From a modern viewpoint, it is not clear that possessive compounds should comprise a class of their own distinct from the class of determinative compounds. (Whitney 1993: 481 concedes that possessive compounds have the structure of determinative compounds but "with the idea of *possessing* added".) Today, a number of linguists would argue that the possessive interpretation of these compounds arises on the basis of their determinative structure via a metonymic shift in meaning (for example, Fleischer and Barz 2012: 179; Schmid 2011: 125; Motsch 2004: 376; Olsen 2012: 2121), an idea which can apparently be traced back at least to Coseriu (1977). Metonymic shift is a semantic process that applies freely to (both simplex and complex) words; just as it is possible to say *the suits* referring to 'persons wearing suits', one can use *hardhat* as a metonymic epithet for 'a person wearing a hardhat'. The shifted word identifies the intended referent as the possessor of the particularly salient property that it expresses. A different view is held by Marchand (1969), however, who assumes that an actual morpheme without phonetic content (i.e. a zero morpheme) performs the function of shifting the reference away from the actual head to a metonym of the head so that *birdbrain* 'one having a birdbrain' would have the structure [[bird + brain] Ø] parallel to *pigtailer* [[pig + tail] er] where the overt morpheme *-er* signals possessive meaning. Hence, Marchand does not consider *birdbrain* a compound, but terms such constructions "pseudo-compounds", and classifies them as derivations (Marchand 1969: 13–14).

2.2 Co-compounds vs. coordinative appositive compounds

The category of copulative compounds has recently experienced a necessary and important clarification as well. Arcodia, Grandi and Wälchli (2010), based on earlier work in Wälchli (2005) (see also Bauer 2008; Fanselow 1981), point out that the class of copulative compounds actually instantiates two different general types of coordination cross-linguistically, termed by the authors "co-compounds" and "coordinative appositional compounds". Co-compounds denote a hyperonym of their constituents, or a superordinate concept. Coordinative appositional compounds, on the other hand, express a hyponym of the denotation of their constituents and, hence, denote subordinate concepts. The minimal pair in (3) illustrates the contrast, cf. Arcodia, Grandi and Wälchli (2010: 178):

(3)   a. *dāo-qiāng*   'weapons; lit. sword-spear'
     b. *lanza-espada*   'spear which is also a sword'

The co-compound in (3a) from Mandarin Chinese names two co-hyponyms 'sword' and 'spear' and in doing so triggers their common hyperonym 'weapons' as its meaning. The meaning of the coordinative appositional Spanish compound in (3b) with the same constituents is, in contrast, hyponymic. In this case we conceive of a more specific concept than either 'spear' or 'sword', one that unites the properties of both constituents and functions as a subordinate to each. Arcodia, Grandi and Wälchli (2010) show further that co-compounds express natural coordination; i.e. they typically denote a coherent unit made up of objects that naturally occur together or are otherwise understood as belonging together such as 'mother-father' in the meaning 'parents' or 'hand-foot' denoting 'limbs'. Coordinative appositional compounds, on the other hand, express accidental coordination. English with its productive class of coordinative compounds (cf. Olsen 2001, 2004) provides good examples of combinations of concepts that do not necessarily condition one another, cf. *movie star-politician*, *philosopher-mechanic*, *scientist-educator* or *witchdoctor-acrobat*. It is furthermore claimed that the dichotomy between hyperonymic and hyponymic coordinative compounds correlates with a characteristic areal distribution for each type. Co-compounds are found primarily in the languages of East and South East Asia, New Guinea and Mesoamerica, while coordinative appositional compounds are typical of the languages occupying the Central European region.

    The Sanskrit *dvandvas* exemplify the class of co-compounds; in fact, the Sanskrit grammarians excluded appositional compounds from the class of *dvandvas* and assigned them to the class of *karmadhārayas*. In several languages of easternmost Europe coordinative compounds are found as well, cf. the additive subtype of co-compound in Georgian *da-dzma* 'siblings; lit. sister-brother' and in Chuvash *xut-kărantaš* 'writing material; lit. paper-pencil', the collective subtype in Chuvash *šet-sú* 'dairy products; lit. milk-butter', Avar *ber.k'al*; 'face; lit. eye-mouth' and Crimean Tatar *savut-saba* 'dishware; lit. vessels-containers' as well as the alternative subtype from Mordvinic *vest'-kavkst* 'once or twice'. Co-compounds represent – to different degrees – loose word structures as can be seen by the fact that they can carry inflection on both constituents indicating that both stems are visible to the syntax (cf. the Mordvinic nominal co-compound *ponks.t-panar.t* 'clothes; lit. trouser.PL-shirt.PL' with the *t*-suffix encoding plural and as well as the verbal *kuź.i-valg.i* 'fly up and down; lit. ascend.PRES.SG-descend.PRES.SG' with the *i*-suffix indicating present singular). Other functional categories can accompany both stems as well. For example, the generalizing co-compound in Mari *jüd.et-keč.et* 'day and night; lit. night.also-day.also' has an additive focus particle *et* 'also' repeated after each stem. These co-compounds are described in Wälchli (2005: 137–158). Furthermore, Arcodia, Grandi and Wälchli (2010: 180) mention cases where co-compounds display even more clearly a discontinuous structure like that found in the East Asian language Hmong Daw, cf. (4):

(4)   *kuw lub teb   lub chaw*
       I   CL land CL land

Here the classifier *lub* precedes the two nominal heads *teb* and *chaw*, both meaning 'land', that together with *kuw*, a possessive pronoun in the 1st person, glossed by the authors as 'I', give the meaning 'my land', an example of a synonymic co-compound.

Such properties are not shared by the coordinative appositional compounds of the more western European languages. The view is often expressed in the literature that they have two semantic heads, e.g., Plag (2003: 146), but formally speaking, at any rate, coordinative appositive compounds have a unique head. The neuter gender of German *Zeuge-Opfer*, as an example, demonstrates this; it correlates with the neuter gender of the second constituent and not with that of the masculine first constituent. The formal head is also unique in Romance coordinative appositives where the compounds are in general left-headed: the gender of *coche casa* 'van; lit. car-house' matches that of the masculine left constituent, not the feminine second constituent. The picture is complicated somewhat in Romance due to the fact that the appositive compounds quite strictly inflect for plural on both stems, cf. Sp. *poetas-pintores* 'painter-poets'. But it needs to be kept in mind that compounding in Romance is less typically morphological than in Germanic. Double inflection for plural can even occur with nominal determinative compounds whose second constituent functions much like an adjective as in Pg. *palavra-chave* → *palavras-chaves* 'key word'. With their left-headed structure and productive "improper" or "syntagmatic" NPrepN patterns (cf. Fr. *pomme de terre*), there appears to be more syntactic influence present in the compounds of the Romance languages, even though these compounds must be considered lexical (cf. Rainer and Varela 1992; Kornfeld 2009; Fradin 2009) and not syntactic (DiSciullo and Williams 1987: 81) patterns, cf. section 3.

2.3 Endocentric vs. exocentric compounds

Bloomfield (1933) did not adopt the traditional classes of Sanskrit compounds as the basis of his discussion. Instead, he proposes a general classification according to whether the compound has the same grammatical structure found in the phrases of the language (cf. *blackbird* and *a black bird*), in which case it is termed "syntactic", or whether there is no parallel construction in the syntax, in which case the compound is considered "asyntactic", cf. *door-knob*. Intermediate cases in which an equivalent phrasal structure is present but the word order of the compound is different (*to housekeep* vs. *to keep house*) or in which the compound lacks a functional category necessary in the syntax like an article (*turnkey* vs. *to turn the key*) are termed "semi-syntactic". Copulatives like *bittersweet* are "semi-syntactic" because of the missing conjunction, cf. *bitter and sweet* (Bloomfield 1933: 233–235).

In addition to these classes, Bloomfield proposes another fundamental distinction that crosscuts the previous classification, namely whether the compound has a head or not. Compounds like *blackbird*, *doorknob* and *bittersweet* that as a whole have the same semantic "function" as their head constituents (*bird*, *knob* and *sweet*) are termed "endocentric"; but *turnkey* 'jailer; lit. one who turns a key' and *bittersweet* (the name of a plant) that do not are "exocentric". *Red-head* and *longhorn* are also exocentric because their referent is not understood as belonging to the semantic category of the head. Examples like *chimney-sweep* and *clambake*, on the other hand, must be considered endocentric due to the fact that their nominal head arises on the basis of the regular process of conversion (*to sweep/bake* → *a sweep/bake*).

2.4 Synthetic vs. primary/root compounds

In the course of his discussion of exocentric structures like *loudmouth*, Bloomfield touches on endocentric nominal constructions that carry the same possessive meaning as the exocentric *redhead* type, but whose possessive meaning is signaled by an overt morpheme such as *-ed*, *-d* or *-t* as exemplified by *blue-eyed*, cf. Bloomfield (1933: 231–233). He terms this structural type *synthetic* and their deverbal counterparts *meat eater semi-synthetic* because of the word order difference to the phrase *to eat meat*. Marchand (1969: 15–18) uses the same terms for his *hunchbacked* and *watchmaker* types. The term *synthetic compound* apparently originates with von Schroeder (1851–1920) where it was coined to describe the formation process of German examples like *Machthaber* ('power holder') that seem to involve a synthesis of compounding and derivation in their genesis: neither the compound **machthab* 'to power hold' nor the derivation **Haber* 'holder' exist as words in German – the construction arises only when all three morphemes join together. From the start, the discussion of these structures has revolved around the question of their correct analysis. Are they to be considered compounds with the structure in (5a) or derivations as in (5b)? The original term *synthetisches Kompositum* is, in fact, no longer in use in German linguistics, but was replaced by the term *Zusammenbildung* in order not to prejudice the issue by referring to such structures as compounds (Leser 1990). Although both Bloomfield and Marchand see a parallel between the deverbal type *meat eater, watchmaker* and an underlying sentence structure, they nevertheless consider these composites to be compounds, structured similarly to the primary compounds that contain purely nominal constituents like *steamboat*, *oilwell*, cf. Marchand (1969: 18).

(5) a. $[[watch]_N [make_V + er]_N]_N$
    b. $[[watch_N make_V]_V$ -$er]_N$

Many linguists including Allen (1978), Selkirk (1982), Lieber (2004), Jackendoff (2009), ten Hacken (2010) and Olsen (2012) have espoused the analysis in (5a) as well. The disadvantage of the alternative analysis in (5b) is that the derivation of synthetic compounds from a NV base cannot account for their extreme productivity, since NV compounds are not productive in Germanic (cf. Booij 1988). If the compound structure in (5a) is supplemented with the idea of argument inheritance, however, the awkwardness of the deverbal head alone can be explained along the same lines as the use of a transitive verb without its obligatory argument: the deverbal noun *maker* inherits a modified version of the argument structure of the transitive verb *make* (cf. Fanselow 1988, Bierwisch 1989) and assigns the inherited object to its first constituent. Without the satisfaction of its argument, *maker* is as incomplete as the verb phrase **he makes*. It was most likely the insights of this early discussion that opened the way for modern theories of word-formation to extend the content of the term *synthetic compound* from its original sense as a synthesis of compounding and derivation to become equated with the class of compounds based on a verbal interpretation, i.e. those compounds whose first constituent is understood as an argument of their deverbal head, regardless of whether the head can occur alone (*programmer – computer programmer*) or not (??*keeper – house keeper*). Due to the verbal nature of their head, synthetic compounds (also termed *verbal compounds*) have a narrow range of unambiguous interpretations that can be contrasted with the more open and often ambiguous meanings of compounds whose heads are not deverbal, but consist of nominal roots or stems called *primary* (or *root*) *compounds*. This can be illustrated by comparing the verbal interpretations of *cost reduction, snow removal, law enforcement, oil spillage* and *window installer* with the semantically more variable interpretational possibilities of primary or root compounds like *dance music, merit pay, designer drug, sweetheart contract* and *monsoon wedding*. Synthetic compounds are also found in Slavic, cf. Cz. *dřev-o-rub-ec* 'woodcutter' and R. *kanat-o-chod-ec* 'ropewalker' where they represent a more productive alternative to the less productive nominal root compounds (see Ohnheiser (2015).

3 Exceptions to the head generalization

3.1 No overt head, formal or semantic

The class of synthetic compounds is lacking in Romance. The Romance languages, rather, display a pattern of agentive and instrument compounds that are semantically similar to the synthetic compounds of Germanic and Slavic, but without a derived head:

(6) a. *cuentachistes*   'joke teller; lit. tell jokes'   Spanish
     b. *rabat-joi*   'spoil sport; lit. reduce joy'   French
     c. *cantastorie*   'street singer; lit. sing stories'   Italian
     d. *limpa-chaminés*   'chimney cleaner; lit. clean chimneys'   Portuguese
     e. *fura-becuri*   'tall person; lit. steal lightbulbs'   Romanian

Remnants of this pattern are found in English as well where they were most likely borrowed during Middle English times from French (cf. Kastovsky 2009), for instance: *scofflaw* 'law violator', *spoilsport, sawbones* 'surgeon', *daredevil* 'recklessly bold person', etc. This VN pattern cannot be considered synthetic because it does not contain an overt signal of derivation, but consists of the combination of the (3rd person singular or imperative) stem of a verb together with a noun marked for plural if it is a count noun (cf. Fr. *coupe-légumes* 'vegetable cutter; lit. cut-vegetables') or as an indefinite singular if it belongs to the category of mass nouns (cf. Sp. *quitaesmalte* 'polish remover; lit. remove-polish') that is understood as the object of the verb. The nature of the stem can be more precisely determined in Italian where a few unambiguous cases are found that show it to be formally identical to the imperative. An interesting aspect of the productive VN pattern is that the words are headless, both formally and semantically: Sp. *abrepuertas* denoting a 'doorman' (lit. 'open-doors') is not a feminine plural noun as *puertas* but carries the default gender of masculine singular; furthermore it denotes neither a subcategory of the constituent lexeme 'open' nor of 'door'. Rainer (2016: 2622) reports that the pattern creates nouns even when no noun is present as in *matasiete* 'braggart; lit. kill-seven' and *mandamás* 'boss; lit. order-more'. Such headless composites constitute an exception to the generalization formulated in section 1.2 that compounds are headed structures. In fact, these structures are both formally and semantically headless. Formally they are assigned the default gender masculine and semantically they are perhaps best interpreted as examples of coercion, i.e. a shift from the property they denote (e.g., to open doors) to the person or instrument that is typically associated with this property (cf. Olsen 2012). Using Bloomfield's terminology, they are "exocentric" since neither constituent functions as the head of the compound.

The term "exocentric" in Bloomfield's sense is broader than the Sanskrit term *bahuvrīhi* introduced in section 2.1 in that it was conceived to encompass both the semantically and formally headless VN compounds (Bloomfield's examples are E. *pickpocket* and *lickspittel* 'a fawning subordinate') as well as semantically headless AN compounds such as *redhead* and *longhorn* (cf. Bloomfield 1933: 235–237) with a metonymically shifted meaning. The term *bahuvrīhi* is defined more narrowly as NN or AN compounds of the descriptive determinative type "with the idea of possession added, turning them from nouns into adjectives" (Whitney 1993: 481). Bloomfield's notion "exocentic", moreover, includes two further Sanskrit classes beyond the *bahuvrīhis*, namely the numeratives (*dvigu*) such as *sixpense, fortnight* and adverbials with a nominal head (*avyayībhāva*) like *bareback, uphill* (Bloomfield 1993: 237).

The PN pattern of Romance as in Sp. *sinvergüenza* '(one) without shame', Fr. *sans-coeur* '(one) without heart' and It. *senzatetto* '(one) without roof' must be considered "exocentric" as well: the property expressed by a preposition together with a noun that is understood as its object is coerced into a reading as a person who exemplifies this property (Olsen 2012: 2142). Another class of exocentric, or semantically and formally headless word structures, are the scalar co-compounds characteristic of East and South East Asia. In this case, two adjectives that denote the opposite poles on a scale hyponymically express the quality that names the scale; thus a noun arises on the basis of two adjectives, cf. Wälchli (2005: 152–154).

(7) a. *srab-mthug*   'density; lit. thin-thick'   Tibetan
     b. *xaluun xüjten*   'temperature; lit. heat-cold'   Khalkha
     c. *tsopats mkältö*   'size; lit. big-small'   Tokharian

3.2 Formal, but no semantic head

The pure possessives or core cases of *bahuvrīhis*, like E. *tenderfoot* 'newcomer, beginner' or G. *Dickbauch* lit. 'fat-belly', are exocentric in Bloomfield's sense because their second constituents *foot* and *Bauch* have a different function in the combinations which mean 'inexperienced person' and 'fat person', respectively, than when they occur as independent words. They are not the semantic heads of the construction. On the other hand, they do function as the formal heads of the word: that is the nouns *foot* and *Bauch* determine the gender and plural class of the whole compound (*tenderfeet*, *Dickbäuche*). Such cases as these demonstrate the necessity of distinguishing between the semantic and the formal notion of head.

3.3 Left-headed compounds

Another deviation from the head generalization are the left-headed compounds of the Romance languages. Morphologically speaking, these structures do not represent the default case because – when considering the NN pattern – pluralization disrupts the structural integrity of the words, cf. Fr. *timbres poste* 'postage stamps', Sp. *hombres rana* 'frogmen', and It. *vagoni letto* 'sleeping cars'. This is even more obvious in the productive NPrepN pattern of so-called "improper" or "syntagmatic" compounds, exemplified by the following forms where a semantically bleached remnant of a functional category from syntax signals the subordination of the modifying constituent to the head.

(8) a. *bota de lluvia*   'rain boot'   Spanish
     b. *chemin de fer*   'railroad'   French
     c. *mulino a vento*   'windmill'   Italian
     d. *casa de banho*   'bathroom'   Portuguese

The literature reports cases of such NPrepN combinations that have been reduced to the more typical NN structure such as Sp. *tren de mercancías* → *tren mercancías* 'freight train' (Rainer and Varela 1992: 120) and Fr. *stylo à bille* → *stylo-bille* 'ballpoint pen' (Fradin 2009: 433), demonstrating a tendency to level the marked to the unmarked word form. There have been attempts to view the syntactically opaque preposition as a linking morpheme similar to the opaque case markings in German compounds *Freundeskreis* 'circle of friends' or *Sonnenschein* 'sun shine', cf. Ralli (2008). This view, however, is highly controversial since the prepositions, although weakened semantically, still define clear semantic patterns among the compounds. In fact, Romance has a true linking morpheme that does parallel the Germanic linking morphemes in function, namely the *-i-* as in Sp. *puticlub* 'hostess club' and It. *fruttivendolo* 'fruit seller', see Rainer and Varela (1992: 124).

4 Bound compound constituents

4.1 Combining forms of neoclassical compounds

Neoclassical compounds differ from regular compounds in a number of ways. First, in defiance of the definition of compounds in section 1.1, their constituents are not freely occurring lexemes. Rather, they consist of combinations of elements taken over from the Classical languages, Greek and Latin, that do not occur freely in the modern languages. However, the combinations themselves are formed according to modern compounding rules, hence the term "neo"classical. Neoclassical compounds are usually comprised of simple combinations of two elements; the recursion found in regular compounding is usually absent. They appear in all the language families of Western Europe and are so prevalent in the international terminologies of science, technology, scholarship, etc., that they are often referred to as "internationalisms" (cf. Bauer 1998). Examples are E. *neurology, democracy, stethoscope, suicide* (Bauer 1998), Fr. *aérodrome, géographe, anthropomorphe, pathogène* (Zwanenburg 1992), Polish *neofita* 'neophyte', *poligamia, ksenofobia* 'xenophobia', *neurologia* (Szymanek 2009) and Basque *telefono, mikrobiologia, filologia, elektromagnetismo* (Artiagoitia 2016: 3330–3331).

Because the lexemes involved in neoclassical compounds represent a class of forms that do not occur freely in the compounding languages, they are often termed *combining forms*. In their formal aspects, combining forms seem to have much in common with prefixes and suffixes. The majority are specialized to either the initial or final position of a combination; e.g., *astro-, bio-, electro-, geo-, gastro-, tele-* occur initially while *-cide, -cracy, -graphy, -phobe, -scope* occur finally (cf. Plag 2003: 155 ff.). They are also transparent in meaning and form the basis of productive patterns, cf. *anthropology, astrology, geology, pathology, psychology,* etc., and *geology, geography, geometry, geophagy,* etc. Nevertheless, combining forms cannot be equated with affixes because prefixes and suffixes do not combine with one another as the combining forms typically do. Their lexical category and, in the case of nouns, their gender and inflectional class are not set at a default for the entire set of patterns, but vary with the particular head. Although they do not constitute free lexemes, the individual combining forms (at least those that appear in head position) are lexically marked for these features which they project onto the whole word, cf. the German nouns *die Biologie*, pl.: *die Biologien; der Psychologe*, pl.: *die Psychologen; das Pathogen*, pl.: *die Pathogene*. The righthand head structure of these internationalisms is taken over even into languages whose native compounds typically display lefthand heads: e.g., Port. *gastropatia,* Fr. *biologie,* It. *termometro.*

The combining forms of the class of neoclassical compounds differ in their transparency and productivity from the bound roots of the Latinate vocabulary in English as represented by *-ceive* in *conceive, deceive, perceive, receive, -mit* in *omit, submit, transmit, remit* and *-duce* in *deduce, induce, reduce,* etc. The most pronounced difference between the two is that the bound roots of the Latinate vocabulary do not share a common semantic component: *-tain,* for example, does not have a uniform meaning in *contain, detain, retain,* etc. And, secondly, whereas the combining forms of neoclassical compounds are productive and continually spawn new forms, the Latinate patterns do not permit novel creations. These verbs entered the English language from Romance early on as complete words in specialized meanings so that a transparent preposition + root structure was never reconstructed. Even though speakers may be aware subconsciously that the roots of these verbs represent a morphological unit (they share the same allomorphic form under suffixation, cf. *conception, deception; submission, remission; deduction, reduction* and *detention, retention,* cf. Aronoff 1976), their semantic opacity prohibits speakers from identifying them as morphemes capable of new combinations.

4.2 Positionally bound lexemes

Another type of bound lexeme not only occurs regularly in native compounds, but is in actual fact very typical of compounding. What is at issue here are not the results of the grammaticalization processes by which certain types of compound constituents evolve over time into affixes or even affix-like units that are classified in word-formation grammars as "semi-affixes; semi-prefixes, semi-suffixes" (G. "Affixoide; Präfixoide, Suffixoide"). Rather, what is central to this section is another phenomenon that has come to light as a matter of interest in the structure of the mental lexicon. Psycholinguistic experimentation has demonstrated that both transparent and opaque constituents of compounds can be primed and, hence, are psychologically available to speakers, cf., e.g., Zwitserlood (1994), Libben, Buchanan and Colangelo (2003) and Libben et al. (2003). In theories of parsing that assume dual access to entries in the mental lexicon such that decomposition and whole-word access are simultaneously employed in the retrieval of compound meaning, the activation of constituent meaning together with the whole-word meaning will lead to conflicting information whenever a compound contains a nontransparent constituent. For example, if both *air* and *line* are activated while processing *airline* (or *Hand* and *Schuh* in G. *Handschuh*), incongruous information is called up because the compound constituent *-line* (or *-schuh*) does not correspond in meaning to the independent lexeme *line* (or *Schuh*). Conflicting information requires a resolution. Since meaning specialization is widespread in compounds, access to both the individual lexemes and the whole-word meaning of the compound will result in the activation of superfluous information. Solutions to this problem have been sought that include missing links as well as inhibition processes that do not allow access to or suppress the irrelevant meaning of the free lexeme. Libben (2010) proposes an alternative suggestion that circumvents much of the problem: the specialization in meaning of a compound constituent (what he terms "morphological transcendence") encourages the creation of a positionally bound variant of that constituent that corresponds to its specialized meaning in the context of the compound. This means, for example, that in addition to the entry for the independent word *line*, the mental lexicon would contain a positionally bound entry *-line* which would be targeted during the decomposition of *airline*. This bound constituent would then cover *busline*, *shipline*, *cruiseline* as well. The same would apply to *-lace* in *necklace, shoelace, bootlace*, etc., vis-à-vis the related, but no longer relevant, free word *lace*. Positionally bound constituents will differ in their degree of opacity. For example, *industry* refers in its core meaning to the production of goods or resources within an economy. Typical compounds with this lexeme are *metal industry, petroleum industry, iron industry, auto industry, meatpacking industry, electronic industry*, etc. In recent creations like *entertainment industry* and *happiness industry*, the head lexeme deviates from its core meaning in as far as *entertainment* and *happiness* denote concepts too abstract to fall under its usual production output. The lightly bleached meaning of the constituent *-industry* might therefore at some time establish its own entry in the mental lexicon, allowing further compound creations with the same meaning extension.

Positionally bound constituents often spawn larger patterns: *-free* in *sugar-free, fat-free, salt-free, gluten-free, caffein-free, error-free, toll-free*, etc. is related to its free counterpart *free*, but is not used in its core sense since it simply signals absence of an unwanted object. Likewise, *smart-*, which implies the presence of information-based technology in *smart phone, smart card, smart key, smart board*, etc., is related to, but simultaneously differs from, the independent adjective *smart*. More opaque cases like E. *pig* and G. *Schwein* 'pig' could have the positionally bound variants *pig-* and *schweine-* with the semantics of an intensifier as in E. *pig ignorant, pig arrogant* and G. *schweineteuer* 'extremely expensive', *schweinekalt* 'extremely cold'. Seen in this light, these lexemes would not have to be – implausibly – classified as *prefixoids*. Positionally bound entries in the mental lexicon would capture speakers' knowledge of regular patterns and relations in their inventory of words. First constituents in German compounds suggest the need for an independent entry of compound constituents at any rate, due to the fact that they occur in unpredictable combinatorial variants.

5 Compound meaning

5.1 Compound template

Earliest studies of compound meaning attempted to capture the general semantic patterns instantiated by established compounds and use these relatively fixed sets of meaning as a basis for predicting the meanings that are possible in novel compounds. The patterns were described in the form of underlying syntactic relations (subject, object, object of preposition, attribute, predicate, etc.) or basic semantic-thematic roles (purpose, location, instrument, material, and so on). Most often a combination of the two were used, cf. Jespersen (1909), Hatcher (1960), Marchand (1969), Lees (1970), Adams (1973), Levi (1978) and Warren (1978). Work by Zimmer (1981) and Downing (1977) shifted the focus away from classifying the relations that held between the constituents to the idea that compound meanings could arise on the basis of any relation that was "appropriately classificatory". Bauer (1978: 122) captured the basic intuition of this new approach by postulating a single covert PRO-verb that was understood as establishing a plausible relation. Allen (1978: 93) introduced her "variable R condition" in an attempt to characterize the range of possible compound meanings by requiring a matching of semantic features between the constituents. Dowty (1979: 316) formalized the idea of an open relation between the constituents by relating the external arguments of the two predicates involved by means of an unspecified relation variable R indexed with the feature "appropriately classificatory". Around the same time, Fanselow (1981) isolated the class of "Rektionskomposita" [governed compounds], i.e. compounds with relational heads whose interpretation was based on the inherent argument structure of the nominal or deverbal head, from two further sets, namely those displaying basic relations ('and', 'location' and 'part of') and those with numerous options available. For the latter he formalized a series of semantic rules that allowed stereotypical relations to be inferred on the basis of the semantic content of the constituents. Jackendoff (2009: 122) postulates two general compound schemata – one based on argument structure yielding the class of synthetic interpretations and another based on modification allowing for the "unlimited set of possibilities" exemplified by primary compounds.

Olsen (2012: 2138–2140), on the other hand, proposes that compound interpretation proceeds by means of a uniform reasoning strategy that relates the predicates of a compound without distinguishing between *primary* and *synthetic* interpretations. These different meaning types are simply the result of the specific choices made during the instantiation of the unspecified relation connecting the component predicates. A compound template, adopted from the modification templates of Higginbotham (1985), Maienborn (2003) and Bücking (2009, 2010), is used to implement this strategy. This compound template can be thought of as a lexical schema in the grammar that combines two arbitrary predicates and relates their referential arguments by means of an unspecified relation. In the transition from the grammar to an actual utterance, the content of the implicit relation will be fleshed out. As an example of such a specification, the relation 'made of' might be inferred on the basis of the predicates *chocolate* and *cake* in (9a), yielding the interpretation 'cake made of chocolate'. For the predicates *pepper* and *grind* in (9b) the cognitively most prominent relation is already found in the semantic structure of *grind* producing the probable reading 'something that grinds pepper':

(9) a. chocolate cake
    b. pepper grinder
    c. waitress-actress

Hence, the template does not enforce an artificial distinction between two classes of meaning, the so-called primary and synthetic interpretations. Many borderline cases exist between the two reading types that make clear-cut decisions notoriously difficult. For example, are relations such as 'synthesize', 'certify', 'steal', 'trap', 'cover' and '(to) pilot' in *speech synthesis, death certificate, car thief, bear trap, bed cover* and *airplane pilot* argument relations or are their readings based on modification? Furthermore, a single structure can receive both types of meaning: *horse rescuer* can be 'one who rescues horses' or 'one who rescues something on horseback' and a *shop corner* can be 'corner of a shop' or 'corner with a shop located on it'.

The proposed interpretative strategy accommodates coordinative appositive interpretations as well. Since the predicates in (9c) carry information about career types, the most plausible relation will be the identity relation, identifying the referential arguments of the two predicates, resulting in the meaning 'one who is a waitress and an actress'. Thus, the argument reading of the synthetic compounds as well as the coordinative reading of the coordinative appositive compounds comes about by means of the same general inferential strategy that is responsible for the broad scope of relations that are in principle possible and that also account for primary compounds. Hence, all regular meanings can be traced back to a general reasoning process that fleshes out for each compound a covert relation that holds between the constituents. Thus, the predicate-argument relation and the identity relation do not constitute different compound types alongside of the primary compounds, but simply instantiate different specific choices among the many possible. They are triggered by the highly relational nature of the deverbal head in the case of argument readings and by a common type of typical referent in the case of appositive readings. In the creation of a novel compound, a particular utterance or situation may help to narrow down the range of options made possible by the template. Disambiguation can result as well from the institutionalization of a novel compound in a specific reading by a speech community or as a consequence of semantic shifts in the vocabulary. Such cases of idiosyncratic meaning will be listed in the collective "lexicon" (or vocabulary) of the speech community.

5.2 Loose word structures

The compound meanings just discussed presuppose unmarked lexical structures (morphological objects) in which one of the constituents functions as the morphological head of the word, while the nonhead modifies the head in a number of plausible ways. The meaning of a morphologically headed compound, therefore, will always be a hyponym of the head. It has been pointed out by Downing (1977: 823), Warren (1978: 257), Bücking (2009, 2010) and Olsen (2004, 2012), among others, that morphological structures serve the primary function of naming categories in a speaker's conceptual space (as opposed to syntactic phrases that, roughly, describe states of affairs) and that compounds in particular provide a label for complex concepts, or subordinate concepts. Thus, for the headed compounds of Germanic, Romance and Slavic, hyponymic meanings are predicted. This is what Arcodia, Grandi and Wälchli (2010) found to be the case for coordinative appositive structures such as the example (3b) from the discussion in section 2.2, i.e. Sp. *lanza-espada* 'spear which is also a sword'.

Structures that are not clearly morphological, i.e. not structured via a unique morphological head, on the other hand, will not be forced into a hyponymic meaning. When such a situation obtains, for instance in the case of coordination, we would expect the default function of coordination as group formation to apply as it does in the syntax. Consequently, a "loose" coordinative combination, as Arcodia, Grandi and Wälchli (2010) describe the structure of co-compounds, in which both constituents are visible to the syntax as heads (such as is exemplified in the Mordvinic nominal co-compound from section 2.2, namely *ponks.t-panar̄.t* 'clothes; lit. trouser.PL-shirt.PL' in which each nominal head carries a plural marking; see also example (4) of that section) should demonstrate the unmarked case of coordination, or group formation. More specifically, work on the semantics of coordination has shown that the meaning of a conjoined syntactic structure is not obtained by simply adding the meanings of the conjuncts together to form an arbitrary group, but rather by subsuming the conjuncts under a common conceptual frame which Lang (1991: 605) terms a "common integrator" and which is integrated into the semantic structure of the sentence. Co-conjuncts that are formally and semantically similar will be easily assimilated to a common integrator. In such cases, a more natural and direct interpretation is possible. This is the case in the Mordvinic example where the common integrator of 'trousers and shirts' is clearly 'clothes', supplying the meaning of the co-compound. Interestingly, the additive, collective, generalizing and scalar interpretation groups of the co-compounds postulated by Wälchli (2005) and discussed in section 2.2 and section 3.1, provide confirmation of this. Their compound meaning is equivalent to the common integrator of their constituents and is, therefore, hyperonymic. Furthermore, the directness of the common integrator as the superordinate category of the constituents is the source of their naturalness: the Mordvin combination *t'et'a.t-ava.t* 'father.PL-mother.PL' denotes the hyperonymic concept 'parents', Chuvash *sĕt-śu* 'milk-butter' picks out the superordinate concept 'dairy products', Vietnamese *bàn ghê* 'table-chair' refers to 'furniture' and Chinese *gāo ǎi* 'high-low', conveys the meaning 'height', etc. (cf. Olsen 2014). Hence, Arcodia, Grandi and Wälchli's (2010: 182) assumption that co-compounds may have originated via the grammaticalization of an asyndetic phrasal coordination is a highly plausible explanation for the source of their meaning.

5.3 Pragmatic considerations

The simple, non-formal, open and ambiguous character of the basic compound template discussed in section 4.1 yields basic morphological objects that are assumed here to be the default case of compounding. But in spite of their pragmatic flexibility, even these structures are subject to clear restrictions. In the previous sections the influence of the morphological head on the interpretation possibilities of a compound was shown. There are further restrictions of a pragmatic nature that are placed on a compound's interpretation by virtue of its function in communication and as a name for a relevant category in the speaker's experience. The most general restriction requires, in accordance with the cooperation principle of Grice (1975), the interpretation of a compound to be inferable on the basis of the overt information present. If it is not possible to find a plausible interpretation, the compound fails to fulfill its communicative purpose. For example, the novel compound *weed bicycle* would require a great deal of context or common background in order to make sense. In addition, several linguists have noted that, although the range of possible relations between the constituents is very broad, relations based purely on negation, absence or dissimilarity are nevertheless not possible, cf. Zimmer (1971: C11), Downing (1977: 825) and Dowty (1979: 316). Notions such as 'not located at', 'not similar to' or 'not for', open up such a large number of possibilities that they would not provide a clear basis for classification. A reading based on an inferred relation that contains an element of negation, on the other hand, will be possible (cf. *mud guard* 'guards against mud'). Next, a plausible referent needs to be chosen from one of the domains in the human ontological system. Hence, *cowboy hat* cannot have a coordinative appositive denotation *'x is a cowboy and a hat' although the determinative meaning 'hat worn by cowboys' is fine. And, as Olsen (2004: 23) further explains, the coordinative reading of *father-daughter* is permissible in the nonhead (modifier) position of a compound as in *father-daughter dance*, but it cannot occur in an unembedded position in a coordinative interpretation without violating the Principle of Ontological Coherence, cf. *father-daughter, because no single individual can simultaneously be a father and daughter. Hence, speakers do not entertain a coordinative interpretation for German *Vatertochter*, but immediately construe either a determinative 'daughter favored by her father' or an argument reading 'daughter of the father'. On the other hand, E. *actress-daughter* and G. *Schriftsteller-Freund* can have both a coordinative ('actress and daughter', 'writer and friend') and a determinative reading ('daughter of an actress', 'friend of a writer'), depending on the context. Such considerations demonstrate the openness of interpretation predicted by the underspecified relation of the compound template: It is not the combination of the lexemes *father* and *daughter* that is deviant – such combinations are structurally possible. But restrictions – pertaining both to the human conceptual system and the context of use – apply to limit the set of possible meanings of a combination, cf. Meyer (1993: 171 ff.).

Furthermore, since the function of a modifier is to restrict the meaning of the head that it modifies, a headed compound violating this endocentric structure will be deviant. Compounds like ??*water fish* or ??*building house* are extremely odd for this reason, unless a context can be construed revealing a set of alternatives which would allow the recovery of a sensible hyponymic reading. In order to pick out a subcategory that is relevant to the speaker's cognitive organization in a coherent manner, the modifier must make reference to a property that is not necessarily shared by all members of the head category. Thus, **whisker cat* has no *raison d'être*, unless it can be contrasted with a type of cat that has no whiskers. Changes in society allow combinations to emerge that once would have had no function: a generation ago *cord telephone* would most likely have been eschewed, but is possible today due to the contrast with cordless phones. Again, such examples attest to the correctness of the open pragmatic interpretation strategy sketched in section 4.1.

Subsumptive, clarifying, redundant and synonymous compounds, on the other hand, serve a function, namely to make the unclear or demotivated meaning of one constituent more perspicuous, cf. E. *tuna fish, pebble stone* or G. *Maultier* 'mule; lit. mule animal', where the meaning of *Maul* 'mule' is now unclear to speakers. Also the word *pea* was added to E. *chick* < ME *chick* 'pea' to clarify its meaning, cf. *chick pea*, and G. *Kichererbsen* 'chick pea' was created for the same reason from MHG *kicher* 'pea' and *Erbse* 'pea'. Furthermore, synonymic (cf. E. *pathway, courtyard*, G. *Zeitalter* 'time age', *Streifzug* 'tract passage'), imitative (*nap schmap* 'not a real nap'), rhyming and alliterative (*razzle-dazzle, teeny-weeny, topsy-turvy*, G. *Techtelmechtel* 'flirtation') and reduplicating compounds (*hush-hush, goody-goody*, G. *Pinkepinke* 'money') may occur sporadically. Their use in emphatic or playful language allows them to circumvent the pragmatic restrictions that are operative in normal discourse.

5.4 Origin of compounds in a protolanguage?

It has been suggested that compounds originated, as far as their evolution is concerned, outside of grammar proper in a primitive pragmatic system of communication. Fanselow (1985), for example, recognized that the free adjunction of two lexemes in compounds differs quite distinctly from the combinatorial properties of derivational and inflectional structures that obey strict grammatical, selectional and phonological constraints placed on them by the grammar. Furthermore, compounds display a degree of semantic openness and flexibility that is not found in other morphological or syntactic structures and the functional categories and grammatical requirements (e.g., agreement, congruence and argument satisfaction) of syntax are absent in them as well. After considering further neurocognitive and evolutionary evidence, Fanselow concludes that compounds may have originated in a rudimentary system of symbols that was a precursor to grammar. This symbolic ability formed the basis for the production and transmission of simple, conceptually motivated, messages before modern syntax developed. Remnants of the primitive code are still present and can be identified in the elliptical structures of discourse and telegraphic speech. This code can also surface as a means of communication when the more sophisticated structures of human linguistic competence are absent or impaired, as in the earliest stages of child language acquisition, the language taught to nonhuman primates, the language of linguistically deprived children and in agrammatic aphasic speech. Compounds will be taken over into the linguistic system by a language learner according to the strength of their presence in the primary linguistic data that serves as the basis for language acquisition. Their formal and semantic structure is simple enough to be learned without the help of universal grammar. Fanselow draws a parallel between compounds and the earliest two-word stage of language acquisition before the development of grammar takes effect. This stage is universally characterized by a strong presence of nominal elements whose combinations implement basic conceptual patterns like agent and action, action and patient, object and location, etc. Their interpretations are dependent on general reasoning strategies and anchored in basic knowledge about how objects interrelate.

Jackendoff (1999, 2002, 2009), in his work on the evolution of language, has argued similarly. Basing his discussion on Bickerton's (1990) hypothesis that an earlier protolanguage made up of a vocabulary and pragmatic knowledge preceded our modern language, Jackendoff sees remnants of the early protolanguage in phenomena like the two-word stage of child language, pidgins, late language learning as in the case of Genie, the sign language of apes, agrammatical aphasia, home sign of deaf children, the steady state of second language by immigrant learners and compounding. In all these cases, simple agrammatical structures interface directly with conceptual semantics and their meaning results from inferences made by the communication partners on the basis of the content of the symbols employed.

These ideas lend support to the analysis of compound meaning as envisioned by the compound template in section 4.1: the conjunction of two predicates carries the implicit assumption that they are somehow related. Comprehension of a novel compound proceeds by means of a simple interpretative strategy anchored in our conceptual system and based on general pragmatic principles that allows us to infer a sensible relation between the two predicates that are actually expressed.

6 Conclusion

In spite of appearing on the surface to encompass an inexplicably wide range of irregular structures, diverse formal types and complex meanings, at a deeper level of closer inspection a broad spectrum of compound structures conforms to quite simple basic principles of concatenation and meaning constitution: two predicates conjoin and – guided by the formal modifier-head structure which they instantiate – result in the designation of a hyponymic or subordinate concept. One type of exception to this generalization occurs via the application of the regular semantic process of metonymic shift to a headed morphological structure. A shift in reference, but not in category, results yielding an exocentric interpretation. Nonheaded morphological structures are also subject to the semantic process of metonymic shift or coercion and in this case a new category results that is not represented in the formal structure of the base. In all these cases, general ontological and pragmatic principles are at play, placing restrictions on the process of inference and guaranteeing the comprehensibility of the resulting structures. Loose word structures that differ from the default case of morphological structures in that they make more than one head visible to the syntax, on the other hand, are subject to different principles. They result in hyperonymic meanings, the choice of which is guided by the hierarchical organization of the human conceptual system.

7 References

Adams, Valerie (1973): *An Introduction to Modern English Word Formation*. London: Longman.
Allen, Margaret (1978): Morphological investigations. Ph.D. dissertation, University of Connecticut.
Arcodia, Giorgio F., Nicola Grandi and Bernhard Wälchli (2010): Coordination in compounding. In: Sergio Scalise and Irene Vogel (eds.), *Cross-Disciplinary Issues in Compounding*, 177–197. Amsterdam/Philadelphia: Benjamins.
Aronoff, Mark (1976): *Word Formation in Generative Grammar*. Cambridge, MA: MIT Press.
Artiagoitia, Xabier, José Ignacio Hualde and Jon Oritz de Urbina (2016): Basque. In: Peter O. Müller, Ingeborg Ohnheiser, Susan Olsen and Franz Rainer (eds.), *Word-Formation. An International Handbook of the Languages of Europe*. Vol. 5, 3327–2248. Berlin/Boston: De Gruyter Mouton.
Bauer, Laurie (1978): *The Grammar of Nominal Compounding with Special Reference to Danish, English and French*. Odense: Odense University Press.
Bauer, Laurie (1998): Is there a class of neoclassical compounds, and if so is it productive? *Linguistics* 36: 403–422.
Bauer, Laurie (2001): Compounding. In: Martin Haspelmath, Ekkehard König, Wulf Österreicher and Wolfgang Raible (eds.), *Language Universals and Language Typology*. Vol. 1, 695–707. Berlin/New York: de Gruyter.

Bauer, Laurie (2005): The borderline between derivation and compounding. In: Wolfgang U. Dressler, Dieter Kastovsky, Oskar E. Pfeiffer and Franz Rainer (eds.), *Morphology and its Demarcations*, 97–108. Amsterdam/Philadelphia: Benjamins.
Bauer, Laurie (2008): Dvandva. *Word Structure* 1: 1–20.
Bauer, Laurie (2017): Compounds and Compounding. Cambridge: Cambridge University Press.
Bickerton, Derek (1990): *Language and Species*. Chicago, IL: The University of Chicago Press.
Bierwisch, Manfred (1989): Event nominalizations: Proposals and problems. In: Wolfgang Motsch (ed.), *Wortstruktur und Satzstruktur*, 1–73. Berlin: Akademie Verlag.
Bloomfield, Leonard (1933): *Language*. Chicago: University of Chicago Press.
Booij, Geert (1988): The relation between inheritance and argument linking: Deverbal nouns in Dutch. In: Martin Everaert and Arnold Evers (eds.), *Morphology and Modularity. In Honour of Henk Schultink*, 57–73. Dordrecht: Foris.
Bücking, Sebastian (2009): How do phrasal and lexical modification differ: Contrasting adjective-noun combinations in German. *Word Structure* 2: 184–204.
Bücking, Sebastian (2010): German nominal compounds as underspecified names for kinds. In: Susan Olsen (ed.), *New Impulses in Word-Formation*, 253–281. Hamburg: Buske.
Coseriu, Eugenio (1977): Inhaltliche Wortbildungslehre (am Beispiel des Types „coupe-papier"). In: Herbert E. Brekle and Dieter Kastovsky (eds.), *Perspektiven der Wortbildungsforschung*, 48–61. Bonn: Bouvier.
Downing, Pamela (1977): On the creation and use of English compounds. *Language* 53: 810–842.
Dowty, David (1979): *Word Meaning and Montague Grammar*. Dordrecht: Kluwer.
Dressler, Wolfgang U. (2006): Compound types. In: Gary Libben and Gonia Jarema (eds.), *The Representation and Processing of Compound Words*, 23–44. Oxford: Oxford University Press.
DiSciullo, Anna Maria and Edwin Williams (1987): *On the Definition of Word*. Cambridge, MA: MIT Press.
Erben, Johannes (1983): *Einführung in die deutsche Wortbildungslehre*. 2nd ed. Berlin: Schmidt.
Fanselow, Gisbert (1981): *Zur Syntax und Semantik der Nominalkomposition*. Tübingen: Niemeyer.
Fanselow, Gisbert, (1985): Die Stellung der Wortbildung im System kognitiver Module. *Linguistische Berichte* 96: 91–126.
Fanselow, Gisbert (1988): Word syntax and semantic principles. In: Geert Booij and Jaap van Marle (eds.), *Yearbook of Morphology*, 95–122. Dordrecht: Foris.
Fleischer, Wolfgang (1969): *Wortbildung der deutschen Gegenwartssprache*. Tübingen: Niemeyer.
Fleischer, Wolfgang and Irmhild Barz (2012): *Wortbildung der deutschen Gegenwartssprache*. 4th ed. Tübingen: Niemeyer.
Fradin, Bernard (2009): IE, Romance: French. In: Rochelle Lieber and Pavol Štekauer (eds.), *The Oxford Handbook of Compounding*, 417–435. Oxford: Oxford University Press.
Giegerich, Heinz (2009): Compounding and Lexicalism. In: Rochelle Lieber and Pavol Štekauer (eds.), *The Oxford Handbook of Compounding*, 178–200. Oxford: Oxford University Press.
Grice, Herbert P. (1975): Logic and conversation. In: Peter Cole and Jerry L. Morgan (eds.), *Syntax and Semantics*. Vol. 3: *Speech acts*, 41–58. New York: Academic Press.
Grimm, Jacob (1826): *Deutsche Grammatik, 2. Theil: Ableitung und Zusammensetzung*. Göttingen: Dieterich.
Hatcher, Anna (1960): An introduction to the analysis of English noun compounds. *Word* 16: 356–373.
Henzen, Walter (1947): *Deutsche Wortbildung*. Tübingen: Niemeyer.
Higginbotham, James (1985): On semantics. *Linguistic Inquiry* 16: 547–593.
Hoeksema, Jack (1985): *Categorial Morphology*. New York: Garland.
Jackendoff, Ray (1999): Possible states in the evolution of the language capacity. *Trends in Cognitive Sciences* 3: 272–279.
Jackendoff, Ray (2002): *Foundations of Language*. Oxford: Oxford University Press.

Jackendoff, Ray (2009): Compounding in the parallel architecture and conceptual semantics. In: Rochelle Lieber and Pavol Štekauer (eds.), *The Oxford Handbook of Compounding*, 105–128. Oxford: Oxford University Press.

Jespersen, Otto (1909): *A Modern English Grammar on Historical Principles*. Part 1: *Sounds and Spelling*. London: George Allen & Unwin.

Johansson, Stig (1980): *Plural Attributive Nouns in Present-Day English*. Lund: LiberLäromedel.

Kastovsky, Dieter (2009): Diachronic perspectives. In: Rochelle Lieber and Pavol Štekauer (eds.), *The Oxford Handbook of Compounding*, 323–340. Oxford: Oxford University Press.

Kornfeld, Laura Malena (2009): IE, Romance: Spanish. In: Rochelle Lieber and Pavol Štekauer (eds.), *The Oxford Handbook of Compounding*, 436–452. Oxford: Oxford University Press.

Lang, Ewald (1991): Koordinierende Konjunktionen. In: Arnim von Stechow and Dieter Wunderlich (eds.), *Semantics. A Handbook*, 597–623. Berlin/New York: de Gruyter.

Lees, Robert (1970): Problems in the grammatical analysis of English nominal compounds. In: Manfred Bierwisch and Karl-Erich Heidolph (eds.), *Progress in Linguistics*, 174–186. The Hague: Mouton.

Leser, Martin (1990): *Das Problem der 'Zusammenbildungen'. Eine lexikalistische Studie*. Trier: Wissenschaftlicher Verlag Trier.

Levi, Judith (1978): *The Syntax and Semantics of Complex Nominals*. New York: Academic Press.

Libben, Gary (2010): Compound words, semantic transparency, and morphological transcendence. In: Susan Olsen (ed.), *New Impulses in Word-formation*, 318–330. Hamburg: Buske.

Libben, Gary, Lori Buchanan and Annette Colangelo (2003): Morphology, semantics and aphasia: The failure of inhibition hypothesis. *Logos and Language* 4(1): 45–53.

Libben, Gary, Martha Gibson, Yeo Bom Yoon and Dominiek Sandra (2003): Compound fracture: The role of semantic transparency and morphological headedness. *Brain and Language* 84: 50–64.

Lieber, Rochelle (2004): *Morphology and Lexical Semantics*. Cambridge: Cambridge University Press.

Lieber, Rochelle and Pavol Štekauer (2009): *The Oxford Handbook of Compounding*. Oxford: Oxford University Press.

Maienborn, Claudia (2003): Event-internal modifiers: Semantic underspecification and conceptual interpretation. In: Ewald Lang, Claudia Maienborn and Cathrine Fabricius-Hansen (eds.), *Modifying Adjuncts. An Introduction*, 475–509. Berlin: Mouton de Gruyter.

Marchand, Hans (1967): Expansion, transposition, and derivation. In: Dieter Kastovsky (ed.), *Studies in Syntax and Word-Formation. Selected articles by Hans Marchand*, 322–337. München: Fink.

Marchand, Hans (1969): *The Categories and Types of Present-Day English Word-Formation. A Synchronic-Diachronic Approach*. 2nd ed. München: Beck.

Mayrhofer, Manfred (1965): *Sanskrit-Grammatik mit sprachvergleichenden Erläuterungen*. Berlin: de Gruyter.

Meibauer, Jörg (2007): How marginal are phrasal compounds? Generalized insertion, expressivity, and I/Q-interaction. *Morphology* 17: 233–259.

Melloni, Chiara (2020): Subordinate and synthetic compounds in morphology. In: Rochelle Lieber (ed.), *Oxford Encyclopedia of Morphology*, 700–726. Oxford: Oxford University Press.

Meyer, Ralf (1993): *Compound Comprehension in Isolation and in Context*. Tübingen: Niemeyer.

Motsch, Wolfgang (2004): *Deutsche Wortbildung in Grundzügen*. 2nd ed. Berlin/New York: de Gruyter.

Ohnheiser, Ingeborg (2015): Compounds and multi-word expressions in Slavic. In: Peter O. Müller, Ingeborg Ohnheiser, Susan Olsen and Franz Rainer (eds.), *Word-Formation. An International Handbook of the Languages of Europe*. Vol. 1, 757–799. Berlin//Boston: De Gruyter Mouton.

Olsen, Susan (2001): Copulative compounds. A closer look at the interface between morphology and syntax. In: Geert Booij and Jaap van Marle (eds.), *Yearbook of Morphology 2000*, 279–320. Dordrecht: Kluwer.

Olsen, Susan (2004): The case of copulative compounds. In: Alice ter Meulen and Werner Abraham (eds.), *The Composition of Meaning. From Lexeme to Discourse*, 17–37. Amsterdam/Philadelphia: Benjamins.
Olsen, Susan (2012): Semantics of compounds. In: Claudia Maienborn, Klaus von Heusinger and Paul Portner (eds.), *Semantics. An International Handbook of Natural Language Meaning*. Vol. 3, 2120–2150. Berlin/Boston: De Gruyter Mouton.
Olsen, Susan (2014): Coordinative structures in morphology. In: Antonio Machicao y Priemer, Andreas Nolda and Athina Sioupi (eds.), *Zwischen Kern und Peripherie. Untersuchungen zu Randbereichen in Sprache und Grammatik*, 269–286. Berlin/New York: de Gruyter.
Paul, Hermann (1920): *Deutsche Grammatik*. Vol. 5: *Wortbildungslehre*. Halle/S.: Niemeyer.
Plag, Ingo (2003): *Word-Formation in English*. Cambridge: Cambridge University Press.
Rainer, Franz (2016): Spanish. In: Peter O. Müller, Ingeborg Ohnheiser, Susan Olsen and Franz Rainer (eds.), *Word-Formation. An International Handbook of the Languages of Europe*. Vol. 4, 2620–2640. Berlin/Boston: De Gruyter Mouton.
Rainer, Franz and Soledad Varela (1992): Compounding in Spanish. *Rivista di linguistica* 4(1): 117–142.
Ralli, Angela (2008): Compound markers and parametric variation. *Language Typology and Universals* 61: 19–38.
Ralli, Angela (2020): Coordination in compounds. In: Rochelle Lieber (ed.), *Oxford Encyclopedia of Morphology*, 726–742. Oxford: Oxford University Press.
Sandra, Dominiek (1990): On the representation and processing of compound words: Automatic access to constituent morphemes does not occur. *The Quarterly Journal of Experimental Psychology* 42a: 529–567.
Scalise, Sergio and Irene Vogel (eds.) (2010): *Cross-Disciplinary Issues in Compounding*. Amsterdam/Philadelphia: Benjamins.
Schlücker, Barbara (2013): The semantics of lexical modification. Meaning and meaning relations in German A+N compounds. In: Pius ten Hacken and Claire Thomas (eds.), *The Semantics of Word Formation and Lexicalization*, 121–139. Edinburgh: Edinburgh University Press.
Schlücker, Barbara (2016): Adjective-noun compounding in Parallel Architecture. In: Pius ten Hacken (ed.), *The Semantics of Compounding*, 178–191. Cambridge: Cambridge University Press.
Schmid, Hans-Jörg (2011): *English Morphology and Word-Formation. An Introduction*. Berlin: Schmidt.
Selkirk, Elisabeth (1982): *The Syntax of Words*. Cambridge, MA: MIT Press.
Szymanek, Bogdan (2009): IE, Slavonic: Polish. In: Rochelle Lieber and Pavol Štekauer (eds.), *The Oxford Handbook of Compounding*, 464–477. Oxford: Oxford University Press.
ten Hacken, Pius (2010): Synthetic and exocentric compounds in a parallel architecture. In: Susan Olsen (ed.), *New Impulses in Word-Formation*, 233–251. Hamburg: Buske.
Wälchli, Bernhard (2005): *Co-Compounds and Natural Coordination*. Oxford: Oxford University Press.
Warren, Beatrice (1978): *Semantic Patterns of Noun-Noun Compounds*. Lund: Acta Universitatis Gothoburgensis.
Whitney, William Dwight (1993): *Sanskrit Grammar*. Delhi: Motilal Banardsidass.
Williams, Edwin (1981): On the notions 'lexically related' and 'head of a word'. *Linguistic Inquiry* 12(2): 245–274.
Wilmanns, Wilhelm (1896): *Deutsche Grammatik. Gotisch, Alt-, Mittel- und Neuhochdeutsch. Zweite Abteilung: Wortbildung*. 2nd ed. Straßburg: Trübner.
Zimmer, Karl (1972): Appropriateness conditions for nominal compounds. *Working Papers on Linguistic Universals* 8: 3–10.
Zwanenburg, Wiecher (1992): Compounding in French. *Rivista di Linguistica* 4(1): 221–240.
Zwitserlood, Pienie (1994): The role of semantic transparency in the processing and representation of Dutch compounds. *Language and Cognitive Processes* 9(3): 341–368.

Bernard Fradin
15 Blending

1 Introduction
2 Characteristic properties of blends
3 Blending and grammar
4 Phonological conditioning
5 Semantic conditioning
6 Delimiting blending
7 References

Abstract: In this article, the most typical features of blending are first presented and the way they shape the status of blending relative to grammar is discussed. The issue of the phonology of blends, which plays a crucial role in the way their parts are combined, is then addressed. Many of the approaches that have been proposed are discussed and the main conclusion to be drawn is that neither purely categorical nor purely statistical treatments can cope with all the data. These approaches must be viewed as complementary rather than as alternatives. The various interpretations observed in blends are sorted out and some descriptive proposals are made. The last section aims at disentangling blends from the constructs they are often confused with.

1 Introduction

On a first approximation, blends (Ger. *Kontamination, Wortverschmelzung*, Fr. *mots-valises, amalgames*, It. *parole macedonia, incroci*) are lexemes formed by means of fusing two already existing lexemes into a new one, where the stems of the initial lexemes have often been shortened. English *smog ← smoke × fog* is an example of a blend. Blending shares with compounding the fact that it takes two lexemes as bases (rarely more). To that extent, both processes contrast with derivation, which involves one base lexeme only. This proximity makes it worthwhile to undertake a systematic comparison of blending with compounding in order to bring to light the properties that uniquely characterize blending (section 2). In addition, this will allow us to address the controversial issue of the status of blending in rela-

---

Bernard Fradin, Paris, France

https://doi.org/10.1515/9783111420561-015

tion to grammar (section 3). Insofar as blends are complex linguistic signs, albeit not straightforward ones, the subsequent sections of this article will be devoted to each of the dimensions constituting a sign in turn. I refer to Cannon (1986) for a discussion of terminological issues.

Giving a general, but accurate enough, picture of blending is not an easy task for several reasons. The first one is that any serious study of this phenomenon has to rely on attested examples. However, as blends do not fit the regular patterns of word-building morphology, they will not be detected by an automatic processing system. Therefore, we must resort to the lists of blends mentioned in previous studies, which include, for English: Pound (1914), Bauer (1983), Kelly (1998), Cannon (1986), Algeo (1991), Cannon (2000), Enarsson (2006), Hong (2005); for German: Grésillon (1984), Ronneberger-Sibold (2006), Friedrich (2008), Reischer (2008), Müller and Friedrich (2011); for Italian: Thornton (1996), Bertinetto (2001), Thornton (2004); for Spanish: Pharies (1987), Piñeros (2004); for Hebrew: Bat-El (1996); for French: Galisson (1987), Léturgie (2012), Grésillon (1984) and the annex of Bertinetto (2001). Data from other languages will be provided by the works referred to in the text. Note that in many languages, blending is (almost) non-existent, e.g., Finnish (M. Kaunisto p.c.), Czech (J. Strnadová p.c.). The second reason is that blending is very dependent on the prosodic structure of the word in each distinct language, which makes it difficult to express cross-linguistic generalizations (cf. section 4). The third reason is that the blends that circulate in the literature are very heterogeneous, because the sources they come from (literary texts, medical reports, newspapers and journals, advertisement, and even fictional dictionaries of blends (17 of them have been published for French between 1979 and 2008; cf. Léturgie 2011)) are heterogeneous too; moreover, some of them are mixed up with expressions which should not be regarded as blends (section 5). The fourth reason is that the blends in question are not considered equally felicitous, or even acceptable, by native speakers, a fact sometimes acknowledged (Thornton 1993; Piñeros 2004: 234) but never seriously taken into account. Therefore, trying to elaborate a fair account of blending is probably out of reach for the time being.

Blending is not generally recognized as a legitimate word-formation process in Slavic. It is dealt with in one article on Russian (Janko-Trinickaja 1975) and mentioned, together with other units of word-formation, in Uluxanov (1996: 52 ff., 192). There are no monographs dealing directly with blends and blending is neither mentioned in the Russian Academy Grammar (Švedova 1980) nor in a monograph on recent tendencies in Polish word-formation (Jadacka 2005) that otherwise provides a good discussion of the development of Polish word-formation. Since blends that arise in Slavic are predominately stylistically marked occasionalisms, blending is usually considered a type of playful word-creation (cf., e.g.,

Il'jasova and Amiri 2009). Recent works document the fact that blending is active in contemporary Russian (Xruščeva 2011).

2 Characteristic properties of blends

Let's admit the uncontroversial claim that word-building processes belonging to the grammar of a given language L normally satisfy the properties stated in (1). The first clause expresses compositionality, the second one guarantees that a given morphological process is embodied in a fixed phonological pattern, and the third one states that the association of sound with meaning is stable for any given morphological process.

(1) (i) The meaning of a morphological construct is the regular combination of the meaning of the source lexemes together with the instruction associated with the rule itself.
 (ii) In a given morphological process, the phonological link between the input unit(s) and the output unit (the construct) is held constant for each construct which belongs to the process in question.
 (iii) There is a link between the way phonological parts are combined, on the one hand, and the way semantic contents are, on the other, and this linking is held constant for each construct exemplifying the process.

If we agree that compounding belongs to plain morphology (Booij 2005: ch. 4), then compounds should meet the requirements in (1). Indeed, French VN compounds satisfy properties (i) and (iii) since they are interpreted in 90 % of cases as 'x such that x V' N'', where V' is the semantic counterpart of V, and N' that of N, e.g., *garde-barrière* 'level-crossing keeper' = 'x such that x keeps level-crossing'. The same is true of Germanic nominal determinative compounds, even though their construction meaning often remains largely underspecified. Their interpretation follows their structure (Olsen 2000: 898) which, in turn, depends on the position of stress; then, in certain varieties of German, while *Lebensmittelpunkt*, the structure of which is 'N_1 (N_2 N_3)', means 'centre of life', *Lebensmittelpunkt*, the structure of which is '(N_1 N_2) N_3', is interpreted as 'marker on groceries' (Neef 2009: 394). The compounds just mentioned also satisfy property (ii) insofar as the phonology of the compound results from the concatenation of the appropriate stems associated with the lexemes involved in the compounding process, following the order lexeme$_1$, lexeme$_2$ (lexeme$_{n+1}$). If we compare these compounds with French binominal blends *hippidémie*, *élevache*, and *ordinosaure* given in Table 15.1,

Tab. 15.1: Form meaning combination in blends.

Lexeme 1	Gloss	Lexeme 2	Gloss	Phonol.	Meaning
hippie	'hippie'	<épi>démie	'epidemic'	1 ⊕ 2	'epidemic of hippies'
éle<vage>	'breeding'	vache	'cow'	1 ⊕ 2	'cow breeding'
ordi<nateur>	'computer'	<di>nosaure	'dinosaur'	1 ⊕ 2	'very old computer'

we see that the latter do not satisfy (iii) because the linear adjustment of the segments correlated to the base-lexemes does not allow us to predict the way these lexemes are semantically combined. For instance, whereas the semantic head is lexeme$_2$ in *hippidémie*, it is lexeme$_1$ in *élevache* and *ordinosaure*. In addition, (i) is not satisfied because the semantic combination of the lexemic contents varies: in *hippidémie* the content of lexeme$_1$ is what the epidemic is the vector of; in *élevache*, the content of lexeme$_2$ is the argument of the verb underlying lexeme$_1$, while in *ordinosaure* the connotative content of lexeme$_2$ is predicated of the first unit. Property (ii) is not satisfied either, since the combination of the phonological stems belonging to each of the source lexemes greatly varies (cf. section 4). The more striking feature is that the integrity of the lexical stems corresponding to each of the source units is rarely kept intact in blending, and the part which is kept cannot be known in advance. In most cases, the stems are shortened in a way that depends on strictly local phonological parameters (section 4). As Table 15.1 shows, the suppressed segments, which are between angle brackets, can be part of either one of the source lexemes or of both.

This sample of examples, however small, shows that blending does not comply with the most basic principles of grammatical word-formation, namely (1ii) and (1iii).

If we take into account paradigmatic relations (in the Saussurean sense), we discover another feature distinguishing blending from compounding that we might call the hapactic nature of blends: blends do not constitute series (see section 6.5) and this is all the more true the more the phonological overlap (cf. section 4.1) motivating the original blend has disappeared. For instance, on the model of *élevache* it is utterly awkward to coin *élechien 'dog breeding' or *élanguille 'eel breeding'. But when the overlap is preserved and complete, series may emerge, e.g., Ger. *Fairkehr* (cf. *Verkehr* 'traffic'), *Fairkauf* (cf. *Verkauf* 'selling'), *fairteilen* (cf. *verteilen* 'to divide'). To sum up, blends show three salient properties (in a weak sense, since all are negative properties):

a) No preservation of lexical integrity. In contrast to derivational morphology and compounding, the integrity of the stems corresponding to each of the source units is rarely maintained in blending and, moreover, the manner in

which they are altered does not follow a predetermined pattern. Hence clause (1ii). In most cases, they are shortened in a way that depends on the interaction of one stem upon the other (sections 4.1, 6.3).
b) No fixed pattern of compositionality. Insofar as there is no specific instruction, however coarse, attached to the process of blending (cf. (1i)), the semantic combination of the source units' content is left floating. The absence of clause (1iii) strengthens this effect. It would be inaccurate however to say that blends are not compositional, insofar as their meaning results from the combination of the meaning of their parts. But this combination is constrained only by general conceptual categories. Blends show as much compositionality as the most underspecified compounds do, namely attributive (determinative) N-N compounds, e.g., Ger. (attributive) *Fischfrau* may have half a dozen meanings (Neef 2009: 395) except the 'fish maid' meaning, whereas (coordinate compound) *Kinder-Soldat* means 'child soldier'.
c) Blends are type hapaxes. Unlike derived or compound units, they cannot form series. Each one is a (lexeme) type which is the only one to instantiate the morphological pattern it belongs to.

3 Blending and grammar

3.1 Clarifying the issue

The idea that the way (parts of) lexemes are combined in blending does not follow any explicit grammatical rule indicating how the combination has to be carried out, in contrast to what happens in compounding, has been defended by Dressler (2000) and Bauer (1988: 39) among others. Other linguists, however, hold the view according to which blending is rule-governed and should be considered as a completely grammatical phenomenon on a par with other word-building morphological processes (Kubozono 1990; Bat-El 1996; Plag 2003). These opposing views raise the question of the link between blending and grammar. Actually, the debate involves two separate issues corresponding to the conceptual oppositions regular vs. irregular on the one hand and grammatical vs. extragrammatical on the other. The key point is to determine what the criteria could be that allow one to say whether a given process pertains to grammar or not.

Advocates of the view according to which "blending is part of derivational morphology" (Bat-El 1996: 316) emphasize that the phonology of blends is regular and obeys the general prosodic constraints that apply throughout the lexicon. Plag recalls that truncations (cf. section 4.1) that take place in blends are highly systematic and follow the same patterns as those observed in clipping (cf. definition section 6.3), which shows that blending is "part of the morphological competence of the speakers" (Plag 2003: 177). Plag (2003: 123) claims that rule (2) may account for the most frequent types of blends in English, e.g., *guess* × *estimate* → *guestimate* (B or C may be null).

(2)   A B + C D → A D

Actually, the fact that the phonology of blends is not completely special is not disputed by anybody. Dressler even says that "universal preferences" are expected to apply more consistently to extragrammatical phenomena than to the morphological rules encapsulated within grammar (Dressler 2000: 6). Saying that blending pertains to extragrammatical morphology does not mean that it lies out of the realm of linguistic mechanisms, especially the phonological ones (Fradin, Montermini and Plénat 2009), or that it is governed by a "distorted version of them" (Piñeros 2004: 209). Assuming that a given process is extragrammatical only entails that it includes properties which do not match the grammar of the language in question, or that it lacks properties regularly associated with processes of similar type (in the language in question). (Extra)grammaticality should be measured against the grammar of a particular language, not in general. From this perspective, besides (i) regular vs. irregular, the other relevant dimension to take into account is (ii) universal vs. specific. The grammar of a particular language may include phenomena which are:

a) regular and specific: Constraints applying in lexeme-building morphology are such, either because they simultaneously bear on several levels of the linguistic signs, e.g., "suffix /X/ to the phonology of the base if it is a V and if its first argument denotes an agent" or because they reflect a deeply entrenched historical conditioning, e.g., the monosuffix constraint in English, which says that suffixes that select Germanic bases select unsuffixed bases (Aronoff and Fuhrhop 2002: 473). By nature, morphophonology includes constraints which are very specific as illustrated by English *-al*, *-ance* which "need to occur next to syllables that have main stress", e.g., *relúct-ance*, *refús-al* vs. *deep-en-ance (Plag 2003: 174–175; also Pierrehumbert and Nair 1995: 95). Similar constraints are common in compounding too. French VN compounds are a case in point, since their verbal base is required to be monosyllabic (Villoing 2012) and it always corresponds to the 'indicative present singular' stem of the verb (Bonami, Boyé and Kerleroux 2009).
b) regular and universal: Constraints such as the obligatory contour principle (OCP) illustrate this case (McCarthy 1986; Prince and Smolensky 1993).
c) irregular and specific: e.g., the plural of *ox* in English.

The fourth case (irregular and universal) cannot exist. As for extragrammatical phenomena, the claim is that they are the concern of very general mechanisms only, those of type b) and the less specific of those of type a), e.g., the phonotactic constraints of a given language (cf. section 4.3) (but not of very specific constraints such as those exemplified in a) above). This position has been endorsed by linguists describing extragrammatical phenomena other than blending, such as hypocoristic clipping (cf. section 6.3), e.g., It. *Vico* ← *Lodovico* (Thornton 1996; Montermini 2007) or secret languages, e.g., French *verlan* [ridako] ← *corrida* [korida] 'corrida' (Plénat 1995). As hinted before, blending qualifies as extragrammatical also because it may include processes which are not present elsewhere in the morphology of the language in question. These can be phonological operations which never occur in the language, as internal replacement, e.g., Fr. *mét<amour>phose* ← *métamorphose* 'metamorphosis' × *amour* 'love', E. *s<lith>y* ← *slimy* × *lithe* (L. Carroll) or combinations of units which are never used as bases in normal compounding. For French this includes proper names, e.g., *Bokhassan II* ← *Bokassa* × *Hassan II*, adverbs, e.g., *intelligentiment* ← *intelligemment* 'cleverly' × *gentiment* 'kindly', verbs, e.g., *se barricaner* ← *se barricader* 'to barricade onself' × *ricaner* 'to snigger', onomatopoeia and adverbial phrases, e.g., *turlututête* ← *turlututu* 'onomatopeia imitating flute's song' × *tue-tête* '(to sing) at the top of one's voice'. The fact that blends are conscious creations has been given as an additional argument in favour of considering them extragrammatical (Ronneberger-Sibold 2010), insofar as ordinary morphological rules are executed unconsciously but with perfect mastery by speakers and yield expressions indistinguishable from already existing lexemes (van Marle 1985; Baayen 1993). Blends resulting from slips of tongue will be discussed in section 6.1.

3.2 Unexpected behaviour

When the semantic aspect of blends is taken into account, it becomes clear that blends never show some properties that one would expect them to exhibit if they instantiate plain word-formation. For instance, quite often compounds develop special meanings. In Dutch NA compounds, the N provides a point of comparison with respect to the property expressed by the adjective, e.g., *boter-zacht* 'as soft as butter; lit. butter-soft', *ijzer-sterk* 'as strong as iron; lit. iron-strong' (Booij 2002: 155–156). But the N can function as a mere intensifier, in which case it bears the main stress of the word, e.g., *boterzacht* 'very soft; lit. butter-soft', etc. Meaning specializations of this sort presuppose the emergence of a compounding subpattern which is the basis out of which the variation grows. No such patterns can emerge with blends because each blend is by nature a hapax.

3.3 Consequences of a major gap

There is one property constitutive of blending which strongly supports the extragrammatical view, namely the non-satisfaction of (1iii). To fully acknowledge this point, it is worth recording that, if we leave aside the issue of shortening, the phonology of blends is rule-governed (by very general rules or constraints) and their semantics is underspecified (as it is for some compounds) but not at all specific (section 5). The crucial point is that no sound/meaning correlation is stated contrarily to what is required in morphology (Zwicky 1992). The first consequence is the fact that the burden of combining the (parts of) source units hinges on phonology. The second is the fact that the well-formedness of blends qua signs is referred to semiotic principles, inasmuch as no morphological rules state the correlation between the phonological and the semantic plane (cf. section 3.4). This has an immediate impact on category and (gender) assignment. This assignment is stable and well-defined for any word-building process. For instance, in Romance VN compounds are always masculine Ns, while N-N compounds inherit their category and gender from the first noun, e.g., Fr. *camion-citerne* 'tanker-truck' is a masculine noun (as *camion*) but *émission-phare* 'flagship program; lit. program lighthouse' is a feminine noun (as *émission*). In blends, this assignment is not fixed. When it involves two nouns, lexeme$_2$ is the morphological head, e.g., *hippidémie, ordinosaure* but sometimes there is a conflict between the semantic and the morphological head: *suicidérurgie* (← *suicide* 'suicide' × *sidérurgie* 'steel metallurgy') is a feminine noun as *sidérurgie*, yet it means 'suicide of steel metallurgy'. Lexeme$_1$ is the semantic head, as in normal compounds, e.g., *chou-fleur* 'cauliflower; lit. cabbage flower', but in *hippidémie*, it is lexeme$_2$.

The position assumed here entails that blending should not be considered a word-formation process, contrary to what is claimed in the majority of studies devoted to blending (Pharies 1987; Kubozono 1990; Gries 2004a: 639; Renner 2006). What is true, nevertheless, is that blends quite often enter the lexicon of languages as the result of lexicalization. But this is not special to blends, since almost any kind of expression, be it constructed by morphology or syntax, may eventually be lexicalized (Hohenhaus 2005). Lexicalization is orthogonal to word-formation and this is why erratic formations can enter the lexicon and become well-behaved lexemes, e.g., Fr. *chandail* '(thick) jumper' by aphaeresis of *marchand d'ail* 'garlic retailer'. If blending is no more a word-formation process, it becomes meaningless to speak of the productivity of blending, let alone of blends, because there is no way to measure it. Following Baayen and his colleagues, many people agree that metric *P*, based on *hapax legomena*, gives a fairly good approximation of morphological productivity in the narrow sense (Baayen 1992, 1993). Therefore a given word-formation rule, e.g., the formation of *-bar* suffixed adjectives in

German (Riehemann 1998), will be said to be productive only if the number of new lexemes that fit the pattern increases, and the measure of productivity is necessarily relative to a (well-balanced) corpus (Baayen and Lieber 1991; Gaeta and Ricca 2003). In the case of blends, we have neither the pattern, nor the corpus. Speaking of productivity only amounts then to loosely say that blends, on the whole, are numerous vs. scarce in some varieties of discourse.

3.4 The semiotic tension in blending

Many authors (Thornton 1993: 148; Kelly 1998; Gries 2004a; Ronneberger-Sibold 2006) have noted in various ways that blending has to accommodate two contradictory requirements, namely a) the shortening of the source lexemes in order to make the blend resemble a single lexeme, and b) the preservation of as many segments (Bat-El 2006: 66–67) or relevant phonological properties from the source lexemes as possible (Ronneberger-Sibold 2006) in order to maximize the semantic transparency of the blend. Compounds are not put under a similar strain, since their base lexemes need not be shortened. But blends give the speakers something that compounds do not, namely the opportunity to show their capacity to play with language, which is a socially praised ability, creating an unconventional, witty semantic association between two (or *n*) lexical meanings packed in one word. Coining blends is part of the epilinguistic competence of native speakers, which also manifests itself through puns, spoonerisms, witticisms, and other language games. From a semiotic point of view, (a) diminishes understanding (while possibly enhancing social rewarding), whereas (b) maximizes it. Diminution vs. maximization may involve three operations: A) truncation, B) linearization and C) overlap, which can be used as parameters to classify blends (section 4.1).

4 Phonological conditioning

4.1 Phonological issues in blending

In contradistinction to what happens in regular morphology, in blending phonology is not strictly limited to phonological matters (viz. to determine the phonic shape of derived lexemes) since it has a direct bearing on the way the source constituents combine to form the blend. The fact "that prosodic and other phonological constraints have the power to determine even the order of the elements [in blends]" is rightly underlined by Bat-El (1996: 317). This power, which never shows up in syntax, directly follows from the fact that blending is an extragrammatical process, that is a process without a combinatorics of its own (no clause (1iii)). To see what is at stake, let's start from the two words W_1 *smoke* and W_2 *haze*. Kelly (1998: 580) says that they can be blended to form either *smaze*, *hoke*, or *smoze*, but that the first one is arguably better than the two others. If we agree with Kelly, this means (i) that the order 'W_1 before W_2' has to be selected by some instance, and (ii) that the switching point, i.e. the point where the first constituent of the blend ends and the second begins, has also to be determined by a mechanism sensitive to fine-grained phonological distinctions at the level of syllable or below. Phonologically oriented approaches assume that both tasks (i) and (ii) are in the realm of phonology (Bat-El 1996: 288; Kubozono 1990). This assumption is probably founded for what regards (ii), but it is much more controversial for what regards (i). Actually, even though the decision about (i) is based on information concerning the phonology of W_1 and W_2 (number of syllables, etc.), the conditions allowing one to choose the best order are not strictly phonological (cf. section 4.3). In order to have a better grasp of the mechanisms carrying out tasks (i) and (ii), we must have an idea of the variety of blends that may exist. To achieve this goal, we shall classify blends according to their use of the three operations mentioned above, A) truncation, B) linearization and C) overlap. If we assume that the commonest blends involve two source units only, the combination of these parameters results in Table 15.2, which corresponds to Gries's classification of blends (Gries 2004a: 646; see also Pharies 1987: 284). Actually this classification is a two-lexeme combination classification. It is helpful precisely because it allows us to delimit what place blending occupies among the morphological phenomena involving two (or more) lexemes. The notation follows Bat-El's (1996): non-occurring material is enclosed in angle brackets, similar segments are underlined, and the bullet indicates a lexeme boundary.

Tab. 15.2: The classification of blends and two-lexeme units (cf. Gries 2004: 646).

	A. Trunc. = both	B. Trunc. = 1	C. Trunc. = 2	D. Trunc. = 0
+OV +LIN	daxpór daxáf × laxpór	knáuros knástos × áuros	wildschön wild × bildschön	Paradiesel Paradies × Diesel
+OV −LIN	dialügisch dialogisch × Lüge	carnibbleous carniverous × nibble	–	hypocritiquement hypocritement × critique
−OV +LIN	brunch breakfast × lunch	klafúda klára × fúda	smothercate smother × suffocate	sálkal sál × kál
−OV −LIN	–	–	–	rajolivissant ravissant × joli

a) Truncation (±trunc) can be distributed over the constituents of the blend or limited to just one. *Truncation* means here that a segment of a source lexeme is without a correlate in the blend. For instance, in A1 Table 15.2 the segments /áf/ and /lax/, present in *daxáf* and *laxpór* respectively, have disappeared from *daxpór*. But *dies* /di:z/ in D1 has not since this segment occurs in the blend. What we have instead here is a case of overlap (cf. below).
b) Linearization of constituents. The constituents of a blend are linearly ordered (+lin) when no part of a blend correlated to the first source lexeme needs to be processed after parts belonging to the second source lexeme have been processed (where a part includes at least one onset). This usually corresponds to configuration PART1 <...•...> PART2. Otherwise, the order is non-linear (–lin). Parameters involved in ordering can be tied either to the source units, or to systemic constraints on blending, which impose restrictions on the output or take advantage of the phonotactics of the language (section 4.3).
c) Overlap of constituents (±ov). Two phonologically similar segments overlap when both appear in the source lexemes whereas only one remains in the blend. The overlap can be local or global (section 4.4). Although overlap includes contiguous segments (+con) in most languages, this is not always so (section 4.5.2). Overlap is the same as haplology.

A1) Heb. *daxpór* 'bulldozer' ← *daxáf* 'to push' × *laxpór* 'to dig', da<x̱áf•la>x̱pór
A2) Ger. *dialügisch* ← *dialogisch* 'dialogal' × *Lüge* 'lie', dia<lo>•Lü<ge>•gisch
A3) E. *brunch* ← *breakfast* × *lunch*, br<eakfast•l>unch. *Agitprop* ← *agitation* × *propaganda*, agit<tation>•prop<aganda> would illustrate this case too.
A4) no attested example
B1) Gr. *knáuros* 'ripe but green' ← *knástos* 'ripe' × *áuros* 'unripe', kn<ástos>•áuros
B2) E. *carnibbleous* ← *carniverous* × *(to) nibble*, car<niver>•nibble•ous (Pound 1914: 45)
B3) Gr. *klafúda* 'branch with a tuft' ← *klára* 'branch' × *fúda* 'tuft', kla<ra>•fúda
B4) no attested example
C1) Ger. *wildschön* ← *wild* 'wild' × *bildschön* 'beautiful', wild•<bild>schön
C2) No attested example (most intercalated blends show no truncation cf. 4.4)
C3) E. *smothercate* ← *smother* × *suffocate*, smother•<suffo>cate
C4) no attested example
D1) Ger. *Paradiesel* ← *Paradies* 'paradise' × *Diesel* 'diesel', Para<dies>•diesel
D2) Fr. *hypocritiquement* (Rabelais) ← *hypocritement* 'hypocritically' × *critique* 'critical', hypo<crite>•critique•ment (**critiquement* does not exist by itself).
D3) Heb. *sálkal* 'baby car seat' ← *sál* 'basket' × *kál* 'easy, light', sál•kal
D4) Fr. *rajolivissant* ← *ravissant* 'charming' × *joli* 'pretty', ra•joli•vissant

Not all cells of Table 15.2 correspond to widespread patterns, neither cross-linguistically nor language internally. The prevalent ones are those that combine overlap and contiguity (line 1), most of which including a truncation (A1 = rule (2), B1, C1). The patterns in line 2 illustrate "intercalative blends", which are also quite common unlike patterns without overlap (lines 3 and 4). These blends strongly prefer overlapping (section 4.5.1), hence their absence in C2. Actually, cell D3 may include expressions whose pattern is outside of the blending system, namely compounds, e.g., E. *bow-tie*; *sálkal* is not a compound in Hebrew (Bat-El 1996: 287). This is also the case of patterns in cell A4 (section 4.4). Cell D4 includes untypical blends, which "are not very witty" precisely because their components have not been shortened but "just stuck together" (Gries 2006: 538–539). These are hardly blends, which is confirmed by the fact that they are sparse and even non-existent in most languages with blends (more examples in Fradin 2000). Table 15.2 provides us with a systematic classification of blends but gives no information about the actual possibilities or impossibilities we observe in languages. These possibilities depend on fine-grained phonological constraints and structural (segmental and prosodic) preferences (section 4.4). Moreover, some patterns allow variations on overlap or truncation which seem to be language dependent (section 4.5.2).

The classification of blends in Table 15.2 does not preclude one from distinguishing among blend classes based on other properties, such as the interlocutor's capacity to understand the blend. The most widely accepted distinction among linguists is the one between telescope (Piñeros, Ronneberger-Sibold)/overlap (Kemmer) blends on the one hand, e.g., A1, A3, B1, B3, C3, and substitute (Kemmer)/portemanteau (Piñeros)/intersective (Ronneberger-Sibold) blends on the other, e.g., B2, C1, D1, D2 (section 3.4.2). This classification is based on semiotic instead of formal properties. In telescope/overlap blends (= A blends), the source lexemes are juxtaposed like in a phrase or compound, in intersective/substitute/portemanteau blends (= B blends), one source lexeme includes (part of) the other as part of its sound chain.

4.2 General constraints on source units

The issue of the nature of sources has seldom been addressed, although it should be once one assumes the distinction between word-form (the inflected form) and lexeme (the abstract unit) (Matthews 1991). Some linguists claim that the bases of blends are "full surface forms" (Bat-El 1996: 290) and many speak of "source words" (SW), but it is not certain that they are referring to "word-form", since the above distinction is not operative in their works. Even though attested examples support the idea that the sources of blends are word-forms, e.g., It. *Alitalia* (company name) ← *ali* wing:PL × *Italia* 'Italy', it is difficult to elaborate an undisputed argument for this view, because the number (or gender) feature can be an inherent inflectional feature and as such may appear in derivation, e.g., Nld. *helden-dom* hero:PL-NZR 'heroism' (Booij 2002: 84). What is sure, is that the sources of blends are full-fledged forms generated by morphology and endowed with prosodic structure. For lack of evidence to the contrary, I will continue to assume that blends are formed with lexemes even though, for reasons of convenience, I will make use of *word* when discussing the views of authors who use this term.

Kubozono contends that the source lexemes must be of the same category (Kubozono 1990: 3). This is certainly not a mandatory requirement. There are many cases where the constituents are N and A, e.g., Ger. *dämondän* ← *Dämon* 'demon' × *mondän* 'chic', or N and V, e.g., Fr. *giraffoler* ← *girafe* 'giraffe' × *raffoler* 'to be crazy about'. Cross-linguistic differences are expected to exist for this parameter.

The fact that blending does not confine itself to strict phonology but, in many cases, involves the graphemic dimension has been noticed by several authors (Grésillon 1984; Cannon 2000 and Gries 2004a). For instance, Cannon (2000: 954) notes that in *smog* the shared 'o' is pronounced differently in *smoke* and *fog*, which implies that the overlap is graphemically licenced by the spelling conventions of the language. Blends uniquely motivated by graphemic aspects are those where the pronunciation of the blend is identical to the pronunciation of the longer source lexeme, e.g., Fr. *fessetival* ← *fesse* 'buttock' × *festival* 'festival', E. *jewbilee* ← *Jew* × *jubilee*. They are sometimes called "inclusive blending", e.g., Ger. *alternatief* ← *alternativ* 'alternative' × *tief* 'deep' (Ronneberger-Sibold 2006). Although they are quite numerous, these blends will be left aside in this article since I consider the phonemic dimension as the fundamental one.

4.3 Ordering issues

Several authors have suggested that the order of occurrence of the source lexemes within a blend is correlated to their length. Kubozono observes that in 86% of the error blends in English and 80% of blends in his database "the righthand source word and the resultant blend form consist, in most instances, of the same number of syllables" (Kubozono 1990: 12). Even though many counter-examples can be found, e.g., Ger. *Denkmaler* ← *Denkmal* 'monument' × *Maler* 'painter', E. *ambisextrous* ← *ambidextrous* × *sex*, Kubozono's observation indicates that the shorter source lexeme tends to come first, a view that is explicitly advocated by Kelly on a basis of a statistical study of 320 two-word English blends (where the source units co-occur sequentially as if they were coordinated, e.g., *scandalous* × *ridiculous* → *scandiculous*). He demonstrates that length effect may combine with frequency and even prototypicality effects, whereby the source lexeme which denotes the most prototypical entity in a given domain appears in the first position, e.g., *spoon, fork* → *spork* vs. *foon (Kelly 1998). In the same vein, Bat-El argues that segmental maximization determines the order of the base lexemes in exocentric blends (i.e. without a semantic head), since it leads speakers to adopt "the number of syllables from the longer rather than the shorter base word" (Bat-El 2006: 67–68). When the number of syllables is identical, segments are substituted for syllables. The maximization of the number of segments makes a lexeme with a complex onset occur first and a lexeme with a complex coda second. Hence the contrast: *glaze* ← *glare* × *gaze* vs. *gare ← *gaze* × *glare*. Piñeros argues contra Kelly that, in Spanish, phonological resemblance between source words is what determines their order in the blend (Piñeros 2004: 226).

The order of elements in blends can also be determined by systemic constraints following from the lexical integrity constraint or from higher level constraints. The Linearity Constraint, which guarantees that the respective order of the subparts of the source lexemes is preserved in the blend, is of the first type. It aptly rules the order of subparts in blends. For instance, since /by/ preceeds /sefal/ in *Bucéphale* and /lobil/ in *Buffalo-Bill*, the only possible blend will be *Bucéphalo-Bill*. Phonotactic constraints belong to the second type and any blend must comply with them, e.g., E. *bang, smash* → *bash* vs. *smang. Since English does not allow the sequence CVC where the two C are nasal (Bat-El 2006: 68), the only licit order is *bang* × *smash*. A very general constraint prohibits a process from having an output phonologically similar to its input (Bauer 1983). It has been restated by Bat-El as the Uniqueness Constraint (Bat-El 1996: 288), e.g., Heb. *mešuxzár* 'reconstructed' × *mešupác* 'renovated' → *mešuxpác* vs. *mešupác, which excludes the reverse order (other examples in Koutita-Kaimaki and Fliatouras 2001: 128). A similar constraint is in force in derivation too, e.g., Fr. *papier* 'paper' (Agent nominal derivation) → *papier-ier* paper-AGT 'paper-maker' (haplology) → *papier 'paper-maker' (the actual form is *papet-ier*).

4.4 Maximization

The semiotic challenge any blend has to face is to allow the listener to recover the source units while having no access to their integral phonological form. Among the means available to the speakers to help them reach this goal, and thereby to further maximization, there are length limitations, segment sharing, similarity in prosodic structure and phonemic/graphemic clues associated with lexical items (the situation is slightly different for blends which are trademarks). Many authors have claimed that limitations are imposed on the length of blends. They must not have more syllables than the longer of two source elements (Cannon 2000), which "facilitates the semantic recoverability of the base word" (Bat-El 2006: 67–68). Piñeros notes that Spanish blends tend to be faithful to the source lexeme that functions as the head with regards to prosodic structure (Piñeros 2004: 219). Exceptions to the above-mentioned proposals are numerous however (cf. B2, D2).

Overlap at the edges is the more common segment sharing phenomenon in blending. Overlap clearly weakens the effect of shortening since it allows one to shorten the outcome without truncating the source lexemes, which makes them readily identifiable, e.g., Ger. *Fantasiegel* ← *Fantasie* 'imagination' × *Siegel* 'seal'. For many authors (Grésillon, Plag, Piñeros), overlap is a crucial feature of blending and for some a typical blend must have an element that has correspondents in both source lexemes (Bat-El, Cannon). The fact that overlapping acts as a driving force in blending can be deduced from several facts: (i) there are more patterns with overlap than without, (ii) these patterns exhibit many examples, (iii) overlap furthers the creation of intercalated blends allowing the insertion of a segment of which it is a subpart, e.g., Fr. *autoimmobiliste* ← *automobiliste* 'driver' × *immobile* 'immobile' auto•im<u>mobile</u>•<<u>mobil</u>>iste, (iv) there are no intercalated blends without overlap (cf. A2, B2; D4 is highly marked), (v) examples without overlap are less numerous and more contrived (in a given language) (cf. also Piñeros 2004: 234–235). However, overlap depends on the language. From a comparative study, Bertinetto concludes that it is more frequent in German and French than in English or Italian (Bertinetto 2001). The overlap need not be completely faithful (Pharies's "imperfect overlapping"). Segments may not be identical in all their features, e.g., Sp. *čándafé* ← *čánda* 'lousy' × *Santafé* 'a Bogota soccer team', čánda•<santa>fé [d ≠ t] (Piñeros 2004: 219), E. *smog*. Even metathesis is licensed in some languages (but not in others as Hebrew), e.g., Fr. *caveaubulaire* ← *caveau* 'sepulcher' × *vocabulaire* 'vocabulary', ca<u>veau</u>•<<u>voca</u>>bulaire [kav ≠ voka] (more examples in Fradin 2000). These data show the importance of taking into account the whole phonological/prosodic structure instead of just the segments. According to Kemmer "speakers are operating with a facility for global pattern-matching that allows similarities on many different dimensions to count, as long as there are many of them" (Kemmer 2003: 77), and the more familiar the patterns, the easier the recovering of the source lexemes is. The necessity of adopting a global viewpoint to deal with the communicative transparency of blends also motivates the introduction of "contour blends" which are characterized by their "overall rhymical contour defined by its number of syllables and the place of its main stress" (Ronneberger-Sibold 2006: 170–173). Contour blends are reminiscent of an earlier proposal stating that blends must retain the same stress that occurs in one of the source words (Cannon 2000).

The idea according to which the match between a blend and its source lexemes has to be globally and not locally evaluated has been taken up again by Gries in a more cognitive perspective (Gries 2004a). Starting from the claim made by Kaunisto that the shorter lexeme in a blend contributes a larger percentage of itself to the blend than the longer lexeme in order to preserve its recognizability (Kaunisto 2000), Gries proposes to calculate how much each source word (SW) contributes to the blend. The contribution is based on the respective number of phonemes or graphemes each SW share with the blend. He argues that the graphemes (phonemes) taken into account should not be limited to the switching point area, as most authors do, but extended to elements similar in the whole SW. According to this method, the contribution of both source lexemes is very similar in *chunnel*, whereas limiting the similarity around the switching point (noted by '|'), the contribution of *channel* drops to 28.6% (only the letters <ch> are shared). For *brunch*, the same method shows that *lunch* contributes 80% of itself to the blend (viz. <unch>) whereas *breakfast* only contributes 22.2% (viz.
). On the basis of a list of 585 English blends, Gries determined statistically the graphemic/phonemic contribution of each SW to the blend as well as their graphemic/phonemic length. He demonstrated that when SW_1 is longer, then SW_2 contributes more, and when SW_2 is longer, the opposite is true (which supports Kaunisto's hypothesis). He also found that both sources contribute equally to the blend when they are equally long. In a second case study, Gries shows that blend coiners choose source words that are more similar to each other than one would expect on the basis of mere chance. This result is very important because it empirically supports, for the first time, the hypothesis that the similarity between source words and the blends plays a decisive role in blending. I refer to Gries's study for more results and details. Gries also investigates whether the coiners of blends make use of the recognition point (RP) of the source words in order to ensure that the blend is neither too long, and hence not very witty, nor too short to be recognized in the first place (Gries 2006). The recognition point is the empirical estimate of the uniqueness point (*UP*) of a word W, the *UP* being "the point at which W can be uniquely identified from a set of candidate words". Three results of this study are worth mentioning here. The first is that for both source words of blends, the average cut-off for SW_1 is nearly exactly the random cut-off point to the *RP*, but the average cut-off point for SW_2 is half an element (letter, phoneme) earlier in comparison with the random

Tab. 15.3: Quantitative contribution of source words in *chunnel* (Gries 2004: 652).

SW$_1$	a		⇒ 1/7 not in the blend	= 14.0 %
channel	c h	|n n e l	⇒ 6/7 in the blend	= 85.7 %
SW$_2$		|u n n e l	⇒ 5/6 in the blend	= 83.3 %
tunnel	t		⇒ 1/6 not in the blend	= 16.7 %

cut-off point. The second is that the data indicate that blends make an extensive use of overlap, which makes the retrieval of source words easier and obviates the need for adhering to the *RP* for SW$_2$. The third is that "complex clippings" (e.g., *agitprop*) behave totally differently (cf. section 5.3). Their cut-off points to the *RP* are three times as high as the ones expected by chance, and they greatly underuse overlap (Gries 2006: 547–548).

4.5 Phonological splicing

4.5.1 Fine tuning

Although quantitative approaches to lexeme formation offer invaluable insights into the splicing of blends, some of these splicings involve phonological intricacies that lie beyond their reach for the time being. Those tied to syllable structure are the case in point. Assuming constituents On(set), Nu(cleus), Co(da), syllable structure can be (i) flat viz. [On Nu Co], (ii) left-branching viz. [[$_{Bo(dy)}$ On Nu] Co]], or (iii) right-branching [On [$_{Rh(yme)}$ Nu Co]]. Contrary to English, which by far favors structure (iii) (but see Pierrehumbert 2012), Italian gives a very strong advantage to final elements over initial ones and is therefore not oriented towards structure (iii) (Bertinetto 1999). The major switching point in Italian natural blends is localized at the juncture of two whole syllables. The other major switching point is after the On of SW$_1$, e.g., *polstrada* ← *polizia* 'police' × *strada* 'road', po.l<i.zia>•stra.da, which in very few cases corresponds to structure (iii), e.g., *farmitalia* ← *farmacia* 'pharmacy' × *Italia* 'Italy', far.m<a.ci.a>•i.ta.lia. In conclusion, Italian would be weakly oriented toward type (iii), English strongly, and Korean would illustrate type (ii). In a subsequent comparative study Bertinetto (2001) shows that in lexical blends without overlap English prefers structure (iii), which is the second choice for the other languages. For additional results illustrating the interaction of fine-grained phonological parameters with the switching point, I refer to Bertinetto (2001).

4.5.2 Extended haplology

Haplologic overlap is not the exclusivity of blends. This phenomenon also occurs in learned compounding, e.g., Fr. *minéralogie* 'mineralogy' ← *minéral-o-logie* 'mineral-RFX-logy' (Corbin and Plénat 1992). In this case, the suppressed part is limited to the adjacent edges of base lexemes, a fact that can be attributed to the contiguity constraint: haplology is limited to contiguous segments. In Fradin, Montermini and Plénat (2009), it has been claimed that in French, and probably some other languages, a key property of blending is the extension of haplology to non-contiguous segments. The behaviour of many blends stems from the relaxation of the contiguity constraint. Let's take a few examples. When the source lexemes have an identical segment on opposite edges, as in (3a), they can be combined in the two ways illustrated in (3b, c). In (3b), the two similar segments overlap and a blend of type D1 obtains. In (3c) however, no overlap is possible and the result is not a blend but just two lexemes stuck together. *Mystiquoptimiste* is unpalatable (too long, unwitty) and runs afoul the constraints we have seen up to now (sections 4.3, 4.4).

(3)   a. *optimiste* /ɔpti̱mist/ 'optimist', *mystique* /mi̱stik/ 'mystical'
      b. *optimiste + mystique* /ɔpti̱mist + mi̱stik/ → *optimystique*
      c. *mystique + optimiste* /mi̱stik + ɔpti̱mist/ → **mystiquoptimiste*

When the source lexemes have an identical segment located on the same side, they can combine in the two ways illustrated in (4b–c). While (4b) is a perfect and attested blend, (4c) is markedly worse and unattested.

(4)   a. *chérubin* /ʃerybɛ̱̃/ 'cherubim', *bambin* /bãbɛ̱̃/ 'small child'
      b. *chérubin + bambin* /ʃerybɛ̃ + bãbɛ̃/ → *chérubambin*
      c. *bambin + chérubin* /bãbɛ̃ + ʃerybɛ̃/ → **banchérubin*

The fact that examples such as (4b) exist supports the idea that the internal segment (<bin>, /bɛ̃/) has been deleted under identity with the final segment of the other source lexeme. The hypothesis defended in Fradin, Montermini and Plénat (2009) is that this deletion is an instance of haplology, which can take place because the Contiguity constraint has been relaxed: in *chérubambin*, the segment /chéru/ is separated from segment /bin/ by one syllable (/bam/), whereas in (3b) the segment /opti/ is not separated from segment /mist/ even in the blend (for convenience, I use plain writing conventions). The very low acceptability of (4c) shows that the violation of the contiguity constraint cannot be extented to two or more syllables. The same pattern of acceptability is observed with other blends based on source lexemes ending in similar segments, e.g., *marron* 'chesnut', *potiron* 'pumpkin' → *potimarron* vs. ***mapotiron*. The same phenomenon is observed when the source lexemes share the same beginning: *cinéma* 'cinema', *cyber* 'cyber' → *cybernéma*, c̲y.ber•<c̲i>.né.ma vs. **sinémaber,* c̲i.né.ma•<c̲y>.ber. It has been pointed out that source lexemes beginning with a similar segment cannot yield acceptable blends in French (Fradin 2000: 28, fn. 27). Actually three cases have to be distinguished. The first one has to do with examples that violate the contiguity constraint in the same way as **banchérubin* does, e.g., *imbécile* 'stupid', *important* 'important' → **imbécileportant*, vs. **importantbécile*. The part belonging to the second source lexeme is too far from the initial segment of the blend. The second case is illustrated by *cobaye* 'guinea-pig', *copain* 'pal' → **cobayepain*, c̲o.baye•<c̲o>.pain and **copainbaye*, c̲o.pain•<c̲o>.baye. Since the contiguity constraint cannot be invoked (cf. *chérubambin*), it can be suggested that the remaining part of the second source lexeme is too small (one syllable) for the latter to be identified. Maximization would require two consecutive syllables at least from each source lexeme (two-syllable constraint). This constraint also accounts for the contrast between *Rocardbespierre* vs. **Robespierrecard*, formed on the name of political leaders *Robespierre* and *Rocard*. The third case concerns blends formed on source lexemes such as *citoyen* 'citizen', *cynique* 'cynical'. Whereas the unacceptability of **citoyenique* /s̲i.twa.jɛ̃•<s̲i>.nik/ is predicted on the basis of both the contiguity and the two-syllable constraints, the unacceptability of **cyniquetoyen* /s̲i.nik•<s̲i>.twa.jɛ̃/ is unaccounted for. A possible explanation (which I originally owe to E. Ronneberger-Sibold) could be that after the first two syllables the word *cynique* has been identified and the procedure stops in spite of the fact that the part corresponding to the second source lexeme has not been decoded. This would also explain the unacceptability of Fr. **mélassemé* vs. *mémélasse* ← *mémé* 'grandma' × *mélasse* 'muck'. German seems to behave as French for source lexemes exhibiting parallel edge similarity, e.g., *Laufbahnmasche* ← *Laufbahn* 'career' × *Laufmasche* 'ladder, run'. For reasons that cannot be discussed here, some intercalated blends may not obey the contiguity constraint, e.g., Fr. *emmiterrantouflé* ← *emmitouflé* 'wrapped up' × *Mitterrand*, even though most do. In all examples involving similar initial vs. final segments, the linearity constraint is never violated and therefore cannot be adduced to account for the observed impossible cases. To sum up, the fact that some blends are unacceptable proves that everything is not possible in blending contrary to what is sometimes assumed. The discussion of French data has shown that, all in all, blends are rather faithful to their source lexemes as the contiguity constraint itself shows: when it is infringed, it tends to be minimally infringed (more in Fradin, Montermini and Plénat 2009).

5 Semantic conditioning

5.1 General considerations

All types of semantic relations observed with compounds in a given language should be found with blends. Actually, there are even more, since blending puts no ban on the categories that may combine, in contradistinction to compounding (section 2). The formal pattern of blends, i.e. the way the (splinters of) source lexemes are phonologically combined, is not supposed to have an impact on their interpretation and it has none (section 2). On the contrary, the category of the source lexemes plays a crucial role. In brief, the semantic combinations we come across are those usually allowed by grammar with units exhibiting the categories in question. Some of these combinations correspond to the linguistic material that (conceptual) blends, put forward by cognitive linguists, are made of (Fauconnier and Turner 2002). Finally, the semiotic perspective according to which a blend is coined seems to have a bearing on the way it is interpreted. At least two such "semiotic perspectives" come to mind. According to the first, the scope of blending is to give a name to (new) objects or substances; according to the second, it amounts to introducing a word into the discourse without any particular prerogative except to be a witty substitute of an ordinary lexical unit. From the first perspective, blends may be coined and used outside discourse, simply as objects' names occurring on labels, catalogs or posters. Blends of this type are frequent in advertising, e.g., Fr. *Olympiaf* [name of a show] ← *Olympia* [name of music hall] × E. *Piaf*, and some of them function as trademarks (Ronneberger-Sibold 2006). Blends created with the communicative purpose of providing an entity with a name are eagerly promoted by language planners and generally have a coordinative reading, e.g., E. *quasar, pulsar*, Fr. *rurbain* 'rural urban'.

5.2 Semantic patterns

Four major patterns of interpretation can be tentatively proposed for blends. In the first, the two lexemes are on an equal footing and their semantic import is equivalent. This type corresponds to co-compounding (dvandvas). But whereas co-compounds express a natural coordination of items closely related by meaning and forming a conceptual unit (Wälchli 2005: 5), the coordination in blends is always artificial and the units are fused instead of being kept conceptually distinct. Even though blends are not co-compounds strictly speaking, some of the meanings Wälchli mentions for them are widespread in blends as the additive and synonym readings.

Tab. 15.4: Pattern (I). Coordinated interpretation.

		Lg	Blend	P'_Q'(x)
a)	A	Fr.	*optimystique*	optimist'_mystical'(x)
		Gr.	*psidrós*	slender'_fat'(x)
	N	E.	*smog*	smoke'_fog'(x)
		Heb.	*šezifarsék*	plum'_peach'(x)
	V	E.	*smothercate*	to smother'_to suffocate'(x)
		Fr.	*bavardîner*	to chat'_to dinner'(x)
	PN	E.	*Oxbridge*	Oxford'_Cambridge'(x)
		Fr.	*Bokhassan II*	Bokassa'_Hassan II'(x)
b)	N	Gr.	*frímos*	horror'_terror'(x)

a) additive reading: the blend denotes "pairs, each consisting of the parts A and B" (Wälchli 2005: 137). More generally, the meaning of the blend is the union of the meanings of its source lexemes (Bauer 2008). But for categories other than Ns, this union may be controversial. Here are the glosses of the newly mentioned blends: Gr. *psirós* ← *psilós* 'slender' × *xodrós* 'fat'; Heb. *šezifarsék* 'nectarine' ← *šezík* 'plum' × *ʔafarsék* 'peach'.

b) synonym reading: the parts A, B and the whole blend have almost the same meaning (Wälchli 2005: 143), e.g., Gr. *frímos* 'more than terror' ← *fríci* 'horror' × *trómos* 'terror'.

The second pattern (II) corresponds to intersective meaning. Such interpretation occurs in what Wälchli (2005) calls appositional compounds, e.g., Ger. *berühmt-berüchtigt* 'famous and ill-famed'. The semantics of many blends follows this pattern.

Tab. 15.5: Pattern (II). Intersective interpretation.

	Lg	Blend	P'(x) ∧ Q'(x)
A, N	E.	*fantabulous*	fantastic'(x) ∧ fabulous'(x)
	Fr.	*autoimmobiliste*	car_driver'(x) ∧ immobile'(x)
	Sp.	*brujeres*	witch'(x) ∧ women'(x)
V	Gr.	*saxlaburízo*	to talk_nonsense'(x) ∧ to make_jokes'(x)

Glosses: Sp. *brujeres* ← *bruja* 'witch' × *mujeres* 'women'; Gr. *saxlaburízo* 'to make nonsense jokes' ← *saxláro* 'to talk nonsense' × *kalaburízo* 'to make jokes' (Koutita-Kaimaki and Fliatouras 2001: 123–124; cf. also Ralli 2009).

Pattern (III) includes blends where one of the source lexemes provides the second lexeme with a predicate of which this second lexeme is an argument. The predicate can be the source lexeme itself or a verb inferable from the source lexeme. Variable *e* is Davidson's (1967) eventuality variable.

Tab. 15.6: Pattern (III). Argumental interpretation.

	Lg	Blend	P'(x_1, ..., x_n, e) ∧ Q'(x_i)
N, N	Ger.	Witzenschaft	science'(x) ∧ object_of'(x, y) ∧ joke'(y)
N, V	E.	sneakret	to sneak'(x, y, e) ∧ secret'(y)
	Fr.	élevache	to breed'(x, y, e) ∧ cow'(y)

Glosses: Ger. *Witzenschaft* (E. Jandl) ← *Witz* 'joke' × *Wissenschaft* 'science'.

The fourth pattern (see Tab. 15.7) involves a causal relation between an event, of which one of the source lexemes is an argument, and a causer, which may be an agent or another event. The relation can appropriately be recast in terms of a result relation, but for simplicity reasons I refrain from modifying the proposed formulation.

Tab. 15.7: Pattern (IV). Causal interpretation.

Lg	Blend	CAUSE(x, e) ∧ P'(y_1, ..., y_n, e) ∧ Q'(x)
Fr.	s'étrangueuler	CAUSE(e_1, e_2) ∧ to have_a_row'(x, y, e_1) ∧ to choke'(x, e_2)
Heb.	ricpáz	CAUSE(x, e_1) ∧ to shine'(y, e_1) ∧ floor'(y)

Glosses: Fr. *s'étrangueuler* ← *s'engueuler* 'to have a row' × *s'étrangler* 'to choke'; Heb. *ricpáz* 'floor cleaning detergent' ← *ricpá* 'floor' × *páz* 'shining'.

A fifth minor pattern (see Tab. 15.8) involving the equative relation 'isa' could be added to the preceding relations. This relation makes explicit the class of the referent of the second source lexeme, which hence must be a proper noun. It has a strong connotative flavour since it introduces a side predication, actually an implicature (Potts 2005), about the referent denoted by the blend. Using *Chirouette* the speaker both (i) refers to Chirac and (ii) says that he is somebody who always changes his mind (metaphorical sense attached to *girouette* 'weathercock'). Such blends illustrate the conceptual integration exhibited by conceptual blends (according to cognitive linguistics), where the blend's denotatum belongs to a mental space sharing properties of the two input spaces containing the source referents (Fauconnier and Turner 2002; Kemmer 2003).

Tab. 15.8: Pattern (V). The equative interpretation.

	Lg	Blend	isa'(x, y) ∧ P'(x) ∧ Q'(y)
N, N	Fr.	*Chirouette*	isa'(x, y) ∧ Chirac'(x) ∧ weathercock'(y)

Two final remarks. First, as evidenced long ago by Lehrer (1996), blends are more easily identified in context, and when the context proves to be indispensable, it means that the blend is too opaque to stand by itself (cf. *magalog* (magazine, catalog) quoted in Brdar-Szabó and Brdar 2008: 175). Second, blending permits interpretive combinations not allowed by grammatical morphology. Fr. *élevache* (*élevage, vache*) is a case in point since N-N compounds such as Ger. *Schiffbau* 'shipbuilding', where one of the Ns is a deverbal of which the semantic content of the other N is an argument, are generally not well-formed in Romance languages, e.g., Fr. **traitement-données* 'data processing' (although the model *trasporto latte* 'milk transportation' is speading in Italian).

6 Delimiting blending

6.1 Blending and speech errors

Gries has shown that speech-error blends (also called interference blends, or contaminations), e.g., E. *stragedy* ← *strategy* × *tragedy* differ significantly from intentional blends in a way predicted by Kaunisto's hypothesis (section 4.4; Gries 2004a, b). This reason is sufficient to treat them separately (cf. also Pharies 1987).

6.2 Neoclassical compounds

Blends differ from neoclassical compounds, e.g., *anthropomorphous* in several properties. In the majority of cases the sources for the former are lexemes belonging to the native language, while the parts stem from the classical languages in the case of neoclassical compounds; the former have no interfix while the latter generally have one, e.g., /o/ in *cardi-o-logy*; their parts may be absolute forms, e.g., Ger. *spät* in *Spätnik* ← *spät* 'late' × *Sputnik* whereas neoclassical compounds' forms are conjunct forms, e.g., E. *-logy*; the order of constitutive elements is ruled by the phonology in blends (section 4.3) but by the semantics in neoclassical compounds, e.g., E. *techn-o-logy, pyr-o-technics*.

6.3 Blending and shortening

Since blending involves shortening (section 4.1), shortening techniques used by speakers (cf. article 13 on clipping) have often been considered non-distinct in blending and elsewhere (Bauer 1988: 40). These techniques come in two types, depending on whether they take the formal structure of the source into account (acronymy) or not (clipping). While the source of shortening is normally a well-formed existing expression (word or phrase), e.g., *lab* ← *laboratory*, *VAT* ← *value added tax*, the same does not necessarily hold for blends: neither *fantastic fabulous* (cf. *fantabulous*), nor *sneak secret* (cf. *sneakret*) are possible English phrases. Since shortening only affects the phonological or graphemic aspect of the sign, the shortened expression denotes the same entity as this source (Kreidler 2000: 959). This is not true of blends, which combine the meaning of their sources in various ways (section 4.2). We have then principled reasons to distinguish blends from any variety of shortenings.

Acronyms are formed from the initial letters of a phrase used as a name. Only acronyms that can be pronounced as words (rather than by letter-naming) could possibly be considered as blends. Taking advantage of this, many authors assume that, e.g., E. *modem* ← *mod<ulator>, dem<odulator>*, It. *afoterm* ← *afo<no>* 'aphone', *term<ico>* 'thermic', are blends. But these constructs are syllabic acronyms (Bertinetto 2001: 19) rather than blends (or clipped compounds (Cacchiani 2011)) because (i) they have the same meaning as their source, (ii) they do not behave like blends (cf. section 4.4), and (iii) "they do not leave enough of the etymon intact so that it can be recognizable" (Pharies 1987: 283). While acronyms can be derivational bases, e.g., Fr. *ONU* 'UNO' → *onus-ien* ONU-AZR, blends cannot.

A clipping is an expression resulting from the suppression of a phonological subpart of a word, the meaning of the source word being kept intact. The process of clipping exists in two versions, fore-clipping (apocope), e.g., *professor* → *prof* and back-clipping (aphaeresis), e.g., Fr. *capitaine* 'captain' → *pitaine*. Phonologically, clipping is the mapping of a base onto a template which coincides with the minimal prosodic word of the language (Kilani-Schoch 1996; Plénat 1984; Thornton 1996). This is illustrated by Italian *pattu* ← *pattum-iera* 'garbage bin', where the minimal word for nouns is a disyllabic trochaic foot ending in a vowel. The minimal word requirement predicts that clippings will always be absolute forms, which they are. This is not the case of the constitutive subparts of blends: E. /unch/ cf. *brunch*, /sm/ cf. *smog*, It. /llo/ cf. *zebrallo* ← *ze.bra* 'zebra' × *ca.val.lo* 'horse' do not constitute minimal words. The suppression observed in blends originates neither in mapping onto a template, as in clipping, nor in circumscription, as in prosodic morphology (cf. McCarthy and Lombardi 1991), but in a mere truncation. To that extent it is misleading to claim that blends are formed through clipping as some authors do (Lehrer 1996; Clas 2001).

The so-called "stump compounds", illustrated in (5) with Russian data, consist in the juxtaposition of two or more words, of which one at least is shortened (Mel'čuk 1997: 93). The shortened elements are mapped onto the template of the minimal prosodic word in Russian, which is a bimoraic (closed) syllable (Arcodia and Montermini 2012). Only apocope seems to be allowed.

(5) a. *sovxoz* ← *sov<et-skoe> xoz<jajstvo>* soviet-AZR farm 'Soviet farm'
 b. *zavsektorom* ← *zav<ed-ujuščij> sektor-om* to_direct-ACT.PRSPT sector-INS 'sector director'

The fact that a prosodic mapping takes place indicates that these constructs are not blends. They should rather be considered reduced phrases since, as in acronyms, (i) the order of the elements follows the order of the constituents of the source, and (ii) they have no meaning of their own.

6.4 Blending and secreted affixation

Blending has often been endowed with the capacity to trigger processes leading to the apparition of new elements, such as E. *-burger, -gate, -(a)holic* or Fr. *-stroïka* (Cannon 2000: 734; Bauer 1983: 236). These elements have received various names: *splinters* (Lehrer 1996), *fractomorphemes* (Tournier 1985).

(6) a. *Irangate, Inkhatagate, Westlandgate, Monicagate, Rubygate* ...
 b. *Workaholic, spendaholic, shopaholic, cleanaholic, fruitaholic* ...

Many authors assume that there is a genetic link between these elements and blends, the clearest expression of which is given by Tournier: "We remark that *telecast* is actually a blend of *television broadcast*. [...] the difference between a fractomorpheme and a part of a blend is that the part of a blend may occur only in one form (e.g., *og* in *smog*). It becomes a fractomorpheme when it is reused in other forms" (Tournier 1985: 87, fn. 7; my translation). This hypothesis adequately captures the idea that blends are by nature at odds with series. However, it supposes that the elements ending the constructs in (6) arose out of blending, which is wrong: none of the forms in (6a) has a two-lexeme source, the second lexeme of which would be *Watergate*. Facing *telecast*, a production pattern such as *Irangate* ← *Iran* × *Watergate* does not correspond to reality. The elements under discussion originate instead from a unique model lexeme (*Watergate, alcoholic*) through a process of secretion. For this reason they will be called secreted affixes. Secretion can be characterized as the combination of three operations. On the phonological plane, a shortening takes place whereby the output is associated with a segmental string F_2 which is a substring of the input string F_1: (i) $|F_2| < |F_1|$, e.g., /watergate/ → /gate/. On the semantic plane, an operation of selection keeps certain salient meaning units of the meaning of the input lexeme and discards others (this is secretion proper (cf. Warren 1990: 119)): (ii) $|S_2| < |S_1|$, (S_i = semantic unit). In parallel, (iii) an operation of abstraction replaces one argument constant by a variable, transforming the expression into a function (i.e. a lambda expression) (see Fradin 2000). In the present case, this function would be the semantic correlate of the exponent -gate. The secretion process results in new lexeme formation rules which then apply to any relevant lexemes, e.g., IRAN. Hence *Irangate* = 'scandal connected with Iran involving high-ranking people'. Secreted affixation is therefore markedly distinct from blending, since neither operation (ii) nor (iii) is involved in blending. It is also distinct from shortening, insofar as both only share the abbreviation operation (i). Secreted affixation, like all derivational processes, crucially depends on series of forms showing identical correlations, such as (6), since abstraction presupposes repetition. Jespersen is the first one who pointed out the phenomenon of secretion and gave it a name (Jespersen 1922: XIX §13).

6.5 Concealed compounding

Repetition obviously does not always result in a secreted affixation rule. In (7), substrings -*ware*, -*tique*, *san*- are not secreted affixes but subparts of full-fledged lexemes, respectively SOFTWARE, INFORMATIQUE 'computer science', SANITARNYJ 'sanitary' (Mel'čuk 1997: 93).

(7)   a. *fontware, freeware, groupware, shareware, vapourware* ...   English
       b. *bureautique, domotique, éducatique, ludotique, monnétique* ...   French
       c. *sanvrač, sanpunkt, sanobrabotka, sanprosveščenie, santexnika* ...   Russian

Actually, this is the situation we had with *telecast*, where *tele-* abbreviates *television*, e.g., *telefilm, telegenic, teleplay, televisual*. Contrary to what is often claimed, the constructs in (7) cannot be blends because they constitute series and blends are antithetic to series. The only property they share with blending is (i) i.e. shortening. They do not involve secretion proper nor, by the same token, abstraction since the meaning of the substring is equivalent to that of the whole source lexeme. This is confirmed by the fact that their interpretation is the combination of the meaning of the two source lexemes, on the model of what happens in compounding, e.g., E. *fontware* 'software for fonts'; Fr. *bureautique* 'computer science devoted to office'; Rus. *sanvrač* 'sanitary doctor', etc. For this reason, these constructs have been dubbed concealed compounds (more on this in Fradin 2000: 47). Some of them may stem from series based on a source lexeme which is a reduced phrase (Mel'čuk 1996: 58) such as (5b) or even (5a), e.g., Rus. *profsojuz* ← *professional'nyj sojuz* professional union 'trade-union' abbreviated as *prof* in *profsobranie* 'trade-union meeting', *profrabotnik* 'trade-union worker', etc. Concealed compounding is quite common in many languages, especially in technological or administrative speech. In Chinese, this phenomenon seems to be widespread in ordinary language too (Arcodia and Montermini 2012), e.g., *fēijī* fly-machine 'airplane' → *jīchǎng* machine-field 'airport', *jīcāng* machine-cabin 'airplane cabin', where *jī* stands for 'airplane'.

Abbreviations

ACT.PRSPT active present participle
AZR   adjectivizer
INS   instrumental
RFX   interfix

7 References

Algeo, John (ed.) (1991): *Fifty Years among the New Words. A Dictionary of Neologisms*. Cambridge: Cambridge University Press.

Arcodia, Giorgio Francesco and Fabio Montermini (2012): Are reduced compounds compounds? Morphological and prosodic properties of reduced compounds. In: Pierre J.-L. Arnaud, François Maniez and Vincent Renner (eds.), *Cross-Disciplinary Perspectives on Lexical Blending*, 93–114. Berlin/New York: Mouton de Gruyter.

Aronoff, Mark and Nanna Fuhrhop (2002): Restricting suffix combinations in German and English: Closing suffixes and the monosuffix constraint. *Natural Language & Linguistic Theory* 20(3): 451–490.

Baayen, Harald R. (1992): Quantitative aspects of morphological productivity. In: Geert Booij and Jaap van Marle (eds.), *Yearbook of Morphology 1991*, 109–149. Dordrecht: Kluwer.

Baayen, Harald R. (1993): On frequency, transparency and productivity. In: Geert Booij and Jaap van Marle (eds.), *Yearbook of Morphology 1992*, 181–208. Dordrecht: Kluwer.

Baayen, Harald R. and Rochelle Lieber (1991): Productivity and English derivation: A corpus-based study. *Linguistics* 29(5): 801–843.

Bat-El, Outi (1996): Selecting the best of the worst: The grammar of Hebrew blends. *Phonology* 13: 283–328.

Bat-El, Outi (2006): Blends. In: Keith Brown (ed.), *Encyclopedia of Language & Linguistics*. Vol. 2, 2nd ed., 66–70. Oxford: Elsevier.
Bauer, Laurie (1983): *English Word-Formation*. Cambridge: Cambridge University Press.
Bauer, Laurie (1988): *Introducing Linguistic Morphology*. Edinburgh: Edinburgh University Press.
Bauer, Laurie (2008): Dvandvas. *Word Structure* 1(1): 1–18.
Bertinetto, Pier Marco (1999): Psycholinguistic evidence for syllable geometry: Italian and beyond. In: John R. Rennison and Klaus Kühnhammer (eds.), *Phonologica 1996. Syllables!?*, 1–28. The Hague: Holland Academic Graphics.
Bertinetto, Pier Marco (2001): Blends and syllabic structure: A four-fold comparison. In: Mercé Lorente, Núria Alturo, Emil Boix, Maria-Rosa Lloret and Lluis Payrató (eds.), *La gramática i la semántica en l'estudi de la variació*, 59–112. Barcelona: Promociones y Publicaciones Universitarias, S.A.
Bonami, Olivier, Gilles Boyé and Françoise Kerleroux (2009): L'allomorphie radicale et la relation flexion-construction. In: Bernard Fradin, Françoise Kerleroux and Marc Plénat (eds.), *Aperçus de morphologie française*, 103–125. Saint-Denis: Presses Universitaires de Vincennes.
Booij, Geert (2002): *The Morphology of Dutch*. Oxford: Oxford University Press.
Booij, Geert (2005): *The Grammar of Words*. Oxford: Oxford University Press.
Brdar-Szabó, Rita and Mario Brdar (2008): On the marginality of lexical blending. *Jezikoslovije* 9(1–2): 171–194.
Cacchiani, Silvia (2011): On unfamiliar Italian lexical blends from names and nouns. *Linguistica* 51: 105–120.
Cannon, Garland (1986): Blends in English word formation. *Linguistics* 24(4): 725–753.
Cannon, Garland (2000): Blending. In: Geert Booij, Christian Lehmann and Joachim Mugdan (eds.), *Morphology. An International Handbook on Inflection and Word-Formation*. Vol. 1, 952–956. Berlin/New York: de Gruyter.
Clas, André (2001): *Abeille* et *rose-épine*! Mots-valises et méronymie. *Cahiers de Lexicologie* 78(1): 99–106.
Corbin, Danielle and Marc Plénat (1992): Note sur l'haplologie des mots construits. *Langue Française* 96: 101–112.
Davidson, Donald (1967): The logical form of action sentences. In: Nicholas Rescher (ed.), *The Logic of Decision and Action*, 81–120. Hertford: University of Pittsburgh.
Dressler, Wolfgang U. (2000): Extragrammatical vs. marginal morphology. In: Ursula Doleschal and Anna Thornton (eds.), *Extragrammatical and Marginal Morphology*, 1–10. München: LINCOM Europa.
Enarsson, Anna (2006): *New Blends in the English Language*. Karlstad: Karlstads universitet.
Fauconnier, Gilles and Mark Turner (2002): *The Way We Think. Conceptual Blending and the Mind's Hidden Complexities*. New York: Basic Books.
Fradin, Bernard (2000): Combining forms, blends and related phenomena. In: Ursula Doleschal and Anna Thornton (eds.), *Extragrammatical and Marginal Morphology*, 11–59. München: LINCOM Europa.
Fradin, Bernard, Fabio Montermini and Marc Plénat (2009): Morphologie grammaticale et extragrammaticale. In: Bernard Fradin, Françoise Kerleroux and Marc Plénat (eds.), *Aperçus de morphologie du français*, 21–45. Saint-Denis: Presses Universitaires de Vincennes.
Friedrich, Cornelia (2008): Kontamination – Zur Form und Funktion eines Wortbildungstyps im Deutschen. Ph.D. dissertation, Universität Erlangen-Nürnberg. http://www.opus.ub.uni-erlangen.de/opus/volltexte/2008/1174/ [last access 5 Feb 2012].
Gaeta, Livio and Davide Ricca (2003): Italian prefixes and productivity: A quantitative approach. *Acta Linguistica Hungarica* 50: 89–108.

Galisson, Robert (1987): Les mots-valises et les dictionnaires de parodie comme moyen de perfectionnement en langue et culture française. *Etudes de linguistique appliquée* 67: 57–118.
Grésillon, Almuth (1984): *La règle et le monstre. Le mot-valise*. Tübingen: Niemeyer.
Gries, Stefan Th. (2004a): Shouldn't it be *breaklunch*? A quantitative analysis of blend structure in English. *Linguistics* 42(3): 639–667.
Gries, Stefan Th. (2004b): Some characteristics of English morphological blends. In: Mary A. Andronis, Erin Debenport, Anne Pycha and KeikoYoshimura (eds.), *Papers from the 38th Regional Meeting of the Chicago Linguistics Society*. Vol. 2: *The Panels*, 201–216. Chicago: Chicago Linguistic Society.
Gries, Stefan Th. (2006): Cognitive determinants of subtractive word formation: A corpus-based perpective. *Cognitive Linguistics* 17(4): 535–558.
Hohenhaus, Peter (2005): Lexicalization and institutionalization. In: Pavol Štekauer and Rochelle Lieber (eds.), *Handbook of Word-Formation*, 353–373. Dordrecht: Springer.
Hong, Sung-Hoon (2005): An optimality theoretic analysis to English blends. *Korean Journal of Linguistics* 30(3): 535–557.
Iljasova, Svetlana V. and Ljudmila P. Amiri (2009): *Jazykovaja igra v kommunikativnom prostranstve SMI i reklamy*. Moskva: Flinta Nauka.
Jadacka, Hanna (2005): *System słowotwórczy polszczyzny (1945–2000)*. Warszawa: Wydawnictwo naukowe PWN.
Janko-Trinickaja, Nadija (1975): Mežduslovnoe naloženie. In: Elena A. Zemskaja (ed.), *Razvitie sovremennogo russkogo jazyka. Slovoobrazovanie. Členimost' slova*, 254–258. Moskva: Nauka.
Jespersen, Otto (1922): *Growth and Structure of the English Language*. Garden City, NY: Doubleday & Company.
Kaunisto, Mark (2000): Relations and proportions in English blend words. In: *Conference Handbook of the Fourth Conference of the International Quantitative Linguistics Association. Prague – August 24–26*. Prague: Qualico.
Kelly, Michael H. (1998): To "brunch" or to "brench": Some aspects of blend structure. *Linguistics* 36(3): 579–590.
Kemmer, Suzanne (2003): Schemas and lexical blends. In: Hubert Cuyckens, Thomas Berg, Renée Dirven and Klaus-Uwe Panther (eds.), *Motivation in Language. From Case Grammar to Cognitive Lingustics. A Festschrift for Günter Radden*, 69–97. Amsterdam/Philadelphia: Benjamins.
Kilani-Schoch, Marianne (1996): Syllable and foot in French clipping. In: Bernhard Hurch and Richard A. Rhodes (eds.), *Natural Phonology. The State of the Art*, 135–152. Berlin /New York: Mouton de Gruyter.
Koutita-Kaimaki, Myrto and Asimakis Fliatouras (2001): Blends in Greek dialects: A morphosemantics analysis. In: Angela Ralli, Brian D. Joseph and Mark Janse (eds.), *Proceedings of the First International Conference of Modern Greek Dialects and Linguistic Theory*, 117–130. Patras: University of Patras.
Kreidler, Charles W. (2000): Clipping and acronymy. In: Geert Booij, Christian Lehmann and Joachim Mugdan (eds.), *Morphology. An International Handbook on Inflection and Word-Formation*. Vol. 1, 956–963. Berlin/New York: de Gruyter.
Kubozono, Haruo (1990): Phonological constraints on blending in English as a case for phonology-morphology interface. In: Geert Booij and Jaap van Marle (eds.), *Yearbook of Morphology 1990*, 1–20. Dordrecht: Kluwer.
Lehrer, Adrienne (1996): Identifying and interpreting blends: An experimental approach. *Cognitive Linguistics* 7(4): 359–390.
Léturgie, Arnaud (2011): Un cas d'extragrammaticalité particulier: Les amalgames lexicaux. *Linguistica* 51: 87–104.

Léturgie, Arnaud (2012): Prédire la structure des amalgames lexicaux du français. In: Frank Neveu, Valéria Muni-Toke, Peter Blumenthal, Thomas Kingler, Pierluigi Ligas, Sophie Prévost and Sandra Teston-Bonnard (eds.), *3ᵉ Congrès Mondial de Linguistique Française – Lyon, 4–7 juillet 2012*, 1351–1368. Paris: ILF/EDP Science. Available at: www.linguistiquefrancaise.org [last access 20 Jan 2015].

Matthews, Peter Hugoe (1991): *Morphology*. 2nd ed. Cambridge: Cambridge University Press.

McCarthy, John (1986): OCP effects: Gemination and antigemination. *Linguistic Inquiry* 17(2): 207–263.

McCarthy, John J. and Linda Lombardi (1991): Prosodic circumscription in Choctaw morphology. *Phonology* 8(1): 37–71.

Mel'čuk, Igor A. (1993): *Cours de morphologie générale. Première partie: Le mot*. Vol. 1. Montréal: Presses de l'Université de Montréal – CNRS Editions.

Mel'čuk, Igor A. (1996): *Cours de morphologie générale. Troisième partie: moyens morphologiques. Quatrième partie: syntactiques morphologiques*. Vol. 3. Montréal: Presses de l'Université de Montréal – CNRS Editions.

Mel'čuk, Igor A. (1997): *Cours de morphologie générale. Cinquième partie: signes morphologiques*. Vol. 4. Montréal: Presses de l'Université de Montréal – CNRS Editions.

Montermini, Fabio (2007): Hypocoristiques et minimalité en russe. In: Elisabeth Delais-Roussarie and Laurence Labrune (eds.), *Des sons et des sens: données et modèles en phonologie et en morphologie*, 198–213. Paris: Lavoisier/Hermès.

Müller, Peter O. and Cornelia Friedrich (2011): Kontamination. In: Hilke Elsen and Sascha Michel (eds.), *Wortbildung im Deutschen zwischen Sprachsystem und Sprachgebrauch. Perspektiven – Analysen – Anwendungen*, 73–107. Stuttgart: ibidem.

Neef, Martin (2009): IE, Germanic: German. In: Rochelle Lieber and Pavol Štekauer (eds.), *The Oxford Handbook of Compounding*, 386–399. Oxford: Oxford University Press.

Olsen, Susan (2000): Composition. In: Geert Booij, Christian Lehmann and Joachim Mugdan (eds.) *Morphology. An International Handbook on Inflection and Word-Formation*. Vol. 1, 897–916. Berlin/New York: de Gruyter.

Pharies, David A. (1987): Blending in Spanish word-formation. *Romanistisches Jahrbuch* 38: 271–289.

Pierrehumbert, Janet (2012): The dynamic lexicon. In: Abigail Cohn, Mary K. Huffman and Cécile Fougeron (eds.), *Handbook of Laboratory Phonology*, 173–183. Oxford: Oxford University Press.

Pierrehumbert, Janet and Rami Nair (1995): Word games and syllable structure. *Language and Speech* 38(1): 77–114.

Piñeros, Carlos-Eduardo (2004): The creation of portmanteaus in the extragrammatical morphology of Spanish. *Probus* 16(2): 203–240.

Plag, Ingo (2003): *Word-Formation in English*. Cambridge: Cambridge University Press.

Plénat, Marc (1984): Toto, Fanfa, Totor et même Guiguitte sont des ANARS. In: François Dell, Daniel Hirst and Jean-Roger Vergnaud (eds.), *Forme sonore du langage. Structure des représentations en phonologie*, 161–181. Paris: Hermann.

Plénat, Marc (1995): Une approche prosodique de la morphologie du verlan. *Lingua* 95(1): 97–129.

Potts, Christopher (2005): *The Logic of Conventional Implicatures*. Oxford: Oxford University Press.

Pound, Louise (1914): *Blends, their Relation to English Word Formation*. Heidelberg: Winter.

Prince, Alan and Paul Smolensky (1993): *Optimality Theory. Constraint Interaction in Generative Grammar*. Report no. 2, Rutgers University Center for Cognitive Science. Cambridge, MA: MIT Press.

Ralli, Angela (2009): Modern Greek VV dvandva compounds: A linguistic innovation in the history of the Indo-European languages. *Word Structure* 2(1): 48–68.

Reischer, Jürgen (2008): *Die Wortkreuzung und verwandte Verfahren der Wortbildung. Eine korpusbasierte Analyse des Phänomens „Blending" am Beispiel des Deutschen und Englischen*. Hamburg: Kovač.

Renner, Vincent (2006): Dépasser les désaccords: pour une approche prototypiste du concept d'amalgame lexical. In: Miryam Pereiro and Henry Daniels (eds.), *Le désaccord*, 137–147. Nancy: AMAES.

Riehemann, Suzanne Z. (1998): Morphology and the hierarchical lexicon. *Journal of Comparative Germanic Linguistics* 2: 49–77.

Ronneberger-Sibold, Elke (2006): Lexical blends: Functionally tuning the transparency of complex words. *Folia Linguistica* 40(1–2): 155–181.

Ronneberger-Sibold, Elke (2010): Word creation: Definition – function – typology. In: Franz Rainer, Wolfgang U. Dressler, Dieter Kastovsky and Hans Christian Luschützky (eds.), *Variation and Change in Morphology*, 201–216. Amsterdam/Philadelphia: Benjamins.

Švedova, Natalija Ju. (ed.) (1980): *Russkaja grammatika*. Moskva: Nauka.

Thornton, Anna M. (1993): Italian blends. In: Livio Tonella and Wolfgang U. Dressler (eds.), *Natural Morphology: Perspectives for the Nineties*, 143–155. Padova: Unipress.

Thornton, Anna M. (1996): On some phenomena of prosodic morphology in Italian: Accorciamenti, hypocoristics and prosodic delimitation. *Probus* 8: 81–112.

Thornton, Anna M. (2004): Parole macedonia. In: Maria Grossmann and Franz Rainer (eds.), *La formazione delle parole in italiano*, 567–571. Tübingen: Niemeyer.

Tournier, Jean (1985): *Introduction descriptive à la lexicogénétique de l'anglais contemporain*. Paris/Genève: Champion – Slatkine.

Uluxanov, Igor' S. (1996): *Edinicy slovoobrazovatel'noj sistemy russkogo jazyka*. Moskva: Astra sem'.

van Marle, Jaap (1985): *On the Paradigmatic Dimension of Morphological Creativity*. Dordrecht: Foris.

Villoing, Florence (2012): Contraintes de taille dans les mots composés: quand la phonologie entre en concurrence avec les contraintes morphologiques. In: Frank Neveu, Valéria Muni-Toke, Peter Blumenthal, Thomas Kingler, Pierluigi Ligas, Sophie Prévost and Sandra Teston-Bonnard (eds.), *3ᵉ Congrès Mondial de Linguistique Française – Lyon, 4–7 juillet 2012*, 1425–1440. Paris: ILF/EDP Science. Available at: www.linguistiquefrancaise.org [last access 20 Jan 2015].

Wälchli, Bernhard (2005): *Co-compounds and Natural Coordination*. Oxford: Oxford University Press.

Warren, Beatrice (1990): The importance of combining forms. In: Wolfgang U. Dressler, Hans Christian Luschützky, Oskar E. Pfeiffer and John R. Rennison (eds.), *Contemporary Morphology*, 111–132. Berlin/New York: Mouton de Gruyter.

Xruščeva, Oksana A. (2011): Universal'nye i lingvokul'turnye osobennosti blendinga. Ph.D. dissertation, Čeljabinskij gosudarstvennyj universitet, Čeljabinsk.

Zwicky, Arnold M. (1992): Some choices in the theory of morphology. In: Robert Levine (ed.), *Formal Grammar. Theory and implementation*, 327–371. Oxford: Oxford University Press.

Andrew McIntyre
16 Particle-verb formation

1 What is a particle (verb)?
2 Semantic and argument-structural properties of particle verbs
3 The syntax of particle verbs
4 Particle verbs and morphology
5 Particle verbs as morphological objects (complex heads)?
6 References

Abstract: This article provides an overview of the empirical phenomena and theoretical questions associated with particle verbs. We overview the semantic, argument-structural, syntactic and morphological properties of these structures, giving an idea of the issues discussed in the vast literature on the subject.

1 What is a particle (verb)?

The combinations of verbs and preposition-like elements in (1) and (2) are referred to as *particle verbs* (or *verb-particle combinations, phrasal verbs, separable (complex) verbs*). Definitions of "particle (verb)" vary, but (3) provides a template for a definition of "verb particle" which tries to encapsulate the points of consensus and variation.

(1) a. I threw the rubbish OUT.
    b. I threw OUT the rubbish.

(2) a. Ich warf den Müll   WEG.   German
       I   threw the rubbish away
    b. Ich habe den Müll   WEGgeworfen.   German
       I   have the rubbish away.thrown

(3) Properties of verb particles:
    a. Under certain syntactic conditions, particles need not, or may not, be verb-adjacent.

Andrew McIntyre, Berlin, Germany

https://doi.org/10.1515/9783111420561-016

b. Particles differ from other elements fulfilling condition (a) in that they form a "close union" with a verb whose precise nature differs from theory to theory.
c. Most, if not all, particles are (or are at least formally related to) complementless prepositions (or "directional/locational adverbs" in traditional terms).

Effects of (3a) are seen in (1a) and (2a). By (3a), the term "particle" will not be used of (true) affixes. The notion "close union" in (3b) refers to certain phenomena which have led some analysts to treat particle verbs as being morphological, compound-like entities. Examples of "close union" phenomena include the ability of particle verbs to feed morphological processes which otherwise eschew phrasal input (*taker-out-er* vs. **taker-inside-r*) and the ability of the particle in (1b) to intervene between the verb and object, a privilege not enjoyed by other elements in English (in the absence of heavy NP shift effects). In (4) we see examples of constraints on items which can interrupt verb-object adjacency. We will see more "close union" phenomena in sections 3, 4 and 5.

(4) a. push {in/out/up/down/away/over/aside/*inside/*upwards/*through} the box
b. *do well the job, *talk silly the people; *fold flat the boxes; *let leave the people
c. let slip$_V$ a chance, let go$_V$ the rope, cut short$_A$ the meeting, set free$_A$ the captives

To understand (3c), consider (4). (4a) shows that some prepositional elements allow the pre-object placement typical of particles. (4b) illustrates a ban on non-prepositional elements in particle position. (4c) illustrates rare, unsystematic exceptions to this ban. Some apparent exceptions are spurious. For instance, *home* in *take home the books* has independent prepositional properties, say *right*-modification (*run right home*), PP-fronting (*Home ran the children*) and selection by verbs which otherwise only select PPs (*bring it home, traipse home*). German *weg* in (2), though synchronically homophonous with the noun *Weg* 'way', has clearly prepositional traits such as compatibility with *with*-imperatives (*Weg mit ihm!* 'Away with him!') and licensing unaccusative resultatives (*Sie ist weggeschwommen* 'she swam away'), which in German allow PPs as predicates but not other categories (Kaufmann and Wunderlich 1998). Attributing prepositional status to particles lacking complement-taking uses (e.g., *home*, *aside*, German *weg* 'away', *heraus* 'out of that/there') is at variance with the idea from traditional grammar that complementless directional expressions are "adverbs" rather than "prepositions". However, this idea is not well-founded. Making complements a necessary condition for the category "preposition" (or "adposition") is incongruous given that other categories like nouns or verbs are exempt from this requirement and given the existence of adverbs which take complements (*independently of me, unbeknownst to me*). Furthermore, the items in question pattern with P(P)s rather than true (adjective-related) adverbs according to most tests, such as the modifiers they allow, coordination with P(P)s, the syntactic positions they occupy, selection by verbs which otherwise select only PPs, and their frequent propensity to be arguments when true adverbs are nearly always modifiers (cf., e.g., Huddleston and Pullum 2002: 612–617). In sum, we can safely treat particles as complementless prepositions, with the caveats that not all complementless prepositions act like particles (4a) and that there are marginal cases of particles which are not prepositional (4c). For more challenges to an across-the-board characterisation of particles as prepositions, see Cappelle (2005) on English, Toivonen (2003: 246) on Swedish, and Stiebels and Wunderlich (1994) and Zeller (2001b) on German. The latter two studies discuss cases like *staubsaugen* 'to vaccuum-clean; lit. dust-suck' which are sometimes treated as backformations and show varying degrees of resistance to verb movement.

As suggested in (3c), prepositions with (overt) complements do not display normal particle behaviour. (5a) indicates that English transitive prepositions cannot appear in the verb-adjacent particle position. Structures like (5b) do not involve particles. They are simple V+PP constructions ("prepositional verbs"), not particle verbs, because clause-final weak pronouns are excluded from particle verbs (**take out it*) and because the order object-P is either excluded (**walk it over*) or has a different interpretation (*run them through* 'to run a sword through them').

(5) a. *pull off the sticker the box. (= pull the sticker [PP off the box].)
 b. walk [PP over it]; run [PP through them]

The insistence on complementless prepositions in (3c) might have exceptions in certain analyses. Certain particles like those in (6a, b) co-occur with arguments which are thematically arguably grounds (reference objects) of the prepositional relation expressed by the particle, i.e. correspond to complements of prepositions in the glosses. Arguably the objects in such constructions are inserted as complements of prepositions and raise to a structural case position like arguments of passive or unaccusative verbs (Svenonius 2003; McIntyre 2007: section 2.7).

(6) a. wipe the table off/wipe off the table (cf. wipe the dust off the table)
 b. pump the cellar out/pump out the cellar (cf. pump the water out of the cellar)

c. Du solltest dem Mann nicht hinterher laufen   German
   you should the man_dat not after run
   'You shouldn't run after the guy.'
d. [_PP Dem Mann hinterher] ist keiner gelaufen
       the man after   is nobody run
   'Nobody went after the guy.'

A harder case is (6c). The adposition *hinterher* occupies the particle position adjacent to the clause-final verb. The dative *dem Mann* could be analysed as the ground argument of *hinterher*, similarly to the dative in (6d), where *hinterher* is a dative-assigning postposition forming a full PP. Such constructions would be problematic for the particles-qua-*complementless*-prepositions constraint in (3c) only on an analysis which assumes that (6c) contains a PP like that seen in (6d). The non-adjacency between the particle and dative in (c) makes this approach hard to defend; presumably *hinterher* would have to reanalyse with the verb (without incorporating, since V can move away from *hinterher*), allowing the dative to scramble despite German's usual ban on P-stranding. There are alternative analyses which do not counterexemplify (3c). Zeller (2001b: 218–225) adumbrated a non-movement account involving percolation of P's dative feature. Another possibility for at least some such constructions is that the dative is not grammatically represented as an argument of the particle but is a free dative. For more on datives with particle verbs, see McIntyre (2007) and Oya (2009).

2 Semantic and argument-structural properties of particle verbs

Resultative or directional particles like those in (7) predicate a result or direction over a direct argument (i.e. direct object or unaccusative subject). As is often observed with resultative constructions, the direct argument need not correspond to the verb's usual selection restrictions, cf. (7c) and **vote the government* (McIntyre 2007 and references).

(7) a. She put a hat on.   [on her head]
    b. She walked in.   [into a contextually present room/building]
    c. We voted the government in.   [into office/power/parliament, etc.]

In (7) the direct argument is a figure/theme while the ground is implicit. There are three main deviations from this standard type of resultative particle. Firstly, in structures like (6) the ground is realized instead of or along with the figure. Secondly, there is a rare and rarely-discussed type of unergative particle construction like *look in, phone through* where the particle coexists with an agent without predicating over it (McIntyre 2004). Thirdly, (8) shows a "pleonastic" construction, widespread in German and Dutch but missing in English, in which a prepositional element manifests itself both as a particle and as a case-assigning preposition in the same clause (e.g., Olsen 1996).

(8) Aus der Kirche will sie nicht austreten.
out.of the church wants she not out.step
'She doesn't want to leave the church.'

Resultative particles need not have (purely) spatial meanings: *turn off the light* or *put out the fire* have a clearly resultative semantics but do not have spatial-directional content. Various writers (Cappelle 2005; Lindner 1983; McIntyre 2002, 2003; Stiebels 1996) posit resultative meanings for non-spatial particles whose resultative character is not immediately obvious. For instance, Lindner (1983: 80–87, 125–138) analyzed the particles in (9) as metaphorically motivated result predicates expressing cognitive availability.

(9) a. {search/seek/point/pick/find/work/tease/figure} out the answer
    b. {dream/think/bring/summon/call/play/look} up the argument

Several types of particles are commonly referred to as "aspectual" particles since (at first sight) they appear to be aspectual operators or to give information about the temporal contours of the event or its aktionsart. There are two main types. Those in (10) normally require a direct argument (even if the verb does not select one), while those in (11) are atransitive, being incompatible with direct objects. Treatments of aspectual particles include Brinton (1985), Cappelle (2005: ch. 8), McIntyre (2004, 2007), Stiebels (1996), Toivonen (2006), Zeller (2001a).

(10) a. eat the chicken up; think the matter *(through/over)
     b. *Gabi will* {*das Buch anlesen/das Problem *(an)denken*}.
        Gabi wants {the book 'at'.read/the problem 'at'.think}
        'Gabi wants to start {reading the book/thinking about the problem}.'

(11) a. She played (*her guitar) {on/around/away/along}.
     b. hammer (*the metal) around/away (in sense 'hammer around/away on the metal')

A third type of particle is seen in (12). Such particles have neither aspectual nor resultative meanings, but are interpreted like locative or temporal modifiers. See Blom (2005: 132–135, 148–152, 168–173) on Dutch examples.

(12) a. *den Ofen* VOR*heizen;* *ein Bier* MIT*trinken* German
 the oven pre.heat a beer with.drink
 'to preheat the oven' 'to drink a beer with (other people)'
 b. I ate dinner IN; I slept IN

Many particle verbs are idiomatic to some degree. Some are totally opaque (German AUF*hören* 'to stop; lit. to up hear'), while others like (9) are motivated to some extent, but are partly idiosyncratic and at best semi-productive. Subtler problems attend examples like (13), where the implicit ground in (a) is deduced on the basis of contextual knowledge while that in (b) is deduced on the basis of associative relationships (between coats and their wearers). (c) allows either strategy, which makes one wonder whether the interpretations of (a, b) can be derived by pure pragmatic reasoning without the help of any lexical stipulations.

(13) a. I went to the wall and took the sticker off. [off the wall]
 b. I went to the washing line and took my coat off. ['off me', not off the line]
 c. I went to the bag and put my false teeth in. [in my mouth or in the box]

Discussions of the semantics of particles include Blom (2005), Cappelle (2005), Dehé et al. (2002), Lindner (1983), McIntyre (2001, 2002, 2004), Olsen (1998), Stiebels (1996), Zeller (2001b). The argument-structural properties of particles are overviewed in McIntyre (2007).

3 The syntax of particle verbs

Since other overviews of the literature on the structure of particle verbs exist (cf. Haiden 2006), the subject is treated briefly here. The two commonest types of analyses are as follows:

Object-particle analyses assume a stage in a syntactic derivation where the particle forms a constituent with a direct argument (i.e. [the trace of] a direct object or unaccusative subject).

Complex predicate analyses posit a (morphological or syntactic) constituent which includes the verb and particle but not the direct argument.

Object-particle analyses assume that the particle either forms a small clause with the direct argument (den Dikken 1995; Hoekstra 1988; Kayne 1985; Ramchand and Svenonius 2002) or takes the object as its complement (Harley and Noyer 1998; Zeller 2001a). In these analyses the syntax directly reflects the fact that direct arguments are arguments of particles at least in resultative particle constructions. For structures like *turn the light off* the existence of a predicative small clause is independently motivated by, e.g., copula predications (*The light is off*). Often copula predication is excluded (*take the books away* vs. **The books are away*), but this does not refute object-particle analyses, since most directional expressions are incompatible with copulas (**the books are onto the table*; **with the books onto the table ...*).

Object-particle analyses are harder to motivate for non-resultative particles since their argument-structural properties are less clear (McIntyre 2007). Such analyses readily explain unselected objects, see (14), but are implausible for adjunct-like particles like (12) which do not take entities as semantic arguments. One response is to posit object-particle analyses for some particle verbs and complex predicate analyses for others (cf. Wurmbrand 2000).

(14) think the problem through/over / *think the problem

Complex predicate analyses either assume that the verb and particle form a phrasal constituent, e.g., V', (Booij 1990; Lüdeling 2001; Müller 2002; Zeller 2001b, 2002) or that they form a compound-like morphological object (complex head) (Dehé 2002; Farrell 2005; Johnson 1991; Neeleman and Weerman 1993; Stiebels and Wunderlich 1994; Stiebels 1996). There are also hybrid analyses in which particles initially form phrasal constituents with verbs, but reanalyse with, or incorporate into verbs to form complex heads with them (Basilico 2008; Haider 1997; Toivonen 2003; Winkler 1997; Zeller 2002).

Complex predicate analyses require a theory of how the arguments of the particle and verb can be realised outside the particle verb. For resultative particles and others like those in (14), the particle must be able to contribute an argument to the whole structure. Some theories allow the direct argument to be shared by the verb and particle (Haider 1996; Neeleman and Weerman 1993). Such accounts will need to address atransitive particles (11) and other atransitive structures like *phone (*the secretary) through*, *see (*people) into the window*, *shoot (*a bird) into a tree*. Atransitivity follows if verbs cannot link their direct arguments when particles and other secondary predicates are present (McIntyre 2004, 2007; Zeller 2001b).

Some types of analyses are describable neither as complex predicate nor as object-particle analyses. There is a rare type of analysis which assumes that (some) particles are inserted higher in the structure than verbs and direct arguments (cf. Nicol 2002, and Miller 2010 for aspectual particles). Other accounts mix the complex predicate and object-particle analyses, either by applying each analysis to different particle verbs (Wurmbrand 2000), or by allowing particles in object-particle constituents either to incorporate into verbs, forming complex heads (Harley and Noyer 1998), or reanalyse with the verb abstractly (den Dikken 1995). For accounts claiming to capture benefits of both small clause and complex predicate analyses in other ways, see Basilico (2008) and Ramchand and Svenonius (2002).

We return to the structure of particle verbs in section 5, where we assess the idea that particle verbs can be morphologically complex heads. This requires us to discuss the interactions between particle verbs and morphology, which we do in section 4.

4 Particle verbs and morphology

4.1 Particle verbs and inflection

Germanic inflectional exponents are realised on verb stems, not on particles. In English one finds *walked out* but not **walk out-ed*. In languages with head-final particle verbs like German and Dutch inflectional prefixes intervene between the particle and verb, cf. German *weggeschmissen* 'thrown away' (from *wegschmeiß-* 'to throw away'). See, e.g., Müller (2003), Stiebels and Wunderlich (1994) and Zeller (2002) on the German cases.

The irrelevance of particles to inflectional morphology is sometimes taken to show that particle verbs cannot be morphologically complex entities, but such arguments are not telling without a refutation of the idea that the inflectional exponents in question must be realised on heads of words rather than on the edge of X° elements. This idea is hard to exclude given cases discussed in Stump (1995) in which inflectional affixes are realised *both* on the head of a word and on the word's edge (e.g., Breton *bagoúigoú* 'little boats', plural of the left-headed *bagig* 'boat (diminutive)').

4.2 Particle verbs as input to derivational morphology and compounding

In head-final languages like Dutch and German, particle verbs freely feed word-formation processes, as (15) illustrates with German data. (15a, b) are compounds with particle verbs as nonheads (here there is no evidence that the particle verbs have been nominalized; German freely forms compounds with verb stems as nonhead, cf. Gast 2008). Particle verbs inside other types of derviational morphology are seen in (15c–g).

(15) a. ANziehsachen 'on.put.things = clothes'
WEGgehabend 'away.go.evening = evening where someone goes out'
b. ABfahrbereit 'off.go.ready = ready to leave'
WEGwerffreudig 'away.throw.joyful = who likes throwing things out'
c. RUMsteherei 'round.stand.Af = standing around'
ANbieter 'to.offerer = provider'
d. unAUFhörlich 'un.up.hear.ly = unceasing, from AUFhör 'cease; lit. up.hear'
ANnehmbar 'to.take.able = acceptable'
e. RUMgelabere 'around.Af.chat.Af = incessant chatter'
EINgekaufe 'in.Af.buy.Af = negatively evaluated shopping'
f. UMzug 'move$_N$' ← UMzieh- 'move houses/flats'
AUFnahme 'taking up' ← AUFnehm- 'take up'
g. ANkunft 'arrival' ← ANkomm- 'arrive'
UNTERkunft 'accommodation' ← UNTERkomm- 'find/have accommodation'

The types in (15e–g) raise special problems. In (e) the nominalizing circumfix *Ge-...-e* takes the whole particle verb as its semantic input (as is clear from cases where the particle verb is lexicalised), even though *ge-* intervenes between the particle and verb (Lüdeling 2001; Müller 2003; Stiebels and Wunderlich 1994). Structures like (15f–g) ("root nominalizations") do not involve synchronically productive affixation or vowel/consonant mutation. They could be analysed either as idiosyncratic spellouts of the verb roots plus nominalizers, or as allomorphs of the verb roots which surface in nominal environments. In (g) the *-kunft*-nominals show the additional complication that *-kunft* only co-occurs with particles. For more on root nominals, see Stiebels and Wunderlich (1994), Becker (1993: 15 f.).

Here it is expositionally expedient to prefigure the question of section 5 regarding the status of particle verbs as compound-like morphological objects (complex heads). It is often argued that instances of particle verbs feeding affixation or compounding need not show that particle verbs are morphological structures, since clearly phrasal constituents can also feed affixation and compounding. Instances of this include phrasal compounds like *the particle-verbs-are-compounds stance* and nominalizations like *the destruction of the evidence immediately*, where the adverb indicates that the nominalizer attaches to a verb but to a VP or larger constituent (Fu, Roeper and Borer 2001). There are, however, several complications. As part of an argument that particle verbs, though initially merged in phrasal configurations, reanalyze as X° items inside complex verbs, Zeller (2001b: ch. 6) notes that many German affixes disallow phrasal input. One can add that compounds like (15a) do not evince the expressive, jocular or stylistically marked feel of phrasal compounds discussed in Meibauer (2007), and that compounds like (15b) do not have the ungrammatical feel of structures like *nach-Leipzig-fahr-bereit* 'ready to go to Leipzig'. However, Lüdeling (2001) and Lüdeling and de Jong (2002) argue that affixes which allow particle verbs but not uncontroversially phrasal structures as input are sensitive to factors other than the word-phrase distinction, including pragmatic considerations and a requirement that certain affixes attach to lexically listed input (see Müller 2002: 314–337 for criticism). More work will be needed to determine the precise details of the selection restrictions of the affixes in question before their relevance to the complex word view of particle verbs can be established.

Head-initial particle verbs found in languages like English present greater obstacles to derivational suffixes. As (16) suggests, there is tension between attaching the suffix to the head of the particle verb (i.e. to the verb stem), and attaching it outside the particle verb. This tension is sometimes resolved by reduplicating the affix. (Though the reduplications are rejected by some speakers and subject to purist attacks, all data in (16) are too well attested to be dismissed as metalinguistic affix-play.) With few exceptions (notably Cappelle 2010; Walker 2009), the reduplication phenomenon has had surprisingly little attention. If the reasons for the reduplication were better understood it might be possible to use the attachment of suffixes outside the particle verb as an argument for the complex-head analysis of particle verbs.

(16) a. passer-by, hanger-on, foldable up
b. pick-up-able, un-make-up-able, walk-outer
c. taker-outer, fixer-upper, filler-inner of forms, showy-offy
d. present giver-out-er-er
e. taker-out-ee ('one who is taken out')
f. screwed-up-(ed-)ness ← screwed-up(*ed)

Structures like (17) avoid problems associated with adding suffixes to left-headed structures. Nominals like (17a) are common (Fraser 1976: 28 lists dozens). They could be analysed either as stress-shift conversions (cf. *réject* ← *rejéct*) or as exocentric compounds interpreted as lexically related to particle verbs (Olsen 1997; Stiebels and Wunderlich 1994). In the nominals and adjectival participles in (17b, c) the particles appear before the verb stems. Berg (1998) argued that some nominals like (b) are derivationally related to particle verbs. However it is captured theoretically, such a relation is certainly possible in view of the existence of synthetic compounds related to phrasal idioms (*tantrum-throwing / throw a tantrum*; *dummy-spit / spit the dummy*). A final point regarding (17) is that there are formally similar constructions which are not related to (currently existing) particle verbs (*tradeoff, onset*), see, e.g., Marchand (1969: 108–121, 382–386).

(17) a. handout, spellout, sendup, putdown, flashback, bailout, takeoff, takeover, stuffup, workout, turnoff, showoff, dropout, runaway
b. offcut, outtake, outbreak, overpass, outcast, outflow, outcry, income, input
c. incoming, ongoing, upcoming, offputting

Note finally that certain types of affixation attach to the verb stem without reduced acceptability. These include "of-ing" nominalizations (18a) and gerunds (18b) (see, e.g., Harley and Noyer 1998 on the difference) and adjectival participles (18c). An interesting question for future research would concern the reasons for the differing behaviour of the affixes in (18) and (16).

(18) a. the turning {off} of the lights {*off}
b. their turning {off} the lights {off}
c. sawnoff shotguns; un-written-up/under-worked-out ideas; falling-down houses

4.3 Verb stems in particle verbs

We now discuss some problems concerning the types of elements which can function as verb stems (or: non-particle elements) in particle verbs. Firstly consider the English and German examples in (19). Here the non-particle elements lack (relevant) counterparts which can be used as verbs without the particle. Explaining this by treating the particles as heads of the construction is not an option since verbal inflection is realized on the non-particle element and since the particles act like prepositions according to certain tests (e.g., preposition-specific modifier: *dumb it back down, soldier right on*). The alternative is that the structures exploit the conversion (zero derivation) patterns available without particles, with the additional complication that certain conversions are (in some yet-to-be-understood sense) licensed only in the presence of a particle. (The same problem is found in clearly phrasal structures like *worm one's way in*, where *worm* is not independently usable as a verb, and *one's way* is clearly a syntactic entity, cf. *corporations have wormed their insidious way into governments*.) On data like (19) see especially Stiebels (1998), as well as Booij (2002), Kolehmainen (2006: 48–52), McIntyre (2002), Müller (2002: 337 f.), Olsen (1998), Zeller (2001b: 211–215).

(19) a. slot in, ferret/bottom out, muck up/around, soldier on, beaver away, pig out
b. wise up, dumb down
c. AUFbahr- 'to put on a stretcher', EINsack- 'to put in a sack', EINsarg- 'to put in a coffin'
d. AUFfrisch- 'to freshen up', ANreicher- 'to enrich'

Perhaps unsurprisingly, particles do not usually exhibit the types of morphological and phonological restrictions found with affixes. One potential exception is Fraser's (1976: 13–16) observation that most English particle verbs have monosyllabic or forestressed bisyllabic stems, cf. {ring/phone/*telephone} her up. A related observation is that in (20) the non-particle element appears in a clipped form not found without the particle. The theoretical significance of these observations is unclear given the sporadic nature of data like (20) and the existence of exceptions to the tendency: *partition off, separate out, continue on, gallyvant around.*

(20) sum(*marise) up, (*con)fess up, (con)glom(erate) together

Another constraint affecting verb stems in particle verbs is the resistance to morphologically complex stems seen in (21a). Fraser (1976: 15) sees the blockage as phonological, while Keyser and Roeper (1992) assume that particles and prefixes originate in the same syntactic position and are therefore mutually exclusive. Caveats include that some speakers accept some of these structures (Farrell 2005) and that there is no comparable ban on particle-prefix-verbs in Dutch and German (e.g., den Dikken 2003; Stiebels and Wunderlich 1994).

(21) a. *I preheated it up; *I overworked on; %I resent it off
b. push the cart back on in

Another empirical phenomenon which could be seen as relevant to (21a) is the existence of apparent cases of particle recursion like (21b). However, notions like "particle recursion" or "adding particles to particle verbs" do not appear apposite here. The string after the object in (21b) is unproblematically analysable as a complex PP with multiple complementless prepositions, and some elements in such combinations, notably *back*, act like modifiers of particles or prepositions in certain contexts (Cappelle 2008; Svenonius 2010). This does not exclude the possibility of morphologically complex particles, cf. cases like *put aside the problem* and the German double particles discussed in McIntyre (2001).

5 Particle verbs as morphological objects (complex heads)?

Section 1 alluded to the "close union" between particles and verbs. As noted in sections 3 and 4, some linguists capture this phenomenon by treating particle verbs as a type of complex word (compound, morphological object, complex head). This section gives an overview of the pros and cons of this *complex word view* of particle verbs.

Certain arguments sometimes given for the complex word view are inconclusive. Firstly, idiomatic particle verbs are rightly no longer taken to support this view, since it is well-known that clearly phrasal constructions can have idiomatic interpretations (*I could have done without that*). Secondly, we noted in section 4.2 that the ability of particle verbs to feed affixation and compounding will not provide a failsafe argument for the complex word view until the selection restrictions of the affixes involved are fully understood.

Perhaps the best (and least known) presently existing argument for the complex word view in English comes from quotative inversion (Collins and Branigan 1997; Toivonen 2003: 175 f.). (22a) shows a particle appearing with the verb in a pre-subject position. (22b) shows that other VP-internal elements do not have this privilege, which would be hard to explain if (22a) were derived by fronting a VP (remnant) around the subject or by extraposing the subject. These problems disappear if we assume that the particle verb is some type of complex head. Unfortunately, the evaluation of this argument is made harder by the fact that linguists disagreeing with the complex word view have not yet discussed data like (22).

(22) a. 'Get lost!', shouted/cried/blurted OUT Marmaduke.
 b. 'Get lost!', shouted {OUT/*loudly/*at him} Marmaduke {loudly/at him}

The most immediate obstacle to the complex word view is that particles can be separated from verbs in syntax (e.g., (1a), (2a)), whereas normal morphological objects are inseparable and thus obey constraints like lexical integrity (which bans syntactic manipulation of parts of X° items) or the oft-posited ban on excorporation (e.g., Baker 1988: 73). This puts an explanatory burden on the complex word view, but whether this burden breaks its back is another, partly theory-dependent question. To see this, we have to distinguish two types of complex word approaches:

(i) The particle and verb only enter a complex word configuration in *some* of their uses (for instance when the particle incorporates into, or reanalyses

with, the verb). These uses do not include the uses where the particle and verb are separated syntactically.
(ii) The particle and verb are always initially inserted into syntax as a complex word but are separated in certain contexts.

Proponents of (ii) have the harder task given that complex heads are not normally separable. It is not problematic for (ii) that affixes do not separate from their hosts, since any theory would presumably need (the empirical equivalent of) a stipulation in the lexical entry of an affix which makes it inseparable from its base, and one can simply say that particles lack this stipulation. The real challenge to (ii) arises when we compare particle verbs to compounds. Here the options seem to be as follows. One could try to argue that verbs separate from particles in, say, verb-second contexts like (2a) because verb movement (or its empirical equivalents) targets verb stems, and there is no reason to pied-pipe the particle, since it is not an affix. To explain why constituents of compound nouns or adjectives do not normally separate, one could assume firstly that normal compound formation turns one of the constituents into an affix-like element, an operation which is sometimes visible, cf. conjunct forms like *oft* (usable only in compound adjectives: *oft-derided*) or linking morphs (interfixes) like the *-s* in *tradesman*. A second option would be to assume that there are simply no syntactic operations which could legitimately target parts of normal compounds. This would be possible if one assumes that nouns and adjectives do not undergo (the empirical equivalent of) head movement operations, and that compound non-heads cannot undergo phrasal movement (*Car he is not a* [$_{NP}$ t$_{car}$ *driver*]) either because they are not phrases of the appropriate category (e.g., DP) or because such movements would violate island constraints (e.g., the left-branch condition). These positions might be correct, but a satisfying defense would require a substantial cross-linguistic discussion of the reasons for the observation that compounds are cross-linguistically normally inseparable.

The issue of particle modification often crops up in discussions of the complex word view of particles. Particles (or at least complementless prepositions homophonous with particles) can uncontroversially be modified, see (23a). Proponents of position (ii) above would presumably have to assume a phrasal compound [push [right in]] here. This seems hard to defend given that the "close union" phenomena discussed in section 1 are excluded with modified particles: English disallows particle-object order in the presence of a modifier, cf. (23b, c), and it is hard to find convincing examples of particle-verb nominalizations where the particle is modified. If some variant of the complex word analysis of particle verbs is right, then data like (23) seem to favor option (i) above. The modifier would prevent the particle from compounding with, reanalyzing with, or incorporating into, the verb because English simply does not license phrasal compounds of the type [push [right in]], or because the modifier projects some structure which interrupts the adjacency between particle and verb, so that reanalysis would be excluded by the head movement constraint or some empirically equivalent principle.

(23) a. She pushed the pin [right in].
b. *She pushed [right in] the pin.
c. *She pushed in the pin right.   (* if *right* modifies *in*)
d. pin pusher-(*right)-in-er

A final point to note concerning the complex word view of particle verbs is that English-style verb-initial particle verbs violate the right-hand head rule of Williams (1981), see, e.g., den Dikken (1995: 88). To evaluate this point, note firstly that some writers, including Williams himself (1981: 249 f.), do not see this rule as exceptionless. Williams' putative counterexamples include denominal prefix verbs lacking unprefixed verbal counterparts (*enthrone* but *$throne_V$). This argument seems dubious given that particles can also "license" zero derivations or conversions but are clearly not heads of particle verbs, recall (19). Stronger evidence for left-headed morphological structures in English comes from data like (24), which are attested and acceptable to many speakers not influenced by language purism. Here plural -s appears on the right edge of the construction. This suggests that the construction is analysed as a morphological object, since plural -s does not otherwise behave like a phrasal affix (*the discussion(s) yesterday(*s), the car(s) of his daughter(#s)*). Nevertheless, structures like *mother-in-law* and *passer-by* are clearly left-headed, witness, e.g., their semantics and the fact that some speakers additionally attach the affix to the leftmost element, which seems to be a straightforward case of head marking (recall again Stump's 1994 Breton examples).

(24) mother(s)-in-laws, passer(s)-bys, hanger(s)-on(s), fixer(s)-uppers

This section has hopefully clarified some of the issues regarding the debate concerning the complex word view of particle verbs and shown why the last word on the (non)existence of morphological objects consisting of particles and verbs has not been said.

6 References

Baker, Mark (1988): *Incorporation*. Chicago: University of Chicago Press.
Basilico, David (2008): Particle verbs and benefactive double objects in English: High and low attachments. *Natural Language and Linguistic Theory* 26: 731–773.

Becker, Thomas (1993): Back-formation, cross-formation, and 'bracketing paradoxes' in paradigmatic morphology. In: Geert Booij and Jaap van Marle (eds.), *Yearbook of Morphology 1993*, 1–25. Dordrecht: Kluwer.

Berg, Thomas (1998): The (in)compatibility of morpheme orders and lexical categories and its historical implications. *English Language and Linguistics* 2: 245–262.

Blom, Corrien (2005): *Complex predicates in Dutch*. Utrecht: LOT.

Booij, Geert (1990): The boundary between morphology and syntax: Separable complex verbs in Dutch. In: Geert Booij and Jaap van Marle (eds.), *Yearbook of Morphology 1990*, 45–63. Dordrecht: Kluwer.

Booij, Geert (2002): Separable complex verbs in Dutch. In: Nicole Dehé, Ray Jackendoff, Andrew McIntyre and Silke Urban (eds.), *Verb-Particle Explorations*, 21–41. Berlin/New York: Mouton de Gruyter.

Brinton, Laurel (1985): Verb particles in English: Aspect or aktionsart? *Studia Linguistica* 39: 157–168.

Cappelle, Bert (2005): Particle patterns in English. Ph.D. dissertation, University of Leuven.

Cappelle, Bert (2008): The grammar of complex particle phrases in English. In: Anna Ashbury, Jakub Dotlacil, Berit Gehrke and Rick Nouwen (eds.), *Syntax and Semantics of Spatial P*, 103–145. Amsterdam/Philadelphia: Benjamins.

Cappelle, Bert (2010): Doubler-upper nouns. In: Alexander Onysko and Sascha Michel (eds.), *Cognitive Perspectives on Word Formation*, 335–374. Berlin: Mouton de Gruyter.

Collins, Chris and Phil Branigan (1997): Quotative Inversion. *Natural Language and Linguistic Theory* 15: 1–41.

Dehé, Nicole (2002): *Particle Verbs in English. Syntax, Information Structure, and Intonation*. Amsterdam/Philadelphia: Benjamins.

Dehé, Nicole, Ray Jackendoff, Andrew McIntyre and Silke Urban (eds.) (2002): *Verb-Particle Explorations*. Berlin/New York: Mouton de Gruyter.

den Dikken, Marcel (1995): *Particles. On the Syntax off Verb-Particle, Triadic, and Causative Constructions*. Oxford: Oxford University Press.

den Dikken, Marcel (2003): When particles won't part. Ms., Cuny Graduate Center.

Farrell, Patrick (2005): English verb-preposition constructions. *Language* 81: 96–137.

Fraser, Bruce (1976): *The Verb-Particle Combination in English*. New York: Academic Press.

Fu, Jincqui, Thomas Roeper and Hagit Borer (2001): The VP within nominalizations. *Natural Language and Linguistic Theory* 19: 549–582.

Gast, Volker (2008): Verb-noun compounds in English and German. *Zeitschrift für Anglistik und Amerikanistik* 56(3): 269–282.

Haiden, Martin (2006): Verb particle constructions. In: Martin Everaert and Henk van Riemsdijk (eds.), *The Blackwell Companion to Syntax*. Vol. 5, 344–375. Oxford: Blackwell.

Haider, Hubert (1997): Precedence among predicates. *Journal of Comparative Germanic Linguistics* 1: 3–41.

Harley, Heidi and Rolf Noyer (1998): Mixed nominalizations, short verb movement and object shift in English. In: *Proceedings of the North East Linguistic Society*. Vol. 28, 143–158. Amherst: Graduate Linguistic Student Association.

Hoekstra, Teun (1988): Small clause results. *Lingua* 74: 101–139.

Huddleston, Rodney and Geoffrey Pullum (2002): *The Cambridge Grammar of the English Language*. Cambridge: Cambridge University Press.

Johnson, Kyle (1991): Object positions. *Natural Language and Linguistic Theory* 9: 577–636.

Kaufmann, Ingrid and Dieter Wunderlich (1998): Cross-linguistic patterns of resultatives. In: *Theorie des Lexikons. Arbeiten des Sonderforschungsbereichs 282*. Nr. 109. Heinrich-Heine-Universität Düsseldorf.

Kayne, Richard (1985): Principles of particle constructions. In: Jacqueline Guéron, Hans-Georg Obenauer and Jean-Yves Pollock (eds.), *Grammatical Representations*, 101–140. Dordrecht: Foris.
Keyser, Samuel J. and Thomas Roeper (1992): The abstract clitic hypothesis. *Linguistic Inquiry* 23: 89–125.
Kolehmainen, Leena (2006): *Präfix- und Partikelverben im deutsch-finnischen Kontrast*. Frankfurt/M.: Lang.
Lindner, Susan (1983): *A Lexico-Semantic Analysis of English Verb Particle Constructions*. Bloomington, IN: Indiana University Linguistics Club.
Lüdeling, Anke (2001): *On Particle Verbs and Similar Constructions in German*. Stanford: CSLI.
Lüdeling, Anke and Nivja de Jong (2002): German particle verbs and word formation. In: Nicole Dehé, Ray Jackendoff, Andrew McIntyre and Silke Urban (eds.), *Verb-Particle Explorations*, 315–333. Berlin/New York: Mouton de Gruyter.
Marchand, Hans (1969): *The Categories and Types of Present-Day English Word Formation. A Synchronic-Diachronic Approach*. 2nd ed. München: Beck.
Meibauer, Jörg (2007): How marginal are phrasal compounds? *Morphology* 17: 233–259.
McIntyre, Andrew (2001): *German Double Particles as Preverbs*. Tübingen: Stauffenburg.
McIntyre, Andrew (2002): Idiosyncrasy in particle verbs. In: Nicole Dehé, Ray Jackendoff, Andrew McIntyre and Silke Urban (eds.), *Verb-Particle Explorations*, 97–118. Berlin/New York: Mouton de Gruyter.
McIntyre, Andrew (2003): Preverbs, argument linking and verb semantics. In: Geert Booij and Jaap van Marle (eds.), *Yearbook of Morphology 2003*, 119–144. Dordrecht: Kluwer.
McIntyre, Andrew (2004): Event paths, conflation, argument structure and VP shells. *Linguistics* 42: 523–571.
McIntyre, Andrew (2007): Particle verbs and argument structure. *Language and Linguistics Compass* 1: 350–397.
Miller, Gary (2010): On the syntax of morphology. Ms., University of Florida.
Müller, Stefan (2002): *Complex Predicates*. Stanford: CSLI.
Müller, Stefan (2003): Solving the bracketing paradox: An analysis of the morphology of German particle verbs. *Journal of Linguistics* 39: 275–325.
Neeleman, Ad and Fred Weerman (1993): The balance between syntax and morphology: Dutch particles and resultatives. *Natural Language and Linguistic Theory* 11: 433–75.
Nicol, Fabrice (2002): Extended VP-shells and the verb-particle construction. In: Nicole Dehé, Ray Jackendoff, Andrew McIntyre and Silke Urban (eds.), *Verb-Particle Explorations*, 165–190. Berlin/New York: Mouton de Gruyter.
Olsen, Susan (1996): Pleonastische Direktionale. In: Gisela Harras and Manfred Bierwisch (eds.), *Wenn die Semantik arbeitet. Klaus Baumgärtner zum 65. Geburtstag*, 303–329. Tübingen: Niemeyer.
Olsen, Susan (1997): Über den lexikalischen Status englischer Partikelverben. In: Gisa Rauh and Elisabeth Löbel (eds.), *Lexikalische Kategorien und Merkmale*, 45–71. Tübingen: Niemeyer.
Olsen, Susan (ed.) (1998): *Semantische und konzeptuelle Aspekte der Partikelverbbildung mit* ein-. Tübingen: Stauffenburg.
Oya, Toshiaki (2009): Ground arguments in German particle verbs. *Journal of Linguistics* 21: 257–296.
Ramchand, Gillian and Peter Svenonius (2002): The lexical syntax and lexical semantics of the verb-particle construction. In: Lina Mikkelsen and Chris Potts (eds.), *Proceedings of the West Coast Conference on Formal Linguistics* 21, 387–400. Somerville, MA: Cascadilla Press.
Stiebels, Barbara (1996): *Lexikalische Argumente und Adjunkte*. Berlin: Akademie Verlag.

Stiebels, Barbara (1998): Complex denominal verbs in German and the morphology-semantics interface. In: Geert Booij and Jaap van Marle (eds.), *Yearbook of Morphology 1997*, 265–302. Dordrecht: Foris.
Stiebels, Barbara and Dieter Wunderlich (1994): Morphology feeds syntax: The case of particle verbs. *Linguistics* 32: 913–968.
Stump, Gregory (1995): The uniformity of head marking in inflectional morphology. In: Geert Booij and Jaap van Marle (eds.), *Yearbook of Morphology 1994*, 245–296. Dordrecht: Kluwer.
Svenonius, Peter (2003): Limits on P: Filling in holes vs. falling in holes. *Nordlyd* 31: 431–445.
Svenonius, Peter (2010): Spatial P in English. In: Guglielmo Cinque and Luigi Rizzi (eds.), *Mapping Spatial PPs*, 127–160. Oxford: Oxford University Press.
Toivonen, Ida (2003): *Non-Projecting Words*. Dordrecht: Kluwer.
Toivonen, Ida (2006): On continuative on. *Studia Linguistica* 60: 181–219.
Walker, Jim (2009): Double -er suffixation in English. *Lexis. E-Journal in English Lexicology* 1: 5–14.
Williams, Edwin (1981): On the notions 'lexically related' and 'head of a word'. *Linguistic Inquiry* 12: 245–74.
Winkler, Susanne (1997): *Focus and Secondary Predication*. Berlin/New York: Mouton de Gruyter.
Zeller, Jochen (2001a): How syntax restricts the lexicon: Particles as thematic predicates. *Linguistische Berichte* 188: 461–494.
Zeller, Jochen (2001b): *Particle Verbs and Local Domains*. Amsterdam/Philadelphia: Benjamins.
Zeller, Jochen (2002): Particle verbs are heads and phrases. In: Nicole Dehé, Ray Jackendoff, Andrew McIntyre and Silke Urban (eds.), *Verb-Particle Explorations*, 233–267. Berlin/New York: Mouton de Gruyter.

Matthias Hüning and Barbara Schlücker
17 Multi-word expressions

1 Introduction
2 General properties
3 Multi-word expressions and word-formation
4 References

Abstract: Multi-word expressions (MWEs) are complex lexical units, for example verbal idioms (*bite the bullet*) or frozen adverbials (*all at once*). Others, such as particle verbs (*stick out*) or complex nominals (*day-care center*), indicate a close relationship between MWEs and word-formation units. Focusing on this relation, the present article discusses commonalities and differences between MWEs and word-formation units and their mutual relations in the language system and in language use.

1 Introduction

According to a recent definition, MWEs are "lexical units larger than a word that can bear both idiomatic and compositional meanings. [...] the term multi-word expression is used as a pre-theoretical label to include the range of phenomena that goes from collocations to fixed expressions" (Masini 2005: 145). A similar but more detailed definition of MWEs (using different terminology) is given in Sprenger (2003: 4):

> Fixed Expressions refer to specific combinations of two or more words that are typically used to express a specific concept. Typical examples of FEs that are referred to in the literature often have an opaque meaning or a deficient syntactic structure, for example, *by and large* or *kick the bucket*. However, these properties are not essential. The defining feature of a FE is that it is a word combination, stored in the Mental Lexicon of native speakers, that as a whole refers to a (linguistic) concept. This makes FEs "non-compositional" in the sense that the combination and structure of their elements need not be computed afresh, but can be retrieved from the Mental Lexicon. However, the degree of lexical and syntactic fixedness can vary.

Matthias Hüning, Berlin, Germany
Barbara Schlücker, Leipzig, Germany

https://doi.org/10.1515/9783111420561-017

These two definitions illustrate two of the problems one faces when dealing with MWEs. The first one is the abundant terminology related to MWEs, some of the most common terms being *chunk, cliché, collocation, extended lexical unit, fixed expression, formulaic sequence, idiom, idiomatic expression, lexical/lexicalized phrase, multi-word unit, phraseme, phraseologism, phraseological unit, phrasal lexical item, phrasal lexeme, prefabricated chunk, prefab*. Some of these terms can be regarded as synonyms; for the most part, however, their meanings overlap only partially. In addition, the definition of each individual term often varies among scholars. The terms also belong to different levels of description: whereas *extended lexical unit, fixed expression* or *multi-word expression/unit* are relatively general, others, such as *idiom* or *collocation*, have a more restricted meaning. Some studies use continuum models in order to capture different subclasses of MWEs on the basis of their degree of semantic compositionality, syntactic fixedness or lexicalization, cf. Wray (2002). In the following, we will use the term *multi-word expression* as a general term that includes phenomena with different degrees of syntactic fixedness and semantic compositionality. The second problem illustrated by the above definitions is the range of properties relevant for the definition of MWEs in the literature. These include semantic, syntactic, and pragmatic aspects as well as processing and frequency considerations. Again, there is much variation in the literature with respect to the properties relevant for defining MWEs.

Phraseology, the linguistic sub-discipline which deals with MWEs, is a relatively young branch of linguistics. After early phraseological studies in the Soviet Union in the 1940s, the main development of the Western phraseological research took place in the 1970s and 1980s, with Weinreich (1969), Fraser (1970), and Newmeyer (1974) being some of the influential early studies. In addition to structural aspects, research on MWEs has become increasingly important in the fields of lexicography, text linguistics, first and second language acquisition, second language education and machine translation. In particular, research on MWEs has become an important part of (both theoretical and experimental) psycholinguistics, dealing with the comprehension of MWEs, their storage and mental representation, the acquisition and loss of MWEs, and speech production. Furthermore, the development of new methodological approaches as well as the availability of huge electronic corpora has made corpus linguistics extremely important for phraseological research in recent years, as can be seen from the numerous corpus-based/driven studies on MWEs. Corpus linguistic approaches are based on frequency data rather than on predefined linguistic criteria, leading to a much broader view of MWEs than that prevailing in more traditional phraseology. There is a close relation between corpus linguistics and phraseological research in usage-based frameworks, such as constructionist approaches to grammar, as these theories attach great importance to authentic corpus data (cf. section 3.2). Since providing complete references for these aspects of phraseological research would exceed the scope of this article, the reader is referred to recent review articles of psycholinguistic and computational phraseology, cf. Gibbs and Colston (2007), Häcki Buhofer (2007), Heid (2007, 2008), Moon (2007) and Sailer (2007).

The following list gives an overview of the phenomena commonly regarded as MWEs. Importantly, however, it is not intended as a classification of MWEs.

- Proverbs (*A bird in the hand is worth two in the bush*), quotations (*Shaken, not stirred*) and commonplaces (*One never knows*)
- Metaphorical expressions (*as sure as eggs is eggs* / German *so sicher wie das Amen in der Kirche* lit. 'as sure as the amen in the church', *autumn of one's life* / German *Herbst des Lebens*)
- Verbal idioms (*to kick the bucket, to shoot the breeze*, French *marcher sur des œufs* 'to walk on eggshells', German *jemanden nicht riechen können* 'to not be able to stand s.o.; lit. to not be able to smell s.o.', Dutch *iemand met de nek aankijken* 'to look down on s.o.; lit. to look at s.o. with the neck')
- Particle/phrasal verbs (*to make up*, German *ankommen* 'to arrive', Dutch *bijvallen* 'to approve', Italian *mettere giù* 'to put down')
- Light verb constructions / composite predicates (*to have a look*, German *zur Abstimmung bringen* 'to put to the vote', French *faire partie de* 'to be part of')
- Syntactic/quasi noun incorporation (German *Auto waschen* 'to wash car', Dutch *piano spelen* 'to play piano', Danish *købe hus* 'to buy (a) house', Swedish *ha bil* 'to have/own a car')
- Stereotyped comparisons / similes (*as nice as pie, swear like a trooper*, Dutch *koud als steen* 'cold as stone', German *schimpfen wie ein Rohrspatz* 'to rant and rave; lit. to rant like a reed bunting', French *bête commes ses pieds* 'stupid like one's feet')
- Binomial expressions (*shoulder to shoulder* / German *Schulter an Schulter, by and by* / German *nach und nach, nourish and cherish* / German *hegen und pflegen*)
- Complex nominals (*man about town, weapons of mass destruction, sheep's clothing*, French *marché aux puces* 'flea market', Italian *atto di nascita* 'birth certificate', Spanish *silla para niños* 'baby high chair', Russian *universal'nyj magazin* 'department store', *kiosk moroženogo* 'ice cream parlor')
- Collocations (*strong tea, hard frost*, German *Zähne putzen* 'to brush teeth')
- Fossilized/frozen forms (*all of a sudden*, complex prepositions like Dutch *in plaats van* 'instead of', French *en fonction de* 'depending on')
- Routine formulas (*Good morning, How are you doing?, Happy Birthday*)

This list of MWEs is neither complete nor generally applicable as, obviously, the question as to what counts as a MWE depends on the definition used. Also, it confuses semantic, syntactic, pragmatic, and distributional criteria. Thus, for instance, *strong tea* can be regarded as a complex nominal and a collocation at the same time. Nevertheless, these examples are useful as they give an impression of the range of relevant data. Naturally, not all of these kinds of MWEs can be dealt with in this article. In the context of this handbook, the focus is on the relation between MWEs and word-formation. For this reason, sentence-length expressions as well as routine formulas are not considered further. Instead, particular attention is paid to MWEs that have more or less direct counterparts in word-formation. In addition, the reader is referred to article 16 on particle-verb formation.

In the following, we will start by reviewing the most important properties of multi-word expressions as discussed in the literature (section 2). Section 3 then addresses the central topic, i.e. commonalities and differences between MWEs and word-formation units and their mutual relations in the language system and in language use.

2 General properties

Multi-word expressions are complex by definition. Consisting of a minimum of two words, they cut across word boundaries. Some approaches draw a distinction between function words and content words, either in the sense that a MWE should comprise at least one content word, such as in *as far as*, or that a sequence of two function words should also qualify as a MWE, e.g., *up to*. With regard to the upper limit, it is generally assumed that MWEs do not exceed the sentence boundary. It is obvious that a definition of MWEs hinges crucially on the definition of the word and of word boundaries, as will be further discussed in section 3.

MWEs are different from "regular", purely syntactic complex expressions in that they form stable units with respect to various aspects. First, a MWE is a single lexical unit. This means that uttering a MWE involves the reproduction or retrieval of the phrase as a whole from the mental lexicon rather than the production or computation of the individual parts (for discussion, see, e.g., Wray 2008). MWEs are regarded as lexical units because they obviously form semantic units, that is, they function as an expression for a particular concept, just as words do.

Second, in the view of traditional phraseological research, prototypical MWEs by definition have non-compositional (or idiomatic) meaning, e.g., *to keep one's fingers crossed* / German *die Daumen drücken* lit. 'to press the thumbs'. Although this is true for many MWEs, it is nowadays – thanks to the seminal paper by Nunberg, Sag and Wasow (1994) and others – generally accepted that non-compositionality should not count as a defining criterion for MWEs. This is why many approaches distinguish between several degrees of idiomaticity/non-compositionality of MWEs. However, the notion of non-compositionality is usually associated with several aspects of meaning, such as opacity, unanalysability or figurative meaning, which are often confused (or at least not made explicit) in the literature, cf. Svensson (2008). Generally, a distinction is made at least between fully opaque, non-decomposable MWEs (e.g., *red herring*), decomposable MWEs which contain one or several words with an idiomatic meaning (e.g., *black market*) and fully compositional, non-idiomatic MWEs (e.g., *fish and chips*). The latter are often referred to as "collocations" (cf., e.g., Barz 1996; Riehemann 2001; Burger 2010) or as "institutionalised phrases" (cf. Sag et al. 2002; Villavicencio et al. 2005).

Third, MWEs have traditionally often been regarded as syntactically fixed expressions. However, as in the case of semantics, it is widely accepted nowadays that, although many MWEs are indeed syntactically fixed or otherwise deficient, this is not necessarily the case. Instead, MWEs exhibit a continuum of syntactic fixedness, which is often related to the degree of compositionality of meaning (see, for instance, Fellbaum 2011). On the one end, there are, rather infrequently, fully invariant expressions (e.g., English *by and large* / German *im Großen und Ganzen*). Some MWEs contain unique elements, i.e. items that only appear in one particular MWE and do not have a meaning on their own ("cranberry collocations", cf. Moon 1998), e.g., klipp *und klar* 'clear as daylight; lit. (klipp) and clear'. Other MWEs are restricted with regard to syntactic operations such as anaphoric reference, passivization, relative clause formation, topicalization, modification, and others (cf. Nunberg, Sag and Wasow 1994; Dobrovol'skij 1997; Moon 1998; Donalies 2009; Burger 2010, among others). For example, Dutch *rode kool* 'red cabbage' allows (in its MWE meaning) neither the modification of the adjective nor the insertion of another prenominal adjective, cf. *erg rode kool 'very red cabbage', *rode dure kool 'red expensive cabbage', cf. Booij (2009). However, although the word order is fixed in these cases, they are not fully invariant forms, as can be seen from similar examples in German. In spite of the syntactic restrictions, they exhibit regular inflection, e.g., *der blaue Fleck, dem blauen Fleck* 'blue mark, bruise'. On the other hand, many (often relatively complex) MWEs allow occasional variation in creative speech, e.g., by means of adjectival modification (cf. Ernst 1981; Fellbaum and Stathi 2006; Stathi 2007; Burger 2010), e.g., German *etwas unter den politischen Teppich kehren* 'to brush something under the political carpet'. Finally, there are underspecified MWEs, i.e. patterns with open slots. Two subclasses can be distinguished: (i) MWEs with a more or less fixed group of lexical items that may be inserted in these slots, resulting in expressions which are relatively similar semantically (cf. Dobrovol'skij 1988), e.g., *to hit the roof/the ceiling*; German *jemandem eins aufs Dach / auf den Deckel / auf den Hut / auf die Nase / auf die Rübe geben* lit. 'to give somebody something on the roof / on the hat / on the nose / on the conk, to conk somebody'. (ii) Patterns with a variable slot to be filled by a non-restricted group of content words, such as the NPN construction (N *by* N, N *for* N, N *after* N, etc., e.g., *day after day*, cf. Jackendoff 2008). The NPN construction partially coincides with constructions known as binomials in traditional phraseology (e.g., Lambrecht 1984; Moon 1998; Burger 2010), e.g., Danish *to og to* 'pairwise; lit. two and two', *med hud og hår* 'neck and crop; lit. with skin and hair', German *null und nichtig* 'null and void', *Hab und Gut* 'goods and chattels'. Other examples of patterns with open slots are the 'time'-*away* construction (*Bill slept the afternoon away*, cf. Jackendoff 1997) or collocational sequences such as *a/an* N *of* or *at the* N *of* (e.g., *a kind/lot/number of, at the end/time/beginning of*; Renouf and Sinclair 1991; Biber 2009).

Finally, there is another aspect of MWEs' stability as units which has often been referred to in the literature as "habitualness" or "recurrence". MWEs are combinations of a minimum of two words which language users prefer over alternative combinations with an equivalent meaning, so they occur more frequently (cf. Erman and Warren 2000). This criterion is of particular importance for the identification of collocations as they lack other properties such as deviant semantics or syntax. The question as to what should count as "more frequently" as well as methodological questions of measuring frequency have been subject to extensive discussion in the corpus linguistic literature, cf. Bartsch (2004), Biber (2009) for an overview. According to one common view, MWEs are a combination of lexical items whose frequency of co-occurrence is larger than would be expected on the basis of chance alone, cf. Gries (2008).

3 Multi-word expressions and word-formation

The relation between MWEs and word-formation can be considered under three aspects:
(i) The demarcation between MWEs and word-formation units. – Just like MWEs, word-formation units are complex units made up from a minimum of two constituents. Cross-linguistically as well as language-specifically, languages differ greatly with regard to the degree to which the distinction between morphological and syntactic complex entities is formally marked. For instance, while the distinction between nominal compounds and phrases can easily be made on the basis of stress and inflection in German, Dutch and Danish, this is much more difficult in languages like English, French or Spanish. This difference is also reflected by the fact that in the latter languages, compounds are not, or not consistently, written as one word, in contrast to

German, Dutch and Danish, which exhibit a consistent distinction between morphological and phrasal complex nominals in terms of spelling. Particle verbs such as English *to look up*, German *aufgeben* 'to give up' or Dutch *opbellen* 'to phone' are another case in point as they appear either as one single unit or as two words, depending on the kind of sentence they appear in, e.g., *Er will den Plan aufgeben* 'He wants to give up the plan' vs. *Er gab den Plan auf* 'He gave up the plan / gave the plan up'.

(ii) MWEs as alternative forms to word-formation units. – Often, MWEs and word-formation can be regarded as alternative means for naming a particular concept, e.g., German *weiß wie Schnee* 'white as snow' vs. *schneeweiß* 'snow-white', *schwarzer Tee* vs. *Schwarztee* 'black tea'. In contrast to these examples, however, morphological and phrasal forms of this kind do not usually exist side by side. Instead, the existence of one form usually blocks the formation of the other. This raises questions as to the function of lexical entities and the factors determining the choice between word and MWE formation. These aspects have – to our knowledge – been given relatively little attention, both in the morphological and phraseological literature, the works by Fleischer (1982/1997a, 1992, 1996a, 1996b, 1997b) and Barz (1988, 1996, 2007) being exceptions to this.

(iii) Implications for the architecture of the language system. – Studying the processes of both word and MWE formation leads to important insights in the structure of the language system. This applies in particular to the question as to whether these processes can be described as regular and/or productive.

The following sections review the shared properties of multi-word expressions and word-formation units as well as the differences between them while taking the aspects mentioned above into account, in particular the aspect of competition between phrasal and morphological patterns.

3.1 Shared properties of multi-word expressions and word-formation units

Both MWEs and word-formation units are by definition complex expressions. As the constituents of MWEs are words, the parallel between MWEs and word-formation units can be narrowed down to the parallel between MWEs and compounds since compounds are made up of free morphemes (words and stems), whereas derivation involves the combination of free and bound morphemes. This parallel leads to the question as to whether compounds should be regarded as MWEs too, since in English (and other languages) it is relatively difficult to draw a clear distinction between nominal compounds and corresponding phrases on formal grounds, as mentioned above. However, this problem has only rarely been tackled explicitly in phraseological research, as has been pointed out by Granger and Paquot (2008). Whereas Moon (1998) excludes nominal compounds from her study because of their morphological nature, many studies of English MWEs not surprisingly include nominal compounds, e.g., Sag et al. (2002), Villavicencio et al. (2005). Sometimes a distinction is drawn on the basis of the spelling (i.e. a form is considered as a MWE if written as two words, but not if written as one; e.g., Erman and Warren 2000; Copestake et al. 2002). Such a distinction, however, although understandable from the practical viewpoint of conducting a corpus study, is rather unsatisfactory from a theoretical point of view.

The next property shared by MWEs and word-formation units is their status as a lexical unit. More precisely, word-formation units are potential lexical units. That is, although most word-formation units end up in the lexicon, there are also ad hoc forms that are only produced for occasional use in a particular context and therefore do not become lexicalized. MWEs, on the other hand, seem to be lexical by definition: MWEs with deviant semantic or syntactic properties necessarily have to be stored in the mental lexicon. However, in a broad view of MWEs that includes patterns with variable slots (cf. section 2), MWEs must be regarded as potential lexical units, too, rather than as being lexical by definition. Acknowledging phrasal patterns of this kind means that there must also be non-lexicalized MWEs, i.e. MWEs that have been occasionally coined as instantiations from a certain phrasal pattern for use in a particular situation but have not become lexicalized.

Closely related to their lexical status is another property shared by MWEs and word-formation units: their function. Both forms function as linguistic signs for specific concepts, i.e. they are names. However, as has been repeatedly mentioned in the literature, word-formation units – and in particular compounds – may also be used as mere descriptions, i.e. as expressions that describe a concept but do not name it – just like "regular", non-lexicalized phrases do. A case in point is the well-known example *apple juice seat* when used in a particular conversation to indicate a seat in front of which a glass of apple-juice has been placed (cf. Downing 1977). It is obvious that this use of *apple juice seat* does not involve the existence of a corresponding self-contained concept. Accordingly, one may wonder whether MWEs can have a descriptive function, too. However, this question has – as far as we know – not yet been discussed in the literature.

Finally, both MWEs and word-formation units may have compositional or non-compositional semantics, and both may (but need not) contain constituents with a metaphorical meaning.

3.2 Differences between multi-word expressions and word-formation units

The main difference between MWEs and word-formation units is that, while both are complex expressions, MWEs are phrases, i.e. syntactic entities, whereas word-formation units are words, i.e. morphological entities.

A first question related to this difference in status between MWEs and word-formation units has to do with their mutual relations: should MWEs and word-formation units be regarded as alternative means that complement each other or as competitive processes instead? Obviously, lexical categories differ greatly with regard to their attraction to MWE formation and word-formation. According to Fleischer (1996b, 1997b) and Barz (2007), MWEs are abundant in the verbal domain, but they are less frequent with nouns and adverbs and even more infrequent with adjectives in German (and presumably also in other (Germanic) languages). This unequal distribution can be related to the corresponding word-formation processes: whereas verbal compounding does not exist in German, or exists there only marginally, and the number of verbal prefixes is relatively restricted, nominal compounding is highly productive. That is, MWEs and word-formation units seem to complement each other, supporting the view of MWEs and word-formation are alternative means of expanding the lexicon. Of course, other factors are important in this connection, too. For instance, MWEs (especially verbal ones) are often said to exhibit a high degree of expressivity (e.g., *to sweat blood* / German *Blut und Wasser schwitzen*). Likewise, German MWEs seem to include a high proportion of technical terms and proper names (e.g., *Echte Kamille* 'German chamomile', *Totes Meer* 'Dead See'). Thus, stylistic factors also play an important role in the alternation between MWEs and word-formation.

There also seems to be a major difference in between the way in which MWEs and word-formation units come into existence. Word-formation units, we can assume, are the result of regular, more or less productive word-formation rules (or patterns or schemas, depending on the particular framework used). On the other hand, many MWEs are made from existing phrases in a secondary process, i.e. through semantic reinterpretation or specialization, or just by becoming habitual through frequent use (cf. Fleischer 1997b; Barz 2007). These changes may also affect the syntactic properties of the phrase, for example by causing it to lose its syntactic flexibility. Such a view of MWEs and word-formation units in fact implies a fundamental difference between them: word-formation is a primary process, it is regular and – given extralinguistic motivation – it is more or less predictable, whereas MWE formation is a secondary process, i.e. an unsystematic and idiosyncratic lexicalization of phrasal units, and it is not predictable at all. However, in addition to highly idiosyncratic MWEs resulting from the alteration of existing phrases, there are also many MWEs that are obviously based on patterns or schemas. The NPN construction and the 'time'-*away* construction mentioned in section 2 are pertinent examples of this. Also, lexical A+N phrases (e.g., German *blauer Fleck*, Dutch *rode kool*, cf. section 2) can be regarded as instantiations of an abstract lexical schema that is equipped with additional morphosyntactic restrictions (compared to regular, non-lexicalized A+N phrases, cf. Booij 2009; Schlücker 2014).

Under the assumption that MWEs may be formed from abstract underlying patterns or schemas, MWEs become more similar to word-formation units, and the difference between MWEs and word-formation is less fundamental than described above. This view, however, makes important assumptions about the architecture of the language system as it assumes the existence of regular and productive phrasal patterns within the lexicon. Obviously, such a view is incompatible with a modular view of the grammar system, i.e. a strict separation of grammar and the lexicon as set forth in mainstream generative grammar. On the contrary, it is in full agreement with the fundamental assumptions behind a number of related frameworks known as "constructionist" theories (e.g., Goldberg 1995, 2006; Croft 2001; Jackendoff 2002), and, similarly, cognitive grammar (e.g., Langacker 1987, 1991; for an overview of different linguistic frameworks and MWE research, see Wray 2008; Gries 2008). Leaving aside many details and differences, these theories share the assumption that "constructions", i.e. symbolic units that are pairings of form and meaning, constitute the basic elements of the language system, and that there is no such thing as a strict divide between grammar and lexicon. Not surprisingly, much recent work on MWEs is construction-based, for example Riehemann (2001), Masini (2005, 2009), Booij (2002, 2009, 2010), Jackendoff (1997, 2008), Poß (2010). It can be said without doubt that the increased interest of theoretical linguistics in research into MWEs is connected with the development of constructionist frameworks during the past decades: work on specific constructions such as the *let alone* construction in Fillmore, Kay and O'Connor (1988) and the insight that MWEs are central to language and cannot be disregarded as marginal by linguistic theory (e.g., Jackendoff 1995) were fundamental for the further development of constructionist theory. Even earlier, similar ideas of considering MWEs as being variable syntactic patterns with open slots within the lexicon have been developed in more traditional research on phraseology under the name of *Modellbildung* (cf. Häusermann 1977) and *Phraseoschablone* (cf. Fleischer 1982/1997a).

3.3 Competition between phrasal and morphological patterns

Fellbaum (2011: 454) speculates that "perhaps the most important function of many idioms, which may account for their universality and ubiquity, is that they provide convenient, pre-fabricated, conventionalized encodings of often complex messages". In contrast to "regular" phrases, the central functions of MWEs are the encoding of complex messages and the providing of names for (complex) concepts ("naming function", cf. Fleischer 1982: 129). This can be illustrated by comparing the MWE *black market* with its paraphrase (taken from Merriam-Webster): "illicit trade in goods or commodities in violation of official regulations; also: a place where such trade is carried on."

MWEs like *black market* share their naming function with morphologically complex words like compounds (cf. Barz 2007). If, therefore, a clear formal distinction cannot be drawn between complex morphological and phrasal entities, this functional equivalence may lead to the assumption of "mixed" rather than pure morphological or syntactic entities. For instance, it has been proposed that some English A+N sequences might be constructions that are neither fully lexical nor fully syntactic and that there might therefore be a significant area of overlap between syntax and lexicon (cf. Sadler and Arnold 1994; Giegerich 2005).

The shared function of complex morphological and phrasal entities becomes even more significant through language comparison. Comparing English A+N units with their counterparts in Dutch and German reveals that speakers of Dutch very often use MWEs (*zwarte markt* 'black market', *rode wijn* 'red wine') where German has compounds for the same concepts (*Schwarzmarkt, Rotwein*) (cf. section 2 for some criteria for distinguishing phrases from compounds in Dutch and German). Dutch, like German, has A+N compounds (*fijnstof, Feinstaub* 'fine particles', *zuurdeeg, Sauerteig* 'sour dough'), and German, like Dutch, allows for phrases being used as lexical units (*saurer Regen, zure regen* 'acid rain'). However, these forms are not equally distributed in both languages: a great many of lexicalized A+N compounds in German correspond to A+N phrases in Dutch (*Dunkelkammer – donkere kamer* 'darkroom', *Vollmond – volle maan* 'full moon'; cf. Booij 2002; Hüning 2010). Within one language, lexicalization of one form often blocks the other, corresponding form (as indicated by #), e.g., *grüne Welle* 'progressive signal system; lit. green wave' vs. #*Grünwelle*, *die Dunkelkammer* 'darkroom' vs. #*die dunkle Kammer* (although this is a well-formed phrase, it is blocked for the specific interpretation expressed by the compound). The same is true for Dutch, where the potential compound #*zuurregen* and the potential phrase #*dunne druk* are blocked by the existence of *zure regen* 'acid rain' and *dundruk* 'lightface'.

The fact that lexicalization of a phrase can be blocked by the existence of a compound and that compounding can be blocked by the existence of a MWE shows that the syntactic and the morphological pattern are in competition with each other. This has been taken as a further argument against theories in which syntax and lexicon are seen as distinct modules of a language, since blocking only takes place among lexical elements (cf. Booij 2002, 2010, among others).

The question, then, is which factors determine the choice of one of the two patterns for encoding a certain concept. One factor is probably analogy with existing forms. For German A+N sequences, the choice between both patterns seems to be sensitive to type frequency effects, as shown by Schlücker and Plag (2011). The realization of a novel A+N sequence as either a compound or a phrase is largely dependent on the availability and the number of similar constructions in the mental lexicon of the speakers.

Blocking is, however, almost never absolute. Expressions like *grüner Tee* and *Grüntee* 'green tea' or *schwarzer Markt* and *Schwarzmarkt* 'black market' are used side by side, even in one text. The coexistence and use of both the compound and the synonymous phrase might be explained by the need for stylistic variation. It could, however, also indicate a diachronic change. Synchronically, the compound *Schwarzmarkt* is more conventional and more frequent, but diachronically, the meaning was first expressed by the phrase *schwarzer Markt*. This phrase has been gradually replaced by the compound since the middle of the 20th century, cf. Schuster (2016). Thus, the existence of a MWE and a synonymous compound might be an indication for a transitional phase in which one is replaced by the other. This replacement on the lexical level could correspond to the changing degrees of productivity of the patterns.

Thus, the syntactic and the morphological A+N pattern may function as competing categories. This is, however, only true for a subset of all possible A+N combinations because of a restriction on A+N compounding according to which the adjective has to be monomorphemic in A+N compounds. Thus, morphologically complex adjectives may be part of a lexicalized phrase, but not of an A+N compound (*der wissenschaftliche Mitarbeiter* – **der Wissenschaftlichmitarbeiter* 'scientific assistant'; *die treulose Tomate* – **die Treulostomate* 'fair-weather friend; lit. faithless tomato'). A phrase is therefore a much more flexible means of coining a name consisting of an adjective and a noun than a compound as there are no restrictions on its formation.

Greater flexibility and applicability seems to be a general property of phrasal patterns as compared to compounds. This can also be illustrated by what is known as a "phrasal simile" in the literature (other terms are "frozen simile" or "stereotyped comparison", cf. Fiedler 2007: 43). According to Wikberg (2008: 128) a "simile can be defined as a figurative expression used to make an explicit comparison of two unlike things by means of the prepositions *like, (as) ... as* or the conjunctions *as, as if, as though.*" Similes thus can be conceived of as fixed comparative frames, i.e. as patterns with open slots. They have the structure of a typical comparison and can be used predicatively or adverbially.

We will focus on two frequent types of these comparisons, an adjectival type (*(as) strong as a horse, (as) white as snow*) and a verbal type (*to eat like a horse, to sleep like a log*). These phrasal similes can be found in many languages. Fleischer (1992: 63) even states a particular phraseological affinity of comparative structures and binomials.

According to Wikberg (2008), similes have to be distinguished from literal comparisons and from metaphors. While literal comparisons are reversible (*olive oil is like a fine wine – a fine wine is like olive oil*), similes are not (*Kim is like a ray of sunshine – *a ray of sunshine is like Kim*) (examples taken from Wikberg 2008: 129). From a functional point of view, similes resemble metaphors: speakers ascribe some characteristic to something or somebody by making use of a supposed similarity. Similes are, however, more explicit, which explains why metaphors are sometimes seen as elliptical similes. The German MWE *er ist (so) dumm wie ein Esel* 'he is (as) stupid as a mule', in this view, corresponds to the metaphor: *er ist ein Esel*.

In our context, it is interesting that similes and compounds often function as alternative means for expressing a particular concept. Many similes of the adjectival type have a lexical equivalent (an N+A compound): *(so) weiß wie Schnee* 'as white as snow' – *schneeweiß* 'snow-white'. In the compound, the phrasal comparison is compressed into one word. This can therefore be regarded as a case of "univerbation". It is an endocentric compound and the adjective functions as the syntactic and semantic head. As in the phrasal expression, the comparison is made explicit by giving the "tertium comparationis" (the property denoted by the adjective), which is modified by the first element of the compound (the noun). The comparison can thus be expressed syntactically/phraseologically or morphologically without a difference in meaning: *ihre Haut war weiß wie Schnee / schneeweiß* – 'her skin was as white as snow / snow-white'.

This parallel, however, only holds for the adjectival type of phrasal similes. Verbal comparisons cannot be expressed by means of a compound: *frieren wie ein Schneider* 'to be very cold; lit. to freeze like a tailor' – **schneiderfrieren*; *schimpfen wie ein Rohrspatz* 'to rant and rave; lit. to rant like a reed bunting' – **rohrspatzschimpfen*. This type of noun incorporation is ungrammatical, and verbal compounding is in general highly restricted in German. This illustrates once more (as in the A+N case above) that the syntactic patterns are less restricted, and accordingly more flexible, than the morphological ones.

For the adjectival type, the coexistence of both the MWE and the compound is well-established in many cases. Pairs like *flink wie ein Wiesel* 'as quick as a flash; lit. as nimble as a weasel' – *wieselflink* or *schlank wie eine Gerte* lit. '(as) slender as a whip' – *gertenschlank* are well-known to native speakers of German. In many other cases, however, the compound is not conventionalized. Words like *haubitzenvoll* (< *voll/blau wie eine Haubitze* 'as drunk as a skunk; lit. drunk like a howitzer') or *bohnenstrohdumm* (< *dumm wie Bohnenstroh* 'as thick as a brick; lit. dumb like bean straw') are grammatical and can be found via Google, but they are not conventionalized and their use is highly marked. The relationship between the two patterns is asymmetrical: all compounds expressing a stereotyped comparison have a corresponding phrasal comparison but not vice versa. There are many phrasal similes without a corresponding compound.

Another difference concerns the syntactic behaviour of similes and compounds. Both can be used predicatively or as an adverbial, but only the compound can be used prenominally as an attribute in an NP (*der Kleinwagen war wieselflink / flink wie ein Wiesel* 'the compact car was as nimble as a weasel' – *der wieselflinke Kleinwagen*). MWEs, on the other hand, can only be used in postnominal position to modify a noun (as an apposition): *der Kleinwagen, flink wie ein Wiesel*.

Thus, as in the A+N case, the morphological and the phrasal comparative pattern are competitive only with regard to a relatively small subset of all possible similes. Compounding is, again, much more restricted than MWE formation. On the other hand, compounds are words, and this makes them more versatile with regard to their syntactic range of use.

3.4 Constructionalization

In phrasal similes the noun tends to lose its literal meaning. The comparison often seems to be "strange" or far-fetched (Donalies 2009: 76). Why is *Bohnenstroh* 'dumb' (*dumm wie Bohnenstroh sein* 'to be as thick as a brick; lit. dumb like bean straw')? What has drunkenness to do with a skunk (*as drunk as a skunk*)? Other comparisons seem to be motivated. For instance, it seems reasonable to consider a weasel as agile (*flink wie ein Wiesel*). In most comparisons, however, the intensifying meaning dominates the meaning of the expression as a whole. This seems to be true for MWEs as well as for compounds: *dumm wie Bohnenstroh* means 'very dumb' and *wieselflink* means 'very agile'.

This kind of abstract intensification of meaning suggests the existence of abstract "models" (Burger 2010: 44) or "constructional schemas" (in the sense of construction grammar, cf. Booij 2010 and article 6 on word-formation in construction grammar) for intensifying MWEs and compounds in German:

MWE: [(*so*) A *wie* N] ↔ 'very A'
Compound: [N + A]_A ↔ 'very A'

These schemas can be seen as subschemas of a more general literal comparison schema (in the MWE case) and of a more general schema for N+A compounding. In German, most N+A compounds express a comparison, but there are also other meaning relations, e.g., *lebensfremd* 'remote from everyday life; lit. life foreign', *knielang* 'knee-length; lit. knee long', etc. The comparative subschemas in question inherit some of their general properties from the general schemas for the MWEs and the compounds. However, they add the intensifying meaning which is part of the construction itself rather than of the constituent words.

This idea can be related to the variability found in many of the MWEs. As Fiedler (2007: 43–44) points out, many phrasal similes can be filled very flexibly with lexical material:

[as happy as X]: *(as) happy as Larry/a clam/a lark/a pig in muck/a sandboy*
[work like X]: *work like a horse/a dog/a slave/a Trojan/a black/a nigger/like stink*

Phrasal similes also allow for (limited) variation and modification, for example by means of adjectival modification, if this can be interpreted as a further signal of intensification, e.g., *dumm wie <u>altes</u> Brot* 'as dumb as (old) bread', *schwarz wie die <u>finstre</u> Nacht* 'as black as the (dark) night'. Compounds, on the contrary, do not allow such modifications, since they are words. Variation and modification can be seen as aspects of the greater expressivity of phrases as compared to compounds.

The constructional meaning accounts for the fact that the meaning of a phrasal simile can be inferred even in the case of modified or unknown comparisons. Although a speaker/hearer does not always know the meaning of the noun someone/something is compared with, he or she is able to understand the meaning of the utterance. For instance, even without knowing the meaning of *Haubitze* 'howitzer' it is obvious that somebody who is *blau/voll/betrunken wie eine Haubitze* lit. 'blue/full/drunk like a howitzer' is very drunk. The constructional schema also accounts for the interpretability of unknown loan translations like *besoffen wie ein Molch* (from *as drunk as a newt*) and of occasional ad hoc comparisons (*Nerven dünn wie Zahnseide* 'nerves on edge; lit. nerves as thin as dental floss'; Donalies 2009: 76). Novel nonsense comparisons are also interpreted according to the constructional meaning, such as *er stinkt wie ein Gartenzwerg* 'he stinks like a skunk; lit. he stinks like a garden gnome'.

Comparative compounds, on the other hand, also tend to lose the comparison as an element of their meaning when intensification becomes the central aspect of the compound's semantics. N+A compounds expressing a gradation or intensification of the adjective usually go back to formations expressing a comparison. The German compound *stocksteif* lit. 'stickstiff', for example, got its meaning 'very stiff' through the comparison *steif wie ein Stock* 'as stiff as a stick'. By analogy, new compounds with the constituent *stock* have been coined (cf. Fleischer and Barz 1995: 231): *stockblind* 'stone-blind', *stockkonservativ* 'conservative to the core', *stockbürgerlich* 'philistine to the core', *stockkatholisch* 'catholic to the core', *stockreaktionär* 'extremely reactionary', etc. This use of *stock-* might also be related to the existence of adjectival participle *verstockt* 'obdurate' and related words. In any case, the literal meaning of the noun *Stock* has been lost in these adjectives. They can be accounted for by assuming a subschema of the one given above, in which the position of the N is lexically filled: [*stock* + A]$_A$ ↔ 'very A / extremely A / A to the core', cf. Hüning and Booij (2014).

The element *stock* is no longer (synchronically) identical to the noun *Stock*, it has become a "prefixoid" or even a "prefix" (for a discussion of the concept of "affixoid", see, e.g., Stevens 2005; Booij and Hüning 2014). The comparison is no longer part of the meaning, so these compounds do not correspond to a MWE expressing a stereotyped comparison. In a case like this, the phrasal simile can be seen as a starting point for the development of a new morphological pattern. Through "univerbation", the comparison can be expressed by a compound. The compound becomes lexicalized, the meaning may become more abstract (intensification), and the relation to the meaning of the corresponding noun becomes opaque. Through the use in a series of compounds, the first element (the noun) is reinterpreted and eventually becomes a bound morpheme. Ultimately, this can change the status of the compounds in question. They are interpreted as instantiations of a productive derivational word-formation process rather than as examples of compounding.

Summing up, the developments outlined here strongly support the idea of a hierarchical lexicon, containing words, MWEs, constructions and constructional schemas on different levels of abstraction (cf. Jackendoff 2008; Booij 2010). Subschemas allow for generalizations of subsets of words and MWEs within a morphological category or within a certain phrasal construction. The examples presented here show that there is a functional overlap between syntax and morphology (and the lexicon). MWEs and compounds often share certain functions and meanings, but as a result of their different origin and structural status (syntactic phrase vs. morphological compound) they also differ with respect to their range of use. The two patterns compete such that it sometimes is not really possible to make a distinction between an MWE and a complex word, as in the case of English A+N constructions. The overall picture is, however, that MWEs and compounds are largely a complementary means for creating lexical units.

4 References

Bartsch, Sabine (2004): *Structural and Functional Properties of Collocations in English. A Corpus Study of Lexical and Pragmatic Constraints on Lexical Co-occurrence*. Tübingen: Narr.

Barz, Irmhild (1988): Wortbildung und Nomination. *Zur Theorie der Wortbildung im Deutschen. Dem Wirken Wolfgang Fleischers gewidmet*, 19–24. (Sitzungsberichte der Akademie der Wissenschaften der DDR 4/G). Berlin: Akademie Verlag.

Barz, Irmhild (1996): Komposition und Kollokation. In: Clemens Knobloch and Burkhard Schaeder (eds.), *Nomination – fachsprachlich und gemeinsprachlich*, 127–146. Opladen: Westdeutscher Verlag.

Barz, Irmhild (2007): Wortbildung und Phraseologie. In: Harald Burger, Dimitrij Dobrovol'skij, Peter Kühn and Neal R. Norrick (eds.), *Phraseology. An International Handbook of Contemporary Research*. Vol. 1, 27–36. Berlin/New York: de Gruyter.

Bauer, Laurie (2019): Compounds. In: Bas Aarts, Jill Bowie and Gergana Popova (eds.), *The Oxford Handbook of English Grammar*, 261–280. Oxford University Press.

Belica, Cyril and Rainer Perkuhn (2015): Feste Wortgruppen/Phraseologie I: Kollokationen und syntagmatische Muster. In: Ulrike Haß and Petra Storjohann (eds.), *Handbuch Wort und Wortschatz*, 221–225. Berlin/Boston: De Gruyter.

Biber, Douglas (2009): A corpus-driven approach to formulaic language in English: Multi-word patterns in speech and writing. *International Journal of Corpus Linguistics* 14: 275–311.

Booij, Geert (2002): Constructional idioms, morphology, and the Dutch lexicon. *Journal of Germanic Linguistics* 14: 301–329.

Booij, Geert (2009): Phrasal names: A constructionist analysis. *Word Structure* 2: 219–240.

Booij, Geert (2010): *Construction Morphology*. Oxford: Oxford University Press.

Booij, Geert and Matthias Hüning (2014): Affixoids and constructional idioms. In: Ronny Boogaart, Timothy Colleman and Gijsbert Rutten (eds.), *Extending the Scope of Construction Grammar*, 77–105. Berlin/Boston: De Gruyter Mouton.

Burger, Harald (2010): *Phraseologie. Eine Einführung am Beispiel des Deutschen*. 4th ed. Berlin: Schmidt.

Copestake, Anne, Fabre Lambeau, Aline Villavicencio, Francis Bond, Timothy Baldwin, Ivan Sag and Dan Flickinger (2002): Multiword expressions: Linguistic precision and reusability. In: *Proceedings of the Third International Conference on Language Resources and Evaluation (LREC 2002)*, 1941–1947. Las Palmas: European Languages Resources Association.

Croft, William (2001): *Radical Construction Grammar*. Oxford: Oxford University Press.

Dobrovol'skij, Dmitrij (1997): *Idiome im mentalen Lexikon. Ziele und Methoden der kognitivbasierten Phraseologieforschung*. Trier: Wissenschaftlicher Verlag Trier.

Dobrovol'skij, Dmitrij (1988): *Phraseologie als Objekt der Universalienlinguistik*. Leipzig: VEB Verlag Enzyklopädie.

Donalies, Elke (2009): *Basiswissen deutsche Phraseologie*. Tübingen/Basel: Francke.

Downing, Pamela (1977): On the creation and use of English compound nouns. *Language* 53: 810–842.
Erman, Britt and Beatrice Warren (2000): The idiom principle and the open choice principle. *Text – Interdisciplinary Journal for the Study of Discourse* 20: 29–62.
Ernst, Thomas (1981): Grist for the linguistic mill: Idioms and "extra" adjectives. *Journal of Linguistic Research* 1: 51–68.
Fellbaum, Christiane (2011): Idioms and collocations. In: Claudia Maienborn, Klaus von Heusinger and Paul Portner (eds.), *Semantics. An International Handbook of Natural Language Meaning*. Vol. 1, 441–456. Berlin/New York: De Gruyter Mouton.
Fellbaum, Christiane and Ekaterini Stathi (2006): Idiome in der Grammatik und im Kontext: Wer brüllt hier die Leviten? In: Kristel Proost and Edeltraut Winkler (eds.), *Von Intentionalität zur Bedeutung konventionalisierter Zeichen. Festschrift für Gisela Harras zum 65. Geburtstag*, 125–146. Tübingen: Narr.
Fiedler, Sabine (2007): *English Phraseology. A Coursebook*. Tübingen: Narr.
Fillmore, Charles J., Paul Kay and Mary Catherine O'Connor (1988): Regularity and idiomaticity in grammatical constructions. *Language* 64: 501–538.
Finkbeiner, Rita and Barbara Schlücker (2019): Compounds and multi-word expressions in the languages of Europe. In: Barbara Schlücker (ed.), *Complex lexical units. Compounds and multi-word expressions*, 1–44. Berlin/Boston: De Gruyter.
Fleischer, Wolfgang (1982): *Phraseologie der deutschen Gegenwartssprache*. Leipzig: VEB Bibliographisches Institut.
Fleischer, Wolfgang (1992): Konvergenz und Divergenz von Wortbildung und Phraseologisierung. In: Jarmo Korhonen (ed.), *Phraseologie und Wortbildung – Aspekte der Lexikonerweiterung*, 53–65. Tübingen: Niemeyer.
Fleischer, Wolfgang (1996a): Phraseologische, terminologische und onymische Wortgruppen als Nominationseinheiten. In: Clemens Knobloch and Burkhard Schaeder (eds.), *Nomination, fachsprachlich und gemeinsprachlich*, 147–170. Opladen: Westdeutscher Verlag.
Fleischer, Wolfgang (1996b): Zum Verhältnis von Wortbildung und Phraseologie im Deutschen. In: Jarmo Korhonen (ed.), *Studien zur Phraseologie des Deutschen und des Finnischen II*, 333–344. Bochum: Brockmeyer.
Fleischer, Wolfgang (1997a): *Phraseologie der deutschen Gegenwartssprache*. 2nd ed. Tübingen: Niemeyer.
Fleischer, Wolfgang (1997b): Das Zusammenwirken von Wortbildung und Phraseologisierung in der Entwicklung des Wortschatzes. In: Rainer Wimmer und Franz-Josef Berens (eds.), *Wortbildung und Phraseologie*, 9–24. Tübingen: Narr.
Fleischer, Wolfgang and Irmhild Barz (1995): *Wortbildung der deutschen Gegenwartssprache*. 2nd ed. Tübingen: Niemeyer.
Fraser, Bruce (1970): Idioms with a transformational grammar. *Foundations of Language* 6: 22–42.
Gibbs, Raymond W. and Herbert L. Colston (2007): Psycholinguistic aspects of phraseology: American tradition. In: Harald Burger, Dmitrij Dobrovol'skij, Peter Kühn and Neal R. Norrick (eds.), *Phraseology. An International Handbook of Contemporary Research*. Vol. 2, 819–836. Berlin/New York: de Gruyter.
Giegerich, Heinz J. (2005): Associative adjectives in English and the lexicon-syntax interface. *Journal of Linguistics* 41: 571–591.
Giegerich, Heinz J. (2015): *Lexical structures: compounding and the modules of grammar*. Edinburgh: Edinburgh University Press.
Goldberg, Adele (1995): *Constructions. A Construction Grammar Approach to Argument Structure*. Chicago: University of Chicago Press.

Goldberg, Adele (2006): *Constructions at Work. The Nature of Generalization in Language*. Oxford: Oxford University Press.

Granger, Sylviane and Magali Paquot (2008): Disentangling the phraseological web. In: Sylviane Granger and Fanny Meunier (eds.), *Phraseology. An interdisciplinary perspective*, 27–49. Amsterdam/Philadelphia: Benjamins.

Gries, Stefan Th. (2008): Phraseology and linguistic theory: A brief survey. In: Sylviane Granger and Fanny Meunier (eds.), *Phraseology. An interdisciplinary perspective*, 3–25. Amsterdam/Philadelphia: Benjamins.

Häcki Buhofer, Annelies (2007): Psycholinguistic aspects of phraseology: European tradition. In: Harald Burger, Dmitrij Dobrovol'skij, Peter Kühn and Neal R. Norrick (eds.), *Phraseology. An International Handbook of Contemporary Research*. Vol. 2, 836–853. Berlin/New York: de Gruyter.

Häusermann, Jürg (1977): *Phraseologie. Hauptprobleme der deutschen Phraseologie auf der Basis sowjetischer Forschungsergebnisse*. Tübingen: Niemeyer.

Heid, Ulrich (2007): Computational linguistic aspects of phraseology II. In: Harald Burger, Dmitrij Dobrovol'skij, Peter Kühn and Neal R. Norrick (eds.), *Phraseology. An International Handbook of Contemporary Research*. Vol. 2, 1036–1044. Berlin/New York: de Gruyter.

Heid, Ulrich (2008): Computational phraseology. In: Sylviane Granger und Fanny Meunier (eds.), *Phraseology. An interdisciplinary perspective*, 337–360. Amsterdam/Philadelphia: Benjamins.

Hüning, Matthias (2010): Adjective + noun constructions between syntax and word formation in Dutch and German. In: Alexander Onysko and Sascha Michel (eds.), *Cognitive Perspectives on Word Formation*, 195–215. Berlin/New York: Mouton de Gruyter.

Hüning, Matthias and Geert Booij (2014): From compounding to derivation: The rise of derivational affixes through 'constructionalization'. *Folia Linguistica* 48(2): 579–604.

Jackendoff, Ray (1995): The Boundaries of the lexicon. In: Martin Everaert, Erik-Jan Van der Linden, André Schenk and Rob Schreuder (eds.), *Idioms. Structural and psychological perspectives*, 133–165. Hillsdale, NJ: Erlbaum.

Jackendoff, Ray (1997): Twistin' the night away. *Language* 73: 534–559.

Jackendoff, Ray (2002): *Foundations of Language*. Oxford: Oxford University Press.

Jackendoff, Ray (2008): Construction after construction and its theoretical challenges. *Language* 84: 8–28.

Lambrecht, Knud (1984): Formulaicity, frame semantics, and pragmatics in German binomial expressions. *Language* 60: 753–796.

Langacker, Ronald (1987): *Foundations of Cognitive Grammar*. Vol. 1: *Theoretical prerequisites*. Stanford, CA: Stanford University Press.

Langacker, Ronald (1991): *Foundations of Cognitive Grammar*. Vol. 2: *Descriptive applications*. Stanford, CA: Stanford University Press.

Masini, Francesca (2005): Multi-word expressions between syntax and the lexicon: The case of Italian verb-particle constructions. *SKY Journal of Linguistics* 18: 145–173.

Masini, Francesca (2009): Phrasal lexemes, compounds and phrases: A constructionist perspective. *Word Structure* 2: 254–271.

Moon, Rosamund (1998): *Fixed Expressions and Idioms in English. A corpus-based approach*. Oxford/New York: Clarendon Press.

Moon, Rosamund (2007): Corpus linguistic approaches with English corpora. In: Harald Burger, Dmitrij Dobrovol'skij, Peter Kühn and Neal R. Norrick (eds.), *Phraseology. An International Handbook of Contemporary Research*. Vol. 2, 1045–1059. Berlin/New York: de Gruyter.

Moon, Rosamund (2015): Multi-word items. In: John R. Taylor (ed.), *The Oxford Handbook of The Word*, 120–140. New York, NY: Oxford University Press.

Newmeyer, Frederick (1974): The regularity of idiom behaviour. *Lingua* 34: 327–342.
Nunberg, Geoffrey, Ivan Sag and Thomas Wasow (1994): Idioms. *Language* 70: 491–538.
Ohnheiser, Ingeborg (2015): Compounds and multi-word expressions in Slavic. In: Peter O. Müller, Ingeborg Ohnheiser, Susan Olsen and Franz Rainer (eds.), *Word-Formation. An International Handbook of the Languages of Europe.* Vol. 1, 757–779. Berlin/Boston: De Gruyter Mouton.
Poß, Michaela (2010): *Under Construction. Cognitive and Computational Aspects of Extended Lexical Units.* Utrecht: LOT.
Renouf, Antoinette and John Sinclair (1991): Collocational frameworks in English. In: Karin Aijmer and Bengt Altenberg (eds.), *English Corpus Linguistics*, 128–143. London/New York: Longman.
Riehemann, Susanne Z. (2001): A constructional approach to idioms and word formation. Ph.D. dissertation, Stanford University.
Roth, Tobias (2014): *Wortverbindungen und Verbindungen von Wörtern. Lexikografische und distributionelle Aspekte kombinatorischer Begriffsbildung zwischen Syntax und Morphologie.* Tübingen: Narr Francke Attempto.
Sadler, Louisa and Douglas J. Arnold (1994): Prenominal adjectives and the phrasal/lexical distinction. *Journal of Linguistics* 30: 187–226.
Sag, Ivan, Timothy Baldwin, Francis Bond, Anne Copestake and Dan Flickinger (2002): Multiword expressions: A pain in the neck for NLP. In: Alexander Gelbukh (ed.), *Computational Linguistics and Intelligent Text Processing*, 1–15. Mexico City/Berlin: Springer.
Sailer, Manfred (2007): Corpus linguistic approaches with German corpora. In: Harald Burger, Dmitrij Dobrovol'skij, Peter Kühn and Neal R. Norrick (eds.), *Phraseology. An International Handbook of Contemporary Research.* Vol. 2, 1060–1071. Berlin/New York: de Gruyter.
Schlücker, Barbara (2014): *Grammatik im Lexikon. Adjektiv+Nomen-Verbindungen im Deutschen und Niederländischen.* Berlin/Boston: de Gruyter.
Schlücker, Barbara (ed.) (2019): *Complex lexical units: compounds and multi-word expressions.* Berlin/Boston: De Gruyter.
Schlücker, Barbara and Ingo Plag (2011): Compound or phrase? Analogy in naming. *Lingua* 121: 1539–1551.
Schulte im Walde, Sabine and Eva Smolka (eds.) (2020): *The role of constituents in multiword expressions: An interdisciplinary, cross-lingual perspective.* Berlin: Language Science Press.
Schuster, Saskia (2016): *Variation und Wandel. Zur Konkurrenz morphologischer und syntaktischer A+N-Verbindungen im Deutschen und Niederländischen seit 1700.* Berlin/Boston: De Gruyter Mouton.
Sprenger, Simone (2003): Fixed expressions and the production of idioms. Ph.D. dissertation, Max Planck Instituut voor Psycholinguïstiek, Nijmegen.
Stathi, Katerina (2007): A corpus-based analysis of adjectival modification in German idioms. In: Christiane Fellbaum (ed.), *Idioms and Collocations. Corpus-based Linguistic and Lexicographic Studies*, 81–108. London: Continuum.
Stevens, Christopher M. (2005): Revisiting the affixoid debate: On the grammaticalization of the word. In: Torsten Leuschner, Tanja Mortelmans and Sarah De Groodt (eds.), *Grammatikalisierung im Deutschen*, 71–83. Berlin/New York: de Gruyter.
Svensson, Maria Helena (2008): A very complex criterion of fixedness: Non-compositionality. In: Sylviane Granger and Fanny Meunier (eds.), *Phraseology. An Interdisciplinary Perspective*, 81–93. Amsterdam/Philadelphia: Benjamins.
Villavicencio, Aline, Francis Bond, Anna Korhonen and Diana McCarthy (2005): Introduction to the special issue on multiword expressions: Having a crack at a hard nut. *Computer Speech and Language* 19: 365–377.

Weinreich, Uriel (1969): Problems in the analysis of idioms. In: Jaan Puhvel (ed.), *Substance and Structure of Language. Lectures delivered before the Linguistic Institute of the Linguistic Society of America, Univ. of California, Los Angeles*, 23–81. Berkeley: University of California Press.
Wikberg, Kay (2008): Phrasal similes in the BNC. In: Sylviane Granger and Fanny Meunier (eds.), *Phraseology. An Interdisciplinary Perspective*, 127–142. Amsterdam/Philadelphia: Benjamins.
Wray, Alison (2002): *Formulaic Language and the Lexicon*. Cambridge: Cambridge University Press.
Wray, Alison (2008): *Formulaic Language. Pushing the Boundaries*. Oxford: Oxford University Press.

Thomas Schwaiger
18 Reduplication

1 Introduction
2 Forms
3 Meanings and functions
4 Reduplication and word-formation
5 Reduplication, word-formation and the languages of Europe
6 References

Abstract: This article gives an overview of general formal and functional properties of reduplication as well as their interpretation in different theoretical approaches. Special emphasis is put on reduplication as a productive and lexical means of word-formation. As it is a relatively marginal phenomenon in European languages and because reduplication theory has thus advanced primarily due to the examination of non-European languages, relevant data from many language families all around the world are adduced throughout the discussion. This broader scope notwithstanding, the article is rounded off by providing an outline of reduplication and word-formation specifically in the languages of Europe.

1 Introduction

"Reduplication" is the systematically and productively employed repetition of words or parts of words for the expression of a variety of lexical and grammatical functions. As a morphological device exhibiting a range of theoretically challenging phonological characteristics, it has been the subject of an ever-growing field of intense linguistic research since the 1970s. Terminologically, besides occasionally also being referred to by the less redundant form "duplication" (e.g., Inkelas 2008; see also Naylor 1986: 175), other labels sometimes attached to the phenomenon in question as well as to related or similar (but nonetheless distinct) phenomena include "(morphological) doubling" (e.g., Inkelas and Zoll 2005), "(re-)iteration" (e.g., Aboh, Smith and Zribi-Hertz 2012), "repetition" (e.g., Gil 2005) and "replication" (e.g., Mel'čuk 2006: 301–302). Notwithstanding this terminological diversity and its potential for causing confusion, over the years the term "redupli-

Thomas Schwaiger, Graz, Austria

https://doi.org/10.1515/9783111420561-018

cation" has proven to be the most stable and most widely-used one among linguists engaged in the topic.

In addition to giving an overview of formal and functional properties (see also article 9 on units of word-formation) displayed by reduplication in spoken languages from all over the world (including creoles; see Kouwenberg 2003) as well as sketching an outline of the phenomenon's interpretation within different theoretical frameworks, this article specifically concentrates on reduplication as a means of word-formation and its status in the languages of Europe (for reduplication in sign language see Pfau and Steinbach 2005 and Wilbur 2005).

2 Forms

In modern twentieth-century linguistics, at the latest since the seminal dissertation by Wilbur (1973), reduplication is commonly recognized as a morphological process characterized by the phonological peculiarity of providing the exponents for various linguistic categories (i.e. the "reduplicants") by full or partial repetition of the respective base forms. During the past four decades the at times surprising formal properties exhibited by different types of the process have been the main theoretical focus of reduplication research.

2.1 General formal properties

"Full (or complete or total) reduplication" is the repetition of any morphological unit, preferably from the root up to the whole word (see below). For example, Basque forms intensive adjectives like *argi~argia* 'very clear' (following the Leipzig glossing rules, from here on a tilde will be used to indicate the boundary between base and reduplicant) by reduplicating the adjectival base form without inflectional suffixes, in the case at hand the singular determiner *-a* (Hualde and Ortiz de Urbina 2003: 360). In Afrikaans, a noun including a plural suffix can be reduplicated to express considerable number, e.g., *bottel-s* 'bottles' → *bottels~bottels* 'bottles and bottles (i.e. many bottles)' (Botha 1988: 92). Falling in line with an apparent privilege of morphological roots to be at least partly repeated in all kinds of reduplication (cf. Inkelas 2012: 358), full reduplication of affixes alone is rather rare; one language exemplifying the phenomenon is Fijian, where a collective or distributive prefix *vēi-* can be reduplicated to express greater number of a noun, e.g., *vanua* 'country' → *vēi-vanua* 'various countries' → *vēi~vēi-vanua* 'larger number of countries' (Schütz 1985: 367; a somewhat more complicated example of prefix reduplication in the European language Hungarian is discussed at length in Kiefer 1995–96).

"Partial reduplication" involves phonological and prosodic categories smaller than the morphological base undergoing the process, offering a number of subtypes and classificatory parameters. Leaving possible but often controversial cases of single-segment reduplication like gemination aside (but see El Zarka 2005), partial reduplication can manifest itself in any way from simply reduplicating a consonant and vowel to the almost complete repetition of a base, while the respective reduplicants can attach initially, internally or finally to the latter. Illustrative examples come from Ngiyambaa attenuation by an initial disyllabic foot reduplicant (cf. Donaldson 1980: 69–70) as in *bara:y* 'fast' → *bara~bara:y* 'more or less fast, fastish' (Donaldson 1980: 72), Mangarayi final consonant-vowel-consonant reduplication as in the plural dyadic kin term *galŋbam~bam-yi* 'spouses' (additionally requiring the proprietive suffix *-yi*) from *galŋbam* 'spouse' (Merlan 1982: 215) and Chamorro medial consonant-vowel continuative reduplication as in *hugándo* 'play' → *hu~gá~gando* 'playing' (Topping 1973: 259; the accent marks primary stress). As can be seen from the first and last example, the prosodic make-up of the base is not necessarily exactly reflected in the reduplicant (the Ngiyambaa foot reduplicant only shows the onset consonant and nuclear vowel of the second base syllable, while in Chamorro the sole reduplicant syllable lacks the base coda), pointing toward an independently fixed shape for partial reduplicants merely to be filled by segmental information from the base (see Moravcsik 1978: 307–308, 311–312, 315).

A further special characteristic when comparing a base and its reduplicant is the structural reduction in terms of markedness occasionally found in partial reduplication. In the example from Ngiyambaa above, vowel length is reduced in the reduplicant; another widespread case of reduced marked structures is the simplification of consonant clusters vis-à-vis the base as in Tagalog so-called proposed verbal forms, exemplified here by *mag-ta~trabáhoh* 'X will work' (the prefix *mag-* indicates agent focus) from *trabáhoh* 'work' (French 1988: 23). The latter example moreover demonstrates the possibility of a discontinuous string of segments in the base to form a partial reduplicant.

Intensive adjective formation in Turkish via partial reduplication as in *sarı* 'yellow' → *sap~sarı* 'yellow like a quince (i.e. bright yellow)' (Müller 2004: 87) reveals important characteristics as well. On the one hand, such an example demonstrates that the reduplicant and base do not necessarily have to appear directly adjacent to one another. On the other hand, it can be seen that what specifically interferes in this case is a so-called "fixed segment" in the reduplicant, i.e. a segmental unit not found in the base. Fixed segments are not restricted to partial reduplication, though; they can also appear as sound substitutions or additions with full reduplication in formations commonly known as "echo-words". Relevant examples for the latter can once again be adduced from Turkish, e.g., *hasta* 'sick' → *hasta~masta* 'sick or so' and *oyun* 'game' → *oyun~moyun* 'games and the like' (Müller 2004: 18).

2.2 Theoretical approaches to reduplication form

Examining cases of the exceptional (non-)application of phonological rules in reduplicative contexts nowadays commonly termed "overapplication" and "underapplication", Wilbur (1973) raised fundamental issues for a generative-derivational architecture of grammar and the proper localization of reduplication in such a model. To better handle said exceptions in a framework of the mentioned type, Wilbur (1973: 58) formulated the identity constraint (basically saying that there is a tendency for a base and reduplicant to preserve identity in a reduplicated form) as a condition on over-/underapplying rules and assigned reduplication wholly to the morphological component (see Wilbur 1973: 64–65), thereby initiating and paving the way for an ensuing dominance of theoretical investigations into the formal nature of reduplication always making use of state-of-the-art concepts and tools offered by linguistics.

In the 1980s, observations like the one in Moravcsik (1978) alluded to in the previous subsection brought about a change from looking at the interaction of reduplication with phonological rules to investigating so-called "reduplicative templates" within the by then popular approaches committed to nonlinear or prosodic morphology (see article 5 on word-formation in generative grammar). Responding to the inadequacy of overgenerating transformational rules in the formalization of reduplication, Marantz (1982) put forth an autosegmental copy-and-association model, in which he treated reduplication as the concatenative affixation of a segmentally underspecified morpheme template later on to be filled by segments from the base via "phonological copying". Addressing theoretical problems arising from the sometimes occurring additional transfer of prosodic information like syllabicity and length to the reduplicant, Clements (1985) subsequently proposed a non-concatenative account instead, claiming that the reduplicative affix is joined to the base in parallel so that prosodic features may be transferred as well before the linearization of the base and reduplicant takes place. In contrast to her above-mentioned predecessors, Steriade (1988: 78) finally rejected the possibility of partial reduplicative templates altogether; in her full-copy approach, partial reduplication always starts out as full reduplication, while the final reduplicant shape is determined by the application of reductional operations implementing requirements of syllable markedness (cf. Steriade 1988: 92).

As a consequence of further pursuing and constantly refining prosodic morphology, the 1990s were marked by a turn to non-derivational, declarative models of language and, especially, the accompanying rise of optimality theory, the general development and success of which are intimately connected with the application of various optimality-theoretic subtheories to cases of reduplication. Essentially going all the way back to Wilbur (1973: 72), (base-reduplicant) correspondence theory (e.g., McCarthy and Prince 1999) revived the central idea behind the identity constraint in terms of "correspondence relations" holding between the underlying stem and surface base as well as between the surface base and the surface reduplicant (see McCarthy and Prince 1999: 232); accordingly, the long-debated instances of overapplication and underapplication are attributed to the high ranking of base-reduplicant identity constraints in this model. Generalized template theory (e.g., McCarthy and Prince 1994), on the other hand, strived to derive reduplicative templates by independent constraints concerning prosody, morphology and their interface (but see Hendricks 2001 for an argument against prosodic templatic constraints). In this approach, the often observed unmarked reduplicant structures already investigated by Steriade (1988) follow from a constraint ranking in which any structural constraint (e.g., a ban against syllable codas or complex onsets) is dominated by general input-output faithfulness but itself dominates base-reduplicant faithfulness (the effects of such a ranking are now commonly known as the emergence of the unmarked or simply TETU). In a similar vein, Alderete et al. (1999) investigated fixed reduplicative segmentism within optimality theory, arguing for two distinct types of the phenomenon; phonologically fixed segments are just regarded as another case of the emergence of the unmarked (i.e. the insertion of an unmarked default segment), while morphologically fixed segments (as found in echo-words) are treated as a kind of affixation realized simultaneously with reduplication and overwriting part of the reduplicated string (cf. Alderete et al. 1999: 328).

Although reduplication research in the new millennium has seen an occasional return to derivational models (e.g., Raimy 2000 and, more recently, Frampton 2009; see also McCarthy, Kimber and Mullin 2012), optimality theory up until today remains the most popular umbrella theory for analyzing reduplication data in terms of their formal characteristics. However, especially studies of the past two decades have also shown a growing interest in reduplication semantics, spawning descriptions and a model of reduplication looked at more closely in the course of the next main section.

3 Meanings and functions

Already the extensive early study undertaken by Pott (1862) had been largely devoted to reduplication meanings and functions in the languages of the world (for a summary and critical evaluation see Stolz, Stroh and Urdze 2011: 78–83). Despite the fact that after that scholars have time and again pointed out cross-linguistic regularities and peculiarities concerning the semantics of reduplicative formations, pertinent investigations (mostly of a typological nature) have always lagged behind form-related studies of the phenomenon since the beginning of generative and post-generative linguistics, and only recently has the meaning component of reduplication found a prominent place also in the more theoretically oriented literature.

3.1 General functional properties

Reduplication can apply to many different word classes and may serve a wide range of meanings and functions some of which have already been exemplified in the previous main section (e.g., simple plurality or considerable/greater number of nouns, continuative aspect of verbs and intensification or attenuation of modifiers). Further examples follow.

Next to the already encountered meanings related to a more general notion of plurality, reduplicated nouns also often express distributivity or totality, e.g., Lavukaleve *mina* 'thing' → *mina~mina* 'everything' (Terrill 2003: 36). Another frequent function of nominal reduplication (though quite distinct from any type of plurality) is diminution as in Malagasy *àlahélo* 'sadness' → *àlahèlo~hélo* 'little sadness' (Keenan and Razafimamonjy 1998: 167; the grave and acute accents mark secondary and primary stress, respectively).

With verbs, the most common meanings expressed by reduplication belong to the broad field of verbal plurality, including continuity or progressivity as in Swahili *-cheka* 'laugh' → *-cheka~cheka* 'keep laughing' (Novotna 2000: 65), repetition or iterativity as in Eastern Oromo *bab~baas-e* 'took out often' (with the past tense suffix *-e*) from the verbal base *baas* 'to take out' (Owens 1985: 84), frequentativity or habituality as in Hmong Njua *quaj* 'to cry loudly' → *quaj~quaj* 'to always cry' (Harriehausen 1990: 47) and distributivity or dispersion as in Plains Cree *kāh~kīwikē-wak* 'they visit from time to time/here and there' (the *h* indicates devoicing following the long fixed reduplicant vowel, while the ending *-wak* adds specifications for person, number, animacy and transitivity) from the base *kīwikē-* 'to visit' (Ahenakew and Wolfart 1983: 375). Also, reduplicating a verb may intensify its meaning, e.g., Kwaza *kahɛ-* 'to bite' → *kahɛ~kahɛ-* 'to keep on biting (ferociously)' (van der Voort 2003: 75). Furthermore, similarly to diminution in nouns, one frequently finds attenuation of verbal meanings with reduplication too as in Malagasy *mànomé* 'gives' → *mànomè~mé* 'gives a bit' (Keenan and Razafimamonjy 1998: 166).

Adjectives and adverbs often reduplicate for plural reference or agreement as well as for distributivity, e.g., Amele *ben* 'big' → *ben~ben* 'many big things' (Roberts 1991: 121), Somali *fiican* 'good' → *fiic~fiican* 'good (plural)' (Berchem 1991: 159) and Georgian *axal-i* 'new' (with absolutive suffix *-i*) → *axal~axali* 'new (obligatorily distributed over head noun)' (Gil 1988: 1042–1043). Intensification as in Bagirmi *you* 'quickly' → *you~you* 'very quickly' (Stevenson 1969: 161) is also a very common function of adjectival and adverbial reduplication, and as with verbs, attenuation is found as well, frequently in reduplicated colour terms like Modern Hebrew *tsahov* 'yellow' → *tsahav~hav* 'yellowish' (Levkovych 2007: 152; the vowel *a* in the reduplicated syllable is fixed and appears in the base as well).

Minor word classes and certain subclasses of major word classes are also prone to reduplication, with similar semantic effects as found in (and exemplified above with) nouns, verbs, adjectives and adverbs. Pertinent examples are distributive numerals like Lezgian *c'uwad~c'uwad* 'fifteen each' (Haspelmath 1993: 235) and indefinite pronouns as in Gayo *sahan* 'who' → *sahan~sahan* 'whoever' (Eades 2005: 57).

The semantic interpretation of echo-reduplication (called the "Et Cetera interpretation" by Singh 2005: 266) is relatively uniform across different word classes as well as across languages, context-dependently conveying different mixtures of generality, vagueness, plurality, indefiniteness, pejorative connotations and sometimes also intensification (see Keane 2001: 56–58), e.g., Tamil *puli* 'tiger'→ *puli~gili* 'tiger and the like', *vəndu* 'to come' → *vəndu~gindu* 'to come, etc.', *motti* 'fat' → *motti~gitti* 'fat and the like' and *əvən* 'he' → *əvən~givən* 'he, etc.' (Abbi 1992: 21).

There are also reduplicative phenomena with unclear semantic effects. For example, it is hard to tell whether in reduplications with simultaneous affixation as in Lavukaleve reciprocal formations (Terrill 2003: 366–367) showing a suffix *-ria* and initial consonant-vowel reduplication of the stem (e.g., *numa* 'to choose' → *nu~numa-ria* 'to choose each other') the reduplicative part itself contributes any meaning (in the Lavukaleve case this is especially doubtful because reduplication in reciprocal forms is only obligatory with stems longer than two syllables) or if it is rather some kind of stem formation process upon which morphological rules act (cf. Saperstein 1997: 160; see also Niepokuj 1997: 83–86).

It should be noted that most of the above meanings can be summarized as somehow expressing the concept of increased quantity, with the subtypes quantity of referents (loosely plurality) and amount of emphasis or intensification (cf.

Moravcsik 1978: 317). The remaining meanings revolve around the quite opposite notions of diminution and attenuation. The theoretical interpretation of such rather stark semantic contrasts is a strong dividing line between two broad approaches to reduplication semantics to be discussed in the next subsection. There are, however, reduplicative meanings which do not easily fit into any of the above categories too, e.g., perfectivity, future, possession, inchoative and associative qualities (see Moravcsik 1978: 325; Inkelas and Zoll 2005: 14; Rubino 2005b: 20–21). At the same time, some meanings seldom or never seem to occur with any type of reduplication, e.g., gender, case and negation (for a longer list exclusively dedicated to full reduplication see Stolz, Stroh and Urdze 2011: 194).

The above survey has left two important functions of reduplication completely out of the picture, namely the creation of new words and word-class change, both often correlated with an additional change involving plurality, intensity or diminution/attenuation (cf. Moravcsik 1978: 324). As the former functions constitute prime examples of word-formation, they will be described more thoroughly in the remaining main sections (for further cross-linguistic overviews of reduplication semantics see Key 1965; Niepokuj 1997: 65–87; Regier 1998).

3.2 Theoretical approaches to reduplication function

Although Moravcsik (1978) stands out as a notable exception in early modern reduplication research in also containing a detailed discussion of reduplicative meanings, the paper's overall conclusion on this point nevertheless reads as follows: "Given that reduplication is neither the exclusive expression of any one meaning category in languages, nor are the meanings that it is an expression of all subsumable under general classes, *no* [emphasis mine] explanatory or predictive generalization about the meanings of reduplicative constructions can be proposed" (Moravcsik 1978: 325). The author thereby further supported from a functional-typological perspective an opinion which has more or less naturally fallen out from the formally oriented reduplication studies since Wilbur (1973). The latter were either not concerned with reduplicative semantics at all or they saw no reason to regard the meanings occurring with reduplications in different languages as special in any way. This was particularly true in reduplication-as-affixation approaches (e.g., Marantz 1982), in which the assumption of reduplicants as merely being segmentally underspecified affixes could be paralleled without difficulty by the view that the same range of meanings is in principle possible for reduplication and other types of affixation.

Despite her above quotation, Moravcsik (1978: 330) did acknowledge "a tendency […] for languages to use reduplicative patterns – i.e. quantitative form differentiation – for the expression of meanings that have something to do with the quantity of referents", however. This already touched upon a topic of interest which would later on be taken up more seriously especially by functional approaches to morphology (most notably natural morphology) under the heading of iconic form-meaning relationships or "(constructional) iconicity" (for an early example see Mayerthaler 1977). In general, iconicity can be characterized as the non-arbitrary motivation of lexical items, morphological processes and aspects of morphological and syntactic structure, either directly by virtue of a sign's homology with the entity signified or, more abstractly, via diagrammaticity, the latter being the mirroring of relations among concepts or elements of discourse by the make-up of linguistic structures (cf. Downing and Stiebels 2012: 379). Reduplication is special in that it very often reflects both these aspects of iconicity; it exhibits diagrammaticity because more complex concepts are expressed by more complex structures (cf. Mayerthaler 1977: 34), and it additionally shows homology because repetition of form mirrors repetition of meaning (cf. Downing and Stiebels 2012: 394). Observations like these led Kouwenberg and LaCharité (2005: 534) to propose the iconic principle of reduplication: "More of the same form stands for more of the same meaning", where "more of the same meaning" must be interpreted in a metaphorical sense to be able to include meanings like distributivity, continuity and intensification as well (cf. Downing and Stiebels 2012: 395).

The obvious question now arises if and how widespread reduplicative meanings like diminution and attenuation can also be motivated by the above principle. In her semantic study of Malayo-Polynesian noun and verb reduplication, Kiyomi (1995) regarded reduplication as both iconic and non-iconic, with a so-called "consecutive" as well as a "cumulative iconic process" bringing about all sorts of plurality and intensity meanings, respectively (similarly, Fischer 2011: 59 speaks of repetition on a horizontal and a vertical axis here), and a non-iconic process akin to affixation being responsible for sundry notions like diminution. On the other hand, Regier (1998) and Fischer (2011) both took a similar stance in granting reduplication a cognitively grounded iconic base that is semantically extendable via metaphoric and metonymic processes. The two authors also proceeded similarly in deriving the problematic diminutive and attenuative meanings from meanings ultimately connected to the concept of baby (Regier 1998) or the baby-talk register in general (Fischer 2011; see also Niepokuj 1997: 72–73). From a somewhat different angle (and also in slight contrast to their earlier work on reduplication in Caribbean creoles, e.g., Kouwenberg and LaCharité 2001), Kouwenberg and LaCharité (2005: 540) subsumed diminution and attenuation in reduplication under the iconic principle by proposing an extension of dispersive readings from discontinuous occurrence to approximation, e.g., Jamaican Creole *yala~yala* 'yellow-spotted', in which "[t]he real-world effect of such scattered distribution of colour is to tone down rather than intensify the colour, to diminish rather than augment it" (Kouwenberg and LaCharité 2005: 538), ultimately yielding the meaning 'yellowish' (see Abraham 2005 for a critical reaction to Kouwenberg and LaCharité 2005). Finally, invoking a statement going all the way back to Pott (1862: 102), Stolz (2007: 342–345) developed a revised model of reduplicative iconicity, claiming that the latter is not primarily based on diagrammaticity or homology but rather on the conceptual deviation a reduplicated form expresses vis-à-vis the norm or prototype encoded in its unreduplicated counterpart. Obviously, by this the author was not only able to accommodate diminution and attenuation but all kinds of other reduplicative meanings problematic for a traditional conceptualization of iconicity as well (see also Stolz, Stroh and Urdze 2011: 178–191).

A recent theory of growing popularity which considers reduplication as being heavily based on semantics, yet does not concern itself with questions of iconicity at all, is morphological doubling theory (Inkelas 2005, 2008; Inkelas and Zoll 2005). This approach is rooted in optimality theory and construction grammar (see article 6), assigning reduplicative constructions a mother node and two daughter nodes, each node endowed with its own meaning and so-called "co-phonology", the latter in order to capture the general difference between full and partial reduplication as well as all sorts of more specific phonological peculiarities often associated with (especially partial) reduplication. Most importantly, "reduplication results when the morphology calls twice for a constituent of a given *semantic description* [emphasis mine], with possible phonological modification of either or both constituents" (Inkelas and Zoll 2005: 6), meaning that in an extreme case even formally unrelated synonyms can instantiate the construction (as in synonym compounding) and with the effect of downgrading the hitherto defining characteristic of phonological identity to a very common correlate of the process but not a required one (cf. Inkelas 2005: 84). In such a model, both phonological copying to fill a template and correspondence relations holding between segments of a base and its reduplicant are thus replaced by the insertion of two morphological units whose morphosemantic descriptions must match (cf. Inkelas 2005: 65). In contrast to reduplication-as-affixation approaches, morphological doubling theory thus pushes reduplication closer to compounding (see also Saperstein 1997).

4 Reduplication and word-formation

This section looks at reduplication specifically from the perspective of word-formation in a narrower sense. For the discussion to follow it is useful to make a distinction between productive and lexical reduplication. The concept of (morphological) productivity has to be understood in a loose way here, however, productive patterns simply being those in which new words are formed or derived on the basis of existing vocabulary items (i.e. base forms). In contrast, lexical reduplications in fact show a repetitive segmental make-up as well as semantic similarities with (and perhaps diachronic connections to originally) productive reduplications but they crucially lack (at least synchronically) a corresponding unreduplicated base form (see also Vollmann 2009; Mattes 2014). To incorporate the latter formation type in the present discussion obviously entails a deviation from most traditional definitions of reduplication (including the one given at the beginning of this article) but it is nevertheless a common practice of many pertinent studies to discuss these sorts of patterns along with the more productive ones.

4.1 Productive reduplication

4.1.1 Formation of new words

The creation of new words (see also article 19 on word-creation) from existing ones without or only very loosely predictable semantics can be achieved via reduplication in many languages. Relevant examples include, among plenty of others, Afrikaans *kort* 'short' → *kort~kort* 'every now and again' (Botha 1988: 118), Swahili *bata* (denoting a kind of duck) → *-bata~bata* 'waddle' (Novotna 2000: 65) and Portuguese *esconde~esconde* (a traditional game of hide-and-seek), cf. *esconder* 'to hide' (Kröll 1991: 33).

According to the standard interpretation rule of Afrikaans reduplications and a number of additional conceptual devices presented in Botha (1988), *kort~kort* above should mean 'for a very short period', its actual meaning thus being a case of lexicalization, a property also typical of many compounds and derived words (cf. Botha 1988: 118; see also Niepokuj 1997: 68). Apart from an apparent change in word class (see section 4.1.2), the Swahili case, on the other hand, is an example of a transfer of meaning based on similarity (see Novotna 2000: 65), a notion conceptually close to attenuation (cf. Moravcsik 1978: 323), which in turn is very often expressed by reduplication as has already been pointed out in the previous main section. In a similar vein, the Portuguese game-name reduplication can be interpreted as being connected to plurality via the conceptual link that the playing of a game typically (in hide-and-seek especially) involves more than one participant (cf. the discussion of Afrikaans reduplicated game names in Botha 1988: 122–128).

4.1.2 Word-class derivation

Changing the word class of a base is a very common function of reduplication in various languages. It can affect all major word classes and displays all possible directions of change. To give just a handful of examples, Marshallese reduplicates a noun like *bahat* 'smoke' to form a verb *bahat~hat* 'to smoke' (Harrison 1973: 439), while in Papiamentu an adjective like *zeta~zeta* 'very oily' can be formed by reduplicating a noun, cf. *zeta* 'oil' (Kouwenberg and Murray 1994: 21). Similarly, Chamorro verbs like *kanno'* 'to eat' and *hatsa* 'to lift' can be nominalized or changed into a modifier via reduplication, cf. *ká~kanno'* 'eater' (Topping 1973: 182) and *há~hatsa* 'lifting (attributive)' (Topping 1973: 103), respectively. Finally, word-class changing reduplication from adjectival bases can be illustrated by Swahili *-tamu* 'sweet' → *tamu~tamu* 'sweets, confectionary' (Novotna 2000: 63) and Nama (a click language in which morpheme-final nasals can also carry tone) *!óm̀* 'difficult' → *!óm̀~!om* 'to make (something) difficult' (Hagman 1977: 18).

Although in general word-class derivation is functionally quite distinct from the broad meaning categories of plurality, intensification and diminution so often found in reduplication (and discussed in the previous main section), it frequently occurs simultaneously with such notions in reduplicative constructions (cf. Moravcsik 1978: 324), for example in the Papiamentu denominal adjective above which also expresses intensification.

4.1.3 Intra-category changes and other functions

Reduplication can also bring about clearly derivational changes within a given word class, a typical intra-category change of this kind being one that affects the transitivity of a verb as in Mokilese *koso* 'to cut (transitive)' → *kos~kos* 'to cut (intransitive)' (Harrison 1973: 415). Another clear example of reduplicative derivation is the diminution of nouns which has already been exemplified in the previous main section. However, many cases of reduplication can pose problems when trying to classify them in terms of their morphological function.

It has long been noted in linguistics that the difference between inflection and derivation is not necessarily a clear-cut one (see article 8 on the delimitation of derivation and inflection). While the previous main section showed that the meanings and functions of reduplication are at least to a great extent easily characterized in a general fashion (theoretically in terms of iconicity, for example, if one subscribes to such a concept), the question as to whether morphologically these meanings and functions are inflectional or derivational in nature is often much harder to answer (see also Inkelas 2014). Typically problematic instances are all sorts of meanings pertaining to plurality (cf. number in nouns and adjectives as well as certain aspectual differentiations in verbs) and intensification (cf. the degree of adjectives) but also less common reduplicative functions like forming the perfect (i.e. tense) as in some Latin and Ancient Greek verbs. However, it should be pointed out that many of these meanings can be related to inherent (i.e. derivation-like) inflectional categories in the sense of Booij (1993, 1996). What is more, even at first sight clearly inflectional meanings like plural agreement often turn out to lack some decisive properties like obligatoriness when expressed by reduplication (e.g., Owens 1985: 93 on Eastern Oromo). The question thus arises if indeed there is unambiguous reduplicative inflection at all in the languages of the world (see also Saperstein 1997: 161–163).

4.2 Lexical reduplication

Lexical reduplicative formations (often called frozen, fossilized or pseudo-reduplications) lack an unreduplicated counterpart but may nevertheless exhibit striking formal and functional parallels to productive reduplication. Many of the forms in question probably hail from a once productively used pattern, others may have a more spontaneous and transparent origin (for general diachronic aspects of reduplication, including possible scenarios of grammaticalization, see Bybee, Perkins and Pagliuca 1994: 166–174; Niepokuj 1997; Hurch and Mattes 2005; Stolz 2008; Stolz, Stroh and Urdze 2011: 147–204).

4.2.1 Inherent plurality and other semantic fields

There is a cross-linguistic tendency for words containing some degree of inherent plurality to be formally reduplicated, especially zoological expressions, certain kinds of movement and botanical terms, e.g., Welsh *pilipala* 'butterfly', Koasati *wananátlin* 'to shiver' (Kimball 1988: 438) and Portuguese *lemba-lemba* (a local term from São Tomé) meaning 'liana, cord' (Kröll 1991: 28), respectively.

Further semantic fields found fairly frequently in lexical reduplication relate to human beings or bodyparts, e.g., Bagirmi *ṭiṭik* 'bowels' (Stevenson 1969: 18), nature or natural phenomena, e.g., Lavukaleve *lamulam* 'storm' (Terrill 2003: 106), diseases or sickness, e.g., Ngiyambaa *giraŋgira* 'sickly' (Donaldson 1980: 37), and colours, e.g., Mokilese *imwpwilapwil* 'pink' (Harrison 1973: 437), to name just a few (for a systematic compilation of Portuguese lexical reduplications according to such categories see Kröll 1990, 1991).

4.2.2 Expressive formations

Expressives of all sorts, often with negative connotations, are also prone to be lexically reduplicated, e.g., German *plemplem* (*sein*) '(to be) nuts' (see also Wiese 1990; Schindler 1991), Portuguese *xexé* 'ridiculous person' (Kröll 1991: 40) and Swahili *halahala* 'immediately!, at once!' (Novotna 2000: 68).

Especially widespread are reduplicated expressive forms of a sound-symbolic nature, i.e. onomatopoeia and ideophones, e.g., Danish *klipklap* (the sound of wooden shoes or horseshoes), Spanish *cucú* (cry of the cuckoo), Polish and Slovak *chi-chi* (laughter), Albanian *bu(m)bullin* 'to thunder', Ossetic *c'ip-c'ip* (sound produced by young chickens), Tat *jiv-jiv zere* 'to chirp' (ideophonic coverb; see article 174 on Tat), Udmurt *zup-zup* (heartbeat), Mari *vrek-vrek* (a cat or hare jumping) and Chuvash *čuččʼu* 'swing' (noun based on sound imitation).

5 Reduplication, word-formation and the languages of Europe

Putting the focus on Europe, striking observations on the status of reduplication in general as well as the phenomenon's specific connection to word-formation can be made. As the examples provided throughout the previous main sections have already suggested, reduplication is normally found with onomatopoeia in European languages, next to some expressive forms and words relatable to certain common semantic fields. Compared to such cases of lexical reduplication, productive reduplication of whatever kind seems to be rare in this part of the world (see also article 10 on derivation). This state of affairs is normally related to the fact that the predominant language family spoken in Europe is (western) Indo-European, which is generally believed to lack reduplicating languages in a narrow sense. In additional support of this, important exceptions to the above characterization of Europe as an essentially reduplication-free area typically come from languages like Basque (an isolate) and Hungarian (Uralic) as well as from other non-Indo-European family members encountered when moving towards or straddling the outer borders of the continent (e.g., Turkish, Georgian and Modern Hebrew).

The occurrence of productive reduplication thus appears to become markedly higher with an increasing distance from uncontroversial mainland Europe and western Indo-European languages. In principle, all kinds of reduplicative forms and functions show up, e.g., fully reduplicated plurality in Komi *łun* 'day' → *łun-łun* 'every day', partially reduplicated intensification (with fixed segmentism) in

Gagauz *koca* 'big' → *kos~koca* 'huge', attenuating echo-word formation in Akhwakh *ʒemada* 'liquid' → *ʒema~ʒemada* 'more or less liquid' as well as word-class derivation, cf. Tat *para* 'piece' → *para~para* 'scattered', Karaim *jyrach* 'far' → *jyrach~jyrach* 'far away' and Sardinian *curre* 'run' → *curre curre* 'in a hurry'. In coming from a Romance language, the latter example is hinting at a controversial topic which has only recently gained fresh interest to be discussed below.

In line with the mainstream opinion presented above, the typological map of *The World Atlas of Language Structures* (Haspelmath et al. 2005) pertaining to reduplication portrays Europe as a more or less blank spot concerning this feature (see Rubino 2005a: 116–117). Among other things as a reaction to the methods reflected in Rubino (2005a), Stolz, Stroh and Urdze (2011) set out to redraw the European reduplicative landscape in an extensive areal-typological study concentrating on full reduplication. By quantitatively and qualitatively investigating a large corpus of literary texts instead of solely relying on written grammars, the authors take up several languages of Europe into the productively reduplicating class which more or less have been excluded before, but their approach crucially involves the expansion of the definition of reduplication so as to also include what many other researchers would rather count as syntactic repetition (see Stolz, Stroh and Urdze 2011: 26). Also, the reduplicative functions they discover often straddle the line between emphasis and intensification, i.e. they make it hard to unambiguously assign certain forms as belonging to either pragmatics or grammar (see Stolz, Stroh and Urdze 2011: 137–147). What is more, their results indeed only pertain to full reduplication as the authors explicitly state themselves that they find "no compelling evidence of P[artial]R[eduplication] as a systematically employed grammatical device in Europe" (Stolz, Stroh and Urdze 2011: 490; see also article 10 on derivation). It thus remains an open question to what extent reduplication in most European languages is really comparable to reduplication as it is found in the rest of the world, be it from a formal or from a functional perspective.

Acknowledgements

Many thanks are due to Bernhard Hurch for his suggestions concerning the overall outline of this article as well as some points of detail. Furthermore, much is owed to my former position as a research assistant in Hurch's Graz reduplication project (duration 2005–2010) funded by the Austrian Science Fund (project number P18173-G03), a main outcome of which was the Graz database on reduplication (see Hurch and Mattes 2007, 2009) from where most of the examples given here have been drawn (http://reduplication.uni-graz.at/).

6 References

Abbi, Anvita (1992): *Reduplication in South Asian Languages. An Areal, Typological and Historical Study*. New Delhi: Allied Publishers.

Aboh, Enoch Oladé, Norval Smith and Anne Zribi-Hertz (eds.) (2012): *The Morphosyntax of Reiteration in Creole and Non-Creole Languages*. Amsterdam/Philadelphia: Benjamins.

Abraham, Werner (2005): Intensity and diminution triggered by reduplicating morphology: Janus-faced iconicity. In: Bernhard Hurch (ed.), *Studies on Reduplication*, 547–568. Berlin/New York: Mouton de Gruyter.

Ahenakew, Freda and H. Christoph Wolfart (1983): Productive reduplication in Plains Cree. In: William Cowan (ed.), *Actes du Quatorzième Congrès des Algonquinistes*, 369–377. Ottawa: Carleton University.

Alderete, John, Jill Beckman, Laura Benua, Amalia Gnanadesikan, John McCarthy and Suzanne Urbanczyk (1999): Reduplication with fixed segmentism. *Linguistic Inquiry* 30(3): 327–364.

Berchem, Jörg (1991): *Referenzgrammatik des Somali*. Köln: OMIMEE.

Booij, Geert (1993): Against split morphology. In: Geert Booij and Jaap van Marle (eds.), *Yearbook of Morphology 1993*, 27–49. Dordrecht: Kluwer.

Booij, Geert (1996): Inherent versus contextual inflection and the split morphology hypothesis. In: Geert Booij and Jaap van Marle (eds.), *Yearbook of Morphology 1995*, 1–16. Dordrecht: Kluwer.

Botha, Rudolf P. (1988): *Form and Meaning in Word Formation. A Study of Afrikaans Reduplication*. Cambridge: Cambridge University Press.

Bybee, Joan L., Revere Dale Perkins and William Pagliuca (1994): *The Evolution of Grammar. Tense, Aspect, and Modality in the Languages of the World*. Chicago/London: University of Chicago Press.

Clements, George N. (1985): The problem of transfer in nonlinear morphology. *Cornell Working Papers in Linguistics* 7: 38–73.

Donaldson, Tamsin (1980): *Ngiyambaa. The Language of the Wangaaybuwan*. Cambridge: Cambridge University Press.

Downing, Laura J. and Barbara Stiebels (2012): Iconicity. In: Jochen Trommer (ed.), *The Morphology and Phonology of Exponence*, 379–426. Oxford: Oxford University Press.

Eades, Domenyk (2005): *A Grammar of Gayo. A Language of Aceh, Sumatra*. Canberra: The Australian National University.

El Zarka, Dina (2005): On the borderline of reduplication: Gemination and other consonant doubling in Arabic morphology. In: Bernhard Hurch (ed.), *Studies on Reduplication*, 369–394. Berlin/New York: Mouton de Gruyter.

Finkbeiner, Rita and Ulrike Freywald (eds.) (2018): *Exact Repetition in Grammar and Discourse*. Berlin/Boston: Mouton de Gruyter.

Fischer, Olga (2011): Cognitive iconic grounding of reduplication in language. In: Pascal Michelucci, Olga Fischer and Christina Ljungberg (eds.), *Semblance and Signification*, 55–81. Amsterdam/Philadelphia: Benjamins.

Frampton, John (2009): *Distributed Reduplication*. Cambridge, MA/London: MIT Press.

French, Koleen Matsuda (1988): *Insights into Tagalog Reduplication, Infixation and Stress from Nonlinear Phonology*. Dallas: Summer Institute of Linguistics.

Gil, David (1988): Georgian reduplication and the domain of distributivity. *Linguistics* 26(6): 1039–1065.

Gil, David (2005): From repetition to reduplication in Riau Indonesian. In: Bernhard Hurch (ed.), *Studies on Reduplication*, 31–64. Berlin/New York: Mouton de Gruyter.

Hagman, Roy S. (1977): *Nama Hottentot Grammar.* Bloomington, IN: Indiana University Publications.
Harriehausen, Bettina (1990): *Hmong Njua. Syntaktische Analyse einer gesprochenen Sprache mithilfe datenverarbeitungstechnischer Mittel und sprachvergleichende Beschreibung des südostasiatischen Sprachraumes.* Tübingen: Niemeyer.
Harrison, Sheldon P. (1973): Reduplication in Micronesian languages. *Oceanic Linguistics* 12(1–2): 407–454.
Haspelmath, Martin (1993): *A Grammar of Lezgian.* Berlin/New York: Mouton de Gruyter.
Haspelmath, Martin, Matthew S. Dryer, David Gil and Bernard Comrie (eds.) (2005): *The World Atlas of Language Structures.* Oxford: Oxford University Press.
Hendricks, Sean (2001): Bare-consonant reduplication without prosodic templates: Expressive reduplication in Semai. *Journal of East Asian Linguistics* 10(4): 287–306.
Hualde, José Ignacio and Jon Ortiz de Urbina (2003): *A Grammar of Basque.* Berlin/New York: Mouton de Gruyter.
Hurch, Bernhard and Veronika Mattes (2005): Über die Entstehung von partieller Reduplikation. In: Gertraut Fenk-Oczlon and Christian Winkler (eds.), *Sprache und Natürlichkeit. Gedenkband für Willi Mayerthaler,* 137–156. Tübingen: Narr.
Hurch, Bernhard and Veronika Mattes (2007): The Graz database on reduplication. In: Alexis Michaud and Aliyah Morgenstern (eds.), *La Réduplication,* 191–202. Paris: Ophrys.
Hurch, Bernhard and Veronika Mattes (2009): Typology of reduplication: The Graz database. In: Martin Everaert, Simon Musgrave and Alexis Dimitriadis (eds.), *The Use of Databases in Cross-Linguistic Studies,* 301–327. Berlin: Mouton de Gruyter.
Inkelas, Sharon (2005): Morphological doubling theory: Evidence for morphological doubling in reduplication. In: Bernhard Hurch (ed.), *Studies on Reduplication,* 65–88. Berlin/New York: Mouton de Gruyter.
Inkelas, Sharon (2008): The dual theory of reduplication. *Linguistics* 46(2): 351–401.
Inkelas, Sharon (2012): Reduplication. In: Jochen Trommer (ed.), *The Morphology and Phonology of Exponence,* 355–378. Oxford: Oxford University Press.
Inkelas, Sharon (2014): Non-concatenative derivation: Reduplication. In: Rochelle Lieber and Pavol Štekauer (eds.), *The Oxford Handbook of Derivational Morphology,* 169–189. Oxford: Oxford University Press.
Inkelas, Sharon and Cheryl Zoll (2005): *Reduplication. Doubling in Morphology.* Cambridge: Cambridge University Press.
Kallergi, Haritini (2015): *Reduplication at the Word Level. The Greek Facts in Typological Perspective.* Berlin/Boston: Mouton de Gruyter.
Keane, Elinor (2001): Echo words in Tamil. Ph.D. dissertation, Merton College, Oxford.
Keenan, Edward L. and Jean Paulin Razafimamonjy (1998): Reduplication in Malagasy. In: Matthew Pearson (ed.), *Recent Papers in Austronesian Linguistics. Proceedings of the Third and Fourth Meetings of the Austronesian Formal Linguistics Association (AFLA), Los Angeles, 1996–1997,* 159–183. Los Angeles: UCLA Department of Linguistics.
Kentner, Gerrit (2022): DO NOT REPEAT: Repetition and reduplication in German revisited. In: Matthias Eitelmann and Dagmar Haumann (eds.), *Extravagant Morphology. Studies in Rule-Bending, Pattern-Extending and Theory-Challenging Morphology,* 181–205. Amsterdam/Philadelphia: Benjamins.
Key, Harold (1965): Some semantic functions of reduplication in various languages. *Anthropological Linguistics* 7(3): 88–102.
Kiefer, Ferenc (1995–96): Prefix reduplication in Hungarian. *Acta Linguistica Hungarica* 43(1–2): 175–194.

Kimball, Geoffrey (1988): Koasati reduplication. In: William Shipley (ed.), *In Honor of Mary Haas. From the Haas Festival Conference on Native American Linguistics*, 431–442. Berlin: Mouton de Gruyter.

Kiyomi, Setsuko (1995): A new approach to reduplication: A semantic study of noun and verb reduplication in Malayo-Polynesian languages. *Linguistics* 27(6): 1145–1167.

Kouwenberg, Silvia (ed.) (2003): *Twice as Meaningful. Reduplication in Pidgins, Creoles, and other Contact Languages*. London: Battlebridge Publications.

Kouwenberg, Silvia and Darlene LaCharité (2001): The iconic interpretations of reduplication: Issues in the study of reduplication in Caribbean creole languages. *European Journal of English Studies* 5(1): 59–80.

Kouwenberg, Silvia and Darlene LaCharité (2005): Less is more: Evidence from diminutive reduplication in Caribbean creole languages. In: Bernhard Hurch (ed.), *Studies on Reduplication*, 533–545. Berlin/New York: Mouton de Gruyter.

Kouwenberg, Silvia and Eric Murray (1994): *Papiamentu*. München/Newcastle: LINCOM Europa.

Kröll, Heinz (1990): Beitrag zu den Reduplikationen im Portugiesischen. *Lusorama* 11: 31–39.

Kröll, Heinz (1991): Beitrag zu den Reduplikationen im Portugiesischen (II). *Lusorama* 15: 25–44.

Levkovych, Nataliya (2007): Totale Reduplikation im modernen Hebräischen. In: Andreas Ammann and Aina Urdze (eds.), *Wiederholung, Parallelismus, Reduplikation. Strategien der multiplen Strukturanwendung*, 109–163. Bochum: Brockmeyer.

Marantz, Alec (1982): Re reduplication. *Linguistic Inquiry* 13(3): 435–482.

Masini, Francesca and Jacopo Di Donato (2023): Non-prototypicality by (discontinuous) reduplication: The N-*non*-N construction in Italian. *Zeitschrift für Wortbildung/Journal of Word Formation* 7(1): 130–155.

Mattes, Veronika (2014): *Types of Reduplication. A Case Study of Bikol*. Berlin/Boston: Mouton de Gruyter.

Mattes, Veronika (2017): Iconicity in the lexicon: The semantic categories of lexical reduplication. *Studies in Language* 41(4): 813–842.

Mattes, Veronika and Thomas Schwaiger (2024): Reduplication. In: Alexander Adelaar and Antoinette Schapper (eds.), *The Oxford Guide to the Malayo-Polynesian Languages of Southeast Asia*, 749–772. Oxford: Oxford University Press.

Mayerthaler, Willi (1977): *Studien zur theoretischen und zur französischen Morphologie. Reduplikation, Echowörter, morphologische Natürlichkeit, Haplologie, Produktivität, Regelteleskoping, paradigmatischer Ausgleich*. Tübingen: Niemeyer.

McCarthy, John J. and Alan S. Prince (1994): The emergence of the unmarked: Optimality in prosodic morphology. In: Mercè Gonzàlez (ed.), *Proceedings of the North East Linguistics Society 24*, 333–379. Amherst: GLSA.

McCarthy, John J. and Alan S. Prince (1999): Faithfulness and identity in prosodic morphology. In: René Kager, Harry van der Hulst and Wim Zonneveld (eds.), *The Prosody-Morphology Interface*, 218–309. Cambridge: Cambridge University Press.

McCarthy, John J., Wendell Kimper and Kevin Mullin (2012): Reduplication in harmonic serialism. *Morphology* 22(2): 173–232.

Mel'čuk, Igor (2006): *Aspects of the Theory of Morphology*. Berlin/New York: Mouton de Gruyter.

Merlan, Francesca (1982): *Mangarayi*. Amsterdam: North-Holland Publishing Company.

Moravcsik, Edith A. (1978): Reduplicative constructions. In: Joseph H. Greenberg (ed.), *Universals of Human Language*. Vol. 3: *Word Structure*, 297–334. Stanford: Stanford University Press.

Müller, Hans-Georg (2004): *Reduplikationen im Türkischen. Morphonologische Untersuchungen*. Wiesbaden: Harrassowitz.

Naylor, Paz Buenaventura (1986): On the semantics of reduplication. In: Paul Geraghty, Lois Carrington and Stephen Adolphe Wurm (eds.), *FOCAL I. Papers from the Fourth International Conference on Austronesian Linguistics*, 175–185. Canberra: The Australian National University.
Niepokuj, Mary (1997): *The Development of Verbal Reduplication in Indo-European*. Washington: Institute for the Study of Man.
Novotna, Jana (2000): Reduplication in Swahili. *Afrikanische Arbeitspapiere* 64: 57–73.
Owens, Jonathan (1985): *A Grammar of Harar Oromo (Northeastern Ethiopia)*. Hamburg: Buske.
Pfau, Roland and Markus Steinbach (2005): Backward and sideward reduplication in German Sign Language. In: Bernhard Hurch (ed.), *Studies on Reduplication*, 569–594. Berlin/New York: Mouton de Gruyter.
Pott, August Friedrich (1862): *Doppelung (Reduplikation, Gemination) als eines der wichtigsten Bildungsmittel der Sprache, beleuchtet aus Sprachen aller Welttheile*. Lemgo/Detmold: Verlag der Meyer'schen Hofbuchhandlung. http://reduplication.uni-graz.at/pott/index.html [last access 18 Apr 2013].
Raimy, Eric Stephen (2000): *The Phonology and Morphology of Reduplication*. Berlin/New York: Mouton de Gruyter.
Regier, Terry (1998): Reduplication and the arbitrariness of the sign. In: Morton Ann Gernsbacher and Sharon J. Derry (eds.), *Proceedings of the Twentieth Annual Conference of the Cognitive Science Society, University of Wisconsin-Madison, August 1–4, 1998*, 887–892. Mahwah: Erlbaum.
Roberts, John R. (1991): Reduplication in Amele. In: Tom Dutton (ed.), *Papers in Papuan Linguistics No. 1*, 115–146. Canberra: The Australian National University.
Rossi, Daniela (ed.) (2015): The Why and How of Total Reduplication. Current Issues and New Perspectives. [Special issue]. *Studies in Language* 39(4).
Rubino, Carl Ralph Galvez (2005a): Reduplication. In: Martin Haspelmath, Matthew S. Dryer, David Gil and Bernard Comrie (eds.), *The World Atlas of Language Structures*, 114–117. Oxford: Oxford University Press.
Rubino, Carl Ralph Galvez (2005b): Reduplication: Form, function and distribution. In: Bernhard Hurch (ed.), *Studies on Reduplication*, 11–29. Berlin/New York: Mouton de Gruyter.
Saperstein, Andrew D. (1997): A word-and-paradigm approach to reduplication. Ph.D. dissertation, Department of Linguistics, The Ohio State University.
Schindler, Wolfgang (1991): Reduplizierende Wortbildung im Deutschen. *Zeitschrift für Phonetik, Sprachwissenschaft und Kommunikationsforschung* 44(5): 597–613.
Schütz, Albert J. (1985): *The Fijian Language*. Honolulu: University of Hawaii Press.
Schwaiger, Thomas (2018): The derivational nature of reduplication: Towards a Functional Discourse Grammar account of a non-concatenative morphological process. *Word Structure* 11(1): 118–144.
Singh, Rajendra (2005): Reduplication in Modern Hindi and the theory of reduplication. In: Bernhard Hurch (ed.), *Studies on Reduplication*, 263–281. Berlin/New York: Mouton de Gruyter.
Steriade, Donca (1988): Reduplication and syllable transfer in Sanskrit and elsewhere. *Phonology* 5(1): 73–155.
Stevenson, R. C. (1969): *Bagirmi Grammar*. Khartoum: University of Khartoum.
Stolz, Thomas (2007): Re: duplication: Iconic vs counter-iconic principles (and their areal correlates). In: Paolo Ramat and Elisa Roma (eds.), *Europe and the Mediterranean as Linguistic Areas. Convergencies from a Historical and Typological Perspective*, 317–350. Amsterdam/Philadelphia: Benjamins.
Stolz, Thomas (2008): Grammatikalisierung ex nihilo: Totale Reduplikation – Ein potentielles Universale und sein Verhältnis zur Grammatikalisierung. In: Thomas Stolz (ed.), *Grammatikalisierung und grammatische Kategorien*, 83–109. Bochum: Brockmeyer.

Stolz, Thomas, Cornelia Stroh and Aina Urdze (2011): *Total Reduplication. The Areal Linguistics of a Potential Universal*. Berlin: Akademie Verlag.

Terrill, Angela (2003): *A Grammar of Lavukaleve*. Berlin/New York: Mouton de Gruyter.

Topping, Donald M. (1973): *Chamorro Reference Grammar*. Honolulu: University of Hawaii Press.

Urdze, Aina (ed.) (2018): *Non-Prototypical Reduplication*. Berlin/Boston: Mouton de Gruyter.

Vollmann, Ralf (2009): Reduplication in Tibetan. *Grazer Linguistische Studien* 71: 115–134.

Voort, Hein van der (2003): Reduplication of person markers in Kwaza. *Acta Linguistica Hafniensia* 35: 65–94.

Weijer, Jeroen van de, Weiyun Wei, Yumeng Wang, Guangyuan Ren and Yunyun Ran (2020): Words are constructions, too: A construction-based approach to English ablaut reduplication. *Linguistics* 58(6): 1701–1735.

Wiese, Richard (1990): Über die Interaktion von Morphologie und Phonologie: Reduplikation im Deutschen. *Zeitschrift für Phonetik, Sprachwissenschaft und Kommunikationsforschung* 43(5): 603–624.

Wilbur, Ronnie Bring (1973): *The Phonology of Reduplication*. Bloomington, IN: Indiana University Linguistics Club.

Wilbur, Ronnie Bring (2005): A reanalysis of reduplication in American Sign Language. In: Bernhard Hurch (ed.), *Studies on Reduplication*, 595–623. Berlin/New York: Mouton de Gruyter.

Elke Ronneberger-Sibold
19 Word-creation

1   Definition: word-creation versus word-formation
2   Creative techniques
3   Functions of word-creation
4   Word-creation in a cross-linguistic perspective
5   References

Abstract: The term *word-creation* refers not only to the coining of new lexemes not based on any previously existing meaningful linguistic elements. It also covers linguistic operations such as shortening, blending, alienation, and so-called extragrammatical derivation, which are deliberately performed on the basis of existing words or phrases, but outside the productive models or rules of word-formation. The present article discusses the differences between word-creation and regular word-formation and presents an overview of the basic creative techniques, their functions and their cross-linguistic implementation.

1 Definition: word-creation versus word-formation

The term *word-creation* is traditionally reserved for the coining of a new lexeme without using any previously existing meaningful linguistic element (German *Urschöpfung*, cf. Paul 1920: 174–175, taken up, e.g., in Fleischer and Barz 2012: 18–20). In a wider sense, which is adopted in this article, the term word-creation also refers to linguistic operations such as shortening, blending, alienation, and others, which are deliberately performed on the basis of existing words or phrases, but outside the productive models or rules of word-formation. In contradistinction to the latter, such operations are here called creative techniques. In this article, the focus is on those techniques which are not treated in separate articles in this volume (see articles 13 on clipping and 15 on blending).

The distinction between regular word-formation and word-creation is a matter of debate among morphologists, mostly argued out with respect to blending and/or clipping (Ronneberger-Sibold 2010).

Elke Ronneberger-Sibold, Eichstätt, Germany

The major arguments in favor of a principled difference between regular word-formation on the one hand and word-creation on the other are the following:

a) The output of a creative technique is not predictable from its input, because the way in which a technique is applied is not fixed in every detail. E.g., blending *flimsy* and *miserable* could result in (attested) *mimsy* as well as in (unattested) *fliserable* (Bauer 2003: 47).
b) Because of this indeterminacy, the output of a creative technique cannot be evaluated according to its grammaticality. It makes no sense to ask native speakers of English whether *mimsy* or *fliserable* are acceptable or non-acceptable as blends of *flimsy* and *miserable*. All they can possibly evaluate is the efficiency of these words in fulfilling their purpose as an amusing word play, and in this respect, *mimsy* might be the better solution.
c) The transparency of word-creations with respect to their linguistic input is reduced as compared to regular formations, for most creative techniques shorten or modify their linguistic input in a way that impedes its recoverability (Marchand 1969: 2–3). Even if all input elements are contained in full in the output, they are combined in an unexpected manner, hampering the semantic interpretation of the output. Regular word-formational operations, in contrast, are normally not designed in a way to make their input difficult or impossible to recover. In fact, this would run counter to the very purpose of normal linguistic utterances which is to make oneself understood.
d) Unlike with regular word-formation, the products of some important creative techniques such as shortening and alienation are not new words with respect to form and meaning/part of speech, but with respect to their form only (Bauer 2003: 40). E.g., *ad* has the same denotation as *advertisement*. Only the stylistic value may be changed, cf. below.

In contrast to this, the following arguments have been put forward against a principled difference between regular word-formation and word-creation:

a) The phonetic outputs of creative techniques are most often regular (frequently even preferred or minimal) sound patterns of the respective language, especially as far as prosody is concerned (cf. section 4). Note, however, that this in no way implies the regularity of the techniques producing these patterns (see also article 15 on blending).
b) The products of word-creation are often integrated into the inflectional system of the respective language (though with certain licenses, cf. Barz 2009: 736). Of course, this argument also applies to the products, but not to the techniques of word-creation.

c) Like creative techniques, even regular operations such as suffixation can be output-driven, for the resulting words have to fulfill certain prosodic requirements (cf., e.g., Plag 2003: 116 with respect to English deadjectival abstract nouns in *-ity*).
d) Although a certain reduction of transparency, e.g., through clipping, cannot be denied, the respective techniques are devised in such a way as to maximize the recoverability of the source form by different constraints (for a discussion cf. Lappe 2007: 171–205).
e) Even though creative techniques such as shortening do not change the denotation of their source forms, they nevertheless provide a special stylistic value of sloppiness, confidentiality or expressiveness (Zwicky and Pullum 1987: 335), which normally qualify the creations for special pragmatic functions. Occasionally they may even modify the denotation of their source forms (Lappe 2007: 20–29).

Taking into account some or all of these arguments, several views on the relation between word-formation and word-creation have been advanced:
a) Both word-formation and word-creation are based on regular rules or models (cf., e.g., Soudek 1978, Plag 2003: 116 and the articles cited in section 4.1), the only problem being that the rules or models of word-creation have not yet been completely discovered and described. Many manuals of word-formation (including this handbook) treat at least some creative techniques on a par with regular word-formational operations without or with only little discussion of the problem. E.g., in the standard grammar of German, shortening is explicitly classified as regular word-formation together with compounding, derivation and conversion (Barz 2009: 660), whereas blending and other creative techniques follow as "other kinds of word-formation" (Barz 2009: 669–673).
b) Neither word-formation nor word-creation is based on regular rules or models, but both are directly founded on cognitive principles. This is assumed in the schema-based approach within cognitive grammar, which deliberately renounces any "'building-block' style theories of morphology" even for regular word-formation (Kemmer 2003: 69). This approach quite efficiently describes certain types of transparent blends which crucially rely on a formal similarity between words. However, nowhere nearly all creative techniques are of this kind.
c) Only productive word-formation is regular and therefore relevant to the linguistic system proper. Word-creation, on the contrary, is a matter of performance in general or at best of stylistics in particular. This is the view of "pure" structuralist morphology (cf., e.g., Marchand 1969: 441 with respect to

clipping and 451 to blending) and of generative morphology (e.g., Aronoff 1976: 20).
d) Only productive word-formation is completely regular, but word-creation is not completely irregular. Rather, it is a borderline phenomenon between regular morphology and phonology or between regular word-formation and an (unspecified) kind of irregularity. This view is held by many morphologists, e.g., Grésillon (1984), Cannon (1986).
e) Word-creation is a subtype of extragrammatical morphology, characterized by intentionality. This is the view of natural morphology (cf., e.g., Dressler 2000, 2005). In this theory, "extragrammatical" is a cover term for different morphological operations "outside of grammar", governed entirely (at the first, pre- and protomorphological stages of language acquisition) or in part (at later stages) by cognitive principles such as iconicity or figure vs. ground. The fact that these principles remain available to language users even after the acquisition of grammatical morphology explains why similar creative techniques are applied and their products understood with some consistency in many different languages, although these techniques are not part of the linguistic systems proper. (This effect is explained by a kind of metalinguistic competence for stylistic effects assumed by Sobkowiak 1991; cf. also section 4.)

2 Creative techniques

For a complete typology of creative techniques exemplified by product names see Ronneberger-Sibold (2010: 209). In the following, only the structure of this typology will be sketched and the techniques not covered by articles 13 on clipping, 15 on blending, and 18 on reduplication will be described in some detail. Given the principled creative freedom of the techniques, this description can only cover their basic features, such that every non-basic instance of word-creation can be interpreted as a variation or combination of these features.

Moreover, it is important to note that the techniques are described from the viewpoint of the creator only, for, as a consequence of the reduced transparency of word-creations, the perspective of the receiver is not simply the converse of the creator's perspective. For instance, the hearer or reader of an opaque word-creation such as *Persil*, name of a washing powder, cannot decide whether this word was created by shortening, blending, or some other technique. For the creator, on the contrary, these techniques exhibit important differences. (For the perspective of the receiver cf. Ronneberger-Sibold 2004: 590 ff.)

2.1 Word-creation without a linguistic input: phonetic symbolism

On the highest level of the proposed typology, a distinction is made between creative techniques which are based on a morphological input and others which are not. The latter produce free creations in the traditional sense mentioned in section 1 (German *Urschöpfungen*).

Free creations are, strictly speaking, not new words but new roots not assigned to any particular part of speech, e.g., German *husch*, English *woosh*. The integration of these roots into grammar as interjections (*husch!*), verbs (*huschen* 'to dart', *huscheln* 'to do something sloppily'), nouns (*das* or *der Husch* '(the) jiffy') or adjectives (*huschelig* 'sloppily') and possible conversions between these parts of speech concern regular derivational and inflectional morphology as well as syntax, but not the creative technique as such (Paul 1920: 183). The same applies *mutatis mutandis* to semantic shifts frequently accompanying grammatical integration, e.g., the metonymic use of a sound-iconic root depicting a bird's call, such as German *Uhu* [u:.hu:] 'eagle owl' for the bird itself.

Most free creations are motivated by what is currently called "phonetic symbolism", e.g., by Marchand (1969: 397) and Hinton, Nichols and Ohala (1994: 5), subdivided by the latter into a) "imitative phonetic symbolism", i.e. onomatopoeia imitating an auditory sensation (e.g., *bang*, *splash*, *miaow*), b) "synaesthetic phonetic symbolism" imitating a visual and/or haptic sensation (e.g., *dump*, *plump*), and c) "conventional phonetic symbolism", imitating the sound shape of other words. As with respect to a) and b) the use of the term symbolism is at variance with Peircian semiotic terminology (cf. Jakobson and Waugh 1979: 178), they are here called sound-iconic, the third, conventional one sound-symbolic.

Synaesthetic sound-iconic creations are based on (universal?) associations between certain sound shapes or even individual sounds and sensory concepts such as 'bright' or 'dark', 'hard' or 'soft', 'strong' or 'weak', 'big' or 'small', etc., e.g., between the vowel /i/ and 'small size' (Jespersen 1933). For an excellent overview of the problem and the older literature cf. Jakobson and Waugh (1979: 177–204), including milestones such as Grammont (1901), Sapir (1929) and Jespersen (1933). An in-depth empirical psycho-linguistic study is presented by Ertel (1969), a variety of languages are contrasted in Fischer-Jørgensen (1978) and Ultan (1978), cf. also O'Boyle, Miller and Rahmani (1987) with further references. For different psychological explanations of synaesthesia based on auditory inputs cf. Tsur (2006).

Sound-iconic imitations of haptic sensations often depict movements, especially if they are accompanied by sounds. Thus, German *husch*, English *woosh* imitate the sensation and sound of an airflow produced by a quick, furtive movement. In an even more iconic variant of haptic sound-iconicity the speaker's mouth while pronouncing the sound-iconic word imitates the depicted movement (Marchand 1969: 397). E.g., in pronouncing the name *Maoam* the speaker automatically imitates the movements of the lower jaw when chewing this sweet. Moreover, the bilabial closure of the initial and final bilabial resonant [m] imitates the movement of the lips during swallowing and intensive tasting, thus indirectly even imitating a gustatory experience.

An important device for depicting rhythmically recurring sounds or movements or both is sound-iconic reduplication, possibly accompanied by vowel alternations, especially between high and non-high vowels in so-called ablaut combinations, e.g., English *ding-dong* rendering bell chimes and at the same time the swinging movement of the bell, or English and French *zigzag* for a movement in opposite directions. As pointed out by Marchand (1969: 436), the motivating factor in ablaut combinations is the polarity of the vowels in an identical consonantal frame. E.g., in *zigzag*, the identity of the movements is rendered by [z...g], their opposite direction by the opposition between the highest English short vowel [ɪ] and its lowest counterpart [æ]. Another variant with a similar motivation are rhyme combinations such as English *helter-skelter*.

Of course, sound-iconic reduplication is a free creation only if it is not based on any existing morpheme. Cases such as German *Zickzack* 'zigzag', synchronically and probably also etymologically based on *Zacke* 'sharp point' (Dressler 2000: 5), though not according to a regular let alone a productive model, are better classified as a type of extragrammatical derivation (cf. section 2.3). Moreover, reduplication as a creative technique has to be kept apart from regular derivational and inflectional reduplication found in many languages (but cf. Malkiel 1977 on the difficulty of delimitation).

Sound-symbolic free creations (i.e., instances of "conventional phonetic symbolism" according to Hinton, Nichols and Ohala 1994: 5), are motivated by a phonetic resemblance to the sound shapes characteristic of certain groups of words in the lexicon sharing certain semantic features. Two types of such lexical groups are to be distinguished:

The first group contains prototypical loanwords from a certain language or language group sharing a number of phonetic and semantic (mostly connotative) features. E.g., in German, comparatively recent, unadapted loanwords and proper names from Italian, Spanish, or Portuguese such as *Milano, Espresso, Polenta, Spaghetti, Torero, Veranda*, etc. are phonetically characterized by three or more syllables with full vowels, the last of which ends in [-o], [-a], or [-i], and by penultimate stress (Ronneberger-Sibold 2002). As semantically most of these words belong (for Germans) in the context of Mediterranean holidays, elegance and enjoyment of life, the above-mentioned sound shape is capable of evoking these associations even in completely meaningless free creations often used as names for products designed for making life pleasant, elegant and easy, such as *Zafira, Meriva, Antara* (names of car models made by Opel, artificially created by a computer program, cf. Lötscher 2007).

In the second type of sound symbolic words serving as models for free creations, the common phonetic features are not abstract sound shapes, but so-called phonaesthemes (Firth 1957: 39: "phonaesthetic function"), also called submorphemes (Dressler 1990), i.e., concrete sounds or sound clusters recurring in a number of words which share a common semantic feature without, however, allowing for a morphological analysis. A famous English example is the initial cluster [gl-] in words such as *gleam, glimmer, glisten, glitter, glow, gloss*, etc. All of them share a semantic feature 'light, shine', but a segmentation of a morpheme *[gl-] 'light, shine' is impossible, because the remaining parts such as *-eam, -immer, -isten*, etc. do not exist as separate morphemes (Marchand 1969: 411; Tournier 1985: 139). Free creations containing a phonaestheme [-on], suggesting a scientifically developed chemical substance are, e.g., artificially created German names for synthetic fibers such as *Dacron, Orlon, Antron*, probably by an original analogy with *Nylon* (Lötscher 1992: 84). (In an alternative analysis, *-on* would be considered as a suffix, in which case only the bases *Dacr-*, etc. would be free creations, whereas the suffixation by *-on* would be an instance of extragrammatical derivation, cf. section 2.3.)

Of course, free creation is not the only way in which sound-iconic or sound-symbolic sound shapes may come into being. In many cases, they are created by other techniques, relying on previously existing morphological material. E.g., in the German name *Eduscho* [e.ˈduː.ʃo] for a coffee brand the above-mentioned "Italian" sound shape has been created by shortening *Eduard Schopf*, name of the founder of the firm. Moreover, they may also be borrowed or result from diachronic change (Marchand 1969: 398; Meier 1975: 13–17). In fact, the production of such sound shapes "on demand" is an important motive for word-creation in cases where no borrowed or diachronically arisen word is available (Ronneberger-Sibold 2001).

All free creations cited so far are motivated by their sound shape. In fact, contrary to what is sometimes claimed (e.g., in Bußmann 2008: 800), it is extremely difficult to find examples of totally unmotivated new free creations. (Incidentally, both examples given in Bußmann are in fact based on morphological material.) Even artificially created product names such as *Meriva*, etc., mentioned above, were selected because of their sound-symbolic sound shape. Only creations in nursery rhymes such as *eeny-meeny-miny-moe* are completely unmotivated, because they lack any meaning with respect to which they could possibly be motivated (Zelinsky-Wibbelt 1983: 38).

Of course, the original motivation of free creations may be lost by diachronic change (Jespersen 1922: 406). This seems to have occurred in many so-called expressive interjections such as *ouch*, *ugh*, etc. or orders such as *whoa!* Although they are today highly conventionalized, they possibly originated in "natural" gestures and expressions of feelings (cf. Paul 1920: 179–180 and, for a typology of interjections, Kleiber 2006).

2.2 Modification of an existing source form: shortening and alienation

As for the creative techniques based on a linguistic input, the linguistic elements of this input may either be combined for the first time by extra-grammatical word-formation in order to create a word which is new regarding its meaning and form, or the input may be a previously existing word or phrase, here termed source form, which is merely modified with respect to its phonological and/or graphical shape, but not with respect to its meaning (except for its stylistic register). Two important techniques of the latter type are shortening and alienation. Shortening has been studied for various languages and in different theoretical frameworks (see articles 13 on clipping). Contrary to this, alienation is only touched upon in investigations of different linguistic varieties such as the language of advertising, journalism, the new media, etc., but, to my knowledge, there is no typology, let alone a comprehensive study of this phenomenon. In the following, a typology will be sketched, based on Ronneberger-Sibold (2004) and Ronneberger-Sibold, Kazzazi and Potsch-Ringeisen (2016).

Alienation (German *Verfremdung*) is a cover term for different techniques reducing the recoverability of a source form without, however, shortening it. Contrary to shortening, alienation aims less at simplifying the task of the speaker or writer than at surprising and impressing the hearer or reader. The proposed typology distinguishes between three types: orthographical alienation, orthographical and phonetic alienation, and phonetic alienation.

In an orthographical alienation, only the orthography of the source form is modified, leaving its pronunciation intact. (Note that purely graphical variation of graphemes within the same orthography is not covered by this definition.) There are two subtypes: plain orthographical alienation and alienation by homophones. An example of a plain orthographical alienation is the German brand name *Vileda* for an artificial chamois leather from the German phrase *wie Leder* 'like leather', spelt in the IPA system and thus giving the impression of an Italian or Spanish loan word. This type of alienation is quite common in bi- or multilingual and -scriptal speech communities where words of one language may be written in the orthography or even the script of another language for humorous or euphemistic purposes or for camouflage. In alienation by homonyms, the source form is replaced by a previously existing or regularly formed new homophone word. E.g., the German phrase *(was) kostet das?* '(How much) does this cost?' in colloquial pronunciation is replaced by the Greek name *Kostas* in a German advertisement for Greek specialties by McDonalds (Wabner 2003: 113). Although the homophone word (in this case *Kostas*) is not new with respect to its form, it is new with respect to its meaning. Therefore, such cases may be considered as word-creations, provided that the two meanings are indeed entirely different from each other, i.e., are neither synchronically in any metaphorical, metonymic, generalizing, etc. relation, nor combined in the creation like in a compound. (In the latter case the creation is better considered as a blend, cf. below.)

Alienation by homophones may be combined with plain orthographical alienation in rebus-like creations, where numbers or alphabet names of letters written as ciphers or letters respectively replace homophone (parts of) words, thus yielding a graphical shortening at the same time. This shortening effect makes the technique especially attractive for texting or advertising, e.g., in English *CU* for *see you*, *U2* for *you too* or *Car2Go* for *car to go* (Crystal 2008).

An orthographical and phonetic alienation may proceed from a modification of the sound shape or of the spelling of the source form. The sound shape can be alienated by extending it or by replacing part of it by elements without a morphological function, as in German *Schauma*, name of a shampoo, from *Schaum* 'foam' and German *Wella* from *Welle* 'wave', a brand name for hair cosmetics, respectively. Moreover, elements of a sound shape such as syllables, may be mixed up, e.g., in French *verlan* from *(à) l'envers*, name of a special jargon popular among young people, which consists in modifying the order of syllables in a word (cf., e.g., Goudailler 2002). The orthographic alienation precedes the phonetic one in anagrams, where the letters of the source form are "read backwards" or mixed up, e.g., in *Lycra*, name of a fabric, from *Acryl*).

A mere phonetic alienation without a corresponding orthographical change is performed in word plays obscuring the morphological structure of the source form, e.g., by a stress shift in German puns such as [bluˈmɛntopfeɐdə] instead of [bluːməntopfeɐdə] *Blumentopferde* 'flower-pot soil'. Although the output of the alienation sounds like a compound with the word *Pferde* 'horses' as its second member, it is not designed to talk about an obscure kind of horses, but simply to conceal the source form in a playful way, by alienating its sound shape.

2.3 Extra-grammatical word-formation: blending and extra-grammatical derivation

Contrary to shortening and alienation, the techniques subsumed here under the term extra-grammatical word-formation do not modify a given source form, but combine lexical and derivational morphemes into new words, thereby breaking the rules or models of regular word-formation. If the combined morphemes are lexemes, the respective techniques are different kinds of blending; if lexical bases are combined with affixes or combining forms, we call this extra-grammatical derivation. As blending is treated in article 15, the present article focuses on extra-grammatical derivation.

In extra-grammatical derivation, regular derivatives are used outside their regular functions. For instance, the German loan suffix *-al* is regularly used to form relational denominal adjectives, (e.g., *phänomenal* from *Phänomen*), possibly nominalized, especially in professional jargons (e.g., *Chloral* for a chemical substance containing chlorine, German *Chlor*). However, in the name *Veronal* for a barbiturate, the suffixation by *-al* neither produces an adjective meaning 'related to Verona' nor a noun meaning 'a substance containing Verona', but has simply been chosen because it provides the name with a sound shape characteristic of Latin and Greek loan words, associated by Germans with scientific reliability. I.e. for the hearer or reader, *-al* here functions more as a phonaestheme comparable to *-on*, mentioned above, than as a genuine suffix. This is why such "derivations" are here considered as extra-grammatical creations.

A similar argument can be made for creations with combining forms (German *Konfixe*), such as *therm* 'warm' or 'warmth' (Marchand 1969: 131–132, Donalies 2000). In regular use, they have full lexical meanings, but, unlike lexemes, they do not occur as free forms. Moreover, most of them are fairly productive, like affixes. Their principal domain is neoclassical word-formation, where they occur in initial or final position (e.g., *Thermometer* lit. 'measure of warmth', *endotherm* lit. 'inside warm') or even as bases (*Thermik*). In extra-grammatical use, this distribution is superficially imitated, but without a clear structural and semantic function of the combining forms, especially if these forms were themselves created through shortening, such as *flex* from *flexible*, *tex* from *textile* or *text*, *med* from *medicine* or *medical*, *mat(ic)* from *automat(ic)*, etc. (Cf. Thornton 2000; Ronneberger-Sibold 2009 for a delimitation between regular and extra-grammatical use; Schmitt 1996 on the international use of such elements; Fradin 2000 on the process of their creation.) Examples are brand names such as *Blend-a-med* for a toothpaste, combining the ideas of brilliance (German *blendend*) and medicine, but not according to the regular models of German or neoclassical word-formation.

As mentioned in section 2.1, even reduplication, possibly accompanied by "Ablaut", might be considered as an instance of extra-grammatical derivation, if it is based on existing morphemes but not derived by regular rules or models (e.g., German *Zickzack*).

3 Functions of word-creation

The most basic function of word-creation is an extension of the lexicon by words exhibiting two characteristics which, normally, may result from diachronic change or borrowing, but not from regular word-formation. These are a) specific sound shapes and b) specific degrees of morphosemantic transparency. In regular word-formation, a) is impossible because the phonetic shape of the output is governed by the input and the word-formational rule or model, whereas, in word-creation, it is the desired phonetic characteristics of the output such as a specific rhythmical contour or the presence/absence of certain segments which govern the choice of an input and the selection and application of a technique. b) is impossible with regular word-formation, because all regularly formed words are initially morphosemantically transparent (cf. section 1). It is only through subsequent change that they may lose their transparency. Whereas the phonetic advantage of word-creation is generally recognized, especially with respect to shortening, the lack of transparency is frequently considered as an inevitable side-effect, which has to be kept to a minimum, e.g., by "truncation-specific faithfulness constraints" (Lappe 2007: 56). There are, however, certain lexical domains and communicative purposes which, for pragmatic or semiotic reasons, are better served by totally or partially opaque words labeling their referents than by transparent formations describing them (Seiler 1975; Ronneberger-Sibold 2001).

Pragmatic purposes of a partial or total reduction of morphosemantic transparency are

a) excluding outsiders of a social group by using words which can be understood by insiders only in secret languages and certain social jargons, occasionally also in professional jargons,
b) avoiding social taboos by replacing descriptive nominations of things or persons considered as unpleasant in a society by an opaque label, e.g., *water closet* by *WC* in euphemistic speech,
c) amusing or impressing listeners or readers by giving them a "riddle" to solve in humorous (especially satirical) texts and in literature for children (Grésillon 1984; Sobkowiak 1991), as well as in advertising texts (Forgács and Göndöcs 1997) and in commercial names.

A semiotic purpose of transparency reduction through word-creation is an iconic symbolization of holistic concepts most iconically symbolized by unmotivated, simple, internally unstructured labels. Such concepts are, e.g.,
a) denominations of things or substances consisting of several amalgamated ingredients such as *smog* for an amalgam of *smoke* and *fog* (Meid 1977; Kemmer 2003),
b) denominations of concepts which are highly familiar to language users, e.g., in professional jargons (Bellmann 1980), but also in the general lexicon (Ronneberger-Sibold 2001) – cf. also the optimization of sound shapes mentioned below,
c) proper names, for they present their referents as individual, i.e. undivided, self-contained entities (cf. Nübling, Fahlbusch and Heuser 2012: 20). Nevertheless, some transparency may be helpful for mnemonic reasons (Nübling 2000) or for an advertising purpose in commercial names (Ronneberger-Sibold 2000). Word-creation is an ideal means for the production of such finely tuned intermediate degrees of transparency.

As far as the creation of specific sound shapes is concerned, important pragmatic purposes are
a) saving effort, time, and space through shortness in the social media and certain formats of the mass media as well as in high frequency words in the general lexicon and professional jargons requiring short sound shapes which are at the same time maximally distinctive and easy for production and perception (Kobler-Trill 1994; Ronneberger-Sibold 1996; Steinhauer 2000; Balnat 2011),
b) a gain in prestige through the imitation of typical sound shapes of prestige languages (cf. section 2.1).

A semiotic purpose of specific sound shapes is the imitation of sensory impressions by phonetic iconism, used in literary texts in the widest sense including literature for children and comics (e.g., Kayser 1932; Nodier 2008: 15–20 and passim; Grünewald 2000: 14).

4 Word-creation in a cross-linguistic perspective

If word-creation is not entirely governed by the word-formational rules or models of individual languages, but, at least in part, based on universal cognitive principles (cf. section 1), a cross-linguistic survey should be of particular interest for research on linguistic universals and typology, because it allows for the study of the interaction between universal tendencies and language-specific features more directly than the grammars of individual languages. In the following, some examples of this interaction will be discussed separately for the creative techniques and for their products.

4.1 Products of word-creation

Research on the sound shapes of word-creations, especially of clippings and blends, has to a great deal focussed either on their congruence with the minimal or at least the preferred prosodic patterns of the language in question, thus emphasizing the language-specific character of word-creations (e.g., Monnot 1971 for English and French; Plénat 1993 for French; Wiese 1996 and Féry 1997 for German; Bat-El 2000 for Hebrew), or, on the contrary, on the emergence of universally unmarked structures in word-creations, thus stressing their universal properties (e.g., Kubozono 1990 for English and Japanese; Kilani-Schoch 1996 for French; Montermini 2007 for Russian). A median position is taken in Ronneberger-Sibold (1996) on the basis of a detailed comparative study of German and French shortenings. It seems that word-creation serves, among other things, to re-establish an optimal balance between different universal tendencies in cases where this balance has been upset by diachronic change in the normal vocabulary of a language. E.g., in the history of French, repeated deletion of final consonants due to a continuous pursuit of the universal preference for open syllables has yielded numerous homophones, thereby coming into conflict with the universal need for distinctiveness. In the historical development of German phonology, on the contrary, final consonants were far more stable. Therefore, somewhat perversely at first sight, the preference for open syllables is stronger in German than in French shortenings (cf. also Nübling 2001 on German and Swedish).

A field where language-specific phonology interacts with universally identical patterns is onomatopoeia. Although the imitated sounds, e.g., certain birdcalls (Callebaut 1985), are universally (almost) identical, their linguistic imitation has to take into account the segmental inventories and dominating prosodic features as well as the phonotactics of individual languages (Marchand 1969: 402), even though sound-iconic words (e.g., in comics) can be less constrained in these respects than the normal lexicon (Trubetzkoy 1977: 230). As for the universal character of synaesthetic associations cf. section 2.1.

4.2 Creative techniques

The creative techniques have been less in the focus of contrastive research, although they, too, reflect an interaction of universal faculties based on cognitive principles, on the one hand, and the regular grammar and word-formation, as well as the script of individual languages, on the other. In fact, a contrastive analysis of creative techniques applied in three typologically extremely different languages, namely German, Farsi, and Chinese (Ronneberger-Sibold 2012 and 2014) has revealed that the creative techniques summarized in section 2 seem to form a kind of international pool from which users of different languages select techniques which appear attractive to them. In the first place, this choice is determined by the compatibility with their respective linguistic system and their script. (Cf. also López Rúa 2005 with respect to shortening in text messaging.) E.g., in Chinese word-creation on a native base, all techniques operating within syllables are systematically excluded because of the strict syntagmatic 1:1 correspondence between syllables, morphemes, and ideographic characters in this isolating language.

However, among the available techniques, closeness to universal, cognitively based faculties favours their selection. For instance, in Chinese, two types of blending are theoretically possible (Ronneberger-Sibold 2012): telescope blending of integral words, strongly resembling regular compounding as in *Workoutfit*, a brand name composed of *outfit* and *workout* overlapping in *-out-*, and contour blending as in *Bonn Juan* 'a Don Juan in Bonn', where *Don Juan* is recovered among other things by its rhythmic contour, although its first morpheme has been replaced by a phonetically similar one. Although telescope blending is closer to Chinese regular compounding, only contour blending is actually implemented, probably precisely because it relies less on the grammar of Chinese, which hardly allows for any infringements other than on the universal faculty of language users to recognize a word by certain elements of its sound shape (Ronneberger-Sibold 2012).

A further factor influencing not so much the selection of creative techniques from the international "pool", but the extent and the functions of their use are social norms concerning the linguistic behaviour in different speech communities. For instance, in Farsi, contour blending is active as well, but only in a special milieu or in very colloquial style, because blends are considered as not sufficiently serious for general use, let alone for journalistic or even literary texts.

Beyond such cultural preferences, the primary criterion determining the use of creative techniques seems, however, to be the transparency of their products: If different creative techniques are available in a speech community, then the less transparent ones are preponderantly used with proper names, the more transparent ones in the non-onymic lexicon (cf. Ronneberger-Sibold 2014). This finding underlines the very basic function of word-creation as a means for fine-tuning the transparency of words.

5 References

Aronoff, Mark (1976): *Word-Formation in Generative Grammar.* Cambridge, MA: MIT Press.
Balnat, Vincent (2011): *Kurzwortbildung im Gegenwartsdeutschen.* Hildesheim: Olms.
Barz, Irmhild (2009): Die Wortbildung. In: Dudenredaktion (ed.), *Duden. Die Grammatik*, 634–762. 9th ed. Mannheim: Dudenverlag.
Bat-El, Outi (2000): The grammaticality of "extragrammatical" morphology. In: Ursula Doleschal and Anna M. Thornton (eds.), *Extragrammatical and Marginal Morphology*, 61–84. München: LINCOM Europa.
Bauer, Laurie (2003): *Introducing Linguistic Morphology.* 2nd ed. Edinburgh: Edinburgh University Press.
Believa, Natalia (2019): Blending creativity and productivity: on the issue of delimiting the boundaries of blends as a type of word formation. *Lexis* 14: 1–22.
Bellmann, Günther (1980): Zur Variation im Lexikon: Kurzwort und Original. *Wirkendes Wort* 30: 369–383.
Bußmann, Hadumod (ed.) (2008): *Lexikon der Sprachwissenschaft.* 4th ed. Stuttgart: Kröner.
Callebaut, Bruno (1985): Onomatopées et noms d'oiseaux en français. *Le Français Moderne* 53(1–2): 49–77.
Cannon, Garland (1986): Blends in English word-formation. *Linguistics* 24: 725–753.
Crystal, David (2008): *Txtng. The Gr8 Db8.* Oxford: Oxford University Press.
Donalies, Elke (2000): Das Konfix. Zur Definition einer zentralen Einheit der deutschen Wortbildung. *Deutsche Sprache* 28: 144–159. [Reprinted in: Müller, Peter O. (ed.) 2005 *Fremdwortbildung. Theorie und Praxis in Geschichte und Gegenwart*, 179–198. Frankfurt/M.: Lang.]
Dressler, Wolfgang U. (1990): Sketching submorphemes within natural morphology. In: Julian Méndez Dosuna and Carmen Pensado (eds.), *Naturalists at Krems*, 33–41. Salamanca: Ediciones Universidad de Salamanca.
Dressler, Wolfgang U. (2000): Extragrammatical vs. marginal morphology. In: Ursula Doleschal and Anna M. Thornton (eds.), *Extragrammatical and Marginal Morphology*, 1–10. München: LINCOM Europa.
Dressler, Wolfgang U. (2005): Word-formation in natural morphology. In: Pavol Štekauer and Rochelle Lieber (eds.), *Handbook of Word-Formation*, 267–84. Dordrecht: Springer.
Ertel, Suitbert (1969): *Psychophonetik.* Göttingen: Hogrefe.
Féry, Caroline (1997): Unis und Studis: Die besten Wörter des Deutschen. *Linguistische Berichte* 172: 461–89.
Firth, John R. (1957): The use and distribution of certain English sounds. In: John R. Firth, *Papers in Linguistics 1934–1951*, 34–46. Oxford: Oxford University Press.
Fischer-Jørgensen, Eli (1978): On the universal character of phonetic symbolism with special reference to vowels. *Studia Linguistica* 32: 80–90.
Fleischer, Wolfgang and Irmhild Barz (2012): *Wortbildung der deutschen Gegenwartssprache.* 4th ed. Berlin/Boston: de Gruyter.

Forgács, Erzsébet and Ágnes Göndöcs (1997): Sprachspiele in der Werbung. *Studia Germanica Universitatis Vesprimiensis* 1: 49–70.
Fradin, Bernard (2000): Combining forms, blends and related phenomena. In: Ursula Doleschal and Anna M. Thornton (eds.), *Extragrammatical and Marginal Morphology*, 11–59. München: LINCOM Europa.
Goudaillier, Jean-Pierre (2002): De l'argot traditionnel au français contemporain des cités. *Linguistique* 38(1): 5–23.
Grammont, Maurice (1901): Onomatopées et mots expressifs. *Revue des langues romanes* 44 (5ème série, tome 4ème): 97–158. [Reprint Nendeln: Kraus 1970.]
Grésillon, Almuth (1984): *La règle et le monstre. Le mot-valise. Interrogations sur la langue, à partir d'un corpus de Heinrich Heine*. Tübingen: Niemeyer.
Grünewald, Dietrich (2000): *Comics*. Tübingen: Niemeyer.
Hinton, Leanne, Johanna Nichols and John J. Ohala (eds.) (1994): *Sound Symbolism*. Cambridge: Cambridge University Press.
Jakobson, Roman and Linda R. Waugh (1979): *The Sound Shape of Language*. Bloomington/London: Bloomington University Press.
Jespersen, Otto (1922): *Language. Its Nature, Development and Origin*. London: Allen & Unwin.
Jespersen, Otto (1933): Symbolic value of the vowel *I*. In: Otto Jespersen, *Linguistica. Selected Papers in English, French and German*, 283–303. Copenhagen: Levin & Munksgaard, London: Allen & Unwin.
Kayser, Wolfgang (1932): *Die Klangmalerei bei Harsdörffer. Ein Beitrag zur Geschichte der Literatur, Poetik und Sprachtheorie der Barockzeit*. Leipzig: Mayer & Müller.
Kemmer, Suzanne (2003): Schemas and lexical blends: Studies in honor of Günter Radden. In: Hubert Cuyckens, Thomas Berg, René Dirven and Klaus-Uwe Panther (eds.), *Motivation in Language*, 69–97. Amsterdam/Philadelphia: Benjamins.
Kilani-Schoch, Marianne (1996): Syllable and foot in French clipping. In: Bernhard Hurch and Richard Rhodes (eds.), *Natural Phonology. The State of the Art*, 261–292. Berlin/New York: Mouton de Gruyter.
Kleiber, Georges (2006): Sémiotique de l'interjection. *Langages* 161: 10–23.
Kobler-Trill, Dorothea (1994): *Das Kurzwort im Deutschen. Eine Untersuchung zu Definition, Typologie und Entwicklung*. Tübingen: Niemeyer.
Kubozono, Haruo (1990): Phonological constraints on blending in English as a case for phonology-morphology interface. In: Geert Booij and Jaap van Marle (eds.), *Yearbook of Morphology 1990*, 1–20. Dordrecht: Foris.
Lappe, Sabine (2007): *English Prosodic Morphology*. Berlin: Springer.
Lötscher, Andreas (1992): *Von Ajax bis Xerox. Ein Lexikon der Produktenamen*. 2nd ed. Zürich: Artemis & Winkler.
Lötscher, Andreas (2007): Von *Mercedes* zu *Xsara* – Modellnamen für Automobile in geografisch-historischer Perspektive. In: Ludger Kremer and Elke Ronneberger-Sibold (eds.), *Names in Commerce and Industry. Past and Present*, 115–129. Berlin: Logos.
López-Rúa, Paula (2005): Shortening devices in text messaging: A multilingual approach. *Neuphilologische Mitteilungen* 106: 139–155.
Malkiel, Yakov (1977): From phonosymbolism to morphosymbolism. In: Michel Paradis (ed.), *The Fourth Lacus Forum*, 511–529. Columbia, SC: Hornbeam Press. [Reprinted in: Yakov Malkiel 1990: *Diachronic problems in Phonosymbolism. Edita and Inedita, 1979–1988*. Vol. 1, 157–175. Amsterdam/Philadelphia: Benjamins.]
Marchand, Hans (1969): *The Categories and Types of Present-Day English Word-Formation. A Synchronic-Diachronic Approach*. 2nd ed. München: Beck.

Mattiello, Elisa (2013): *Extra-grammatical morphology in English. Abbreviations, blends, reduplicatives, and related phenomena*. Berlin/Boston: De Gruyter Mouton.

Mattiello, Elisa (2023): *Transitional morphology. Combining forms in Modern English*. Cambridge: Cambridge University Press.

Meid, Wolfgang (1977): Beziehungen zwischen äußerer und innerer Sprachform: Verschränkte Zeichen und fusionierte Inhalte. *Veröffentlichungen der Kommission für Linguistik und Kommunikationsforschung. Anzeiger der philosophisch-historischen Klasse* 114(6): 294–304. Wien: Verlag der Österreichischen Akademie der Wissenschaften.

Meier, Harri (1975): *Primäre und sekundäre Onomatopöien und andere Untersuchungen zur romanischen Etymologie*. Heidelberg: Winter.

Monnot, Michel (1971): Examen comparatif des tendances de syllabation dans les mots abrégés de l'anglais et du français. *Le Français Moderne* 39: 191–206.

Montermini, Fabio (2007): Hypocoristiques et minimalité en russe. In: Élisabeth Delais-Roussarie and Laurence Labrune (eds.), *Des sons et des sens*, 198–213. Paris: Lavoisier/Hermès.

Nodier, Charles (2008): *Dictionnaire raisonné des onomatopées françaises*. Edition établie, présentée et annotée par Jean-François Jeandillou. Genève/Paris: Droz [Original edition 1808].

Nübling, Damaris (2000): Auf der Suche nach dem idealen Eigennamen. *Beiträge zur Namenforschung* 35: 275–302.

Nübling, Damaris (2001): Auto – bil, Reha – rehab, Mikro – mick, Alki – alkis: Kurzwörter im Deutschen und im Schwedischen. *Skandinavistik* 31: 167–199.

Nübling, Damaris, Fabian Fahlbusch and Rita Heuser (2012): *Namen. Eine Einführung in die Onomastik*. Tübingen: Narr.

O'Boyle, Michael W., David A. Miller and Fahim Rahmani (1987): Sound-meaning relationships in speakers of Urdu and English: Evidence for a cross-cultural phonetic symbolism. *Journal of Psycholinguistic Research* 16(3): 273–288.

Paul, Hermann (1920): *Prinzipien der Sprachgeschichte*. 5th ed. Tübingen: Niemeyer.

Plag, Ingo (2003): *Word-Formation in English*. Cambridge: Cambridge University Press.

Plénat, Marc (1993): Observations sur le mot minimal français: L'oralisation des sigles. In: Bernard Laks and Marc Plénat (eds.), *De natura sonorum. Essais de phonologie*, 143–172. Saint-Denis: Presses Universitaires de Vincennes.

Ronneberger-Sibold, Elke (1996): Preferred sound shapes of new roots: On some phonotactic and prosodic properties of shortenings in German and French. In: Bernhard Hurch and Richard Rhodes (eds.), *Natural Phonology. The State of the Art*, 261–292. Berlin/New York: Mouton de Gruyter.

Ronneberger-Sibold, Elke (2000): Creative competence at work: The creation of partial motivation in German trade names. In: Ursula Doleschal and Anna M. Thornton (eds.), *Extragrammatical and Marginal Morphology*, 87–105. München: LINCOM Europa.

Ronneberger-Sibold, Elke (2001): On useful darkness: Loss and destruction of transparency by linguistic change, borrowing, and word creation. In: Geert Booij and Jaap van Marle (eds.), *Yearbook of Morphology 1999*, 97–120. Dordrecht: Kluwer.

Ronneberger-Sibold, Elke (2002): On the phonostylistic function of prototypical nonnative sound shapes in contemporary German: Evidence from the history of brand names. In: Katarzyna Dziubalska-Kołaczyk and Jarosław Weckwerth (eds.), *Future Challenges for Natural Linguistics*, 211–231. München: LINCOM Europa.

Ronneberger-Sibold, Elke (2004): Warennamen. In: Andrea Brendler and Silvio Brendler (eds.), *Namenarten und ihre Erforschung. Ein Lehrbuch für das Studium der Onomastik*, 557–603. Hamburg: Baar.

Ronneberger-Sibold, Elke (2009): Thermodur, Blend-a-med, Sivitrex: Konfixe in deutschen Markennamen: Typen – Geschichte – Funktionen. In: Peter O. Müller (ed.), *Studien zur Fremdwortbildung*, 141–193. Hildesheim: Olms.

Ronneberger-Sibold, Elke (2010): Word creation: Definition – function – typology. In: Franz Rainer, Wolfgang U. Dressler, Dieter Kastovsky and Hans Christian Luschützky (eds.), *Variation and Change in Morphology. Selected Papers from the 13th International Morphology Meeting (Vienna, February 2008)*, 201–216. Amsterdam/Philadelphia: Benjamins.

Ronneberger-Sibold, Elke (2012): Blending between grammar and universal cognitive principles: Evidence from German, Farsi, and Chinese. In: Vincent Renner, François Maniez and Pierre J. L. Arnaud (eds.), *Cross-Disciplinary Perspectives on Lexical Blending*, 115–143. Berlin/Boston: Mouton de Gruyter.

Ronneberger-Sibold, Elke (2014): Tuning morphosemantic transparency by shortening: A cross-linguistic perspective. In: Franz Rainer, Francesco Gardani, Hans Christian Luschützky and Wolfgang U. Dressler (eds.), *Morphology and Meaning. Selected Papers from the 15th International Morphology Meeting, Vienna, February 2012*, 275–287. Amsterdam/Philadelphia: Benjamins.

Ronneberger-Sibold, Elke, Mir Kamaladin Kazzazi and Stefanie Potsch-Ringeisen (2016): Markiertheitsabbau durch intendierte morphologische Irregularität. Schriftbasierte Wortschöpfung im Deutschen, Farsi und Chinesischen. In: Andreas Bittner and Klaus-Michael Köpcke (eds.), *Regularität und Irregularität in Phonologie und Morphologie. Diachron, kontrastiv, typologisch*. Berlin: De Gruyter, 263–301.

Sapir, Edward (1929): A study in phonetic symbolism. *Journal of Experimental Psychology* 12: 225–259. [Reprinted 1949 in: David G. Mandelbaum (ed.), *Writings of Edward Sapir in Language, Culture and Personality*, 61–72. Berkeley, CA: University of California Press.]

Schmitt, Christian (1996): Euromorphologie: Perspektiven einer neuen romanistischen Teildisziplin. In: Wolfgang Dahmen, Günter Holtus, Johannes Kramer, Michael Metzeltin, Wolfgang Schweickard and Otto Winkelmann (eds.), *Die Bedeutung der romanischen Sprachen im Europa der Zukunft*, 119–146. Tübingen: Narr.

Seiler, Hansjakob (1975): Die Prinzipien der deskriptiven und der etikettierenden Benennung. In: Hansjakob Seiler (ed.), *Linguistic Workshop III*, 2–57. München: Fink.

Sobkowiak, Włodzimierz (1991): *Metaphonology of English Paronomasic Puns*. Frankfurt/M.: Lang.

Soudek, Lev I. (1978): The relation of blending to English word-formation: Theory, structure, and typological attempts. In: Wolfgang U. Dressler and Wolfgang Meid (eds.), *Proceedings of the Twelfth International Congress of Linguists*, 462–466. Innsbruck: Institut für Sprachwissenschaft.

Steinhauer, Anja (2000): *Sprachökonomie durch Kurzwörter. Bildung und Verwendung in der Fachkommunikation*. Tübingen: Narr.

Thornton, Anna M. (2000): On -ex and -tex. In: Ursula Doleschal and Anna M. Thornton (eds.), *Extragrammatical and Marginal Morphology*, 107–126. München: LINCOM Europa.

Tournier, Jean (1985): *Introduction descriptive à la lexicogénétique de l'anglais contemporain*. Paris/Genève: Champion & Slatkine.

Trubetzkoy, N[ikolaj] S[ergeevič] (1977): *Grundzüge der Phonologie*. 6th ed. Göttingen: Vandenhoeck & Ruprecht.

Tsur, Reuven (2006): Size-sound symbolism revisited. *Journal of Pragmatics* 38(6): 905–924.

Ultan, Russell (1978): Size-sound symbolism. In: Joseph H. Greenberg (ed.), *Universals of Human Language*. Vol. 2: *Phonology*, 525–568. Stanford, CA: Stanford University Press.

Wabner, Matthias (2003): *Kreativer Umgang mit Sprache in der Werbung. Eine Analyse der Anzeigen- und Plakatwerbung von McDonald's*. Networx, Nr. 32. <http://www.mediensprache.net/networx/networx-32.pdf>.

Wiese, Richard (1996): *The Phonology of German*. Oxford: Oxford University Press.
Zelinsky-Wibbelt, Cornelia (1983): *Die semantische Belastung von submorphematischen Einheiten im Englischen. Eine empirisch-strukturelle Untersuchung*. Frankfurt/M.: Lang.
Zwicky, Arnold M. and Geoffrey K. Pullum (1987): Plain morphology and expressive morphology. In: Jon Aske (ed.), *Proceedings of the Thirteenth Annual Meeting (14-16 February 1987). General Session and Parasession on Grammar and Cognition*, 330-340. Berkeley, CA: Berkeley Linguistics Society.

Wolfgang U. Dressler
20 Allomorphy

1 Introduction
2 General overview
3 Conditions of allomorphy
4 Exclusion of zero allomorphs
5 Word-creation
6 Conclusion
7 References

Abstract: Allomorphy, which violates biuniqueness and canonical word-formation, has to be restricted. This is true more for word-formation than for inflection but is otherwise rather similar in stem vs. affix allomorphy and in types of conditioning. Allomorphy is rare in most types of extragrammatical word-creation.

1 Introduction

Allomorph (of a morpheme) and *allomorphy* are terms created by Nida (1948: 420) in analogy to the terms *allophone* and *allophony* with the primary purpose of conceptualising stem variation and affix variation in inflectional morphology (cf. Carstairs-McCarthy 2005). Allomorphs thus form a set of formal variants of the same morpheme but must have an identical content in terms of syntactic, semantic and (I must add) pragmatic features, which is more precise than Bloomfield's (1933) principle of identical function and complementary distribution. Thus the German adjective-forming suffixes *-ig, -lich, -isch* (cognate to E. *-y, -ly, -ish*) are not only formally similar but also have the same syntactic and semantic content as heads of derived adjectives, except for the fact that *-isch* adjectives may be pejorative, as in *weib-lich* 'woman-ly' vs. pejorative *weib-isch*, *kind-lich* 'child-like' vs. *kind-isch* 'child-ish', and inherently pejorative adjectives have also adopted the pejorative suffix *-isch* in their diachronic development, as in former *neid-ig* > *neid-isch* 'envious'. Because of these differences in meaning, the three similar German suffixes are not to be considered allomorphs of the same morpheme but rather competing and functionally overlapping morphemes. For the same rea-

Wolfgang U. Dressler, Vienna, Austria

sons, the Spanish adjective-forming suffixes -*ado*, -*udo*, -*ido* cannot be classified as allomorphs (pace Malkiel 1966: 335 f.). But when semantic differences occur only rarely, then we are in a transition zone between allomorphy and morphematic contrast, as in Štekauer, Valera and Körtvélyessy's (2012: 137–138) Slovak instances of contrast between the prefix forms *pre-* and *prie-* in predictable derivations, e.g., *pre-beh-nú-t* 'to run (perfective)' → verbal noun *prie-beh* 'course (of events)' vs. the unpredictable contrast between deverbal *pre-chod* 'transition' and *prie-chod* 'gangway'.

Content identity holds only for word-formation meanings (Marchand 1969; cf. also Corbin's 1987 concept of "sens construit"), usually not for word meanings. Thus the word-formation meaning of E. (*a*) *build-ing* is 'something which has been/is being built', where the meaning of *build-* is identical with the lexical meaning of the verb *build*, whereas the word meaning of (*a*) *building* has idiosyncratic meaning restrictions in respect to the verbal base. As a consequence not everything that has been or is being built can be called *a building*. And such deviation of word meaning from its word-formation meaning holds for all result nouns, and, at least to a certain degree, for all derivations in general. In other words, the word-formation meaning of a complex/derived word is fully compositional, whereas the word meaning is never fully compositional (cf. Frege 1892).

Another criterion of allomorphy advanced by many (e.g., Thornton 2005: 40; cf. also Mugdan 1994: 2547) is complementary distribution. But since allophony is not necessarily in complementary distribution, allowing also for free allophones (e.g., several rhotic variants of the same /r/ phoneme in the same context), it is not self-evident why complementary distribution should be obligatory for allomorphs. English examples of free variation between allomorphs are *dependence* and *dependency, expectance* and *expectancy* (Plag 2003: 87; further examples in Štekauer, Valera and Körtvélyessy 2012: 193). On the other hand, the presence of complementary distribution is an argument for allomorphy, such as Plag's (2003: 29) example of English adjectivizing -*al* vs. -*ar* (after base-final -*l*) in *caus-al* vs. *pol-ar*.

What remains, in any case, as a distinctive criterion for allomorphy is non-contrastive distribution in meaning, a consequence of the above-mentioned identity-of-content constraint, as in *dependence* – *dependency*.

So far we have treated allomorphy in terms of alternation in representation. But process models, such as some generative word-formation models treat it, at least partially, in terms of adjustment rules, including allomorphy rules. For example, Aronoff (1976 and later; cf. also Štekauer 2000: 146) derives complex forms such as *electri-fic-ation* from *electri-fy* with an allomorphy rule which replaces the suffix -*fy* with its allomorph -*fic*- (cf. Scalise 1984: 57–69).

For quite some time, allomorphy in word-formation has not been the only or the main topic of any single publication, but it has been dealt with together with other basic concepts of morphology in all introductory books and handbooks of morphology (albeit with a focus on inflectional morphology). This holds also for the most formal classification of allomorphy in Mel'čuk 1993–2000 Vol. 4: 214–228).

2 General overview

2.1 Generalities

This article focuses on word-formation as part of grammatical morphology; operations of extragrammatical morphology (cf. Dressler 2001) will be mentioned only marginally, such as abbreviations, blends or sophisticated terminography, as in the truncated base of *laps+o+logy* 'error analysis' from *lapsus*.

Allomorphy violates the general preference for biunique relationships between meaning and form (Dressler 2005: 274, 1987: 111), i.e. between the meaning and the form of a morpheme. Since biuniqueness is difficult to attain in morphology and since it plays a greater role in (especially scientific and juridical) terminology, allomorphy should be less frequent in sophisticated, conscious terminology than in ordinary language. But this is hardly the case, because the different types of conditioning of allomorphy (studied in section 3) can hardly be avoided even in very sophisticated terminology.

In Corbett's approach to canonical typology, allomorphy inherently deviates from canonical derivational morphology (implicit in Corbett 2010). Allomorphy also provides a problem for learnability, insofar as it presents a problem for young children, which so far has only been investigated systematically for inflectional morphology, cf. Bernhardt and Stemberger (1998: 658 ff.), Peters (1997: 169 ff.). But in the acquisition of diminutives and hypocoristics (Savickiene and Dressler 2007), at least Russian, Italian, Spanish and Hungarian children do not seem to have particular problems acquiring competing suffixations with stem allomorphy, nor do Flemish children with Dutch suffix allomorphy. Also Austrian children produce nearly no errors in the selection of the umlauted base accompanying umlaut-inducing suffixes.

Evidently, children's learning task becomes more difficult the more allomorphs there are. But this aspect is not only underinvestigated for acquisition, but even in theoretical morphology where no upper bound for allomorphy has been found and explained (Bonet and Harbour 2012: 218 f.).

This leads us to the criterion of phonological similarity important for allomorphy in word-formation but not in inflection. Whereas the English participle suffixes -ed and -en (as in *work-ed* vs. *giv-en*) are generally considered to be allomorphs of the same participle morpheme, the synonymous English derivational suffixes -ness and -ity (as in *opaque-ness* vs. *opac-ity, odd-ity* vs. *odd-ness*) are generally considered to be different, though synonymous, morphemes. Carstairs-McCarthy (2005: 18–21) justifies this difference to inflectional morphology by the patchiness (or "gappiness") of derivational morphology as well as its greater tolerance for homophony and polysemy (thus to its much greater disregard for biuniqueness). To this I would add the great importance of the notion of the paradigm in inflectional morphology and its absence or near-absence in models of derivational morphology. This is also the reason why in Corbett's canonical typology (2010) the ideal of biuniqueness plays a central role in inflection but none in derivation.

Phonological similarity between derivational allomorphs, a notion not yet sufficiently studied, may be of at least two types:

1. Allomorph A includes allomorph B, as in E. /si/ vs. /s/ in *dependence* vs. *dependency* (cf. section 1) or in the Dutch diminutive suffixes -je vs. -tje, -pje, -kje vs. -etje (Booij 1995, Booij and van Santen 1995). Such cases of longer affix variants must be distinguished from sequences of an interfix plus a suffix as in the diminutive It. *volp-ic-ino* 'little fox' (Dressler and Merlini Barbaresi 1994).
2. The allomorphs A and B are related by a phonological or morphophonological rule (or alternation), as in the case of E. -al and -ar in *caus-al* vs. *pol-ar* and in the stem alternation of *divine* [di'vaɪn] and *divin-ity* [di'vinɪti]. Clearly the assumption of such rules must be justifiable within a theory of phonology or morphophonology (see section 3). The rule/alternation may also be fossilized, as in the case of weak suppletion, e.g., in the stem allomorphy between *Wales* and *Wel-sh*. In contrast, strong suppletion does not relate allomorphs but different, synonymous stems, as in E. *bellic-ose, belli-gerent* and *war*. Also /luːn/ in *lun-ar* is not an allomorph of *moon*, although they rime and are thus phonologically similar (the reason will be given in section 3.1).

Also the extreme case of phonological similarity, i.e. phonological identity, must be excluded from allomorphy, because allomorphy, as well as allophony, presupposes formal difference (cf. section 4 for the exclusion of conversion).

Allomorphs are easier to identify, the more compositional a word-formation is (for natural morphology see Dressler 1987, 2005 and for canonical typology Corbett 2010). This means iconicity between meaning and form insofar as addition of meaning in a derivative is paralleled by the addition of an affix. Conversion, which is non-iconic because its meaning change is not paralleled by a formal change, does not produce allomorphy (cf. section 4), whereas anti-iconic subtraction can produce stem allomorphy in a loose sense (see below) in inflectional instances, such as in a Franconian dialect: *hond* 'dog' → plural *hon*, with subtraction of the word-final consonant of a word-final consonant cluster. No good corresponding example has been found in word-formation as part of morphological grammar (cf. Dressler 2000). In extragrammatical word-formation subtractive stem allomorphy is frequent, such as in hypocoristics (e.g., E. *Edward* → *Ed*) and in abbreviations of all sorts. But subtractive, grammatical stem allomorphy may occur in combination with the iconic means of compounding and derivational affixation. Such instances are usually called truncations, as in E. *nominate* → *nomin-ee* (cf. Iacobini 2000: 872). Truncation, though, is often not easy to distinguish from root-based morphology. For example, many German nouns ending in *e*-schwa, such as masc. *Friede* 'peace', have either root-based derivations and compounds, such as *fried-lich* 'peaceful', the synonymous compounds *fried-voll, fried-fertig, fried-liebend* 'peace-loving', morphosemantically opaque *Fried-hof* 'cemetery' or the weak-stem-based compounds with the interfix /s/, as in *frieden-s-liebend, Frieden-s-engel* 'peace angel', *Frieden-s-vertrag* 'peace treaty'. Similarly *Kirsche* 'cherry' has the synonymous compounds *Kirsch-baum* and *Kirschen-baum* 'cherry tree'. Thus one can identify stem variation between the word-based plural *Kirsche-n* and either root- or stem-based word-formation. The alternative is to assume both truncation and interfixation. Similarly Scalise (1984; cf. also Scalise and Bisetto 2008; Iacobini 2000) postulates truncation only for Italian nominal and adjectival morphology, as in *volpe* 'fox' → augmentative *volp-one* and adjectival *volp-ino*, but an interfix such as *-ic-* in the diminutive *volp-ic-ino*, whereas he assumes root-based derivation in verb morphology as in the diminutives *cant-erellare, cant-icchiare* from *cant-a-re* 'to sing', with generally assumed stem allomorphy between the root / kant/ and the stem /kant+a/.

Second, morphotactic (also called phonological or formal) transparency enhances the identifiability of allomorphs. Full transparency means that there is no change of the morpheme shape. For example, the nominalising allomorph E. *-ation* is transparent in, e.g., *starv-ation* and also the lexical base remains fully transparent. In contrast, the (orthographic and putatively phonological) allomorph *-ion* is opaque in, e.g., *nomination* [nomiˈneɪʃən], due to fusion between the stem-final /t/ of the verb *nominate* and the putative initial phoneme of the suffix allomorph, which opacifies both the lexical base or stem and the suffix. Plag (2003: 90) assumes even a third allomorph *-ification*, as in *ident-ification* derived from the verb *identify*, but the co-existence of the adjective *specific* with the verb *spec-ify* and its derivation *spec-ific-ation* suggests a different analysis of *-ific-*, i.e. as being a very opaque allomorph of the suffix *-ify*. A detailed analysis of the similar Italian allomorphy between the suffixes *-zione* (e.g., in *ammini-stra+zione* 'administr+ation') and *-ione* (e.g., in *percuss+ione* 'percuss+ion') can be found in Scalise and Bisetto (2008: 215–222). For the cognate French suffix *-ion* see Bonami and Kerleroux (2009).

2.2 Stem allomorphy and affix allomorphy

There is a basic distinction between stem allomorphy and affix allomorphy:

Affix allomorphy may refer to prefixes, as in the English negative prefix *in-* with its allomorphs in *im-pure, ir-religious, il-legal* (see section 3.2) or to suffixes, as in above-mentioned E. *-al, -ar*, to interfixes, as in G. *Garage-n-besitzer* 'proprietor of a garage' vs. *Schwan-en-hals* 'swan's neck', or to inflectional (but apparently not to truly derivational) infixes.

Stem allomorphy refers to variants of the stem, which is prototypically the lexical base, affix allomorphy to affix variants, as in the above examples. This difference is, however, blurred in opaque cases of multiple affixation as in E. *person-ific-ation*, where the verb *person-ify* is the base and thus the complex stem of *person-ific-ation*. Derivational morphology has both types of allomorphy, whereas compounding has only stem allomorphy, if at all: for the first member of compounds note Fuhrhop's (1998) analysis of the first part of G. *Garagen-platz* 'garage place (of a car)' as stem allomorph of the noun *Garage*. But an alternative, traditional analysis is the assumption of an interfix or linking element /n/ inserted between the two compound members. An undisputed case of stem allomorphy in compounding is constituted by the following change from *-a* to *-i* in earlier Chicago Lithuanian, which is even applied to English loan words, e.g., masc.nom.sg. *kara-s* (< E. *car*) → *street-kari-s* 'street-car, tram'. The same stem change, inherited from Proto-Indo-European, occurs in Latin derivatives of the type *in-ermi-s* 'unarmed', from *arma* 'arms', genitive *armorum*.

In Latin and many other Indo-European (incl. modern Romance and Slavic) languages, stem allomorphy has been assumed (predominately since Aronoff 1994), not only for inflectional but also derivational deverbal morphology, starting with the participial stem as an allomorph of the present and perfect stems, such as in Latin action and agent nouns: *ora-re* 'to speak out, pray', perf. *oravi*, past participle *oratus* → *orat-io* 'speech', *orat-or* 'speaker', *auge-re* 'to increase', perf. *aux-i* 'I increased', past participle *auct-us* → *auct-io* 'auction', *leg-e-re* 'to read', perf. *lēg-i*, past participle *lect-us* → *lect-io* 'reading', *lect-or* 'reader'. Aronoff (1994) calls this participial stem allomorph of derivational morphology "morphomic", i.e. a stem variant implying no semantic change, whereas an older, alternative name is "parasitic", i.e. morphosemantically opaque derivation.

We can speak of stem allomorphy in the strict sense, if a single stem change is not the only morphological change involved. Thus we can establish English stem allomorphy in *bread+th* vs. *broad*, *drunk+ard* vs. *drink*, *divin+ity* vs. *divine* (with vowel change in the second syllable). Here the addition of a suffix is the primary signal of derivation, stem vowel change the secondary signal, which can therefore be classified as stem allomorphy in the strict sense. In contrast, the German partially synonymic deverbal nouns *Trank*, *Trunk* 'drink, potion' from *trink+en* 'to drink' do not fulfil this criterion and thus can be classified only as allomorphs in a loose sense, whereas we can identify stem allomorphy in the strict sense in the partial synonym *Ge+tränk* 'beverage'.

All cases of allomorphic changes discussed so far, have been cases of segmental allomorphy. But prosodic changes may accompany or even determine segmental changes in allomorphy (cf. Drachman, Kager and Malikouti-Drachman 1995). For example, the adjective *manager-ial* derived from the noun *manager* shows two allomorphic stem changes: segmental change in the vowel of the last stem syllable plus stress shift from the first to the last stem syllable (cf. Kaisse 2005: 32). A prosodically automatic constraint also affects derivational suffixes in Slovak, due to its often discussed rhythmic law, which prohibits a sequence of long vowels in adjacent syllables at the word level, as in the allomorphic contrast between the long basic variant *-ík* and the shortened variant *-ik*, e.g., *rečník* 'speak-er' vs. *básn-ik* 'poet' (Štekauer, Valera and Körtvélyessy 2012: 189–190).

Prosodic changes occur in ancient Indo-European languages together with the stem allomorphy of ablaut (apophony) which can change vowel duration and vowel quality. For example, in Ancient Greek (classical Attic dialect) the word for mother shows the following five allomorphs /méːteːr/ (nom.sg. with rising acute pitch-accent on the first syllable) vs. /metér/ in the acc.sg. /meːtér+a/ (with accent shift to the second syllable) vs. /mêter/ (voc.sg. with rising-falling circumflex) vs. /meːtr/ in several oblique cases, e.g., gen.sg. /meːtr+ós/ (with accent shift and deletion of the second stem vowel) vs. adjective derivations /a+méːtoːr/ 'without a mother' and /dys+méːtoːr/ 'of a bad mother' (with final vowel change).

This Ancient Greek example illustrates the fact that, at least in ancient Indo-European languages, stem allomorphy is much richer in inflection than in word-formation. The opposite is true in Semitic morphology. Note the Standard Arabic stem allomorphy of the root /ktb/ 'to write' in derivational morphology: *kātab-a* 'corresponded', *a-ktab-a* 'dictated', *kitb-a* 'book's transcription', *kitāb* 'book', *kutub-i* 'book-seller', *katib-a* 'written document, diploma', *kātib* 'writer', *kuttāb* 'writing school', *mu-kattib* 'master of writing', *ma-ktūb* 'letter' vs. the inflectional allomorphs of the verb, as they appear in *katab-a* 'he wrote', imperfect *ya-ktub(u)*, and either inflectional or derivational in the participle *kātib* (also agent noun, see above) or in the causative *kattab-a*. Thus the relative amount of stem allomorphy is a typological criterion.

Due to the much greater morphological richness in English of Latinate derivational morphology than of inflectional morphology, English also has, in absolute numbers, more stem allomorphy in derivation than in inflection, i.e. in strong verbs, as in *keep – kept+t, rise – ris-en* (and *rose* as a stem allomorph in the loose sense, because vowel change is here the only signal of the category of preterit). In derivational morphology, we have many more instances of stem allomorphy, such as in *deep – dep+th, divine – divin+ity, manager – manager+ial, porous – poros+ity*, etc. Prosodic change in terms of stress shift, as in *éxport ← to expórt* are instances of stem allomorphy in the loose sense, because it is the only signal of word-formation.

2.3 Primary vs. secondary allomorphs

Among both stem and affix allomorphs we can distinguish between primary vs. secondary allomorphs. Primary (also called basic or principal) allomorphs are the basic or major variants in allomorphy (Mel'čuk 1993–2000 Vol. 4: 217–218), most clearly when they represent the default in derivation, i.e. the least restricted variant (cf. Scalise 1984: 60). Instances in affix allomorphy are E. *-able* as primary vs. *-ible* as secondary or minor allomorph, analogically adjectival *-al* vs. *-ar* (cf. sections 1 and 3.2), cf. G. +*heit* in *Frei+heit* 'free+dom' vs. its secondary allomorphs in *Bitter+keit* 'bitter+ness' and *Neu+igkeit* 'new+ness'. In stem allomorphy, however, the essential criterion for the dichotomy between primary and secondary allomorphs is their occurrence in underived bases vs. derived stems. Thus E. *electric* with word-final /k/ is considered as primary allomorph vs. secondary stem allomorphs in *electric+ity* [elekˈtrisiti], *electric+ian* [elekˈtriʃən], because these secondary allomorphs occur only in affixed forms. The occurrence of the primary allomorph in other derivations, such as *electric+al*, is of minor importance for justifying its status as primary. Obviously often both occurrence in the base of derivations and frequency of occurrence in derivations may converge, as in the case of the primary stem allomorph in the base *elect* and in the derivations *elect+or, elect+ress, elect+ive* vs. the secondary allomorph in the fusional derivation *elect+ion* [eˈlekʃən].

3 Conditions of allomorphy

3.1 Phonological conditioning

Phonological conditioning of either affix or stem allomorphy entails, first of all, the application of phonological rules (Booij 2000: 336 ff.; Dressler 1985a: 41 ff.;

Kaisse 2005). First, their optional application in casual speech must be mentioned, but need not be discussed in detail. For example, in casual speech, final /n/ of the first member of a compound can be assimilated to the initial obstruent of the second member, as in E. *sun-burn, rain-coat*. Or the final nasal of the English (and German, etc.) negative prefix *un-* can be assimilated in place of articulation to a following obstruent, phonemically (i.e. neutralizing) before labials, as in E. *un-pleasant, un-believable, un-married*, allophonically before labiodentals, as in *un-faithful*, and velars, as in *un-committed*. Also the Latinate negative prefix *in-* (cf. section 3.5) shows the same optional allophonic assimilation to word-initial velars (e.g., *in-credible*) and labiodentals (e.g., *in-frequent*). Before labials assimilation is obligatory (e.g., *im-possible*), and it depends on the respective phonological approach whether this conditioning is classified as phonological or morpho(pho)nological (see section 3.2). In any event such cases should not be simply collapsed (as in Štekauer, Valera and Körtvélyessy 2012: 192).

Obligatory phonological conditioning can be illustrated with Bauer's (1983: 126; cf. also Plag 2003: 28) examples of stress-change-induced stem allomorphy between diphthongs and schwa and between tense and lax vowels in *photograph – photograph-y, cremate – cremat-orium, regal – regal-ia*. Of course, such alternations occur only in word-formation. For quantitative conditioning of allomorphs in Slovak cf. section 2.2.

Phonological conditioning of allomorphy is often used, when there are also phonological conditions for the application of morphonological rules or even for suppletion, as in the allomorphy of the English indefinite article *a/an* (Plag 2003: 27; cf. Iacobini 2000: 874, and sections 3.2, 3.4, and 3.5).

3.2 Morpho(pho)nological conditioning

Morphophonological conditioning of allomorphy can be defined as a phonological change which occurs only in certain morphological alternations (cf. Booij 2000: 336 f.), such as the English alternations which go back historically to the Great Vowel Shift, as in the stem allomorphy of *divine – divin-ity, wild – wild-er-ness* (many examples in Bauer 1983: 126 ff.).

Following the approach of Dressler (1985a), which is partially comparable to that of lexical phonology and morphology (Kiparsky 1982; Mohanan 1986), I define, more precisely, morphonological conditioning of allomorphy as the application of morphonological rules. These represent an interface between phonology and morphology insofar as they possess many properties of neutralising phonological rules (such as phonetic basis and plausibility) but do not apply automatically to the relevant phonological input, being limited to certain morphological conditions. Thus, among Bauer's (1983: 126) examples we can identify shortening monophthongization (so-called trisyllabic laxing) in polysyllabic *divin-ity, profan-ity, profund-ity* vs. the shorter diphthongal bases *divine, profane, profound* as a morphonological rule, but not the vowel change in *broad, long* → *bead-th, leng-th*. (see section 3.3). Such rules can be productive, as shown in the rule of English velar softening (with parallels in Romance and Slavic languages) in *electric – electric-ity*, cf. the neologism *formulaic-ity*, where the change /k/ > /s/ is at least optional.

Now we can identify the obligatory assimilation of /n/ in the negative prefix *in-* to word-initial phonemes in *im-possible, im-mature, il-legitimate, ir-respective* as a case of morphophonological conditioning, because the assimilation to word-initial liquids and rhotics takes place only in this prefix but not in the prefix *un-* nor in sentence phonology in the homophonous preposition *in* (plus *within*). Furthermore the assimilation to labials is obligatory, whereas in all the other cases mentioned it is only optional (see section 3.1).

Morphological restrictions on rule application occur in the Basque morphonological rules of postnasal plosive lenition, restricted to the two derivational suffixes *-tar, -ta*, to the homophonous clitic *+ta* and a few inflectional suffixes (Mascaró 2007), e.g., in *Irun-dar* vs. *Bilbo-tar* 'inhabitant of Irun/Bilbao'. An English example is the deletion of /t/ in the clusters /ft/ and /st/ in the derived verbs *soft-en, fast-en* (Plank 1994: 1673).

A dissimilatory morphonological rule occurs in the already mentioned allomorph *-ar* of the suffix *-al* (Plag 2003: 29; see section 1). The antecedent of this English morphonological rule was a Latin phonological rule of liquid dissimilation. And quite in general, morphonological rules go back diachronically to earlier phonological rules, whereas synchronically they resemble phonological rules only to a limited extent (Dressler 1985a). Thus, *lun-ar* (mentioned in section 2.2), which contains the dissimilatory allomorph *-ar* and can be related to a Latin base which occurs also in *lun-atic*, cannot be derived from the noun *moon* because there is no phonological rule /m/ > /n/ __/u/ to which the assumed allomorphy could be associated (cf. also section 3.5).

Vowel harmony is a morphonological rule producing allomorphy in inflection and derivation, i.e. it is restricted in most languages, notably agglutinating ones, to suffix harmony (cf. Dressler 1985a: 340–341). A case in point is palatal and velar harmony in Hungarian (Kenesei, Vago and Fenyvesi 1998: 419–425), e.g., for the abstract-noun-forming suffix *-sé/ág*, as in: *vezér-ség* 'leader-ship' vs. *igazgató-ság* 'director-ate'. But whereas morphonological rules are typically difficult to acquire by children and easily impaired in aphasia, vowel harmony is easily acquired and rarely impaired, similar to phonological rules, as has been abundantly shown for Turkish and Hungarian (Dressler 1985a: 231; Savickiene and Dressler 2007).

3.3 Morphological conditioning

Postponing cases of morphological and idiosyncratic lexical conditioning to section 3.4, we come to purely morphological conditioning, without any synchronic trace of phonologicity. If we can find a subregularity, then we can postulate a rule of allomorphy or an allomorphic rule modelling such parallel allomorphies (Dressler 1985a). A case in point is stem vowel change in E. *broad, long, strong, deep, wide* → *bread-th, leng-th, streng-th, dep-th, wid-th* (cf. Plag 2003: 36 f.), where only the last two cases could be compared with the morphonological rule of trisyllabic laxing (section 3.2).

German umlaut, which goes back to an Old High German phonological rule of vowel palatalisation before /i/ in the following syllable, has scattered into many different synchronic rules (Janda 1982): before an /i/ in the suffix, umlaut in stem allomorphy may still be considered to be morphonologically conditioned, as in *Hund* 'dog' → adj. *hünd-isch,* fem. *Hünd-in* 'bitch', *Koch* '(male) cook' → fem. *Köch-in.* But if the following vowel is the central vowel schwa, then umlaut rules must be allomorphic, as in the diminutives *Hünd-chen* 'doggy', *Mütter-chen* from *Mutter* 'mother' or in the attenuatives *köch-el-n* 'to cook a little and slowly', and *läch-el-n* 'to smile', derived from *koch-en* 'to cook', and *lach-en* 'to laugh' respectively, or in the adjectival derivatives of *Erde* 'earth' → *ird-en* 'earthen' (e.g., ware), *ird-isch* 'terrestrial' vs. *erd-ig* 'earthy'.

Such allomorphic rules, in contrast to automatic phonological rules and possibly productive morphonological rules, are usually unproductive. This is not true of morphologically conditioned stem allomorphy in Semitic languages, for example in the Classical Arabic deverbal derivations from the root /ktb/, basic stem /katab/ 'to write': verbal noun *kitāb-a-t* 'activity of writing', agent noun *kātib* 'writer', causative *a-ktab-a* 'dictated', etc. (for Hebrew, cf. Werner 1983).

Clearly the device of level ordering, often used for contrasting Latinate and non-Latinate derivation (cf. Giegerich 1999) cannot be used for the differentiation of phonological vs. morphonological vs. morphological allomorphy (cf. Laurie Bauer p. 376 f. vs. Stephen Anderson p. 399 in Štekauer 2000). What is more successful is the already older, but often renewed and refined, device of cyclic derivation, as in stratal optimality theory.

3.4 Predominant lexical conditioning

Usually there exists some lexical co-conditioning in many cases of morphonological conditioning (section 3.2) and in most cases of morphological conditioning of allomorphy (section 3.3), for example in German umlauting (section 3.2) not all the umlautable vowels are actually umlauted, as in feminine motion: *Herzog* 'duke' → *Herzog-in* 'duchess' vs. *Wolf* 'wolf' → *Wölf-in* 'she-wolf'.

But often lexical conditioning becomes predominant, which results in very small and always unproductive series of parallel examples. Instances already mentioned are vowel changes in E. *broad* → *breadth*, G. *Erde* → *ird-en* (section 3.3), nasal assimilation of the negative prefix *in-* (section 3.2).

An often discussed French example is the addition of final consonants (with dentals as default) in deadjectival derivation, where the same consonant is used as in feminine formation and in phrase phonology, e.g., masc. *petit* 'small' (where the final orthographic <t> is not realised phonologically) vs. appearance of word-final *-t* in "liaison" in *petit ami,* fem. *petite,* in the derived adverb *petite-ment* and in the noun *petit-esse* 'smallness', similarly in the antonym *grand, grand ami, grande, grand-eur* or in numbers: *trois* 'three' (without a final consonant in pronunciation) vs. *trois enfants* 'three children', *trois-ième* 'third', where <s> is realized as /z/. This relation between liaison and word-formation was already observed by the ancient Indian grammarian Pāṇini (1989) in his conception of external vs. internal sandhi.

Free phonological allomorphy, such as in the word-initial vowel variation between [ɪ] and [ɛ] in *explain* (Plag 2003: 28), is usually always lexically restricted.

Another type of lexical condition has been attributed to analogical lexical influence in output patterns within optimality theory, also subsumed under the concept of external allomorphy (cf. Mascarò 2007; Lloret 2011). For example prosodic stem allomorphy in E. *bureáucrat-ism* vs. *búreaucrat* can be regarded as influenced by parallel accent shift in *bureáucrac-y*, i.e. by analogy within an actual word family.

A further type of lexical condition lies in the appurtenance to different lexical strata. Thus in English, there is the default restriction that Latinate derivation is limited to Latinate bases. This is clearly the case with the suffixation of adjectivising *-ive* (phonologically restricted to stems ending in the dentals /t, s/ and only partially transforming /t/ into /s/, as in *permit* → *permiss-ive*) or with velar softening (cf. section 3.2). The German counterpart is much more restricted, namely to Latinate nouns ending in *-ik*, when transformed into a verb with the derivational suffix /iːr/, as in *Fabrik* 'industrial plant', *Rubrik* 'rubrique' → *fabriz-ier-en, rubriz-ier-en.* But this constraint is looser than in English, because also the Hungarian loan-word *Paprika* 'peppers' was derived to *papriz-ier-en.*

A similar lexical division is responsible for the allomorphy in French quality noun formation in -té vs. -ité, as in étrange-té 'strange-ness' vs. banal-ité 'banality' (Koehl 2012).

3.5 Suppletive allomorphy

Lexical conditioning is at its extreme in suppletion, i.e. in the combination of a high degree of morphosemantic transparency and formal irregularity usually accompanied by a high degree of morphotactic opacity (cf. Mel'čuk 1993–2000 Vol. 2: 349, 392, 397; Vol. 4: 361, 369–392; Dressler 1985b), as in Russian suppletive stem allomorphy between *xolod-n-yj* 'cold' and its prefixed verbal derivatives *o-xlad-et'* 'to get cold', *o-xlad-it'* 'to cool' (Mel'čuk 1993–2000 Vol. 2: 349). In weak suppletion sometimes high morphotactic transparency remains as in the stem allomorphy of G. *Risiko* 'risk' vs. *risk-ant* 'risky' or in G. *Insel* 'island' vs. adj. *insul-ar* and in the outdated (translational) name of Indonesia *Insul-inde*. The relation between the English and French correspondents, E. *island* → *insular*, Fr. *île* → *insul-aire*, is already more opaque. More important than word-final or word-internal identities in weakly suppletive allomorphy are word-initial identities and especially prosodic identity of identical segments as in the above examples. Thus stem allomorphy in Fr. *éponge* 'spunge' vs. adj. *spong-ieux*, E. *moon* – *lun-ar* is more opaque, although it is difficult to rank opacity in regard to E. *law* vs. *leg-al* or even also morphosemantically deviant *loy-al*. And the suppletion between the French toponym *Fontainebleau* and its inhabitant name *Bellifontain* must already by considered as an instance of strong suppletion, inspite of having seven or eight identical segments. Of course, suppletion is strongest in cases such as Fr. *aveugle* 'blind' and acephalous *céc-ité* 'blindness'. Since the criterion of phonological similarity (section 2.2) is lacking in this strongest type of suppletion, it should be excluded from the set of derivational allomorphies.

4 Exclusion of zero allomorphs

One might postulate derivational zero allomorphs in cases of haplology, such as in the German deverbal agent nouns *Zauber-er* 'magician' (where the final agent suffix *-er* is realized as an a-schwa) and its feminine derivative *Zauber-in* (where the agent suffix would be realized as an e-schwa plus /r/, such as the preceding biphonemic right-edge sequence). If Menn and McWhinney's (1984) analysis as the avoidance of adding a suffix which is homophonous with an immediately preceding phonological sequence is correct, then we have rather an overlap of suffix and the right edge of the lexical base than a zero realisation which could be identified as a zero allomorph of the suffix.

Also conversions cannot be classified as zero allomorphs: the German triplets masc. *Trank, Trunk*, neuter *Ge-tränk* 'drink, beverage' have already been rejected as cases of allomorphy in the strict sense (cf. section 2.2). This holds also for the fourth, now obsolete, synonym masc. *Trink* 'drink' converted from the root of *trink-en* 'to drink' (cf. Manova and Dressler 2005; Manova 2011). English examples would be $code_N \rightarrow code_V$ and *en-code*.

For the same reason, i.e. the restriction of derivational stem allomorphy to secondary properties in addition to a primary signal of derivation, conversions, such as E. $drink_N$ converted from the verb *drink* cannot be classified as allomorphs of each other in the strict sense, in contrast to morphological conditioning of voicing in word-final stem allomorphy of E. *house → to house* (see section 3.3). Moreover it makes little sense to identify in conversion allomorphs in the loose sense, since there is no difference at the level of expression, which is a requirement for the establishment of allomorphy in analogy to allophony.

One could object that there are formal differences in terms of syntactic distribution. This would mean an extension of the notion of word-formation allomorphy from the word level to the sentence level, comparable to phrase or sentence phonology, which to my knowledge has never been done in theoretical morphology.

This is different from accepting zero allomorphy in the case of variation in distribution within the word domain. A clear case has been reported for Austronesian Nakanai, where the deverbal nominalization affix *il* occurs as a prefix in *il-au* 'steering' and as an infix in *p-il-eho* 'death'. The difference between the status of a prefix and of an infix fulfils the criterion of formal variance of allomorphy. The Spanish variation between normal suffixation and much rarer infixation of the diminutive affix /it/, as in the hypocoristic variants of *Carlos* 'Charles', *Carlos-ito* vs. *Carl-it-os*, also establishes allomorphy (cf. also *azúcar* 'sugar' → dim. *azuqu-i-ar*; other instances in Yu 2007).

5 Word-creation

Allomorphy exists also in various (extragrammatical) strategies of word-creation (cf. article 19), to which much less space is devoted here than to grammatical word-formation in the preceding sections.

5.1 Backformation and popular etymology

Backformation creates non-existing bases in order to motivate polysyllabic words, i.e. words which have more syllables than usual simple words and whose word length thus resembles the length of morphologically complex words. It tends towards maximisation of morphosemantic transparency but allows low degrees of morphotactic transparency. This may lead to the creation of irregular allomorphs, as in E. *beggar > beg*, where the noun has been reanalysed as containing an irregular allomorph of the suffix *-er*. In contrast, the backformation *editor > edit* has been formed in analogy to the normal allomorph *-or* after stem-final /t/, as in *creat-or*. This allomorph is not simply an orthographic variant of *-er* (Plag 2003: 189), in view of the derivations *manag-er-ial* vs. *edit-or-ial*.

In contrast, popular etymology, which also creates motivation of longer words, tends towards partial or full morphotactic transparency, thereby caring little for morphosemantic transparency. Thus it avoids allomorphy. A case in point is Hock's (1991: 203) example of Old French *a(u)ndier*, borrowed into Middle English as *aundyre* 'fire dog', and then first motivated morphotactically in its second part as *and-iron* and finally fully motivated as *hand-iron* (*and-* could have been regarded as a Cockney variant of *hand*, thus not allowing stem allomorphy). In contrast to the production of popular etymologies, the secondary interpretation of words, which represents an evaluative subpart of popular etymology, may allow for irregular allomorphy (Olschansky 1996: 193 ff.), as in G. *Attentat* 'assault', when related by popular etymology to *Attacke* 'attack' and *Tat* 'deed'.

5.2 Blending

In blends (cf. article 15) allomorphic variants are rare but possible, e.g., Fr. *technoval* and *technival* from *techno* and *festival*, *tigron* and *tiglon* (from *tigre* 'tiger' and *lion* 'lion'). Allomorphy due to alternative order of constituents does not seem to exist in adult blends, because one of the conceivable two variants is more salient. Thus E. *smog* from *smoke* and *fog* is more salient than the conceivable variant **foke*. But in early acquisitional stages of child language such variants exist, e.g, Fr. *Pama/Mapa* (← *Papa* and *Maman* 'Daddy-Mama'; Russian *Bama, Maba* (← *babuška* and *mama* 'Granny-Mama'). These blends have the meaning of coordinate compounds.

5.3 Abbreviatory devices

In extragrammatical word-formation subtractive stem allomorphy occurs by definition by means of abbreviation (cf. article 13 on clipping), as in Fr. *professeur* → *prof* 'professor', but due to official or at least social norming there is little variation in the forms of the abbreviatory targets. This contrasts with the large amount of allomorphy in hypocoristic abbreviations, e.g., E. *Elizabeth* → *Liz, Bet, Eliza* (plus the possibility of adding hypocoristic suffixes: *Lizz-y, Bett-y*), G. *Elisabeth* → *Lisa, Liese, Ella*, plus a great variety via hypocoristic suffixes: *Lies-l, Lis-i, Lieschen, Iss-i, Siss-i* (cf. below), *Ell-i, Bett-i*.

Variants exist much less in other abbreviations, e.g., Fr. *procu/proc(ureur)* 'prosecutor', *super-prod/super-produc(tion)* 'superproduction'.

Hypocoristic abbreviation plus subsequent reduplication, derived from proper names has generally several variants, e.g., Fr. *Sophie* → *Soso, Fifi, Dominique* → *Dodo, Mimi, Valérie* → *Vévé, Lili*.

6 Conclusion

The notion of allomorphy has fuzzy boundaries, particularly in the transition to strong suppletion (section 3.5), to overlapping competing morphemes (section 2.1), to zero allomorphy (which we excluded for derivation but not for inflection: section 4). And in Amerindian languages there may be even fuzzy boundaries between stem and affix allomorphy. Although syntax may condition affix competition, it apparently does not condition allomorphy in word-formation. This fact can be derived from assumptions on modularity which allow for morphological, morpho(pho)nological, phonological and lexical conditioning. Apparent semantic and pragmatic conditioning can be reduced to lexical and sociolinguistic conditions.

7 References

Aronoff, Mark (1976): *Word Formation in Generative Grammar.* Cambridge, MA: MIT Press.
Aronoff, Mark (1994): *Morphology by Itself. Stems and inflectional classes.* Cambridge, MA: MIT Press.
Bauer, Lauri (1983): *English Word-formation.* Cambridge: Cambridge University Press.
Bernhardt, Barbara H. and Joseph P. Stemberger (1998): *Handbook of Phononological Development.* San Diego: Academic Press.
Bloomfield, Leonard (1933): *Language.* London: Allen & Unwin.

Bonami, Boyé and Françoise Kerleroux (2009): L'allomorphie radicale et la relation flexion-construction. In: Bernard Fradin, Françoise Kerleroux and Marc Plénat (eds.), *Aperçus de morphologie du français*, 103–126. Paris: Presses Universitaires de Vincennes.

Bonet, Eulalia and Daniel Harbour (2012): Contextual allomorphy. In: Jochen Trommer (ed.), *The Morphology and Phonology of Exponents*, 195–235. Oxford: Oxford University Press.

Booij, Geert (1995): *The Phonology of Dutch.* Oxford: Clarendon Press.

Booij, Geert (2000): Morphology and phonology. In: Geert Booij, Christian Lehmann and Joachim Mugdan (eds.), *Morphology. An International Handbook on Inflection and Word-formation.* Vol. 1, 335–343. Berlin/New York: de Gruyter.

Booij, Geert and Ariane van Santen (1995): *Morfologie. De Woordstructuur van het Nedelands.* Amsterdam: Amsterdam University Press.

Carstairs-McCarthy, Andrew (2005): Basic terminology. In: Pavol Štekauer and Rochelle Lieber (eds.), *Handbook of Word-Formation*, 5–23. Dordrecht: Springer.

Corbett, Greville G. (2010): Canonical derivational morphology. *Word Structure* 3: 141–155.

Corbin, Danielle (1987): *Morphologie dérivationnelle et structuration du lexique.* Tübingen: Niemeyer.

Drachman, Gaberell, René Kager and Angelika Malikouti-Drachman (1995): Greek allomorphy: An optimality account. *University of Trondheim Working Papers in Linguistics* 28: 345–361.

Dressler, Wolfgang U. (1985a): *Morphonology.* Ann Arbor: Karoma.

Dressler, Wolfgang U. (1985b): Sur le statut de la suppléance dans la morphologie naturelle. *Langages* 78: 41–56.

Dressler, Wolfgang U. (1987): Naturalness in word formation. In: Wolfgang U. Dressler, Willi Mayerthaler, Oswald Panagl and Wolfgang U. Wurzel (eds.), *Leitmotifs in Natural Morphology*, 99–126. Amsterdam/Philadelphia: Benjamins.

Dressler, Wolfgang U. (2000): Subtraction. In: Geert Booij, Christian Lehmann and Joachim Mugdan (eds.), *Morphology. An International Handbook on Inflection and Word-formation.* Vol. 1, 581–587. Berlin/New York: de Gruyter.

Dressler, Wolfgang U. (2001): Extragrammatical vs. marginal morphology. In: Ursula Doleschal and Anna Thornton (eds.), *Extragrammatical and Marginal Morphology*, 1–10. München: LINCOM Europa.

Dressler, Wolfgang U. (2005): Word-Formation in Natural Morphology. In: Pavol Štekauer and Rochelle Lieber (eds.), *Handbook of Word-Formation*, 267–284. Dordrecht: Springer.

Dressler, Wolfgang U. and Lavinia Merlini Barbaresi (1994): *Morphopragmatics.* Berlin: Mouton de Gruyter.

Frege, Gottlob (1892): Über Sinn und Bedeutung. *Zeitschrift für Philosophie und philosophische Kritik* N.F. 100: 25–50.

Fuhrhop, Nanna (1998): *Grenzfälle morphologischer Einheiten.* Tübingen: Stauffenburg.

Giegerich, Heinz J. (1999): *Lexical Strata in English.* Cambridge: Cambridge University Press.

Hock, Hans Henrich (1991): *Principles of Historical Linguistics.* Berlin: Mouton de Gruyter.

Iacobini, Claudio (2000): Base and direction of derivation. In: Geert Booij, Christian Lehmann and Joachim Mugdan (eds.), *Morphology. An International Handbook on Inflection and Word-formation.* Vol. 1, 865–576. Berlin/New York: de Gruyter.

Janda, Richard D. (1982): On limiting the form of morphological rules: German *umlaut*, diacritic features, and the 'cluster-constraint'. *Proceedings of the Annual Meeting of the North Eastern Linguistic Society* 12: 140–152.

Kaisse, Ellen M. (2005): Word-formation and phonology. In: Pavol Štekauer and Rochelle Lieber (eds.), *Handbook of Word-Formation*, 25–47. Dordrecht: Springer.

Kenesei, István, Robert M. Vago and Anna Fenyvesi (1998): *Hungarian.* London: Routledge.

Kiparsky, Paul (1982): From cyclic phonology to lexical phonology. In: Harry van der Hulst and Norval Smith (eds.), *The Structure of Phonological Representations I*, 131–175. Dordrecht: Foris.
Koehl, Aurore (2012): La construction morphologique des noms désadjectivaux suffixés en français. Ph.D. dissertation, ATILF; Université de Lorraine.
Lloret, Maria-Rosa (2011): La alomorfía en la teoría de la optimidad. In: José Pazó, Irene Gil and María Ángeles Cano (eds.), *Teoría morfológica y morfología del español*, 133–161. Madrid: Ediciones Universidad Autónoma de Madrid.
Malkiel, Yakov (1966): Genetic analysis of word formation. In: Thomas A. Sebeok (ed.), *Current Trends in Linguistics* 3, 305–369. The Hague/Paris: Mouton.
Manova, Stela (2011): *Understanding Morphological Rules. With special emphasis on conversion and subtraction in Bulgarian, Russian and Serbo-Croatian*. Dordrecht: Springer.
Manova, Stela and Wolfgang U. Dressler (2005): The morphological technique of conversion in the inflecting-fusional type. In: Laurie Bauer and Salvador Valera (eds.), *Approaches to Conversion/Zero-Derivation*, 67–101. Münster: Waxmann.
Marchand, Hans (1969): *The Categories and Types of Present-Day English Word Formation. A Synchronic-Diachronic Approach*. 2nd ed. München: Beck.
Mascarò, Joan (2007): External allomorphy and lexical representation. *Linguistic Inquiry* 38: 715–735.
Mel'čuk, Igor (1993–2000): *Cours de morphologie générale*. 4 Vol. Montréal: Les Presses de l'Université de Montréal.
Menn, Lise and Brian McWhinney (1984): The repeated morph constraint. *Language* 60: 519–541.
Mohanan, Karuvannur P. (1986): *The Theory of Lexical Phonology*. Dordrecht: Reidel.
Mugdan, Joachim (1994): Morphological units. In: Robert E. Asher (ed.), *The Encyclopedia of Language and Linguistics*, 2543–2553. Oxford: Pergamon Press.
Nida, Eugene (1948): The identification of morphemes. *Language* 24: 414–441.
Olschansky, Heike (1996): *Volksetymologie*. Tübingen: Niemeyer.
Pāṇini (1989): *Aṣṭādhyāyī*. Roman Transliteration and English Translation by Sumitra M. Katre. Delhi: Byanarsidass.
Peters, Ann M. (1997): Language typology, prosody, and the acquisition of grammatical morphemes. In: Dan Slobin (ed.), *The Crosslinguistic Study of Language Acquisition*. Vol. 5, 135–197. Hillsdale: Erlbaum.
Plag, Ingo (2003): *Word-Formation in English*. Cambridge: Cambridge University Press.
Plank, Frans (1994): Inflection and derivation. In: Robert E. Asher (ed.), *The Encyclopedia of Language and Languages*. Vol. 5, 1671–1678. Oxford: Pergamon Press.
Savickiene, Ineta and Wolfgang U. Dressler (eds.) (2007): *The Acquisition of Diminutives*. Amsterdam/Philadelphia: Benjamins.
Scalise, Sergio (1984): *Generative Morphology*. Dordrecht: Foris.
Scalise, Sergio and Antonietta Bisetto (2008): *La struttura delle parole*. Bologna: il Mulino.
Štekauer, Pavol (2000): *English Word-Formation. A history of research (1960–1995)*. Tübingen: Narr.
Štekauer, Pavol, Salvador Valera and Lívia Körtvélyessy (2012): *Word-Formation in the World's Languages. A typological survey*. Cambridge: Cambridge University Press.
Thornton, Anna M. (2005): *Morfologia*. Roma: Carocci.
Werner, Fritz (1983): *Die Wortbildung der hebräischen Adjektive*. Wiesbaden: Harrassowitz.
Yu, Alan C. L. (2007): The phonology-morphology interface from the perspective of infixation. In: Matti Miestamo and Bernhard Wälchli (eds.), *New Challenges in Typology*, 35–54. Berlin: Mouton de Gruyter.

Index

ablaut 67, 69, 72, 206, 240, 267, 430, 435, 451
acronym 138, 301, 302
– alphabetic 301, 302
– orthoepic 301, 302
– syllabic 297
activation 124, 125, 128–132, 321
adjacency condition 85, 86
adjustment rules 446
affix 4, 8, 43, 44, 51, 73, 80, 83, 85, 87, 94, 95, 113, 114, 140, 141, 143, 147, 150, 157, 163, 165, 172, 176, 179, 183–202, 204, 205, 207–212, 221, 235, 240, 243–246, 249, 284, 286, 287, 289, 374, 378, 379, 445, 448, 450, 452, 458, 460
– adfix 191
– ambifix 192, 197
– ambiguous 140
– circumfix 190–193, 197, 373
– class I 142, 255
– class II 245
– duplifix 204, 205
– exfix 191
– extrafix 191
– infix 190, 191, 194–198, 207, 458
– mobile affix 197
– multifix 191
– parafix 191, 204
– postfix 191
– semi-affix 185
– simulfix 191, 192, 200, 207, 210
– superfix 200
– suprafix 200
– synaffix 191
– variable-direction affix 197
– zero affix 201, 202
affix order 243
affixation 88, 110, 133, 146, 189, 203–207, 209, 210, 239, 240, 246, 261, 272, 273, 284, 285, 297, 358, 373, 375, 377, 408, 409, 411–414, 449, 450
affixoid 5, 68, 69, 103, 185, 398
aktionsart 192, 244, 249, 250, 369
alienation 425, 426, 432–434
– alienation by homophones 432, 433
– orthographical alienation 432
– orthographical and phonetic alienation 432, 433
– plain orthographical alienation 432, 433
allolex 179
allomorph 17, 165–169, 179, 180, 210, 245, 250, 445, 446, 448–450, 452, 454, 459
– opaque allomorph 449
– primary allomorph 452
– secondary allomorph 452
– stem allomorph 450, 452
– zero allomorph 458
allomorphy 12, 84, 165–167, 169, 212, 245, 253, 445–460
– suppletive allomorphy 457
a-morphous morphology 92, 93
analogy 14, 37, 39, 48, 49, 107, 121, 132, 164, 179, 247, 283, 284, 288, 289, 394, 398, 431, 445, 456, 458, 459
anti-iconic subtraction 449
apophony 206, 240, 254, 451
archiphoneme 167
aspect 11, 69, 72, 73, 81, 88, 90, 91, 106, 139, 143, 176, 178, 192, 195, 200, 204, 205, 236, 243, 271, 295–297, 304, 317, 339, 356, 388, 389, 398, 410, 447
asyndetic phrasal coordination 325
atom condition 85, 86
atomicity thesis 84
attenuation 407, 410–415
augmentative 249, 251, 282, 449
autosegmental phonology 88
autosemantic 5, 184

backformation 8, 208, 209, 236, 262, 279–291, 294, 298, 459
base 4, 10, 15, 16, 69, 79, 80, 83, 85, 86, 89, 94, 95, 100, 102, 104, 105, 111, 113, 143, 153, 190, 192, 194–197, 200, 203–205, 207–210, 212, 213, 220, 221, 235, 236, 238, 239, 241, 243, 245–249, 253–256, 259, 264–266, 268, 273, 274, 282, 288, 291, 297, 315, 329, 333, 338, 341, 346, 347, 350, 356, 378, 406–411, 413–416, 438, 446, 447, 449, 450, 452, 454, 458

base form 35, 181, 254, 259, 268, 406, 415
binary branching 6, 189, 247, 310
biuniqueness 445, 447, 448
blend 298, 333, 336, 339, 341–355, 357, 433
– interference 355
– intersective 344, 354
– recognition point 348
– speech-error 355
blending 9, 294, 298, 333–345, 347, 348, 350–352, 355–358, 425–428, 434, 438
– contour blending 438
– inclusive 345
– telescope blending 438
blocking 19, 107, 394
bracketing paradox 111

canonical derivational morphology 255, 447
citation form 141, 176, 181, 182, 190, 202, 218, 265, 268
cline 137, 143, 153
clipping 9, 132, 138, 208, 209, 212, 282, 286, 287, 291, 293–304, 338, 356, 357, 425, 427, 428, 432, 460
– back clipping 299, 300, 303
– complex 295, 299, 302
– fore-clipping 299, 300, 356
– middle clipping 299, 300
– syllabic 297, 338, 356
clitic 175, 242, 249, 454
co-compound 312, 313, 325
– additive 312, 325, 352, 353
– alternative 313
– collective 53, 325
– concealed 358, 359
– generalizing co-compound 313
– imitative 327
– scalar 317, 325
– synonymic co-compound 313
coercion 237, 317, 329
combining form 5, 216
common integrator 325
complex lexeme 5, 11, 19, 302
complex predicate 370–372
composition 8, 9, 12, 25–33, 35–39, 47–51, 54, 55, 84, 183, 297, 307–310
composition vowel 44, 50
compositionality 5, 37, 38, 172, 215, 335, 337, 384, 386, 387

compound 8, 12, 31, 32, 34, 37, 39, 44, 53, 68, 79, 87, 88, 91, 102, 103, 105, 107, 110, 113, 114, 120, 124, 127, 129, 131–133, 172, 175, 177, 185, 194, 197–199, 213–218, 223, 248, 280, 282, 286, 287, 302, 303, 307, 309–312, 314, 315, 317, 318, 320–326, 328, 329, 335, 337, 344, 377, 378, 393–396, 398, 433, 450, 453
– asyntactic 68, 314
– *amredita* 310
– *avyayībhāva* 53, 317
– *bahuvrīhi* 32, 53, 54, 311, 317
– clarifying 327
– coordinative appositional 312, 313
– copulative 30, 31, 53, 54, 70, 310–312, 314
– determinative 8, 28, 29, 31, 53, 54, 70, 300, 310, 311, 313, 317, 326, 335, 337
– *dvigu* 53
– endocentric 395
– esocentric 55
– exocentric 8, 55, 70, 105, 314, 317, 318, 329, 374
– improper 31, 70, 314, 318
– *karmadhāraya* 53, 54, 310, 312
– neoclassical 5, 319, 320, 355, 434
– phrasal 109, 212, 378
– possessive 32, 53, 54, 310, 311, 314, 318
– reduplicating 327
– redundant 327
– subsumptive 327
– synonymous 394
– syntactic 39, 55, 314, 322, 325
– syntagmatic 314, 318
– synthetic 55, 89, 92, 213, 315
– *tatpuruṣa* 53, 54, 310
compounding 4, 8, 12, 48, 50, 51, 53, 54, 78, 79, 84, 88, 92–94, 102–104, 108–110, 120, 145, 172, 175, 177, 183, 185, 188, 198, 199, 203, 214, 215, 218, 219, 238, 271–273, 289, 303, 307, 309, 310, 313, 315, 319, 320, 325, 328, 333, 335–339, 350, 352, 359, 373, 377, 378, 391, 394–398, 414, 427, 438, 449, 450
comprehension 62, 120, 121, 128, 132, 134, 328, 384
conditioning 165–167, 169, 187, 282, 338, 445, 447, 453, 454, 456, 460
– grammatical conditioning 165

– lexical conditioning 165, 455–457, 460
– morphological conditioning 164–167, 455, 456, 458
– phonological conditioning 165, 167, 168, 452, 453
confix 185, 190, 192
consonant mutation 88, 240, 373
constituent 5, 6, 8, 30, 31, 59, 64, 66, 79, 102, 103, 105, 107, 109, 124, 126, 128–130, 133, 153, 171, 173, 177, 199, 213, 217, 219, 309, 310, 313, 315–318, 321, 327, 342, 370, 371, 373, 397, 398, 414
construction 39, 68, 73, 80, 99, 101, 114, 132, 142, 146, 172, 182, 214, 215, 236, 241, 252, 254, 290, 314, 315, 318, 335, 369, 375, 379, 388, 392, 397, 398, 414
– construction grammar 13, 99, 101, 104, 114, 222, 255, 397, 414
– construction morphology 99, 101, 105, 106, 115
constructional iconicity 207, 279, 289
constructional idiom 103, 106
constructional schema 100, 101, 103, 105, 106, 254, 397
contextual inflection 146
continuity 410, 413
conventionalization 19, 20, 108
conversion 8, 38, 78, 94, 142, 145, 161, 202, 207, 216, 220, 222, 223, 237, 239, 246, 252, 259–274, 279, 282, 285–287, 314, 375, 427, 448, 458
coordination 106, 178, 312, 325, 352, 367
– natural coordination 312, 352
Copenhagen school 60, 63
cranberry morph 160
creation 34–36, 49, 123, 124, 130, 131, 133, 208, 250, 266, 295, 321, 324, 347, 412, 415, 433, 434, 436, 459

decomposition 70, 121, 126, 221, 321
derivation 2, 4, 8, 10, 12, 19, 25–38, 48–51, 78–80, 84, 91–94, 104, 108, 120, 137, 139–148, 150, 152, 153, 161, 164, 176, 177, 182, 183, 188–190, 193, 198, 201, 202, 207–209, 214, 215, 218, 219, 222, 223, 235–241, 243, 246, 249, 251, 252, 254–256, 259, 261–263, 266, 270–273, 279, 281, 286, 291, 307, 308, 315, 316, 333, 345, 346, 370, 375, 389, 416, 418, 419, 427, 434, 435, 448–452, 454–456, 458, 460
derivational morphology 13, 137, 138, 142–148, 163, 193, 207, 208, 235, 236, 239, 252, 279, 336, 337, 448, 450–452
derivational paradigm 149
derivative 28, 30, 32, 34, 35, 140, 186, 213, 218, 223, 259, 264–266, 268, 270, 273, 283, 448, 457
– phrasal derivative 212
determinant 73, 151, 308
determinatum 6, 73, 151, 308
diachrony -4, 62, 67, 70, 122, 209
diagrammaticity 207, 279, 413, 414
diminutive 33, 52, 144, 198, 211, 212, 220, 243, 244, 249, 251, 255, 256, 282, 372, 413, 448, 449, 458
directionality 266, 273, 285
dispersion 410
distributionalism 66
distributivity 410, 411, 413
dual access 321

embedded productivity 104
expansion 38, 147, 419
exponence 93, 179, 211
– cumulative exponence 144, 164, 169
– extended exponence 211
exponent 179, 203, 207, 209, 211, 212, 239, 358
extragrammatical derivation 425, 430, 431
extragrammatical word-formation 449, 460

facilitation 131
feature 36, 81, 85, 93, 94, 128, 140, 151, 159, 163–165, 179, 181, 188, 202, 211, 216, 221, 223, 249, 262, 322, 336, 345, 347, 368, 383, 419, 431
figura 26, 27, 29, 47
formative 6, 51, 307
fractomorpheme 357
free creation 430, 431
frequency 9, 18, 19, 123, 125–127, 131, 149, 207, 208, 261, 264, 282, 346, 384, 388, 394, 436, 452
frequentativity 410
fuzziness 138, 140, 223

gender 26, 34, 54, 110, 111, 144, 145, 165, 178, 181, 182, 197, 202, 220, 223, 236, 248, 255, 260, 270, 271, 299, 313, 317, 318, 320, 340, 345, 412
generative grammar 12-14, 70, 77-83, 89, 92, 189, 235, 284, 392, 408
Geneva school 60, 63
gerundive 80, 89
glossematics 64
grammaticalization 240, 320, 325, 417
grammeme 169, 178

habituality 410
hapax 19, 339, 340
haplology 343, 346, 350, 457
head 1, 6, 8, 14, 63, 73, 85, 91, 102, 105, 107, 110, 111, 113, 114, 131-133, 151, 222, 240, 241, 246, 248, 267, 300, 307, 309-311, 313-318, 320, 321, 323-327, 329, 336, 340, 346, 347, 368, 371, 372, 374, 377-379, 395, 411
– lefthand 320
– righthand 14, 320
headedness 151
head-initial particle verbs 374
hierarchical lexicon 99, 101, 104, 115, 398
hierarchical structure 176, 190, 247
historical-comparative grammar 13, 30, 43. 46, 47, 49, 50, 61, 70, 310
holistic property 105
homology 413, 414
hyperonym 49, 178, 312
hypocoristic 209, 300, 458, 460
hypocoristic clipping 339
hyponym 178, 263, 309, 312, 324

iconicity 207, 413, 414, 416, 428, 430, 448
idiomaticity 387
idiomatization 19, 20
implicit derivation 207
incorporation 90, 91, 175, 289-291
inflection 2, 31, 32, 36, 37, 44-46, 50, 84, 87, 90, 92-94, 107, 111, 120, 137, 140-148, 150, 153, 158, 165, 167, 176, 178, 181-183, 189, 190, 194, 201, 207, 212, 214, 215, 219, 222, 236-238, 240, 241, 243, 253, 256, 263, 268, 270, 271, 274, 309, 310, 313, 375, 387, 388, 416, 417, 445, 447, 448, 451, 452, 454, 460

inflectional morphology 1, 2, 137, 138, 142-148, 158, 163, 210, 256, 372, 429, 445, 447, 448, 452
inherent inflection 146, 216, 251
inherent plurality 417
institutionalization 19, 20, 324
intensification 396-398, 410, 411, 413, 416-419
interference 123, 131, 355
interfixation 449
internal modification 191, 206, 267
item-and-arrangement 67, 73
item-and-process 67
iterativity 410

langue 33, 35, 37, 38, 61, 62, 164
lexeme 4, 8, 18, 20, 94, 103, 133, 169, 173, 179-182, 187, 188, 199, 211, 216, 218, 219, 222, 223, 235-238, 243, 246-249, 253-256, 265, 266, 282, 293, 298, 307, 308, 317, 320, 321, 333, 335-337, 340-351, 354, 357-359, 384, 425
lexical access 126
lexical association 121
lexical category 105, 260, 320
lexical creativity 13, 127, 128
lexical integrity 77, 84, 110, 247, 336, 346, 377
lexical item 173, 384
lexical phonology and morphology 86, 87, 453
lexical relatedness 235, 236, 251, 252
lexical relisting 261
lexicalist hypothesis 84, 89, 90
– strong lexicalist hypothesis 84
– weak lexicalist hypothesis 84
lexicalization 1, 19, 20, 144, 262-264, 340, 384, 391, 393, 394, 415
lexicon 3, 13, 35, 37, 38, 69, 70, 80-82, 100-102, 108, 124, 149, 158, 165, 172, 173, 181, 193, 208, 209, 215, 224, 236, 287, 301, 324, 337, 340, 383, 390-394, 398, 430, 435-438
linking element 198, 199, 217, 450
– non-paradigmatic 199
– paradigmatic 199

marker 15, 83, 140, 151, 174, 179, 194, 197, 212, 215, 216, 241, 249, 250, 335
maximization of opportunity 124, 130-132
mental lexicon 78, 95, 119, 122-131, 133, 321, 322, 386, 390, 394

mental representation 78, 120
metaphor 37, 125, 235, 236, 265, 395
mirror principle 90, 91
modifier 6, 102, 110, 133, 177, 214, 252, 309, 326, 327, 375, 378, 379, 416
morph 157, 160–164, 168, 169, 178, 180, 195, 204, 210, 240
- blocked morph 160
- cranberry 160, 239, 253
- pseudomorph 160, 161
morpheme 4, 5, 13, 45, 66, 68, 69, 71, 78, 82, 83, 85, 90, 93, 94, 103, 119, 131, 133, 143, 144, 157, 160, 162–164, 166–170, 178, 180, 195, 198, 199, 201, 206, 210, 267, 280, 281, 299, 308, 311, 315, 319, 408, 430, 431, 438, 445, 447–449
- base morpheme 184
- bound morpheme 8, 71, 398
- core morpheme 184
- grammatical morpheme 2
- lexical morpheme 143
- bound lexical morpheme 8, 10
- free lexical morpheme 5, 10
morphological alteration 271
morphological decomposition 128
morphological doubling 414
morphological object 371, 377, 379
morphological structure 11, 45, 84, 100, 110, 111, 119, 121, 122, 131, 132, 259, 284, 309, 329, 433
morphological transcendence 321
morphology 32, 33, 35, 45, 46, 59, 64–66, 71, 78, 80, 82, 84–95, 100, 101, 110, 126, 133, 137, 146, 150, 153, 157, 164, 169, 197, 200, 210, 211, 213, 235, 238, 240, 241, 246, 247, 252, 253, 255, 262, 266, 268, 270, 273, 287, 334, 335, 338–341, 345, 372, 373, 398, 409, 413, 414, 427, 428, 447, 449–451, 453, 458
- distributed morphology 93
- evaluative morphology 235, 237, 239, 243, 255, 256
- extragrammatical morphology 296, 338, 428, 447
- grammatical morphology 355, 428, 447
- natural morphology 13, 150, 279, 289, 413, 428, 448
- prosodic morphology 86, 88, 296, 297, 299, 356, 408, 409

- root-based morphology 449
- subtractive morphology 208, 289
morphomic stem 238
multifunctional suffix 265
multifunctionality 202, 261
multimorphemic word 124, 126, 134
multi-word expression 2, 116, 173, 240, 331–384, 386, 388, 389, 391, 401, 402

naming 109, 288, 289, 301, 324, 356, 389, 393
natural class 188, 221
neoclassical word-formation 434
neurocognitive research 119–121, 131, 133, 134
no phrase constraint 84, 214
noun incorporation 91, 175, 289, 290, 385, 395

onomasiological approach 11
onomasiological perspective 11
onomatopoeia 72, 339, 418, 429, 437
orthoepic pronunciation 298, 302
over-activation 130
overlap 9, 81, 262, 336, 341–345, 347, 349, 350, 384, 393, 398, 457

paradigm 13, 63, 92, 93, 121, 133, 140, 142, 144, 181–183, 199, 216, 219, 236, 251, 264, 448
paradigmatic derivation 8, 269
paradigmatic opposition 246
paradigmatic relation
- paradigmatic lexical relationship 246
paradigmatic word-formation 209, 284
parasynthesis 38, 192
parole 61, 62, 164, 333
parse 124, 129
particle 2, 6, 106, 112–114, 173, 240, 313, 365–379, 383, 385, 389
- aspectual 369, 370, 372
- resultative particle 368, 371
particle verb 112–114, 371, 373, 374, 377
particle-verb formation 365, 375, 377, 386
perception 100, 101, 161, 436
periphrastic 175, 248
periphrastic form 182
phonaestheme 6, 431, 434
phonological copying 408, 414
phraseology 2, 384, 385, 388, 392
polysemous variants 237

portmanteau morpheme 144
positionally bound 133, 320–322
possessive adjective 248, 252
Prague school 60, 61, 64, 65, 166
prefab 384
prefix 5, 6, 8, 85, 86, 90, 100, 122–124, 129, 150, 176, 183, 190–198, 200, 202, 221, 241, 244, 245, 247, 250, 253, 254, 308, 379, 398, 406, 407, 446, 450, 453, 454, 456, 458
– attenuative 244, 478
– intensive 242, 478
– supra-lexical 244
prefixation 8, 11, 15–18, 27–29, 38, 172, 241, 242, 244, 279, 308
prefixoid 185, 398
preverb 241
processing 119–134, 235, 304, 321, 334, 355, 384
production 100, 101, 120, 128, 134, 321, 328, 357, 384, 431, 436, 459
productivity 1, 3, 10, 12, 15, 19, 53, 68, 72, 80, 95, 103, 145, 146, 185, 262–265, 268, 269, 272, 273, 284, 286, 289–291, 315, 320, 340, 341, 394, 415
progressivity 410
prosodic changes 451
prosodic word 171
– minimal prosodic word 297, 356, 357
prototype 261, 299, 414
PRO-verb 322
psycholinguistics 3, 12, 21, 95, 119–122, 124, 125, 130, 131, 133, 134, 149, 217, 245, 246, 321, 360, 384, 385, 400, 401

quantification 244
quasi-inflectional affixes 140

recursion 243, 309, 319, 376
reduplicant 204, 205, 406–410, 414
reduplication 9, 88, 105, 157, 195, 203–206, 239, 240, 374, 405–419, 428, 430, 435, 460
– adverbial reduplication 411
– echo- 408, 409, 411, 419
– full reduplication 406, 408, 412, 419
– lexical reduplication 415, 417
– partial reduplication 204, 407, 408, 414
– sound-iconic reduplication 430

reduplicative affix 204, 408
reflexive 193, 197, 241, 242, 252–254
regularity 34, 68, 80, 145, 182, 209, 426, 428
reinterpretation 210, 283, 284, 291, 391
repetition 9, 18, 140, 192, 204, 205, 358, 405–407, 410, 413, 419
righthand head rule 85, 151, 309
root 4, 8, 11, 13, 27–31, 37, 43–45, 50, 80, 88, 100, 106, 143, 144, 150, 157, 161, 182–185, 189, 190, 194–197, 200, 214, 218, 219, 223, 224, 236, 238–240, 244, 245, 253, 270, 307, 316, 320, 373, 406, 429, 449, 451, 455, 458
– bound root 5

schema 15, 16, 18, 66, 100–106, 112, 222, 285, 323, 392, 397
– subschema 102, 398
secreted affixation 357, 358
secretion 358
semantic specification 103
semasiological perspective 11
semiotic perspective 352
separation hypothesis 93, 94
series 9, 36, 63, 79, 86, 149, 189, 281, 298, 323, 336, 337, 357–359, 398, 456
shortening 9, 132, 208, 240, 293–299, 302, 304, 340, 341, 347, 356, 358, 425–428, 431–435, 438, 454
sign 32, 36, 37, 60–62, 64, 65, 71, 72, 114, 158–161, 183, 198, 214, 328, 334, 356, 406, 413
– linguistic sign 60, 63, 159, 164, 201, 210
– minimal sign 160–162, 168, 178, 183, 185, 195
signifiant 64, 158
signifier 34, 64, 158
simile 394, 397, 398
small clause 371, 372
species 26, 27, 29, 32–34, 47, 54, 241
splinter 6, 352, 357
stem 4, 5, 8, 12, 39, 43–45, 49, 50, 54, 59, 71, 83, 84, 90, 103, 112, 113, 123, 124, 157, 165, 167, 175, 182, 184, 186–190, 192, 195–202, 204, 207, 210, 212, 216–219, 235, 238–240, 243, 244, 253, 270, 289, 301, 313, 316, 317, 337, 338, 355, 359, 409, 411, 445, 447–453, 455–460
– allostem 187
– portmanteau stem 188

- word stem 4
- word-formation stem 4, 218, 219
stem alternants 187, 188
stem variation 445, 449
stem-based conversion 270
storage 107, 114, 126, 133, 384
stress shift 200, 240, 266, 267, 433, 451, 452
structuralism 59–61, 63, 65, 67, 163, 296
substitution 157, 203, 206, 207, 210, 211
subtraction 157, 203, 206, 208–211, 268, 279, 449
suffix 2, 8, 10, 31, 34, 38, 52, 68, 85, 86, 89–91, 94, 103, 108, 111–113, 122, 139, 140, 144, 145, 148, 150, 151, 153, 175, 176, 181–183, 190–200, 202, 207–213, 217, 220, 240, 243–249, 251, 253, 255, 281, 282, 284, 285, 287, 289, 300, 313, 338, 374, 406, 407, 410, 411, 431, 434, 445–451, 454–459
- cumulative 244
- distributive 244, 251
- evaluative 244
superstate 133
suppletion 167, 168, 203, 246, 453, 457
- allomorphic suppletion 167
- full suppletion 167
- portmanteau suppletion 167
- strong suppletion 167, 448, 457, 460
- weak suppletion 167, 448, 457
suppletive 167, 169, 238, 457
symbolism 429
- conventional phonetic symbolism 429, 430
- phonetic symbolism 429
synchrony 35, 37, 39, 62, 67, 68, 70, 122, 209
synsemantic 5, 184
syntactic fixedness 383, 384, 387
syntagma 151
syntax-morphology interaction 106

template 113, 150, 189, 190, 197, 205, 214, 239, 297, 323–326, 328, 356, 357, 365, 408, 409, 414
theme 44, 129, 140, 194, 220, 238, 368
theoretical frameworks 13, 77, 150, 406, 432
- categorial grammar 13
- cognitive grammar 13, 392, 427
- optimality theory 13, 409, 414, 455, 456
transfix 190, 191, 196, 197

transfixation 196, 240
transflexion 142, 146, 269
transparency 114, 131, 144, 320, 341, 347, 426–428, 435, 436, 438, 439, 449
- morphosemantic transparency 291, 435, 457, 459
- morphotactic transparency 457, 459
transposition 202, 252, 262
truncation 83, 209, 211, 212, 293, 341–344, 357, 449

umlaut 188, 189, 206, 211, 212, 254, 455
underspecified relation 326
unified schema 104
unitary base hypothesis 14, 85, 86, 220, 221
unitary output hypothesis 14, 85, 86, 220, 221
univerbation 50, 395, 398
Urschöpfung 425

valency-changing word-formation 271
variable R condition 322
verb 2, 9, 11, 29, 45, 67, 68, 73, 79, 80, 86, 88–91, 106, 112, 113, 141, 142, 145, 148, 150, 152, 153, 164, 174, 176, 179, 180, 182, 189, 192–196, 200, 202, 207, 208, 211, 216, 220, 222, 223, 236–238, 240–242, 244, 245, 248, 249, 251–254, 261–267, 269, 270, 274, 281–284, 287–289, 315–317, 336, 338, 354, 365–379, 385, 386, 410, 413, 416, 446, 449–451, 456, 458
verb stem 202, 204, 205, 241, 244, 374, 375

whole-word access 321
whole-word processing 126
word 2, 4, 6, 9, 13, 20, 25–30, 32–35, 38, 46–48, 54, 60, 63, 67–70, 73, 80–85, 88, 89, 94, 99–101, 103–108, 110, 111, 115, 119–123, 126–131, 133, 134, 138, 142, 143, 147–149, 157, 159, 160, 165, 168–180, 182, 183, 185, 186, 189, 191, 192, 194, 195, 197, 200, 201, 208, 211, 213–224, 236, 240, 243–245, 247, 248, 253, 255, 256, 261, 262, 264–266, 268, 270–274, 280, 283, 286–288, 291, 293–304, 307, 309–311, 313–315, 317, 318, 320, 321, 324, 327–329, 334, 339, 341, 344–348, 351, 352, 356, 372, 374, 377–379, 383, 384, 386–389, 395, 399, 406, 410, 411, 416, 419,

426, 428, 430–433, 438, 446, 451, 456, 458, 459
- morphosyntactic word 173–175, 178
- orthographic word 171
- phonological word 171, 172
word class 8, 26, 29, 32, 139, 146, 159, 182, 183, 190, 192, 202, 212, 219–224, 236, 252, 255, 256, 259, 261–266, 268, 270, 273, 274, 415, 416
- word-class change 260, 261, 264, 265, 268–270, 272, 412
- word-class underspecification 261, 265
word form 132, 149, 179, 180, 188, 199, 211, 218, 236, 247, 319
word meaning 321, 446

word structure autonomy condition 84
word-based 4, 82, 83, 93, 269, 270, 449
word-creation 2, 212, 334, 415, 425–428, 431, 435–439, 445, 458
word-formation 2, 4, 26, 45, 46, 49, 52, 69, 72, 93, 95, 128, 158, 269, 293, 294, 334, 427
- word-formation meaning 446
- word-formation pattern 3, 73, 194, 284, 289
- word-formation rule 3, 100, 157, 213, 218, 219, 243, 247, 284, 340

zero-derivation 8, 266, 281, 282, 285, 286
zero-morpheme 8, 72
Zusammenbildung 315

www.ingramcontent.com/pod-product-compliance
Lightning Source LLC
Chambersburg PA
CBHW031540300426
44111CB00006BA/124